olume 2

nall Groups and Social Interaction

Volume 2

Small Groups and Social Interaction

Edited by

Herbert H. Blumberg
University of London Goldsmiths' College

A. Paul Hare
Ben-Gurion University of the Negev, Israel

Valerie Kent
University of London Goldsmiths' College

and

Martin F. Davies
University of London Goldsmiths' College

JOHN WILEY & SONS

Chichester · New York · Brisbane · Toronto · Singapore

Library of Congress Cataloging in Publication Data:

Main entry under title:
Small groups and social interaction.

   Includes index.
   1. Small groups—Addresses, essays, lectures.
2. Social interaction—Addresses, essays, lectures.
3. Interpersonal relations—Addresses, essays, lectures.
4. Social change—Addresses, essays, lectures.
5. Personality—Addresses, essays,
lectures. I. Blumberg, Herbert H.
HM133.S65   1983   302.3'4   82-8558

ISBN 0 471 90091 5

British Library Cataloguing in Publication Data

Small groups and social interaction.
   1. Social interaction
   I. Blumberg, Herbert H.
   302   HM291

ISBN 0 471 90091 5

Typeset by Pintail Studios Ltd., Ringwood, Hampshire.
Printed by Page Bros., Norwich.

Acknowledgements

We would like to thank those colleagues and students who kindly read portions of the proposals and manuscript and offered suggestions—in particular, Paul Webley, Duncan Cramer, and a number of the represented authors.

Acknowledgements for permission to reprint various extracts are shown at the relevant places in the text.

We especially wish to thank our publishers—particularly, Celia Bird, Linda Burden, Amanda Gray, Wendy Hudlass and Vivienne Squire—for their advice and help in a variety of major and minor matters.

Contributors to Volume 2

Nicholas Albery, *London, England*
Robert F. Bales, *Harvard University, USA*
Robert R. Blake, *Scientific Methods Inc., Austin, Texas, USA*
Eugene Burnstein, *University of Michigan, USA*
Jerome M. Chertkoff, *Indiana University, USA*
James H. Davis, *University of Illinois, USA*
Morton Deutsch, *Teachers College, Columbia University, USA*
Julian J. Edney, *Los Angeles, California, USA*
Gerard Egan, *Loyola University of Chicago, USA*
James K. Esser, *Indiana University, USA*
Claude Faucheux, *Institut Européen d'Administration des Affairs, Fontainebleau, France*
Erving Goffman, *University of Pennsylvania, USA*
Clem Gorman
Susanne Gowan, *Movement for a New Society, Philadelphia, USA*
A. Paul Hare, *Ben-Gurion University of the Negev, Israel*
Wayne Harrison, *University of Nebraska at Omaha, USA*
Elaine Hatfield, *University of Hawaii at Manoa, USA*
R. G. Havelock, *American University, Washington DC, USA*
L. Richard Hoffman, *University of Chicago and Rutgers University, USA*
Roger Holmes, *London School of Economics and Political Science, England*
Irving L. Janis, *Yale University, USA*
Rosabeth Moss Kanter, *Goodmeasure Inc., Cambridge, Massachusetts, USA*
Linda J. Keil, *University of California, Santa Barbara, USA*
Harold H. Kelley, *University of California, Los Angeles, USA*
Valerie Kent, *University of London Goldsmiths' College, England*

S. S. Komorita, *University of Illinois, Urbana-Champaign, USA*
David A. Kravitz, *University of Kentucky, USA*
George Lakey, *Movement for a New Society, Philadelphia, USA*
Martin Lakin, *Duke University, USA*
John T. Lanzetta, *Dartmouth College, USA*
Leon H. Levy, *University of Maryland, Baltimore County, USA*
Morton A. Lieberman, *University of Chicago, USA*
Svenn Lindskold, *Ohio University, USA*
Elizabeth Lorentz, *Yale University, USA*
J.Richard McCallum, *Catawba College, Salisbury, North Carolina, USA*
Charles G. Mclintock, *University of California, Santa Barbara, USA*
Gerald Marwell, *University of Wisconsin, Madison, USA*
Frederick D. Miller, *New York University, USA*
Serge Moscovici, *École des Hautes Études en Sciences Sociales, Paris, France*
Jane S. Mouton, *Scientific Methods, Inc., Austin, Texas, USA*
William Moyer, *Movement for a New Society, Philadelphia, USA*
Tom Murton
Thich Nhat Hanh, *Les Patates Douces, Estissac, France*
Jozef M. Nuttin, Jr., *Universiteit te Leuven, Belgium*
Steven Penrod, *University of Wisconsin, USA*
Dean G. Pruitt, *State University of New York at Buffalo, USA*
Jaap M. Rabbie, *Rijksuniversiteit, Utrecht, Netherlands*
Rosemary Randall, *Milton Keynes, Buckinghamshire, England*
John Rowan, *Independent Consultant, London, England*
Sheila Rowbotham, *London, England*
Seymour B. Sarason, *Yale University, USA*
Marshall Sashkin, *University of Maryland, USA*
Davis R. Schmitt, *University of Washington, USA*
Yaacov Schul, *University of Michigan, USA*
Will Schutz, *Muir Beach, California, USA*
Joseph Shepher, *University of Haifa, Israel*
Lynne Shivers, *Movement for a New Society, Philadelphia, USA*
Gerald H. Shure, *University of California, Los Angeles, USA*
John Southgate, *Polytechnic of North London, England*
R. Timothy Stein, *A. T. Kearney, Inc., Chicago, USA*
Ivan D. Steiner, *University of Massachusetts, Amherst, Massachusetts, USA*
Richard Taylor, *Movement for a New Society, Philadelphia, USA*
John W. Thibaut, *University of North Carolina at Chapel Hill, USA*
Lionel Tiger, *Harry F. Guggenheim Foundation, New York City, USA*
R. Scott Tindale, *University of Illinois, USA*
Uhuru Collective, Oxford, England
Jacobo A. Varela, *Montevideo, Uruguay*
Alvin F. Zander, *University of Michigan, USA*

Contents

ix

Preface

Most of the papers in this work have been specially prepared. When we set out to edit a new revision of *Small Groups*, it quickly became clear that there has been so much major material since the mid-1960s that it would be best to let the 1965 revision—edited by Hare, Borgatta, and Bales—stand as a collection of main work up to that time and to compile a new work, with virtually no overlap of actual content. After preparing a 'draft anthology' as described below, we invited the represented authors to contribute new papers, consolidating their present perspectives. It is these new papers that constitute the bulk of the present volumes. In some cases, though, we have simply reprinted existing work from journals and books.

As was true even for the 1965 edition, probably most of the articles have to do with social interaction in general or with the individual in a social situation, rather than being limited to the small group. However, the results are all applicable to the analysis of behaviour in small groups.

For an overview and extensive bibliography, readers might like to refer to Hare's (1976) *Handbook of Small Group Research*. To identify current works in this field, one could also use the sources from our own search, described below. For example, one could look under 'small groups' (and, for longer lists, 'social psychology' and the other headings described by Blumberg, 1977) in the *Subject Guide to Books in Print* and (for longer lists) the other sources noted in (d), below, plus the Library of Congress cumulative subject catalogues. See also the *Annual Review of Psychology*, for example, the chapters on intergroup relations and group research in Volume 33 (1982).

The present work was planned, in its initial stages, by Paul Hare and Herbert Blumberg, who were then joined by Valerie Kent and Martin Davies. All major decisions have been made jointly. The primary responsibilities for selecting and editing were as follows: Volume 1—Part I, MD; Parts II and III, VK (Chapters 7 and 8, MD); Volume 2—Parts I and II, HB; and Part III, VK and APH.

In proposing selections for the present work, we have used various criteria and carried out a number of searches. We have tried to give coverage to the entire field—including major developments and areas that have 'remained active'—since the early 1960s. (However, social behaviour among non-human primates is among topics not dealt with here—see, for example, Chalmers, 1979.) We have tried for a reasonable mix (both within and among papers) of theory, review, empirical studies, and applications. In preparing shortlists of authors, papers, and topics, we paid special attention to a number of sources, some of which were: (a) authors and specific items heavily cited in any two of the following three—Hare (1976), relevant topics in Middlebrook (1980) (a particularly recent and comprehensive text), and the 1978 *Social Sciences Citation Index* (for this set of names, the results would not have been substantially different if, for example, the 1980 SSCI or the 1971–75 SSCI 5-year cumulation had been used instead of 1978)—to look at particularly 'seminal' work; (b) 1977–79 *Psychological Abstracts* to 'update' the searches; (c) about 15 key journals, especially 1979, plus various convention programmes, also for 'updating'; (d) scan of all books on social psychology (and selected other topics) in various reference libraries and bookshops, and of listings in the *Subject Guide to Books in Print, Subject Guide to Forthcoming Books*, and *British National Bibliography*; (e) work cited in Blumberg (1976 and also 1977—works which were themselves compiled on the basis of various literature searches); and (f) a variety of personal recommendations and miscellaneous notices, etc. (Also, in retrospect, virtually all of the names heavily cited by Wrightsman and Deaux, 1981, came to notice in the course of the foregoing search.) We have wanted to include a variety of approaches, even though we do not necessarily agree with all of them.

On the basis of these various searches we compiled a 'draft anthology' and where possible, as noted above, invited the represented authors to contribute new or specially revised selections for the current book. As some other editors once said of a work, 'We are happier about what is included than about what is left out.' It might have been easier to edit two works than one.

The overall organization of this work roughly follows the simple rationale of progressively 'bringing more things on stage,' starting with the physical space (Volume 1, Chapter 1), then the backgrounds and personalities that people bring with them (Chapter 2), and members' impressions of the group and the fact of being part of it (Chapter 3). Part II deals with influence: the mere presence of other people (Chapter 4), effects of interacting with them (Chapter 5) and, especially, positive and negative interaction (Chapter 6) and the formation of close relationships (Chapter 7). Part III focuses on social interaction itself and broad differences among groups (Chapter 8); social interaction often shows specialization into roles (Chapter 9), and particular attention may be devoted to 'leadership' roles (Chapter 10). In Volume 2, complex processes are dealt with explicitly in Part I: group decision making (Chapter 1) plus a special focus on cooperation and conflict resolution (Chapter 2) and on interpersonal negotiations treated in a systematic quantified way (Chapter 3). By this point, complete, functioning groups are now 'on stage.' In Part II some general concerns of this book are explicitly highlighted: personal growth (Chapter 4), living together in harmony (Chapter 5) and social action and change (Chapter 6)—as these emerge from, or are manifest in, experience in small groups. Various theoretical approaches comprise Part III. We were not sure whether to place these at the beginning or end of the volumes (or perhaps between the lines of the other sections!), since a knowledge of theory would be helpful in understanding the other parts and vice versa. Since most of the selections in the volumes could in any event be read independently—and many refer to various theoretical orientations—readers may wish to cover Part III after they have read some but not all of the other parts.

References

Blumberg, H. H. (1976). 'Group processes,' in H. J. Eysenck and G. D. Wilson (eds.), *A Textbook of Human Psychology*, ch. 13, MTP, Lancaster, Lancashire.

Blumberg, H. H. (1977). 'Bibliographic guide,' in A. P. Hare and H. H. Blumberg (eds.), *Liberation without Violence: A Third Party Approach*, pp. 288–341, Rex Collings, London.

Chalmers, N. (1979). *Social Behaviour in Primates*, Edward Arnold, London.

Hare, A. P. (1976). *Handbook of Small Group Research*, Second Edition, Free Press/Collier-Macmillan, New York and London.

Hare, A. P., Borgatta, E. F., and Bales, R. F. (eds.) (1965). *Small Groups: Studies in Social Interaction*, Revised Edition, Knopf, New York.

Middlebrook, P. N. (1980). *Social Psychology and Modern Life*, Second Edition, Knopf, New York.

Wrightsman, L., and Deaux, K. (1981). *Social Psychology in the 80s*, Third Edition, Brooks/Cole, Monterey, CA.

Part I
Processes

Introduction

In Chapter 1 the general question of group decision making is reviewed. Tindale and Davis (sub-Chapter 1.1) draw on examples from research on 'jury' verdicts. The conditions which facilitate or hinder high-quality decisions in policy-planning groups—sometimes with major international ramifications—are described in Janis's paper (sub-Chapter 1.2) 'Groupthink.' Penrod (sub-Chapter 1.3) provides a review of models of jury decision making. Readers with limited training in mathematics may find this a difficult paper in places (the same is true of portions of the paper by Tindale and Davis). However, both the method and the content are of interest; some background references are provided; and the paper is clear and succinct. Lastly, how do individuals in groups come to modify their opinions? Burnstein and Schul (sub-Chapter 1.4) describe 'group polarization' or choice shift, formerly viewed as 'risky shift.'

The papers in Chapter 2 focus on a representative significant topic, cooperation and conflict resolution. Deutsch (sub-Chapter 2.1) describes a versatile game for exploring experimentally the likelihood that, for example, various strategies will elicit cooperative behaviour. Schmitt and Marwell (sub-Chapter 2.2) use a different procedure to investigate the effects of risk and inequity. An absorbing tale of the 'commons dilemma'—with urgent implications—is told by Edney (sub-Chapter 2.3), who goes on to cover research on problem solving in groups having a scarce pool of resources (cf. 'social traps'). Lindskold (sub-Chapter 2.4) contrasts intergroup and interindividual conflict resolution. 'The conflict grid' by Blake and Mouton (sub-Chapter 2.5) provides a straightforward scheme for integrating and comparing various ways of managing conflict.

Perhaps it is worth noting here that Lindskold bases his approach on Osgood's 'GRIT' strategy—Graduated and Reciprocated Initiatives in Tension reduction. Osgood (1981) believes more strongly than ever that a most urgent application of GRIT strategy is in the reduction of international tension. He feels that if humanity is to survive, disarmament—especially nuclear disarmament—is essential, as is a much strengthened United Nations. He adds that, as far as is now known, reactors for nuclear-powered energy also need to be curtailed, for their waste products are very dangerous and need to be kept separate from the rest of the world's ecological systems essentially forever. (For small-group and general procedures toward social change, see also Chapters 5 and 6 in this book.)

The introductory paragraphs in Pruitt's paper (sub-Chapter 3.1) cover the rationale for the whole of Chapter 3 (games, bargaining, and coalitions), and the body of the paper deals particularly with matrix games and also with negotiation. Separate reviews of experiments in explicit bargaining and in coalition formation are provided, respectively, by Chertkoff and Esser (sub-Chapter 3.3) and by Komorita and Kravitz (sub-Chapter 3.5). Two detailed examples 'complete' the chapter. McClintock and Keil (sub-Chapter 3.2) describe the developmental study of social values—using matrix games. And Shure *et al.* (sub-Chapter 3.4) carried out a comparative study of bargaining. These are both 'double papers', dealing partly with content and partly with developmental and/or comparative methods.

Additional reading

In addition to the works represented or cited in these chapters (and general sources such as those indicated in the Preface), some further items which readers may wish to consult are as follows. *Chapter 1*: Gerbasi *et al.* (1977), Lieberman (1971), Maple (1977), and Petrovskii (1976). Also, in connection with simulation and other modeling: Hart and Sung (1976), Kempf and Repp (1977), Mayer (1975), Raser (1978), and Shane (1979). *Chapter 2*: Boulding (1978), Brehmer (1976), Bryan (1975), Burton (1979), Cohen *et al.* (1977), Curtis *et al.* (1979) (a self-teaching guide), Helm *et al.* (1979), Houlden *et al.* (1978), Isard and Smith (1982); Levi and Benjamin (1977), Likert and Likert (1976), Lind *et al.* (1978), McCarthy (1977), Miller and Simons (1974), Oltman *et al.* (1975), Reychler (1979), Sharan *et al.* (1980) (cf. Aronson and Yates in Volume 1, sub-Chapter 3.3, and Gibson, cited in the introduction to Part II, below), Smith (1971), Tolor (1970), and Wilkinson (1976). *Chapter 3*: Grzelak (1976), Ingram and Berger (1977), Ofshe and Ofshe (1970), Orbell and Wilson (1978), Wagner (1979), and Walcott and Hopmann (1978).

References

Boulding, K. E. (1978). 'Future directions in conflict and peace studies,' *Journal of Conflict Resolution*, **22**, 342–354.

Brehmer, B. (1976). 'Social judgment theory and the analysis of interpersonal conflict,' *Psychological Bulletin*, **83**, 985–1003.

Bryan, J. H. (1975). 'Children's cooperation and helping behaviors,' in E. M. Hetherington (ed.), *Review of Child Development Research*, Vol. 5, pp. 127–181, University of Chicago Press, Chicago.

Burton, John. (1979). *Deviance, Terrorism and War; The Process of Solving Unsolved Social and Political Problems*, Martin Robertson, Oxford.

Cohen, S. P., Kelman, H. C., Miller, F. D., and Smith, B. L. (1977). 'Evolving intergroup techniques for conflict resolution: an Israeli–Palestinian pilot workshop,' *Journal of Social Issues*, **33** (1), 165–189.

Curtis, D. B., Mazza, J. M., and Runnebohm, S. (1979). *Communication for Problem-Solving*, Wiley, New York.

Gerbasi, K. C., Zuckerman, M., and Reis, H. T. (1977). 'Justice needs a new blindfold: a review of mock jury research,' *Psychological Bulletin*, **84**, 323–45.

Grzelak, J. (1976). 'Game theory and its applicability to the description of prosocial behavior,' *Polish Psychological Bulletin*, **7**, 197–205.

Hart, E. W., and Sung, Y. H. (1976). 'Systems simulation; computer and experimental simulation of triad decision making,' *Behavioral Science*, **21**, 532–47.

Helm, B., Constable, M. A., and Rivers, W. J. (December 1979). 'Interpersonal dispute resolution: the role of social psychology,' *SASP Newsletter* (Society for the Advancement of Social Psychology), **5** (6), 18–20.

Houlden, P., LaTour, S., Walker, L., and Thibaut, J. (1978). 'Preference for modes of dispute resolution as a function of process and decision control,' *Journal of Experimental Social Psychology*, **14**, 13–30.

Ingram, B. L., and Berger, S. E. (1977). 'Sex-role orientation, defensiveness, and competitiveness in women,' *Journal of Conflict Resolution*, **21**, 501–18.

Isard, W., and Smith, C. (1982). *Conflict Analysis and Practical Conflict Management: An Introduction to Peace Studies*, Ballinger, Cambridge, MA.

Kempf, W. F., and Repp, B. H. (eds.) (1977). *Mathematical Models for Social Psychology*, Wiley, Chichester.

Levi, A. M., and Benjamin, A. (1977). 'Focus and flexibility in a model of conflict resolution,' *Journal of Conflict Resolution*, **21**, 405–425.

Lieberman, B. (ed.) (1971). *Social Choice*, Gordon and Breach, New York.

Likert, R., and Likert, J. G. (1976). *New Ways of Managing Conflict*, McGraw-Hill, New York.

Lind, E. A., Erickson, B. E., Friedland, N., and Dickenberger, M. (1978). 'Reactions to procedural models for adjudicative conflict resolution,' *Journal of Conflict Resolution*, **22**, 318–341.

McCarthy, H. (1977). 'Some situational factors improving cognitive conflict reduction and interpersonal understanding,' *Journal of Conflict Resolution*, **21**, 217–234.

Maple, F. F. (1977). *Shared Decision Making*, Sage, Beverly Hills, Calif.

Mayer, T. F. (1975). *Mathematical Models of Group Structure*, Bobbs-Merrill, Indianapolis.

Miller, G. R., and Simons, H. W. (eds.) (1974). *Perspectives on Communication in Social Conflict*, Prentice-Hall, Englewood Cliffs, NJ.

Ofshe, L., and Ofshe, R. (1970). *Utility and Choice in Social Interaction*, Prentice-Hall, Englewood Cliffs, NJ.

Oltman, P. K., Goodenough, D. R., Witkin, H. A., Freedman, N., and Friedman, F. (1975). 'Psychological differentiation as a factor in conflict resolution,' *Journal of Personality and Social Psychology*, **32**, 730–36.

Orbell, J. M., and Wilson, L. A. (1978). 'Institutional solutions to the N-prisoners' dilemma,' *American Political Science Review*, **72**, 411–21.

Osgood, C. E. (1981). 'Psycho-social dynamics, "GRIT" strategy and the prospects for mankind,' Paper at the Annual Meeting of the American Psychological Association.

Petrovskii, A. V. (1976). ['On some phenomena of interpersonal relations in a collective'], *Voprosy Psikhologii*, No. 3, 16–25. *Psychological Abstracts*, **60**, 3046.

Raser, J. R. (1978). 'Simulating social systems: philosophical and methodological considerations, in R. T. Golembiewski (ed.), *The Small Group in Political Science: the Last Two Decades of Development*, pp. 282–302, University of Georgia Press, Athens, Ga.

Reychler, L. (1979). 'The effectiveness of a pacifist strategy in conflict resolution,' *Journal of Conflict Resolution*, **23**, 228–260.

Shane, B. (1979). 'Open and rigid communication networks; a reevaluation by simulation,' *Small Group Behavior*, **10**, 242–262.

Sharan, S., *et al.* (eds.) (1980). *Cooperation in Education*: . . . , Brigham Young University Press, Provo, Utah.

Smith, C. G. (ed.) (1971). *Conflict Resolution*, University of Notre Dame Press, Notre Dame, Indiana.

Tolor, A. (1970). 'The "natural course" view of conflict resolution,' *Psychological Reports*, **26**, 734.

Wagner, R. H. (1979). 'On the unification of two-person bargaining theory,' *Journal of Conflict Resolution*, **23**, 71–101.

Walcott, C., and Hopmann, P. T. (1978). 'Interaction analysis and bargaining behavior,' in R. T. Golembiewski (ed.), *The Small Group in Political Science: The Last Two Decades of Development*, pp. 251–258, University of Georgia Press, Athens, Ga.

Wilkinson, D. (1976). *Cohesion and Conflict: Lessons from the Study of Three-Party Interaction*, Pinter (for Richardson Institute), London.

Reference note

The reader may wish to consult the following papers in other parts of Volumes 1 and 2 which seem particularly relevant to the chapters in Part 1 of this volume:

Chapter 1. See Volume 1: Nemeth (2.2), Moscovici and Paicheler (5.4).
            See Volume 2: Hoffman and Stein (7.5).
Chapter 2. See Volume 1: Tajfel (3.2), Aronson and Yates (3.3), the whole of Chapter 6.
            See Volume 2: The whole of Chapters 5 and 6, Hatfield (7.2), Harrison and McCallum (7.3).
Chapter 3. See Volume 2: Harrison and McCallum (7.3).

1 Group Decision Making and Choice Shift

Small Groups and Social Interaction, Volume 2
Edited by H. H. Blumberg, A. P. Hare, V. Kent and M. Davies
© 1983 John Wiley & Sons Ltd

1.1 Group Decision Making and Jury Verdicts

R. Scott Tindale, and James H. Davis   *University of Illinois*

Introduction

The important role most societies have accorded small group problem solving and decision making has been especially marked when fundamental or socially significant issues were involved. Corporate boards, cabinets, advisory councils, planning commissions, school boards, etc., are all central to the functioning of the various organizations and institutions in which they exist, and often wield substantial power. Such confidence in small groups may be partly due to political factors such as the representation of constituency interests or the balancing of divergent opinions. However, other reasons for their popularity have to do with assumptions about effective performance.

Until recent years, there has been little evidence to support or refute faith in the superiority of small groups, although a number of intuitive arguments can be generated to support such a notion. Most people have probably observed that a given individual may not be able to solve all problems correctly, may have certain biases concerning specific topics, and may hold rather extreme positions on at least some issues. However, small groups may be perceived as minimizing such problems. Besides mutual error checking, the apparently greater information storage processing, and retrieval capacities attributable to groups would seem to increase the probability of their coming to optimal solutions or decisions. Moreover, consensus pressures should moderate extreme positions on a given issue, producing group outcomes more cautious than positions of individuals. The desirability of group action seems quite salient in democratic societies, where judgments and decisions made by several, rather than one, are seen as especially fair and equitable.

Even though the rationale for the above assumptions seemed intuitively plausible for a long time, such conventional wisdom was eventually questioned in light of subsequent empirical evidence. A wide variety of such common-sense 'intuitions' have now been qualified and it is perhaps instructive to focus on two such incidents (one in the area of group problem solving and the other related to group risk taking) as particularly excellent examples. Prior to the mid-1950s, it was widely held that, on the average, *ad hoc* groups were better problem solvers than individuals working alone. One of the major sources of support for these notions was the classic study by Shaw (1932) in which interacting groups and isolated individuals worked on a variety of word puzzles. Her results showed that a higher percentage of groups solved the problems than did individuals. These findings were on the face of it consistent with the results of later studies on 'brainstorming' (Osborn, 1953; Parnes and Meadow, 1959), where groups were said to produce more and better ideas than individuals.

However, Taylor (1954) and Lorge and Solomon (1955), proposed models that lacked group facilitation assumptions, but which yielded predictions at or *above* the level of group task performance actually observed—results counter to prevailing intuition. In fact, such models, later referred to as 'truth wins' models (Steiner, 1966, 1972), assume that group interaction has no effect on the probability of an individual achieving a correct solution; members act independently. The chief assumption of a 'truth wins' model is that the group solves if at least one individual solves. Consequently, this model can be seen as defining one kind of a baseline for optimal group performance.

More recent research on group problem solving has shown that groups typically do not attain the 'truth wins' optimal level of performance (Davis, 1969a,b). Thus, it would seem that small groups under such conditions may not even be as proficient as their best member. Failures of task-oriented groups to perform optimally have been taken by Steiner (1972) to define losses due to faulty social processes. Restle and Davis (1962) formulated a general stochastic model of group problem solving to account for process losses in groups. Two extreme forms were: (a) The Equalitarian Model that assumed members took their proportionate share of the group's working time, whether or not they were on the right track; and (b) the Hierarchical Model that assumed only those members on the right track consumed any of the group's work time. Restle and Davis originally assumed that the Equalitarian Model would be more or less a lower bound, yet when compared to the data, this model could be retained as an accurate description of the social solution process, while the Hierarchical Model could be confidently rejected (Davis and Restle, 1963; Davis, 1969b). Results such as these do not demonstrate that individuals are better problem solvers than groups, but they do tend to refute the overall superiority routinely attributed to groups prior to the mid-1950s.

Another plausible intuition underlying the importance attributed to groups, has been that groups will tend to counter the influence of extreme individuals, thus producing relatively moderate decisions, more prudent positions, etc. However, an immense body of research over the past two decades has shown that group moderation is not necessarily the outcome. In the seminal study by Stoner (1961), groups tended, on the average, to endorse response alternatives regarded as riskier choices than did individuals acting alone. Originally called the 'risky shift,' the effect is now more commonly labeled 'choice shift' since groups have also been observed to shift toward caution, depending on the particular task scenario. Subsequently demonstrated in a variety of different settings and cultures, the choice shift is one of the more robust findings in small group research (for reviews, see Dion *et al.*, 1970; Davis *et al.*, 1976a). Even though various criticisms concerning experimental design and procedure have arisen, the basic counterintuitive finding is empirically well established: groups in at least some situations will make more extreme decisions, on the average, than individuals responding privately.

The foregoing discussion stresses that research findings concerning small group performance have not always been consistent with conventional wisdom and popular beliefs. Such findings demonstrate the need for research on topics, practices, policies, etc., that are usually governed by widely-shared and long-accepted assumptions about human social behavior. Moreover, proposals for or against important institutional changes might usefully be evaluated, at least in part, against some form of empirical data. The US criminal justice system, in particular the jury, is one such significant institutional system and will be the major focus of this paper.

The jury

The citizen jury is probably held in higher esteem, yet surrounded by more con-- troversy, than any other small decision-making group. It has been an important cornerstone for administering justice in the United Kingdom and in the United States, although the precise nature of its role has been changing in recent years. A number of countries have drastically altered the way in which juries are used (e.g. France), abandoned them altogether (e.g. India), or declined to use them at all (e.g. Israel). However, the jury in the United States criminal justice system is still held in high regard by the citizenry and large controversies have surrounded a variety of proposals aimed at reducing its importance or restricting its function.

Recent increases in research activity addressing law and justice matters have tended to develop two avenues. Research applying such notions as equity theory (Walster and Walster, 1975) or the 'just world' hypothesis (Lerner, 1965; Rubin and Peplau, 1975) to the concept of justice has been focused on the way in which rewards and consequences are distributed or apportioned. This line of research has thus been focused on questions of distributive justice in that the actual or perceived distribution of just outcomes is in question. The other body of research has been directed at the technical or procedural aspects of the justice system. Much of the work in this area was stimulated by legislation and Supreme Court decisions concerning such things as representativeness of jury pools, juror selection procedures, reliability of eyewitness testimony, and numerous other research topics (see Shoben, 1977, 1978 and Van Dyke, 1977, for illustrative discussions). A particularly good example comes from the Supreme Court decisions (*Apodaca et al.* v. *Oregon*, 1972; *Ballew* v. *Georgia*, 1978; *Johnson* v. *Louisiana*, 1972; and *Williams* v. *Florida*, 1970) which essentially relaxed the permissible jury size from 12 to as few as 6, and the assigned decision rule from a unanimous verdict to a two-thirds majority. The effects of these procedural changes were basically unknown at the time most of the decisions were rendered; the apparent assumption of the Court that changes in size and decision rule would not affect the administration of justice was based primarily on conventional wisdom rather than on empirical evidence.[1] Given the counterintuitive nature of research findings associated with group performance we discussed earlier, the implications of such procedural changes may be far different from those routinely expected.

Unfortunately, the empirical evidence required in order to make informed social policy decisions of this kind is in many cases extremely difficult if not impossible to obtain by direct observation. Jury deliberations are conducted in total privacy, and for good reason. Most people would agree that allowing observers into a deliberation room would undoubtedly hamper the jury's ability to come to an unbiased and just verdict. Yet, this necessary privacy obviously precludes obtaining direct empirical data on the processes involved in jury decision making. Of course, many small groups other than juries are equally resistant to *in situ* study. Corporate boards, tenure committees and the like are seldom, if ever, open to the public for practical as well as ethical reasons. These same considerations rule out the direct manipulation of relevant variables, such as group size and assigned decision rule, that would seem on the face of it to be the most straightforward research strategy for answering such questions.

In addition to the problems mentioned above, engineering institutional changes faces two serious handicaps which are not shared by the physical engineer. First, physical engineers often construct small-scale functional models of complex systems in order to obtain information of sorts on the working system or structure. Social engineers, on the other hand, rarely have a suitable analogical model with which to work, and those they might construct are usually far removed from the actual entity of interest. Second, the physical sciences have established a fairly strong foundation of theory, an important aid to constructing relevant analytical models for special cases of interest. Such theoretical models permit one at least to draw some implications for instances poorly documented by empirical data, and to 'run through' changes prior to implementing them. Unfortunately, in many situations, the theoretical base necessary for tests pertaining to social policy change has not yet been developed. Although some theory does exist, little is applicable to the types of social questions at issue here. (Exceptions are discussed below.) Such problems are not unique to research on procedural justice, but they are highly salient when dealing with such a sensitive area.

However, three strategies have proved useful for addressing questions of jury performance. The first, typified by the pioneering work of Kalven and Zeisel (1966), has been to gather data about juries through indirect methods, such as interviewing ex-jurors or reviewing court records. A second method has used the field/laboratory experiment, either as simulation or demonstration of possibilities. 'Mock juries' are composed and studied in simulated trial settings (e.g. Davis *et al.*, 1975; Davis *et al.*, 1981a). Some of these studies take place in actual courtrooms (Diamond and Zeisel, 1974), use subjects from actual jury rolls (Crossen, 1967), and otherwise attempt various degrees of verisimilitude short of intervening in an actual trial. The third strategy makes use of the general theoretical and empirical work in the area of small group performance to set up 'thought experiments' (Davis, 1980), whether as formal analytical models or as computer simulations, to obtain some notion of jury behavior under various conditions—especially those largely inaccessible and remote from inspection of any sort. Although each of these strategies has its own problems, it seems fair to conclude that, taken as a whole, they have provided a variety of useful insights into jury performance.

Mock juries have constituted the most popular research strategy (see Davis *et al.*, 1977a, for a more thorough discussion of this topic). Cost and ease of implementation are especially prominent among the several reasons why mock jury research has predominated. Interestingly enough, most studies of small group performance have used *ad hoc* groups, and the lack of a temporal dimension (no history of mutual experiences or prospects of future association) has often seemed at variance with important societal analogs. Yet, there also exist a great many decision-making bodies in which the only common bond among the members is the specific task at hand, and the group as a whole has no past or future. The jury is an important example of such a group. The individual members have no interpersonal relationships with each other at the outset, and usually have none at the termination of service. These same characteristics typify the *ad hoc* groups used in most laboratory research. Members are assembled at random and have had little or no contact prior to the experiment. These individuals then interact as a group only for the duration of the experiment, and are again dispersed with no commitments for future interaction. The positive consequences of this similarity between *ad hoc* experimental groups and juries are thus realized for two purposes. Since mock juries by definition have many of the same qualities as real juries, they provide a good medium for addressing procedural justice questions (at least in the sense of 'demonstration'). Moreover, since most experimental subjects have a moderate knowledge of how a jury is supposed to function, the jury paradigm provides an excellent setting in which more basic questions concerning small group processes in general can be assessed.

Again, mock jury research is not without difficulties, some as serious as those facing other methods. Although real and mock juries may share some characteristics in common, they are also quite different. At the most basic level, a population made up largely of undergraduates is not much like the typical jury pool (the subjects are on the average younger, better educated, less mature, more intelligent, and so on). At a more process-oriented level, the consequences of a decision made by a real jury are obviously of greater moment than those associated with a mock jury. Thus, the seriousness with which the task is undertaken and perhaps a number of social attitudes as well are not closely comparable.

On the other hand, mock jury studies do not usually reach the level of control necessary for a careful, internally consistent, laboratory experiment. In fact, increasing restrictions (experimental controls) placed on such things as trial evidence, length of discussion time, and the like, actually decrease the generalizability of results obtained from mock jury research. Thus, most mock jury studies attempt to control or manipulate only a few variables of particular interest by way of a compromise in aims. Such studies are perhaps more demonstrations than experiments, and provide less precise, but more general, information about the processes involved in jury decision making.

However, even as demonstrations mock jury studies are limited due to extreme costs in subjects, time, and materials. Thus, there is a strong need in this, as in many other areas of social research with a potential for application, to extrapolate from existing empirical evidence to areas which cannot be studied empirically. It is for just such extrapolation (or interpolation between data sets) that computer simulations or thought experiments (Davis, 1980) are most useful. The idea is to explore both theoretical notions and empirical implications in areas where data collection is either severely limited or functionally impossible.

The remaining portions of this sub-chapter will be a discussion of research, using both laboratory and simulation techniques to address problems in jury behavior as well as small group performance in general. The section immediately following presents an outline of the theory of social decision schemes (Davis, 1973) which provided the structure for the studies discussed later. The remaining sections will be devoted to describing some of the research associated with this theory and various implications derived from the results. A final section will also discuss some 'side benefits' to be realized from a programmatic approach and some interesting implications related to one such set of studies.

Social decision scheme theory[2]

When a set of individuals decides on some course of action, the social consensus may follow some sort of decision rule that is explicitly stated, informally understood, or even an inadvertent consequence of discussion. In some cases, as in an army unit, one person makes a decision and the others obey. In many other situations, such as many city councils, legislative bodies, committees of various sorts, a majority rule of some order (simple, two-thirds, and four-fifths, majority are examples) applies. For juries, unanimity is required in most cases by law; every juror must agree on the same verdict alternative (e.g. guilty or not guilty in a criminal case) before that alternative is accepted. The unanimity rule as it relates to juries is an explicit decision rule, in that there is formal statutory provision for its exercise. However, the process by which groups decide on an alternative may be summarizable in somewhat different form than the explicit decision rule. For instance, even though a jury must unanimously agree on a verdict, the route to that level of consensus from initial disagreement may be the interesting issue. Such a social decision process might effectively be due to a simple majority or some other order of majority, yet all jurors agree (concur) concerning the jury's verdict. In groups where there is more than one alternative (e.g. civil litigation) very complex social decision rules, perhaps involving various types of compromise, might be required to describe the social decision process. It is also possible that a 'second order' or contingency decision rule goes into effect when the main decision rule cannot be achieved. For example, if a majority could not be reached by a given group, it may be equally likely that any alternative advocated by at least one member is subsequently chosen. Such a decision rule could be labeled as simple majority wins, equiprobability otherwise.

The ideas presented above form the conceptual basis for social decision scheme theory (Davis, 1973). In essence, the theory provides for models, or social decision schemes, which map members' preferences into a group response. In the general case, let us imagine that an individual decision maker must select one of n mutually exclusive and exhaustive response alternatives, $A_j, j = 1, 2, 3, \ldots, n$. We assume that individual decisions are characterized by a discrete probability distribution, $p = (p_1, p_2, \ldots, p_n)$, over the A_j alternatives, and similarly for groups, $P = (P_1, P_2, \ldots, P_{n'})$. Observe, however, that in some situations (e.g. jury decisions) $n \neq n'$, in that the number of response outcomes defined for groups, $n' = 3$, (i.e. guilty, not guilty, hung) may differ from the number, $n = 2$, defined for individuals (i.e. guilty or not guilty).

Prior to discussion, the r individual group members may array themselves over the n response alternatives in

$$m = \binom{n + r - 1}{r} \tag{1}$$

different ways. For example, guilt preferences in a six-person jury may at the outset be distributed over the two possible alternatives (guilty, not guilty) in seven different ways, i.e. $(6, 0), (5, 1), \ldots, (0, 6)$. Such an array will be referred to as a distinguishable distribution, where response alternatives but not individual people are distinguishable. The probability, π_i of the ith distribution, $i = 1, 2, \ldots, m$, of member preferences occurring may be estimated in two different ways. Some applications allow for a direct estimate by counting the relative frequency, $\hat{\pi}_i$, with which the ith distribution is observed to occur (e.g. inspecting predeliberation ballots). In other cases, π_i, must be estimated indirectly using the multinomial distribution,

$$\pi_i = \begin{pmatrix} r \\ r_1, r_2, \ldots, r_n \end{pmatrix} p_1^{r_1} p_2^{r_2} \ldots p_n^{r_n} \tag{2}$$

and substituting appropriately the observed relative frequencies, $(\hat{p}_1, \hat{p}_2, \ldots, \hat{p}_n)$ observed for a sample of individual decisions. In the two alternative case, this distribution collapses to the more familiar binomial distribution.

Given a particular distribution of opinions in a group, the relevant problem is to ascertain the probability that the group will choose a given alternative. This process is obviously a function of the social interaction as well as various prescribed rules or laws governing the particular group. Although the process is probably rather complex, it can be given an explicit summary form by defining the conditional probability, d_{ij}, of the group choosing the jth response alternative given the ith distinguishable distribution. The general statement of the theoretical relation between the initial preference distribution and the final group outcome may be cast as a $m \times n'$ stochastic matrix, D, called a social decision scheme matrix. (Some examples of social decision scheme matrices for 6- and 12-person groups are presented in Table 1.)

The D matrices presented in Table 1 are defined in two parts: (1) a primary scheme which predicts the group outcome under certain conditions; and (2) one or more subschemes, which predict group outcomes when the conditions specified by the primary scheme do not hold. For example, D_7 in Table 1 is defined as two-thirds majority prevails, hung otherwise. The primary scheme specified that whenever a two-thirds majority exists, the alternative favored by that majority will be chosen with probability very near 1.0. If, however, a two-thirds majority does not exist, the subscheme predicts that the group will not come to a decision. (In popular terms, the jury is hung.)

Given the social decision scheme matrix, D, the group probability distribution, $P = (P_1, P_2, \ldots, P_n)$, is obtained from

$$P = \pi D \tag{3}$$

where $\pi = (\pi_1, \pi_2, \ldots, \pi_m)$. This model can be used in two different ways in relation to research on small groups. First, group outcomes predicted by social decision schemes, D, given *a priori* definitions, like those presented in Table 1, may be tested against empirical outcome distributions obtained from performing groups. Thus, a variety of initially plausible models can be tested against a data set. A second approach emphasizes the estimation of the entries $[d_{ij}]$ from empirical data. Such an estimate, $\hat{D}$, may be regarded as a description of the social decision processes within the groups from which it was estimated. Of course, inferred social decision schemes may themselves be valuable descriptions, but they may also be tested against data sets from other experiments or demonstrations in order to assess their generality. (For a more detailed and comprehensive discussion of model testing comparing *a priori* predictions against data and model fitting

Table 1 Selected examples of social decision scheme matrices for 12- and 6-person juries, showing the probability, d_{ij}, of the jth verdict given the ith distribution of member preferences

Distribution of jurors		Verdict distribution														
		D_1			D_3			D_4			D_7			D_8		
G	NG	G	NG	H	G	NG	H	G	NG	H	G	NG	H	G	NG	H
12	0	1.0	0	0	1.0	0	0	1.0	0	0	1	0	0	1	0	0
11	1	1.0	0	0	1.0	0	0	1.0	0	0	1	0	0	1	0	0
10	2	1.0	0	0	1.0	0	0	1.0	0	0	1	0	0	1	0	0
9	3	0	0	1.0	.75	.13	.13	.75	.13	.13	1	0	0	0	1	0
8	4	0	0	1.0	.67	.17	.17	.67	.17	.17	1	0	0	0	1	0
7	5	0	0	1.0	.58	.21	.21	.58	.21	.21	0	0	1	0	1	0
6	6	0	0	1.0	.50	.25	.25	0	0	1.0	0	0	1	0	1	0
5	7	0	0	1.0	.21	.58	.21	0	0	1.0	0	0	1	0	1	0
4	8	0	0	1.0	.17	.67	.17	0	0	1.0	0	1	0	0	1	0
3	9	0	0	1.0	.13	.75	.13	0	0	1.0	0	1	0	0	1	0
2	10	0	1.0	0	0	1.0	0	0	1.0	0	0	1	0	0	1	0
1	11	0	1.0	0	0	1.0	0	0	1.0	0	0	1	0	0	1	0
0	12	0	1.0	0	0	1.0	0	0	1.0	0	0	1	0	0	1	0

continued

Table 1 *continued*

Verdict distribution

Distribution of jurors		D9			D10			D11			D16			D17		
G	NG	G	NG	H	G	NG	H	G	NG	H	G	NG	H	G	NG	H
12	0	1	0	0	1.0	0	0	1.0	0	0	1	0	0	1	0	0
11	1	0	0	1	1.0	0	0	1.0	0	0	1.0	0	0	1	0	0
10	2	0	0	1	1.0	0	0	1.0	0	0	1	0	0	1	0	0
9	3	0	0	1	.75	.13	.13	0	0	1.0	1	0	0	1	0	0
8	4	0	0	1	.67	.17	.17	0	0	1.0	1	0	0	1	0	0
7	5	0	0	1	.58	.21	.21	0	0	1.0	1	0	0	1	0	0
6	6	0	1	0	.25	.50	.25	0	0	1.0	0	0	1	0	0	1
5	7	0	1	0	.21	.58	.21	0	0	1.0	0	1	0	0	0	1
4	8	0	1	0	.17	.67	.17	0	.67	.33	0	1	0	0	1	0
3	9	0	1	0	.13	.75	.13	0	.75	.25	0	1	0	0	1	0
2	10	0	1	0	0	1.0	0	0	1.0	0	0	1	0	0	1	0
1	11	0	1	0	0	1.0	0	0	1.0	0	0	1	0	0	1	0
0	12	0	1	0	0	1.0	0	0	1.0	0	0	1	0	0	1	0

Distribution of jurors		D1			D2			D3			D4			D6		
G	NG	G	NG	H	G	NG	H	G	NG	H	G	NG	H	G	NG	H
6	0	1.00	.00	.00	1.00	.00	.00	1.00	.00	.00	1.00	.00	.00	1.00	.00	.00
5	1	1.00	.00	.00	1.00	.00	.00	1.00	.00	.00	1.00	.00	.00	.50	.50	.00
4	2	.00	.00	1.00	.33	.33	.33	.67	.17	.17	.67	.17	.17	.50	.50	.00
3	3	.00	.00	1.00	.33	.33	.33	.50	.25	.25	.00	.00	1.00	.50	.50	.00
2	4	.00	.00	1.00	.33	.33	.33	.17	.67	.17	.00	.00	1.00	.50	.50	.00
1	5	.00	1.00	.00	.00	1.00	.00	.00	1.00	.00	.00	1.00	.00	.50	.50	.00
0	6	.00	1.00	.00	.00	1.00	.00	.00	1.00	.00	.00	1.00	.00	.00	1.00	.00

Split (G, N)	D_7 (G)	D_7 (H)	D_7 (N)	D_{12} (G)	D_{12} (H)	D_{12} (N)	D_{13} (G)	D_{13} (H)	D_{13} (N)	D_{14} (G)	D_{14} (H)	D_{14} (N)	D_{15} (G)	D_{15} (H)	D_{15} (N)
6 0	1.00	.00	.00	1.00	.00	.00	1.00	.00	.00	1.00	.00	.00	1.00	.00	.00
5 1	1.00	.00	.00	.83	.17	.00	1.00	.00	.00	1.00	.00	.00	1.00	.00	.00
4 2	1.00	.00	.00	.67	.33	.00	1.00	.00	.00	1.00	.00	.00	1.00	.00	.00
3 3	.00	1.00	.00	.33	.33	.33	.00	.50	.50	.50	.00	.50	.00	.25	.75
2 4	.00	.00	1.00	.00	.33	.67	.00	.00	1.00	.00	.00	1.00	.00	.00	1.00
1 5	.00	.00	1.00	.00	.17	.83	.00	.00	1.00	.00	.00	1.00	.00	.00	1.00
0 6	.00	.00	1.00	.00	.00	1.00	.00	.00	1.00	.00	.00	1.00	.00	.00	1.00

Note Some entries (d_{ij}) are given as .00 or 1.00 for convenience; the true corresponding parameter values should be regarded as very near but not equal to .00 or 1.00. The subscript, h, for D_h refers to an arbitrary catalogue as listed in Nagao (1978).

Notes

D_1: 5/6 majority, hung otherwise.
D_2: 5/6 majority, equiprobability otherwise.
D_3: 5/6 majority, otherwise proportionality and equiprobability mixture.
D_4: 5/6 majority, proportionality and hung otherwise mixture.
D_5: Equiprobability.
D_6: 2/3 (simple) majority, hung otherwise.
D_7: A not-guilty advocate supported 'wins.'
D_8: Unanimity for guilty, simple majority for not guilty, hung otherwise.
D_9: 5/6 majority, proportionality and equiprobability asymmetrical mixture.
D_{10}: 5/6 majority, hung-equiprobability mixture.
D_{11}: Proportionality-hung mixture, equiprobability otherwise.
D_{12}: 2/3 (simple) majority, equiprobability otherwise.
D_{13}: 2/3 (simple) majority, doubt and hung mixture otherwise.
D_{14}: 2/3 (simple) majority, otherwise guilty or not guilty with equiprobability.
D_{15}: 2/3 (simple) majority, defendant protection-hung otherwise mixture.
D_{16}: Simple majority, hung otherwise.
D_{17}: 2/3 majority for guilty, simple majority for not guilty, hung otherwise.

(estimating the most descriptive scheme from data), from the perspective of social decision scheme theory, see Kerr *et al.*, 1979.)

Jury size and assigned decision rule

As mentioned earlier, much of the recent research on questions of legal procedure has been stimulated by proposed changes in the current system. Two changes directed specifically at juries were the result of a number of Supreme Court rulings concerning the jury size and decision rule that may be allowed by legislation (e.g. *Williams* v. *Florida*, 1970; *Ballew* v. *Georgia*, 1978). Although a few investigations into these issues had been carried out prior to the Court decisions, the empirical results were inconsistent and difficult to interpret due to a variety of methodological problems (see Davis, 1980; Davis, *et al.*, 1977a; Ziesel and Diamond, 1974). However, none of the research had attempted to look at both size and decision rule in the same study. The importance of looking at both variables together stems from the fact that certain decision rules function differently or have different definitions for groups of various sizes. For example, even a simple majority rule will produce different outcomes depending on whether the number of group members is odd or even, since even-sized groups allow possibilities of a 'tie' (subgroups of equal numbers).

In order to assess the general implications of group size (6 or 12) in conjunction with social decision rule (two-thirds majority or unanimity), Davis *et al.* (1975) observed mock juries deliberating a verdict after viewing a reenactment of an actual rape trial (edited) recorded on videotape. Considerable effort was devoted to creating a courtroom trial atmosphere (e.g. courtroom settings, dress and comportment of participants, formality of proceedings, etc.). In this spirit, subjects first filled out a brief questionnaire containing items which might have been asked during *voir dire*, a formal pretrial examination of jurors to determine their suitability for service. Next, subjects watched the videotaped trial which included opening statements, examinations and cross-examinations of witnesses, final summations by both prosecution and defense attorneys, and the judge's instructions to the jury. Groups were then randomly composed of either 6 or 12 members, and moved into secluded rooms for deliberation. Prior to discussion, participants were asked to record privately their personal verdict preferences (guilty or not guilty), and then to estimate the probability of the defendant's actual guilt (given the evidence), using an 11 point scale.

Juries received two types of instructions. One set instructed juries to continue deliberations until a poll of the jury members indicated that at least two-thirds of them (4 in 6-person juries, 8 in 12-person juries) agreed on a verdict. The second set was the same as the first except all members were to agree in order to establish a verdict. Deliberations continued until a verdict was reached, or until 30 minutes had elapsed, at which time undecided juries were declared hung. Finally, the 'exjurors' were again asked to record privately their personal verdicts and probability-of-guilt judgments. A separate sample of subjects experienced the same sequence of events with the exception that these individuals paralleled the group condition, 'reflected' on the evidence, and did not interact.

The proportion of subjects who favored a guilty verdict prior to deliberations, $\hat{p}_G$, was .22, indicating a relatively strong, but not overwhelming sentiment for acquittal. Interestingly enough, none of the juries in any of the conditions rendered a guilty verdict, although 14% were declared hung. Another interesting finding was that the proportion of guilty, not guilty, and hung verdicts did not differ significantly due to either group size or assigned decision rule. However, juries assigned a unanimous decision rule took significantly longer on the average to reach verdicts than those assigned a two-thirds majority rule, consistent with the finding that a larger proportion of unanimity-assigned than two-thirds-majority-assigned juries 'hung' (.19 and .08 respectively).

Besides assessing empirically the effects of size and decision rule, the observed verdict distributions $(\hat{P}_G, \hat{P}_{NG}, \hat{P}_H)$ were compared with the distributions predicted by various social decision scheme models. The relevant social decision scheme matrices $(D_1, \ldots)$ are given in Table 1. Not all were equally plausible, a priori, but as a set illustrate how conjectures about social decision processes may be translated into explicit predictions. Verdicts from the second test session of the individual sample were used to obtain $(\hat{p}_G, \hat{p}_{NG})$, and together with Equation (1) yielded $\hat{\pi} = (\hat{\pi}_1, \hat{\pi}_2, \ldots, \hat{\pi}_m)$, the estimated probability of each possible initial array of guilt opinion at the beginning of deliberation. Separate predictions were made for both 6- and 12-person juries under each of the models. Only the two-thirds majority, otherwise hung model (D_7 in Table 1) could not be confidently rejected as a sufficient model for describing the social decision process. Not only did this single model provide the best fit for both 6- and 12-person juries, it also provided that best fit for juries under both decision rule conditions. Thus, it would seem that even when a unanimity rule was assigned, the actual social process could be more accurately described by a two-thirds majority rule. In relation to our earlier discussion, the unanimity rule was the *explicit* (assigned) decision scheme, yet the *implicit* (actual) scheme may have been a two-thirds majority (otherwise hung), or some very similar scheme that yielded the same outcome distribution. (See Kerr *et al.*, 1979 for a discussion of the lack of uniqueness in social decision scheme predictions.)

One problem with drawing conclusions about social process based on this study is that none of the juries rendered a guilty verdict. It is, therefore, possible to assume that for a case where the evidence is more evenly distributed, the social process may take on a different form. However, another study by Davis *et al.* (1977b) used the same mock trial to which they added some moderately incriminating evidence with the result that now a higher proportion of individuals, $\hat{p}_G = .53$, initially favored a guilty verdict. All of the juries were assigned a unanimous decision rule and the changes in the trial produced a distribution of jury verdicts of 41% guilty, 54% not guilty, and 5% hung, i.e.

$(\hat{P}_G, \hat{P}_{NG}, \hat{P}_H) = (.41, .54, .05)$. Even with a distribution of verdicts that differed considerably from the first study, a two-thirds majority decision scheme still provided the best fit to the data.[3] Evidence for a majority type process of some sort had also been reported by Kalven and Zeisel (1966) who gathered data from actual juries, and concluded, 'The jury tends to decide in the end which ever way the initial majority lies' (p. 496).

Jury size revisited: a thought experiment

The lack of significant differences between mock juries of 6 and 12 persons discussed above is quite consistent with other empirical studies of the problem. (See Vollrath and Davis, 1980 for a summary of recent research on size and rule.) Yet, is such an outcome reasonable? Apparently, the empirical evidence along with whatever conventional wisdom applies was sufficient to support the Supreme Court decisions (see above) permitting legislation to reduce the minimum jury size to as low as six. However, given that juries in fact use a two-thirds majority decision rule, which the empirical data also seem to indicate, an anomaly exists, albeit a rather subtle one. It can be shown that for groups of 6 and 12 randomly composed from the same population the verdict distributions *must differ*, given a two-thirds majority social decision scheme. (Actually, the result holds for groups of any size and for various types of majority or plurality social decision schemes; Vollrath and Davis, 1980.) The resolution of this apparent contradiction comes from the recognition that the empirical results are based on statistical inference; the failure to reject the null hypotheses does *not*, of course, imply its validity. Thus, questions of statistical power and 'true' differences in the various empirical studies become of considerable importance to interpretation.

In an attempt to demonstrate the nature and consequences of these conceptual inconsistencies, verdict distributions were simulated for 6- and 12-person juries (P_G, P_{NG}, P_H), across all possible values of juror preferences (p_G, p_{NG}), using a two-thirds majority, otherwise hung social decision scheme (Davis *et al.*, 1975). The results of the simulations for all three verdict possibilities are presented in Figure 1. The differences due to size are nowhere very large, and of course they vary with p_G in a way having implications for the design of studies as well as for interpretations of empirical results. For example, if we take $\hat{p}_G = .22$ in the study discussed above, and set $\hat{p}_G \equiv p_G = .22$, then inspection of Figure 1 suggests that those empirical results failing to show size effects may not be so surprising. Even at the points of maximum differences between the two curves for each decision outcome, the sample size needed to detect with confidence differences of such small magnitude would be considerably larger than 2,000 subjects! (The study discussed earlier used 720 subjects, and is one of the largest known to us.) From a cost–benefit viewpoint, these differences may not seem important, but from the perspective of the defendant, scientist, or ethician the contrary is likely.

The apparent inconsistencies between the theoretical and empirical findings

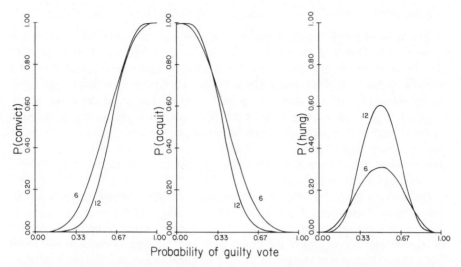

Figure 1 Probability of conviction, acquittal, and hung jury under a two-thirds majority decision scheme for 6- and 12-person juries as a function of the probability of an individual guilty vote. (From Davis *et al.*, 1975. Copyright American Psychological Association. Reproduced with permission.)

above bring up two important points:

1. Social research, like research in other areas, requires both empirical *and* theoretical effort. Such a reminder seems especially pertinent where results may have relatively immediate potential for application. Implications of empirical results are always limited by subject population, social context, and time. Moreover, in many cases, and research on juries is but one instance, results found in one laboratory cannot be easily replicated in another or in actual settings, or across all possible (interesting) combinations of relevant variables. We have just noted above how limited samples can fail to detect effects of considerable importance. Plausible theory, as guided by data, offers the very practical possibility of assessing extrapolations beyond and interpolations between existing data sets—prior to social policy implementation.

2. Institutional changes, alterations of social policy, and the like that are based on one or a few studies are imprudent in the extreme. Not only do the problems discussed above constitute a hazard, there are numerous social, historical, and political forces that put social research results in a sensitive position. Thus, it is especially important that results *and* interpretations be thoroughly worked and carefully cast if they are to be useful to those actually involved in engineering changes (or the *status quo*) in social institutions and policy.

Further applications of thought experiments: the grand jury

The focus of the discussion to this point has been the *petit* jury, particularly in a criminal trial. However, there is another citizen group that figures importantly in the US legal system: the grand jury. Often a highly controversial institution, the grand jury has wide powers and relatively few procedural constraints—the latter being something of an anomaly in the Anglo-Saxon legal tradition which emphasizes procedural protection for the defendant. An investigatory mechanism in some states and in the Federal judicial system, the decision options of the grand jury are often 'indict' (bind over for trial) or 'not indict' (do not bring to trial). Most change proposals attack some issue of procedure, but occasionally address the structure of the group itself.

One such proposal (HR94) was introduced in the 95th Congress, at which time little empirical data existed to evaluate the likely effects of the changes proposed. Two of the proposed changes (the only provisions we consider) dealt with the size (minimum and maximum) of the grand jury, and the type of decision rule to be used. Under the current system, at least 12 proindictment votes are needed for an indictment to be issued, and the minimum and maximum number of jurors are 16 and 23 respectively. An interesting consequence of this system is that a 'sliding' decision rule results, ranging from a simple (i.e. 12/23) to a $12/16 = 3/4$ majority, depending on the number of members present. Bill HR94 proposed that the minimum and maximum sizes be changed to 9 and 16, and that a two-thirds majority be required to return an indictment regardless of the number of grand jurors present.

In view of the absence of directly relevant data from even mock grand juries, Vollrath and Davis (1979) constructed a hypothetical system (i.e. thought experiments) in order to aid evaluation of the size and decision rule proposals. The entire set of simulations run by Vollrath and Davis is too large to be included here, but the results from one of the more informative thought experiments appear in Figure 2. The three curves give probability of indictment under the present system, P; the system proposed by HR94, P^*; and a 'mixed' system, P^{**} as hypothesized by Vollrath and Davis—one in which a fixed, two-thirds majority rule was paired with the size range $(16, \ldots, 23)$ currently allowed. Each curve represents the probability of an indictment, given the probability any given juror will vote for indictment, p, as aggregated across the group sizes allowed under that system with each size weighted relative to its probability of occurrence.[4] As can be seen, the current system produces the highest probability of indictment across all values of p, with the other differences between the other two systems depending upon the particular value of p. Thus, when the probability, p, of an individual voting for indictment is low, we see that $p^{**} < p^*$. However, this difference changes direction, such that $p^{**} > p^*$ when p is large.

These results again emphasize the important distinction between distributive and procedural justice. The three systems investigated by Vollrath and Davis have

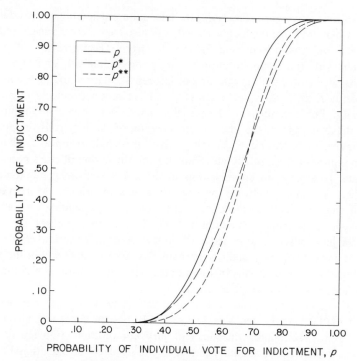

Figure 2 The probability of indictment by a grand jury as a function of the individual probability of indictment under each system, using the available minimum data. The current system is represented by P, the proposed system (HR 94) by P^*, and a composite system by P^{**}. The abscissa represents the probability of an individual vote for indictment, p. (From Vollrath and Davis, 1979. Copyright Plenum Press. Reproduced with permission.)

different qualities, and result in different indictment probabilities. However, none is inherently superior to the others. Whether higher or lower indictment probabilities are desired is a question of distributive justice, political realities, and so on, and should be answered by the relevant legal and political decision makers. However, the social researcher (before or even after implementation) can assist in evaluating the procedural justice question of which system best approaches the desired results.

Juror bias and jury performance

The general issue of bias (in hiring, promotion, housing, etc.) usually on the basis of race, sex, religion, etc., has been at the center of numerous controversies

in the US for many years. The *petit* jury has, quite predictably, received its share
of such attention; there the highly valued notions of representativeness and 'a jury
of one's peers' has served as a focus of concern. (For a review of problems
associated with 'fair' representation in jury composition, see Van Dyke, 1977.)
The concepts involved in the question of fair representation and jury bias are not
easily defined, and can involve sampling and selection problems of surprising
complexity. For example, non-representativeness may come about in several
ways—departures from the ideal in composition of the jury rolls, inappropriate
sampling mechanisms, or even sampling error for a single group so small as a jury
(and small juries are especially vulnerable). Even the notion of one's peers is open
to debate. Not only are combinations of criteria conceivable, but there is the
possibility of conflict between two or more sets of criteria. Moreover, most
criminal trials are held in the city, county, or state (depending on the type of
offense) where the crime was committed. Yet, in a number of cases, the composition of the jury rolls in an area may contain few members of certain ethnic groups;
they may have been 'excluded,' or perhaps few are residents within the jurisdic-
tion. Thus, how could 'a jury of one's peers' actually be formed if some type of
ethnic balance is an important criterion?

We do not have the space here to treat in further detail such complex philosophical matters (again, see Van Dyke, 1977), but the foregoing illustrates the
difficulties in investigating questions of jury composition. (Obviously, not all
procedural justice issues are independent of philosophical or definitional entangle-
ments.) In any event, there is a problem propaedeutic to further inquiry concerning the notions of representativeness and peers: the basic relation of composition
to verdict. Compositional variations that do not influence actual outcome would
seem trivial and likely to be only of cosmetic interest. Thus, we will confine
ourselves to the composition–verdict relation, and restrict attention as well to
individual difference variations likely to be encountered in actual practice.

Excluding obviously aberrant personalities, prospective jurors with preconceived notions of the particular defendant's guilt, those with specific personal
involvements, and similar pretrial inclinations *specific* to the principals, there
remain numerous *general* opinions associated with one or another person 'type,'
population member, etc., that may be in some sense relevant to a trial.
Apparently, the idea that any 12 (or now perhaps as few as 6) 'rational' people
will come to the same verdict as any other 12 is not uniformly held; even the law
allows a change in the location of the trial at least partly as a function of local
opinion. Again, the fundamental question is whether or not more general opinions, or demographic features (social class, region, group memberships, etc.) can
influence verdict preference. Layman and professional alike suspect that such
classifications or distinctions may be predictive of verdict, despite the widely
touted counterbalancing and error-correcting virtues of discussion and debate.

The *voir dire* examination of jurors before acceptance for service is common in the US legal system and may with some probability detect and excuse those forthrightly confessing to prejudice or possessed of some clear conflict of interest. But, more general, less explicit, attitudes (perhaps in turn associated with some membership group or community) are largely unexplored as predictors of jury verdicts. (Remember, it is not only the relationship between some opinion and individual verdict preference that is of interest, but also any association between the weight of individual opinion in a jury and the final verdict—a group phenomenon.)

For example, considerable controversy arose when a number of social scientists attempted to aid the defense during several widely publicized trials involving civil unrest (e.g. the 'Harrisburg Seven' and the 'Gainesville Eight'). Charging the government had chosen trial sites where general opinion favored conviction, a major effort was directed, among other things, at providing the defense attorneys with information (from opinion surveys and community observers) likely to be predictive of how various subpopulations would vote in the event of jury service (see Christie, 1976; Schulman, 1973; Kairys, 1975). Unfortunately, empirical data do not exist that would permit a judgment on the efficacy of such efforts, and opinion is divided. Saks (1976) has concluded that the trial verdicts were probably not significantly influenced by the social data provided the defense, and suggests the approach in general is not promising.

One approach to the basic question has been to investigate any general opinion–verdict relationship under conditions of only minimal realism, but considerable experimental control, replication, etc.—the mock trial. Observe that it is the general opinion–verdict relationship that now is at issue, rather than 'bias' *per se*. A defendant is either guilty or not, but we cannot really be expected to know the correctness of a verdict. Even from a statistical perspective, we might define the parameter, P_G, as the probability a subject is guilty, *given the evidence*. For estimates, $\hat{P}_G$, from samples of juries to be unbiased, it is necessarily true that $E(\hat{P}_G) = P_G$, otherwise the processes would be biased, namely, $E(\hat{P}_G) \neq P_G$.

Davis *et al.* (1978) used an experimental set-up similar to the one described earlier (Davis *et al.*, 1975). Now, however, juries were carefully composed on the basis of subjects' responses to a question, among several 'information' items, concerning the likelihood that defendants in rape trials were, in general, actually guilty. (Such information might well be elicited during *voir dire*, but would hardly result in a juror being excused.) The six-point response scale was trichotomized creating three 'kinds' of jurors labeled 'pro-prosecution, moderate, and pro-defense.' Thus, three kinds of (six-person) juries were constructed by sampling randomly within the three regions of the distribution. Actual assignments to juries followed the (closed-circuit) televised trial. Participants were not aware of their subpopulations' categories. All other procedures were the same as those described earlier.

The results showed that jurors' pretrial opinions indeed affected guilt judgments, both at the individual and the group level. The proportions, $\hat{p}_G$, of jurors preferring guilty verdicts were .70, .68, and .52 for those classified as pro-prosecution, moderate, and pro-defense respectively. These values were significantly related to pretrial opinions, χ^2 (2) = 18.383, $p < .001$. This same trend, though not statistically significant, was observed for jury verdicts as well, where $\hat{P}_G = (.49, .48,$ and .28) for the same three conditions. However, significant correlations were found between pretrial opinion and verdict choices for *both* jurors and juries.

The social decision schemes estimated from individual and group responses for the three types of juries appeared to be quite similar. (Note that earlier studies had *tested* social decision scheme models thought to be plausible *a priori*; the present application sought to infer the best-fitting scheme. See Kerr *et al.*, 1979, for a discussion of model testing and model fitting.) Thus, the locus of the bias leading to different verdicts seems to be at the individual level rather than in the social decision process responsible for aggregating juror verdict preferences.

The above results demonstrate that sampling jurors from populations with different pretrial biases can, in fact, produce different jury verdict distributions. Unfortunately, a simple study of this sort can neither show the possible patterns of effects when sampling from a *variety* of differently disposed populations, nor assess the degree to which such different dispositions may actually be manifested in any given situation. On the other hand, thought experiments using plausible assumptions from past research allow us at least to explore additional possibilities. One such effort was a thought experiment with three different hypothetical populations with different guilt preference dispositions and different sampling probabilities. The results are presented in Figure 3. For each population, a particular individual verdict preference distribution was assumed—conditions which might arise from holding a given trial in an area actually composed of three different populations labeled A, B, and C. The relevant parameters assumed are (A) $p_G = .60$, $p_{NG} = .40$; (B) $p_G = .40$, $p_{NG} = .60$; and (C) $p_G = .50$, $p_{NG} = .50$. Based on these hypothetical population values, the predicted verdict distributions for both 6- and 12-person juries were calculated using three different social decision schemes that might be plausible in one situation or another.

Figure 3 shows some rather obvious differences in verdict distributions due to differences in the individual population distributions. Also of interest here are the patterns due to jury size and social decision schemes. Even though some patterns seem consistent with intuition, other intuitive population—jury size—decision scheme combinations produced rather surprising distributions. Very large differences were found between the hung categories for 6- and 12-person juries under D_7 (two-thirds majority—otherwise hung) while for D_{15} (two-thirds majority—defendant protection, otherwise hung mixture) these differences are quite small. Also, 6-person juries produced a much smaller proportion of not guilty verdicts than 12-person juries under D_7. Matrix D_3, which contains a rather complex subscheme, produced very divergent patterns of results across group sizes, especially for populations A and C. Since all three decision schemes are

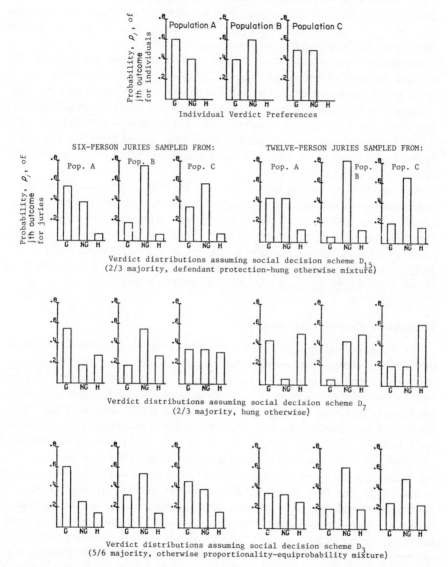

Figure 3 Predicted distributions of verdict outcomes for 6- and 12-person juries, sampled from each of three different populations, and assuming in turn three different social decision schemes. (From Davis, 1980. Copyright Lawrence Erlbaum Associates. Reproduced with permission.)

based on a majority process, the differences among them point out the strong effects attributable to different subschemes, *especially* for 12-person juries. Obviously, a defense attorney would prefer to encounter a social decision process such as D_{15} to one like D_7, even though the primary decision scheme for *both* models is a two-thirds majority wins process.

The results from both the empirical and theoretical experiments illustrate why bias and representativeness have been issues in recent controversies concerning juries. The initial selection and the *voir dire* examination of jurors take on a new importance in light of the surprisingly *large effects* that relatively *small individual differences* can have on jury verdicts. Also, the sometimes considerable effort aimed at securing a change in venue may indeed be justified according to whether the local population(s) are inclined toward defense or prosecution—general and subtle though such tendencies may be.

Much is yet to be learned before proposals for refining procedures addressing bias problems may be seriously advanced or entertained. Yet, it already seems prudent to view with considerable skepticism conclusions that jury composition is essentially cosmetic and that one set of ('rational') jurors is much like another. Likewise, efforts at influencing who is selected should be taken seriously at this point. In any event, the questions of procedural justice here at issue are likely to be unavoidably entangled with matters of distributive justice.

Implications of temporal inconstancies

The dangers of extrapolation from a single study have been stressed throughout this chapter—a particular problem where the application is far removed from the data-gathering situation. The variance attributable to undefined, uncontrolled, and often uncontrollable variables in any given situation surely requires multiple assessments and wide investigation of a particular phenomenon before much generalization becomes attractive. The problem is particularly acute in light of social behavior which may change over culture or region. The thought experiment described earlier illustrated the change in verdict possible for even slight population differences in guilt dispositions. Another inconstancy relevant to our concern is that which may take place over time. Pollsters have sometimes documented apparent temporal changes in attitudes, beliefs, norms, and so on over a period of even a few years (e.g. Uniform Crime Reports, 1976). Unfortunately, it is difficult to explore the implication of such temporal trends because repeating studies has not been popular. Even laboratory studies, which, despite the problems associated with verisimilitude, verdict responsibility, etc., at least offer some possibility of replication, have been discouragingly expensive in time, subjects, and opportunities.

Fortunately, it is sometimes possible to inspect comparable parts of experiments carried out under constant conditions over time, and treat them as levels of a temporal factor. For example, the empirical studies described earlier were part of a larger sequence of mock jury experiments taking place between 1973 and 1976, all of which used the same rape trial (videotape), procedure, and conditions (Davis *et al.*, 1981a; Davis *et al.*, 1975; Davis *et al.*, 1977b; Davis *et al.*, 1978; Davis *et al.*, 1976b; Kerr *et al.*, 1976; Davis *et al.*, 1981b). Even though different experimental manipulations were involved in each study, some portions remained constant; subjects were always asked to record their individual guilt preferences after the mock trial but prior to experimental manipulations. In comparing the values of $\hat{p}_G$ observed across seven such studies, a consistent and significant upward trend was evident (Nagao and Davis, 1980). In other words, subjects' preference for conviction in this particular case *increased* over time. Figure 4 shows this trend for both males and females, as well as the total sample. At least part of the large increment between the first two studies may have been due to some minor modifications in the trial tape, but the remaining change, a 16% increase

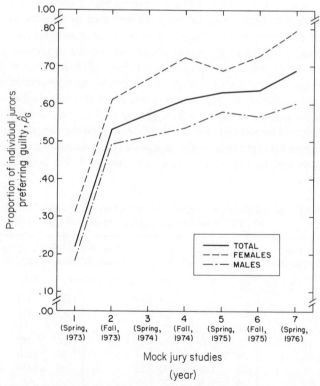

Figure 4 Proportion of guilty verdicts favored by predeliberation jurors over successive semesters, 1973–1976. (From Nagao and Davis, 1980. Copyright Academic Press. Reproduced with permission.)

from Fall 1973 to Spring 1976, occurred although *exactly* the same trial was used throughout the remainder.

The temporal trend noted above, of course, pertains to individual preferences, rather than to mock jury verdicts *per se*. Unfortunately, experimental treatments for the various studies were typically administered to the group conditions and are thus confounded with any temporal drift in actual verdicts. However, Studies 2 and 5 are exceptions—two comparable jury conditions separated only in time. Table 2 presents the observed social decision scheme matrices, $\hat{D}$, for Studies 2 and 5 (Davis *et al.*, 1977b, and Davis *et al.*, 1981a, respectively). As can be seen, although the two matrices are fairly similar, there are also some interesting differences. A much larger percentage of hung juries occurred in Study 5, and this seems to have come at the expense of the not guilty tendency—at least relative to the Study 2 findings. Such increased 'severity' under constant conditions appears to be consistent with the values of $\hat{p}_G$ which were higher for Study 5 than for Study 2. Although a defendant-protection norm seems to be in operation for both experiments, it is partially offset in Study 5 by the higher disposition toward guilt, producing a larger proportion of hung rather than not guilty juries. Taken together, the preceding results suggest that both the individual juror guilt preference, indexed by $\hat{p}_G$, and the social consensus process aggregating individual votes, indexed by $\hat{D}$, may have changed over time—and toward conviction.

Temporal changes bear several important implications for social research. One such implication involves the replication of empirical findings. Replication failures are often attributed to sampling error, sloppy procedures or the fundamental capriciousness of human behavior. Where coupled with the rarity of opportunities for genuine research replication in the first place, the pessimism prevalent in social psychology during the early 1970s (e.g. see Gergen, 1973; Schlenker, 1974) is

Table 2 Social decision scheme matrices observed in Study 2 (Davis *et al.*, 1977b) and Study 5 (Davis *et al.*, 1981b)

	Observed relative frequences Study 2 (Davis *et al.*, 1977b)			Observed relative frequences Study 5 (Davis *et al.*, 1981b)		
($N = 90$)	G	NG	H	($N = 48$) G	NG	H
(6, 0)	—	—	—*	1.00	.00	.00
(5, 1)	.93	.07	.00	.82	.00	.18
(4, 2)	.84	.16	.00	.47	.11	.42
(3, 3)	.16	.68	.16	.14	.00	.86
(2, 4)	.06	.94	.00	.00	1.00	.00
(1, 5)	.00	1.00	.00	.00	1.00	.00
(0, 6)	.00	1.00	.00	—	—	—*

*No juries with this initial distribution were observed.
(Adapted from Nagao and Davis, 1980. Copyright Academic Press. Reproduced with permission.)

perhaps not surprising. Yet, the apparent drift in p_G (as implied by Figure 3) is 'orderly' and may be due to larger national trends in opinions about crime and punishment (including, in the present case, changes in the perception of rape), suggested by Nagao and Davis (1980), that we cannot easily document. For example, suppose we assume a constant social decision scheme (viz. D_7, in Table 1) and explore the implications for P_G of the changes in p_G for the question of jury size. The results of such a thought experiment are given in Figure 5 for jury sizes 6 and 12. Also shown there are points along the p_G continuum where each of the studies fell that provided individual guilt preference estimates over time. The vertical differences between the curves are the theoretical gaps between the population conviction probabilities in juries of 6 and 12 that would have obtained *if* those empirical studies would have included the suitable size variations. Given size differences of the magnitude graphed in Figure 5, the large gaps at the time of Studies 2 and 3 might well have yielded results unlikely to have been replicated at the time of Studies 1, 5, 6, or 7 where the population differences are very small. Although this discussion is only hypothetical, the implications for empirical research and its potential applications are quite clear. In the case at hand, the small magnitude of the theoretical differences (given the assumptions of this thought experiment) and the usual sample sizes available to detect such differences together again suggest caution in relying on a single empirical study or a few such studies. Moreover, the social and ethical importance of attending to the

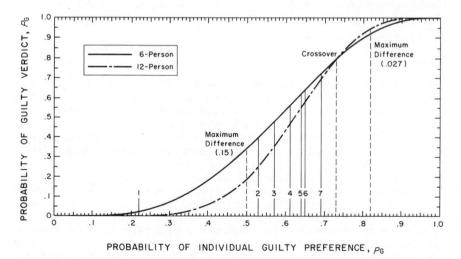

Figure 5 Probability of conviction under a two-thirds majority decision scheme (D_7 and D_{15}) for 6- and 12-person juries as a function of the probability of an individual guilty vote. Also shown are the maximum size differences on each side of the crossover and the relative location of studies 1–7 on the p_G continuum. (From Nagao and Davis, 1980. Copyright Academic Press. Reproduced with permission.)

consequences of such effects does not permit the usual dismissal of very small theoretical differences as lacking 'practical significance.'

The possibility of parameter change over time (or area, cultures, etc.) is probably characteristic of a number of research areas in social psychology, and should be given much greater consideration in the future. However, suggestions that such changes render the methods used in other sciences inappropriate for social research (e.g. Gergen, 1973) seem to overstate the problem while missing the major point. Given that social parameters and processes do change over time, such changes may constitute much of the very stuff to be studied. Viewed in this light, temporal variability becomes an interesting variable to be investigated rather than an unsolvable problem.

Concluding remarks

This chapter's major concern has been to show how social research can be applied to selected questions of procedural justice. The role of such research in relation to relevant policy decisions will probably become more important in the future, as the costs as well as the benefits for implementing social changes are recognized. We have argued here, however, that care must be taken in any application of relevant research findings. Both theory and data are important in order to achieve a comprehensive and informative picture. Empirical studies, in many cases, might be usefully viewed as demonstrations of possibilities and should be supplemented by theoretical work illustrating further implications, side effects, extensions, and so on.

Notes

1. An exception to this was the *Ballew* v. *Georgia* decision which was rendered after empirical and theoretical research concerning these issues had been carried out. In fact, portions of the research reported herein were cited in some of the actual opinions.

2. Our purpose here is not to engage in a comprehensive discussion of this theory, but rather to provide a brief overview as a framework for interpreting the research presented in the subsequent sections. For a more complete exposition of relevant theory, see Davis (1973), Stasser, *et al.* (1980), and Stasser and Davis (1981).

3. The most accurate social decision scheme model in both studies assumed that a two-thirds majority, if it existed, determined the verdict. However, the subschemes differed somewhat. In the first study the most predictive model had a subscheme that assumed a 6-person jury split 3-3 between conviction and acquittal was likely to 'hang,) whereas the second model assumed a substantial inclination in a 3-3 split to acquit the defendant. (See Davis *et al.*, 1975 and 1977b for a more comprehensive discussion.)

4. The assumptions and subsequent derivations involved in the weighting plan for the models of Figure 2 are discussed at length in Vollrath and Davis (1979).

References

Apodaca et al. v. *Oregon.* (1972). *United States Supreme Court Reports*, **406**, 404–415.
Ballew v. *Georgia.* (1978). *The United States Law Week*, **46**, 4217–4224.

Christie, R. (1976). 'Probability vs. precedence: The social psychology of jury selection,' in G. Bermant, C. Nemeth, and N. Vidmar (eds.), *Psychology and the Law*, Lexington Books, Lexington, Mass.

Crossen, R. F. (1967). 'An investigation into certain personality variables among capital trial jurors,' *Dissertation Abstracts*, 1967, **27**, 3668B–3669B.

Davis, J. H. (1969a). 'Individual-group problem solving, subject preferences, and problem type,' *Journal of Personality and Social Psychology*, **13**, 362–374.

Davis, J. H. (1969b). *Group Performance*, Addison-Wesley, Reading, Mass.

Davis, J. H. (1973). 'Group decision and social interaction: A theory of social decision schemes,' *Psychological Review*, **80**, 97–125.

Davis, J. H. (1980). 'Group decision and procedural justice,' in M. Fishbein (ed.), *Progress in Social Psychology*, Vol. 1, Erlbaum, Hillsdale, NJ.

Davis, J. H., Bray, R. M., and Holt, R. W. (1977a). 'The empirical study of social decision processes in juries: A critical review,' in J. Tapp and F. Levine (eds.), *Law, Justice, and the Individual in Society: Psychological and Legal Issues*, Holt, New York.

Davis, J. H., Holt, R. W., Spitzer, C. E., and Stasser, G. (1981a). 'The effects of consensus requirements and multiple decisions on mock juror verdict preferences,' *Journal of Experimental Social Psychology*, **17**, 1–17.

Davis, J. H., Kerr, N. L., Atkin, R. S., Holt, R., and Meek, D. (1975). 'The decision processes of 6- and 12-person juries assigned unanimous and 2/3 majority rules,' *Journal of Personality and Social Psychology*, **32**, 1–14.

Davis, J. H., Kerr, N. L., Stasser, G., Meek, D., and Holt, R. (1977b). 'Victim consequences, sentence severity, and decision processes in mock juries,' *Organizational Behavior and Human Performance*, **18**, 346–365.

Davis, J. H., Laughlin, P. R., and Komorita, S. S. (1976a). 'The social psychology of small groups: Cooperative and mixed-motive interaction,' in M. Rosenzweig, and L. Porter (eds.) *Annual Review of Psychology*, Vol. 27, pp. 501–541.

Davis, J. H., Nagao, D. H., Spitzer, C. E., and Stasser, G. (1981b). 'Decisions in mock juries with multiple minorities and majorities' (Tentative title). Manuscript in preparation, University of Illinois.

Davis, J. H., and Restle, F. (1963). 'The analysis of problems and prediction of group problem solving,' *Journal of Abnormal and Social Psychology*, **66**, 103–116.

Davis, J. H., Spitzer, C. E., Nagao, D. H., and Stasser, G. (1978). 'The nature of bias in social decisions by individuals and groups—An example from mock juries, in H. Brandstatter, J. H. Davis, and H. C. Schuler (eds.), *Dynamics of Group Decisions*, Sage, Beverly Hills, Calif.

Davis, J. H., Stasser, G., Spitzer, C. E. and Holt, R. W. (1976b). 'Changes in group members' decision preferences during discussion: An illustration with mock juries,' *Journal of Personality and Social Psychology*, **34**, 1177–1187.

Diamond, S. S., and Zeisel, H. (1974). 'A courtroom experiment on juror selection and decision making,' Paper presented at the annual meeting of the American Psychological Association, New Orleans.

Dion, D. L., Baron, R. S., and Miller, N. (1970). 'Why do groups make riskier decisions than individuals?' in L. Berkowitz (ed.), *Advances in Experimental Social Psychology*, Vol. 5, Academic Press, New York.

Gergen, K. J. (1973). 'Social psychology as history,' *Journal of Personality and Social Psychology*, **26**, 309–320.

Johnson v. *Louisiana*. (1972). *United States Supreme Court Reports*, **406**, 356–403.

Kairys, D. (ed.), Schulman, J. and Harring, S. (co-eds.). (1975). *The Jury System: New Methods for Reducing Prejudice*, Philadelphia Resistance Print Shop, Philadelphia.

Kalven, H., and Zeisel, H. (1966). *The American Jury*, Little, Brown, Boston.

Kerr, N. L., Atkin, R. S., Stasser, G., Meek, D., Holt, R. W., and Davis, J. H. (1976). 'Guilt beyond a reasonable doubt: Effects of concept definition and assigned decision rule on the judgments of mock jurors,' *Journal of Personality and Social Psychology*, **34**, 282–294.

Kerr, N. L., Stasser, G., and Davis, J. H. (1979). 'Model testing, model fitting, and social decision schemes,' *Organizational Behavior and Human Performance*, **23**, 399–410.

Lerner, M. J. (1965). 'Evaluation of performance as a function of performer's reward and attractiveness,' *Journal of Personality and Social Psychology*, **1**, 355–360.

Lorge, I., and Solomon, H. (1955). 'Two models of group behavior in the solution of Eureka-type problems,' *Psychometrika*, **20**, 139–148.

Nagao, D. H. (1978). 'SCHEME: IBM 360 and Cyber Batch versions, program description, and use,' Unpublished manuscript, Department of Psychology, University of Illinois.

Nagao, D. H., and Davis, J. H. (1980). 'Some implications of temporal drift in social parameters,' *Journal of Experimental Social Psychology*, **16**, 479–496.

Osborn, A. F. (1953). *Applied Imagination*, Scribners, New York.

Parnes, S. F., and Meadow, A. (1959). 'Effects of "brain storming" instructions in creative problem solving by trained and untrained subjects,' *Journal of Educational Psychology*, **50**, 171–176.

Restle, F., and Davis, J. H. (1962). 'Success and speed of problem solving by individuals and groups,' *Psychological Review*, **69**, 520–536.

Rubin, Z., and Peplau, L. A. (1975). 'Who believes in a just world?' *Journal of Social Issues*, **31** (3), 65–89.

Saks, M. (1976). 'The limits of scientific jury selection: Ethical and empirical,' *Jurimetrics Journal*, **17**, 3–22.

Schlenker, B. R. (1974). 'Social psychology as science,' *Journal of Personality and Social Psychology*, **29**, 1–15.

Schulman, J. (1973). 'A systematic approach to successful jury selection,' *Guild Notes*, (November).

Shaw, M. E. (1932). 'Comparison of individuals and small groups in the rational solution of complex problems,' *American Journal of Psychology*, **44**, 491–504.

Shoben, E. W. (1977). 'Probing the discriminatory effects of employee selection procedures with disparate impact analysis under Title VII,' *Texas Law Review*, **56**, 1–45.

Shoben, E. W. (1978). 'Differential pass/fail rates in employment testing: Statistical proof under Title VII,' *Harvard Law Review*, **91**, 793–813.

Stasser, G., and Davis, J. H. (1981). 'Group decision-making and social influence: A social-interaction sequence model,' *Psychological Review*, **88**, 523–551.

Stasser, G., Kerr, N. L., and Davis, J. H. (1980). 'Influence processes in decision making: A modeling approach,' in P. Paulus (ed.), *Psychology of Group Influence*, Erlbaum, Hillsdale, NJ.

Steiner, I. D. (1966). 'Models for inferring relationships between group size and potential group productivity,' *Behavioral Science*, **11**, 273–283.

Steiner, I. D. (1972). *Group Process and Productivity*, Academic Press, New York.

Stoner, J. A. F. (1961). 'A comparison of individuals and group decisions involving risk,' Unpublished master's thesis, Massachusetts Institute of Technology.

Taylor, D. W. (1954). 'Problem solving by groups,' in *Proceedings XIV, International Congress of Psychology, 1954*, North Holland Publishing, Amsterdam.

Uniform Crime Reports for the United States (Federal Bureau of Investigation Department of Justice). (1976). US Government Printing Office, Washington, DC.

Van Dyke, J. M. (1977). *Jury Selection Procedures*, Ballinger, Cambridge, Mass.

Vollrath, D. A., and Davis, J. H. (1979). 'Evaluating proposals for social change with minimal data: An example from grand jury reform proposals,' *Law and Human Behavior*, **3**, 121–134.

Vollrath, D. A., and Davis, J. H. (1980). 'Jury size and decision rule,' in R. V. Simon (ed.), *The Jury: Its Role in American Society*, Lexington Books, Lexington, Mass.
Walster, E. and Walster, G. W. (1975). 'Equity and social justice,' *Journal of Social Issues*, **31** (3), 21–43.
Williams *v*. Florida. (1970). *Supreme Court Reporter*, **90**, 1893–1914.
Zeisel, H. and Diamond, S. S. (1974). 'Convincing empirical evidence on the six-member jury,' *University of Chicago Law Review*, **41**, 281–295.

Summary Note

Small groups, especially the citizen's jury, play an important and fundamental role in society. Their role in administering justice is widespread in the United States, yet the social and psychological processes underlying their functioning are still not well understood. This lack of understanding is partly a function of the difficulties surrounding the direct observation of groups, such as juries, in situ. The present sub-chapter discusses a program of research that has attempted to investigate some of the basic questions about how the preferences of a set of individuals are combined or integrated into a group product or outcome. The joint use of theoretical and empirical 'denominations' was a special emphasis throughout. Theoretical ideas relied heavily on social decision scheme theory (Davis, 1973), and data came largely from mock juries.

Small Groups and Social Interaction, Volume 2
Edited by H. H. Blumberg, A. P. Hare, V. Kent and M. Davies
© 1983 John Wiley & Sons Ltd

1.2   Groupthink*

Irving L. Janis   *Yale University*

One of the first requirements for carrying out research on errors in policy planning is to specify criteria that can be used as dependent variables. In earlier research (Janis, 1972; Janis and Mann, 1977), I have reviewed the extensive literature on decision making and have extracted seven major criteria to use in judging whether a decision made by a person or group is of *high quality*. Such judgments pertain to the decision-making *procedures* that lead up to the act of commitment to a final choice (see Etzioni, 1968; Hoffman, 1965; Maier, 1967; Simon, 1976; Taylor, 1965; Wilensky, 1967; Young, 1966). As applied to policy-planning groups, the seven procedural criteria are as follows: The group (1) thoroughly canvasses a wide range of policy alternatives; (2) takes account of the full range of objectives to be fulfilled and the values implicated by the choice; (3) carefully weighs whatever is found out about the costs or drawbacks and the uncertain risks of negative consequences, as well as the positive consequences, that could flow from each alternative; (4) intensively searches for new information relevant for further evaluation of the policy alternatives; (5) conscientiously takes account of any new information or expert judgment to which the members are exposed, even when the information or judgment does not support the course of action they initially prefer; (6) re-examines the positive and negative consequences of all known alternatives, including those originally regarded as unacceptable, before making a final choice; and (7) makes detailed recommendations or provisions for implementing and executing the chosen policy, with special attention to contingency plans that might be required if various known risks were to materialize.

*This paper is based on Janis, *Groupthink*, Houghton Mifflin, Boston, 1982, and on the paper published in *Group Decision Making*, Academic Press, New York, 1982 (Janis, 1982b).

Janis and Mann (1977) point out that although systematic data are not yet available on this point, it seems plausible to assume that failure to meet any of the seven criteria is a defect in the decision-making process. When policy planners display many such defects before committing themselves, they are likely to undergo unanticipated setbacks and fail to achieve their goals.

One major source of defective decision making has been described in my analysis of fiascos resulting from foreign policy decisions made by presidential advisory groups (Janis, 1972, 1982a). I call attention to a *concurrence-seeking tendency* that occurs among moderately or highly cohesive groups. When this tendency is dominant, the members use their collective cognitive resources to develop rationalizations in line with shared illusions about the invulnerability of their organization or nation and display other symptoms of concurrence seeking (referred to as 'groupthink').

A number of historic fiascos appear to have been products of defective policy planning on the part of misguided government leaders who obtained social support from their ingroups of advisers. My analysis of case studies of historic fiascos suggests that the following groups of policy advisers were dominated by 'groupthink': (1) Neville Chamberlain's inner circle, whose members supported the policy of appeasement of Hitler during 1937 and 1938, despite repeated warnings and events indicating that it would have adverse consequences; (2) Admiral Kimmel's ingroup of Naval Commanders whose members failed to respond to warnings in the fall of 1941 that Pearl Harbor was in danger of being attacked by Japanese planes; (3) President Truman's advisory group, whose members supported the decision to escalate the war in North Korea despite firm warnings by the Chinese Government that United States entry into North Korea would be met with armed resistance from the Chinese; (4) President John F. Kennedy's advisory group, whose members supported the decision to launch the Bay of Pigs invasion of Cuba despite the availability of information indicating that it would be an unsuccessful venture and would damage relations between the United States and other countries; (5) President Lyndon B. Johnson's 'Tuesday luncheon group,' whose members supported the decision to escalate the war in Vietnam despite intelligence reports and other information indicating that this course of action would not defeat the Viet Cong or the North Vietnamese and would entail unfavorable political consequences within the United States. In all these 'groupthink'-dominated groups, there were strong pressures toward uniformity, which inclined the members to avoid raising controversial issues, questioning weak arguments, or calling a halt to soft-headed thinking.

Other social psychologists (Green and Conolley, 1974; Raven, 1974; Raven and Rubin, 1977) have noted similar symptoms of groupthink in the way Nixon and his inner circle handled the Watergate cover-up. Drawing on their work and my own detailed analyses of the unedited Nixon tapes, I have recently completed an additional case study of the Watergate cover-up and have used it to elaborate on the theory of concurrence seeking (Janis, 1982a).

Eight main symptoms of groupthink run through the case studies of historic decision-making fiascos. Each symptom can be identified by a variety of indicators, derived from historical records, observers' accounts of conversations, and participants' memoirs. The eight symptoms of groupthink are:

1. An illusion of invulnerability, shared by most or all the members, which creates excessive optimism and encourages taking extreme risks;
2. Collective efforts to rationalize in order to discount warnings which might lead the members to reconsider their assumptions before they recommit themselves to their past policy decisions;
3. An unquestioned belief in the group's inherent morality, inclining the members to ignore the ethical or moral consequences of their decisions;
4. Stereotyped views of rivals and enemies as too evil to warrant genuine attempts to negotiate, or as too weak and stupid to counter whatever risky attempts are made to defeat their purposes;
5. Direct pressure on any member who expresses strong arguments against any of the group's stereotypes, illusions, or commitments, making clear that this type of dissent is contrary to what is expected of all loyal members;
6. Self-censorship of deviations from the apparent group consensus, reflecting each member's inclination to minimize to himself the importance of his doubts and counterarguments;
7. A shared illusion of unanimity concerning judgements conforming to the majority view (partly resulting from self-censorship of deviations, augmented by the false assumption that silence means consent);
8. The emergence of self-appointed mindguards—members who protect the group from adverse information that might shatter their shared complacency about the effectiveness and morality of their decisions.

Hypotheses concerning the conditions that foster concurrence seeking were formulated on the basis of inferences from the case studies of groupthink and from two other comparative case studies (Janis, 1982a). The two other case studies involve well worked-out decisions made by similar groups whose members made realistic appraisals of the consequences. One of these is the main decision made by the Kennedy administration during the Cuban missile crisis in October 1962. The second deals with the hardheaded way that planning committees in the Truman administration evolved the Marshall Plan in 1948. These two case studies indicate that policy-making groups do not always suffer the adverse consequences of group processes, that the quality of the group's decision-making activities depends upon current conditions that influence the group atmosphere.

Janis and Mann (1977) have elaborated on the theory of concurrence seeking, or groupthink, as a defective pattern of decision making. Their assumption is that the symptoms of groupthink are behavioral consequences of a coping pattern of *defensive avoidance*, which is mutually supported by the group members.

The schematic analysis in Figure 1, which includes the determinants of defensive avoidance, shows the major antecedent conditions that foster concurrence seeking, manifested by the symptoms of groupthink. This figure lists the main independent and dependent variables that need to be investigated in comparative case studies, field experiments, and other systematic investigations of groupthink.

A study that illuminates some of the politically relevant consequences of groupthink was carried out by Phillip Tetlock, (1979). He reinvestigated the Bay of Pigs fiasco and two other historic fiascos in US foreign policy that were analyzed in the main case studies presented in Janis's *Victims of groupthink* (1972). Tetlock carried out systematic content analyses of the relevant public speeches made by the President of the United States and by the Secretary of State during the period when each of the three policy decisions was being made, which presumably would reflect the quality of their thinking at that time. He compared the content analysis results from the three groupthink decisions with those obtained from comparable public speeches made during the time when two non-groupthink decisions were being made (the Marshall Plan and the Cuban Missile Crisis). Using a measure of cognitive complexity developed by Peter Suedfeld, Tetlock found that when the groupthink decisions were being made, the public speeches obtained significantly lower scores than when the non-groupthink decisions were being made. In future research on defective decisions of policy-making groups the comparative method used in Tetlock's study could be applied to other verbal products prepared in connection with group meetings, including memoranda, memoirs, minutes, and verbatim transcripts of the sessions.

A somewhat different type of comparative study, using a systematic content analysis procedure to code statements of agreement and disagreement, was initiated by William Wong-McCarthy (1977). He compared two samples of unedited Watergate tapes from two different periods. One sample was from the period when Nixon and his main White House advisers (Haldeman, Ehrlichman, and Dean) were keenly aware of the threat of public exposure, felt little hope for finding a better solution than to continue the cover-up policy, and displayed coordinated group action. The other sample was from the period when the in-group was disintegrating as more and more devastating revelations implicated one member after another. He found that the transcripts of the meetings held during the period of coordinated action contained significantly more supportive statements that are symptomatic of groupthink than those of the meeting held when the participants were no longer a cohesive group. This comparative method, in which each policy-making group is used as its own control, could be extended to obtain objective data on the relationship between various external conditions and blind ratings of the symptoms of groupthink—provided, of course, that the investigators can obtain detailed minutes or, better yet, tape recordings of group meetings (such as those made for hundreds of meetings in the White House by Presidents Kennedy and Johnson, as well as by President Nixon).

Not all cohesive groups suffer from groupthink, though all may display some of

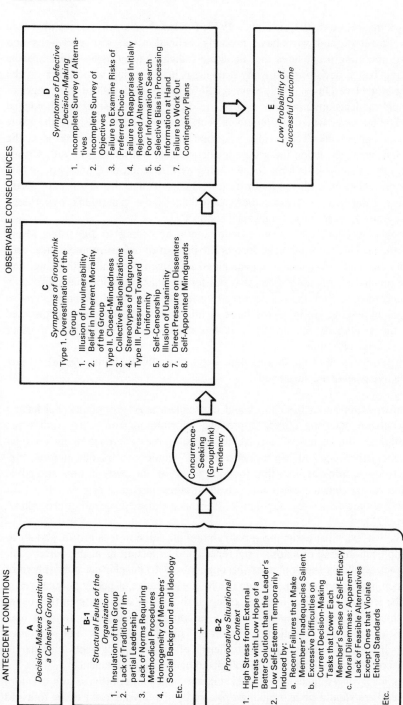

Figure 1 Theoretical analysis of groupthink based on comparisons of high-quality with low-quality decisions by policy-making groups. (From *Groupthink: Psychological Studies of Policy Decisions and Fiascos* by I. L. Janis. Reproduced with permission of Houghton Mifflin.)

its symptoms from time to time (Janis, 1972, 1982a). A group whose members are highly competent and who have properly defined roles, with traditions and standard operating procedures that facilitate critical inquiry, is probably capable of making better decisions than any individual in the group who works on the problem alone (see Davis, 1969; Steiner, 1966, 1982). And yet the advantages of having policy decisions made by groups are often lost because of psychological pressures that arise when the members work closely together, share the same values and, above all, face a crisis situation in which everyone realizes at the outset that whatever action the group decides to take will be fraught with serious risks and that there is little hope for obtaining new information that will point to a satisfactory solution. In these circumstances, the leader and the members of his in-group are subjected to stresses that, according to the groupthink hypothesis, generate a strong need for mutual social support.

As conformity pressures begin to dominate, according to Janis and Mann (1977), the striving for unanimity fosters the pattern of defensive avoidance, with characteristic lack of vigilance, unwarranted optimism, sloganistic thinking, and reliance on shared rationalizations that bolster the least objectionable alternative. That alternative is often the one favored by the leader or other influential persons in the policy-making group on the basis of initial biases that remain uncorrected despite the availability of impressive evidence showing it to be inferior to other feasible courses of action.

From the analysis of conditions that foster groupthink (Janis, 1982a) 10 prescriptive hypotheses are suggested:

1. Information about the causes and consequences of groupthink will have a beneficial deterring effect. Impressive information from case studies can augment the members' resolve to curtail group encroachments on their critical thinking and can increase their willingness to try out antidote prescriptions, 'provided ... that they are aware of the costs in time and effort and realize that there are other disadvantages they must also watch out for before they decide to adopt any of them as a standard operating procedure'; (p. 275).
2. The leader, when assigning a policy-planning mission to a group, should be impartial instead of stating preferences and expectations at the outset. This practice allows the conferees the opportunity to develop an atmosphere of open inquiry and to explore impartially a wide range of policy alternatives.
3. The leader of a policy-forming group at the outset should assign the role of critical evaluator to each member, encouraging the group to give high priority to airing objections and doubts. This practice needs to be reinforced by the leader's acceptance of criticism of his own judgments in order to discourage the members from soft-pedaling their disagreements.
4. At every meeting devoted to evaluating policy alternatives, one or more members should be assigned the role of devil's advocate. In order to avoid domesticating and neutralizing the devil's advocates, the group leader will

have to give each of them an unambiguous assignment to present his arguments as cleverly and convincingly as he can, as a good lawyer would,
challenging the testimony of those advocating the majority position.

5. Throughout the period when the feasibility and effectiveness of policy alter-
    natives are being surveyed, the policy-planning group should from time to
    time divide into two or more subgroups to meet separately, under different
    chairmen, and then come together to hammer out their differences.

6. Whenever the policy issue involves relations with a rival organization or
    out-group, a sizable block of time (perhaps an entire session) should be
    spent surveying all warning signals from the rivals and constructing alterna-
    tive scenarios of the rivals' intentions.

7. After reaching a preliminary consensus about what seems to be the best
    policy alternative, the policy-planning group should hold a 'second chance'
    meeting at which every member is expected to express as vividly as he can
    all his residual doubts and to rethink the entire issue before making a defini-
    tive choice.

8. One or more outside experts or qualified colleagues within the organization
    who are not core members of the policy-planning group should be present at
    each meeting on a staggered basis and should be encouraged to challenge
    the views of the core members.

9. Each member of the policy-planning group should discuss periodically the
    group's deliberations with trusted associates in his own unit of the organiza-
    tion and report back their reactions.

10. The organization should routinely follow the administrative practice of
    setting up several independent policy-planning and evaluation groups to
    work on the same policy question, each carrying out its deliberations under
    a different chairman.

All of these prescriptive hypotheses must be validated before they can be
applied with any confidence. Each of the proposed remedies may prove to have
undesirable side effects and other drawbacks. But these hypotheses appear sufficiently promising to warrant the trouble and expense of being tested as
potentially useful means for counteracting groupthink whenever a small number
of policy planners or executives in any organization meet with their chairman or
chief executive to work out new policies (see Janis, 1982b). Some of the anti-
groupthink procedures might also help to counteract initial biases of the members,
prevent pluralistic ignorance, and eliminate other sources of error that can arise
independently of groupthink.

References

Davis, J. H. (1969). *Group Performance*, Addison-Wesley, Menlo Park, Calif.
Etzioni, A. (1968). *The Active Society*, Free Press, New York.
Green, D., and Conolley, E. (1974). '"Groupthink" and Watergate,' Paper presented at
the annual meeting of the American Psychological Association.

Hoffman, L. R. (1965). 'Group problem solving.' in L. Berkowitz (ed.), *Advances in Experimental Social Psychology*, Vol. 2, pp. 99–132, Academic Press, New York.

Janis, I. L. (1972). *Victims of Groupthink*, Houghton Mifflin, Boston.

Janis, I. L. (1982a). *Groupthink: Psychological Studies of Policy Decisions and Fiascos*, (Revised and enlarged edition of *Victims of Groupthink*, 1972), Houghton Mifflin, Boston.

Janis, I. L. (1982b). 'Counteracting the adverse effects of concurrence-seeking in policy-planning groups: Theory and research perspectives,' in H. Brandstatter, J. Davis, and C. Stocker-Kreichgauer (eds.), *Group Decision Making*. Academic Press.

Janis, I. L., and Mann, L. (1977). *Decision-making: A Psychological Analysis of Conflict, Choice and Commitment*, Free Press, New York.

Maier, N. (1967). 'Group problem solving,' *Psychological Review*, **74**, 239–249.

Raven, B. (1974). 'The Nixon group,' *Journal of Social Issues*, **30** (4), 297–320.

Raven, B. H., and Rubin, J. Z. (1977). *Social Psychology: People in Groups*, Wiley, New York.

Simon, H. A. (1976). *Administrative Behavior: A Study of Decision-Making Processes in Administrative Organizations*, 3rd edn, Free Press, New York.

Steiner, I. D. (1966). 'Models for inferring relationships between group size and potential group productivity,' *Behavioral Science*, **11**, 273–283.

Steiner, I. D. (1982). 'Heuristic models of groupthink,' in H. Brandstatter, J. H. Davis, and G. Stocker-Kreichgauer (eds), *Group Decision-Making*, Academic Press, New York.

Taylor, D. W. (1965). 'Decision making and problem solving,' in J. March (ed.), *Handbook of Organizations*, Rand McNally, Chicago.

Tetlock, P. E. (1979). 'Identifying victims of groupthink from public statements of decision makers,' *Journal of Personality and Social Psychology*, **37**, 1314–1324.

Wilensky, H. L. (1967). *Organizational Intelligence*, Basic Books, New York.

Wong-McCarthy, W. (1977). 'Symptoms of groupthink in the Watergate tapes: Results of a content analysis,' unpublished paper.

Young, S. (1966). *Management: A Systems Analysis*, Scott, Foresman, Glenview Ill.

Small Groups and Social Interaction, Volume 2
Edited by H. H. Blumberg, A. P. Hare, V. Kent and M. Davies
© 1983 John Wiley & Sons Ltd

1.3 Mathematical and Computer Models of Jury Decision Making

Steven Penrod *University of Wisconsin*

From the point of view of the social scientist, the jury is an unusual institution. Certain features of the jury distinguish juries from other small groups studied by social scientists: juries have a limited life span (one trial); they are typically composed of strangers; the jurors are not 'experts' and their decisions involve determinations of 'fact' rather than responses to problems which have objectively correct solutions. Two other notable features also distinguish juries from other types of small groups: the size of the jury is fixed (generally at 6 or 12 members) and the decision rules employed are also fixed (generally jurors must deliberate to unanimity, although some states employ non-unanimous rules such as 5 of 6 or 10 of 12 decision rules).

The fact that jury sizes and decision rules are fixed has made juries an attractive type of group for researchers interested in developing and testing formal models of group decision-making processes. Interest in such models has been further stimulated by the fact that laws governing jury size and decision rules have been the subject of a number of cases decided by the Supreme Court (Roper, 1980; Sperlich, 1980). Partly in response to the Supreme Court cases, a number of researchers developed formal models of decision making that addressed jury size and decision rule issues. More recent models have examined issues such as juror accuracy and the deliberation process itself.

The present review provides an overview of the jury models that have appeared since 1970. These models are divided into four general classes: (a) *single-parameter binomial* models that examine jury size and decision rule effects and jury 'accuracy;' (b) *two-parameter binomial* models that examine prior probabilities that defendants are guilty, juror accuracy detecting guilt and juror satisfaction; (c) *multinomial* models that examine the implicit decision rules governing jury decision making; and (d) *Markovian* models that examine the jury decision-making process.

Single-parameter binomial models

If a few simple conditions are met, the binomial theorem can easily be used to characterize jury voting at the conclusion of a trial and prior to deliberation: if jurors can be drawn at random from a pool in which a specified proportion of jurors are prepared to vote for conviction (and the remainder for acquittal) and these jurors have arrived at their judgments independently, the binomial expansion may be used to compute the probability that a jury will have sufficient votes to convict on the first ballot:

$$p(C) = \sum_{i=Q}^{n} \binom{n}{i} c^i (1-c)^{n-i} \qquad (1)$$

where the probability of conviction by an entire jury, $p(C)$, is a function of: the jury size, n; the criterion for conviction, Q (e.g. unanimous decision rules where $Q = n$ or non-unanimous decision rules where $Q < n$); and the probability a randomly selected juror will vote for conviction, c, or acquittal, $(1-c)$. Because this model includes values for both jury size and decision rule, it allows straightforward assessments of the relationship between jury size, decision rule, and $p(C)$ for different values in the individual juror parameter c. By consulting tables for the cumulative binomial distribution it is possible to determine the probability of conviction for various jury sizes, decision rules, and juror probabilities. For example, the probability that a 12-member jury will unanimously vote to convict, $p(C)$, when $c = .8$ is .07 (or, $.8^{12}$) compared to .26 for a six-member jury ($.8^6$). Readers unfamiliar with the binomial theorem will find useful readings in any text on probability theory and in many introductory statistics texts such as Hays (1973).

Smoke and Zajonc (1962) discussed a binomial model of decision making in an early paper. More recently, Friedman (1972) and Saks and Ostrom (1975) used the model in jury contexts to explore questions raised by the Supreme Court. With respect to first ballot behavior, the model indicates that as jury size is reduced and the decision criterion relaxed, the probability of conviction on the first ballot increases. As Friedman (1972) noted, such relaxations hurt most those defendants who appear to be guilty or who are unable to present a strong defense. Saks and Ostrom (1975) observed that in instances where the pool of jurors would be evenly divided on a case ($c = .5$), juries with nine or more members have a very small probability (less than .0002) of reaching a first ballot verdict of conviction *or* acquittal with a unanimous decision rule compared to a probability of .031 for a 6 of 6 rule and .22 for a 5 of 6 rule. Saks and Ostrom argued that such verdicts (rendered with minimal deliberation) might be characterized as irrational and random. The remedy is obvious—large juries using unanimous decision rules virtually guarantee that no such first ballot verdicts will be obtained.

What if there is no first ballot verdict? Walbert (1971) argued that the basic binomial model could be extended to model verdicts obtained after deliberation. Walbert's approach was to assume that first ballot majorities always prevail and that juries which are evenly split on the first ballot will ultimately divide equally for conviction and acquittal. With these assumptions Walbert demonstrated that whenever c was greater than .5, 12-member juries using unanimous decision rules are more likely to convict than are unanimous six-member juries. Under Walbert's assumptions, larger juries are more likely to produce verdicts consistent with trial evidence. However, Walbert's assumptions are not entirely acceptable, for his model ignores phenomena such as hung juries (4.4% of all cases in Kalven and Zeisel's, 1966, study) and juries in which minorities ultimately persuade majorities (3.1% of Kalven and Zeisel's cases).

Two-parameter binomial models

Extended analyses of two-parameter binomial models have been offered by Gelfand and Solomon (1973, 1974, 1975, 1977) and Grofman (1976, 1980). The basic model was developed to assess the prior probability that defendants are guilty and juror accuracy in assessing that guilt. The model is expressed as follows:

$$p(A_{n,i}) = \sum_{j=0}^{i} \binom{n}{i} \{GV^{n-i}(1-V)^i + (1-G)V^i(1-V)^{n-i}\} \tag{2}$$

where $p(A_{n,i})$ is the probability that at least i jurors in a jury of n members will vote for acquittal (A) on the first ballot. G is the probability that the weight of the trial evidence will indicate that the defendent is guilty or 'convictable' on the trial evidence and V is the probability that jurors will accurately assess the trial evidence. Gelfand and Soloman used several sources of data to estimate general values of G and V across trials. Their 1973 analyses of data collected by Poisson (1837) yielded estimates of .64 for G and .75 for V. In 1975, Gelfand and Solomon used the data from Kalven and Zeisel's (1966) classic jury study. For that set of data, the estimates (using several methods of estimation) clustered around .7 for G and .9 for V. Gelfand and Solomon also tested a 'final-ballot' model that represented a refinement of Walbert's (1971) single-parameter model. The refined model was evaluated using the Kalven and Zeisel data and yielded further confirmation of the $G = .7$ and $V = .9$ estimates.

Grofman (1976) argued that the basic Gelfand and Solomon model (Equation (2)) could be simplified by ignoring 'error' portions of the expression (the $1 - V$ terms) because they contribute very few cases. Furthermore, if only first ballot distributions were examined then the following expressions could be easily evaluated:

$$p(C) = V^n G \tag{3}$$

$$p(A) = V^n(1 - G) \tag{4}$$

$$p(H) = 1 - V^n \tag{5}$$

where $p(C)$ is, once again, the probability of conviction, $p(A)$ is the probability of acquittal, and $p(H)$ is the probability that a jury will hang.

Penrod and Hastie (1979) used these simplified expressions and the Kalven and Zeisel (1966) data to estimate $G = .62$, $V = .91$ for convictable defendants and $V = .92$ for acquittable defendants. In another two-parameter binomial model, Grofman (1976) used a parameter for juror accuracy and a parameter representing a trade-off ratio (R) of the number of guilty defendants a juror would be willing to acquit in order to avoid one erroneous conviction of an innocent defendant (see also Feinberg, 1971, and Nagèl and Neef, 1975). Grofman demonstrated that when a juror is willing to set R defendants free to avoid one erroneous conviction, and the probability a defendant is guilty is greater than $1/2$, the desired decision rule approaches unanimity as the ratio of $R/R + 1$ approaches 1.0.

Multinomial models

The one- and two-parameter binomial models have been characteristically deficient in their ability to model and analyze the effects of jury deliberation on jury verdicts. A model that has quite successfully tackled this problem is a multinomial model first advanced by Davis (1973). Davis's model explicitly addresses the relationship between first ballot vote distributions and final jury verdicts. The model represents the first ballot vote by final verdict distributions in an m by s stochastic (probabilistic) matrix. The multinomial expansion is used to obtain the m possible initial vote distributions that can be generated by r jury members, each of whom has n verdict alternatives available—thus:

$$m = \binom{n + r - 1}{r} \tag{6}$$

which for a six-member jury deciding guilt or innocence yields

$$\binom{2 + 6 - 1}{6} = 7$$

possible distributions ranging from 6 votes for convictions and none for acquittal (6, 0) to 0 votes for conviction and 6 votes for acquittal (0, 6). If these juries can produce one of three ($s = 3$) outcomes—conviction, acquittal, or hung—the $m \times s$ stochastic matrix contains $(7 \times 3) = 21$ cells. These cell entries specify the probability that any particular initial distribution will result in one of the available outcomes. (Gillett, 1980a, 1980b, has provided an extended discussion of the formal mathematical properties of Davis's model.)

The entries in an $m \times s$ matrix (which Davis has termed Social Decision Scheme Matrix) may be estimated from empirical data or specified on theoretical grounds and then tested against data. One notion underlying Davis's approach is that the decision schemes may capture the decision rules that juries (or other small groups) *implicitly* employ. The implicit rules may differ significantly from the explicit rules prescribed for the group. A variety of decision schemes have been tested against empirical data by Davis and his colleagues (e.g. Davis, 1973; Davis *et al.*, 1975; Kerr *et al.*, 1976; Davis, *et al.*, 1977; Davis *et al.*, 1978 [and Sub-Chapter 1.1]) and others (e.g. Saks, 1977; Grofman, 1980; Gelfand and Solomon, 1977).

Davis (1980) has observed that much of the existing research supports what he has termed 'a 2/3 majority, otherwise hung' (p. 177) decision scheme. Essentially, this social decision scheme implies that if two-thirds of the jurors agree on a verdict in their first ballot, that verdict alternative will prevail. If a two-thirds majority is not obtained, the jury is likely to hang. This general, *implicit* decision rule has received support in studies that have used both 6- and 12-member juries and both unanimous and non-unanimous *explicit* decision rules. Further confirmation of this implicit rule has been supplied by researchers using Markovian models.

Markovian models of jury deliberation

Contemporary jury deliberation models have been influenced by research dating back nearly 70 years. Among the earliest research on group decision making in the legal domain were experiments by Münsterberg (1914) and Burtt (1920). Early researchers such as Thorndike (1938) and Timmons (1942) also investigated 'majority influence' in group decision making. However, Asch's (1951) research on conformity effects precipitated one of the first formal models of group influences on individual behavior. Cohen (1958, 1963) offered a formal mathematical model of Asch-type conformity effects by mathematically representing 'subjects' in a four-state Markov process model (Kemeny and Snell, 1962, Bartos, 1967, and Hewes, 1980 provide introductions to Markov models).

Cohen's model is worthy of a brief explanation because it embodies features characteristic of Markov models. Very simply, the subjects who are mathematically simulated in Cohen's Markov model could occupy one of four states during a series of Asch trials: (1) a correct-response state that the subject would not leave on subsequent trials; (2) a correct-response state a subject might leave (thereby rendering an incorrect response on a subsequent trial); (3) an incorrect-response state the subject might leave; and (4) an incorrect-response state that subjects would not leave. The object of Cohen's research was to estimate the 'transition probabilities' that characterized subject movements from one state to another under the influence of the other Asch subjects. These probabilities were represented in a four by four matrix specifying the probability of a transition from one state to another. Lee (1972) and Cohen and Lee (1975) have reported further developments in the Markov model of Asch-type conformity.

In related research, Godwin and Restle (1974) used a Markov model of group influence to trace the development of group consensus on multiple choice problems. Godwin and Restle used data on the decision making of actual groups with 3, 4, 5, and 6 members to estimate the transition probabilities between the states of their model. Each possible state in their model was defined by the number of group members preferring the first, second, third, and fourth most popular choice alternatives. Godwin and Restle observed that the attractiveness of a subgroup preferring a particular alternative (that is, its ability to attract further members) was a nonlinear function of the subgroup's size: once a subgroup obtained a majority of group members, holdouts quickly joined the majority and subgroups confronting single holdouts were found to be particularly attractive.

Stasser and Davis (1977) reported the first investigation to explicitly employ a Markovian model of jury decision making. Their analysis addressed two types of questions: (1) Do jurors change opinions (verdict preferences) at a *stationary* rate during deliberation or are opinion changes concentrated in particular periods (such as the end stages) of deliberation? (2) Are opinion changes unrelated to the relative sizes of the coalitions in a jury (a 'random walk' model) or are opinion changes a *linear function* of the proportion of jurors advocating a verdict—such that a coalition's 'attractiveness' increases as the proportional size of the coalition increases. Stasser and Davis tested four models (stationary versus non-stationary and random walk versus linear function) with data collected from 140 six-member mock juries. The states in the Stasser and Davis model represented the seven possible configurations of votes in a six-member jury—these states ranged from 6 votes for conviction and 0 for acquittal (6, 0) to 0 for conviction and 6 for acquittal (0, 6). When the jury deliberations were used to estimate the probabilities in the 7 by 7 transition matrix, Stasser and Davis found support for the stationary rate model and (in contrast to Godwin and Restle) the linear function model.

Klevorick and Rothschild (1979) also examined several Markovian jury models. Perhaps the most interesting of these was a discrete-time proportional change Markov model in which it was assumed (a) that one juror at a time changed opinion during each fixed-length Markov trial and (b) that transition probabilities were a linear function of the proportion of jurors in a coalition. Klevorick and Rothschild used this model to compare unanimous and non-unanimous decision rules. They found that the change in decision standard would affect less than six-tenths of 1% of the cases decided under the two rules. In contrast to the Godwin and Restle and Stasser and Davis approaches, Klevorick and Rothschild's model was not evaluated with empirical data.

Penrod and Hastie (1979, 1980) developed a computer simulation (DICE) of jury decision making built around a discrete time Markov model of opinion change. The model has several major parameters including a vote transition function that governs the probabilities of opinion change; an individual difference function reflecting individual juror's resistance to persuasion and a ballot counter that determines whether a jury hangs. Values for the model's parameters were fitted through a series of Monte Carlo simulations—that is, repeated tests of the model in which the values of the parameters were systematically manipulated. For each combination of parameter values, the output of the model (such as verdict distributions, deliberation times, and rates of vote changes by jurors) was compared to the results from empirical jury studies.

Penrod and Hastie's model was evaluated using data from jury studies conducted by Padawer-Singer and Barton (1975) and Davis et al. (1977). These studies employed 6- and 12-member juries and unanimous and non-unanimous decision rules. Best-fitting parameter values indicated that opinion change in juries is an exponential function of coalition sizes such that larger coalitions are disproportionately attractive or persuasive to members opposing coalitions (a result consistent with Godwin and Restle's findings) and that jurors do differ in their 'resistance' to persuasion by opposing jurors (i.e. jurors are non-homogeneous with respect to transitions).

In recent research, Kerr (1981a, 1981b) used data from student juries to obtain precise estimates of the probabilities for 7×7 transition matrices associated with six-member juries. Kerr (1981a) addressed two important questions. First, he estimated transition probabilities at different points in deliberation to determine whether the probabilities are stationary throughout deliberation or whether the persuasion process changes as deliberation proceeds. Secondly, Kerr examined the 'order' or path independence (Hewes, 1980) of opinion transitions. Briefly, a first-order Markov model is one in which transitions between states at time t and $t + 1$ depend only on the configuration of states at t. In higher order models, transitions may depend on the history of the group prior to t (e.g. the Penrod and Hastie model assumes that jurors are less likely to change opinions a second time after having once changed opinions). Kerr (1981a) obtained evidence that jury deliberations were non-stationary (partly disconfirming the Stasser and Davis, 1977, results but providing support for results obtained by Davis et al., 1976). Kerr also observed evidence of path dependence (a coalition that just acquired a new member was more likely to acquire another new member than to lose a member—what Kerr termed a 'momentum' effect). However, Kerr (1981a) reported that both effects were weak and a model that ignored both effects would still provide good fits to empirical data.

Conclusion

This review of jury models has traced the evolution of formal models of jury decision making and emphasized the recent development of Markovian models. Binomial and multinomial models initially shed substantial light on the relationships among jury size, explicit and implicit decision rules, defendant guilt, and juror accuracy. The binomial models established the extent to which stricter decision rules (e.g. unanimity versus a five-sixths non-unanimity) reduce the probability that a jury will produce a verdict with little or no discussion; [showed] the relative advantage of larger juries with respect to producing verdicts that are consistent with trial evidence, and provided a basis for assessing the accuracy of juror judgments. The recently developed Markovian models are building on these foundations and have provided additional insights into the deliberation processes that produce jury verdict. These models suggest that jury decision making can be characterized as a conformity process in which conformity may be indexed by the relative sizes of jury coalitions. This conformity process is largely path independent and stationary but is influenced by individual differences in jurors.

References

Asch, S. E. (1951). 'Effects of group pressure upon the modifications and distortion of judgments,' in H. Guetzkow (ed.), *Groups, Leadership and Men*, Carnegie Press, Pittsburgh.

Bartos, O. J. (1967). *Simple Models of Group Behavior*, Columbia University Press, New York.

Burtt, H. E. (1920). 'Sex differences and the effect of discussion,' *Journal of Experimental Psychology*, **3**, 390–395.

Cohen, B. P. (1958). 'A probability model for conformity,' *Sociometry*, **21**, 69–81.

Cohen, B. P. (1963). *Conflict and Conformity: A Probability Model and its Application*, MIT Press, Cambridge, Mass.

Cohen, B. P., and Lee, H. (1975). *Conflict, Conformity and Social Status*, Elsevier Scientific Publishing Company, New York.

Davis, J. H. (1973). 'Group decision and social interaction: A theory of social decision schemes,' *Psychological Review*, **80**, 97–125.

Davis, J. H. (1980). 'Group decision and procedural justice,' in M. Fishbein (ed.), *Progress in Social Psychology*, Erlbaum, Hillsdale, NJ.

Davis, J. H., Kerr, N. L., Atkin, R. S., Holt, R., and Meek, D. (1975). 'The decision processes of 6- and 12-person mock juries assigned unanimous and 2/3 majority decision rules,' *Journal of Personality and Social Psychology*, **32**, 1–14.

Davis, J. H., Kerr, N. L., Stasser, G., Meek, D., and Holt, R. (1977). 'Victim consequences, sentence severity, and decision processes in mock juries,' *Organizational Behavior and Human Performance*, **18**, 346–365.

Davis, J. H., Spitzer, C. E., Nagao, D. H., and Stasser, G. (1978). 'Bias in social decisions by individuals and groups: An example from mock juries,' in H. Brandstatter, J. H. Davis, and H. Schuler (eds.), *Dynamics of Group Decisions*, pp. 33–52, Sage Publications, Beverly Hills.

Davis, J. H., Stasser, G., Spitzer, C. E., and Holt, R. W. (1976). 'Changes in group member's decision preferences during discussion: An illustration with mock juries,' *Journal of Personality and Social Psychology*, **34**, 1177–1187.

Feinberg, W. E. (1971). 'Teaching the type I and type II errors: The judicial process,' *American Statistician*, **25**, 30–32.

Friedman, H. (1972). 'Trial by jury: Criteria for convictions, jury size, and type I and type II errors,' *American Statistician*, **26**, 21–23.

Gelfand, A. E. and Solomon, H. (1973). 'A study of Poisson's models for jury verdict in criminal and civil trials,' *Journal of the American Statistical Association*, **68**, 241–278.

Gelfand, A. E. and Solomon, H. (1974). 'Modeling jury verdicts in the American legal system,' *Journal of the American Statistical Association*, **69**, 32–37.

Gelfand, A. E., and Solomon, H. (1975). 'Analyzing the decision-making process of the American jury,' *Journal of the American Statistical Association*, **70**, 305–309.

Gelfand, A. E., and Solomon, H. (1977). 'An argument in favor of 12-member juries,' in S. S. Nagel (ed.), *Modeling the Criminal Justice System*, Sage, Beverly Hills, California.

Gillett, R. (1980a). 'Complex social decision scheme models,' *British Journal of Mathematical and Statistical Psychology*, **33**, 71–83.

Gillett, R. (1980b). 'Probability expressions for simple social decision scheme models,' *British Journal of Mathematical and Statistical Psychology*, **33**, 57–70.

Godwin, W. F., and Restle, F. (1974). 'The road to agreement: Subgroup pressures in small group consensus processes,' *Journal of Personality and Social Psychology*, **30**, 500–509.

Grofman, B. (1976). 'Not necessarily twelve and not necessarily unanimous,' in G. Bermant and N. Vidmar (eds.), *Psychology and the Law*, Heath, Lexington, Mass.

Grofman, B. (1980). 'Some preliminary models of jury decision making,' in C. Tullock (ed.), *Frontiers of Economics*, Vol. 4, Nijhoff, The Hague, Netherlands.

Hays, W. L. (1973). *Statistics for the Social Sciences*, 2nd edn, Holt, Rinehart and Winston, New York.

Hewes, D. (1980). 'Stochastic modeling of communication processes,' in P. Monge and J. N. Cappella (eds.), *Multivariate Techniques in Human Communication Research*, Academic Press, New York.

Kalven, H., and Zeisel, H. (1966). *The American Jury*, Little, Brown, Boston.

Kemeny, J. G., and Snell, J. L. (1962). *Mathematical Models in the Social Sciences*, Ginn & Co., Boston.

Kerr, N. L. (1981a). 'Social transition schemes: Charting the group's road to agreement,' *Journal of Personality and Social Psychology*, **41**, 684–702.

Kerr, N. L. (1981b). 'Social transition schemes: Model, method, and applications,' in H. Brandstatter and J. H. Davis (eds.), *Group Decisionmaking Processes*, Academic Press, New York.

Kerr, N. L., Atkin, R. S., Stasser, G., Meek, D., Holt, R. W., and Davis, J. H. (1976). 'Guilt beyond a reasonable doubt: Effect of concept definition and assigned decision rule on the judgments of mock jurors,' *Journal of Personality and Social Psychology*, **34**, 282–294.

Klevorick, A. K., and Rothschild, M. (1979). 'A model of the jury decision process,' *Journal of Legal Studies*, 141–164.

Lee, H. E. (1972). 'A Markov chain model for Asch-type experiments,' *Journal of Mathematical Sociology*, **2**, 131–142.

Münsterberg, H. (1914). Cited in R. L. Thorndike (1938).

Nagel, S. S., and Neef, M. (1975). 'Deductive modeling to determine an optimum jury size and fraction required to convict,' *Washington University Law Quarterly*, 933–978.

Padawer-Singer, A., and Barton, A. H. (1975). *Interim Report: Experimental Study of Decision Making in the 12- versus 6-man Jury Under Unanimous versus Non-Unanimous Decisions*, Columbia Bureau of Applied Social Research, New York.

Penrod, S., and Hastie, R. (1979). 'Models of jury decision making: A critical review,' *Psychological Bulletin*, **86**, 462–492.

Penrod, S., and Hastie, R. (1980). 'A computer simulation of jury decision making,' *Psychological Review*, **87**, 133–159.

Poisson, S. D. (1837). *Recherches sur la Probabilite des Jugements en Matiere Criminelle et en Matiere Civile, Precedees des Regles Generales du Calcul des Probabilites*, Bachelier, Imprimeur-Librairie, Paris.

Roper, R. T. (1980). 'Jury size and verdict consistency: "A line has to be drawn somewhere"?' *Law and Society*, **14**, 977–995.

Saks, M. J. (1977). *Jury Verdicts*, Heath, Lexington, Mass.

Saks, M. J., and Ostrom, T. M. (1975). 'Jury size and consensus requirements: The laws of probability v. the laws of the land,' *Journal of Contemporary Law*, **1**, 163–173.

Smoke, W. H., and Zajonc, R. B. (1962). 'On the reliability of group judgments and decisions,' in J. J. Criswell, H. Solomon, and P. Suppes (eds.), *Mathematical Methods in Small Group Processes*, Stanford University Press, Stanford, California.

Sperlich, P. W. (1980). '. . . and then there were six: The decline of the American jury,' *Judicature*, **63** (6), 262–279.

Stasser, G., and Davis, J. H. (1977). 'Opinion change during group discussion,' *Personality and Social Psychology Bulletin*, **3**, 252–256.

Thorndike, R. L. (1938). 'The effect of discussion upon the correctness of group decisions, when the factor of majority influence is allowed for,' *The Journal of Social Psychology*, **9**, 343–362.

Timmons, W. M. (1942). 'Can the product superiority of discussors be attributed to averaging or majority influences?' *The Journal of Social Psychology*, **15**, 23–32.

Walbert, T. D. (1971). 'Note: Effect of jury size on probability of conviction—An evaluation of *Williams* v. *Florida*,' *Case Western Law Review*, **22**, 529–555.

Note

Preparation of this chapter was aided by grant SES 80-12331 from the Law and Social Sciences Program of the National Science Foundation.

Small Groups and Social Interaction, Volume 2
Edited by H. H. Blumberg, A. P. Hare, V. Kent and M. Davies
© 1983 John Wiley & Sons Ltd

1.4   Group Polarization

Eugene Burnstein and Yaacov Schul   *The University of Michigan*

Introduction

Studies of polarization compare the opinion that group members hold before discussion (prior opinions) with those they hold after discussion (posterior opinions). The polarization phenomenon itself refers to instances in which these posterior opinions are *more extreme* than the prior ones. Such an effect usually occurs if a majority of individuals initially favors a particular position. The direction of polarization, therefore, often can be forecast from the distribution of prior opinion.[1] This holds over a very wide range of issues (e.g. see Davis, 1969; Gurnee, 1937a, b; Hall *et al.* 1963; Lorge and Solomon, 1955; Steiner, 1972; Thomas and Fink, 1961; Thorndike, 1938a, b; Zajonc, 1962; Zaleska, 1976; 1978). To illustrate Moscovici and Zavalloni (1969) found individuals who disapprove of American foreign policy or who admire Gaullist policies will express even greater disapproval or admiration, respectively, after group discussion of these issues (also see Doise, 1969; Myers and Bishop, 1970, 1971). Similar observations have been repeatedly made with several hypothetical real-life decisions, called Choice-Dilemmas (Kogan and Wallach, 1964), that involve opinions about what is an acceptable probability of success for pursuing an uncertain (rather than a certain) course of action. Some dilemmas reliably elicit a prior preference for low probability events (e.g. 'He should go to the best school even if there is only a small chance of graduating.') On others, individuals initially demand high probabilities (e.g. 'They shouldn't get married unless they're quite sure that their marriage will succeed'). The former produce posterior preferences for still lower probabilities, a shift toward 'risk,' while the latter give rise to posterior preferences for considerably higher probabilities, a shift toward 'caution.'

Because researchers happened to observe that the group opinion becomes increasingly 'risky' before discovering that under other conditions it also will become increasingly 'cautious,' polarization on the Choice-Dilemmas was dubbed the 'risky-shift.' The notion of risk or its desirability, however, is now seen as irrelevant to understanding group polarizations in general or the 'risky shift' in particular. There is much evidence on this point. First, we have already noted that prior-to-posterior differences often occur in respect to opinions which have little connection with probability levels (also see Fraser *et al.* 1971; Gouge and Fraser, 1972) and that among the standard Choice-Dilemmas several give reliable and robust shifts toward caution (Burns, 1967; Myers, 1967; Nordhoy, 1962; Stoner, 1968). Moreover, shifts toward either high or low probabilities were found to fit a subjective expected utility model that assumes individuals do *not* value riskiness *per se* (Burnstein, *et al.*, 1971; Vinokur, 1971); indeed, it has been directly shown that following the polarization of opinion, group members perceive their posterior opinion to be *no* more risky than their prior opinion (Kahan, 1975). Nor do content analyses of discussions reveal a concern about the desirability of riskiness (Vinokur *et al.*, 1975). Hence, the term 'risky' (or 'cautious') is a misnomer and it is no surprise that theories explaining group polarization in terms of collective risk taking, such as diffusion of responsibility (see below), have turned out to be inadequate even when they limited themselves to probability preferences.

Conditions for polarization

The first explanation of polarization which stimulated considerable research was proposed by Wallach *et al.* (1964). They maintained that a collective choice will be riskier than one made by an individual because in a group situation the decision is shared and, thus, the sense of personal responsibility for the results of decision is diffused. On the whole, this interesting hypothesis received meagre empirical support and has been abandoned as an explanation of group polarization. While diffusion of responsibility attributed the shifts to normative processes—the group reduces uneasiness about being blamed by others for a mishap—it does require discussion in order for the perception of collective accountability to develop. There is a more popular set of explanations for polarization which does *not* require discussion. It is merely assumed that each person learns the initial opinion of others and is able to *compare* his or her own opinion to theirs. These explanations for the shift have been called *value* theories or interpersonal *comparison* theories. They, like the diffusion of responsibility, assume shifts in opinions can be explained primarily in turns of normative processes (see Sanders and Baron, 1977, for a recent statement of this position).

The earliest formulation of interpersonal comparison theories was made by Brown (1965). He assumed that when confronted with certain kinds of problems, Western man values riskiness and wants to appear appropriately risky; given other kinds of problems, he values caution and desires the appearance of caution. Nevertheless what is appropriately risky or cautious in a concrete situation may be unclear. Thus, to the extent that individuals happen to be thinking about riskiness or caution as a value, they initially will prefer a daring or a prudent course, depending on the problem. In a group, however, not only are these people likely to be confronted by others who are more extreme than they, but also, probably as a result of this perceived difference, the value criteria become salient. Thus a comparison between their own opinion and those of the other members quickly informs them that they have been too moderate; believing that risk (or caution) will gain them social approval, they accept a more extreme course of action.

Moscovici and his co-workers have taken a different approach which is reminiscent of a well-known theorem from dissonance theory: the more effort expended in forming an opinion, the greater the commitment to that opinion. According to the commitment hypothesis, people ordinarily do not analyze their opinion intensively until they have to argue its pros and cons. Thus, prior preferences are relatively broad and tentative. Discussion, however, induces group members to evaluate painstakingly their own position against the position other members might hold. As a result, he or she is said to become committed to a more specific choice than was the case prior to discussion. For Moscovici, this commitment implies a narrowing of the latitude of acceptance (a range of (possible) positions perceived as similar to the one actually chosen) and '... a shift of judgment and opinion toward extremity (i.e. polarization). The direction of ... [polarization] ... is a function of dominant social ... [norms]' (Moscovici and Zavalloni, 1969). Although no particular mechanism is posited to explain how group norms determine the direction of polarization (but see Paichler, 1976, 1977), these researchers give intuitively reasonable examples of when this will occur. For instance, Doise (1969) suggests that knowledge of the opinion prevalent in a *rival* group increases the commitment of members in one's own group to the contrary opinion and thereby enhances polarization.

Persuasive argumentation

Set against the interpersonal comparison and commitment formulations, our own approach, persuasive arguments theory, explains polarization in terms of informational influence. It assumes that when a group member evaluates alternative positions, say, J versus K, he generates arguments describing the attributes of J and K. This means there exists in memory a relevant knowledge structure, that is, an organized pool of arguments speaking to each alternative. The arguments vary in number, availability or accessibility (the probability of their coming to mind), direction (pro-J or pro-K), and persuasiveness. To judge the relative merits of these alternatives, the person assembles arguments from this pool and integrates them into an opinion.[2] In outline form the theory says that (1) when the preponderance of arguments in the collective pool favors a particular alternative, the average prior opinion reflects the direction and magnitude of this preponderance; (2) further thought or discussion on the issue leads to the polarization of opinion toward the alternative that elicits more and/or better arguments; and (3) the extent of polarization will depend on whether the initial samples of arguments that members access either overlap with each other or exhaust the collective pool. To the degree that these samples do not overlap or exhaust the larger pool, there will remain important arguments that many members have not yet considered when they come either to rethink the issue in private or to discuss it with others in the group.

A persuasive arguments analysis of *discussion* effects may be illustrated with a simple example. Consider a choice in which the culturally given pool contains six pro-*J* arguments, *a*, *b*, *c*, *d*, *e*, and *f*, and three pro-*K* arguments, *l*, *m*, and *n*. One of several distinct outcomes would be expected, as a function of the distribution of arguments among members. Suppose all three of our discussants had thought of the very same arguments. In this case, their prior opinion about *J* would be identical and discussion would produce no change. On the other hand, if *a*, *b*, and *m* were retrieved by one discussant, *c*, *d*, and *m* by the second, and *e*, *f*, and *m* by the third (i.e. if each had assembled different pro-*J* arguments, but the same pro-*K* arguments), then, although they again hold identical prior opinion, the discussion would produce marked polarization toward *J*. Finally, polarization toward *K* would be predicted if one member had retrieved *a*, *b*, and *l*, another *a*, *b*, and *m*, and the third *a*, *b*, and *n* (i.e. if each had initially thought of the same pro-*J* but different pro-*K* arguments).

Much of our past research has attempted to determine the relative merits of persuasive argument versus comparison explanations of group polarization. Since the two theories often disagree, they were pitted against each other in several experiments. When this was done, it was shown, first, that if group members could argue but not compare their own opinion with that of others, polarization still occurred (Burnstein and Vinokur, 1973); second, if they could compare opinions but not openly argue about them, polarization disappeared (Burnstein and Vinokur, 1973, 1975) or was attenuated (Burnstein *et al.*, 1973); yet, third, even in attenuated form, polarization depended directly on *tacit* argumentation (Burnstein and Vinokur, 1975), that is, in the absence of discussion, information about the opinions of others seemed to guide or bias the person in retrieving arguments while forming his or her opinion. To further demonstrate the latter point, Burnstein and Sentis (1981) set up a conformity situation in which they varied the amount of time available to retrieve arguments by allowing the person either a long or a short interval to consider the majority position before indicating his or her own. They found that the longer the interval and the larger the bias (i.e. majority size), the greater the conformity; when the person was allowed either a long or short interval to think about his or her own position in an unbiased fashion, namely, *before* observing the majority, considerably less conformity was found under the former (long interval) than the latter.

To explain polarization in terms of informational influence we must take into account that group members generate arguments that are implied by, but go beyond, those given in the discussion. The same point is made in past studies that find that while opinion change is only weakly related to retention of the explicit content of an argument (e.g. Greenwald, 1968), it is strongly influenced by the ideational embellishment that occurs either in comprehending an argument (e.g. Brock, 1967; Cacioppo and Petty, 1979; Greenwald, 1968; Keating and Brock, 1974; McGuire, 1964; Petty and Cacioppo, 1977; Petty et al., 1976) or in merely thinking about the issue (e.g. Burnstein and Vinokur, 1977; Tesser, 1978; Tesser and Conlee, 1975). A reasonable conjecture, therefore, is that the persuasiveness of an argument depends on how much the person elaborates upon it during encoding, that is, the extent to which associations are established between the arguments given in the communication and those represented in prior knowledge. Presumably as a result of elaborative encoding, hitherto inaccessible propositions come to mind and are integrated to form an opinion. In brief, an argument is persuasive because it activates other arguments that would not have been made otherwise.[3]

Conclusion

Group discussion often leads members to polarize. There are two classes of explanations for this effect. One says that polarization is due to affective (normative) processes. It assumes that in many circumstances extreme opinions are socially desirable. Thus, moderate members will shift to an extreme position to avoid social disapproval. The second holds that polarization is the result of cognitive (informational) processes. Such an effect occurs when members deciding between alternative courses gain access to arguments that are persuasive with respect to one of the alternatives. Opinions are especially likely to polarize as a result of group discussion because often there are persuasive arguments that initially come to mind in only a few individuals; naturally, when shared with others, these arguments produce a marked shift in opinions. Of primary interest were the different conditions specified by these two approaches for the occurrence of group polarization—for example, with respect to whether or not polarization will occur under conditions in which each member argues for his or her true opinion while believing that the others are not, the persuasive arguments formulation suggests that it will and interpersonal comparison suggests the opposite (cf. Burnstein and Vinokur, 1973). Our analysis of the findings on questions of this kind indicates that theories based on cognitive processes offer a more adequate explanation of polarization than those based on affective processes. From a broader theoretical perspective, however, the relationship between cognition and affect in respect to opinion change might be conceptualized as one in which the former deals with the more immediate determinants of polarization and the latter, with relatively remote determinants. Thus, for instance, the information gained from comparisons with other group members may have influence by biasing the argument sample a person retrieves during opinion formation. From this perspective comparisons process could still exert considerable control, albeit indirectly, over group polarization.

Notes

The research from our laboratory that is reported here was supported by grants from the National Institute of Mental Health and the National Science Foundation.

1. We will argue later (a) that the distribution of opinions in a group corresponds to the distribution of persuasive information among members and (b) that shifts in the former, such as polarization, are due to changes in the latter. It will also be shown that the *same* distribution of prior opinions may be produced by several *different* distributions of information. Only a few of the latter, however, lead to a shift in opinion following discussion. Since these 'few' occur more frequently than other distributions of information, it is fair to say that the shift '... often can be forecast from the distribution of prior opinions'—but not always.

2. It might be useful to imagine a hypothetical collective pool that contains all the available arguments. An individual argument pool would then, on the average, constitute a representative sample of information from the collective one. Naturally, some individual argument pools will be biased or exhaustive, that is, they will include certain arguments that are generally unavailable. This restricted availability of information prior to discussion is assumed to be a necessary condition for polarization following discussion.

3. For example, one of the Choice-Dilemma items widely used in research on polarization (Kogan and Wallach, 1964) has the group decide whether some one should attend a university that is highly distinguished but extremely rigorous, so that a sizable number of students fail to receive their degree, or a university that is considerably less distinguished but easy enough that virtually every student who enters receives his degree. In group discussions of this problem there are a few arguments that are extraordinarily cogent. One of these is: 'He can always transfer if he's failing.' This proposition is persuasive because once it is asserted an important inference is automatically accessed: 'Going to the better school and flunking is not much worse than going to the lesser school to begin with.' This inference constitutes new information that increases the attractiveness of the uncertain alternative and, thereby, polarizes opinions in the group toward the latter (Vinokur and Burnstein, 1978a, b; Vinokur *et al.*, 1975). Notice also that 'He can always transfer' follows from relating the facts of the dilemma to relevant prior knowledge, that is, it comes to mind effortlessly when these facts are encoded within a schema about 'moving from one American university to another.'

References

Brock, T. C. (1967). 'Communication discrepancy and intent to persuade as determinants of counterargument production,' *Journal of Experimental Social Psychology*, **3**, 296–309.

Brown, R. (1965). *Social Psychology*, Free Press of Glencoe, New York.

Burns, J. F. (1967). 'An extremity-variance analysis of group decisions involving risk,' Unpublished doctoral dissertation, Sloan School of Management, Massachusetts Institute of Technology, Cambridge, Mass.

Burnstein, E., Miller, H., Vinokur, A., Katz, S., and Crowley, J. (1971). 'The risky-shift is eminently rational,' *Journal of Personality and Social Psychology*, **20**, 462–471.

Burnstein, E., and Sentis, K. P. (1981). 'Why Asch found that a majority of three was just as powerful as a majority of fifteen,' Manuscript in preparation.

Burnstein, E., and Vinokur, A. (1973). 'Testing two classes of theories about group induced shifts in individual choice,' *Journal of Experimental Social Psychology*, **9**, 123–137.

Burnstein, E. and Vinokur, A. (1975). 'What a person thinks upon learning he has chosen differently from others: Nice evidence for the persuasive-arguments explanation of choice shifts,' *Journal of Experimental Social Psychology*, **11**, 412–426.

Burnstein, E., and Vinokur, A. (1977). 'Persuasive argumentation and social comparison as determinants of attitude polarization,' *Journal of Experimental Social Psychology*, **13**, 315–332.

Burnstein, E., Vinokur, A., and Trope, Y. (1973). 'Interpersonal comparison versus persuasive-argumentation: A more direct test of alternative explanations for group induced shifts in individual choice,' *Journal of Experimental Social Psychology*, **9**, 236–245.

Cacioppo, J. T., and Petty, R. E. (1979). 'Effects of message repetition and position on cognitive response, recall, and persuasion,' *Journal of Personality and Social Psychology*, **37**, 97–109.

Davis, J. H. (1969). *Group Performance*, Addison-Wesley, Reading, Mass.

Doise, W. (1969). 'Intergroup relations and polarization of individual and collective judgments,' *Journal of Personality and Social Psychology*, **12**, 136–143.

Fraser, C., Gouge, C., and Billig, M. (1971). 'Risky shifts, cautious shifts, and group polarization,' *European Journal of Social Psychology*, **1**, 7–30.

Gouge, C., and Fraser, C. (1972). 'A further demonstration of group polarization,' *European Journal of Social Psychology*, **2**, 95–97.

Greenwald, A. G. (1968). 'Cognitive learning, cognitive response to persuasion and attitude change,' in A. G. Greenwald, T. C. Brock, and T. M. Ostrom (eds.), *Psychological Foundation of Attitudes*, Academic Press, New York.

Gurnee, H. (1937a). 'A comparison of collective and individual judgments of fact,' *Journal of Experimental Psychology*, **21**, 106–112.

Gurnee, H. (1937b). 'Maze learning in the collective situation,' *Journal of Psychology*, **3**, 437–444.

Hall, E., Mouton, J., and Blake, R. (1963). 'Group problem solving effectiveness under conditions of pooling vs. interaction,' *Journal of Social Psychology*, **59**, 147–157.

Kahan, J. P. (1975). 'A subjective probability interpretation of the risky shift,' *Journal of Personality and Social Psychology*, **31**, 977–982.

Keating, J. P., and Brock, T. C. (1974). 'Acceptance of persuasion and the inhibition of counterargumentation under various distraction tasks,' *Journal of Experimental Social Psychology*, **10**, 301–309.

Kogan, N. and Wallach, M. A. (1964). *Risk Taking: A Study in Cognition and Personality*, Holt, Rinehart and Winston, New York.

Lorge, I., and Solomon, H. (1955). 'Two models of group behavior in the solution of Eureka-type problems,' *Psychometrika*, **20**, 139–148.

McGuire, W. (1964). 'Inducing resistance to persuasion,' in L. Berkowitz (ed.), *Advances in Experimental Social Psychology*, Vol. I, Academic Press, New York.

Moscovici, S. and Zavalloni, M. (1969). 'The group as a polarizer of attitudes,' *Journal of Personality and Social Psychology*, **12**, 125–235.

Myers, D. G. (1967). 'Enhancement of initial risk taking tendencies in social situations,' unpublished doctoral dissertation, University of Iowa.

Myers, D. G., and Bishop, G. D. (1970). 'Discussion effects on racial attitudes,' *Science*, **169**, 778–779.

Myers, D. G., and Bishop, G. D. (1971). 'Enhancement of dominant attitudes in group discussion,' *Journal of Personality and Social Psychology*, **20**, 386–391.

Nordhoy, F. (1962). 'Group interaction in decision-making under risk,' Unpublished master's thesis, School of Industrial Management, Massachusetts Institute of Technology.

Paicheler, G. (1976). 'Norms and attitudes change I: Polarization and styles of behavior,' *European Journal of Social Psychology*, **6**, 405–427.

Paichler, G. (1977). 'Norms and attitude change II; The phenomenon of bipolarization,' *European Journal of Social Psychology*, **7**, 5–14.

Petty, R. E. and Cacioppo, J. T. (1977). 'Forewarning, cognitive responding and resistance to persuasion,' *Journal of Personality and Social Psychology*, **35**, 645–655.

Petty, R. E., Wells, G., and Brock, T. C. (1976). 'Distraction can enhance or reduce yielding to propaganda: Thought disruption versus effort justification,' *Journal of Personality and Social Psychology*, **34**, 874–884.

Sanders, G., and Baron, R. S. (1977). 'Is social comparison irrelevant for producing choice shifts?' *Journal of Experimental and Social Psychology*, **13**, 303–314.

Steiner, I. D. (1972). *Group Process and Productivity*, Academic Press, New York.

Stoner, J. A. F. (1968). 'Risky and cautious shifts in group decisions. The influence of widely held values,' *Journal of Experimental Social Psychology*, **4**, 442–459.

Tesser, A. (1978). 'Self-generated attitude change,' L. Berkowitz (ed.), *Advances in Experimental Social Psychology*, Vol. 11, pp. 289–339. Academic Press, New York.

Tesser, A., and Conlee, M. C. (1975). 'Some effects of time and thought on attitude polarization,' *Journal of Personality and Social Psychology*, **31**, 262–270.

Thomas, E. J., and Fink, C. F. (1961). 'Models of group problem solving,' *Journal of Abnormal and Social Psychology*, **63**, 53–63.

Thorndike, R. L. (1938a). 'On what type of task will a group do well?' *Journal of Abnormal and Social Psychology*, **33**, 409–413.

Thorndike, R. L. (1938b). 'The effect of discussion upon the correctness of group decisions, when the factor of majority is allowed for,' *Journal of Social Psychology*, **9**, 343–362.

Vinokur, A. (1971). 'Review and theoretical analysis of the effects of group processes upon individual and group decisions involving risk,' *Psychological Bulletin*, **76**, 231–250.

Vinokur, A., and Burnstein, E. (1978a). 'Depolarization of attitudes in groups,' *Journal of Personality and Social Psychology*, **36**, 872–885.

Vinokur, A., and Burnstein, E. (1978b). 'Novel argumentation and attitude change: The case of polarization following group discussion,' *European Journal of Social Psychology*, **8**, 335–348.

Vinokur, A., Trope, Y., and Burnstein, E. (1975). 'A decision making analysis of persuasive-argumentation and the choice-shift effect,' *Journal of Experimental Social Psychology*, **11**, 127–148.

Wallach, M. A., Kogan, N., and Bem, D. J. (1964). 'Diffusion of responsibility and level of risk taking in groups,' *Journal of Abnormal and Social Psychology*, **68**, 263–274.

Zajonc, R. B. (1962). A note on group judgments and group size. *Human Relations*, **15**, 177–180.

Zaleska, M. (1976). 'Majority influence on group choices among bets,' *Journal of Personality and Social Psychology*, **33**, 8–17.

Zaleska, M. (1978). 'Some experimental results: Majority influence on group decisions,' in H. Brandstatter, J. H. Davis and H. Schuler (eds.), *Dynamics of Group Decisions*, Sage Publications, Beverly Hills, California.

2 Cooperation, Competition, and Conflict Resolution

Small Groups and Social Interaction, Volume 2
Edited by H. H. Blumberg, A. P. Hare, V. Kent and M. Davies
Published by John Wiley & Sons Ltd 1983

2.1 Conflict Resolution—Strategies Inducing Cooperation*

Morton Deutsch   *Teachers College, Columbia University*

Subjects

... The Ss used in this experiment consisted of a fairly diverse group of thirty-eight men and sixty-seven women who were randomly selected from the subject pool and randomly assigned to the various experimental conditions.

Experimental situation and instructions

... Recorded instructions for the game were played to the Ss over a tape recorder. A transcript of the instructions follows.

> There are two of you who are going to play a game in which you can either win money or lose money. I want you to earn as much money as you can regardless of how much the other earns. This money is real and you will keep whatever you earn. I am going to give you each thirty cents to begin with—that is, at this time you each have thirty cents. You can lose this thirty cents or earn more money, depending on how you play the game. This game consists of a series of trials; you each have a pegboard in front of you. This board is divided into two areas: a resource area and an allocation area. Your task on each of these trials will be to select one peg from the resource area and

* Abridged from Morton Deutsch (1973). *The Resolution of Conflict*, Yale University Press, New Haven and London: pp. 316–335, 346–347. Reprinted by permission of Yale University Press and the author. Copyright © 1973 Yale University Press. This experiment was done in collaboration with Yakov Epstein, Donna Canavan, and Peter Gumpert. For a fuller account, readers are referred to the original work and to additional items cited there.

place it in the allocation area. At the end of each trial, you will be told what the other has chosen for that trial and how much money you have each won or lost on that trial.

Now let me tell you something about these pegs; there are five different kinds of pegs: black, white, blue, red, and green. In addition, there are two specially shaped markers—orange and beige—and they each have pins on the top of them. [The values of pegs in this experiment were as follows: black = 6¢; blue = 1¢ (9¢ if other also chooses blue); white = 7¢ to other; red = 6¢ from other (if later used in attack); green = 6¢ from other (if later used to defend against attack); orange = 'attack'—for every red peg held by attacker, other pays 6¢ to attacker; but also, attacker gives 6¢ to other for every green peg held by other; pegs thus 'used' cannot be used again later. Beige = 'disarm'—to indicate that you have destroyed all of your red pegs accumulated so far.]

Now let me describe how the game is actually played. At the beginning of each trial, we will announce the trial number. At that time, you will choose one peg of any color from the resource area and place it in the allocation area. Put the peg in the row number corresponding to the trial number. That is, on trial one, place the peg in row 1. On trial two, row 2, and so on. Make sure to place the peg in the hole which is the same color as the peg. Blue pegs go in blue holes, black pegs in black holes, and so on. After you have made your choices, we will announce the results of that trial to both of you. On the table, there is a paper which can be used to keep a record of the game. This paper is used to record the other's choice, also what you expect the other to choose, and also the amount of money that you have each won or lost on that trial. When we announce the trial number, write down the color peg that you intend to choose for that trial in the column entitled *My Choice*. Next, write down the color peg that you expect the other player to choose in the column entitled *I Expect Other to Choose*. Then make your choice on the board. When you have both made your choices, we will announce the results of that trial to each of you. You will then record your gains or losses in the column entitled *My Gains or Losses*, and you will record the other's gains or losses in the column entitled *Other's Gains or Losses*. ... You have a summary sheet which describes the various pegs and what they are worth...

Ss were then run through a series of practice trials ...

Experimental design

Five experimental conditions and one control condition were run. In the control condition, two true Ss played the game with one another. In the five experimental conditions, Ss were paired with an accomplice of the experimenter who played in accordance with one of the predetermined strategies.

1. *Turn the other cheek.* The accomplice chose blue on the first trial, white on the second trial, and blue on the third trial—no matter what the actual S chose. Thereafter, he chose blue, except that he chose white if the S had chosen red or orange on the preceding trial.
2. *Nonpunitive.* The accomplice chose blue on the first three trials. Thereafter, he matched what the S chose on the preceding trial, with the following exceptions: if the S chose red or orange, the accomplice chose green; if the S chose to disarm (beige), then the accomplice chose blue; if the S chose green, the accomplice chose blue.
3. *Deterrent.* The accomplice chose blue on the first trial and whenever the S chose blue, white, or beige. To a choice of black, green, or red by the S, he responded with red; if S chose orange (attack), he counterattacked with an orange on the next trial.
4. *Reformed sinner–turn the other cheek.* The accomplice attacked by choosing orange on the third, ninth, and twelfth trials; otherwise, he chose red during the first fifteen trials. On the sixteenth trial, he disarmed completely by choosing beige, and, thereafter, he chose blue, white, and blue and followed the turn-the-other-cheek strategy (as described in point (1) above).
5. *Reformed sinner–nonpunitive.* For the first sixteen trials, the accomplice behaved in exactly the same manner as indicated in point (4) above. On the seventeenth, eighteenth, and nineteenth trials, he chose blue and, thereafter, followed the nonpunitive strategy described in point (2).

Although fifteen Ss were run in each of the experimental conditions (with twenty pairs in the control condition), an examination of our data soon revealed that not all the Ss in each condition were exposed to the strategy we had assigned for them. For example, in the first three conditions, Ss who made blue choices both initially and throughout received exactly the same responses from the accomplices, and, hence, they were not exposed to different treatments. For this reason, we decided to eliminate from our analysis of results those Ss who did not get exposed, differentially, to the strategy to which they were assigned.[1] In the turn-the-other-cheek strategy, we eliminated four Ss who did not experience a white choice after the first three trials; in the nonpunitive condition, nine Ss were eliminated because they did not experience a green choice in response to their red or orange choice; in the deterrent treatment, five Ss were lost because they did not experience a red choice at any time. In the reformed sinner–turn-the-other-cheek condition, three Ss were eliminated who did not experience a white choice after the first three trials of reformed behavior by the accomplice. In the reformed sinner—nonpunitive condition, eight Ss were eliminated because they did not experience a green choice in response to red or orange choices.

By the criteria we used for eliminating Ss from the experimental conditions, any S who chose blue throughout would have been taken out of our sample. These, of course, were the Ss who behaved most cooperatively. To produce a parallel reduction in our control groups of paired true Ss, we eliminated nine of twenty control pairs who chose blue throughout the game. For analytic purposes, one member of each control pair was then randomly assigned to be compared with the true Ss in the various experimental conditions, and the other member was assigned to be compared with the accomplices.

Results

The meaning of the pegs.   To obtain measures of the emotional meaning of the various moves available to the Ss in the game, they were asked to rate, in a post-experimental questionnaire, each of the different-colored pegs on three nine-point scales: bad–good, strong–weak, active–passive. Analysis of variance indicates that the pegs differed significantly from one another in the ratings they received; this is so for each of the three scales. . .

The ratings of the pegs (in Table 1) seem consistent with our *a priori* conceptions of their interpersonal meanings. Further support for the appropriateness of our *a priori* conceptions came from the names that the Ss ascribed to them. On the post-experimental questionnaire, we asked the Ss to select from a list the two names that would 'best capture the meaning of moving that particular peg' for the black, blue, white, red, and green pegs. Below is a list of the three most frequently selected names for each peg, with the number of Ss selecting each name being given in parenthesis:

Black peg: cautious (30), independent (29), selfish (18)
Blue peg: cooperative (43), mutual (35), co-working (26)
White peg: benevolent (32), philanthropic (30), foolish (19)
Red peg: aggressive (52), combative (26), hostile (17)
Green peg: protective (45), antiweapon (27), self-preservative (26)

Financial outcomes

In a game that permits a variety of behavior, one of the best measures of the overall process is the outcome of behavior. Our data provide four measures of outcome, all of which are relevant to a comparison of the effectiveness of the different behavioral strategies. These measures are: the joint outcome of the two players, the outcome of the S, the outcome of the accomplice, and the difference between the outcomes of the S and the accomplice. Figures 1–4 graph these different outcome data for each of the six conditions by blocks of fifteen trials.

Joint outcomes.   It is evident from Figure 1 that joint outcomes improved with the number of trials in almost all conditions. However, analyses of variance reveal

Table 1 Mean ratings of the pegs ($n = 85$)

	Bad (1)–Good (9)[a]	Active (1)–Passive (9)	Strong (1)–Weak (9)
Black (individualistic)	6.54	5.27	4.67
Blue (cooperative)	7.87	3.17	3.21
White (altruistic-ingratiating)	5.47	6.39	6.13
Red (aggressive)	3.49	2.30	3.40
Green (defensive)	5.77	5.65	5.29
Orange (attack)	3.82	2.22	2.98
Beige (disarm)	5.12	6.16	5.52

Note The data represent the ratings by all Ss who participated in the experiment, including those who were not exposed to the strategies, who completed the post-experimental questionnaire.
[a] The numbers in parentheses indicate the numerical values associated with each end of the bipolar scales.

that there were differences among the conditions in the initial and final outcome levels as well as in the amount of change in outcomes between the initial and final trial blocks.[2] The turn-the-other-cheek strategy produced a high initial joint outcome, which did not improve consistently over trials. The nonpunitive strategy also resulted in a relatively high initial joint outcome, but it got higher with each succeeding trial block. In contrast, the deterrent strategy had a relatively low initial joint outcome, and, although it increased with trials, the increase was comparatively small. As might be expected, the joint outcomes in the first fifteen trials

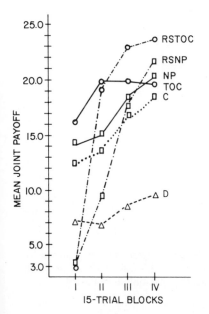

Figure 1 Mean joint payoffs (in cents, divided by 10) for subjects and accomplices, by 15-trial blocks. Conditions are indicated as follows: RSTOC, reformed sinner–turn the other cheek ($N = 12$); RSNP, reformed sinner–non-punitive, ($N = 7$); NP, non-punitive ($N = 6$); TOC, turn the other cheek ($N = 11$); C, control ($N = 11$); D, deterrent ($N = 10$)

were quite low in both reformed sinner conditions. However, after the 'reform' took place on the sixteenth trial, there was a substantial and rapid improvement in outcomes. The improvement was more rapid and the joint outcomes reached a higher level in the turn-the-other-cheek rather than in the nonpunitive–reformed sinner strategy. It is of interest to note that the turn-the-other-cheek strategy produced higher outcomes in the last two blocks of trials when preceded by aggressive behavior during the first block of fifteen trials than if employed from the very start of the game. The control groups, composed of paired true Ss, had joint outcomes that were about midway between those obtained in the deterrent and the nonpunitive strategies.

The subject's outcome. From Figure 2, it is evident that the Ss had the best outcomes in the turn-the-other-cheek condition (as could be expected from the accomplice's behavior in this strategy) and the worst outcomes when the accomplice was employing the deterrent strategy. The control groups of naive Ss did not do as well as the Ss who were exposed to the nonpunitive strategy, but they did better than those who experienced the deterrent strategy.[3]

The accomplice's outcome. Figure 3 gives the answer to the question of which strategy benefited the accomplice most. Evidently, the nonpunitive strategy was considerably more rewarding than either the turn-the-other-cheek or the deterrent strategy. Although the outcomes for the accomplice who employed the deterrent

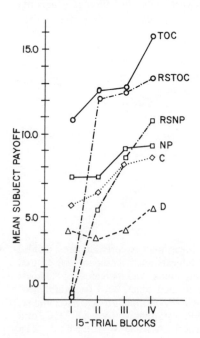

Figure 2 Mean subject payoffs (in cents, divided by 10) by 15-trial blocks. Conditions indicated by initials as in Figure 1

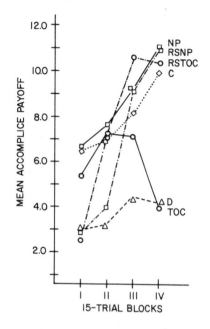

Figure 3 Mean payoffs of accomplices (in cents, divided by 10) by 15-trial blocks. Conditions indicated by initials as in Figure 1

strategy were, on the average, worse than those for the turn-the-other-cheek strategist, the outcomes for the former improved over the last several trial blocks but worsened for the latter. The 'sinners who reformed' did relatively well after they reformed (but poorly while being aggressive). The turn-the-other-cheek–reformed sinner had a faster improvement rate than did the non-punitive–reformed sinner. Also, it is of interest to note that the differences between the two turn-the-other-cheek strategies were substantial and increased with succeeding trial blocks, while the opposite was true for the two nonpunitive strategies. Here, the differences were small and they decreased with trials.[4]

Differences in outcomes between the subject and the accomplice. It is evident from Figure 4 that the Ss did much better, and consistently so, than the accomplices *only* in the turn-the-other-cheek condition. A similar trend was found in the reformed sinner–turn-the-other-cheek condition once the accomplice had 'reformed.' Otherwise, the differences between the Ss and the accomplices were insubstantial and did not necessarily favor the Ss.[5]

Choices made by the subjects

Figure 5 charts the choices made in each condition for each of the four trial blocks. Over all the conditions and trials, the blue pegs were chosen most frequently, and then came the black, red, green, orange, and white pegs in descending order of frequency. The frequencies with which the different pegs were chosen

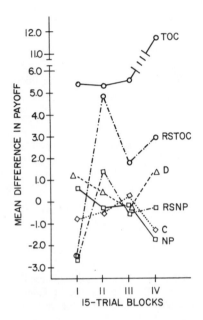

Figure 4 Difference between subject and accomplice payoffs (in cents, divided by 10) by 15-trial blocks. Conditions indicated by initials as in Figure 1

varied, of course, as an interacting function of both the strategy to which the Ss were exposed and the trial block in which the choices were made. Thus the turn-the-other-cheek strategy induced the Ss to make relatively more aggressive moves (red and orange choices) and to decrease the relative frequency of their defensive (green) and individualistic (black) actions as the trials proceeded. On the other hand, the nonpunitive strategy led the subjects to increase the proportion of their

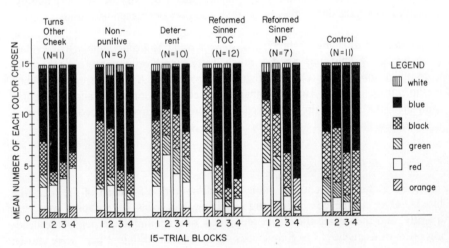

Figure 5   Mean numbers of each color chosen by 15-trial blocks

cooperative (blue) moves as they decreased their individualistic (black) and aggressive (orange and red) choices. The deterrent strategy elicited from the Ss a gradual decrease in individualistic choices, an increase in and then a subsidence of aggressive activity, and finally an increase in cooperative choices. In the 'sinner' stage of the reformed sinner strategies, the subjects reacted with a relatively high level of aggressive, defensive, and individualistic behavior and a low frequency of cooperative choice. After the reform by the accomplice, the turn-the-other-cheek–reformed sinner elicited a rapid increase in cooperative behavior, which was paralleled by a decrease in individualistic, aggressive, and defensive actions. The increase in the frequency of cooperative choices and the accompanying decrease in the noncooperative behaviors did not occur so rapidly after the reform in the nonpunitive–reformed sinner strategy. The control groups of paired true Ss showed a gradual increase in cooperative activity with a gradual decrease in defensive and aggressive behaviors. Their level of individualistic activity did not alter much over the trials.

Analyses of variance were made on the frequency data for each type of choice by condition and trial block. Separate analyses were done excluding and including the first block of trials (i.e. the trials before the accomplice reformed in the reformed sinner conditions). A brief description of the results of these analyses for each type of choice follows.[6]

White pegs.   Relatively few of the Ss made this type of move in any of the conditions, and no significant differences were obtained among the conditions. There was a significant decrease in the use of these pegs during the last three trial blocks.

Blue pegs.   There was a significant overall increase in cooperative choices per trial block the more times the game had been played. There was also a significant interaction between conditions and trial blocks for the last three trial blocks as well as for all trial blocks. Apart from the responses to the reformed sinners before they reformed, the fewest cooperative choices were elicited by the deterrent strategy. The most frequent cooperative responses were made to reformed sinner–turn the other cheek. All strategies except the deterrent strategy ended up eliciting more cooperative behavior than the control condition of paired true Ss.

Black pegs.   There was a significant overall decrease in the number of individualistic choices made over the course of the four trial blocks. No decrease occurred in response to the nonpunitive and the turn-the-other-cheek strategies.

Green pegs.   There was a significant overall decrease in the number of defensive weapons used by the Ss over the last three trial blocks as well as over all four blocks. The decrease over the four blocks is most marked in the reformed sinner conditions and not evidenced in the deterrent and nonpunitive conditions. During the last three trial blocks, significantly more defensive weapons were chosen by the Ss in response to the deterrent strategy than to any other condition.

Red pegs. There was a significant overall decrease in the choice of aggressive weapons over the block of four trials and for the last three trials. However, in the turn-the-other-cheek condition, the frequency of red choices increased from trial block to trial block. Aggressive weapons were chosen most frequently by the Ss who were exposed to the deterrent and the turn-the-other-cheek strategies and least frequently by the Ss in the control condition.

Orange pegs. In general, few attacks were made by the Ss; attacks decreased significantly over all four trial blocks and also over the last three blocks. However, there was a slight increase in attacks over the four trial blocks in response to the deterrent and turn-the-other-cheek strategies; the largest decrease between the initial and final blocks occurred in the Ss exposed to the reformed sinner strategies.

Other findings

Table 2 presents some data obtained from the post-experimental questionnaires about the impressions that the Ss formed of the accomplices in the various experimental conditions. The Ss perceived the accomplices in the nonpunitive condition as the most cooperative, most stable, and most fair; they were also perceived as being relatively kind, generous, and peaceful. The accomplices using the turn-the-other-cheek strategy were also perceived relatively favorably on the just-mentioned characteristics; they were viewed as the most kind, generous, and peaceful. The deterrent strategists were rated as the most uncooperative, least kind, and most selfish of the accomplices; they were also considered to be relatively unstable and almost as aggressive as the reformed sinners. Not surprisingly, the highest instability was attributed to the accomplices employing the

Table 2   Means of Ss ratings from the Post-experimental Questionnaire

	TOC	Non-P	Det.	RS–TOC	RS–Non-P	Control	Sig.[a] level
Ratings of Other as:							
Aggressive (1)–Peaceful (9)	7.73	6.60	4.90	4.42	4.29	6.00	$p < .10$
Fair (1)–Unfair (9)	3.09	1.60	3.77	3.75	4.42	3.75	not sig.
Kind (1)–Cruel (9)	2.30	2.80	4.60	4.33	3.86	4.00	$p < .10$
Stable (1)–Unstable (9)	2.30	1.20	4.60	5.33	4.44	3.88	$p < .005$
Selfish (1)–Generous (9)	7.70	5.60	4.90	4.92	5.14	5.13	$p < .05$
Cooperative (1)–Uncooperative (9)	2.90	1.00	6.20	4.50	3.29	4.38	$p < .001$
Own desire to play again (1)	1.81	1.60	5.33	2.00	2.00	2.20	$p < .005$

[a] Based on one-way analyses of variance with df for F usually being 5/47. Not all Ss filled out the questionnaire.

reformed sinner–turn-the-other-cheek strategy. Finally, it is of interest to note that the Ss who were exposed to the deterrent strategy expressed the least desire to play the game again.

Discussion of results

The results of the present experiment are consistent with, and extend, the findings of other investigators. Solomon [see Ch. 8 of Deutsch, 1973] studied the effects of three strategies upon the development of interpersonal trust in a two-person Prisoner's Dilemma game: an *unconditionally benevolent* strategy (the accomplice always chose to cooperate no matter what the S chose), a *conditionally benevolent* strategy (the accomplice chose cooperatively on the first trial and, after, matched the choice made by the S on the preceding trial), and an *unconditionally malevolent* strategy (the accomplice always chose non-cooperatively, no matter what the S chose). The turn-the-other cheek and unconditionally benevolent strategies resemble one another in that they are both unconditionally cooperative and they both appeal to conscience. The nonpunitive and conditionally benevolent strategies both stress reciprocation—with the exception that the former strategy defends itself against threat and aggression but does not reciprocate them. (In the Prisoner's Dilemma game, it is impossible to tell whether a noncooperative action is defensive or aggressive in intent.) The unconditionally malevolent strategy was not matched by any of our strategies, except during the first fifteen trials of both the reformed sinner strategies.

Solomon found that his Ss exploited the accomplices who were unconditionally benevolent and were puzzled by their behavior; the Ss responded competitively to the unconditionally malevolent strategy and liked these accomplices least; and they responded most cooperatively to the conditionally benevolent accomplices and liked them most. Our results parallel Solomon's: our Ss behaved most competitively during the fifteen trials when the accomplices in the reformed sinner conditions were being threatening and aggressive; they tended to exploit the turn-the-other-cheek accomplices; and they behaved most cooperatively in the nonpunitive treatment.[7]

Bixenstine and Wilson (1963), in a study also employing the Prisoner's Dilemma game, have reported a finding similar to the result that we obtained with our turn-the-other-cheek and reformed sinner–turn-the-other-cheek strategies. They compared two strategies that used the same overall percentage of cooperative choices (50 percent) during 200 trials but that differed in their sequencing of choices. In one strategy, the accomplices chose cooperatively in 95 percent of the first 40 trials, while in the other they chose cooperatively in only 5 percent of these trials; in both strategies, they chose cooperatively in 50 percent of the next 20 trials, i.e. trials 41–60. Although their Ss responded slightly more cooperatively during the first 40 trials, to the accomplices who were programmed to choose cooperatively in 95 percent of the initial trials they responded considerably more favorably in the next 20 trials to the accomplices who had initially chosen a low rather than a high level of cooperation. These results paralleled our findings that the reformed sinner–turn-the-other-cheek strategist elicited more cooperation after the reform than did the accomplice who employed the turn-the-other-cheek strategy initially and throughout the game.

Shure, Meeker, and Hansford (1965) studied the effectiveness of a 'pacifist' strategy in a bargaining game modeled after our Acme-Bolt trucking game [see Ch. 9 of Deutsch, 1973]. In their experiment, they induced the real Ss to adopt a dominating rather than a cooperative strategy by having each S play the game as a representative of a team, i.e. as one who would share the game's outcome equally. The two teammates of the S were, in fact, confederates of the experimenters and they, by majority vote, pressured the S to adopt a dominating strategy before the start of the game; during the initial trials, they sent messages to the S to get him to maintain a dominating strategy. The S was exposed to an accomplice who always acted cooperatively and who required the S to use force (which the S thought would cause a painful electric shock to the accomplice) if the S wished to exploit him. In one experimental condition, the pacifist accomplice communicated his conciliatory intent, presented a statement of fair demands, and emphasized his refusal to use the shock and his intention to force the other to shock him if the other was going to remain unfair. In another condition, no direct communication was allowed among the players.

The results of this effort indicate that only a small proportion of the Ss did not exploit the pacifist accomplice; the proportion of Ss who switched from a dominating, exploitative strategy to a cooperative one increased significantly under the communication condition, but it was not a large increase. Further findings showed that it made little difference whether the pacifist accomplices explicitly disarmed or not, and it made little difference whether or not the Ss received information about the accomplices that indicated that the accomplices were Quakers who were morally committed to a position of nonviolence.

Our results with the turn-the-other-cheek strategy were consistent with the findings obtained by Shure et al. in their study of the pacifist strategy, although their results were considerably more extreme than ours. (In our experiment, the accomplices using the turn-the-other-cheek strategy elicited as much cooperation as the control Ss and had outcomes that were about as good as these Ss.) The extremity of their results was undoubtedly due to their having 'fixed' their Ss into a dominating strategy by the group pressures under which they were placed. This was not the case for our Ss. Shure et al. viewed their results as supporting the 'harsh and unflattering' judgment that the pacifist's tactics invited exploitation and aggression even among those who did not begin with such intentions. Their interpretation is too unqualified. Not only does it ignore the group pressures upon the subjects to be exploitative, but it also ignores the social reality of the experiment. From the experimenter's instructions, the Ss could assume that both players had the experimenter's approval and encouragement to seek 'selfish' outcomes and, also, that the experimenter's provision of means to attempt to dominate the other invited and legitimized their usage. In a sense, the pacifist was violating the implicit norms of the experimental situation as established by the experimenter and was appealing to exterior social values whose relevance had been deliberately minimized by the arrangements and paraphernalia of the experiment. (Ss were isolated in separate cubicles; they had no personal contact; they didn't know each other's names; if they communicated at all, it was through a computer; etc.) In such a context, the pacifist strategy might have been experienced as puzzling or even incredible, and as saintly but inappropriate. And, in fact, the turn-the-other-cheek strategy was often puzzling to *our* Ss; moreover, it was the only one in which some felt that they were not playing with a real person.

It is interesting to note that the reformed sinner–turn-the-other-cheek strategy was considerably more effective in eliciting cooperation than the simple turn-the-other-cheek strategy. The data of Table 2 suggest that, in the former condition, the initially aggressive behavior of the accomplice served to create an image of a relatively unstable and potentially aggressive person whom it was wise not to provoke lest he be tempted to revert to his aggressive ways. It seems likely, however, that, if we had run this condition for a longer series of trials, the cooperation by the Ss would have started to decrease.

The deterrent strategy was ineffective apparently because the Ss tended to perceive the threats made by the accomplice as aggressive rather than as deterrent in intent. Table 2 indicates that the accomplice using this strategy was rated relatively high in aggressiveness, selfishness, cruelty, and uncooperativeness. On the other hand, the nonpunitive strategy, which used defensive rather than threatening tactics to handle noncooperation by the Ss, was quite effective in eliciting cooperation and favorable evaluations from the Ss. It is of interest to note that the reformed sinner–nonpunitive strategy also elicited considerable cooperation, despite the relatively unfavorable ratings that the accomplices received. Unlike our expectation for the other reformed sinner strategy, we would not expect cooperation to deteriorate in a longer series of trials. . .

Conclusion

[In several experiments, the first of which is reprinted above] we have studied several basic types of strategies for inducing cooperation. It is well to stress that each type has many different variants and that it would be mistaken to conclude that the results obtained in our experiments for a given type would hold for all its variants. For example, the less threatening variant of the deterrent strategy used in the third and fourth experiments elicited considerably less negative attitudes, although rather similar behavior, than the harsher variant used in the first two experiments. Also, it is well to recognize that the impact of a given strategy may be great or small, depending on the social context and circumstances in which it is employed. Thus it seems likely that the effectiveness of the turn-the-other-cheek strategy is very much influenced by the competitiveness of the situation; the more competitive the incentives of the other, the more likely it is that such a strategy will be massively exploited. However, it should be noted that this strategy was consistently exploited in all our experiments except when it had been preceded by a show of strength (the reformed sinner variant) in the first experiment. On the other hand, if we consider the deterrent strategy—in comparison with the control situation—it seems plausible to speculate that such a strategy may become relatively more effective as the conditions become more competitive. Under relatively cooperative conditions, it induces the other to see the accomplice as being hostile and aggressive, and provocatively so. On the other hand, when the circumstances strongly elicit competitive behavior, then the deterrent strategist is less aggressive than the control subject, who is operating on unsystematic impulse rather than on deliberate plan and tends to be vindictive.

The effectiveness of the nonpunitive strategy varied least from situation to situation. In none of the experiments was any of the other strategies more effective than the nonpunitive one in eliciting cooperation and reducing aggression. Only under the extremely competitive conditions of the fourth experiment was this strategy no more effective than the deterrent strategy, and, even then, when the accomplice had equal power with the subject, he elicited less competitive behavior when he employed a nonpunitive rather than a deterrent strategy.

It is the task of future investigations to specify more precisely and in greater detail the conditions under which the various strategies of inducing cooperation are most effective and to identify strategies that are effective over a wide range of conditions. It is often man's lot to need to obtain another's cooperation under conditions that are unclear and in situations when little is known about the other.

Notes

1. ... A preliminary analysis of various data, comparing the overall results for males and females without regard to experimental conditions, revealed no statistically significant differences. . . .

2. Here, as with most of our measures, two separate two-way analyses of variance were done: conditions × trial blocks (using all four trial blocks), and conditions × trial blocks (using the last three trial blocks only). Each trial block consisted of 15 trials. For the four trial block analysis of *joint outcomes* the effects of conditions ($F = 4.69$, $df = 5/51$, $p < .001$), trial blocks ($F = 67.70$, $df = 3/153$, $p < .001$), and the interaction ($F = 9.03$, $df = 15/153$, $p < .001$) were all clearly significant. Similarly, for the three trial block analysis of *joint outcomes*: conditions ($F = 5.18$, $df = 5/51$, $p < .001$), trials ($F = 23.09$, $df = 2/102$, $p < .001$), and interaction ($F = 2.90$, $df = 10/102$, $p < .005$) were all significant.

3. For the four trial block analysis of *Ss outcomes*, the effects of conditions ($F = 14.25$, $df = 5/51$, $p < .001$), trial blocks ($F = 63.15$, $df = 3/153$, $p < .001$), and interaction ($F = 9.03$, $df = 15/153$, $p < .001$) are all significant. For the three block analysis, conditions ($F = 13.99$, $df = 5/51$, $p < .001$) and trial blocks ($F = 15.96$, $df = 2/102$, $p < .001$) are significant but not their interaction ($F = .78$, $df = 10/102$).

4. For the four trial block analysis of *the accomplices' outcomes*, there are significant effects of conditions ($F = 20.15$, $df = 5/51$, $p < .001$), trial blocks ($F = 20.81$, $df = 3/153$, $p < .001$), and interaction ($F = 37.91$, $df = 15/153$, $p < .001$). For the three trial block analysis, there are significant effects of conditions ($F = 14.9$, $df = 5/51$, $p < .001$), trial blocks ($F = 9.91$, $df = 2/102$, $p < .001$), and also of the interaction ($F = 3.22$, $df = 10/102$, $p < .005$).

5. For the four trial block analysis of *the differences between the outcomes of the Ss and their paired accomplices*, significant differences were obtained for conditions ($F = 4.13$, $df = 5/51$, $p < .01$), trial blocks ($F = 4.00$, $df = 3/153$, $p < .01$), and the interaction ($F = 2.05$, $df = 15/153$, $p < .01$). For the three trial block analysis, significant differences were found only for the conditions ($F = 3.34$, $df = 5/51$, $p < .025$).

6. To conserve space, we shall not present the details of the analyses of variance performed on the usage of each of the colored pegs but rather only the significant differences. We note that the 'beige' pegs were not employed at all by the subjects. As Table 1 indicates, this peg was not viewed with much favor by our subjects, and they could signal their good intentions through the use of the blue peg.

7. Lave (1965), also using the Prisoner's Dilemma game, studied three strategies: *Unconditionally Benevolent* (called 'Gandhi' by Lave), *Unconditionally Malevolent* (called 'Stalin'), and a seductive strategy (called 'Khrushchev') which was malevolent but occasionally chose cooperatively to seduce the S into cooperation. The 'Gandhi' strategy elicited most cooperation, the 'Khrushchev' next most, and the 'Stalin' least.

References

Bixenstine, V. E. and Wilson, K. V. (1963). 'Effects of level of cooperative choice by the other player on choices in a prisoner's dilemma game. Part II,' *Journal of Abnormal and Social Psychology*, **67**, 139–147.

Deutsch, M. (1973). *The Resolution of Conflict: Constructive and Destructive Processes*. Yale University Press, New Haven and London.

Lave, L. B. (1965). 'Factors affecting cooperation in the prisoner's dilemma,' *Behavioral Science*, **10**, 26–38.

Shure, G. H., Meeker, R. J., and Hansford, E. A. (1965). 'The effectiveness of pacifist strategies in bargaining games,' *Journal of Conflict Resolution*, **9**, 106–117.

Small Groups and Social Interaction, Volume 2
Edited by H. H. Blumberg, A. P. Hare, V. Kent and M. Davies
© 1983 John Wiley & Sons Ltd

2.2 Cooperation: An Experimental Analysis*

David R. Schmitt   *University of Washington*

and

Gerald Marwell   *University of Wisconsin—Madison*

Problem

A vast array of tasks require that people assist one another. When that assistance is motivated by mutual reward, promised or previously received, the activity is termed 'cooperative.' A long-standing research tradition in social psychology has documented conditions under which cooperation is superior to other modes of organization, notably competition and individual activity (for reviews see Schmitt, 1981 and Johnson *et al.*, 1981). The likelihood of cooperation depends upon more than its productive potential, however. Because rewards are divided and resources frequently shared, other factors can come into play which may also have a marked effect on the desire to cooperate. Two such factors, reward inequity and interpersonal risk, were selected for attention in a research program of over 30 experiments investigating conditions affecting the initiation and maintenance of cooperation. The first, reward inequity, occurs when rewards for identical task contributions are unequal. The second, interpersonal risk, occurs when cooperation entails joint access to and control of resources, for example, when capital is pooled in a partnership. Participants run the risk that others may expropriate (i.e. 'take') their resources or rewards.

Method

The experiments used an operational definition of cooperation that included the following characteristics: (a) goal-directed behavior; (b) rewards for each

*The work summarized in this paper is contained in Marwell and Schmitt (1975). Further discussion may also be found in Schmitt and Marwell (1977). Support for this program of research came primarily from the National Science Foundation (Grants GS-834, GS-1695, and GS-28087).

participant; (c) distributed responses (division of labor); (d) coordination of responses using social cues (direct observation of another's behavior).

In the initial experimental setting, two subjects seated in separate laboratory rooms each faced a panel containing a knob, stimulus lights, switches, and counters which registered own and partner's earnings. Subjects could choose between two types of activity—cooperation and individual responding—by using the switch on the panel. Cooperation required that knob pulls be coordinated in a specified manner. Knob pulls constituted the behavioral alternative to cooperation, which was *not* competition. Instead, subjects could each work on an individual task that required no coordination of responses.

The cooperative task was available only if it was chosen by both subjects. If either or both subjects chose to work alone, both subjects could work only on the individual task. Counter points (which were exchanged later for money) were added to each successful cooperative or individual response. In some later experiments conducted in Norway and the United States, a second, less complex apparatus was developed. Subjects were seated in the same room but were concealed from each other by a partition. Task responses and task choice were made on a small panel in front of each subject, and task choice and earnings were registered on a single large panel facing both subjects. The cooperative response was simpler than that required on the first apparatus.

All experiments followed an intra-pair replication procedure to investigate the effects of inequity or risk. In a typical procedure, a baseline condition was established in which cooperation paid more than individual responding. For pairs who were cooperative (most were), a condition predicted to disrupt cooperation was then introduced. In some experiments this condition was followed by another which was predicted to reduce or eliminate the disruption. Finally, baseline conditions were reinstated. In some experiments this sequence was repeated several times over several sessions. The principal dependent measure for each pair was the proportion of total responses that was cooperative.

Equity

Initial studies of inequity investigated the effects of inequity size on the likelihood of withdrawal from cooperation. The experiments began with both subjects able to earn more money by cooperating than by working individually. The rewards for both subjects were equal. Inequity was then introduced by arbitrarily raising the rewards of one of the subjects for cooperation. In 'small,' 'moderate,' and 'large' inequity variations one subject received two, three, or five times as much money as the other subject for cooperation. Thus, when the two subjects were cooperating, they were receiving unequal amounts for the same work, but more than they could by working alone. When working alone, both subjects received equal amounts. The following results were obtained with college students as subjects:

1. Some persons withdrew from an inequitably rewarded cooperative task to a less profitable individual one.
2. The number of pairs withdrawing from cooperation, and the extent of each pair's withdrawal, increased with inequity size.
3. When the inequity was moderate or large, withdrawal from cooperation was initiated by the underpaid subject.
4. Removal of the inequity for noncooperative pairs generally led to the resumption of cooperation.

The disruptive effect of small inequity was found with children (ages 9 to 12) as well.

Next, experiments were conducted in which subjects could rectify the inequity by transferring money. A cover on each subject's panel was removed to reveal a button that could be used to transfer counter points. In one variation pressing the button *gave* money to the other subject. In the other variation it *took* money from the other. Each button press gave or took one count (0.1¢). Transfer was studied only under moderate inequity. Results indicated that the opportunity to transfer rewards (either giving or taking) generally led to cooperation in pairs who were noncooperative when transfer was not available, and led to some disruption in previously cooperative pairs if no transfers were made.

Risk

Initial studies of risk investigated the effects of risk size on cooperation. To create risk a cover on each subject's panel was removed to reveal a button which could be pressed to take money from the other. Money could be taken *only* when both subjects had switched to cooperation. In a 'small' risk variation each button press took one count (0.1¢). In a 'large' risk variation each press took 1,000 counts ($1). Following initial experiments which demonstrated the disruptive effects of risk, additional ones investigated the generality of the risk effect and conditions that could reduce or eliminate the disruption. In all experiments college students served as subjects. The basic effects of risk can be summarized as follows:

1. The addition of interpersonal risk to cooperation typically produced taking, then withdrawal to the less profitable individual task. Disruption was substantial when the risk was small, almost total when the risk was large.
2. Removal of risk generally led to the resumption of cooperation.
3. The effect of large risk was similar for Norwegian and American subjects.
4. The effect of large risk on cooperation did not change substantially with time.

5. Large risk remained disruptive for the majority of pairs even when (a) the difference in rewards for cooperating and working individually was increased threefold; (b) risk was present as little as 7% of the time when subjects were cooperating; and (c) only one subject in each pair was able to take.
6. Large risk did not appreciably disrupt cooperation when 'taking' removed money from the victim but did not reward the taker.

At the level of the group response the control exercised by the manipulation of risk was nearly complete. However, on the individual level there were a variety of behavior patterns which culminated in withdrawal. One principle, though, can be used to explain most of the eventual disruption: subjects faced with a choice of responses initially made the one that was followed by the largest immediate reward. The most profitable single response—taking—occurred in most pairs soon after it was possible. Eventually, at least one of the subjects withdrew to the no-risk individual task, either to protect newly won gains or to avoid further loss. Evidence that the behavior of isolated subjects was, in fact, a product of the reward structure, and not a procedural artefact was shown by the greatly reduced disruption when the rewards for taking were eliminated.

Dominance of reward maximization was one of the ways in which behavior in the risk situation differed importantly from that in the inequity setting. While reward maximizing was also evident for a number of pairs under inequity, for other pairs some behavior was clearly a function of other previously learned social responses.

Several situational and individual characteristics mitigated the effects of large risk. Situational factors included the opportunity to communicate (cooperation typically followed only after an agreement to cease taking), a warning procedure (where an impending take was signaled and could be avoided), the opportunity to avoid risk (by making an additional response at frequent intervals), and past relations (friendship, marriage). On the individual level results indicated that a pacifist strategy could induce a substantial number of persons to cooperate in the face of risk. Other factors were examined which did not prove as useful. Visibility, the invocation of moral norms, and making risk intermittent did not foster high rates of cooperation.

Comments

Methodologically, this research pioneered procedures in which subjects in social settings worked for extended time periods for rewards provided solely by alternative tasks. A choice among alternative activities is much more common in everyday life than single opportunities, and allows clearer inferences with regard to the motives which govern behavior. Similar choice procedures have been used recently to study exchange (Burgess and Neilsen, 1974; Matthews and Shimoff, 1979; Molm, 1979), cooperation and competition (Schmitt, 1976), and reward inequity (Shimoff and Matthews, 1975). Our as yet uncommon strategy of obtaining large samples of behavior over several experimental sessions has been given greater recognition recently as a major means for remedying the persisting problem of unreplicable generalizations in social psychology (see Epstein, 1980).

A major theoretical feature of this research is its molar level of analysis—collectivities are viewed as actors, and their behaviors are analyzed as responses to environmental options or contingencies. Cooperation, in which a single group output is rewarded or not, provides an ideal setting for such an approach. Our research demonstrates that the relationships between a variety of contingencies and group behavior can be strong and reliable. Thus, although molar level analyses have not been common, there is considerable promise in viewing groups as more than simply arenas for individual interaction.

References

Burgess, R., and Neilsen, J. (1974). 'An experimental analysis of some structural determinants of equitable and inequitable exchange relations,' *American Sociological Review*, **39**, 427–443.

Epstein, S. (1980). 'The stability of behavior: II. Implications for psychological research,' *American Psychologist*, **35**, 790–806.

Johnson, D., Maruyama, G., Johnson, R., and Nelson, D. (1981). 'Effects of cooperative, competitive, and individualistic goal structures on achievement: A meta-analysis,' *Psychological Bulletin*, **89**, 47–62.

Marwell, G., and Schmitt, D. R. (1975). *Cooperation: An Experimental Analysis*, Academic Press, New York.

Matthews, B., and Shimoff, E. (1979). 'Expansion of exchange: Monitoring trust levels in an ongoing exchange relation,' *Journal of Conflict Resolution*, **23**, 538–560.

Molm, L. (1979). 'The effects of reinforcement differences and disruption of social exchange in an alternative task situation,' *Social Psychology Quarterly*, **42**, 158–171.

Schmitt, D. R. (1976). 'Some conditions affecting the choice to cooperate or compete,' *Journal of the Experimental Analysis of Behavior*, **25**, 165–178.

Schmitt, D. R. (1981). 'Performance under cooperation or competition: Fifty years of experimental research,' *American Behavioral Scientist*, **24**, 649–679.

Schmitt, D. R., and Marwell, G. (1977). 'Cooperation and the human group,' in R. L. Hamblin and J. H. Kunkel (eds.), *Behavioral Theory in Sociology*, pp. 171–191, Transactions Books, New Brunswick, NJ.

Shimoff, E., and Matthews, B. (1975). 'Unequal reinforcer magnitudes and relative preferences for cooperation in the dyad,' *Journal of the Experimental Analysis of Behavior*, **24**, 1–16.

Small Groups and Social Interaction, Volume 2
Edited by H. H. Blumberg, A. P. Hare, V. Kent and M. Davies
© 1983 John Wiley & Sons Ltd

2.3   The Commons Dilemma: A Cautionary Tale

Julian J. Edney

Los Angeles, California

Imagine for a moment that you are one of a band of, say, 20 people who are traveling in the desert and who unfortunately have got lost. You are miles from anywhere in an inhospitable environment; worse still, you have run out of food. In fact all told, your collective prospects do not look very good. And at this point, after another day of aimless wandering through the wilderness, you go to sleep at nightfall feeling hungry, worried, and rather pessimistic about things in general.

After a rather fitful night's sleep you and the rest of your band wake up the next morning, and you are stunned to discover that a small miracle has occurred. There, not a few feet from the campsite, is a small amount of bread which seems to have appeared out of nowhere and which is lying on the ground. With the food, strangely enough, is a small piece of paper, on which is penned (in beautiful, fine gothic script) a message, explaining the situation.

It seems that in this time of crisis, the food has been freely provided for your group; and it could actually be provided again. But, the message goes on, there is a small catch. The bread will in fact be replenished for the band once a night while in the wilderness unable to secure its own food, but only if a portion of it is left by the group in the same place on the ground each evening. Specifically, the note continues, the amount replenished each night will equal the amount that the group leaves.

You and your fellows do some quick counting, and you all realize that the night's fall would be enough to feed only 5 of the band of 20. If the food is left untouched, the note promises that by the next morning there would be enough to feed 10. But you and the others are very hungry, and there is some animated discussion over the meaning of the whole event, and even over the reliability of the message on the small piece of paper.

You notice that your groupmates keep their eyes on the precious windfall steadfastly. It is agonizing to leave good food just *lying* there, and by late after-noon a certain amount of nasty and very secular bickering has replaced the initial wonderment. Members of the band have started quibbling about how the next night's providence could be divided up. But through an admirable collective exercise in self-restraint, the food is left untouched throughout the day, and the next morning it has in fact doubled (though the beautifully written little note is gone). There is now enough food to feed half the group; but the group is also another day starved, and feeling very hungry indeed.

Now a formal discussion session is called, at which the group members argue what should be done. Prominent in this discussion is your leader (a sharp character, well muscled) who directs the debate. Various proposals are made.

One is to divide up the existing food equally, right then and there, and to eat it; after all, you all need food pretty badly. Someone makes the correct counter-argument that while everybody would indeed get some food, and while this option would also preserve the basic sense of fairness, sharing, and egalitarianism which has always been part of the spirit of the group, it also means almost certainly that you would all also perish afterwards because there would be no food left to double that night. So the proposal is rejected.

Another member then suggests that since some of you seem weaker than others, the most needy should be given *some* of the food now, and a portion be left on the ground to double. To this someone else objects (rather prosily) that it is actually difficult to tell who is most in need. In fact, some members of your band have been complaining of hardship for some time on this journey, while others have stoically suffered in silence. Who should determine who is most in need? A good bit of testy debate follows this point. Somebody in the group uses the phrase 'to each according to his need;' it seems to catch on, and it gets bandied around quite a bit (the leader watches this part of the discussion very carefully). But in the end, the second day's food is left untouched.

The next morning, the group awakens again, and pandemonium breaks out. Instead of the expected amount of food, there is in fact only a fraction—and a new note, explaining. That night, under cover of darkness, one person in your band had surreptitiously helped himself, leaving only a bit of the food to double. The replenishment rules, as originally set forth, were followed precisely; that morning's amount is exactly twice the amount left untouched.

Nobody owns up to the theft; and at this point most people look pretty dazed. Another discussion is organized, and again various proposals are made. One is that everyone be interrogated, the offending person be identified, and punished. Another is to forget the misdeed, and for everybody to eat the remaining food anyway because who knows whether there would be any the next morning. And another: a new variation of the idea that some of the food be given to some, but not to others. (There is a hush after this last suggestion; it now seems to strike most of the band as somehow fair that some are probably more deserving than others.) Then suddenly everyone starts arguing at once, louder than ever. Who is to get some of the food, and who will go without, risking possible starvation?

Order is finally re-established, and more suggestions forwarded. Perhaps women and children only should get food. Perhaps the oldest members of your band. Perhaps those who have held prominent roles and who have rendered conspicuously good service to the group in the past. Each of these ideas is argued at length, and during all of this some members talk very animatedly, but some now are beginning to sit quietly, thinking and watching closely.

Finally the group leader stands up. He raises his gaze, pauses solemnly and waits for undivided attention. When he speaks at last, he proposes that *as* leader, it should really be up to him to take on the responsibility and burden for the group. He will both guard the food at night and allocate it in the morning. He says he will prevent the previous night's tragedy; he will also take it upon his own conscience the awful decision of who will get what, and how much.

After mulling this over, many people finally nod their heads in agreement. Actually, most members of the group seem to be relieved that at least *somebody* will take over these anguishing decisions for them. The leader then takes a deep breath, looks carefully over the group, and continues. He explains that in all fairness his new burden would of course merit a slightly bigger portion of the food for himself each morning. This gets him a number of very hard looks; but there is little actual argument. And so it is settled, at least for the time being. And that night the group waits in hunger and agitated meditation; for it is almost impossible to sleep.

Of course, this story doesn't really stop there. It has several possible endings, and readers may invent a few for themselves. Actually, as over half the world's population of over 4 billion would tell us (that portion which, according to World Health Organization estimates, is underfed or starving), this is a fairy tale with a bite to it. It is also a metaphor, and one which, on larger scales (all involving naturally produced food) has profoundly occupied such thinkers as Malthus, Charles Darwin, and Karl Marx, as well as many contemporary population biologists, ecologists, economists, and food production experts. The story is hardly a new one. And while food is the focal concern here, one can imagine permutations where the scarce resource is water, drugs, oil, gasoline, cattle, money, or any other desirable good which is subject to scarcity and which slowly replenishes or regenerates over time, and which is jointly managed by a group. The story illustrates in miniature a problem which has plagued most societies since the dawn of history; it is the social problem arising from a shared small supply of a valuable resource, and large collective demand.

Psychologists have only recently addressed themselves to it, and mainly in terms of Garrett Hardin's (1968) formulation of the 'tragedy of the commons' and John Platt's (1973) 'social traps,' both of which deal as much with the way original scarcity develops as how the group handles the scarcity (and actually, neither theory really addresses the problem of allocation of the scarce goods). But both approaches predict that tragedy is likely to come to the group in which all members are equally free to consume from a limited common pool of goods, because the pool is quite likely to be destroyed through overuse. But Hardin's and Platt's formulations, together with the game theory approach (Dawes, 1980), tell us that this 'commons problem' can be examined psychologically as a group problem-solving one which involves a conflict of interest between the individual's needs and the group's needs, over time. What is good (or rewarding) for the individual consumer is bad for the group in the long run, and vice versa (the group itself can be treated as both an agent and a recipient of effects). Furthermore, the overall problem is one which, according to Hardin, has no real technical solution. Solutions, he argues, must involve changes in social ethics and morality.

Actually there are many variations of the commons problem, large and small scale (Schelling, 1978). And clearly it can be analyzed in a number of different ways: in its larger forms it is sometimes held to be a problem of overpopulation, or too many consumers, who destroy the source by overconsuming. Sometimes it is held to be a problem of economic mismanagement and exploitation (Fife, 1971); sometimes an effect of political or administrative failure in the group (Crowe, 1969). One point which exacerbates the social dilemma is that in most large commons, such as national and international ones, the resources may be both produced and consumed by the same group (or different members of it)—here the situation can actually take on saturnine overtones of deliberately *planned* shortages which are created for profit or political benefit of one person or sub-group at the expense of another (Calabresi and Bobbitt, 1978; see also Edney, 1981). In this case, the community faces some stony choices. Should it put the general welfare of the whole group above, say, the spirit of competitive economic enterprise among members, or vice versa? If it decides to move against free enterprise, at what point should it *coerce* its members into acting for the common good? In fact there are situations, especially when the resources are vital, and the scarcity a severe one, in which the community through its government may be forced into heavy handed intervention, and where compromise of its own democratic structure may even be necessary to preserve the commons (Arrow, 1951; Edney, 1980; Orbell and Wilson, 1978), essentially because careful and concerted conservation action of the whole group is required, and because individual self-determination, competitive or otherwise, can sometimes ruin the beneficial efforts of the rest.

The commons dilemma is a concept that can be applied to study energy crises, pollution problems, even the overcrowding of cities (where space is the common resource). At some point, however, each of these involves the basic conflict between individual (or subgroup) and the group good.

It should be apparent that concepts familiar to social psychologists such as equity (in the apportioning of the scarce goods), conflict and cooperation, perception of a 'just' world (or a just commons), and freedom of choice and its restriction, all come into play, but in a new context which places a rather different shading on them, because the focus is not so much on short-term individual perceptions and behaviors, as usually studied in social psychology, but on their contributions to *functional outcomes*, in terms of the longer survival of the whole. It also tends to place these concepts more squarely in a systems framework where they interact with each other, and sometimes conflict, and in which they are tied teleologically to some collective eventuality for the group. Concepts newly appearing in the experimental literature such as trust (Rotter, 1980) and social loafing (Latané *et al.* 1979) are also closely entwined, and of course well established ones like altruism and leadership (e.g. Edney and Harper, 1978a) are involved.

To study this many-faceted topic a number of us have devised some new experimental techniques which attempt to capture the processes of commons crises in short periods in the laboratory. These are small group simulations of the commons, some of which are computer based (e.g. Brechner, 1977; Cass and Edney, 1978) and some of which use simpler apparatuses. Two of the latter type are actually very brief and simple to run. Harper's apparatus (Harper, in press; Edney and Harper, 1978a) uses a common pool consisting of slowly regenerating points, from which individuals in small groups can 'harvest' for personal gain. The Nuts Game (Edney, 1979) is an alternative: a short but exciting group exercise which uses tangible goods—metal nuts. But all these methods show how rapidly commons crises develop and how difficult they are to prevent, even when you first tell experimental subjects how to prevent them (Cass and Edney, 1978; Edney and Harper, 1978b).

Feelings often run very high in these experiments; some of the basic value conflicts occurring in real-world commons problems are captured rather clearly. From the first of our studies it seemed too that one could pick out several different personality types among players (some of these are colloquially described in the tale above). One focus of our current research is to look at these individual differences more methodically, with special attention to the 'free rider,' or exploiter of the group good (Edney, 1979) on the one hand, and the cooperative 'good commoner' on the other. Another is to determine the correlations among different methods of analyzing the phenomenon experimentally. Early returns from an ongoing research project indicate, for instance, that the Nuts Game and the N-person Prisoners's Dilemma game correlate reasonably well.

Another focus is the direct problem-solving one: what kinds of things can be done to help prevent these collective tragedies? A few preliminary answers seem to be emerging from our work and that of other experimenters, such as territorial division of the pool, encouraging communication among members, and keeping group sizes small.

But at this point we are just scratching the surface, and there are many intriguing component puzzles to be tackled and solutions to be tried. As new theory is developed (Buckley, *et al.*, 1974; Cross and Guyer, 1980; Edney, 1981; Dawes,

1980; Hardin, and Baden, 1977) more hints emerge. Among other enticements to this new topic, the commons researcher can be assured that any solutions generated in either laboratory or field settings could eventually be of considerable interest to environment managers and planners, policy makers, and social problem scholars alike.

References

Arrow, K. J. (1951). *Social Choices and Individual Values*, 2nd edn, Yale University Press, New Haven, Conn.

Brechner, K. C. (1977). 'An experimental analysis of social traps,' *Journal of Experimental Social Psychology*, **13**, 552–564.

Buckley, W., Burns, T., and Meeker, L. D. (1974). 'Structural resolutions of collective action problems,' *Behavioral Science*, **19**, 277–297.

Calabresi, G., and Bobbitt, P. (1978). *Tragic Choices*, Norton, New York.

Cass, R. C., and Edney, J. J. (1978). 'The commons dilemma: A simulation testing resource visibility and territorial division,' *Human Ecology*, **6**, 371–386.

Cross, J. G., and Guyer, M. J. (1980). *Social Traps*, University of Michigan Press, Ann Arbor.

Crowe, B. (1969). 'The tragedy of the commons revisited,' *Science*, **166**, 1103–1107.

Dawes, R. M. (1980). 'Social dilemmas,' *Annual Review of Psychology*, **31**, 169–193.

Edney, J. J. (1979). 'The nuts game: A concise commons dilemma analog,' *Environmental Psychology and Nonverbal Behavior*, **3**, 252–254.

Edney, J. J. (1980). 'The commons problem: Alternative perspectives,' *American Psychologist*, **35**, 131–150.

Edney, J. J. (1981). 'Paradoxes on the Commons: Scarcity and the Problem of Equality,' *Journal of Community Psychology*, **9**, 3–34.

Edney, J. J., and Harper, C. S. (1978a). 'Heroism in a resource crisis: A simulation study,' *Environmental Management*, **2**, 523–527.

Edney, J. J., and Harper, C. S. (1978b). 'The effects of information in a resource management problem: A social trap analysis,' *Human Ecology*, **6**, 387–395.

Fife, D. (1971). 'Killing the goose,' *Environment*, **13**, 27–31.

Hardin, G. J. (1968). 'The tragedy of the commons,' *Science*, **162**, 1243–1248.

Hardin, G., and Baden, J. (1977). *Managing the Commons*, Freeman, San Francisco.

Harper, C. S. (In press). 'The use of laboratory simulations to study resource management dilemmas,' in J. B. Calhoun (ed.), *Perspective on Adaptation, Environment and Population*.

Latané, B., Williams, K., and Harkins, S. (1979). 'Many hands make light the work: The causes and consequences of social loafing,' *Journal of Personality and Social Psychology*, **37**, 822–832.

Orbell, J. M., and Wilson, L. A. (1978). 'Institutional solutions to the N-person prisoner's dilemma,' *The American Political Science Review*, **72**, 411–421.

Platt, J. (1973). 'Social traps,' *American Psychologist*, **28**, 641–651.

Rotter, J. B. (1980). 'Interpersonal trust, trustworthiness, and gullibility,' *American Psychologist*, **35**, 1–7.

Schelling, T. C. (1978). *Micromotive and Macrobehavior*, Norton, New York.

Small Groups and Social Interaction, Volume 2
Edited by H. H. Blumberg, A. P. Hare, V. Kent and M. Davies
© 1983 John Wiley & Sons Ltd

2.4 Conflict and Conciliation with Groups and Individuals

Svenn Lindskold   *Ohio University*

Most recent studies of conflict resolution in social-psychological laboratories have examined the actions of individual actors in opposition. Seldom have the acts of groups *vis-à-vis* other groups or individuals been studied, although many of the conflicts in life do involve groups on one or both sides. There is, of course, a strong tradition within social psychology to study group formation and organization and group influences on individual members (Shaw, 1976). Frequent comparisons have been made of group and individual performance on various tasks, in brainstorming, in making judgments and decisions (Lamm and Myers, 1978), and in intervening in emergencies (Latané and Darley, 1970). There are also some data indicating that observers consider groups more stable and consistent and less likely to be persuaded than individuals (Foster and Lindskold, 1975; Lindskold *et al.*, 1974).

The findings that both the actions of, and others' perceptions of, groups and individuals do differ in a variety of ways does suggest that conflict resolution may also differ in the group and individual cases. For example, if groups polarize individual judgments (Lamm and Myers, 1978) and there is a general tendency for individuals to be competitive in a given situation, the group would be expected to be more competitive. A similar result might be expected if groups develop stronger negative or hostile orientation to 'outgroups' than do individuals (Dion, 1979; Worchel, 1979). If groups engage in groupthink (Janis, 1972), simplistic and moralistic reasoning by group members may intensify the image of the other party as evil, thereby demanding and justifying coercive action.

There is also a trend in social psychology to consider groups as more antisocial or counternormative in general than individuals—even without conflict with an outside party. Concepts such as diffusion of responsibility and deindividuation (Diener, 1980; Zimbardo, 1970) have been used to describe the presumed state or process leading to the difference. Experimental findings involving group and individual comparisons in this literature, however, are not consistent enough to support the proposition. Actually the group atmosphere and other features of the environment often prescribe the norms for the situation and have the effect of cueing the members regarding the appropriate behavior, defining it for them as desirable or undesirable for that situation, and supporting them in it (Lindskold and Propst, 1981). Jaffe and Yinon (1979), for example, found that groups displayed more 'retaliatory aggression' on a Buss aggression machine in the typical bogus learning setting than did individuals. The authors, however, acknowledged the possibility that the groups helped define the behavior for the members more clearly as altruistic aid to science rather than antisocial aggression (Baron and Eggleston, 1972; Zabrack and Miller, 1972). Thus, we cannot invariably expect greater hostility from groups than from individuals; but the presence of conflict with an outgroup can provide the cues to set the stage for intensification of hostilities.

Conflict studies—groups and individuals

The results of the relatively few experimental conflict studies comparing group and individual performance tend to support the hypothesis that groups are more competitive and hostile. Lindskold *et al.* (1969) found triads to be less trustworthy in the Prisoner's Dilemma (making the cooperative choice on the trial following cooperation by both parties) than individuals when opposing an individual simulated opponent who followed a 50% cooperative, noncontingent strategy. The findings of Pylyshyn *et al.* (1966) were somewhat at variance. Dyads were more cooperative than individuals opposing a tit-for-tat strategy; however, the dyads were less repentant (cooperating after being exploitative on the preceding trial) and less trusting (cooperating after both parties competed on the preceding trial) than were the individuals.

Lindskold *et al.* (1977) reported two studies in a Prisoner's Dilemma setting which involved comparisons of groups and individuals not only in terms of their game choices but also in terms of their preferences for forms of communication. In one study they opposed a live individual 'target;' in the second study they opposed a simulated individual target who was 50% cooperative on nonmessage trials but who was either highly cooperative or 50% cooperative in response to the communications. Each time (15 in all) the experimenter signalled that the communication channel was open, subjects in the 'source' role could send either a promise to cooperate on the next trial or a threat to take 10 points from the target if the latter did not cooperate on the next trial. As a third option, they could decline to communicate. Summarizing the findings from the two studies, groups were less cooperative than individuals and this difference was most consistent in the first five trials, suggesting an initial orientation to competition by groups which may become modified over time as the strategy of the other becomes apparent and relatively more influential in comparison with one's own orientation. Perhaps most significantly, there was a difference between groups and individuals in both studies in the preference for promises or threats. The groups demonstrated a stronger preference for threats, indicating a more coercive and nonconciliatory orientation than that demonstrated by the individuals.

Recent evidence, therefore, has become quite convincing that groups are more competitive and coercive than individuals when in conflict. No matter the theoretical explanation, the group/individual difference does raise questions regarding the generalizability of the literature bearing on the success of various conciliatory approaches to conflict management if the empirical studies have focused on individual rather than group actors. One of the empirically most well-supported proposals for achieving conciliation is Osgood's Graduated and Reciprocated Initiatives in Tension-reduction (GRIT) proposal (Lindskold, 1978).

GRIT

The GRIT proposal involves making a series of conciliatory initiatives as part of a clearly announced program to reduce tensions. It entails a risk of exploitation, but part of the program involves maintaining both the capability and willingness to retaliate against exploitation of initiatives (or other escalation). Persistence in taking initiatives is necessary because the prevailing atmosphere of hostility and suspicion makes early trust of the initiator's intentions and acts unlikely. Assuming only that conflict management is in the self-interest of both parties, it is presumed that trust of the initiator will eventually develop and that conciliatory reciprocation will occur. Future negotiated reductions in tension as well as cooperation in the service of mutual and individual self-interest become more likely.

In terms of specifics, the GRIT initiator first makes a general statement of intent and the reasons for initiating such a proposal. Then a series of acts are announced, one at a time, indicating exactly what is to be done and when, where, and why. Reciprocation is not made a condition. The acts are then carried out precisely as announced. Any third-party witnesses will provide an audience which could both attest to the credibility of the announcements and apply some pressure on the target eventually to reciprocate. If exploitation or escalation occurs, retaliation carefully graded to restore the *status quo*, but not to appear escalatory in itself, is to be made (Lindskold *et al.*, 1976). Then the initiator returns to conciliatory initiatives.

With some limitations owing to restricted responses available, the essence of this proposal may be captured in the laboratory (Lindskold and Aronoff, 1980; Lindskold and Finch, 1981). Using a Prisoner's Dilemma situation Lindskold and Collins (1978) did so with either three-person groups or individuals as the targets of GRIT and three other comparison strategies which were initiated by an individual opponent who was simulated by the experimenter. A total of 48 college women and 48 men served as subjects in the groups; 16 women and 16 men participated as individuals. The payoff matrix indicated that if both parties cooperated (designated as Choice 1) each would gain four points. If both competed (Choice 2) each would lose four points. If one cooperated and the other competed the former would lose five points and the latter would gain five. The points had no extra-experimental value.

In all strategy conditions the experiment consisted of 30 trials. The first 10 were random 50% cooperation by the simulated player to acquaint subjects with the interaction and to create some conflict. In the GRIT condition, the experimenter, consistent with earlier instructions that the communications channel would be opened from time to time, gave the simulated player, who had been designated the sender (apparently by lot), options to send messages prior to the next 10 trials. Three messages were posted on the subjects' game panel. A system of pushbuttons and signal lights was used to transmit the messages from one cubicle to the other. The experimenter controlled events from a central control room from which, additionally, the choices of the simulated player could be signaled. The three messages read 'I will make Choice 1 on the next trial,' 'I will make Choice 2 on the next trial,' and 'I want to write a note.'

Prior to trial 11 the simulated player sent the third message. According to earlier instructions, the experimenter thereupon went to the simulated player's room, supposedly picked up the handwritten note, and took it into the subjects' room quickly—avoiding either verbal or nonverbal communication with the subjects. The note read: 'I will be making Choice 1's. It's what we have to do to get our most points.'

Then, prior to trials 11 through 20, the simulated player used the other two messages to signal truthfully the choice he or she would make on that trial. Choice 1 was made on trial 11 and on each succeeding trial unless the subject had made Choice 2 on the preceding trial. In that case the simulated player made Choice 2—with the added restriction that the latter never made two Choice 2's in a row. That is, after each retaliation in response to exploitation, the simulated player returned *noncontingently* to promising and making Choice 1 on the following trial so as to persist with the conciliatory initiatives and not surrender control to the subject (as would be true of a strict tit-for-tat approach). The last 10 trials in the GRIT condition, as with all other conditions, consisted of all Choice 1's, not announced with messages because the experimenter gave no further message options after trial 20. Hence the last 10 trials represented a test of the persistence of any cooperative tendency developed in block two under conditions in which the simulated player neither communicated nor retaliated to exploitation.

In the *competitive strategy* condition, procedures identical to those in the GRIT condition were followed except that the simulated player lied on trial 11—making Choice 2 after sending the first message—and thereafter was only 50% truthful when promising cooperation while being 100% truthful when promising to make Choice 2.

In the *tit-for-tat condition* no messages were provided so there was no explicit communication. The simulated player made on trials 11 through 20 the choice that the subject had made on the preceding trial.

In the *control condition*, the simulated player continued the same random 50% cooperation strategy followed in the first 10 trials on trials 11 through 20.

The results showed that groups were slightly less cooperative than individuals during the first five trials, across all conditions, but the difference was not statistically reliable. The differing strategies were introduced during trials 11–20; and, during these trials, the subjects in the GRIT condition, both groups and individuals, were more cooperative than those in each of the other three conditions, which did not differ significantly from one another. This difference persisted into the final block of trials during which the simulated other was 100% cooperative; but, during the last three trials the GRIT subjects were significantly more cooperative than only the subjects in the competitive condition. Non-responsive, 100% cooperation has been shown repeatedly in the literature to tempt exploitation (Oskamp, 1971).

In conclusion, we cannot invariably expect groups to be less cooperative than individuals. They do, however, seem to prefer to use coercion rather than conciliation in their explicit communications with the other side. Thus we would expect them to be less favorable toward employing such a conciliatory strategy as GRIT than would individuals. Nevertheless, the GRIT strategy can be used effectively when directed against either groups or individuals. It appears to be a potent means of encouraging reciprocation and has been shown to work in such 'difficult' situations as when there is some power imbalance between the parties (Lindskold and Aronoff, 1980) and when the parties are choosing sequentially rather than simultaneously, including the case in which the GRIT initiator carries out the initiatives before the target is required to choose—making exploitation even more tempting (Lindskold, 1979).

References

Baron, R. A., and Eggleston, R. J. (1972). 'Performance on the "aggression" machine: Motivation to help or harm,' *Psychonomic Science*, **26**, 321–322.

Diener, E. (1980). 'Deindividuation: The absence of self-awareness and self-regulation in group members,' in P. Paulus (ed.), *The Psychology of Group Influence*, Erlbaum, Hillsdale, NJ.

Dion, K. L. (1979). 'Intergroup conflict and intragroup cohesiveness,' in W. G. Austin and S. Worchel (eds.), *The Social Psychology of Intergroup Relations*, Brooks/Cole, Monterey, CA.

Foster, S., and Lindskold, S. (1975). 'Effects of group and relationship on perceptions of stability,' *Perceptual and Motor Skills*, **40**, 223–229.

Jaffe, Y., and Yinon, Y. (1979). 'Retaliatory aggression in individuals and groups,' *European Journal of Social Psychology*, **9**, 177–186. [See also, Vol. 1, Sub-Chapter 6.4.]

Janis, I. L. (1972). *Victims of Groupthink*, Houghton Mifflin, Boston. [See also, Sub-Chapter 1.2.]

Lamm, H., and Myers, D. G. (1978). 'Group induced polarization of attitudes and behavior,' in L. Berkowitz (ed.), *Advances in Experimental Social Psychology*, Vol. 11, Academic, New York.

Latané, B., and Darley, J. M. (1970). *The Unresponsive Bystander*, Appleton-Century-Crofts, New York.

Lindskold, S. (1978). 'Trust development, the GRIT proposal, and the effects of conciliatory acts on conflict and cooperation,' *Psychological Bulletin*, **85**, 772–793.

Lindskold, S. (1979). 'Conciliation with simultaneous or sequential interaction,' *Journal of Conflict Resolution*, **23**, 704–714.

Lindskold, S., and Aronoff, J. R. (1980). 'Conciliatory strategies and relative power,' *Journal of Experimental Social Psychology*, **16**, 187–198.

Lindskold, S., Bennett, R., and Wayner, M. (1976). 'Retaliation level as a foundation for subsequent conciliation,' *Behavioral Science*, **21**, 13–18.

Lindskold, S., and Collins, M. (1978). 'Inducing cooperation by groups and individuals,' *Journal of Conflict Resolution*, **22**, 679–690.

Lindskold, S., and Finch, M. (1981). 'Styles of announcing conciliation,' *Journal of Conflict Resolution*, **25**, 145–155.

Lindskold, S., Gahagan, J., and Tedeschi, J. T. (1969). 'The ethical shift in the Prisoner's Dilemma game,' *Psychonomic Science*, **15**, 303–304.

Lindskold, S., McElwain, D. C., and Wayner, M. (1977). 'Cooperation and the use of coercion by groups and individuals,' *Journal of Conflict Resolution*, **21**, 531–550.

Lindskold, S., Price, R., Rubinstein, M., Bennett, R., and Foster, S. (1974). 'The perception of individual and group stability,' *Journal of Social Psychology*, **93**, 211–218.

Lindskold, S., and Propst, L. R. (1981). 'Deindividuation, self-awareness, and impression management,' in James T. Tedeschi (ed.), *Impression Management Theory and Social Psychological Research*, Academic, New York.

Oskamp, S. (1971). 'Effects of programmed strategies on cooperation in the Prisoner's Dilemma and other mixed-motive games,' *Journal of Conflict Resolution*, **15**, 225–259.

Pylyshyn, Z., Agnew, N., and Illingworth, J. (1966). 'Comparison of individuals and pairs of participants in a mixed-motive game,' *Journal of Conflict Resolution*, **10**, 211–220.

Shaw, M. E. (1976). *Group Dynamics*, McGraw-Hill, New York.

Worchel, S. (1979). 'Cooperation and the reduction of intergroup conflict: Some determining factors', in W. G. Austin and S. Worchel (eds.), *The Social Psychology of Intergroup Relations*, Brooks/Cole, Monterey, CA.

Zabrack, M., and Miller, N. (1972). 'Group aggression: The effects of friendship ties and anonymity,' *Proceedings of the 80th Annual Convention of the American Psychological Association*, **7**, 211–212.

Zimbardo, P. G. (1970). 'The human choice: Individuation, reason, and order versus deindividuation, impulse, and chaos,' in W. J. Arnold and D. Levine (eds), *Nebraska Symposium on Motivation*, Vol. 17, University of Nebraska Press, Lincoln.

Small Groups and Social Interaction, Volume 2
Edited by H. H. Blumberg, A. P. Hare, V. Kent and M. Davies
Published by John Wiley & Sons Ltd

2.5   The Conflict Grid®*

Robert R. Blake and Jane S. Mouton

Scientific Methods, Inc., Austin, Texas

What is needed is a sharply increased understanding by every person of the roots of conflict and the human skills of gaining resolution of differences in a sound manner. This kind of deepened skill in the direct resolution of differences can do much to provide a realistic prospect that antagonisms, cleavages, or injustices, real and imagined, can be reduced if not eliminated. It offers the promise that the sicknesses of alienation and apathy, destructive aggressions, yielding and ingratiation, and the go-along-to-get-along organization-man mentality can be replaced by involvement and commitment to sound decision making and problem solving.

The Conflict Grid in Figure 1 is a way of identifying basic assumptions in situations where differences are present, whether disagreement is openly expressed or silently present (Blake and Mouton, 1978).

Whenever a person meets a situation of conflict, there are at least two basic considerations in mind. One of these is the **people** with whom one is in disagreement. Another is **production of results**, or resolving the disagreement. The amount and kind of emphasis placed on various combinations of each of these concerns determine how conflict is dealt with.

Basic attitudes toward people and toward results are visualized on nine-point scales. These form the Grid in Figure 1. The nine-point scale representing concern for producing a result provides the horizontal axis for the Grid. The same applies on the vertical concern for people dimension. The phrase 'concern for' denotes degree of emphasis. The **1** end represents low concern, and the **9** end represents

*This article is adapted from 'The fifth achievement,' by Robert R. Blake and Jane Srygley Mouton (1970), *Journal of Applied Behavioral Science*, **6**, 413–426. Reprinted by permission of the author.

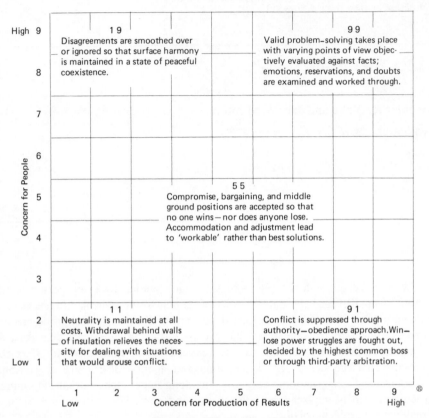

Figure 1   The Conflict Grid

the highest possible concern. Considering the interactions of these two scales, there are 81 possible positions. Each describes an intersection between the two dimensions. Five points of intersection are of key importance.

The following discussion is of strategies of managing conflict according to five theories. These appear at the four corners and the center of the Grid figure. When these basic styles are understood, one can predict how a person operating under each style is likely to handle conflict. There are eight additional important theories composed from various mixtures of these five, but basic issues of conflict resolution can be seen in dealing with these 'pure' theories, and one other to be introduced later.

No one style is exclusively characteristic of one person in comparison with another, although one style may be dominant in a person's actions. Furthermore, even though one may be dominant for a time, it may be abandoned and replaced by another when the first has been ineffective in achieving resolution.

What are some of the ways of dealing with conflict?

Conflict can be controlled by overpowering it through suppression (9, 1 in the lower right corner of the Grid). Extracting compliance by authority–obedience is possible when the conflict can be cut off. 'Yours is not to question why!' When rank is not available, a win–lose basis expresses the same set of assumptions. Winning for one's own position predominates over seeking a valid solution.

Another strategy is to smooth conflict by yielding or ingratiation through letting a person know that with a little patience he or she will find that all is right (1, 9 in the upper left corner). The assumption of sweetness and light often leads to resolution by retraction of previously held positions. This can promote accord and harmony, but solution validity, as well as conviction and insight into causes of differences, may be sacrificed in preference to gaining personal acceptance by being responsive.

Staying out of situations that provoke controversy or turning away from the topics that promote disagreement represents a set of assumptions about how to live in a conflict-free way (1, 1 in the lower left corner). Then one need not be stirred up even though the issue may need resolution. A person can remain composed if not drawn into controversy; it is avoided by remaining neutral. This kind of 'see no disagreement, hear no disagreement, and speak no disagreement' represents withdrawal from social responsibility where resolution of differences is the key to sound solution. It is the ultimate in alienation.

A fourth set of assumptions leads to a middle-of-the-road solution to differences through accommodation, adjustment, and compromise. Disagreement is settled through bargaining a compromise solution (5,5 in the middle of the Grid). The assumptions underlying compromise of one's convictions are at the root of this approach. It means agreeing to be agreeable, even to the point of sacrificing sound action. It represents settling for what one can get rather than working to get what is sound in the light of the best available facts and data. The mental attitude behind the one-person-one-vote approach often leads to the endorsement of positions calculated to produce majority support even though this means giving up solutions of deeper validity.

Paternalism is a fifth approach to conflict resolution. It involves extracting compliance from another person by imposing demands in a 9,1-oriented way, and then rewarding compliance through acceptance, support, gifts, etc., in a 1,9-oriented way. Though disagreement may be felt, conflicts are unlikely to surface because the expression of differences results in loss of reward and, for many people, the need for acceptance dominates the need to be 'right.' This is a powerful tactic of conflict management that produces a peaceful surface even though it may mask underlying resentments and turmoil.

Under a 9,9 orientation, disagreement is valued as an inevitable result of strong-minded people having convictions about what is right. A person says, 'Nothing is sacrosanct. What are the facts? What are the causes? What are the conclusions?' Reservations and emotions that interrupt agreement based on logic and data are confronted through candid discussion of them directly with the person involved in the disagreement. Then insight and resolution are possible. This involves maturity and real human skill. This approach may be time-consuming in the short run but time-conserving over the long term. It permits people to disagree, to work out their disagreements in the light of facts and emotions, and ultimately to understand one another. Such problem-solving constructiveness in conflict situations is fundamental to individual and team effectiveness.

Reference

Blake, Robert R. and Mouton, Jane Srygley (1978). *The New Managerial Grid*, Gulf Publishing Company, Houston.

3. Games, Bargaining, and Coalitions

Small Groups and Social Interaction, Volume 2
Edited by H. H. Blumberg, A. P. Hare, V. Kent and M. Davies
© 1983 John Wiley & Sons Ltd

3.1 Experimental Gaming and the Goal/Expectation Hypothesis[1]

Dean G. Pruitt   *State University of New York at Buffalo*

An experimental game is a laboratory task involving interaction between two or more parties and having the following characteristics: (a) each party's decisions affect both his[2] own and the other's welfare; (b) feedback about the effect of these decisions is in numerical form; and (c) the numbers (the so-called 'payoffs') associated with each decision or combination of decisions are chosen beforehand by the experimenter. The term 'game' is used because the development of these tasks was inspired by the Theory of Games (Luce and Raiffa, 1957), a branch of mathematics that tries to prescribe the rational approach to be taken to any interpersonal situation in which the outcomes are defined numerically. These tasks are not presented as 'games' to the subjects but as serious forms of social inter-action.

The five types of experimental games most often used are as follows:

1. *Matrix games.* In these, the decisions available to one party are represented by the rows of a matrix and those available to the other party, by the columns. The outcomes of each pair of decisions are given by numbers in the cell of the matrix corresponding to these decisions. A matrix game is illustrated by the payoff schedule in Figure 1. The first number in each cell corresponds to the row player's outcome and the second number to the column player's outcome. The game shown is an example of the prisoner's dilemma. In this game, each party has a choice between cooperation (C) and noncooperation (D, for 'defection'). Noncooperation is more profitable than cooperation for each party viewed individually, but paradoxically joint cooperation (CC) is more profitable for both parties than joint noncoopera-tion (DD). In most matrix game studies, there are a series of trials, on each of which both subjects make a decision between responses C and D. Summaries

COLUMN PLAYER

		C	D
ROW	C	10,10	-10,15
PLAYER	D	15,-10	-5,-5

Figure 1   Example   of   a   prisoner's dilemma

of research involving matrix games will be found in Davis *et al.* (1976), Deutsch (1973), Pruitt and Kimmel (1977), Rapoport (1973), Rubin and Brown (1975) and Vinacke (1969).

2. *Negotiation games.* In these, the parties communicate with each other in an effort to reach a joint decision among a set of alternatives. Each alternative has a numerical value to both parties, and there is a divergence of interest such that different alternatives are favorable to each party. Summaries of research involving negotiation games will be found in Chertkoff and Esser (1976), Druckman (1977), Magenau and Pruitt (1979), Pruitt (1981), Rubin and Brown (1975) and Sauermann (1978a).

3. *Coalition games.* These involve three or more parties, who can communicate with one another about the formation of coalitions. A different numerical outcome is associated with each possible coalition, so that some are more likely to be formed than others. Research on coalition formation is summarized in Gamson (1964), Sauermann (1978b), and Vinacke (1969).

4. *Locomotion games.* In these, the parties must move from starting point to destination on an actual or conceptual game board. The better paths can only be traversed by one party at a time, creating a divergence of interest. Research on these games is described by Deutsch (1973) and Kelley (1965).

5. *Social trap games.* In these, the parties compete for resources at a certain cost to themselves. The games simulate certain 'traps,' in which there is a strong temptation to compete and yet the typical cost of competition is greater than the fruits of that competition. Research on various traps is described by Linder (1982), Rubin *et al.* (1980), and Teger (1980).

All of these techniques can be seen as useful for studying strategic interaction, in the sense of the strategies (techniques) people employ in social settings and the impact of these strategies on outcomes.

There are several advantages to employing emperimental games to study strategic interaction rather than tasks involving non-numerical feedback. The main advantage is that games permit a mathematically precise definition of *reward structure*, a term referring to the relationships between the decisions people make and the benefits they receive. Many theorists (e.g. Kelley, 1979; Kelley and Thibaut, 1978; Rapoport and Guyer, 1966; Snyder and Diesing, 1977) have argued that reward structure has a big impact on social behavior and that subtle differences in reward structure have enormous significance. Experimental games allow the investigator to vary reward structure and to study the impact of other variables in the context of particular reward structures. Other advantages are that these tasks: (a) yield behavioral measures of such elusive variables as 'extent of cooperation;' (b) are easy to employ; (c) are unaffected by many sources of random error found in more realistic settings; and (d) allow study of heavily competitive or hostile behavior in a safe setting (Pruitt and Kimmel, 1977).

The rest of this article will focus on the prisoner's dilemma and negotiation, the areas in which there has been the most research.

Social psychology is a fad-ridden discipline that moves rapidly from one crest of interest to another (Baron, 1980). In the late 1960s and early 1970s, there was a great enthusiasm for research on the prisoner's dilemma, but studies of this topic are few and far between today. The impulse that initiated this research was probably a good one. The prisoner's dilemma is a very common reward structure that underlies many social problems, including nonpayment of taxes and arms races. But the research spawned by this enthusiasm was a relatively arid tradition. For the most part, it was neither theoretically guided nor contributory to theory. Also the researchers in this area seldom tried to extrapolate their findings to real-life prisoners' dilemmas. The result was a method-bound field of inquiry with little clear relevance beyond itself. It is not clear that this was the fault of gaming methodology. It should have been possible to develop an initial theory of behavior in the prisoner's dilemma, based on observations of real-life events, to test and develop this theory in laboratory simulations, and to return periodically to real life (in imagination if not empirically) for the purpose of extending the findings beyond the laboratory. But such a procedure was not followed, at least in part because of the leadership of Anatol Rapoport (Rapoport, 1973; Rapoport and Chammah, 1965), a game theorist with a different philosophy of science.

By contrast, research on negotiation has developed along a healthier course. The hypotheses tested have often been consonant with real-life observations of formal negotiation (e.g. the writings of Blake and Mouton, 1961; Follett, 1940; Stevens, 1963, 1966; Walton and McKersie, 1965) and are sometimes related back to this sphere (Pruitt, 1982). Theoretical syntheses of the empirical findings are not uncommon (e.g. Chertkoff and Esser, 1976; Pruitt, 1981; Rubin and Brown, 1975), and theoretically derived hypotheses have frequently been tested. Research on negotiation has also been less dependent on experimental gaming tasks (e.g. Johnson, 1971) than has research on the prisoner's dilemma.

The biggest problem with experimental research on negotiation is that it is hard to know exactly how far to extrapolate the findings. Gaming settings usually put subjects into a formal, economic relationship with one another. Hence we can, presumably, be most confident in generalizing to business-like settings such as those between merchant and customer or labor and management. Can the same principles be extended to bargaining between intimates in informal settings? The question is hard to answer because informal negotiation has not, by and large, been studied. But there is research on bargaining by intimate couples in formal settings suggesting that they behave differently from ordinary laboratory dyads in certain respects. Married couples have been found to place less emphasis than stranger dyads on extreme initial demands and slow concession making (Schoeninger and Wood, 1969), and dating couples are less likely to maintain high aspirations in a bargaining setting (Fry *et al.*, 1979).

The goal/expectation hypothesis

In an effort to inject some theory into study of the prisoner's dilemma, the author and a colleague (Pruitt and Kimmel, 1977) have developed a goal/expectation hypothesis which fits a large number of findings. This hypothesis also helps interpret several results from research on negotiation.

The goal/expectation hypothesis provides an interpretation of C (cooperative) responses in the prisoner's dilemma. The origin of C responses is generally much easier to interpret than that of D (noncooperative) responses. D may be chosen for any of three reasons: (a) for individualistic reasons, because it offers a larger profit than C regardless of what the other party does; (b) for competitive reasons, because it offers the possibility of achieving more profit than the other party; or (c) for defensive reasons, because choice of D means that the other party cannot achieve a higher outcome than the self. The C response, on the other hand, has only one easy interpretation: as an effort to achieve mutual cooperation (to get into the CC cell) over a series of future trials. There is little else to recommend a choice of C. The CD outcome[3] is unattractive because it produces the lowest possible outcome for oneself while allowing the other party to do extremely well. Hence this cannot be the reason for choosing C. Altruism, in the sense of trying to maximize the other party's outcomes regardless of one's own, could theoretically produce a choice of C. But the subjects in most experiments are instructed to maximize their own benefits, and it is the uncommon subject who deviates to such a great extent from these instructions. The only remaining possibility is that the subject is choosing C in order to achieve CC.

While C responses can be interpreted as resulting from a goal of achieving mutual cooperation, people who have this goal do not always choose C. There must be some reason for expecting the other party to choose C, if not immediately then after one has chosen C a time or two. Otherwise a choice of C will only open one to exploitation, placing one in the CD cell.

In short, a cooperative response can be interpreted as indicating the existence of *both* a goal of achieving mutual cooperation *and* an expectation that the other will also cooperate. This is the goal/expectation hypothesis. This hypothesis is shown in Figure 2. Cooperative responding can only be expected in cell W, where both goal and expectation are present.

EXPECTATION OF COOPERATION
FROM THE OTHER

		Present	Absent
GOAL OF ACHIEVING	Present	W	X
MUTUAL COOPERATION	Absent	Y	Z

Figure 2   Schematic version of the goal/expectation hypothesis. Cooperative behavior is expected in situation W

Another name for the expectation of cooperation from the other party is 'trust.'
The rationale underlying the goal/expectation hypothesis can be logically
deduced by means of a transformational analysis of the type developed by Kelley
and Thibaut (1978; see also Kelley, 1979). Assume repeated play of the matrix
shown in Figure 1. If the row player looks simply at the numbers in the matrix, a
strategy of choosing D is clearly indicated, since D dominates C (provides higher
profit than C regardless of what the column player does). Now transform this
matrix by giving row some incentive for achieving mutual cooperation (CC). This
can be represented by the 'effective matrix' shown in Figure 3A, which
corresponds to Cell X in Figure 2. Note that row should still prefer D over C,
Because D still dominates C for the column player and row's proper response to
column's D is D. Now transform the original matrix by giving row some reason to
expect column to choose C if he (row) chooses C. The result is shown in Figure
3B, which corresponds to cell Y in Figure 2. It will be noted that D still dominates
C for row. Clearly trust is not enough to elicit cooperation. Only if *both*
transformations are made, i.e. row both has the goal of achieving mutual cooperation and expects column to cooperate, is row's rational response to choose C. This
situation is shown in Figure 3C. The preferred outcome CC can easily be
achieved by choosing C, since column is motivated to follow suit. Hence we can
expect row to choose C. The transformations shown in this last matrix correspond
to the two conditions specified in the goal/expectation hypothesis, i.e. to cell W in
Figure 2.

Extension of the goal/expectation hypothesis to negotiation is straightforward.
In negotiation, mutual cooperation involves a joint search by the bargainers for a
mutually acceptable alternative (Magenau and Pruitt, 1979). Such collaboration
can take two forms: (a) concession exchanges, in which the parties move arm-in-
arm toward a compromise; and (b) problem solving, in which they seek a novel

20, 10	−10, 15		10, 20	−10, 15		20, 20	−10, 15
15,−10	−5, −5		15,−10	−5, −5		15,−10	−5, −5

A   B   C

Figure 3   Derivation of the goal/expectation hypothesis by means of a transformational analysis

alternative that provides higher joint benefit than those currently available. Efforts to achieve or contribute to mutual cooperation are analogous to C playing in the prisoner's dilemma. These can take many forms, including suggesting a possible compromise, providing information about the goals underlying one's demands so as to help the other party locate a jointly acceptable alternative, signaling a willingness to make contingent concessions, participating in an informal problem-solving meeting with the other party, and cooperating with a mediator. The goal/expectation hypothesis postulates that such behavior results from having a goal of achieving mutual cooperation and having some measure of trust that the other party will cooperate in return. An auxiliary hypothesis recently developed (Pruitt, 1981b) holds that more trust is needed the riskier the coordinative action contemplated. The actions just mentioned were listed in order of riskiness, with the most risky being suggestion of a possible compromise and the least risky being cooperation with a mediator.

Findings with respect to the goal/expectation hypothesis

The goal/expectation hypothesis is supported by a number of studies in which an interaction was demonstrated between a variable that can plausibly be seen as affecting the goal of achieving mutual cooperation and one that can plausibly be seen as affecting trust. For example, studies of the prisoner's dilemma (Komorita et al., 1968; Lindskold and Bennett, 1973) have shown that a party who has lower threat capacity than his adversary is more likely to imitate that adversary's cooperative initiatives than is a party with greater threat capacity. Low threat capacity presumably encourages a goal of mutual cooperation, since one cannot easily get what one wants by pushing the other around; the other's cooperative initiatives presumably engender trust; and the two conditions together presumably cause the subject to behave cooperatively. Another example is a study of negotiation (Gruder, 1971) in which it was shown that people who anticipate interacting with the adversary in the future are especially likely to concede if the other is portrayed as an unselfish person. The expectation of future interaction can be assumed to encourage development of a mutual cooperation goal, and perceived unselfishness to encourage trust. In these and many other studies, the conditions that plausibly put people into cell W of Figure 2 produce the most cooperative behavior.

Interestingly, many studies (e.g. Gruder, 1971; Lindskold and Bennett, 1973; McClintock et al., 1970) have shown that cooperation is *lowest* in cell X of Figure 2. In this condition, the mutual cooperation goal is strong but the other party is seen as noncooperative. This result is not predicted by the goal/expectation hypothesis but does not contradict it. One possible explanation for this finding is that 'the other's noncooperation is particularly frustrating when one has a goal of mutual cooperation. Hence one is especially punitive if the other fails to cooperate' (Pruitt and Kimmel, 1977, p. 383).

The next two sections will summarize findings with respect to the antecedents of the mutual cooperation goal and of trust. Any condition producing C playing in the prisoner's dilemma is assumed to encourage one or both of these states. The same interpretation will be given to clearly coordinative moves in negotiation (such as asking for mediator assistance or providing information about the goals underlying one's demands) and to some instances of concession making. Also where two variables interact to produce C playing in the prisoner's dilemma or cooperation in negotiation, one variable will usually be interpreted as an antecedent of the mutual cooperation goal and the other as an antecedent of trust. Whether a variable is viewed as antecedent to the mutual cooperation goal or to trust will be determined by logical considerations, i.e. by whether it is plausible to make one or the other interpretation.

Antecedents of the mutual cooperation goal

Conditions producing a goal of achieving mutual cooperation can operate either directly on this goal, or indirectly by making other goals seem unattractive or unobtainable.

Among the conditions that make mutual cooperation attractive *per se* are: (a) reward structures in which each party controls the other's largest outcomes (Pincus and Bixenstine, 1977; Pruitt, 1967, 1970); (b) reward structures in which mutual cooperation provides roughly equal benefit to both parties (Marwell and Schmitt, 1975; Tedeschi *et al.*, 1969); (c) friendship with the other party (Oskamp and Perlman, 1966); (d) perceived racial similarity with the other party (Hatton, 1967); (e) the anticipation of future interaction with the other party (Gruder, 1971; Marlowe *et al.*, 1966); (f) positive mood (Carnevale and Isen, 1981).

It also appears that certain people are especially oriented toward achieving high joint benefit in their interactions with others. These people are more likely to choose C in the prisoner's dilemma, presumably in an effort to achieve mutual cooperation (Kuhlman and Marshello, 1975).

Among the indirect sources of the mutual cooperation goal are a number of conditions that reduce the perceived feasibility of dominating or exploiting the other party. In the prisoner's dilemma, exploitation means getting into the DC cell, where one's own outcomes are high and those of the other party are low. It is hard to stay in this cell (which is the lower left cell in Figure 1) for very long, because the other party is likely to shift to D for self-protection. Hence, in the long run, it often becomes clear that the choice is between the CC and DD cells, with CC (mutual cooperation) clearly winning in such a comparison. The conditions in question speed up this process and make it more likely to occur. In negotiation, a unilateral concession from the other party is analogous to the DC cell in the prisoner's dilemma. Similar conditions reduce the perceived likelihood that the other party will make unilateral concessions, thereby enhancing attraction to the goal of mutual cooperation, which is the only other way of achieving one's objectives. If the other party cannot be dominated, one must try to work with him to get a favorable agreement.

The conditions in question include: (a) having weaker threat capacity than the other party (Komorita *et al.*, 1968; Lindskold and Bennett, 1973; Michener *et al.*, 1975); (b) perceiving that the other party represents a firm constituent (Wall, 1977a); (c) having an adversary who employs the reformed sinner strategy, i.e. is initially uncompromising or competitive and then switches to cooperative behavior (Bixenstine and Wilson, 1963; Cialdini *et al.*, 1975; Harford and Solomon, 1967; Wilson, 1971)—the adversary's initial firmness presumably makes it clear that he cannot be exploited and hence encourages the mutual cooperation goal and his later flexibility presumably fosters trust; (d) having an adversary who employs a matching (tit-for-tat) strategy, i.e. cooperates when one is cooperative and competes when one is competitive (Deutsch, 1973; Esser and Komorita, 1975; Komorita and Esser, 1975; Kuhlman and Marshello, 1975; Wall, 1977b). Again, his competitive behavior presumably fosters a recognition that he cannot be exploited and his cooperative behavior fosters trust. Esser and his colleagues (Chertkoff and Esser, 1976; Komorita and Esser, 1975) argue that use of this strategy causes the other to be seen as 'firm but fair,' a formulation that is compatible with the goal/expectation hypothesis.

In negotiation, conditions that discourage one from making unilateral concessions can logically be viewed as another indirect source of the mutual cooperation goal. Unilateral concessions are a means of moving toward agreement and thus avoiding the dangers associated with breaking off negotiation. If this route is blocked, mutual cooperation offers the most obvious alternative path in this direction. Having high limits (ultimate fallback positions) is one impediment to unilateral concession making. This implies a finding by Kimmel *et al.* (1980) that high limits produce problem-solving behavior when the other is trusted. The problem-solving behavior that appeared in this study was exchange of information about the goals underlying one's demands. High aspirations may well have the same impact. Being highly accountable to one's constituents also impedes concession making (Benton, 1972). This implies a finding by Bartunek *et al.* (1975) that highly accountable bargainers are especially likely to seek help from a mediator, a low risk form of cooperative behavior. However, it seems somewhat doubtful that highly accountable representatives will easily adopt *high* risk cooperative strategies, since such strategies are likely to make them suspect to the constituents they represent. Instead they are likely to prefer competitive strategies if these are feasible (Pruitt *et al.*, 1978).

Evidence from case studies of negotiation (Douglas, 1962; Morley and Stephenson, 1977; Snyder and Diesing, 1977) suggests that the goal of achieving mutual cooperation often becomes stronger on both sides as negotiation progresses. What presumably happens is that the situation seems progressively more deadlocked to both parties. Both parties have made all the unilateral concessions that are easy and have become increasingly pessimistic about being able to dominate one another. Time pressure is beginning to mount. Hence each of them begins to think seriously about trying to collaborate with the other in an effort to locate a mutually acceptable solution. However, since trust is usually low at first, the goal of mutual cooperation is likely to be initially expressed in the form of low risk cooperative actions, e.g. a hint of interest in moving to a compromise or an effort to arrange third party intervention. Only after a few such actions will trust grow to the point where it is possible for the parties to take high risk cooperative actions, such as suggesting a possible compromise or providing information about the goals underlying one's demands.

There is also evidence that the goal of achieving mutual cooperation develops over time in the prisoner's dilemma. Part of this evidence is that the percentage of C's chosen increases after an initial decline (Rapoport and Chammah, 1965). In addition, a number of studies have shown that subjects who have reason to trust the other party become especially cooperative as time goes on (Apfelbaum, 1974; McClintock *et al.*, 1970; Pylyshyn, *et al.*, 1966; Swingle and Gillis, 1968; Tornatzky and Geiwitz, 1968). These trends are probably due to increasing awareness that it is impossible to exploit the other party (achieve DC over several trials) and that the only outcomes with any stability are CC and DD, of which CC (mutual cooperation) is the more profitable.

Time out from prisoner's dilemma play (Pilisuk *et al.*, 1971; Pilisuk *et al.*, 1965) and observing others in the DD cell (Braver and Barnett, 1974) also foster cooperation. This is probably because these conditions encourage awareness of the futility of achieving DC and the unproductive outcomes associated with DD in comparison with CC.

Antecedents of trust

Trust, the expectation that the other will cooperate if one does so, makes it possible to act on a goal of mutual cooperation. Trust develops when the other party behaves cooperatively. This is shown by the many studies in which cooperative behavior on the part of a confederate encouraged the subject to cooperate under conditions that could reasonably be construed to produce a desire for mutual cooperation (e.g. Bixenstine and Wilson, 1963; Harford and Solomon, 1967; Benton *et al.*, 1972; Liebert *et al.*, 1968; Michener *et al.*, 1975; Lindskold and Bennett, 1973; Wall, 1977a). More recent cooperation engenders more trust (Kelley and Stahelski, 1970). So too does cooperative behavior that cannot be attributed to external incentives, e.g. cooperative behavior that is (a) costly to the actor (Komorita, 1973), (b) not derived from role requirements (Kimmel, 1974) or surveillance by the other party (Kruglanski, 1970; Strickland, 1958), and (c) taken by an actor who is also seen as firm (Lindskold and Bennett, 1973).

The other party will also be trusted to the extent that his incentives are viewed as encouraging cooperation (Braver and Barnett, 1974). Hence trust will be greater when one has power over the other party (Solomon, 1960), has requested the other's cooperation (Loomis, 1959), or believes that the other has received cooperative instructions from his constituents (Braver and Barnett, 1974).

In addition, there is evidence that one is more trusting of a person whom one likes (McClintock *et al.*, 1970; Swingle and Gillis, 1968), sees as similar to oneself (Apfelbaum, 1974; Tornatzky and Geiwitz, 1968), or to whom one has sent a message of coordinative intent (Loomis, 1959).

Osgood (1962, 1966) has outlined a general strategy for enhancing another party's trust and level of cooperation in an exacerbated conflict situation. He calls this 'Graduated Reciprocation in Tension-reduction' or simply 'GRIT.' The strategist must take a unilateral series of cooperative initiatives observing certain rules. As summarized by Lindskold (1978), these rules are as follows: (1) The series of actions must be announced ahead of time as an effort to reduce tension. (2) Each action should be labeled as part of this series. (3) The initially announced timetable must be observed. (4) The target should be invited to reciprocate each action. (5) The series of actions must be continued for a while even if there is no reciprocation. (6) The actions should be clear-cut and susceptible to verification. (7) The strategist must retain his capacity to retaliate should the other become more competitive during this campaign. (8) The strategist should retaliate if the other becomes competitive. (9) The actions should be of various kinds, so that all they have in common is their cooperative nature. (10) The other should be rewarded for cooperating, the level of reward being graduated to the other's level of cooperation.

Some of these rules have received verification in experimental gaming settings. Rule (1) is supported by Lindskold and Aronoff's (1980) finding that a cooperative initiative is more likely to be reciprocated when preceded by an explanation for why it has been taken. Rule (4) is supported by Deutsch's (1973) finding that a message of intention to cooperate, coupled with a stated expectation that the target will cooperate, induces more cooperation in the prisoner's dilemma than a message of intention alone. Rule (5) is supported by the finding that slow retaliation in the face of the target's noncooperative behavior encourages the target to cooperate more than does fast retaliation (Bixenstine and Gaebelein, 1971). 'Slow' retaliation means that one cooperates for a while in the face of the target's non-cooperation before switching to noncooperation. This strategy presumably helps the target see his own role in encouraging the strategist's switch to noncooperation. Rule (7) is supported by the finding that cooperative actions are more likely to be reciprocated if the strategist is viewed as strong rather than weak (Lindskold and Bennett, 1973; Michener *et al.*, 1975). Rules (8) and (10) taken together imply that a matching strategy should be employed in addition to the unilateral initiatives. Evidence cited earlier supports the value of a matching strategy for eliciting cooperation in the prisoner's dilemma.

Conclusions

The goal/expectation hypothesis and the evidence relating to this hypothesis has been presented in an effort to show that experimental gaming research can contribute to theory building. However, the author does not intend to imply an endorsement of the all too common approach of taking gaming methodology as the starting point of research. The author believes that research should, where possible, be guided by theory and that the method chosen for testing derivations from this theory should be a secondary consideration that is dictated by the nature of the hypotheses to be tested.

A gaming format may well be the best approach to testing certain hypotheses. For example, the author's current research (Pruitt and Carnevale, 1982) deals with the conditions encouraging the development of high joint benefit in negotiation. The numerical aspects of gaming settings lend themselves well to the definition of joint benefit and hence have been employed in this research. Likewise, in an effort to test the hypothesis that group solidarity is a response to temptation to defect from the group, Bonacich (1972) employed a multiperson prisoner's dilemma game that permitted precise definition of the temptation to defect. It should be noted that in both of these theory-based examples, the investigators were flexible in employing gaming methodology, introducing innovations beyond the usual, such as an opportunity for the subjects to talk to one another. Otherwise it would have been impossible to test the hypotheses at issue.

Other hypotheses about strategic interaction do not lend themselves to a gaming format and should be tested in other settings. For example, in a recent nongaming study (Carnevale et al., 1982), we have developed evidence supporting an idea about helping behavior that was derived from the goal/expectation hypothesis. This is that a person will be generous to the extent that he believes the other party has something to offer him in the future (producing a desire for mutual cooperation in the form of an exchange of favors) and finds the other a friendly, open person (producing trust that the other will actually reciprocate his generosity). The fact that the goal/expectation hypothesis was derived from experimental gaming studies did not require that an experimental gaming technique be used to test this derivation.

In short, what is being suggested is that research on strategic interaction should become more theoretical, more concerned about applications, and less method bound. No longer should a scholar define his research interests exclusively in terms of an experimental gaming paradigm.

Notes

1. Preparation of this manuscript was supported by Grant BNS-8014902 from the National Science Foundation.

2. The pronoun 'his' is used in this manuscript because the parties in gaming experiments are usually individuals. However they may be groups. The term 'his' is intended to be gender free. Both men and women can be, and often are, used in experimental gaming studies.

3. The first term in such an acronym refers to the actor's choice and the second to the other's choice. Assuming that the actor is choosing between the rows and the other is

choosing between the columns, the CD outcome refers to the upper right-hand cell in Figure 1.

References

Apfelbaum, E. (1974). 'On conflicts and bargaining,' *Advances in Experimental Social Psychology*, **7**, 103–156.

Baron, R. A. (1980). 'Fads in social psychology,' Presented at a meeting of the Capital Area Social Psychology Association, Washington.

Bartunek, J. M., Benton, A. A., and Keys, C. B. (1975). 'Third party intervention and the bargaining of group representatives,' *Journal of Conflict Resolution*, **19**, 532–557.

Benton, A A. (1972). 'Accountability and negotiations between group representatives,' *Proceedings, 80th Annual Convention, American Psychological Association*, pp. 227–228.

Benton, A. A., Kelley, H. H., and Liebling, B. (1972). 'Effects of extremity of offers and concession rate on the outcomes of bargaining,' *Journal of Personality and Social Psychology*, **23**, 73–83.

Bixenstine, V. E., and Gaebelein, J. W. (1971). 'Strategies of "real" opponents in eliciting cooperative choice in a prisoner's dilemma game,' *Journal of Conflict Resolution*, **15**, 157–166.

Bixenstine, V. E., and Wilson, K. V. (1963). 'Effects of level of cooperative choice by the other player on choices in a prisoner's dilemma game. Part II,' *Journal of Abnormal and Social Psychology*, **67**, 139–147.

Blake, R. R., and Mouton, J. S. (1961). 'Loyalty of representatives to ingroup positions during intergroup conflict.' *Sociometry*, **24**, 177–183.

Bonacich, P. (1972). 'Norms and cohesion as adaptive responses to potential conflict: An experimental study,' *Sociometry*, **35**, 357–375.

Braver, S. L., and Barnett, B. (1974). 'Perception of opponent's motives and cooperation in a mixed-motive game.' *Journal of Conflict Resolution*, **18**, 686–699.

Carnevale, P. J. D., and Isen, A. M. (1981). 'Negotiator mood moderates the barrier effect.' Presented at the annual meeting of the Eastern Psychological Association, New York.

Carnevale, P. J. D., Pruitt, D. G., and Carrington, P. I. (1981). 'Effects of future dependence, liking, and repeated requests for help on helping behavior,' *Social Psychology Quarterly*, **45**, 9–14.

Chertkoff, J. M., and Esser, J. K. (1976). 'A review of experiments in explicit bargaining,' *Journal of Experimental Social Psychology*, **12**, 464–487. [See also Sub-Chapter 3.3.]

Cialdini, R. B., Vincent, J. E., Lewis, S. K., Catalan, J., Wheeler, D., and Darby, B. L. (1975). 'Reciprocal concessions procedure for inducing compliance: The door-in-the-face technique,' *Journal of Personality and Social Psychology*, **31**, 206–215.

Davis, J. H., Laughlin, P. R., and Komorita, S. S. (1976). 'The social psychology of small groups,' *Annual Review of Psychology*, **27**, 501–542.

Deutsch, M. (1973). *The Resolution of Conflict: Constructive and Destructive Processes*, Yale, New Haven, Conn.

Douglas, A. (1962). *Industrial Peace-Making*, Columbia University Press, New York.

Druckman, D. (ed.) (1977). *Negotiations: Social-Psychological Perspectives*, Sage, Beverly Hills, Calif.

Esser, J. K., and Komorita, S. S. (1975). 'Reciprocity and concession making in bargaining,' *Journal of Personality and Social Psychology*, **31**, 864–872.

Follett, M. P. (1940). 'Constructive conflict,' in H. C. Metcalf and L. Urwick (eds.), *Dynamic Administration: The Collected Papers of Mary Parker Follett*, pp. 30–49, Harper, New York.

Fry, W. R., Firestone, I. J., and Williams, D. (1979). 'Bargaining process in mixed-singles dyads: Loving and losing,' Paper presented at the annual meeting of the Eastern Psychological Assòciation, Philadelphia.

Gamson, W. A. (1964). 'Experimental studies of coalition formation,' *Advances in Experimental Social Psychology*, **1**, 82–110.

Gruder, C. L. (1971). 'Relationship with opponent and partner in mixed-motive bargaining,' *Journal of Conflict Resolution*, **15**, 403–416.

Harford, T., and Solomon, L. (1967). '"Reformed sinner" and "lapsed saint" strategies in the prisoner's dilemma game,' *Journal of Conflict Resolution*, **11**, 104–109.

Hatton, J. M. (1967). 'Reactions of Negroes in a biracial bargaining situation,' *Journal of Personality and Social Psychology*, **7**, 301–306.

Johnson, D. W. (1971). 'Role reversal: A summary and review of the research,' *International Journal of Group Tensions*, **1**, 318–334.

Kelley, H. H. (1965). 'Experimental studies of threats in interpersonal negotiations,' *Journal of Conflict Resolution*, **9**, 77–105.

Kelley, H. H. (1979). *Personal Relationships: Their Structure and Processes*, Erlbaum, Hillsdale NJ.

Kelley, H. H., and Stahelski, A. J. (1970). 'The inference of intentions from moves in the prisoner's dilemma game.' *Journal of Experimental Social Psychology*, **6**, 401–419.

Kelley, H. H., and Thibaut, J. W. (1978). *Interpersonal Relations: A Theory of Interdependence*, Wiley, New York.

Kimmel, M. J. (1974). 'On distinguishing interpersonal trust from cooperative responding in the prisoner's dilemma game,' Ph.D. Thesis, Wayne State University, Detroit.

Kimmel, M. J., Pruitt, D. G., Magenau, J. M., Konar-Goldband, E., and Carnevale, P. J. D. (1980). 'Effects of trust, aspiration and gender on negotiation tactics.' *Journal of Personality and Social Psychology*, **38**, 9–23.

Komorita, S. S. (1973). 'Concession-making and conflict resolution,' *Journal of Conflict Resolution*, **17**, 745–762.

Komorita, S. S., and Esser, J. K. (1975). 'Frequency of reciprocated concessions in bargaining,' *Journal of Personality and Social Psychology*, **32**, 699–705.

Komorita, S. S., Sheposh, J. P., and Braver, S. L. (1968). 'Power, the use of power, and cooperative choice in a two-person game,' *Journal of Personality and Social Psychology*, **8**, 134–142.

Kruglanski, A. W. (1970). 'Attributing trustworthiness in supervisor–worker relations,' *Journal of Experimental Social Psychology*, **6**, 214–232.

Kuhlman, D. M., and Marshello, A. F. J. (1975). 'Individual differences in game motivation as moderators of preprogrammed strategy effects in prisoner's dilemma,' *Journal of Personality and Social Psychology*, **32**, 922–931.

Liebert, R. M., Smith, W. P., Hill, J. H., and Kieffer, M. (1968). 'The effects of information and magnitude of initial offer on interpersonal negotiation,' *Journal of Experimental Social Psychology*, **4**, 431–441.

Linder, D. E. (1982). 'The tragedy of the commons in the laboratory,' in V. Derlega and J. Grzelak (eds.), *Living With Other People*, Academic Press, New York.

Lindskold, S. (1978). 'Trust development, the GRIT proposal, and the effects of conciliatory acts on conflict and cooperation,' *Psychological Bulletin*, **85**, 772–793. [cf. Sub-Ch. 2.4.]

Lindskold, S., and Aronoff, J. R. (1980). 'Conciliatory strategies and relative power,' *Journal of Experimental Social Psychology*, **16**, 187–198.

Lindskold, S., and Bennett, R. (1973). 'Attributing trust and conciliatory intent from coercive power capability,' *Journal of Personality and Social Psychology*, **28**, 180–186.

Loomis, J. L. (1959). 'Communication, the development of trust, and cooperative behavior,' *Human Relations*, **12**, 305–315.

Luce, R. D., and Raiffa, H. (1957). *Games and Decisions*, Wiley, New York.

Magenau, J. M., and Pruitt, D. G. (1979). 'The social psychology of bargaining: A theoretical synthesis,' in G. M. Stephenson and C. J. Brotherton (eds.), *Industrial Relations*, Wiley, London.

Marlowe, D., Gergen, K. J., and Doob, A. N. (1966). 'Opponents' personality, expectation of social interaction, and interpersonal bargaining,' *Journal of Personality and Social Psychology*, **3**, 206–213.

Marwell, G., and Schmitt, D. R. (1975). *Cooperation: An Experimental Analysis*, Academic Press, New York. [See also, Sub-Chapter 2.2.]

McClintock, C. G., Nuttin, J. M., Jr, and McNeel, S. P. (1970). 'Sociometric choice, visual presence, and game playing behavior,' *Behavioral Science*, **15**, 124–131.

Michener, H. A., Vaske, J. J., Schleifer, S. L., Plazewski, J. G., and Chapman, L. J. (1975). 'Factors affecting concession rate and threat usage in bilateral conflict,' *Sociometry*, **38**, 62–80.

Morley, I. E., and Stephenson, G. M. (1977). *The Social Psychology of Bargaining*, Allen & Unwin, London.

Osgood, C. E. (1962). *An Alternative to War or Surrender*, University of Illinois Press, Urbana, Ill.

Osgood, C. E. (1966). *Perspective in Foreign Policy*, Pacific Books, Palo Alto, Calif.

Oskamp, S., and Perlman, D. (1966). 'Effects of friendship and disliking on cooperation in a mixed-motive game,' *Journal of Conflict Resolution*, **10**, 221–226.

Pilisuk, M., Kiritz, S., and Clampitt, S. (1971). 'Undoing deadlocks of distrust: Hip Berkeley students and the ROTC,' *Journal of Conflict Resolution*, **15**, 81–95.

Pilisuk, M., Potter, P., Rapoport, A., and Winter, J. A. (1965). 'War hawks and peace doves: Alternative resolutions of experimental conflicts,' *Journal of Conflict Resolution*, **9**, 491–508.

Pincus, J., and Bixenstine, V. E. (1977). 'Cooperation in the decomposed prisoner's dilemma game,' *Journal of Conflict Resolution*, **21**, 519–530.

Pruitt, D. G. (1967). 'Reward structure and cooperation: The decomposed prisoner's dilemma game,' *Journal of Personality and Social Psychology*, **7**, 21–27.

Pruitt, D. G. (1970). 'Motivational processes in the decomposed prisoner's dilemma game,' *Journal of Personality and Social Psychology*, **14**, 227–238.

Pruitt, D. G. (1981). *Negotiation Behavior*, Academic Press, New York.

Pruitt, D. G. (1982). 'Creative conflict management: How bargainers develop integrative agreements,' in G. B. J. Bomers and R. B. Peterson (eds.), *Industrial Relations and Conflict Management*, Mouton, The Hague, Netherlands.

Pruitt, D. G., and Carnevale, P. J. D. (1982). 'The development of integrative agreements in social conflict,' in V. J. Derlega and J. Grzelak (eds.), *Living With Other People*, Academic Press, New York.

Pruitt, D. G., and Kimmel, M. J. (1977). 'Twenty years of experimental gaming: Critique, synthesis and suggestions for the future,' *Annual Review of Psychology*, **28**, 363–392.

Pruitt, D. G., Kimmel, M. J., Britton, S., Carnevale, P. J. D., Magenau, J. M., Peragallo, J., and Engram, P. (1978). 'The effect of accountability and surveillance on integrative bargaining,' in H. Sauermann (ed.) *Contributions to Experimental Economics, Vol. 7: Bargaining Behavior*, Mohr, Tübingen.

Pylyshyn, Z., Agnew, N., and Illingworth, J. (1966). 'Comparison of individuals and pairs as participants in a mixed-motive game,' *Journal of Conflict Resolution*, **10**, 211–220.

Rapoport, A. (1973). *Experimental Games and Their Uses in Psychology*, General Learning Press, Morristown, NJ.

Rapoport, A., and Chammah, A. M. (1965). *Prisoner's Dilemma; A Study in Conflict and Cooperation*, Univ. of Michigan Press, Ann Arbor, Mich.

Rapoport, A., and Guyer, M. (1966). 'A taxonomy of 2 × 2 games,' *General Systems*, **11**, 203–214.

Rubin, J. Z., Brockner, J., Small-Weil, S., and Nathanson, S. (1980). 'Factors affecting entry into psychological traps,' *Journal of Conflict Resolution*, **24**, 405–426.

Rubin, J. Z., and Brown, B. R. (1975). *The Social Psychology of Bargaining and Negotiation*, Academic Press, New York.

Sauermann, H. (ed.) (1978a). *Contributions to Experimental Economics, Vol. 7: Bargaining Behavior*, Mohr, Tübingen.

Sauermann, H. (ed.) (1978b). *Contributions to Experimental Economics, Vol. 8: Coalition Forming Behavior*, Mohr, Tübingen.

Schoeninger, D. W., and Wood, W. D. (1969). 'Comparison of married and *ad hoc* mixed-sex dyads negotiating the division of a reward,' *Journal of Experimental Social Psychology*, **5**, 483–499.

Snyder, G. H., and Diesing, P. (1977). *Conflict Among Nations*, Princeton University Press, Princeton, NJ.

Solomon, L. (1960). 'The influence of some types of power relationships and game strategies upon the development of interpersonal trust,' *Journal of Abnormal and Social Psychology*, **61**, 223–230.

Stevens, C. M. (1963). *Strategy and Collective Bargaining Negotiation*, McGraw-Hill, New York.

Stevens, C. M. (1966). 'Is compulsory arbitration compatible with bargaining?' *Industrial Relations*, **65**, 38–52.

Strickland, L. H. (1958). 'Surveillance and trust,' *Journal of Personality*, **26**, 200–215.

Swingle, P. G., and Gillis, J. S. (1968). 'Effects of emotional relationship between protagonists in the prisoner's dilemma,' *Journal of Personality and Social Psychology*, **8**, 160–165.

Tedeschi, J. T., Lindskold, S., Horai, J., and Gahagan, J. P. (1969). 'Social power and the credibility of promises,' *Journal of Personality and Social Psychology*, **13**, 253–261.

Teger, A. I. (1980). *Too Much Invested to Quit*, Pergamon, New York.

Tornatzky, L., and Geiwitz, P. J. (1968). 'The effects of threat and attraction on interpersonal bargaining,' *Psychonomic Science*, **13**, 125–126.

Vinacke, W. E. (1969). 'Variables in experimental games: Toward a field theory,' *Psychological Bulletin*, **71**, 293–317.

Wall, J. A., Jr (1977a). 'Intergroup bargaining: Effects of opposing constituent's stance, opposing representative's bargaining, and representatives' locus of control,' *Journal of Conflict Resolution*, **21**, 459–474.

Wall, J. A., Jr (1977b). 'Operantly conditioning a negotiator's concession making,' *Journal of Experimental Social Psychology*, **13**, 431–440.

Walton, R. E., and McKersie, R. B. (1965). *A Behavioral Theory of Labor Negotiations: An Analysis of a Social Interaction System*, McGraw-Hill, New York.

Wilson, W. (1971). 'Reciprocation and other techniques for inducing cooperation in the Prisoner's Dilemma game,' *Journal of Conflict Resolution*, **15**, 167–196.

Small Groups and Social Interaction, Volume 2
Edited by H. H. Blumberg, A. P. Hare, V. Kent and M. Davies
© 1983 John Wiley & Sons Ltd

3.2 Social Values: Their Definition, Their Development, and Their Impact Upon Human Decision Making in Settings of Outcome Interdependence[1]

Charles G. McClintock and Linda J. Keil

University of California, Santa Barbara

In the present article we will undertake to accomplish four objectives. *First*, we will attempt to define social values as they obtain in settings where there is outcome interdependence between two or more actors. *Second*, we will describe two major procedures that have been employed to assess social values, namely, matrix and decomposed games. In doing so, we will use as examples of these methods studies that have attempted to examine the aetiology and development of various social values. *Third*, we will examine various rules of fairness that may serve as values. And, *fourth* and finally, we will consider how cognitive development may influence the aetiology of social values in general, and the various rules of fairness in particular. In concluding, we will examine some research findings that the present authors have recently collected regarding variations in children's use of fairness rules as a function of age.

Human interdependence and social values

Humans very often make decisions in settings where their behavior has implications not only for their own outcomes but also for the outcomes of others. Moreover, in such settings individuals very often do not have full control over the distributions of outcomes affected by their decisions, because these distributions are frequently co-determined by the behavior of others. These two statements, which define the core components of social interdependence, along with a value maximization assumption, form the basis of a previously proposed model of social motivation (McClintock, 1972, 1977). The value assumption states that human behavior is often governed and directed by the values attached to various behavioral alternatives in such a way that individuals select those alternatives that maximize the value of their outcomes. Stated in a different, but conceptually equivalent way, people are frequently motivated to achieve the goals they value most highly.

The present model thus strongly asserts that actors often perceive and take into account both own and other's outcomes in defining the utility of their outcomes. It is this process which Kelley and Thibaut (1978) and McClintock and Keil (1980) describe as one of transforming own and other's payoffs into social utilities, and which they assume is fundamental to understanding the role of social values in interpersonal behavior.

As implied above, much of our behavior occurs in relationship with others with whom we share outcome interdependence, or what Thibaut and Kelley (1959) have called mutual fate control. In such settings an actor's behavior influences not only his own but the other person's outcomes. For example in Robinson Crusoe's case, the arrival of Friday implied that many of his actions had implications not only for his own but also for his new companion's outcomes. To the extent that Robinson Crusoe was aware that his behavior impacted Friday's outcomes, and to the extent that he was concerned with Friday's outcomes, Crusoe's own values had to become social, that is, to involve the simultaneous consideration of his own and another's outcomes. In effect, then, Crusoe's choices would necessarily reflect his *social values*. The fact of social interdependence or mutual fate control also dictates that *both* actors in a dyad must more or less simultaneously take into consideration the outcomes that their behavior produce for each other. Each must rely to some extent upon the other for the outcomes he or she desires as well as for information which is needed for effective and profitable interactions, processes that Thibaut and Kelley (1959) have defined as 'outcome' and 'information' dependence.

The preference for particular social values in terms of the outcomes they produce for self and other may reflect either (1) the actor's most valued outcome, a *social motive* or *goal*, and/or (2) a *strategic choice* or *move* designed to affect the other's subsequent moves so as to increase the likelihood that actor can subsequently achieve some highly valued outcome. In effect, then, preferences for particular outcomes to self and other may represent social means (interpersonal strategies) or social motives (interpersonal goals). Normally, for example, parents would rationalize punishing their children as an outcome they produce for the child in order to change the child's subsequent choice behavior so that it is more consistent with both the child's and the parent's welfare, a *strategic* act. Of course, there is also the real possibility that if the parent is in a state of frustration at the time of punishment that the act of delivering punitive outcomes to the child may also satisfy the interpersonal *goal* of aggression. We will consider some additional implications of this goal/strategy distinction subsequently.

Social values, then, may be defined as consistent preferences for distributions of outcomes to self and other that may serve a motivational or a strategic purpose. Griesinger and Livingston (1973) describe a two-person spatial model of social values in which the magnitude of actor's outcomes is defined by the horizontal axis, and the magnitude of other's outcomes is defined by the vertical axis. Combinations of own and other's outcomes are represented as points in the two-dimensional space formed by these axes. Values as shown in Figure 1 are then defined as vectors consistent with commonly observed preferences for distributions of outcomes to self and other.

Particular combinations of outcomes to self and to other can be projected on vectors by dropping a perpendicular line from the point to the vector in question. If one considers the two points in Figure 1, 5, 5 (5 to self, 5 to other) and 3, 2 (3 to self and 2 to other), one can easily demonstrate that 5, 5 has a greater projection on the cooperation vector as well as the individualism vector, whereas 3, 2 has a greater projection on the competitive vector. This is obvious given the present vector definitions insofar as cooperation implies a value of maximizing joint outcomes, individualism maximizing own outcomes, and competition maximizing relative advantage. In the present instances, actors who prefer 3, 2 are willing to forego individualistic and cooperative outcomes for competitive ones.

The altruism and aggression vectors in Figure 1 represent preferences for outcomes strictly in terms of their impact upon other's outcomes—altruism implies maximizing other's positive outcomes, aggression minimizing other's positive outcomes. The other vectors martyrdom, masochism and sadomasochism are values associated with either abnormal forms of human motivation or rather strong forms of interpersonal strategy. As strategies, martyrdom implies a symbolically strong altruistic act where one is willing to forego own outcomes for other's; masochism implies preferring negative outcomes to self which might obtain when a child beats his head against a wall as a strategy to gain the attention of his

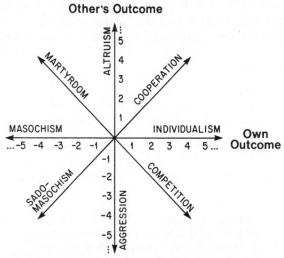

Figure 1   Motivational   vectors   in   a   two-dimensional own/other outcome

parents, and sadomasochism implies preferring outcomes that minimize both own and other's outcomes, a strategy represented by Herman Kahn's once proposed 'doomsday machine' which would blow up the whole world should anyone dare to attack the US with nuclear weapons.

It is also true, of course, that cooperation, competition, and individualism can serve as strategies toward other goals. One may cooperate because access to a valued own outcome is enhanced. Similarly, one person may compete and win a valued outcome in order to persuade another person that the ultimate goal of cooperation would be more rewarding. In effect, any of the vectors defined in Figure 1 may represent preferred strategies or preferred goals.

Assessing social values: matrix games

The major paradigm that social psychologists have employed during the past 20 years to evaluate cooperative and competitive behavior is known as the Prisoner's Dilemma Game (PDG). The game has several advantages. First, it is a situation of mutual outcome interdependence where any given outcome is a function of the behavior of both actors. In effect, there is mutual fate control between actors. A second advantage is that although it is an abstraction of reality, it does have considerable face validity as a setting in which to evaluate cooperation and competition.

Figure 2 presents an example of the dilemma. Player 1 can choose Rows A or B; Player 2, Columns X or Y. By convention, Player 1's outcomes are to the left of the comma in each cell; Player 2's to the right. Which outcome cell is entered on any given trial is a function of the choices of both Player 1 and Player 2. The dilemma is apparent. If both Player 1 and Player 2 attempt to maximize their own outcomes by choosing B and Y respectively, they each obtain 90 points on any given trial. If both attempt to maximize joint gain and select A and X, then they

PLAYER 2

		X	Y
PLAYER 1	A	110, 110	0, 200
	B	200, 0	90, 90

Figure 2 Prisoner's Dilemma Game (PDG). Player 1 makes row choices; Player 2 column choices. Values to left of comma are Player 1 outcomes; those to right are Player 2 outcomes

receive 110 points on each trial. However, if one attempts to maximize joint gain and the other attempts to maximize own, the latter succeeds in maximizing own gain while minimizing the former's outcome. Thus, both individualism and competitive advantage are achieved. Hence, cooperation and long-term own gain maximization require trust. Simultaneous competitive and immediate own gain maximization motives lead to *mutually* disadvantageous outcomes.

We will not attempt to review the massive number of studies that have been performed utilizing the PDG (for a relevant recent review, see Pruitt and Kimmel, 1977). We will, however, comment on the limitations of the PDG as a way of measuring social values. There are two major limitations which led to an early abandonment of the paradigm in the first author's own research program. First, the choices afforded the players are ambiguous as regards the three values under consideration. Obviously, any two choice paradigm will not allow assessment of three values independently; but more importantly, in the PDG it is difficult to prescribe an appropriate choice rule for an actor concerned with maximizing own gain. Obviously, the cell AX provides the greatest short- and long-term joint outcomes, and cells AY and BX the greatest relative advantage to one or the other player. If other can be trusted and is self-interested, then A or X is an obvious own gain choice. If other cannot be trusted and is competitive in orientation, then B or Y is the appropriate own gain choice. A second problem is that given the interdependence structure of a matrix game, such as the PDG, one cannot know whether a given player's choice represents a social goal or strategy. Competition, for example, may be motivated by a desire to win or by a desire to punish the partner's prior competitive choice.

In order to overcome the ambiguity problem, McClintock developed another game matrix paradigm, the Maximizing Difference Game (MDG). Figure 3 provides an example of the MDG, and one can immediately note one major difference between it and the PDG. The AX cell in the MDG not only maximizes

PLAYER 2

		X	Y
PLAYER 1	A	6, 6	0, 5
	B	5, 0	0, 0

Figure 3 Maximizing Difference Game (MDG). Player 1 makes row choices; Player 2 column choices. Values to left of comma are Player 1 outcomes; those to right are Player 2 outcomes

joint and potential long-term own gain, but also immediate own gain. Hence, two of the three social values, individualism and cooperation, dictate one choice, competition uniquely dictates the other. Thus, although two of the three values cannot be distinguished, all values clearly indicate a single choice given that such choices reflect goals rather than strategies. The matrix is still ambiguous in regard to goal-strategy confounding since an actor may make a competitive choice (B or Y) in order to maximize relative gain (achieve a competitive advantage) or to punish the other for previously behaving competitively.

McClintock and several other researchers (Banerjee and Pareek, 1974; Carment, 1974a, b; McClintock and Nuttin, 1969; McClintock, 1974; Toda *et al.*, 1978) have utilized the MDG to examine changes in children's preferences for choices that maximize relative gain, namely, changes in competitive responding, as a function of age across a number of cultures. Figure 4 presents, for example, the relative frequency of competitive choices for five cultures, three age levels, and two outcome display conditions (from Toda *et al.*, 1978). The display conditions were ones where children had information concerning only their own cumulation of points across 100 trials of the MDG (single display) v. children who had information concerning both their own and the other player's cumulative point totals (double display). We anticipated that the double display condition would promote social comparison processes (Festinger, 1954), and increase children's

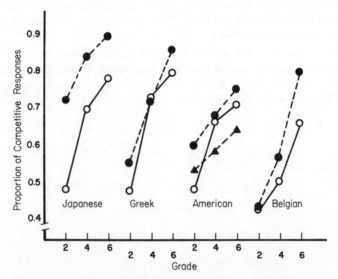

Figure 4 Culture × Grade × Display effects. Solid lines are results from own outcome display condition; dashed from own and other's outcome display. Solid triangles are Mexican–American children in double display (own and other's outcomes) condition. [Grade 2 = about 7 years of age.]

propensities towards competitive values. As indicated in the Figure 4, preferences for competitive outcomes increased sharply with age, were stronger in the double display or social comparison condition, and differed between cultures insofar as Japanese children were the most competitive followed in order by Greek, Anglo-American, and Belgian. The Mexican-American children were observed only in the double display conditions, and, within this condition, displayed the lowest overall level of competition of any of the culture groups. In effect, then, research utilizing the MDG indicates that with increasing age children are more likely to prefer competitive over cooperative and individualistic outcomes, and that this obtains across a large number of Western or Western-influenced cultures. There would seem to be little doubt that both family and schools play a major role in socializing this increase in valuation of competitive outcomes.

Decision making in decomposed games

Messick and McClintock (1968) developed what they term decomposed games[2] in order to obtain a better estimate of the various social motivational vectors or values under conditions where choices are most likely to reflect the chooser's goals rather than his or her strategies. That is, they designed a task where choices are more likely to indicate what distribution of outcomes to self and other the chooser prefers (social goal), rather than representing a choice made to influence some other to behave differently (social strategy). Further, decomposed games could be designed that permitted a clear distinction between the values of cooperation, competition, and individualism.

The choice structure of a decomposed game is illustrated in Table 1. When employed as a means of assessing social values, subjects are informed that they may select alternatives A, B, or C. One's own/other outcome points can be plotted in an outcome space, and the projection of each on the various value vectors can then be determined. Or one can merely ask which point maximizes own, joint, and relative outcomes. In the three choice or triple decomposed game in Table 1, each alternative obviously is dominant in regard to one vector. A maximizes joint outcomes; B maximizes own outcome; and C maximizes relative

Table 1   Three Choice Triple Dominance Decomposed Game Choice Alternatives

	A	B	C
Own outcome	80	90	70
Other's outcomes	80	60	10

A maximizes joint gain (cooperation); B maximizes own gain (individualism); C maximizes relative gain (competition).

gain outcome. Furthermore, it is apparent that the actor has for any single trial complete control over own and other's outcome or what Thibaut and Kelley term 'unilateral fate control.' This control reduces the likelihood of strategic choices. Thus, decomposed games have several clear advantages over matrix games as a way to measure social values.

McClintock and Moskowitz (1976) and McClintock et al. (1977), utilizing decomposed games, conducted two investigations with very young children to trace the development of cooperative, competitive, and individualistic values. Four fundamental expectations served as the conceptual bases for the two studies:

1. Young children initially attempt to maximize their own outcomes regardless of the implications of their acts for the outcomes of others.
2. Through experience, young children learn to take others' outcomes into account in achieving their own. Thus, cooperating or competing become learned strategies in the service of attaining valued own outcomes.
3. Once a child has learned to take others' outcomes into account, the goal structure of a task can affect the likelihood of cooperative or competitive behaviors.
4. Learned strategies that take into account both own and others' outcomes may become autonomous social motives. Thus, given a choice between two outcome distributions, a child may choose the option which affords him/her less of a valued commodity if that option provides him/her more of the commodity than someone else (competition) or if it provides more for self and other jointly (cooperation).

In order to examine the preceding expectations, variations in children's preferences for own (individualistic), joint (cooperative), and relative (competitive) outcomes were examined in three settings. A coordinative setting required

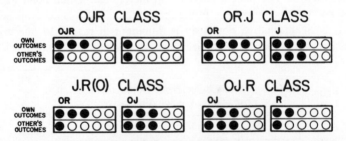

Figure 5 Examples of four two-choice decomposed games. Children must choose between two marble boards (rectangles). Solid circles on each board represent marbles or beads that this choice affords self and other. Values associated with each board are designated: O (own gain maximization); J (joint gain maximization); and R (relative gain maximization)

children to cooperate in order to achieve valued prizes for themselves. A competitive setting required children to outperform each other in order to obtain a valued outcome for self. Finally, an individualistic setting was established such that the child would have to forego own gain maximization in order to achieve a competitive advantage or to maximize joint gain outcomes. Across the two studies, 414

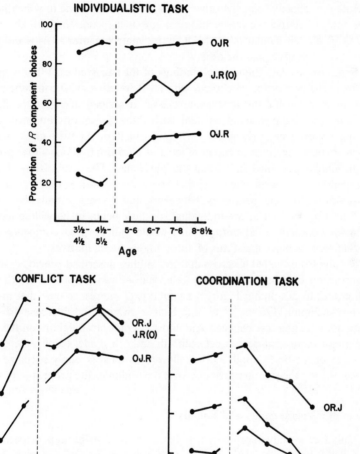

Figure 6 Proportion of R-component choices by task, game class, and age for the two studies of nursery and primary school children. Values defining game class include O (own gain maximization), J (joint gain maximization), and R (relative gain maximization)

children ranging in age from $3\frac{1}{2}$ to 8 years made choices on four kinds of classes of decomposed games. Figure 5 presents examples of one game or choice dilemma for each of these game classes. A brief review of the figure indicates that the OJR game class is one in which own (individualistic), joint (cooperative), and relative (competitive) values dictate the same choice; the OR.J class is one which shares similarity with the PDG matrix game insofar as own and relative preferences dictate one choice, joint the other; the J.R(O) class is one in which joint dictates one choice, relative the other, and own gain is the same for both alternatives; and the OJ.R class is similar to the MDG game matrix insofar as own and joint dictate one choice, relative gain the other.

Figure 6 presents the general findings of the two studies. What is plotted in the figure is the proportion of choices with an R (relative gain) component for each of the three tasks, for the four game classes described above, by children's ages. Overall, the findings are consistent with the expectations outlined above. Very young children are principally own-gain oriented. As they grow older children learn to make choices in the conflict and coordinative tasks that are consistent with achieving valued individualistic outcomes. The acquisition of appropriate competitive strategies occurs earlier, between 4 and 5 years of age, than the acquisition of cooperative ones, between 6 and 7 years. Finally, between the ages of 5 and 6, children in the individualistic task begin to be willing to forego own gain for competitive advantage. This would indicate that competitive values are beginning to achieve the status of autonomous social motives.

Results from the MDG cross-cultural studies described previously indicate that competition continues to develop as an autonomous motive from the 2nd to the 6th grade. In examining Figure 4 again, it is of interest to note that in three of the cultures, Japan, Greece, and the United States, the increase in competitive responding is greatest between 2nd and 4th grade. In Belgium, on the other hand, the major increment occurs between 4th and 6th grade. Hence, there seems to be some evidence that though all the cultures sampled strongly socialize competitive values during the primary school years, the timing of the process may vary.

Rules of fairness: equity and equality

Thus far, we have considered preferences for distributions of outcomes to self and other that can be defined as vectors in a two-dimensional space as illustrated in Figure 1. There are other sets of outcome preferences for self and other that are likely to be dominant in certain settings which cannot be so described, for example, preferences for equitable or equal outcomes. The social values discussed so far can each be represented as a linear vector corresponding to a unique indifference curve. Equity or equality cannot be so defined. An individual intent upon maximizing equity will want the ratio of his own to other's outcomes to be proportional to the ratio of their respective inputs. Such a definition of equity has two implications (Van Avermaet et al., 1978). First, the preference structure is not linear. Second, there is no *unique* cross-situational definition of equity or equity indifference curve because the location of the most preferred indifference curve necessarily varies with different ratios of inputs. At the same time, it is possible to map into our two-dimensional space an equity preference structure for any given ratio of inputs.

Figure 7 presents an instance where an own/other input ratio is perceived to be equal to 1/2, namely, self has contributed half as much as other in terms of inputs. Here, the highest indifference curve has a slope of +2 and can be thought of as a ridge of a mountain. Points on this line should be most preferred. Points equally consistent with equity can fall on different indifference curves on either side of this ridge. Other indifference lines are located on either side of the ridge. Note that the lines are not parallel because equity is defined in terms of the *proportion* of own to other inputs.

An equality preference structure can be similarly defined. Again, the preference structure is not linear. An individual desiring to maximize equality will want to minimize the difference between own and other's outcomes. Figure 8 presents a preference structure for equality. The most preferred indifference curve has a slope of ±1, and can be considered the ridge of the mountain. One would then have equal preferences for outcome points on the ridge, or for points that are on

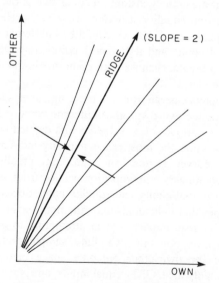

Figure 7   Equity. Most preferred outcomes, given an own/other input ratio of 1:2 and a valuation of equity, fall on the ridge that has a slope of 2 and defines outcomes that are proportional to inputs

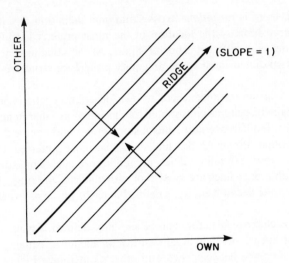

Figure 8 Equality. Most preferred outcomes, given a
valuation of equality, fall on the ridge that has a slope
of 1 and defines equal outcomes to self and other

indifference curves that are equally distant on either side of the ridge. This means,
for example, that given an equality structure, we would prefer an outcome that
affords each of us 4 points, and that we would be indifferent between outcomes
that afford one of us 4 points and the other 3 points, regardless of which of us
received 4 and which 3 points, because both point distributions would be equally
distant from the equality line.

Several important points emerge from the preceding analysis. Given knowledge
of inputs, one can examine two own/other outcome points not only in terms of
their projections on the various social value vectors defined in Figure 1, but also
assess their projection upon the most relevant equity indifference curve and/or
equality indifference curve. Hence, one can conceptually and empirically
discriminate equity or equality maximization values from other social values.
There is no reason, then, that equity and equality cannot be considered as valued
social goals or strategies that individuals may attempt to achieve while interacting
with others. This, of course, implies that in attempting to ascertain the values
underlying human action, one must carefully sample preferences between a
number of points in the own/other outcome space before one can clearly
discriminate the dominant value. Given equal inputs, one player's preference for 4,
4 over 2, 1 may indicate that he/she values equity, or equality, or altruism, or
martyrdom, or cooperation, or own gain maximization. A preference for 2, 1 may
represent the value of competition, or aggression, or sadomasochism, or
masochism. Obviously, one needs to sample more than one choice before one can
begin to attribute particular value orientations. Furthermore, as noted previously,

once one has discriminated the vector that is dominant, one is always confronted with determining whether the rule is being selected for goal attainment or for strategic purposes.

Cognitive prerequisites for the acquisition of values: fairness as an example

Social values are learned goals and strategies that characterize human behavior in settings where actors are interdependent in terms of outcomes. Such values play a major role in structuring the course of human interaction. Differing values by definition imply preferences for different distributions of physical, social, and psychological resources between self and others. In tracing the development of these preferences and the values they reflect, it is essential to recognize that certain cognitive skills are necessary prerequisites for their occurrence.

In fact, social values may be more specifically defined as rules of cognitive or numerical transformation employed in the allocation of outcomes to self and other. (See Messick and McClintock, 1968; Wyer, 1969, 1971; Radzicki, 1976; Kelley and Thibaut, 1978; Van Avermaet *et al.*, 1978; Hook and Cook, 1979; McClintock, 1977; McClintock and Keil, 1980; McClintock and Van Avermaet, in press). The numerical skills required to recognize and express those values we have thus far considered are outlined in Table 2. In tracing the development of fairness as an example of value acquisition, we will be concerned primarily with the final three transformations: equality, ordinal equity, and proportional equity.

Table 2 Choice Rules and Arithmetic Operations that Define Eight Major Social Values: *a* and *b* are alternative own outcomes; *c* and *d* alternative other's outcomes; *i* is input and *o* is outcome

Social value	Choice rule	Arithmetic transformation
Individualism	Maximize own outcome regardless of other's: maximize own gain	$a > b$
Cooperation	Maximize own plus other's outcomes: maximize joint gain	$a + c > b + d$
Altruism	Maximize other's outcomes: maximize other's gain	$c > d$
Competition	Maximize difference between own and other's outcomes: maximize relative gain in one's own favor	$a - c > b - d$
Aggression	Minimize other's outcome: minimize other's gain	$c < d$
Equality	Minimize difference between own and other's outcomes; maximize equality	$\lvert a - c \rvert < \lvert b - d \rvert$
Ordinal equity	Afford more or less outcomes to self or other depending upon whose input is greater	If $i_{self} > i_{other}$ then $o_{self} > o_{other}$
Proportional equity	Afford other outcomes relative to own outcomes in the same ratio as other to own inputs	$\dfrac{i_{self}}{i_{other}} = \dfrac{o_{self}}{o_{other}}$

The development of numerical abilities as they relate to the rules of fairness: theoretical and empirical work to date

Equality is the simplest of the three fairness transformation rules. As a distribution rule, it requires a unidimensional focus of attention, comparing outcomes that accrue to self and to other, and keeping their difference to a minimum regardless of relative input. An *equity* rule necessitates comparisons on two dimensions, both input and outcome. It implies construction of input/outcome ratios for each participant. The rule of *proportional* or *ratio* equity defines a fair distribution as one in which these ratios are equivalent, or where the difference between ratios is minimized. Given the relative difficulty of such calculations for children, Hook and Cook (1979) have proposed an *ordinal equity* rule which implies comparison on both the input and outcome dimensions but requires ordinal correspondence rather than proportionality. Such a rule requires more-than, less-than judgments along the two dimensions simultaneously.

From a developmental perspective, we can identify the numerical operations necessary for application of the above three rules in terms of their similarities and differences. Common to all is comparison, and the ability to make quantitative judgments of more-than, less-than, and equal regarding set sizes. The equality rule, requiring only unidimensional comparisons, is distinct from both forms of the equity rule which require comparisons on two dimensions simultaneously. Equality and ordinal equity are similar insofar as they demand rank ordering capabilities whereas ratio equity alone requires the sophistication of proportional thought.

Under certain circumstances the above distribution rules can be carried out in the absence of some of the numerical abilities cited. A child lacking the ability to make proportional calculations might produce an accurate ratio equity distribution simply by using a one-to-one correspondence rule matching outcome to input sets.

Piaget on the development of numerical abilities

Piaget (1964) has extensively explored the development of numerical abilities within the framework of his developmental stage theory. He first makes a distinction between number skill and number knowledge after observing that a child might demonstrate rotely memorized number skills in the absence of an understanding of the underlying number concepts. Piaget views the developing capability to deal with different set sizes as a second factor important to the assessment of numerical abilities. He calls this 'progressive arithmetization' of the number series, and like Flavell (1977) argues that younger children are more cognitively mature when dealing with very small readily visualizable numbers than when dealing with very large ones. With these two caveats in mind, the relationship between Piaget's three stages of numerical development and various rules of fairness can be considered.

In general, the preoperational child lacks a conceptual understanding of the most basic requirement for application of fairness rules, comparison of set sizes. Prior to the development of conservation of number, which signals the advent of the concrete operational stage, children frequently make errors in judgment of relative set size. For example, they may center their attention on an irrelevant dimension such as spatial arrangement rather than equivalence of number. With very small sets (e.g. two or three objects), even young preoperational children (4–5 years of age) can demonstrate the ability to make successful comparisons (Gelman, 1972), and older preoperational children (5–6 years of age) can construct sets of equivalent number although they would probably fail to conserve this equivalence if the sets were physically rearranged. Children at this age make use of one-to-one correspondence to match sets, but as Piaget notes, this skill is not indicative of an underlying comprehension of the concepts involved. It is merely 'perceptual.' In sum, Piaget's work suggests the stage of concrete operations may be a requisite to making set comparisons.

The development of the concepts of ordinal relations follow a similar pattern. Preoperational children, 4–5-year-olds, generally cannot form a systematic ordinal ordering. By 5 or 6 they do so with difficulty, having trouble focusing on more than one relationship. At 6 or 7, as they enter the concrete operational stage, a good grasp of ordinal relations is achieved given the constraint that the objects are actually present. Dealing with more abstract notions of ordinality, however, proves difficult for the concrete operational child. In fact, when abstract inferences are required, even adolescents may have considerable difficulty.

Piaget studied the development of proportional thought in functional, geometric, and probabilistic relationships. His and others' extensive work is detailed elsewhere. See Hook and Cook (1979) for a concise summary. The findings indicate that a fundamental grasp of proportionality occurs during the formal operational stage beginning at approximately age 13. This conclusion is qualified by what Piaget termed 'vertical décalage,' observing that there are progressive levels of understanding of a concept before its final mastery. In this case, in specific types of tasks, e.g. very simple ratios like 2 : 1, younger children might demonstrate the ability to find the correct solution. Concrete operational children may also be able to solve certain problems of directly manipulating objects. However, they would be unlikely to be able to verbalize the concepts involved. Final attainment of proportional thought according to Piaget includes the ability to verbalize the process, and to deal with abstractions of the material.

The development of fairness rules

In examining the relationship between cognitive development and the development of fairness rules as social values, it is essential to consider what is known regarding the development of fairness rules as well as of numerical abilities. A rather extensive review of the literature may be found in Hook and Cook (1979). Very broadly, research to date indicates very young children (6 and under) often do not employ a fairness rule, but allocate outcomes to themselves regardless of own and other's inputs. In our current research, for example, a sizable number (31 out of 79) of 7-year-olds behaved in a self-interested manner. When asked whether their allocations were fair, more than half acknowledged that they were not. This suggests, of course, that some perceived that their self-interested behavior violates some normative rule of fairness.

Children between 6 and 12 years take into consideration own and other's contribution to a common task, and distribute outcomes using one of three fairness rules: equality, ordinal, or ratio equity. The first two are more frequently reported in the literature than the latter. Research also indicates children at approximately 13 years of age begin to make allocations consistent with a ratio definition of equity. Further, it has been observed that children are more likely to use an equality rule when they are disadvantaged in input than when advantaged probably because this is consistent with self-interest. In our research, the variability in rule use at each age level is higher in the disadvantaged than advantaged condition. Finally, a wide variety of factors have been observed to influence which rules of fairness will dominate within or between age levels. For example, in the authors' current research program, the following have been observed to produce variations in rule use: (a) the degree of behavioral reciprocity that obtains between allocator and other; (b) the public or private nature of the allocator's distribution behaviors; and (c) the cooperative or competitive structure of the task.

On the relationship between the development of numerical abilities and the rules of fairness

In a very compelling analysis of the simultaneous development of fairness rules and various numerical skills, Hook and Cook (1979) assert there may be a direct relation between the development of cognitive abilities and the use of fairness rules. They observe that a review of the cognitive literature indicates that the 'average child under 13 years of age does not solve problems of ratio proportionality.' Since such skills are requisite to making Adams's (1963) form of proportional equity allocations, they conclude children do not have the numerical capabilities before 13 to make such allocations.

Hook and Cook make analogous arguments regarding the appearances of other allocation rules based upon a simultaneous review of the developmental literature on numerical abilities and fairness behavior. Self-interest requires the least cognitive skills and appears earliest (3 years); equality follows in terms of cognitive requisites and in time of appearance (4–6 years). Subsequently, the skills requisite to ordinal equity become available, and it dominates as a rule of fairness during the longest interval of childhood (7–12 years).

Since their assertions are correlational in form, Hook and Cook consider five alternative explanations to account for why children's mean distributions between

7 and 12 years of age are consistent in a large number of empirical studies with the transformational rule of ordinal equity. Their *first* explanation asserts ordinal equity obtains because children may use other inputs than those manipulated by the experimenter to calculate fair allocations. Hence, what appears to be ordinal might be proportional if one knew the 'true' inputs. This initial interpretation is similar to their *second*, that the physical input or outcome scales are not isomorphic with the psychological ones.

A *third* possible interpretation is that ordinal equity may represent an 'intra-allocator norm combination.' This explanation argues that an individual child may simultaneously use more than one rule. This is comparable to Leventhal's (1976) interesting suggestions that a single rule may not be sufficient to represent how humans make judgments regarding fairness. He suggests a summary formula may more adequately portray an actor's view of justice:

Deserved outcomes = $w_c D$ by contributions + $w_n D$ by need + $w_e D$ by equality + $w_o D$ by other rules, where D implies deservingness given a particular criteria, and w the weights observers or actors assign to each criterion.

A *fourth* explanation is that of 'interallocator norm combination: different children at the same age follow different rules and their combination produces a mean allocation consistent with ordinal equity.'

Finally, Hook and Cook reject, partially on the basis of a study by Hook (1978), the preceding four explanations maintaining that children under 13 are typically cognitively unable to solve problems of ratio proportionality, and hence they employ an approximation, ordinal equity, as their dominant rule of fairness.

An evaluation of Hook and Cook's explanation of ordinal equity

In our current research, data have been collected on the allocation behaviors of 2nd, 4th, 6th, and 8th grade children. An input/outcome task was used in which inputs and outcomes were numerically correspondent, namely, inputs were 6/2 and 2/6, and 8 units of outcome were provided for distribution. Hence, abstract numerical skills may not be required for ratio equity distributions, and a fairness rule isomorphic with Adams's notion of proportional equity may be within the numerical capability of most of the children. Table 3 reports results from a condition in which children did not expect others to be able to reciprocate their allocation.

The data reported are different in form than one would expect if children predominantly employed a single distribution rule at each age level, e.g. self-interest, then equality, then ordinal equity, and finally proportional equity. What seems to obtain is that children of the same age use different rules. There is also an obvious change in the overall pattern of rule use as a function of age. It is also quite obvious from the table that most children did not make choices consistent with ordinal equity. Rather, the choices of 2nd graders advantaged in input are trimodal, and distributed in the categories of self-interest, ratio equity, and

Table 3 Children's Outcome Distribution Behaviors as a Function of Input and Grade Level

ADVANTAGED INPUT (Own input 6 strings of beads; other's input 2 strings)

OUTCOME DISTRIBUTION

(First digit in each pair is number child afforded self; second number that afforded other)

GRADE	Generosity (0, 8; 1, 7; 2, 6; 3, 5)	Equality (4, 4)	Ordinal equity (5, 3)	Proportional equity (6, 2)	Self-interest (7, 1; 8, 0)	Total N
2	0.0%	23.1%	12.8%	35.9%	28.2%	39
4	2.5%	62.5%	10.0%	22.5%	2.5%	40
6	7.5%	52.5%	15.0%	25.0%	0.0%	40
8	18.9%	64.9%	5.4%	10.8%	0.0%	37

DISADVANTAGED INPUT (Own input 2 strings of beads; other's input 6 strings)

GRADE	Generosity (0, 8; 1, 7)	Equality (4, 4)	Ordinal equity (3, 5)	Proportional equity (2, 6)	Self-interest (5, 3; 6, 2; 7, 1; 8, 0)	Total N
2	0.0%	42.5%	2.5%	5.0%	50.0%	40
4	0.0%	60.0%	0.0%	17.5%	22.5%	40
6	0.0%	60.0%	5.0%	27.5%	7.5%	40
8	0.0%	41.0%	5.1%	53.8%	0.0%	39

equality; those of the disadvantaged are bimodal, equality and self-interest. The advantaged 8th graders' data are almost unimodal with about 65% of the children distributing the outcomes equally; however, the disadvantaged data are strongly bimodal with two choice rules accounting for about 95% of the choices, equality and ratio equity.

As regards 4th and 6th graders, who according to Hook and Cook should predominantly make ordinal equity choices, in the advantaged input condition their choices are bimodally distributed between equality and proportional equity. In the disadvantaged condition, 4th grade choices are trimodal, equality, proportional equity, and self-interest; 6th grade choices are bimodal, equality and proportional equity. Again it should be stressed that in our study inputs and outcomes were correspondent. Nevertheless, the data reveal multiple rule use at each age level, and suggest that some of the research findings used to support the argument for ordinal equity as a rule may actually reflect an 'interallocator norm combination,' an explanation Hook and Cook discount.

Summary

A model of social values has been presented which emphasizes the influence of outcome interdependence on social decision-making processes. The model asserts that behavior in general is influenced by the value an actor attaches to the outcomes associated with each choice alternative, and that an actor will prefer that choice alternative which affords the most highly valued outcome. In settings of outcome interdependence, each actor's choice impacts not only that actor's own outcome but the outcome(s) of the other(s) with whom he or she shares interdependence. Conversely, other's choice has impact on actor's outcome as well as his/her own. Social values, in this context, are assumed to be defined by the structure of the actor's preferred outcome distribution given this interdependence. Further, an actor's preference on any single choice may reflect the actor's primary social *goal*, a valued end state, or a social *strategy*, a choice designed to influence other's future choices such that actor may reach a valued goal at some future time point.

A spatial representation of the above model as developed by Griesinger and Livingston (1973) illustrates a number of possible value orientations in the two-person interdependence setting. Among the values thus defined and illustrated cooperation, competition, and individualism have been the most thoroughly researched. Two basic approaches to this task are represented by the use of matrix and decomposed games. Matrix games such as the earlier defined PDG and MDG have been extensively used to evaluate the influence of mutual fate control on actor's outcome preferences. In a developmental context, McClintock and his associates using the MDG, have demonstrated a tendency for children to prefer competitive over cooperative and individualistic outcomes with increasing age. This pattern obtains within a number of Western and Western-influenced cultures.

The use of decomposed games allows stronger conclusions about the goal or strategic nature of actor's choices. McClintock and his associates have used this paradigm to establish a developmental progression from the young child's strict self-interest and apparent disregard for or unawareness of outcome interdependence through the development of strategic choice behavior and finally to the internalization of preferences as autonomous social motives.

A more recent topic of inquiry within the social value approach is represented by the redefinition of certain rules of fairness, namely, equality and equity, as unique social values. The inclusion of equity and equality rules within the current framework broadens the focus of decision processes to include consideration of *both* the value of inputs and of outcomes of interdependent actors. Adopting a developmental emphasis, this broadened perspective suggests the importance of an examination of the cognitive prerequisites for the acquisition of social values. To illustrate this importance, some background and preliminary findings from an ongoing study of children's use of fairness rules are described in some detail.

Notes

1. The preparation of this article was supported by NSF Grant #77-003862. Portions of it appeared earlier in McClintock, C. G. 'Social values: their definition, measurement, and development.' *Journal of Research and Development in Education*, 1978, **12**, 121–137.
2. The decomposed game was simultaneously developed by Pruitt (1967).

References

Adams, J. S. (1963). 'Toward an understanding of equity,' *Journal of Abnormal and Social Psychology*, **67**, 422–436.
Banerjee, D., and Pareek, U. (1974). 'Development of cooperative and competitive behavior in children of some subcultures,' *Indian Journal of Psychology*, **49**, 237–256.
Carment, D. W. (1974a). 'Indian and Canadian choice behavior in a maximizing difference game and in a game of chicken,' *International Journal of Psychology*, **9**, 213–221.
Carment, D. W. (1974b). 'Indian and Canadian choice behavior in a mixed-motive game,' *International Journal of Psychology*, **9**, 303–313.
Festinger, L. (1954). 'A theory of social comparison processes,' *Human Relations*, **7**, 117–140.
Flavell, John H. (1977). *Cognitive Development*, Prentice-Hall, Englewood Cliffs, NJ.
Gelman, R. (1972). 'Logical capacity of very young children: Number invariance rules,' *Child Development*, **43**, 75–90.
Griesinger, D., and Livingston, D. (1973). 'Towards a model of interpersonal motivation in experimental games,' *Behavioral Science*, **18**, 173–188.
Hook, J. (1978). 'The development of equity and logicomathematical thinking,' *Child Development*, **49**, 1035–1044.
Hook, J. G., and Cook, T. D. (1979). 'Equity theory and the cognitive ability of children,' *Psychological Bulletin*, **86**, 429–445.
Kelley, H., and Thibaut, J. (1978). *Interpersonal Relations: A Theory of Interdependence*, Wiley, New York.

Leventhal, G. (1976). 'Fairness in social relations,' in J. Thibaut, J. Spence, and R. Carson (eds.), *Contemporary Topics in Social Psychology*, pp. 211–239, General Learning Press, Morristown, NJ.

McClintock, C. G. (1972). 'Social motivation—A set of propositions,' *Behavioral Science*, **17**, 438–454.

McClintock, C. G. (1974). 'Development of social motives in Anglo-American and Mexican-American Children,' *Journal of Experimental Social Psychology*, **29**, 348–354.

McClintock, C. G. (1977). 'Social motivation in settings of outcome interdependence in D. Druckman (ed.), *Negotiation Behavior*, Sage, Beverly Hills.

McClintock, C. G. and Keil, L. (1980). The effects of cognition, reward and social interdependence upon children's fairness behaviors. NSF Proposal #80-63.

McClintock, C. G., and Moskowitz, J. M. (1976). 'Children's preferences for individualistic, cooperative and competitive outcomes', *Journal of Personality and Social Psychology*, **34**, 543–555.

McClintock, C. G., Moskowitz, J. M., and McClintock, E. (1977). 'Variations in preferences for individualistic, competitive, and cooperative outcomes as a function of age, game class and task in nursery school children,' *Child Development*, **48**, 1080–1085.

McClintock, C. G., and Nuttin, J. (1969). 'Development of competitive game behavior across two cultures,' *Journal of Experimental Social Psychology*, **5**, 203–218.

McClintock, C. G. and Van Avermaet, E. (In press). Social values and rules of fairness: A theoretical perspective. In J. Grzelak and V. Derlega (eds.), *Living With Other People: Theory and Research on Cooperation and Helping*, Academic Press, New York.

Messick, D. M., and McClintock, C. G. (1968). 'Motivational bases of choice in experimental games,' *Journal of Experimental Social Psychology*, **4**, 1–25.

Piaget, J. (1964). *The Child's Conception of Number*, Routledge & Kegan Paul, London.

Pruitt, D. G. (1967). 'Reward structure and cooperation: The decomposed prisoner's dilemma game,' *Journal of Personality and Social Psychology*, **14**, 21–27.

Pruitt, D. G., and Kimmel, M. J. (1977). 'Twenty years of experimental gaming: Critique, synthesis, and suggestions for the future,' *Annual Review of Psychology*, **28**, 363–392.

Radzicki, J. (1976). 'Technique of conjoint measurement of subjective value of own and others' gain,' *Polish Psychological Bulletin*, **7**, 179–186.

Thibaut, J. W., and Kelley, H. H. (1959). *The Social Psychology of Groups*, Wiley, New York.

Toda, M., Shinotsuka, H., McClintock, C. G., and Stech, F. (1978). 'Development of competitive behavior as a function of culture, age, and social comparison,' *Journal of Personality and Social Psychology*, **36**, 835–839.

Van Avermaet, E., McClintock, C., and Moskowitz, J. (1978). 'Alternative approaches to equity: Pro-social motivation, strategic accommodation, and dissonance reduction,' *European Journal of Social Psychology*, **8**, 419–437.

Wyer, R. (1969). 'Prediction of behavior in two-person games,' *Journal of Personality and Social Psychology*, **13**, 222–228.

Wyer, R. (1971). 'The effects of outcome matrix and partner's behavior in two person games,' *Journal of Experimental Social Psychology*, **7**, 190–210.

Small Groups and Social Interaction, Volume 2
Edited by H. H. Blumberg, A. P. Hare, V. Kent and M. Davies
Published by John Wiley & Sons Ltd 1983

3.3 A Review of Experiments in Explicit Bargaining*

Jerome M. Chertkoff and James K. Esser   *Indiana University*

In this paper, the term bargaining will be restricted to what Schelling (1963) labeled explicit bargaining. Explicit bargaining is a situation (1) where the parties have divergent interests, at least to a certain extent, and (2) where communication is possible. Three additional conditions are also required for bargaining to occur. First, mutual compromise must be possible. If one side must choose between total victory or yielding completely, no bargaining can occur. Only when intermediate solutions are possible can there be bargaining. Second, the possibility must exist for provisional offers. Third, the provisional offers must not fix the tangible outcomes until an offer is accepted by all sides. This conception fits what is usually meant by bargaining, a situation where parties with certain disagreements confer and exchange ideas about a possible settlement until either a compromise is reached or the bargaining is terminated.

Before beginning the review, it may be helpful to provide a general description of a bargaining paradigm. The typical bargaining experiment involves two people negotiating an economic exchange. The people are given information about the payoffs to their own side for all possible agreements. Sometimes they are also given information about the payoff schedule of the other side. Then the two sides exchange offers. Usually the bargaining is via written offers, though occasionally the bargaining is face-to-face. Usually the bargaining is limited to offers, either because no other form of communication is permitted or because no other bases for communication are provided. Only very rarely are bargainers provided with rationales other than the payoff schedule to use in defending their positions or in persuading the other side.

* Abridged by the authors from *Journal of Experimental Social Psychology*, 1976, **12**, 464–486. Reproduced by permission of Academic Press, Inc.

The vast majority of experiments, then, involve only two people, each representing a different side. Occasionally, the usual paradigm has been extended to include additional people with an interest in the bargaining process, such as a constituent or a mediator.

A major distinction between bargaining experiments is whether the payoff schedule is constant-sum or varying-sum. In a constant-sum schedule, the profits of the respective bargainers always sum to the same amount. An increase in the profit of one bargainer, therefore, always coincides with an equivalent decrease in the profit of the other bargainer. In a varying-sum schedule, the profits of the respective bargainers do not always sum to the same amount. Although the payoff schedules are usually inversely related, a large increase in the profit of one side might coincide with a negligible decrease in profit by the other side.

The typical research paradigm was designed originally to study how economic and structural factors affect the offers that bargainers make. Since other factors are controlled, the paradigm is well suited to this purpose. As researchers shift their emphasis to the persuasive aspects of bargaining, further elaboration of the paradigm will become necessary.

General theories of bargaining

Can all bargaining research be incorporated within some general theory of bargaining? Perhaps, though an attempt to do so would probably appear forced and premature. Let us examine the types of general theories that exist and the limitations of each.

One class of theories is the mathematical utility model. Some utility models of bargaining make predictions about the most likely point of agreement, and some even make predictions about the dynamics of concession making (Cross, 1969; Luce and Raiffa, 1957). Although these models may have been ignored to a certain extent because many social psychologists are not mathematically inclined, there are undoubtedly other reasons. First, the theories contain constructs, like utility, that are difficult to measure. Second, the models usually deal with broad concepts, like the utility of payoffs, without specifying in any detail what variables are related to them, and in what way. A notable exception is the mathematical theorizing of Cross (1969); however, his discussion is restricted to economic variables.

A second general class of theories, such as equity theory (Adams, 1965), emphasizes people's desire to achieve fair outcomes in social exchange. However, when bargainers do advocate an agreement that is fair according to some norm, it may not always be because the bargainers believe that following the norm is, in itself, a good thing to do and feel guilty if they violate it, as is assumed in equity theory. There are at least three alternative reasons why bargainers may accept an agreement in accordance with some norm of fairness. First, a normatively fair settlement may stand out as one possible solution that both sides might accept (Schelling, 1963). Second, bargainers may be interested in establishing or maintaining the friendship of the opponent, and they believe that adhering to a norm of fairness will lead to achievement of this goal (Morgan and Sawyer, 1967). Third, an agreement in accordance with some norm of fairness may yield high material payoffs to at least one of the sides.

The third type of theory emphasizes psychological evaluations of the bargaining process. In this category are face-saving theory, attribution theory, and level of aspiration theory. Face saving is a somewhat ambiguous term. Brown (1971) defined it as the sacrifice of tangible rewards in order to avoid looking foolish or incompetent in public. Defined in this narrow way, the bargaining literature offers only a few examples: (1) the greater willingness of bargainers to accept less favorable terms if offered by a mediator rather than the opponent [the term 'opponent' merely denotes the other side—it does not necessarily imply hostility] (Pruitt and Johnson, 1970) and (2) the tendency for bargainers occasionally to prefer no agreement to terms that yield the bargainer a small profit, but yield the opponent a much greater profit (Chertkoff and Baird, 1971; Lamm and Rosch, 1972). If face-saving were defined more broadly to include any action that creates a positive public image, then almost all bargaining behavior could be viewed as face-saving.

Attributional analyses will be discussed extensively in the section on bargaining strategy. Occasionally attributions will be mentioned elsewhere, but more needs to be known about what affects the attributions of bargainers and when these attributions are crucial before attribution theory can be used broadly to interpret bargaining phenomena.

Level of aspiration theory was used by Siegel and Fouraker (1960) to explain why tough bargaining was advantageous. They proposed that toughness by a bargainer reduces the opponent's level of aspiration, and therefore leads to reduced demands by the opponent. Alternatively, weakness by a bargainer increases the opponent's level of aspiration, and therefore, leads to heightened demands by the opponent. Siegel and Fouraker (1960) attempted to manipulate level of aspiration by varying the amount of profit needed to obtain a bonus. Others (e.g. Hamner and Harnett, 1975) have asked bargainers for their levels of aspiration and have studied the interaction of aspiration level with certain other factors. Occasionally, level of aspiration theory has been evaluated by examining correlations such as that between the bargainer's aspiration level and the level of his immediate demands (e.g. Yukl, 1974a,b). This correlation increases steadily during the course of bargaining to a value of about .7 (Yukl, 1974a) or .9 (Yukl, 1974b). Such a finding seems intuitively obvious.

Early in bargaining, a bargainer's demands are affected by his goals but also by his willingness to follow a strategy of extreme, somewhat unrealistic, demands. As the bargaining proceeds and the likely point of agreement becomes clearer, both the level of aspiration and the demands come to reflect the probable point of agreement.

In conclusion, all of the general theories suffer from one or more of the following problems: (1) There are measurement problems in quantifying the mediating factors. (2) The relations between possible variables and the mediating factors are not spelled out clearly. (3) The theories are stated so broadly and/or with so little precision that very few if any findings could ever lead to rejection or modification of the theories.

Review of experiments

General bargaining predispositions

Two general approaches have been used to study individual differences in the way people bargain. The first approach is to determine to what extent individuals show consistency across bargaining encounters. A second approach to the study of individual differences is to examine the possible effects of demographic and personality factors that might be related to rigidity in bargaining.

To summarize, tougher bargaining occurs by people high in Dogmatism (Druckman, 1967), people with feelings of internal Locus of Control (Harnett, Cummings, and Hamner, 1973), and people with a competitive orientation when competition means personal strength (Kelley, Shure, Deutsch, Faucheux, Lanzetta, Moscovici, Nuttin, Rabbie, and Thibaut, 1970).

What do people with such personality characteristics have in common? Perhaps these persons all feel strongly that obtaining favorable terms signifies personal strength and obtaining unfavorable terms signifies personal weakness. Therefore, to maintain a self-perception of personal strength, they bargain in a tough manner. Consistent with such an interpretation, Druckman (1967) found that on post-experimental questionnaire responses, people high in Dogmatism were significantly more likely to view compromise as a defeat than were people low in Dogmatism. Similarly, a person who perceives himself as internally controlled is likely to feel that his own self-esteem is on the line, since any achievement or lack of it is due to his own actions. Such a person must, therefore, bargain in a tough manner to maintain a self-image of personal strength. In contrast, a person who perceives himself to be externally controlled may tend to attribute any lack of bargaining success to external factors. It seems reasonable to suppose that when yielding is attributed to external events rather than to personal weakness, it should occur more readily. Finally, the research on competitive v. cooperative orientation indicates that it is precisely when this dimension implies personal strength or weakness that a competitive orientation leads to tougher bargaining.

Payoff system

The actual payoff system confronting a bargainer is certainly a major determinant of his bargaining behavior. A number of different factors related to the payoff system have been studied. They include: (1) the amount that has to be exceeded if the bargainer is to realize a profit; (2) the cost of time spent in bargaining; (3) the cost of failure to reach agreement; (4) added benefits achieved by obtaining a specific threshold value; (5) qualitative or quantitative variations in the general level of payoff values; (6) whether payoffs are based solely on one's own profit schedule or are based, in whole or in part, on the degree to which one's profits exceed those of others; (7) whether conflict is constant-sum or varying-sum; and (8) penalties the bargaining opponent (or perhaps a third party) is likely to impose for failure to yield.

Zero profit point. Many names have been used to designate the amount that must be exceeded in order to obtain a profit: breakeven point, zero profit point, minimum necessary share, resistance point, or minimum disposition. In the laboratory research, this value is almost always fixed. As Ikle and Leites (1962) argue, however, the value in natural settings is frequently uncertain, and bargaining often involves an attempt to convince the adversary that he can profitably accept a lower value than the one he maintains is necessary.

The most extensive analysis of the effects of varying the minimum necessary share was performed by Kelley, Beckman, and Fischer (1967). In their theoretical model, a bargainer's resistance to making concessions is assumed to be related positively to both the time required to make a further concession and the probability of withdrawing from the negotiations. The level of resistance is assumed to depend on the distance of a given offer from the minimum necessary share and on the specific value of the minimum necessary share. As a person concedes towards his minimum necessary share, his resistance is assumed to increase. For a given offer, the higher the minimum necessary share, the greater the resistance. For a given level of profit, the lower the minimum necessary share, the greater the resistance. These major assumptions, along with certain other assumptions, form the basis for a model that fits their data reasonably well. Later research (Fischer, 1969; Holmes, Throop, and Strickland, 1971; Kelley *et al.*, 1970; Schoeninger and Wood, 1969) offers further evidence that the location of the zero profit point is extremely important and operates in accordance with the Kelley *et al.* (1967) model.

Time pressure. The greater the time pressure, the faster the concession making (Hamner, 1974; Komorita and Barnes, 1969; Pruitt and Drews, 1969; Pruitt and Johnson, 1970; Yukl, 1974a). Time pressure has been exerted in various ways: (1) high or low probability that the present round of offers would be the last (Pruitt and Drews, 1969; Yukl, 1974a); (2) warning that time was almost up (Pruitt and Johnson, 1970); (3) number of offers remaining before penalties for additional offers (Hamner, 1974); and (4) cost of each trial of offers (Komorita and Barnes, 1969). Undoubtedly, the more rapid yielding under greater time pressures reflects the desire of bargainers to avoid either the undesirable costs associated with making offers or zero profit (which results from no agreement).

Cost of no agreement. In laboratory paradigms, the vast majority of possible terms are usually preferable to no agreement. Under such conditions, warning the subjects that the end of negotiations is imminent will produce extremely rapid concession making, so uniformly rapid, in fact, that any differences in levels of toughness prior to the warning may be obliterated (Benton, Kelley, and Liebling, 1972; Esser and Komorita, 1975).

The research of Thibaut and his associates on the development of contractual norms directly involves the cost of no agreement (Thibaut and Faucheux, 1965; Thibaut, 1968; Thibaut and Gruder, 1969). In this line of research, the payoff associated with no agreement is varied. This payoff is called the external alternative and corresponds to Thibaut and Kelley's (1959) concept of comparison level for alternatives. The higher the alternative value, the more often it is typically chosen.

Bonus threshold. In some instances, a bargainer may either be offered a bonus for attaining some specified outcome, or may face an additional negative payoff for failing to obtain a specific agreement. For example, a bargainer may be promised such added payoffs as a raise, promotion, or a share in the company for obtaining a specified favorable agreement. Or, a bargainer may be threatened with demotion or termination of his employment for failing to obtain certain specified terms.

Siegel and Fouraker (1960) used variation in bonus threshold in operationalizing their concept of level of aspiration. One bargainer had to obtain a rather high payoff in order to receive a bonus, while the other bargainer was offered a bonus for obtaining a much lower payoff. It was possible for both to reach the bonus threshold. The one who had to obtain the higher payoff to receive the bonus was found to average larger payoffs.

Kahan (1968) told players that they would be paid only if they had the highest winnings in their role positions. He then varied the amount allegedly obtained by the best player so far. Cooperation decreased as the sum of the aspiration levels of the two bargainers increased.

In conclusion, when a bonus threshold exists, bargainers obviously try to reach it. When a bargainer can easily reach his own bonus threshold, he will do so. However, when it becomes difficult or impossible for both bargainers to achieve their respective thresholds, the bargainers will exhibit great resistance in concession making.

Payoff level. The magnitude and kind of payoffs may both affect the nature of the bargaining. The payoff levels in most laboratory experiments have been constant across trials (when the experiment involved repeated trials). An exception is the procedure used by Kelley *et al.* (1970), where five consecutive agreements resulted in a marked increase in the payoff levels. This procedure was used in all conditions of the experiment, so its effect was not studied.

Daniels (1967) studied the effects of different incentives in a number of conditions, one of which involved explicit bargaining. Low incentive subjects played for points. High incentive subjects played for small amounts of money and their scores were allegedly to be made public in their psychology class. The game was varying-sum, so that joint outcomes could vary. Joint outcomes in explicit bargaining were higher under high incentive than under low. Kelley et al. (1970) proposed that high incentives lead a person to favor a course of action with low risk. If the value of cooperation is increased without accompanying risk, high incentives should lead to greater cooperation. However, if high risk accompanies attempts at cooperation, high incentives should decrease cooperation. Since in their experiment, engaging in cooperative behavior should appear less risky than engaging in competitive behavior, they predicted that high incentives should lead to greater cooperation. As predicted, cooperation was greater when the subjects played for money rather than points.

Maximizing own gain vs. maximizing difference.   Although subjects in bargaining experiments typically are given the goal of maximizing own gain, they may also be interested in besting the other bargainer. In several studies, the goal of the bargainers has been varied.

Any theoretical model must include assumptions about the goal of bargainers. The utility of a given agreement, the aspiration level of the bargainer, or the magnitude of face maintained may often be in terms of a difference score rather than in terms of own gain. When two bargainers are each trying to maximize difference, tough bargaining is likely (Lamm and Rosch, 1972). When maximizing difference is the goal, failure in this regard leads to tougher bargaining in the future (Esser, 1975).

Constant-sum vs. varying-sum bargaining.   No experiments have attempted to compare directly the behaviors of bargainers when the profit is constant-sum vs. varying-sum. The line of bargaining research launched by Siegel and Fouraker (1960) involves varying-sum bargaining. This research has been mainly concerned with conditions that increase the likelihood of maximizing joint profit. For example, achieving maximum joint profit is more likely if both bargainers know the profits of the opponent than if they do not (Siegel and Fouraker, 1960). On the other hand, if the bargainer's goal is maximization of own gain, knowledge of his opponent's profits is not always advantageous to him. When opposing someone who knew only his own profit schedule, a bargainer with a high initial aspiration level earned more if he also knew only his own profit schedule. However, a bargainer with a low initial aspiration level earned more if he knew the schedules of both himself and his opponent (Hamner and Harnett, 1975).

In several experiments, Kelley and his associates have attempted to analyze the process involved in bargaining using the Siegel and Fouraker paradigm (see Kelley and Schenitzki, 1972, for a review). This analysis indicates that a bargainer typically begins by proposing a contract that gives himself a very high profit. If his initial proposal is rejected, then he proposes, in turn, all possible contracts that yield approximately the same amount of profit as the initial proposal. If all these proposals are also rejected, then he moves to offers that yield a lower level of profit for himself and systematically offers, in turn, all possible contracts yielding the new, lower level of profit. Systematically moving to lower profit levels is crucial in maximizing joint profit. Bargainers who were given a cooperative orientation achieved the maximum joint profit less often than bargainers who were given an individualistic orientation, because the cooperative orientation led bargainers to deviate from a slow, systematic reduction in demands. This deficiency in the performance of cooperatively oriented bargainers held only when the communication was limited to offers. When the bargainers could communicate their evaluative reactions to one another's offers as well as the offers themselves, the orientation of the bargainers had no effect.

Using face-to-face communications and a varying-sum bargaining situation involving the sale of three commodities, Pruitt and Lewis (1975) found that a combination of a problem-solving orientation and high minimum profit levels produced the highest joint profit levels. A failure to reach agreement occurred most often when the orientation was individualistic and there were high minimum profit levels. A process analysis of the bargaining supported the conclusion of Kelley and Schenitzki (1972) that systematic concession making is crucial to maximizing joint profit in varying-sum bargaining.

Taken together, the research of Kelley and Schenitzki (1972) and Pruitt and Lewis (1975) indicates that the form of communication interacts with the orientation of bargainers to affect bargaining performance. When communication is restricted to offers, bargaining pairs with a competitive orientation obtain a higher joint profit. When communication includes the opportunity for evaluative responses as well as offers, orientation has no effect. When communication includes the opportunity for offers, evaluative responses, persuasive attempts, and the exchange of information about one another's profit schedules, bargainers with a cooperative orientation achieve a higher joint profit. Under all types of communication, the mediating process behind maximization of joint profit appears to be systematic concession making.

Threats and promises. If one bargainer (or any ally of his) could punish the opponent or reward him in some way, this might well affect the opponent's bargaining. Tedeschi (1970) has reviewed the research on threats and promises. The effectiveness of threats and promises depends on such factors as the credibility of the threat or promise and the magnitude of punishment or reward. Certainly a bargainer must weigh the magnitude of the possible reward for yielding or punishment for not yielding and the probability that the reward or punishment actually will be delivered against the potential benefit of standing firm.

In the research of Deutsch and Krauss (1960, 1962) using the Acme-Bolt trucking game, threat capacity was detrimental to conflict resolution, even when communciation was permitted or compelled. The threat capacity was used and provoked a spiral of hostile actions which communication could not overcome completely. Shomer, Davis, and Kelley (1966), however, maintained that penalty, not threat alone, evokes increased competitiveness. They noted that in the Deutsch and Krauss research, the use of the gate to obstruct the opponent's truck could represent a penalty as well as a threat. When threat and penalty were separated into distinct behaviors and threat was interpreted as a signal of future intention rather than as a hostile act, threat lead to an avoidance of conflict.

The Shomer *et al.* (1966) research involved tacit rather than explicit bargaining, since no communication was permitted other than the threat and penalty. Smith and Anderson (1975) varied the ability of bargainers to converse and the ability of bargainers both to threaten and to fine the opponent. When subjects were permitted and encouraged to talk to one another, pairs with threat–fine capacity had a lower mean joint profit than pairs without this capacity. However, when no communication was permitted, pairs with threat–fine capacity obtained a higher mean joint profit than those without. While Smith and Anderson (1975) found that threat–fine capacity was detrimental to conflict resolution in explicit bargaining, a crucial factor in determining when this is so may be the language used in transmitting the threat (Rubin and Lewicki, 1973).

In conclusion, various theoretical interpretations can be found in the research on threat. Tedeschi's (1970) research on the magnitude of punishment and the probability of its occurrence seems to fit a subjective utility model. Deutsch and Krauss (1960) emphasized face saving as the psychological mechanism leading to a spiral of hostility in threat situations. Shomer *et al.* (1966) stressed the importance of attributions of intentionality. Perhaps all of these mechanisms can operate, and the important problem is to determine when each mechanism is dominant.

Social relationship with the opponent

One would expect bargaining to be more cooperative when the social relationship between bargainers is more positive. Several experiments clearly support such a prediction (Morgan and Sawyer, 1967; Schoeninger and Wood, 1969).

It is reasonable to suppose that the greater cooperation between friends and between married couples results from the greater concern for the interests of the opponent that exists in such cases. If so, then cooperation should be increased between nonfriends if concern for the interests of the opponent are increased. Such an effect can be seen in an experiment by Dorris (1972), who had people attempt to sell a set of coins to actual coin dealers. The seller explained to the dealer that he had inherited the coins and knew nothing about their worth. Two types of appeals were used. In the moral appeal, the seller needed money to buy textbooks and was sent by a stamp dealer who had recommended the coin dealer as one who could be trusted to give a fair price. In the neutral appeal, no such statements were made. The moral appeal elicited higher initial and final offers.

Social relationship with significant others

The bargainer's relationships with people other than the opponent may also affect his behavior. Several studies have contrasted the effect of planning strategy with members of one's own side with the effect of studying the issues in groups containing members of both sides. A bilateral study session may produce a more positive attitude toward the bargaining opponent if the session is conducted in a friendly, constructive manner. The results of these studies do indicate that unilateral strategy planning leads to more competitive bargaining than does bilateral study (Bass, 1966; Druckman, 1967, 1968; Kahn and Kohls, 1972).

Another line of research has compared the effects of acting as a bargaining representative for others with the effects of bargaining for oneself. This research indicates that being a representative may either increase or decrease toughness, depending on what criteria the constituents are using to evaluate the representative's performance. In the absence of any specific knowledge about such criteria, a bargaining representative will probably assume that he will be evaluated on the basis of how tough he is, since it is usually the bargainer's job to obtain the most beneficial agreement possible for his side. The vast majority of research in this area indicates that representatives do bargain more competitively than nonrepresentatives (Benton, 1972; Benton and Druckman, 1973; Druckman, Solomon and Zechmeister, 1972; Vidmar, 1971). Several experiments (Benton and Druckman, 1974; Gruder and Rosen, 1971; Wall, 1976) do indicate that competitive instructions from the constituents increase toughness and cooperative instructions reduce toughness.

Just as bargainers tend to be responsive to the directives of their constituents, they tend to be responsive to the directives of the experimenter. Instructions that emphasize self-interest and competitiveness will produce greater toughness than instructions that emphasize cooperation and fairness (Deutsch, 1949, 1960; Rubin, 1971).

Sometimes in bargaining, a mediator or arbitrator is called upon to facilitate the settlement process. Pruitt and Johnson (1970) maintain that mediators facilitate agreements because a concession suggested by a mediator can be agreed to without loss of face. 'Presumably many people see concessions in negotiation as a sign of their own personal weakness and are therefore reluctant to make them. But if a mediator suggests that a concession be made, and if he seems reasonable and fair as a person, a negotiator can rationalize a concession by telling himself that he is not being weak but rather intelligent to follow the lead of a worthy consultant. In a sense, the mediator helps him save face with himself' (Pruitt and Johnson, 1970, p. 239). In their experiment on mediation, Pruitt and Johnson (1970) found that concession making was greater when there was a mediator who intervened and recommended a concession. Furthermore, they found an inverse relationship between size of concession and perceived personal strength when there was no mediation, but no such relationship occurred when there was mediation. This supports the notion that when a mediator suggests a concession, concession making can be attributed to his suggestion and not to personal weakness; as a result, concessions are more likely. An experiment by Podell and Knapp (1969) also supports the notion that mediation permits face saving. They found that a bargainer evaluated his opponent as less firm when the opponent conceded on his own rather than at the suggestion of a mediator.

As Pruitt and Johnson (1970) indicated, it is important that the third party be perceived as fair if his recommendations are to be followed or if his binding decisions are to be sought. Johnson and Pruitt (1972) found that if a bargainer is confronted with the possibility of binding arbitration by an arbitrator who is likely to be biased against him, the bargainer will concede rapidly in an effort to avoid intervention by the arbitrator. This effect is similar to the effect produced by the time pressure manipulation of warning bargainers that the bargaining will end very shortly. In both cases, an unsatisfactory result is likely unless rapid concession making occurs.

The intervention of a third party can, of course, involve many activities other than proposing concessions or the terms of agreement (cf. Young, 1967). In a simulation of a pretrial hearing, Erickson, Holmes, Frey, Walker and Thibaut (1974) examined the effects of having the judge (1) identify the issues and (2) suggest that the bargainers either settle the issues one at a time or instead try to develop an overall settlement. They found that identifying the issues had little effect in a low conflict situation but interfered with reaching a solution in a high conflict situation. In contrast, suggesting a wholistic approach rather than a partitive one promoted a settlement in low conflict, but had a negligible effect in high conflict.

The advisability of a wholistic vs. a partitive approach, which Erickson *et al.* (1974) studied, is a question debated by students of conflict resolution. Froman and Cohen (1970), in a varying-sum bargaining experiment, found that discussing two issues simultaneously rather than sequentially led to a higher joint profit and a quicker agreement. They maintain that simultaneous consideration of multiple issues is beneficial in a varying-sum situation, because it permits logrolling. On the other hand, Fisher (1971), while recognizing the potential advantage of coupling issues through logrolling, also sees two potential advantages to fractionating conflict. First, when issues are decided separately, it is more likely that they will be decided on their merits. Second, when many issues are involved, everything cannot be settled at once; in such situations, fractionating the conflict permits progress in certain areas while other matters are being worked out. The research on wholistic vs. partitive approaches to settling multiple issues is limited to a few studies in which only a small number of issues were involved and the approach was either imposed by the experimenter or suggested by a prestigious significant other, but the research findings suggest that a wholistic approach may be advantageous only when there is a low level of disagreement.

Situational factors

First, arrangements can create feelings of differential status. Second, the pleasantness of surroundings can affect the tenor of negotiations. Third, it is advantageous to negotiate in circumstances where you feel comfortable. While there is no relevant research done within the context of bargaining, a number of findings from other areas of research give credence to these conclusions.

Bargaining strategy

In much research, a person is led to believe that he is in a bargaining encounter with another, while actually the experimenter is making the proposals attributed to the opponent. This procedure enables the researcher to learn how people react to different kinds of bargaining behavior by the opponent.

Usually a tougher strategy—a more extreme opening demand, fewer concessions, and/or smaller concessions—has been contrasted with a weaker strategy. In general, this research indicates that an opponent can obtain a more favorable final agreement by being tough (Bartos, 1966, 1970, 1972; Benton *et al.*, 1972; Chertkoff and Conley, 1967; Karras, 1970; Komorita and Brenner, 1968; Liebert *et al.*, 1968; Siegel and Fouraker, 1960; Yukl, 1974a, b). There are limitations to such a conclusion. Excessive intransigence, such as never making a concession, may be responded to by the other side with little concession making throughout the entire bargaining session (Benton *et al.*, 1972; Komorita and Brenner, 1968). When no agreement is likely (as, for example, when time to bargain is very short) and when no agreement is clearly disadvantageous, toughness may be very likely to result in no agreement, thereby making it a poor strategy (Benton *et al.*, 1972). When bargaining becomes deadlocked, toughness is counterproductive (Hamner, 1974).

While tough bargaining is generally a good strategy for obtaining favorable terms, excessive toughness is not beneficial. As a result of several recent experiments in contingent concession making. Esser and Komorita (1975) [and] Komorita and Esser (1975) have concluded that the best strategy is to give the other side the impression that one is tough, but fair. They found that a strategy of always reciprocating both the frequency and magnitude of the other bargainer's concessions is more effective in inducing concessions than strategies involving less reciprocation. They suggest that conceding only in response to a concession by the other side gives the impression that one is strong, while always reciprocating a concession gives the impression that one is fair.

Such an explanation indicates that the dispositions attributed to the other are crucial in mediating yielding. Upon what basis will the attribution be made? According to the theoretical analysis of Jones and Davis (1965), attribution is made on the basis of distinctive effects produced by a given action. Different actions of a bargainer, however, may have numerous possible effects. A bargainer may open with a very high demand because he has a high zero profit level and is only trying to reach a fair agreement, because he is a competitive person who wants to score a decisive victory, because he hates the guts of his adversary and wants to hurt him, etc. A very low opening demand may be made because the person is very cooperative and wants to avoid disagreements, because he has a very low zero profit level and is trying to be fair, because he likes the other bargainer and wants to maintain a friendly relationship, etc.

In most laboratory experiments, the bargainers are strangers and thus do not have a strong affective association. Usually, they are given only limited external factors to consider. Often the only consideration is the profit a given agreement will produce. In such a case, a bargainer's demand is apt to be attributed to general characteristics of his personality, to the profit schedule, or, in demands after the initial one, to the way the other bargainer is behaving. An attributional analysis suggests that for tough bargaining to be successful, a bargainer must become convinced that the toughness being exhibited by the opponent is not due to excessive greed. As long as an opponent shows some willingness to compromise, his protracted toughness may convince a bargainer that he is not trying to win an overwhelming victory, but rather is merely responding to his profit schedule. Hence, yielding finally occurs. Tough bargaining should be more successful, then, if it appears to be caused by economic necessity rather than personal greed. Therefore, if an opponent could convince the bargainer that the cause of his high demand is a high breakeven point, the bargainer should yield more readily. Indeed, Chertkoff and Baird (1971) found that when a high demand was supported by the assertion that one's breakeven point was high, the other side rapidly made substantial concessions.

In conclusion, an attributional analysis suggests that greater yielding is produced when a bargainer receives the impression that his opponent is firm, but fair. The bargainer's inferences about the locus of causality for his opponent's demands may be made on the basis of presumptions or known facts about external factors or on the basis of presumed or known attributes of the opponent. These inferences may be based in part upon observations of the consistency of the opponent's behavior in other bargaining situations or against other people (Kelley, 1967). That is, consistent behavior over situations should lead to the conclusion that the opponent's behavior is due to an attribute of the person. Moreover, behavior that deviates markedly from the behavior of others in a given situation should lead also to the conclusion that the behavior is due to an attribute of the person.

It should be noted, however, that differences in other v. environment attributions may not necessarily lead to differences in responding. For example, whether a bargainer attributes his opponent's tough bargaining to personal hatred, to directives from constituents, or to a competitive personality attribute may make no difference in the kind of offers he makes. In all three cases, he may decide that the appropriate response is toughness. If, however, the opponent's behavior has been attributed to directives from constituents and an opportunity exists either to create better interpersonal attraction with the opponent or to communicate directly to the opponent's constituents, the attribution might well affect the choice of action. If his constituents are responsible for the kind of offers the opponent is making, it might be advisable to try to influence the constituents directly.

Attributions also may not affect bargaining behavior because of pressures that do not allow for freedom of action. For example, specific instructions from constituents or the necessity to obtain certain terms in order to remain solvent may force the bargainer to make certain demands regardless of the perceived cause of the opponent's behavior.

Summary

Bargaining was defined, general theoretical conceptions were evaluated, and the experimental research was reviewed. Most of the research demonstrates the existence of a phenomenon, and some of the research establishes the limiting conditions of a phenomenon; but the research usually has not progressed beyond that. Research identifying the psychological mechanism underlying a phenomenon occurs occasionally, but infrequently. Furthermore, experiments designed to test specific theories of bargaining are rare. The absence of such research may be due to the fact that the theoretical conceptions are often so general that any result can be interpreted as supportive of a theory. What seems to be needed in bargaining research are theories of greater specificity and precision and research of greater theoretical relevance.

References

Adams, J. S. (1965). 'Inequity in social exchange,' in L. Berkowitz (ed.), *Advances in Experimental Social Psychology*, Vol. 2, Academic Press, New York.

Bartos, O. J. (1966). 'Concession making in experimental negotiations,' in J. Berger, M. Zelditch, and B. Anderson (eds.), *Sociological Theories in Progress*, Houghton-Mifflin, Boston.

Bartos, O. J. (1970). 'Determinants and consequences of toughness,' in P. Swingle (ed.), *The Structure of Conflict*, Vol. 1, Academic Press, New York.

Bartos, O. J. (1972). 'Foundations for a rational–empirical model of negotiation,' in J. Berger, M. Zelditch, Jr., and B. Anderson (eds.), *Sociological Theories in Progress*, Vol. 2, Houghton-Mifflin, Boston.

Bass, B. M. (1966). 'Effects on the subsequent performance of negotiators of studying issues or planning strategies alone or in groups,' *Psychological Monographs*, **80** (6).

Benton, A. A. (1972). 'Accountability and negotiations between group representatives,' *Proceedings of the 80th Annual Convention of the American Psychological Association*, pp. 227–228.

Benton, A. A., and Druckman, D. (1973). 'Salient solutions and the bargaining behavior of representatives and nonrepresentatives,' *International Journal of Group Tensions*, **3**, 28–39.

Benton, A. A., and Druckman, D. (1974). 'Constituent's bargaining orientation and intergroup negotiations,' *Journal of Applied Social Psychology*, 4, 141–150.

Benton, A. A., Kelley, H. H., and Liebling, B. (1972). 'Effects of extremity of offers and concession rate on the outcomes of bargaining,' *Journal of Personality and Social Psychology*, 24, 73–83.

Brown, B. R. (May 1971). 'Saving face,' *Psychology Today*, 4 (12), 55–59, 86.

Chertkoff, J. M. and Baird, S. L. (1971). 'Applicability of the big lie technique and the last clear chance doctrine to bargaining,' *Journal of Personality and Social Psychology*, 20, 298–303.

Chertkoff, J. M., and Conley, M. (1967). 'Opening offer and frequency of concession as bargaining strategies,' *Journal of Personality and Social Psychology*, 7, 181–185.

Cross, J. G. (1969). *The Economics of Bargaining*, Basic Books, New York.

Daniels, V. (1967). 'Communication, incentive, and structural variables in interpersonal exchange and negotiation,' *Journal of Experimental Social Psychology*, 3, 47–74.

Deutsch, M. (1949). 'An experimental study of the effects of cooperation and competition upon group process,' *Human Relations*, 2, 199–232.

Deutsch, M. (1960). 'The effect of motivational orientation upon trust and suspicion,' *Human Relations*, 13, 123–140.

Deutsch, M., and Krauss, R. M. (1960). 'The effect of threat upon interpersonal bargaining,' *Journal of Abnormal and Social Psychology*, 61, 181–189.

Deutsch, M., and Krauss, R. M. (1962). 'Studies of interpersonal bargaining,' *Journal of Conflict Resolution*, 6, 52–76.

Dorris, J. W. (1972). 'Reactions to unconditional cooperation: A field study emphasizing variables neglected in laboratory research,' *Journal of Personality and Social Psychology*, 22, 387–397.

Druckman, D. (1967). 'Dogmatism, prenegotiation experience, and simulated group representation as determinants of dyadic behavior in a bargaining situation,' *Journal of Personality and Social Psychology*, 6, 279–290.

Druckman. D. (1968). 'Prenegotiation experience and dyadic conflict resolution in a bargaining situation,' *Journal of Experimental Social Psychology*, 4, 367–383.

Druckman, D., Solomon, D., and Zechmeister, K. (1972). 'Effects of representational role obligations on the process of children's distribution of resources,' *Sociometry*, 35, 387–410.

Erickson, B., Holmes, J. G., Frey, R., Walker, L., and Thibaut, J. (1974). 'Functions of a third party in the resolution of conflict: The role of a judge in pretrial conferences,' *Journal of Personality and Social Psychology*, 30, 293–306.

Esser, J. K. (1975). *Effects of Prior Success or Failure on Subsequent Bargaining*. Unpublished doctoral dissertation, Indiana University.

Esser, J. K., and Komorita, S. S. (1975). 'Reciprocity and concession making in bargaining,' *Journal of Personality and Social Psychology*, 31, 864–872.

Fischer, C. S. (1969). 'The effect of threats in an incomplete information game,' *Sociometry*, 32, 301–314.

Fisher, R. (1971). 'Fractionating conflict,' in J. V. Bondurant (ed.), *Conflict: Violence and Nonviolence*, Aldine-Atherton, Chicago.

Froman, L. A. Jr., and Cohen, M. D. (1970). 'Compromise and logroll: Comparing the efficiency of two bargaining processes,' *Behavior Science*, 15, 180–183.

Gruder, C. L., and Rosen, N. A. (1971). 'Effects of intragroup relations on intergroup bargaining,' *International Journal of Group Tensions*, 1, 301–317.

Hamner, W. C. (1974). 'Effects of bargaining strategy and pressure to reach agreement in a stalemated negotiation,' *Journal of Personality and Social Psychology*, 30, 458–467.

Hamner, W. C., and Harnett, D. L. (1975). 'The effects of information and aspiration level on bargaining behavior,' *Journal of Experimental Social Psychology*, 11, 329–342.

Harnett, D. L., Cummings, L. L. and Hamner, W. C. (1973). 'Personality, bargaining style and payoff in bilateral monopoly bargaining among European managers,' *Sociometry*, 36, 325–345.

Holmes, J. G., Throop, W. F., and Strickland, L. H. (1971). 'The effects of prenegotiation expectations on the distributive bargaining process,' *Journal of Experimental Social Psychology*, 7, 582–599.

Ikle, F. C., and Leites, N. (1962). 'Political negotiation as a process of modifying utilities,' *Journal of Conflict Resolution*, 6, 19–28.

Johnson, D. F., and Pruitt, D. G. (1972). 'Preintervention effects of mediation versus arbitration,' *Journal of Applied Psychology*, 56, 1–10.

Jones, E. E., and Davis, K. E. (1965). 'From acts to dispositions: The attribution process in person perception,' in L. Berkowitz (ed.), *Advances in Experimental Social Psychology*, Vol. 2, Academic Press, New York.

Kahan, J. P. (1968). 'Effects of level of aspiration in an experimental bargaining situation,' *Journal of Personality and Social Psychology*, 8, 154–159.

Kahn, A. S., and Kohls, J. W. (1972). 'Determinants of toughness in dyadic bargaining,' *Sociometry*, 35, 305–315.

Karrass, C. L. (1970). *The Negotiating Game*, World, New York.

Kelley, H. H. (1967). 'Attribution theory in social psychology,' in D. Levine (ed.), *Nebraska Symposium on Motivation*, Vol. 15, University of Nebraska Press, Lincoln.

Kelley, H. H., Beckman, L. L., and Fischer, C. S. (1967). 'Negotiating the division of a reward under incomplete information,' *Journal of Experimental Social Psychology*, 3, 361–398.

Kelley, H. H., and Schenitzki, D. P. (1972). 'Bargaining,' C. McClintock (ed.), *Experimental Social Psychology*, Holt, Rinehart Winston, New York.

Kelley, H. H., Shure, G. H., Deutsch, M., Faucheux, C., Lanzetta, J. T., Moscovici, S., Nuttin, J. M., Jr, Rabbie, J. M. and Thibaut, J. W. (1970). 'A comparative experimental study of negotiation behavior,' *Journal of Personality and Social Psychology*, 16, 411–438. [Also, abridged and reprinted in the present volume.]

Komorita, S. S., and Barnes, M. (1969). 'Effects of pressures to reach agreement in bargaining,' *Journal of Personality and Social Psychology*, 13, 245–252.

Komorita, S. S., and Brenner, A. R. (1968). 'Bargaining and concession making under bilateral monopoly,' *Journal of Personality and Social Psychology*, 9, 15–20.

Komorita, S. S., and Esser J. K. (1975). 'Frequency of reciprocated concessions in bargaining,' *Journal of Personality and Social Psychology*, 32, 699–705.

Lamm, H., and Rosch, E. (1972). 'Information and competitiveness of incentive structure as factors in two-person negotiation', *European Journal of Social Psychology*, 2, 459–465.

Liebert, R. M., Smith, W. P., Keiffer, M., and Hill, J. H. (1968). 'The effects of information and magnitude of initial offer on interpersonal negotiation,' *Journal of Experimental Social Psychology*, 4, 431–441.

Luce, R. D., and Raiffa, H. (1957). *Games and Decisions*, Wiley, New York.

Morgan, W. R., and Sawyer, J. (1967). 'Bargaining, expectations, and the preference for equality over equity,' *Journal of Personality and Social Psychology*, 6, 139–149.

Podell, J. E., and Knapp, W. M. (1969). 'The effect of mediation on the perceived firmness of the opponent,' *Journal of Conflict Resolution*, 13, 511–520.

Pruitt, D. G., and Drews, J. L. (1969). 'The effect of time pressure, time elapsed, and the opponent's concession rate on behavior in negotiation,' *Journal of Experimental Social Psychology*, 5, 43–60.

Pruitt, D. G., and Johnson, D. F. (1970). 'Mediation as an aid to face-saving in negotiation,' *Journal of Personality and Social Psychology*, **14**, 239–246.
Pruitt, D. G., and Lewis, S. A. (1975). 'Development of integrative solutions in bilateral negotiation,' *Journal of Personality and Social Psychology*, **31**, 621–633.
Rubin, J. (1971). 'The nature and success of influence attempts in a four-party bargaining relationship,' *Journal of Experimental Social Psychology*, **7**, 17–35.
Rubin, J. Z., and Lewicki, R. J. (1973). 'A three-factor experimental analysis of promises and threats,' *Journal of Applied Social Psychology*, **3**, 240–257.
Schelling, T. C. (1963). *The Strategy of Conflict*, Oxford University Press, New York.
Schoeninger, D. W., and Wood, W. D. (1969). 'Comparison of married and *ad hoc* mixed-sex dyads negotiating the division of a reward,' *Journal of Experimental Social Psychology*, **5**, 483–499.
Shomer, R. W., Davis, A. H., and Kelley, H. H. (1966). 'Threats and the development of coordination: Further studies of the Deutsch and Krauss trucking game,' *Journal of Personality and Social Psychology*, **4**, 119–126.
Siegel, S., and Fouraker, L. E. (1960). *Bargaining and Group Decision-making*, McGraw-Hill, New York.
Smith, W. P., and Anderson, A. J. (1975). 'Threats, communication and bargaining,' *Journal of Personality and Social Psychology*, **32**, 76–82.
Tedeschi, J. T. (1970). 'Threats and promises,' in P. Swingle (ed.), *The Structure of Conflict*, Academic Press, New York.
Thibaut, J. (1968). 'The development of contractual norms in bargaining: Replications and variation,' *Journal of Conflict Resolution*, **12**, 102–112.
Thibaut, J., and Faucheux, C. (1965). 'The development of contractual norms in a bargaining situation under two types of stress,' *Journal of Experimental Social Psychology*, **1**, 89–102.
Thibaut, J., and Gruder, C. L. (1969). 'The formation of contractual agreement between parties of unequal power,' *Journal of Personality and Social Psychology*, **11**, 59–65.
Thibaut, J. W., and Kelley, H. H. (1959). *The Social Psychology of Groups*, Wiley, New York.
Vidmar, N. (1971). 'Effects of representational roles and mediators on negotiation effectiveness,' *Journal of Personality and Social Psychology*, **17**, 48–58.
Wall, J. A., Jr. (1976). 'Effects of sex and opposing representative's bargaining orientation on intergroup bargaining,' *Journal of Personality and Social Psychology*, **33**, 55–61.
Young, O. R. (1967). *The Intermediaries: Third Parties in International Crises*, Princeton University Press, Princeton, NJ.
Yukl, G. A. (1974a). 'The effects of situational variables and opponent concessions on a bargainer's perception, aspirations, and concessions,' *Journal of Personality and Social Psychology*, **29**, 227–236.
Yukl, G. A. (1974b). 'Effects of the opponent's initial offer, concession magnitude, and concession frequency on bargaining behavior,' *Journal of Personality and Social Psychology*, **30**, 322–335.

Small Groups and Social Interaction, Volume 2
Edited by H. H. Blumberg, A. P. Hare, V. Kent and M. Davies
© 1983 John Wiley & Sons Ltd

3.4 A Comparative Experimental Study of Negotiation Behavior[1]

Gerald H. Shure and Harold H. Kelley   *University of California, L.A.*

Morton Deutsch   *Columbia University*

Claude Faucheux

Institut Européen d'Administration des Affairs, Fontainebleau

John T. Lanzetta   *Dartmouth College*

Serge Moscovici   *École des Hautes Études en Sciences Sociales, Paris*

Jozef M. Nuttin, Jr.   *Universiteit te Leuven*

Jaap M. Rabbie   *Rijksuniversiteit, Utrecht*

John W. Thibaut   *University of North Carolina at Chapel Hill*

Introduction

The experiment reported here investigated several factors determining the course of negotiation behavior in a social relationship. Because the experiment was replicated at three laboratories in Europe and five in the United States, the study had both a comparative and experimental aspect.

Negotiation relationship

The experimental task was designed to simulate a two-party relationship which extends over time and requires for its viability that the two parties satisfactorily negotiate allocations of available rewards. In such relationships, it is in each party's interest both to acquire a large share of rewards at each negotiation, and to make sure the other party is satisfied out of concern for future interaction. The latter was made salient in the experiment by increasing the value of rewards with continued cooperation.

More particularly, on each of a number of trials a joint value (a 'contract') was

163

specified which subjects could obtain if they agreed how to divide it. Each participant also was privately assigned an individual value which he received if they failed to agree. Contract values and individual values varied unpredictably from trial to trial. If individual values were relatively low, it was mutually profitable to divide the contract, but usually it was unprofitable. To provide incentive for agreement, it was specified that both contracts and individual values increased approximately twofold for trials following an uninterrupted and sustained sequence of agreements.

It was to participants' long-run benefit to agree on each contract, but it was often in an individual's short-term interest to take his independent value as it was more than he could gain at that time from agreement.

The task also was characterized by incompleteness of information (Siegel and Fouraker, 1960). Each participant knew the consequences of his failure to cooperate on any given trial (his individual value), but had no objective information about consequences for his partner. Face-to-face and unrestrained interaction allowed a subject to pursue individual interests, by misrepresenting (minimizing) the importance he attached to agreement so he could demand a lion's share. Thus, the relationship could be repeatedly subjected to stress by threat of nonagreement (Kent, 1969) and by misrepresentation and distrust (Deutsch, 1958).

In many respects, the task was like those used in a number of prior studies of bargaining concerned primarily with *distributive* bargaining, that is, with division of more or less fixed rewards (e.g. see Kelley, 1966; Kelley *et al.*, 1967; Siegel and Fouraker, 1960). However, our task also required *integrative* bargaining which enables interdependent parties, if they sufficiently maintain their cooperation, to increase rewards available for allocation (Walton and McKersie, 1965). Thus, the rule which placed a premium on an uninterrupted sequence of cooperation provided an incentive for subjects to free themselves from trial-by-trial variations in their relationship and to establish stabilizing norms and agreements.

Given this complex relationship, participants could pursue trial-by-trial bargaining by employing threats, promises, appeals to the future, references to common interest, honest sharing of information, and deceit and misrepresentation; or they could develop rules or norms about contracts or avoid confrontation by frequent opting for individual values.

Comparative experimental method

This relationship was studied in an experimental design replicated at eight laboratories. This degree of comparative replication is quite unusual, although not without precedent (cf. Schachter *et al.*, 1954). Considerations entering into the design are discussed below.

Generality of functional relationships. The ultimate goal of scientific research is, of course, formulation of laws of general validity. This requires identifying functional relationships between variables which either obtain over various samples of subjects, settings, etc., or which change in known ways with variations in such conditions. In some social psychological research, subjects and laboratory are not assumed to be important variables. Yet evidence to support this assumption is rarely available. Too often, 'replication' is conducted for polemical purposes and is incomplete or questionable as a true replication.

In spite of the accidental sampling of the eight experimental locations, their national and institutional heterogeneity suggested comparison of replications across sites would be valuable.

Definitions of site differences in terms of functional relationships. In contrast to the goal of generality sought in replication studies, the usual reason for conducting comparative studies is to identify differences among various subject populations. This is an especially intriguing possibility in our task as it evokes different values, norms, and roles as well as responses to basic structural and motivational parameters, and, consequently, lends itself to description of differences in orientations to and tactics within a negotiation relationship. Yet, an outcome of our research in terms of site differences obviously is subject to varying interpretations. The most that can be said for our subjects is that they are typical of those from which social psychological generalizations are drawn at our various laboratories. A second source of ambiguity in interpretation of site differences lies in the unknown degree of comparability among procedures, translations, experimenters, etc., at various sites.[2] However, functional relationships, as between independent and dependent variables or as among a number of different dependent variables, probably are less influenced than averages by such procedural differences. For this reason, we chose to conduct an experiment (with manipulation of independent variables) rather than simply to determine, for example, relative frequency of different bargaining styles. For the same reason, we placed considerable emphasis on measurement of perceptions and behaviors at different points in time and in different ways in order to permit comparative analysis of relationships among them.

Site differences and mediating processes. If differences are obtained in replication with different subjects and in different laboratories, and if supplementary information permits differences to be given a theoretical interpretation, the result is a more definitive understanding of processes mediating the relationship under investigation.

A gain of this sort may even be forthcoming when the major functional relationship under study (as between a pair of independent and dependent variables) is found to be the same in all replications. With auxiliary data, one may discover that the underlying reasons for this relationship are different among the sites; that is, two or more different processes mediate a given relationship. This argument has special pertinence to negotiation studies by virtue of the complexity of the situation and the variety of social processes that may intervene between an experimental treatment and a gross outcome variable. The realization of this benefit from comparative replications depends upon having, either by plan or by good luck, appropriate auxiliary indicators of the intervening processes. For a more complete discussion of this point, the interested reader is referred to Shure *et al.*, (1966) and Shure *et al.*, (1969).

Experimental variables and hypotheses

Of the various factors which might affect the manner and success of subjects in our task, we chose three variables for experimentation, based partly on their ease of manipulation and standardization for replication studies. Two of the independent variables are described in this presentation of the study.[3] Their theoretical significance is explained in the following sections.

Type of incentive. Negotiation situations vary greatly in the type and importance of issues at stake. This variable was represented by two conditions in our study. In the money condition, each subject was rewarded with a significant amount of money depending upon the values he accumulated during the experiment. In the points condition, subjects merely accumulated points, as in a game in which they were instructed to make as large scores as possible.

The difference that type of incentive can be expected to make is not at all clear in advance. The money incentive probably represents a more valuable outcome for subjects, so comparison of money and points may be viewed as a variation in *magnitude* of incentive. Thus, increasing the value of the outcomes might be expected to heighten conflict, making more important both the common and individual interest. If this occurs, one would expect an increase in the time required to resolve the matter. If either the cooperative or egoistic course of action is seen as entailing considerable risk, then with heightened incentives the other course will be more frequently adopted.

Whether this higher level of conflict is resolved in favor of cooperation or of striving for personal gain probably depends on other factors. Previous research on incentives in interdependent relationships is generally consistent with this view (Gallo, 1966; McClintock and McNeel, 1966a, 1966b, 1967; Kelley *et al.*, 1965). In this study it seemed likely that subjects would generally find cooperation with equal sharing of rewards to be more certain than maximizing one's individual interests through deceiving and exploiting the other person. The reason is that the success of the latter is contingent upon the other person's explicit compliance. However, it is also possible that money, as a different *type* of incentive, will evoke a different definition of the situation (e.g. as an economic exchange rather than a social game), with a corresponding difference in the behavioral norms seen to be appropriate (Lanto and Shure, 1972). Our data analysis was attuned also to the latter kind of effect—especially, possible site differences in definition of the relationship under the two kinds of incentive.

Problem difficulty. Problem difficulty refers to how difficult it is, on any given negotiation problem, for the two persons to find a satisfactory agreement. The higher are their individual values relative to the contract value, the less profitable is agreement (at least in terms of immediate gains), and the more conflict they are likely to experience trying to achieve it. 'Satisfactoriness' of agreement depends, of course, upon the value the person places upon maintaining an unbroken sequence of agreements in order to enjoy benefits of *Schedule 2*, so we expected the effects of problem difficulty, defined in terms of individual values and contract value, to depend upon the prior sequence of agreements. Problem difficulty was varied across the set of negotiation problems.

Existing investigations pertaining to problem difficulty (Kahan, 1968; Kelley *et al.*, 1967; Shure and Meeker, 1969) are consistent in showing that with higher difficulty of the negotiation problem, time to reach agreement increases and (in the first two studies where nonagreement was possible) frequency of agreement declines. Effects of problem difficulty in the present experiment were expected to follow this same pattern.

Method

Sites and subjects

The experiment was conducted with 10 pairs of subjects in each of four conditions created by crossing two levels of incentive with two levels of dependence. For this presentation, the dependence variable was collapsed.[3] This design was completed at eight social psychological laboratories: Universiteit te Leuven, Leuven, Belgie; Ecole Pratique des Hautes Études, Paris, France; Rijksuniversiteit, Utrecht, Nederland; Teachers College, Columbia University, New York, New York; Dartmouth College, Hanover, New Hampshire; University of California, Los Angeles, California; University of North Carolina, Chapel Hill, North Carolina; and System Development Corporation, Santa Monica, California.

Male university subjects were recruited by way of: (a) subject pools and fulfillment of course requirements: Leuven, Dartmouth, UCLA, and North Carolina; and (b) public announcements and advertisements: Paris, Utrecht, Columbia, and System Development Corporation.

Procedure

In all cases, the experimenter was a male research graduate assistant who followed verbatim standard instruction. After introducing the two subjects (who were strangers), the experimenter seated them at opposite sides of a small table in full view of each other's faces, but separated by low screens behind which each could privately view his cards and make notes. The experimenter began the instructions by telling them that each one's sole goal was to make as many points for himself as possible. At this juncture, in the money incentive condition the monetary value of each point was specified. This amount varied at different sites from 8/10 to 2 cents in equivalent US money. The monetary reward in the money condition was made salient by counting out in cash each person's earnings after each 10 trials. This was done privately for each, so as not to provide information about outcomes.

After describing the goals they were to pursue, the experimenter asked each subject to examine and shuffle one of the two blue decks of playing cards in front of them and one of the two red decks in front of the experimenter, this serving to assure them that the decks were ordinary cards and that the order within each deck was random. The experimenter then described the task as follows:

On each problem you will try to agree on how to divide a certain number of points that we'll call the contract. Your problem is to decide whether it is worthwhile to try to reach an agreement between you. You can split the contract any way you both agree upon. For instance, if the contract on a particular problem is 9 points, you can divide it so one gets all 9 and the other none, or so one gets 8 and the other 1, or 7 and 2, or 6 and 3, or 5 and 4. You are not permitted to divide points in half.

The value of the contract each time will depend on a card I turn up here on the red deck of playing cards. Notice Schedule 1 in front of you. The upper line in this table shows that the contract you can divide is worth 5, 7, 9, or 11 points depending upon the *suit* of the card that I turn up here from the red deck.

Consider next what happens if you both wish to obtain 6 of the 9 available points, and neither will accept the remaining 3. It is obvious that a contract cannot be agreed upon if you both *hold firmly* to your demands for 6 points. Under these conditions, two things may happen. You may revise your own demands, or attempt to get the other person to revise his, or both. This may go on until your two demands add up to no more than the value of the contract. *Second*, either person may refuse to agree to a division. If this is done, then each of you will automatically receive the points assigned to you as your *independent* value for the problem.

Each time, when I turn over a card from the red deck to determine the contract value, you will each turn the top card off your own blue decks. These blue cards tell each of you your independent values. That is, what you can get if you cannot reach agreement on a division of the contract. If you can't get the other person to agree to give you a large enough share of the content, you would probably take your independent value.

Like your contract value, your independent value depends on the suit of the card you turn over, off the top of your blue deck.

By reference again to Schedule 1, the experimenter showed that a person's individual value could be 0, 5, or 10 points, depending on whether he turned up a heart, club, or spade. Diamonds were disregarded. The experimenter then said:

During the experiment each of you will place your stack of blue cards behind your screen so that the other person will not be able to see the top card you turn over. In fact that will be our first important rule: You may never show these blue cards to each other. You may, however, say *anything* you want about these blue cards.

Unlike the contract which, on any problem, is the same for both of you, your two independent values will often be different. Your independent value, of course, will be critical in determining your offers and in evaluating the acceptability of any particular division of the points. The bigger your independent value is, the larger the share of the contract you'd be likely to want.

How would you go about dividing up the contract? You would tell each other how much you want or feel you must get from the contract.

If you have a high card or *can make the other person believe* you have a high one, you can and should try to get a large share of the contract.

If you can't get the share you want or think you should have, then you simply take your independent value.

If one of you decides to take your independent value, then the other must take his too.

With the agreement on a division of the contract or the selection of your independent values, the problem is finished. I then turn up a new red card indicating the contract value for the next problem, and you turn up new blue cards to indicate your new independent values.

The experimenter also briefly explained possible gains and risks associated with exaggerating or telling about their individual values. He then explained the last and important rule:

The values in Schedule 2 apply on all problems where there have been agreements to split the contract on the five *immediately preceding* trials.

The contracts in this table and the independent values both have greater value. Once you are in Schedule 2, you stay there as long as you continue to have agreements, but once either of you takes your independent value, you will be back again at the lower values of Schedule 1.

The contract values on Schedule 2 were shown to be 13, 17, 19, and 23 for diamonds, hearts, clubs, and spades, respectively, and the individual values were 6, 13, and 20 for hearts, clubs, and spades.

Then the subjects were given a brief questionnaire testing their understanding of the game and inducing them to calculate the consequences over trials of various ways of playing it. They were shown that a person might make 5 points per trial on the average (if he always took his individual value), or up to 9 points per trial (by getting on Schedule 2 and taking half of every contract), or up to 10, 11, or even 12 points per trial (by getting on Schedule 2 and getting the other person to accept less than half of every contract).

The subjects were then told they were to complete a predetermined but undisclosed number of problems, and that how long they took did not matter. They then completed a brief pre-experiment questionnaire. They next examined and shuffled what appeared to be the remaining three decks of cards (i.e. the one not shuffled earlier), and combined these with the earlier ones to provide a large red deck for the experimenter and a large blue one for each subject. In fact, the position of the decks had been switched in the meantime, so they merely shuffled again the ones they had examined earlier. The three other decks, as yet untouched but thought by the subjects to have been shuffled earlier, were placed on top of each person's pile, and a prearranged order of cards within each of these provided a standard sequence of problems (defined in contract values and individual values) for all pairs.

They then proceeded through the set of 30 problems. Each subject privately recorded his score on each problem and added up a subtotal after each set of 10. At the end of the third 10-trial block, subjects were given a post-experimental questionnaire, paid any extra money necessary, and informally debriefed on the study. The minor deception entailed in control of the sequence of problems was not revealed.

Problem difficulty and sequence

Certain properties of the allocation problems will be apparent to the reader. All contract values were odd, subjects at the very least had to determine some basis for allocating odd points. In terms of immediate gains, it was not possible on 60% of the trials for both subjects to make as many points from a division of the contract as from taking their individual values. On Schedule 1, the average contract value (with equal occurrence of the four suits) would have been 8, and their respective individual values would have averaged 5 (10 per pair). Thus, while on Schedule 1, agreement was reached at an average cost of 2 points, which one or both of them had to bear. But agreement was the means of reaching the higher level of payoff on Schedule 2, so it was certainly profitable from a long-range point of view, inasmuch as the contract values were more than twice as high. At the same time, once on Schedule 2, the temptation not to agree was increased by virtue of the higher individual values. Accordingly, the short-run cost the pair had to bear on the typical trial to remain on Schedule 2 was 8 points.

The problems varied in the cost the pair must bear to agree. An index of problem *difficulty* is the sum of the two individual values minus the contract value. For Schedule 1 values, this index ranges from −11 (which entails negative costs) for the easiest problem to +15 for the most difficult one (where their joint costs are 15 points). Our method of controlling the sequence of cards in the three decks made it possible to present certain combinations of contract values and individual values, and, thus, to control the difficulty of problems and the order in which they occurred. The problems used sampled a broad range of difficulty so as to permit systematic analysis of the effects of problem difficulty.

Problems representing six levels of difficulty were included in each block of 10 trials, the average difficulty being 1.8, which is close to the value of 2, the expected value for a random distribution of cards.

Measures and data analysis

1. *Pregame ratings* were made by subjects on 7-point scales from the semantic differential, having the following polar–opposite adjectives as end anchors: passive–active, dishonest–honest, hostile–peaceful, wise–foolish, cooperative–competitive, weak–strong, brave–cowardly, and moral–immoral. Each subject used the scales first to rate how he expected the typical person to behave and then how *he* himself expected to behave.

2. *Behavioral observations* were made during each trial by the experimenter. For each player on each trial the following behaviors were tallied: (a) *bargained hard:* the subject argued, attempted to persuade the other, pressured the other, used promises; (b) *bargained hard with threat:* as above, but when the pressures assumed the form of threats; (c) *rule discussed:* the subject initiated a discussion about a rule or procedure; (d) *poor cards claimed:* the subject expressed any feeling that the other's cards were better than his own; (e) *misrepresented individual value:* the subject misrepresented his individual value to make it appear higher. The experimenter also made a tally for each trial for whichever member of the pair, if either, exhibited the following behavior: (f) *did not bargain:* the subject took his independent value without making an offer or counteroffer; (g) *Schedule 2 reference:* the subject made reference to Schedule 2 and was the first to do so during the given problem. Finally, the experimenter also made a tally for the pair on each trial for the following: (h) *rule invoked:* when a previously discussed rule was invoked by either to reach agreement.

3. *Outcome measures* obtained for each trial indicated whether the pair was on Schedule 1 or 2, whether the trial terminated in agreement, and if so, the share of the contract each subject received, and the duration of the trial.

4. *Postgame ratings.* After each trial, each subject estimated the individual value of the other for that trial. After the last trial, the subjects used the same

scales as for the pregame ratings, but this time to describe first, how the *other person* had behaved in the experiment and, then, how *he* himself had behaved. Finally, in separate ratings, they indicated such things as how much they estimated the other player had earned relative to their own earnings, and which person appeared to have had better cards.

These various kinds of data were recorded on 80-column data sheets, and punched on IBM cards. The data were complete except for the behavioral observations which were missing at Dartmouth, where some of the subjects had been run before the final set of observational categories was prepared. Most of the analyses reported used standard ANOVA programs. Special analyses, involving the construction of special indexes and cross-tabulations, were made by means of the TRACE program (Shure *et al.*, 1967).

Results[4]

Overall trends

It is useful to provide a general characterization of the perceptions, expectations, and behavior elicited by our experimental situation as background for examining the effects of the independent variables and the differences among the sites.

The relationship was initially perceived as leaning toward competitiveness. However, a general shift in the opposite direction occurred as the individual's opponent was found to be more cooperative during the game than had been expected. An index using the difference between postgame and pregame ratings of cooperation, increased significantly[5] (and markedly) in both incentive conditions. It increased more, but not significantly so, in the money condition. The evolution toward cooperation seems to reflect basic properties of the game, particularly the structure of the experimental relationship and opportunity it provides for communication.

At the same time, there are various indications that the subjects did not become single-mindedly cooperative. Their self-reports indicate their primary motivation throughout the game was individualistic. The goal of making points for themselves was pursued along with subsidiary interests in minimizing trouble, working out fair shares, and outdoing the other person, a pattern which made possible an interaction generally positive in tone but yet characterized, on the postgame semantic differentials, by 'activity' and 'strength.' Behaviorally, this meant hard bargaining and sometimes taking one's individual value without bargaining, although agreement was the rule.

Effects of problem difficulty and prior agreements

An analysis of details of the interaction process yields evidence of effects of subjects' (a) having low or high individual values relative to the divisible contract value and (b) being at various points in a sequence of consecutive agreements. Each trial for every pair was categorized both as to problem difficulty, with nine different degrees established, and as to the number of consecutive agreements on immediately preceding trials. Then these subcategories of trials were compared on several outcome measures to show the joint effect of the two factors on such variables as frequency of agreement, length of trial, and frequency of hard bargaining. The analysis shows that for easy problems, all pairs agreed and did so quickly. For difficult trials, pairs with a longer history tended to agree (though not always), but used considerable time to do so. In contrast, pairs without the constraint of prior agreements tended not to agree, and one or the other person quickly decided to take his individual value. Thus, in this situation where prior agreements (history) made it especially worth while for the bargainers to avoid nonagreement in order to gain or maintain the more profitable interaction, the effects of problem difficulty were more complex than has been observed in prior experiments where no special penalty was attached to nonagreement. The inverse relation between difficulty and agreement rate was especially marked for pairs with few prior agreements, and the direct relation between difficulty and time was present only for pairs with more than two prior agreements. Finally, history had a suppressing effect on hard bargaining. Even taking duration of trial into account, the longer the run of prior agreements, the less likely it was that the interaction would be judged as involving hard bargaining.

Effects of money versus point incentives

The incentives were described to the subjects before they gave their pregame ratings, so we may first ask whether the incentives affected their initial orientations. The results show that this was indeed the case. In the *money* as compared with the *points* condition, the self was rated as more honest and cooperative, and the typical person as more cooperative.

In the bargaining interaction itself, the behavior under the *money* condition was less conflictive in almost all respects coded by the experimenters. *Rule discussed* and *rule invoked* occurred more often, and less often noted were instances of *bargain hard*, *bargain hard with threat*, and *misrepresent* individual value. These differences are not only statistically significant but rather large in absolute terms. Using the *points* condition as a baseline, the money condition yielded a 44% increase in rule discussion, a 49% increase in rule invocation, and decreases of 15% in bargaining hard, 49% in bargaining hard with threat, and 28% in misrepresenting individual value. As the behavioral results would lead us to expect, agreement was significantly more frequent with *money* than with *points* (79% versus 66%). Moreover, pairs in the *money* condition showed significantly greater efficiency in using their agreements to reach and stay on Schedule 2. These results undoubtedly reflect the effectiveness of the rules which were shown above to have been more frequently discussed and invoked within the *money* condition.

These facts imply that money subjects were less responsive to level of problem difficulty, tending to persist in their agreement even when the individual values were temptingly high. The results are quite consistent with this implication: *points* subjects were about as likely to agree on easy problems as were *money* subjects, but the former sample's rate of agreement dropped more sharply as problem difficulty increased.

Just as agreement was more dependably achieved with the *money* incentive, the trial was more quickly concluded. The average trial lasted 44.5 seconds for *money* pairs and 52.5 seconds for *points* pairs. What, then, of our hypothesis that with more valuable incentives, more time would be required to reach agreement because of the sharper conflict between common and individual interest? It appears that this may have been true during the initial stage of the interaction. The times for *money* pairs were equal to or greater than those for the *points* pairs for the early trials, and the *money* pairs became faster only after the initial six or seven trials. When considered in the light of results already presented, this suggests that the first trials were used by *money* subjects to develop rules about their interaction. The crises for these pairs seem to have occurred on the sixth trial, where they were likely to have been on Schedule 2, but where the temptation to depart was extreme (the contract value was minimal and the individual values large). Once they got past their first few trials on Schedule 2, the *money* pairs seem to have settled down to speedy resolution of their conflict, presumably by appeals to rules evolved during the early trials.

The postgame ratings and questions suggest that although the other player's behavior was generally found to be more positive than had been expected before the game of the typical player, this was particularly true when the monetary incentive was involved. The rating data are quite consistent with the process and outcome results, that the negotiations proceeded more smoothly and with greater attention to the integrative bargaining aspects of the situation when the money incentives were involved.

In general, our expectations about the effects of the money incentives, based on the assumption that they would be regarded as more valuable outcomes, are sustained. Under the *points* incentive condition, the relationship tended to evolve toward cooperation and, as we had expected, this tendency was even more marked under the money incentive. The money incentive decreased the magnitude of the tendency toward competition at the outset and, accordingly, the interaction was characterized by more frequent development of allocation rules, less frequent hard-bargaining tactics (threat and misrepresentation), and readier agreement. The beneficial effects of the money incentive are consistent with similar effects found in previous investigations of relationships such as the present one in which (a) the chances of successful exploitation of one party by the other are small, and (b) cooperative action affords a clear and, by virtue of (a), a relatively risk-free route to better outcomes. In this kind of relationship, increasing the value of the outcomes involved in the negotiation tends to increase the ease and success of that negotiation.

Effects of initial attitudes on outcomes.   According to pregame ratings, money incentives produced more cooperative attitudes before interaction began. The question arises as to whether they had any positive effect over and above this initial effect. This question can be answered to some degree, by determining whether money versus points makes any difference when initial attitudes are held constant, that is, within each incentive condition.

The indicated analysis was made using pregame ratings of the self on the cooperative–competitive scale. Each subject was classified in either the *low* (cooperative), *medium*, or *high* (competitive) third of the total distribution of ratings. Then each pair was assigned a 'pattern' based on its combination of individual orientations, low–low and low–medium pairs classified as *cooperative*, low–high and medium–medium pairs as *intermediate*, and high–high and high–medium pairs as *competitive*. The average number of agreements was then calculated for each type of pair, at each site, this being done separately for the *money* and *points* conditions. The results were subjected to a 2 × 3 × 8 analysis of variance for unequal N's, using the method of unweighted means. This analysis yielded significant main effects for the three factors (site, incentive, and pair pattern; $p < .01$ in each case), a nearly significant Incentive × Pair Pattern interaction ($p = .06$), and a significant Site × Pair Pattern interaction ($p < .01$).

The incentive effects are most readily shown by a plot of the interaction between incentive and pair pattern in Figure 1. The results give a clear answer to the question: money definitely made a difference beyond that reflected in the initial ratings. Thus, whereas there were more cooperative pair patterns with *money* and more competitive ones with *points* (which might have accounted for the higher overall rate of agreement in the former condition), when we hold pair pattern constant, the rates of agreement with *money* were higher for each type of pair. Figure 1 also shows, not surprisingly, that the number of agreements decreased as pregame competitiveness of the pair increased. The marginally significant interaction between pair pattern and incentive apparently reflects a tendency for intermediate pair patterns to do poorly with the point incentives.

The cooperative–competitive self-ratings are the only ones for which the pair patterns show consistent and significant relationships to outcome measures. These pair patterns are related not only to number of agreements but to time and (at a marginal significance level) frequency of misrepresentation of the individual value. The more cooperative pairs were, of course, faster and more honest. Interestingly enough, pair patterns defined in terms of pregame ratings of honesty and morality did not differ in amount of misrepresentation during the game.

Site differences: the meaning of cooperation–competition

An important reason for replicating the experiment at eight sites was to investigate factors mediating between task or condition variations on the one hand, and variations in process and outcome on the other. In the present study

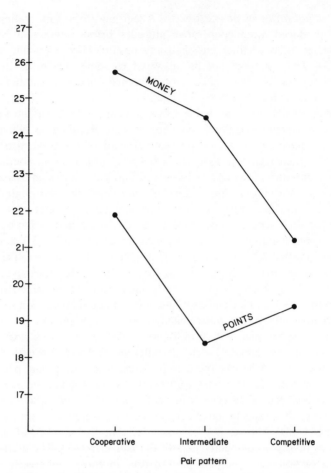

Figure 1   Number of agreements for different types of pairs

variation in type of incentive had a large effect on the amount of agreement reached. By comparing dyads at the different sites, we sought to understand how this came about. As a significant interaction between type of incentive and site was not found for number of agreements, it is inappropriate to compare sites that show improvement under high incentive with those that do not, in order to determine what makes the difference. Rather, the problem becomes one of determining whether the high incentive has its positive effect on agreement in different ways at different sites.

We approached this problem by attempting to discover whether, before the bargaining interaction began, the relationship was defined in different ways at the different sites, particularly in the meaning of cooperation–competition. Such differences were suggested by the significant Site × Pair Pattern interaction in relation to number of agreements, noted earlier, which shows that cooperative–competitive pair pattern had a different relevance for agreement in the different samples.

To investigate this possibility, factor analyses were made of the pregame ratings of 'typical player' and 'self in the game.' This procedure follows the lead of Osgood *et al.* (1957), who obtained ratings of a large number of concepts using bipolar scales (the semantic differential). Their factor analyses of these ratings revealed three major factors of 'connotative' meaning: (a) an *Evaluative* factor, defined best by scales such as good–bad, clean–dirty, and beautiful–ugly; (b) an *Activity* factor, defined by such scales as active–passive, fast–slow, and excitable–calm; and (c) a *Potency* factor, defined by strong–weak, hard–soft, and similar ratings. And importantly for our present research, Osgood and his colleagues found that when persons or person-related concepts were being judged, the activity and potency factors fused into one, which they called the *Dynamism* factor.

The factors resulting from our analyses of the pregame rating scales are remarkably stable and quite similar to those described by Osgood *et al.* In the first analysis, the data for all four sets of measures previously described were utilized. Six factors were extracted, using a Varimax orthogonal solution. Factor loadings of the subject's pregame rating for both self and typical person are presented in the upper part of Table 1 for the two factors identified as Evaluative and Dynamism. Adjective pairs which define the Evaluative factor are dishonest–honest, hostile–peaceful, and moral–immoral. The positive pole of the factor is represented by honest, peaceful, and moral. The Dynamism factor is defined by passive–active, weak–strong, brave–cowardly, and wise–foolish. The (algebraically) positive pole of this factor refers to passive, foolish, weak, and cowardly. Of interest is the fact that in this analysis which extends over all sites, the cooperative–competitive scale does not have high loadings on either factor.

We next made factor analyses separately for each site. Two-factor solutions using only the pregame ratings are presented in the lower part of Table 1. It is apparent that the basic factor structure is defined by these same scales at all eight sites though wise–foolish emerges less consistently on the Dynamism factor. These data also make clear that the factorial definition of cooperative–competitive—its connotative meaning—varies among the sites. In the Columbia and North Carolina data, it loads to a moderate degree on the Dynamism factor (with 'competitive' being *more* dynamic), but relatively little on the Evaluative factor. Just the opposite is the case in the Paris, Leuven, and Dartmouth data. In the UCLA and System Development Corporation data, this scale loads on both factors. The Utrecht data are different yet, with low loadings on both factors. These results are displayed graphically in Figure 2.

Our next step was to investigate whether these different definitions of cooperative–competitive were reflected in the interaction of the pair. For this purpose, we considered only the self-rating loadings (Figure 2) and compared the

Table 1. Factor Loadings of Pregame Ratings

Factor	Passive–Active		Dishonest–Honest		Hostile–Peaceful		Wise–Foolish		Cooperative–Competitive		Weak–Strong		Brave–Coward		Moral–Immoral	
	Typical player	Self	Typical player	Self	Typical player	Self	Typical player	Self	Typical player	Self	Typical player	Self	Typical player	Self	Typical player	Self
For all sites																
Evaluative	46	56	-64	-70	-43	-48	27								64	65
Dynamism							-36	-49		31	47	59	-47	-59		
For each site																
Evaluative																
Paris		38	-45	-53	-30	-40			46	47					65	55
Leuven			-48	-73	-33	-39				52					58	68
Utrecht		41	-75	-68	-48	-48									57	55
Columbia			-74	-86	-35	-33			31	45					59	70
Dartmouth			-64	-70	-57	-61			43						61	73
UCLA			-59	-50		-44			50	31				30	67	60
North Carolina		32	-77	-69	-58	-62			31						78	72
System Development Corp.	37	30	-76	-84	-42	-33			57	58		41			72	51
Dynamism																
Paris	51	59					-57	-54			44	54	-65	-68		
Leuven	37	60						-48			35	73	-36	-59		-30
Utrecht	60	55					-40	-47			55	64	-62	-61		
Columbia	53	66							30	44		67	-40	-45		
Dartmouth	41	55					-60	-54			57	65	-46	-63		
UCLA	55	63			31			-50	38	45	57	62	-34	-57	-35	
North Carolina	40	59					-33	-54	58	49	65	61	-60	-63		
System Development Corp.	31	43					-44	-44	31	49	51	60	-66	-76		

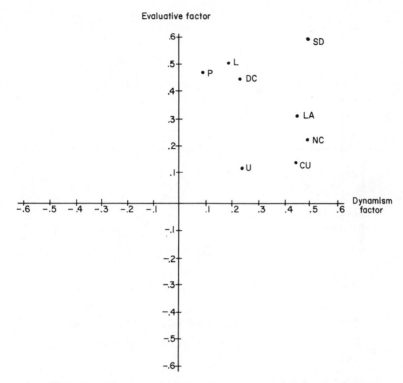

Figure 2   Factor loadings of cooperative–competitive self-ratings

three sites high on the Evaluative factor and relatively low on the Dynamism factor, with the three high on the latter and relatively low on the former. We shall refer to data from the first three (Paris, Leuven, and Dartmouth) as the E sample and that from the second three (Columbia, North Carolina, and UCLA) as the D sample. The reader will note that this comparison must necessarily be quite tentative because of the many possible ways in which the sites may differ. We have tried to reduce the dependence on simple comparisons between sites by examining functional relationships and trends rather than mere averages or percentages. Thus, each dependent variable (reflecting process or outcome) was analyzed in a three-factor analysis of variance design: Sample (E versus D) × Incentive × Pair Pattern. As in our earlier analysis involving pair patterns, the analytic tool was the unweighted-means, unequal N analysis of variance.

For sample comparisons, the major result is shown in Figure 3, which presents the average frequency of agreement in relation to sample and pair pattern. Incentive had a highly significant main effect and no interactions with the other two factors, so it may be disregarded. The main effect of sample is nearly significant ($p < .10$), with the D sample having more agreements on the average (22.2 versus

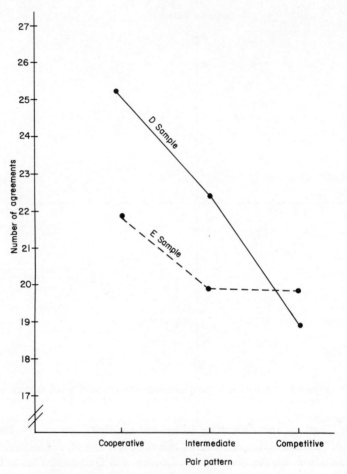

Figure 3   Number of agreements in D and E samples

20.7), and pair pattern has a highly significant main effect. Most interesting for our present purposes is the significant ($p < .05$) interaction between sample and pair pattern. Pair pattern yields a highly significant effect within the D sample ($p < .01$), but a nonsignificant effect in the E sample. Thus, *in the E sample, the initial cooperativeness of the pair has little relation to the rate of agreement.* This is of considerable interest, that the E definition of cooperativeness (moral, honest, peaceful) is such that pairs who described themselves as 'cooperative' at the outset were little more able to agree than those who described themselves as 'competitive.'

A similar analysis of the other major outcome variable, time to reach agreement, yields significant effects only for pair pattern and for E versus D. The E samples average 56 seconds and the D samples, only 43 seconds ($p < .01$).

The comparisons of the two samples in terms of the observational data must be made with some reservations: (a) these data were not obtained for one of the E sites, Dartmouth; (b) it is likely the criteria for the observational categories differed somewhat among sites; (c) differences must be interpreted in the light of the difference between the samples in duration of the negotiation. These reservations noted, we report the following consistent and plausible pattern of results: (a) 'bad' acts (did not bargain, misrepresented individual value, bargained hard, and bargained hard with threat) occurred more frequently in the E sample; (b) 'bad' acts tend to be associated with pair pattern more closely in the E sample; (c) rule use (rule invoked) was more frequent in the D sample; (d) rule was more closely associated with pair pattern in the D sample.

These various results for the two samples are consistent with the notion that the E sample tended to define the bargaining situation in moral terms. Where to be 'competitive' is, relatively speaking, to be 'bad,' the behavioral difference between cooperative and competitive pairs seemed to be in terms of frequency of bad behaviors. In the same moral vein, it was only in the E sample that any sizable number of persons claimed having poor cards, an action that is difficult to understand except possibly as a basis for a moral appeal.

What is most notable about the E sample is the fact that the bad behavior characteristic of the more competitive pairs was little more disruptive of agreement than was the relatively good behavior for pairs who described themselves as cooperative. We may speculate that initially cooperative subjects in the E sample created trouble for themselves by indulging in some misrepresentation (perhaps despite their moral scruples) to which the partners then overreacted. They infrequently used threat so it seems not to have been explicit power tactics which created trouble, but these cooperative pairs in the E sample did have many cases of not bargaining (a mild pressure tactic) which could easily have been another cause of their apparent difficulty.

In the D samples, where to be cooperative is to be passive and weak, the cooperative pairs created and used rules to settle the negotiation problems and were able thereby to achieve high rates of agreement. The psychological significance of the bargaining situation for the D sample seems best described in 'task' or 'instrumental' terms. The subjects describing themselves as cooperators seem to have treated the negotiation problems as tasks to be solved by local and direct arrangements and not (as their counterparts in the E sample) as interactions having wider, moral connotations. The competitive pairs in the D sample were low in rule usage, but they did not, as a substitute, engage in active negotiation with threat and misrepresentation to the same degree as did their E sample counterparts. (In terms of time to reach agreement, the D sample competitors were markedly faster than the E sample competitors.) They appear to have used refusal to bargain and some hard bargaining, and to have done so in a manner which kept both negotiation time and agreement rate at relative low values.

We began this analysis of site differences with the purpose of attempting to determine whether the incentive effects obtained in the experiment were mediated in different ways at the different sites. The evidence as to the role of the money incentive which emerges from the analyses described above (involving the Sample × Incentive × Pair Pattern design) is mixed in its implications. On the one hand, there are several respects in which the money incentive made the E sample like the D one. Whereas in the points condition the E sample was high on *poor cards claimed* and *bargain hard with threat*, in the money condition they were indistinguishable from the D sample. (The Sample × Incentive interactions are both significant.) A similar pattern (though only marginally significant, $p < .10$) occurred for number of agreements. Similarly (though again, the interaction is only marginally significant, $p < .10$), the money incentive produced a sharp drop in negotiation time for the E sample (in the direction of the D averages). On the other hand, whereas money increased rule discussion for the D sample, it *decreased* it for the E sample (interaction significant at $p < .05$).

The implication of these trends is that while money *inhibited* certain behaviors characteristic of the E sample (and thereby decreased time and increased agreement), it *did not encourage* the positive, rule-using behavior more characteristic of the D sample. Thus, of two general possible effects of money (reducing interfering behaviors and increasing agreement-promoting behaviors), the first seems to be more prominent in the E sample and the second, in the D sample.

This tendency for money to change the definition of the situation in the direction of the D sample is suggested by factor analyses of all the data from the United States sites. These were made separately for the money and points conditions. While the basic factor structure is essentially the same for the two conditions, the cooperative–competitive scale loads more on the evaluative factor in the points condition and more on the dynamism factor in the money condition.

Discussion

The results of two of our independent variables were very much as expected. Problem difficulty refers to how difficult it is for the pair of negotiators to satisfy their respective needs within the framework of agreement. Problem difficulty is very similar to what has been called the 'bargaining range,' difficult problems being characterized by a narrow bargaining range (Ikle and Leites, 1962). In the present study as in prior ones (Kahan, 1968; Kelley *et al.*, 1967; Shure and Meeker, 1969), negotiation time generally increased and frequency of agreements decreased as problem difficulty increased. However, the value of agreement had a long-run as well as a short-run component in the present experiment. If the bargainers could manage to withstand the short-run costs required for agreement and develop an unbroken succession of them, their entire interaction became more valuable. This long-term value of agreement complicated the observed relation between problem difficulty and the dependent variables. The decrease in rate of agreement with increasing difficulty was particularly sharp for pairs who had not yet begun to approach the more valuable level of interaction, but the increase in negotiation time with increasing difficulty was particularly marked for pairs who had. Apparently, pairs who had brought under control their individual interest in short-run gains were able to agree even on difficult problems, but reaching agreements required considerable discussion time.

The effects of type of incentive, *money* versus *points*, are generally consistent with the view that an increase in the value of the commodities involved in the negotiation facilitates its course, *if* the relation is one in which cooperative behavior affords a relatively dependable and invulnerable means to attain better outcomes and exploitative or individualistic behavior entails the risk of high costs. And in keeping with the general proposition above, this tendency was stronger under the *money* incentive: initial attitudes were more cooperative, interaction more often involved development and invocation of rules and less often entailed hard bargaining tactics, and agreement was more dependably and quickly reached. Also interest in long-term gain appeared to be higher with the money incentive, shown by better management of integrative bargaining and greater maintenance of unbroken sequences of agreement which increased the general value of the negotiator's relationship.

In addition to the positive effect the money incentive had on preinteraction attitudes, the results suggest that money had a positive effect beyond its initial one. When the effects on subsequent outcomes of initial attitudes were partialed out, the *money* condition still exhibited a more cooperative process and outcome than the *points* condition.

Thus, despite the variations in subjects, experimenter, procedure, etc., among the various laboratories, the advantage of the money over the points condition was evident in all eight sets of data. This is not to say, however, that money had its beneficial effect in the same way at all sites. In fact, it is probable that the across-site consistency reflects exactly this fact—that money has a variety of different effects but, at least in this situation, they all promote ultimate agreement and better outcomes. We have noted the somewhat different effects of money at the D and E sites, which suggest that it acts primarily to inhibit disruptive behaviors in some cases (with E sample subjects), but to promote facilitative behaviors in other cases (with D sample subjects).

It should also be noted that money as compared with points probably does more than merely increase the value to the subjects of the negotiation outcomes. Factor analyses of the meaning of cooperation–competition in the *money* and *points* conditions suggest that the definition of the situation is modified to some degree by the type of incentive. Money tends to make the situation one in which cooperation–competition means *Dynamism* (weak and passive versus strong and active) rather than *Evaluation* (moral and honest versus immoral and dishonest). The situation becomes a more instrumental or task-like one with *money* and more interpersonal or moral in its implications when the incentive is merely *points*.

Site differences

We regard as an important outcome of this research the identification of the two different meanings given to cooperation versus competition. In this and in other research (cf. Kelley and Stahelski, 1970; Shure *et al.*, 1966), the cooperative or competitive orientation a person adopts before the interaction is found to predict his behavior in the interaction. Our present evidence takes us beyond this simple fact and shows that the cooperative–competitive distinction does not have a constant meaning, but rather varies from one situation or set of subjects to another. Presumably, these variations reflect different psychological definitions which may be given to the same objective bargaining situation. In some instances, the situation seems to be defined in moral terms and in this case to be cooperative is to be good (moral, honest). In other instances, the situation seems defined more in task or achievement terms, and to be cooperative is to be weak and passive. Furthermore, behavior associated with a cooperative or competitive outlook depends upon the definition of the situation. Most provocative here is the result that when cooperation is defined in moral evaluative terms, cooperative pairs are little more successful in their negotiations than competitive pairs. Further, this seems particularly to be true in the absence of external monetary incentives—when, perhaps, the outcomes of the bargaining are more symbolic and interpersonal in nature (Lanto and Shure, 1972). The exploration of the implied interplay between type of orientation to the relationship and type of incentive is clearly an important agenda item for future research.

In a study by Flament (1967), striking parallels to the present study are seen, both in the empirically derived groups of sites and in the definitions of the major dimension of individual difference within the two groupings. The two studies seem to reflect the same distinction between different samples of subjects, and the 'Dynamism' versus 'Evaluative' distinction seems to describe the difference rather well. The evidence from Flament's study makes salient two important additional considerations: (a) Certain overall characteristics of the behavior within a given sample (say, the E sample) may reflect in part the general level of the subjects on the other dimension (say, the D factor). (b) The effect of a given dimension may vary from one situation to another. Thus, in the present study, cooperatively inclined subjects in the D sample (that is, the less active) seemed to evolve rules as a means of handling the conflict. In a situation where passive subjects are not able to handle their interpersonal conflicts by rules or by some interpersonal device, they may, as in the Flament study, discontinue responding to one another and, in effect, withdraw from interaction.

Strategy of site comparisons

Certain methodological difficulties are inherent in between-site comparisons of game behavior. As we have noted repeatedly, some of these problems were of considerable importance in the present study and, of course, must be taken into account in the interpretation of site differences noted above. In view of these many problems, the reader may well wonder how we dare to average data over sites, or even worse, try to make sense of differences among sites. The answer, flowing from our experience with the present investigation, can now be given along three lines. *First*, exact replication at different sites is impossible. It is pointless to insist on elimination of all differences in procedure, subject recruitment, meaning of the questions, equivalence of incentives, etc., as a precondition to conducting comparative research. Comparability is, of course, actively to be pursued, but to require a very high level is to delay interminably much needed research. Second, not all of these differences matter. For some problems, the degree of noncomparability we experienced in the present investigation is of little significance. For example, our major independent variable, type of incentive, had quite similar effects on the major outcome variable (rate of agreement) at all eight sites. Third, with sufficient attention to measurement of the psychological mediating variables, it is possible to assess the degree of comparability and to extract meaning from the noncomparability. This point is illustrated by the analysis of the E and D samples. This distinction may very well reflect the different types of subject populations available at the two sets of laboratories, for example, different social or occupational classes. If so, it might be very difficult and perhaps impossible to get comparable kinds of subjects (as through selective recruiting) for a study to be conducted at E versus D sites. But this need not deter us from undertaking such a comparison. Nor, if we undertake it, need we gloss over the problem of incomparability by simply *assuming* the subjects to be comparable. With adequate premeasures (personality, initial perceptions, and orientations) and good luck in their relevance (as illustrated by our own pregame ratings), the degree of comparability can be determined. And to the extent there is incomparability, its meaning and effect can be determined through appropriate classification of subjects and cross-analysis of variables. Undetected incomparability is a danger because it promotes erroneous generalization. Identified incomparability, on the other hand, affords grist for the theoretical mill. If we are ever to be able to generalize from the laboratory to the natural world, and from one real situation to another, we will have to be able to assess and interpret far greater degrees of incomparability than those encountered in any interlaboratory replications. In a real sense, developing a capacity to deal with interlaboratory differences means learning how to make the generalizations which our investigations have as their ultimate goal.

Notes

1. Abridged by G. H. Shure from Kelley, H. H., Shure, G. H., Deutsch, M., Faucheux, C., Lanzetta, J. T., Moscovici, S., Nuttin, J. M., Jr., Rabbie, J. M., and Thibaut, J. W. 'A comparative experimental study of negotiation behavior.' *Journal of Personality and Social Psychology*, 1970, **16**, 411–438. The paper is a report of the Transnational Working Group on the Dynamics of Conflict, a group of European and United States social psychologists with a common interest in an experimental approach to the analysis of social conflict. In addition to the authors, C. Flament, D. G. Pruitt, and H. Tajfel, also members of the group, contributed to the general planning of the study. We are indebted

to Victoria Billings for assistance in abridging the earlier article. The study was made possible by funds from (a) Office of Naval Research, Group Psychology Branch (Contract ONR-3987), (b) System Development Corporation, Santa Monica, California, and (c) Advanced Research Projects Agency (ARPA Order No. 1085). Copyright 1970 by the American Psychological Association. Reprinted by permission.

2. See original paper for procedural variations in sampling and recruitment at different sites.

3. An independent variable creating equal versus unequal dependence of the two parties upon reaching an agreement did not have the anticipated disruptive effect on the interaction or on any of our pair outcome measures. Descriptions of and results for this variable are omitted in this abridged presentation.

4. More detailed results are presented in the original paper.

5. 'Significant' is used throughout this paper to mean that an appropriate statistical test yields a p value of less than .05.

References

Deutsch, M. (1958). 'Trust and Suspicion,' *Journal of Conflict Resolution*, 2, 265–279.

Flament, C. (1967). 'Representations dans une situation conflictuelle: Étude interculturelle,' *Psychologie Francaise*, 12, 297–304.

Gallo, P. J., Jr (1966). 'Effects of increased incentives upon the use of threat in bargaining,' *Journal of Personality and Social Psychology*, 4, 14–20.

Ikle, F. C., and Leites, N. (1962). 'Political negotiation as a process of modifying utilities,' *Journal of Conflict Resolution*, 6, 19–28.

Kahan, J. P. (1968). 'Effects of level of aspiration in an experimental bargaining situation,' *Journal of Personality and Social Psychology*, 8, 154–159.

Kelley, H. H. (1966). 'A classroom study of the dilemmas in interpersonal negotiations,' in K. Archibald (ed.), *Strategic Interaction and Conflict*, University of California, Institute of International Studies, Berkeley.

Kelley, H. H., Beckman, L., and Fischer, C. S. (1967). 'Negotiating the division of a reward under incomplete information,' *Journal of Experimental Social Psychology*, 3, 361–398.

Kelley, H. H., Condry, J. C., Jr., Dahlke, A. E., and Hill, A. H. (1965). 'Collective behavior in a simulated panic situation,' *Journal of Experimental Social Psychology*, 1, 20–54.

Kelley, H. H. and Stahelski, A. J. (1970). 'The social interaction basis of cooperators' and competitors' beliefs about others,' *Journal of Personality and Social Psychology*, 16, 66–91.

Kent, G. (1969). 'Determinants of bargaining outcomes,' *Peace Research Society: Papers*, 11, 23–42.

Lanto, S. and Shure, G. H. (1972). 'Effects of size of payoff and real versus imaginary rewards on prebargaining perceptions,' *Proceedings, 80th Annual Convention of the American Psychological Assocation*, 231–232.

McClintock, C. G., and McNeel, S. P. (1966a). 'Reward and score feedback as determinants of cooperative and competitive game behavior,' *Journal of Personality and Social Psychology*, 6, 606–613.

McClintock, C. G., and McNeel, S. P. (1966b). 'Reward level and game playing behavior,' *Journal of Conflict Resolution*, 10, 98–102.

McClintock, C. G., and McNeel, S. P. (1967). 'Prior dyadic experience and monetary reward as determinants of cooperative and competitive game behavior,' *Journal of Personality and Social Psychology*, 5, 282–294.

Osgood, C. E., Suci, G. J. and Tannenbaum, P. H. (1957). *The Measurement of Meaning*, University of Illinois Press, Urbana.

Schachter, S., Nuttin, J., De Monchaux, C., Maucorps, P. H., Osmer, D., Duijker, H., Rommetveit, R., and Israel, J. (1954). 'Cross-cultural experiments on threat and rejection,' *Human Relations*, 7, 403–439.

Shure, G. H., and Meeker, R. J. (1969). 'Bargaining processes in experimental territorial conflict situations,' *Peace Research Society: Papers*, 11, 109–122.

Shure, G. H., Meeker, R. J., Hansford, E. A., and Moore, W. H. Jr (1969). 'De quelques voles joues par les calculatrices electroniques: Experimentateur, sujet, observateur,' in G. Lemaine and J. Lemaine (eds.), *Psychologie Sociale et Experimentation*, Mortin Press, Paris.

Shure, G. H., Meeker, R. J., and Moore, W. H., Jr (1967). 'TRACE: Time-shared routines for analysis, classification and evaluation,' *Proceedings of Spring Joint Computer Conference*, 30, 525–529.

Shure, G. H., Meeker, R. J., Moore, W. H., Jr, and Kelley, H. H. (1966). 'Computer studies of bargaining behavior: The role of threat in bargaining,' (SP 2916), System Development Corporation, Santa Monica, Calif.

Siegel, S., and Fouraker, L. E. (1960). *Bargaining and Group Decision Making*, McGraw-Hill, New York.

Walton, R. E., and McKersie, R. B. (1965). *A Behavioral Theory of Labor Negotiations*, McGraw-Hill, New York.

Small Groups and Social Interaction, Volume 2
Edited by H. H. Blumberg, A. P. Hare, V. Kent and M. Davies
© 1983 John Wiley & Sons Ltd

3.5 Coalition Formation

S. S. Komorita   *University of Illinois, Urbana-Champaign*

and

David A. Kravitz   *University of Kentucky*

Most social interaction involves a mixture of both cooperation and competition. One important process that occurs in such 'mixed-motive' situations is the formation of coalitions, where a coalition is defined as 'a collection of individuals who have pooled their resources to obtain some desired outcome.' For example, a trade union is a collection of workers who have pooled their resources to obtain better working conditions and wages. Coalition formation is a critical and pervasive process that occurs at all levels of social interaction, from the interpersonal to the international.

A variety of coalition theories have been proposed. Some of these theories only predict which coalitions are likely to form, and others only predict the reward division among the coalition members. This review will be restricted to theories that predict *both* of these variables. This restriction excludes some important normative theories (cf. Luce and Raiffa, 1957; Rapoport, 1970) because they do not predict which coalitions are likely to form, and also excludes Caplow's (1959) theory because it does not predict the reward division.

Coalition situations

Our definition of coalition formation includes a multitude of situations. To be consistent with previous empirical research, we shall assume that resources are votes and outcomes are points to be divided among the coalition members.

The vast majority of empirical studies on coalition formation have used simple weighted majority games. In a *weighted majority game*, each of n players controls a certain number of votes, and a majority of the votes is necessary to form a winning coalition. For convenience, the players will be denoted A, B, C, etc., in decreasing order of the number of votes they control. For example, in the game

9(8-3-3-3) the first number (9) denotes the number of votes required to win, player A controls 8 votes, and players B, C, and D each control 3 votes.

In a *simple game*, all winning coalitions have the same value (say 100 points), and the members of the winning coalition must negotiate the division of the 100 points. All losing coalitions have a different value (say 0). In such games there are two types of winning coalitions: minimal winning and non-minimal winning coalitions. A *minimal winning coalition* is a winning coalition that will become a losing coalition if any of its members defect. The minimal winning coalitions in the above game are: AB, AC, AD, and BCD. A *non-minimal winning coalition* is a winning coalition that can lose at least one member and still be a winning coalition. For example, in the above game ABC is a non-minimal winning coalition because either B or C could be deleted and the remaining two players would still form a winning coalition. Since there is little incentive to add members to a minimal winning coalition, virtually all coalition theories predict that only minimal winning coalitions will form in simple games. This is not true for multi-valued games.

In a simple game all coalitions are assigned one of two values (one each for winning and losing coalitions). In a *multi-valued game* the coalitions are assigned more than two different values. In such games the power of the player is manipulated by varying the values of the coalitions in which he/she is included, and resources are usually not assigned. Consider the following three-person game:

$$v(i) = 0; v(ABC) = 0; v(AB) = 100; v(AC) = 80; \text{ and } v(BC) = 60;$$

where $v(\ )$ denotes the value of a coalition, including the one-person coalition $v(i)$. It can be seen that player A has an advantage because the coalitions that include him/her have greater values than the coalitions that include the other two players.

Theories of coalition formation

There are five theories that predict both coalition likelihood and reward division: (1) minimum resource theory (Gamson, 1961); (2) minimum power theory (Gamson, 1964); (3) bargaining theory (Komorita and Chertkoff, 1973); (4) weighted probability model (Komorita, 1974); and (5) equal excess model (Komorita, 1979). We shall first describe and illustrate the predictions of these theories for the simple weighted majority game, 9(8-3-3-3), and shall then evaluate the theories in both simple and multi-valued games.

Minimum resource theory

The first theory to predict both coalition formation and reward division was Gamson's (1961) minimum resource theory. This theory is based on the proportionality norm (originally called 'parity'), which specifies that rewards be divided in direct proportion to the resources (votes) of the coalition members. In 9(8-3-3-3), for example, reward divisions should be 73-27 in the 8-3 coalition, and

33-33-33 in the 3-3-3 coalition. Since the 3-3-3 coalition mutually maximizes the rewards for players B, C, and D, minimum resource theory predicts that this coalition should form. It can be shown that in simple games minimum resource theory always predicts an inverse relation between coalition frequency and the total resources controlled by the coalition members. The name follows from the fact that the winning coalition with 'minimum resources' is predicted to be most likely.

Minimum power theory

Minimum power theory was also proposed by Gamson (1964), and is based on an index of 'pivotal power' proposed by Shapley and Shubik (1954). In simple games this index is equal to P/T, where T is the total number of permutations of the players, and P is the number of cases in which the individual's resources are pivotal (change a losing coalition into a winning coalition). (For instance, any four-person group has 24 permutations—ABCD, ABDC, etc.—and for each of these, one can ask: adding people one at a time from the left, starting with person A, which person changes a losing coalition to a winning one?) In 9(8-3-3-3), for example, player 8 is pivotal in 12 cases and each of the other players is pivotal in 4 cases. Thus the pivotal power indices are 12/24 for player 8 and 4/24 for each of the others.

Gamson (1964) suggested that rewards might be divided in direct proportion to these indices. Thus, in the 8-3 coalition the reward would be divided 75-25, and in the 3-3-3 coalition the reward would be divided equally (33 each). Since the 3-3-3 coalition mutually maximizes payoffs for players B, C, and D, minimum power theory predicts that this coalition should be most likely. In fact, this theory always predicts an inverse relation between coalition frequency and the sum of the pivotal power indices of the coalition members.

Bargaining theory

The previous two theories are static theories: coalition frequencies and reward divisions are predicted to be constant over all trials of a multi-trial game. In Komorita and Chertkoff's (1973) bargaining theory, the players' expectations and outcomes are assumed to change over trials, as a function of the offers, counteroffers, and outcomes of previous trials.

The bargaining theory assumes that coalition members who are above average in resources will expect and demand a share of the reward based on the proportionality norm, whereas those who are below average will expect and demand an equal share. On the initial trial an outcome midway between proportionality and equality is predicted. In the 9(8-3-3-3) game the predicted division for the 8-3 coalition is 61-39, midway between 73-27 (proportionality) and 50-50 (equality).

At the asymptote (after an indefinite number of trials), the theory assumes that the bargainers will base their demands on their maximum expectations in alternative coalitions (denoted Emax), and the reward will be divided proportionally to these alternatives. In 9(8-3-3-3), if players 8 and 3 are negotiating the division of the reward, player 8's Emax is 73, based on proportionality in the other 8-3 coalitions, and player 3's Emax is 33, based on equality in the 3-3-3 coalition. Direct proportionality of these Emax values yields an asymptotic predicted division of 69-31.

Bargaining theory assumes that the most likely coalition is one which minimizes the sum of the coalition members' temptations to defect from the coalition. The temptation of individual i to defect from coalition j, denoted T_{ij}, is defined as: $T_{ij} = (E\text{max}_{ik} - 0_{ij})/E\text{max}_{ik}$, where $E\text{max}_{ik}$ is player i's maximum expectation in alternative coalitions, and 0_{ij} is the predicted share for player i in coalition j. For the predicted asymptotic split of 69-31 in the 8-3 coalition it can be shown that the temptation value summed over both players is .114. In contrast, the temptation value summed over all three players in the 3-3-3 coalition is 1.00. Thus bargaining theory predicts that the 8-3 coalition will be most likely.

Weighted probability model

All of the previous theories begin by predicting reward division, and then base predictions of coalition formation on the predicted division. This order is reversed in Komorita's (1974) weighted probability model. In addition, this theory yields exact predictions of the probabilities of the coalitions, given by: $P_j = w_j/\Sigma w_k$, where $w_j = 1/(n_j - 1)$; n_j denotes the number of players in coalition j; and the summation is over all minimal winning coalitions. For the 9(8-3-3-3) game, the minimal winning coalitions are AB, AC, AD, and BCD. For the two-person coalitions, $w_j = 1.0$ each, whereas for the BCD coalition, $w_j = .50$. Hence, the probability (P_j) of each of the two-person coalitions is $1/3.5 = 2/7$, while the probability of BCD is 1/7.

The model also assumes that each member's share of the reward is directly proportional to the probability of being included in the winning coalition, given by $P_i = \Sigma P_{ij}$, where the summation is over all the minimal winning coalitions that include individual i. In the above game, the probability that player 8 will be included in the winning coalition is 6/7, and the probability that each of the others will be included in the winning coalition is 3/7. Hence the model predicts a 67-33 split in the 8-3 coalition and equal shares in the 3-3-3 coalition.

Equal excess model

The equal excess model was recently proposed by Komorita (1979) explicitly to deal with multi-valued games. Like the bargaining theory, it is a dynamic model and predicts changes in expectations and outcomes over rounds of bargaining. For simple weighted majority games the equal excess model incorporates the Trial

1 assumptions of the bargaining theory. Although it was originally hypothesized that the Trial 1 assumptions might be substituted for Round 1, we shall substitute them for the initial expectations (E^0_{iS}) of the model. Thus initial expectations are based on splitting the difference between proportionality and equality. For 9(8-3-3-3), it predicts that initial expectations in the 8-3 coalition will be 61 and 39 for players 8 and 3, respectively. Predictions on subsequent rounds of bargaining are based on iterations of the following equation:

$$E^r_{iS} = \max E^{r-1}_{iT} + (1/s)\,[v(S) - \Sigma \max E^{r-1}_{iT}], \quad S \neq T \qquad (1)$$

where E^r_{iS} denotes the expectation of member i in coalition S on round r; $\max E^{r-1}_{iT}$ denotes the maximum expectation of member i in alternative coalitions on the previous round; s denotes the number of persons in coalition S; $v(S)$ denotes the value of coalition S, and the summation is over all s members of coalition S.

Since 9(8-3-3-3) is a simple game, $v(S)$ is constant (100) for all winning coalitions. Substituting the initial expectations (E^0_{iS}) in Equation (1), for round 1 the model predicts that the split in the 8-3 coalition will be 64-36. For the 3-3-3 coalition it can be shown that the expectations of the three players will be 33 each over all rounds of bargaining. Since expectations on round 1 are mutually maximized in the 8-3 coalition, it is predicted that if an agreement is reached the 8-3 coalition is most likely to occur for a division of 64-36.

For successive rounds of bargaining, iterations of Equation (1) yield asymptotic predictions of 67-33 in the 8-3 coalitions and 33 each in the 3-3-3 coalition. At the asymptote the model predicts an equilibrium solution in which none of the players in any of the coalitions is tempted to defect. This implies that the earlier the round on which an agreement is reached, the more likely the 8-3 coalition but the smaller the share received by player 8.

Since no prediction can be derived about the exact round on which an agreement is likely, rounds of bargaining can be conceptualized as a parameter of the model. Hence, Komorita (1979) suggested that round of formation might be directly related to: (1) competitiveness of the players; (2) size of the stakes; (3) subjects' familiarity and experience with the structure of coalition games; and (4) freedom of communication and amount of information available.

Evaluation of theories for simple weighted majority games

An exhaustive review of the empirical literature is clearly beyond the scope of this paper (the interested reader is referred to Stryker, 1972; Murnighan, 1978a; and Miller and Crandall, 1980). Instead, we shall consider only a subset of the available data. We shall discuss separately the results in resource-irrelevant and resource-relevant coalition games.

In *resource-irrelevant* games a player's resources are not related to his/her strategic position relative to the other players in the game. Specifically, all players are included in the same number of minimal winning coalitions, and these coalitions are all of the same size. The most common resource-irrelevant game has been 5(4-3-2). In this game the three minimal winning coalitions are AB, AC, and BC. Since each player is included in two two-person coalitions, the assigned resources are strategically irrelevant. Since all players are in strategically equivalent positions, one might expect all coalitions to be equally likely with reward divisions of 50-50. However, many studies have shown that the BC (3-2) coalition is most likely, and that player B receives more than half the prize (Chertkoff and Braden, 1974; Chertkoff and Esser, 1977; Kelley and Arrowood, 1960; Vinacke and Arkoff, 1957). This is consistent with minimum resource theory, bargaining theory, and equal excess model, but not with minimum power theory and weighted probability model. However, the first three of the above studies also found that the domination of the BC coalition decreased slightly over trials, and reward divisions tended toward equality, though the changes were quite small. Similar findings have been obtained with four-person groups (Miller, 1980).

The changes over trials suggest that coalition formation may partly depend on subjects' familiarity and experience with coalition games (cf. Komorita and Kravitz, 1981). If inexperienced bargainers are used, resource-irrelevant games provide support for minimum resource theory, but if experienced bargainers are used, such games provide support for minimum power theory and weighted probability model. However, since such changes over trials are predicted by bargaining theory and equal excess model, the results of resource-irrelevant games provide the strongest support for these two theories.

In *resource-relevant* games the players' strategic positions depend, in part, on their resources. For example, in 9(8-3-3-3) the player with 8 votes is included in three coalitions of size two, whereas the players with 3 votes are only included in two coalitions, one of size two and the other of size three. In such games differences in the outcomes of players with different resources *and* sets of minimal winning coalitions are quite large (Chertkoff, 1971; Michener *et al.*, 1976; Murnighan, 1978b; Murnighan *et al.*, 1977). The results of such studies tend to support bargaining theory, weighted probability model, and equal excess model; minimum resource theory and minimum power theory perform quite poorly.

The game 9(8-3-3-3) was used for illustrative purposes because it has been used in two different experiments (Chertkoff, 1971; Murnighan *et al.*, 1977), for a combined sample of 32 groups (102 trials). Minimum resource theory and minimum power theory both predict that the 3-3-3 coalition should occur most frequently, whereas the remaining theories predict that the 8-3 coalition should be most frequent. The mean proportion of occurrence of the 8-3 coalition, pooled over all trials of all groups, was .78, while the mean proportion of the 3-3-3 coalition was .17. Non-minimal winning coalitions (e.g. 8-3-3) occurred on 5% of the trials. Thus these data support the predictions of bargaining theory, weighted probability model, and equal excess model. The mean reward division in the 8-3 coalition was 68-32. Although no statistical tests were performed on the pooled data, these values probably do not differ significantly from the predictions of these three theories (69-31 for bargaining theory, 67-33 for weighted probability model, and 64-36 for round 1 of the equal excess model). In contrast, the predicted divisions for the other two theories (73-27 for minimum resource and 75-25 for minimum power) tend to overestimate the outcomes of player 8.

Evaluation of theories in multi-valued games

In a multi-valued game resources typically are not assigned: each coalition has a different value and the power of a given player is based on the values of the coalitions that include him/her. When resources are not assigned, no predictions can be derived from minimum resource theory. This is a severe restriction on the generality of the theory. Similarly, as previously described, predictions for multi-valued games cannot be derived from minimum power theory, bargaining theory, and weighted probability model. However, in recent studies by Komorita and Tumonis (1980) and Miller (1980), extensions of these theories were proposed and tested in multi-valued games.

In the study by Komorita and Tumonis (1980), the predictions of bargaining theory, weighted probability model, and equal excess model were contrasted in simple and multi-valued games, when resources were assigned and not assigned. Their results showed that resource assignment had negligible effects on coalition formation, and provided the greatest support for bargaining theory and equal excess model. The study by Miller (1980) used three games which differed either in terms of coalition values or assigned resources. He too found miniscule effects of resources, and supported bargaining theory and equal excess model over minimum resource theory and minimum power theory. Both of these studies found a strong positive relation between coalition value and coalition frequency.

In addition to the above studies, an important set of coalition experiments with multi-valued games has been conducted by Rapoport and Kahan and their associates (e.g. Kahan and Rapoport, 1974; Rapoport and Kahan, 1976). In general, the results of their studies support Aumann and Maschler's (1964) bargaining set, a normative theory of coalition formation. Since this theory does not predict coalition likelihood, we did not describe it here. However, it can be shown that for many of the multi-valued games used in their experiments, the asymptotic reward division predictions of the equal excess model coincide with the predictions of the bargaining set. Hence, the results of their experiments also provide support for the equal excess model.

Summary and conclusions

Our brief review and evaluation of coalition theories indicates that there is very little support for minimum power theory. This conclusion has also been reached by other reviewers (e.g. Murnighan, 1978a). This does not imply, however, that

Shapley and Shubik's (1954) index of pivotal power is invalid; the problem may lie instead with the assumed rule of reward division—proportionality. Our review also suggests that support for minimum resource theory is restricted to the case of simple resource-irrelevant games, and there is little support for the theory when tested with resource-relevant games (cf. Komorita and Meek, 1978). In addition, this theory has limited generality: predictions cannot be derived for games in which resources are not assigned.

The validity of the remaining three theories can be differentiated on the basis of both simple and multi-valued games. In simple resource-irrelevant games, bargaining theory and equal excess model are superior because they predict the obtained changes over trials and with experience. In simple resource-relevant games the three theories cannot be clearly differentiated, but data from multi-valued games suggest that the weighted probability model may be restricted to simple games. Hence, at present the evidence suggests that bargaining theory and equal excess model are the most promising coalition theories that predict both coalition frequency and reward divisions.

References

Aumann, R. J., and Maschler, M. (1964). 'The bargaining set for cooperative games,' in M. Dresher, L. S. Shapley, and A. W. Tucker (eds.), *Advances in Game Theory*, Princeton University Press, Princeton, NJ.

Caplow, T. (1959). 'Further development of a theory of coalitions in the triad,' *American Journal of Sociology*, **64**, 488–493.

Chertkoff, J. M. (1971). 'Coalition formation as a function of differences in resources,' *Journal of Conflict Resolution*, **15**, 371–383.

Chertkoff, J. M., and Braden, J. L. (1974). 'Effects of experience and bargaining restrictions on coalition formation,' *Journal of Personality and Social Psychology*, **30**, 169–177.

Chertkoff, J. M., and Esser, J. K. (1977). 'A test of three theories of coalition formation when agreements can be short-term or long-term,' *Journal of Personality and Social Psychology*, **35**, 237–249.

Gamson, W. A. (1961). 'A theory of coalition formation,' *American Sociological Review*, **26**, 373–382.

Gamson, W. A. (1964). 'Experimental studies of coalition formation,' in L. Berkowitz (ed.), *Advances in Experimental Social Psychology*, Vol. 1, Academic Press, New York.

Kahan, J. P., and Rapoport, An. (1974). 'Test of the bargaining set and kernel models in three-person games. In An. Rapoport (ed.), *Game Theory as a Theory of Conflict Resolution*, Reidel, Dordrecht, Holland.

Kelley, H. H., and Arrowood, A. J. (1960). 'Coalitions in the triad: Critique and experiment,' *Sociometry*, **23**, 231–244.

Komorita, S. S. (1974). 'A weighted probability model of coalition formation,' *Psychological Review*, **81**, 242–256.

Komorita, S. S. (1979). 'An equal excess model of coalition formation,' *Behavioral Science*, **24**, 369–381.

Komorita, S. S., and Chertkoff, J. M. (1973). 'A bargaining theory of coalition formation,' *Psychological Review*, **80**, 149–162.

Komorita, S. S., and Kravitz, D. A. (1981). 'The effects of prior experience on coalition bargaining, *Journal of Personality and Social Psychology*, **40**, 675–686.

Komorita, S. S., and Meek, D. D. (1978). 'Generality and validity of some theories of coalition formation,' *Journal of Personality and Social Psychology*, **36**, 392–404.

Komorita, S. S., and Tumonis, T. W. (1980). 'Extensions and tests of some descriptive theories of coalition formation,' *Journal of Personality and Social Psychology*, **39**, 256–268.

Luce, R. D., and Raiffa, H. (1957). *Games and Decisions*, Wiley, New York.

Michener, H. A., Fleishman, J. A., and Vaske, J. J. (1976). 'A test of the bargaining theory of coalition formation in four-person groups,' *Journal of Personality and Social Psychology*, **34**, 1114–1126.

Miller, C. E. (1980). 'A test of four theories of coalition formation: Effects of payoffs and resources,' *Journal of Personality and Social Psychology*, **38**, 153–164.

Miller, C. E., and Crandall, R. (1980). 'Experimental research on the social psychology of bargaining and coalition formation,' in P. B. Paulus (ed.), *Psychology of Group Influence*, Erlbaum, Hillsdale, NJ.

Murnighan, J. K. (1978a). 'Models of coalition behavior: Game theoretic, social psychological, and political perspectives,' *Psychological Bulletin*, **85**, 1130–1153.

Murnighan, J. K. (1978b). 'Strength and weakness in four coalition situations,' *Behavioral Science*, **23**, 195–208.

Murnighan, J. K., Komorita, S. S., and Szwajkowski, E. (1977). 'Theories of coalition formation and the effects of reference groups,' *Journal of Experimental Social Psychology*, **13**, 166–181.

Rapoport, Am., and Kahan, J. P. (1976). 'When three is not always two against one: Coalitions in experimental three-person cooperative games,' *Journal of Experimental Social Psychology*, **12**, 253–273.

Rapoport, An. (1970). *N-person Game Theory*, University of Michigan Press, Ann Arbor.

Shapley, L. S., and Shubik, M. (1954). 'Method for evaluating the distribution of power in a committee system,' *American Political Science Review*, **48**, 787–792.

Stryker, S. (1972). 'Coalition behavior,' in C. G. McClintock (ed.), *Experimental Social Psychology*, Holt, New York.

Vinacke, W. E., and Arkoff, A. (1957). 'An experimental study of coalitions in the triad,' *American Sociological Review*, **22**, 406–414.

Part II
Social and Personal Change

Introduction

This section emphasizes personal growth, social action and change, and living together in harmony. Much has been written about these topics in recent years. The present examples emphasize that social and personal change may emerge from, or can be manifest in, experience in small groups. We have tried to include descriptions, analyses, and imaginative ideas—as well as accounts of empirical research. (We do not necessarily agree with all of the viewpoints.)

Chapter 4 begins with Martin Lakin's descriptive overview of experiential helping groups (sub-Chapter 4.1). In the next paper, Leon Levy (sub-Chapter 4.2) describes some of the underlying processes whereby self-help groups accomplish their goals. A brief excerpt from Egan's work (sub-Chapter 4.3) gives some 'rules' which may help to make confrontation within groups a constructive process. Morton Lieberman (sub-Chapter 4.4) is known for his collaborative large-scale studies of encounter groups; in the present paper, he analyses various change mechanisms in groups. Finally, John Rowan (sub-Chapter 4.5) points out that it is worth understanding the 'groups' that are *within* individuals.

Chapter 5 is concerned with 'living together' in both the narrow sense of sharing a household and the broader sense of cooperating with other people in one's community and indeed in the world. An excerpt by Kanter (sub-Chapter 5.1) is concerned with the boundaries that define a group. Gorman (sub-Chapter 5.2) provides some ideas about communal living. As an example of organized rural communities, we have included Shepher and Tiger's (sub-Chapter 5.3) description of the kibbutzim, and a paper in which the authors reconsider their earlier work. A sampling of lively ideas about existing and potential cooperative efforts comprises sub-Chapter 5.4 (compiled by Nicholas Albery). 'Marx and brown rice' (sub-Chapter 5.5, Uhuru) provides a kind of 'case example', a discussion of some of the differences among people who have intentionally lived together in a particular collective which has also had broader social concerns. 'Living the revolution'—by Gowan, Lakey, Moyer, and Taylor (sub-Chapter 5.6)—provides description and analysis of a particular 'multi-generational support community for persons involved in fundamental social change training and activity'. Taken together, these papers are meant to provide a variety of perspectives.

'Social action and social change' are emphasized in Chapter 6, though the boundaries among the chapters in Part II are not sharp ones. Varela (sub-Chapter 6.1) is concerned with 'social technology'—practical examples of how social scientists can help in solving problems. Miller (sub-Chapter 6.2) focuses particularly on group processes in neighbourhood action groups. Sarason and Lorentz (sub-Chapter 6.3) describe and analyse social networks devoted to the 'exchange of resources'—how they develop and what they can accomplish. Next, an excerpted fragment from the work of Sheila Rowbotham (sub-Chapter 6.4) provides a brief idea of 'participatory democracy' and decentralized leadership, as manifest in the women's movement; also excerpted are some comments on consciousness-raising. Lynne Shivers (sub-Chapter 6.5) summarizes suggestions for facilitating the work of small groups—this includes, but is not limited to, leadership, meetings, and conflict resolution in groups concerned with social action. The title of the paper by Havelock and Sashkin (sub-Chapter 6.6) is probably self-explanatory—'a guide to promoting change in groups and organizations,' generally at the invitation or at least agreement of the people concerned. Murton's article (sub-Chapter 6.7) provides a single case study of the direction that social reform can take in a particular setting, in this case a prison where—among other things—some of the decision making was, as far as possible, delegated to small groups, democratically formed. Finally, Nhat Hanh's work (sub-Chapter 6.8) focuses on 'ways of being,' which can have an important effect not only on the individual but also on social action(s) carried out by the individual or group. As with the other chapters in this section, our main hope in Chapter 6 is to provide the reader with a variety of views. Those who are interested in particular areas, such as antipoverty action and disarmament, may also find it useful to consult the suggestions for 'Additional reading,' below.

Some readers may feel that there is a division, in style and approach, between Part II and the rest of this work. A paper such as one by Hall and Watson (1970) may help to bridge part of what has been called the 'soft-helpful'–'hard-abstract' divide.[1]

Additional reading

In addition to the work represented or cited in these chapters (and general sources such as those indicated in the Preface, e.g. see Blumberg, 1977, and Wrightsman and Deaux, 1981, Ch. 20), some further items which readers may wish to consult are as follows. *Chapter 4* (Experiential and self-help groups): Babad *et al.* (1977), Babington Smith and Farrell (1979), Bernstein (1973), Carkhuff (1979), Cavan and Das (1979), Cooper (1975), Glasser *et al.* (1974), Golembiewski and Blumberg (1977), Hartman (1979), Johnstad (1981), Killworth and Bernard (1976), Kravetz (1978), Kreeger (1975), Krupar (1973), Smith (1980), and Yalom (1975). *Chapter 5* (Living together): Abrams and McCulloch (1976), Eiduson and Alexander (1978), Hostetler (1974), Johnson and Johnson (1975), Li and Chieh-yun (1975), Raimy (1979), Shey (1977), Weitzman *et al.* (1976), and Young and Rigge (1979?). *Chapter 6* (Social action and social change): Bender (1979), Birchard and McFadden (1977), Clark (1977), Cohen (1975), Coughlin and Khinduka (1976), Galaskiewicz (1979), Gibbard *et al.* (1974), Gibson (1979), Hastings (1979), Laumann and Pappi (1976), McClelland (1978), Miller *et al.* (1979), Morris (1976), Norton (1977), Rothman (1974), Sinclair *et al.* (1979), and Training/Action Affinity Group (1979).

Readers are also referred to other parts of this book, particularly to Chapter 2 on conflict resolution (and the section introduction for Part I) and to Sub-Chapters 7.7 and 7.8 (see also the Reference Note which follows the References, below).

Of relevance to all of the chapters in this part are the areas of 'evaluation research' and 'quality of life.' See, for example, Cronbach (1982), Bryant and Veroff (1982), and the *Psychological Abstracts* subject indexes under 'evaluation' and 'life experiences'—also see the other main bibliographic sources described in our Preface.

Those who wonder about the various alternative 'futures' which could be influenced, now, by cooperative efforts might like to read—among many other things (cf. Blumberg, 1977)—*Protest and Survive* edited by E. P. Thompson and Dan Smith (1980) (see also *Bombs for Breakfast*, 1981; Calder, 1979; *Common Security*, 1982; *Defence without the Bomb*, 1983; *Nuclear Numbers Game*, 1982) and *Woman on the Edge of Time* by Marge Piercy (1976). For a worldwide list of organizations/groups which are active in various causes, see for example the *World Peace Diary* (1983).

Note

1. We are grateful to Paul Webley for this suggestion. The paper by Hall and Watson is fairly readily available.

As two additional cautionary notes, suggested by P. Freer in the light of the present selections: (a) groups need not make sharp distinctions between 'teachers' and 'followers', and (b) people are not necessarily free to act as they might reasonably wish to do, though some situations may help enable them to do so (cf. Freire, 1972, and the writings of Antonio Grarasci).

References

Abrams, P., and McCulloch, A. (1976). *Communes, Sociology and Society*, Cambridge University Press, Cambridge.

Babad, E. Y., Tzur, A., Oppenheimer, B. T., and Shaltiel, A. (1977). 'An all-purpose model for group work,' *Human Relations*, **30**, 389–401.

Babington Smith, B., and Farrell, B. A. (eds.) (1979). *Training in Small Groups; a Study of Five Methods*, Pergamon, Oxford.

Bender, M. P. (1976). *Community Psychology*. Methuen, London.

Bernstein, S. (ed.) (1973). *Further Explorations in Group Work*, Bookstall (for Boston U. School of Social Work), London.

Birchard, B., and McFadden, D. (1977). 'Peace conversion organizing guide,' *WIN*, **13** (33), (October 6), 23–27.

Blumberg, H. H. (1977). 'Bibliographic guide,' in A. P. Hare and H. H. Blumberg (eds.), *Liberation Without Violence: A Third Party Approach*, Rex Collings, London.

Bombs for Breakfast, (1981). 2nd Ed., Committee on Poverty and the Arms Trade, London.

Bryant, F. B., and Veroff, J. (1982). 'The structure of psychological well-being: a sociohistorical analysis,' *Journal of Personality and Social Psychology*, **43**, 653–673.

Calder, N. (1979). *Nuclear Nightmares: An Investigation into Possible Wars*, BBC, London. (And Penguin, New York, 1981).

Carkhuff, R. R. (1979). *The Art of Helping*; . . . 4th edn., Human Resource Development Press, Amherst, Mass.

Cavan, R. S., and Das, M. S. (eds.) (1979). *Communes: Historical and Contemporary*, Vikas, New Delhi.
Clark, D. (1977). *Basic Communities: Towards an Alternative Society*, SPCK, London.
Cohen, M. W. (1975). 'Development of community action programs through resident participation in an area self-study,' *Dissertation Abstracts International*, **35** (8-B), 4164.
Common Security: A Programme for Disarmament: the Report of the Independent Commission on Disarmament and Security Issues. (1982). Pan, London and Sydney.
Cooper, C. L. (ed.) (1975). *Theories of Group Processes*, Wiley, London.
Coughlin, B. J., and Khinduka, S. K. (1976). 'Social change and social action,' *Journal of Sociology and Social Welfare*, **3**, 322–31.
Cronbach, L. J. (1982). *Designing Evaluations of Educational and Social Programs*, Jossey-Bass, San Francisco.
Defence without the Bomb: the Report of the Alternative Defence Commission. (1983). Taylor and Francis, London.
Eiduson, B. T., and Alexander, J. W. (1978). 'The role of children in alternative family styles,' *Journal of Social Issues*, **34** (2), 149–67.
Freire, P. (1972). *Pedagogy of the Oppressed*, Penguin, Harmondsworth.
Galaskiewicz, J. (1979). *Exchange Networks and Community Politics*, Sage, Beverley Hills.
Gibbard, G. S., Hartman, J. J., and Mann, R. D. (eds.) (1974). *Analysis of Groups*, Jossey-Bass, San Francisco.
Gibson, T. (1979). *People Power; Community and Work Groups in Action*, Penguin, Harmondsworth.
Glasser, P., Sarri, R., and Vinter, R. (eds.) (1974). *Individual Change through Small Groups*, Freee Press, New York.
Golembiewski, R. T., and Blumberg, A. (eds.) (1977). *Sensitivity Training and the Laboratory Approach; Readings about Concepts and Applications*, 3rd edn, Peacock, Itasca, Ill.
Hall, J., and Watson, W. H. (1970). 'The effects of a normative intervention on group decision-making performance,' *Human Relations*, **23**, 299–317.
Hartman, J. J. (1979). 'Small group methods of personal change,' *Annual Review of Psychology*, **30**, 453–76.
Hastings, W. M. (1979). *How to Think about Social Problems: A Primer for Citizens*, Oxford University Press, New York.
Hostetler, J. A. (1974). *Communitarian Societies*, Holt, Rinehart and Winston, New York.
Johnson, D. W., and Johnson, F. P. (1975). *Joining Together: Group Theory and Group Skills*, Prentice-Hall, Englewood Cliffs, NJ.
Johnstad, T. (ed.) (1981). *Group Dynamics and Society: A Multinational Approach*, Ölgeschläger, Munich.
Killworth, P. D., and Bernard, H. R. (1976). 'A model of human group dynamics,' *Social Science Research*, **5**, 173–224.
Kravetz, D. (1978). 'Consciousness-raising groups in the 1970's,' *Psychology of Women Quarterly*, **3**, 168–86.
Kreeger, L. (ed.) (1975). *The Large Group: Dynamics and Therapy*, Constable, London.
Krupar, K. R. (1973). *Communication Games; Participant's Manual*, Free Press, New York.
Laumann, E. O., and Pappi, F. U. (1976). *Networks of Collective Action; A Perspective on Community Influence Systems*, Academic Press, New York.
Li, C., and Chieh-yun, T. (1975). *Inside a People's Commune; Report from Chiliying*, Foreign Languages Press, Peking.

McClelland, D. C. (1978). 'Managing motivation to expand human freedom,' *American Psychologist*, **33**, 201–210.

Miller, F. D., Grega, D., Malia, G., and Tsemberis, S. (1979). 'Community activism and the maintenance of urban neighborhoods,' Paper presented to the Annual Meeting of the American Psychological Association, New York City.

Morris, M. (ed.) (1976). *Instead of Prisons: A Handbook for Abolitionists*, Prison Research Education Action Project, Syracuse, NY.

Norton, M. (1977). *The Directory of Social Change. [Vol. 2.] Community*, Wildwood House, London. [Also: Vol. 1, *Education and play*, 1977, by B. Dinham and M. Norton; and Vol. 3, *Women*, 1978, by W. Collins, E. Friedman, and A. Pivot.]

The Nuclear Numbers Game: Understanding the Statistics Behind the Bombs. (1982). Radical Statistics, London.

Piercy, M. (1976). *Woman on the Edge of Time*, New York, Knopf. (Also, Women's Press, London, 1976; and Fawcett, New York, 1978.)

Raimy, E. (1979). *Shared Houses, Shared Lives; The New Extended Families and How they Work*, Tarcher, Los Angeles.

Rothman, J. (1974). *Planning and Organizing for Social Change; Action Principles from Social Science Research*, Columbia University Press, New York.

Shey, T. H. (1977). 'Why communes fail: a comparative analysis of the viability of Danish and American Communes,' *Journal of Marriage and the Family*, **39**, 605–613.

Sinclair, D., Mentzer, S., and Pike, E. (12 July 1979). 'Beyond simple living: community, alliances and action,' *WIN*, **15** (24), 4–9.

Smith, P. B. (1980). *Group Processes and Personal Change*, Harper & Row, London.

Thompson, E. P., and Smith, Dan. (eds.) (1980). *Protest and Survive*, Penguin, Harmondsworth.

Training/Action Affinity Group. (1979). *Building Social Change Communities*, Movement for a New Society, Philadelphia.

Weitzman, L. J., Eifler, D., Hokada, E., and Ross, C. (1976). 'Sex-role socialization in picture books for preschool children,' in *Sexism in Children's Books*; ..., pp. 5–30, Writers and Readers, London. [See also other items reprinted in the same volume.]

World Peace Diary. (1983). Housmans, 5 Caledonian Rd., London N1, England. (Published annually.)

Wrightsman, L. S., and Deaux, K. (1981). *Social Psychology in the 80s*, Brooks/Cole, Monterey, California.

Yalom, I. D. (ed.) (1975). *The Theory and Practice of Group Psychotherapy*, 2nd Ed., Basic Books, New York.

Young, M., and Rigge, M. (1979). *Mutual Aid in a Selfish Society*, Mutual Aid Press, London.

Reference note

The reader may wish to consult the following papers in other parts of Volumes 1 and 2 which seem particularly relevant to the chapters in Part 3 of this volume:

Chapter 4.   See Volume 2: Schutz (7.8), Bales (7.10).
Chapter 5.   See Volume 1: Broderick (7.3)
          See Volume 2: The whole of Chapter 2, Randall and Southgate (7.7).
Chapter 6.   See Volume 1: Newcomb (5.3), Zimbardo (9.4). See Volume 2: Janis (1.2), the whole of Chapter 2, Randall and Southgate (7.7).

4 Experiential and Self-Help Groups

nall Groups and Social Interaction, Volume 2
dited by H. H. Blumberg, A. P. Hare, V. Kent and M. Davies
ublished by John Wiley & Sons Ltd 1983

.1 Experiential Helping Groups*

Martin Lakin   *Duke University, Durham, North Carolina*

People have always utilized groups to comfort themselves, compare themselves
ith others, and sound out reactions to their own feelings. There is nothing
adically new in using groups for such social–emotional purposes. It is a new
eparture, however, purposefully to join together to generate a mutually support-
ve climate and to exchange reactions frankly designed to be corrective. Such
roups are variously labeled 'therapy,' 'sensitivity training,' 'encounter,' 'personal
rowth,' or 'self help.'

People who consider participating in a group experience for learning, personal
elp, or expressive purposes might want to think about how its processes relate to
heir purposes and their social needs. The practitioner may wish to compare group
rocedures. This paper is written in the conviction that it is better to know what
ne is getting into, to choose a group experience on the basis of realistic expecta-
ons rather than fantasies or hearsay. The counterargument that there is a
iminution in intensity or emotional impact and 'second guessing' when
articipants study group processes before participating is now without merit. The
motional intensity of one's responses often does diminish as a result of greater
wareness of the elements of the process. People who have thought about the
roup process beforehand are also intellectually more critical, because they are, of
ourse, anticipating developments. However, the evocative elements of group
rocesses are usually sufficiently powerful to prevent an 'intellectualized'
pproach. Indeed, one becomes emotionally and intellectually engaged in almost
ny of these experiential helping groups.

*Some of this material appeared in different form within the following work: Martin Lakin (1976),
Experiential groups . . .' in J. Thibaut, J. T. Spence, and R. C. Carson (eds.), *Contemporary Topics*
* Social Psychology*, Ch. 15, General Learning Press, Morristown, NJ. Gerald Midgley provided
ne editors with helpful comments for this paper.

Motivations of participants

Experiential helping groups attract individuals for different reasons. Some perceive the group as an express route to greater interpersonal effectiveness. Others wish to have a corrective emotional experience, to fix something themselves, to eliminate disvalued aspects of personality, or to change their 'personal style.' In a general sense the group serves a therapeutic purpose. Learning about group influences on personal responses and facilitating as well as inhibiting factors in group communication, is another goal of participation. A third purpose can be designated as expressive. This last is unique in that its procedures aim at greater emotional expressiveness for its own sake.

Certain processes are common to all types of experiential helping groups (Lakin, 1972). They are: (a) facilitating emotional expressiveness; (b) generating feelings of belongingness, (c) fostering a norm of self-disclosure as a condition of group membership; (d) sampling personal behaviors; (e) making sanctioned interpersonal comparisons; and (f) sharing responsibility for leadership and direction with the appointed leader (trainer, facilitator, or therapist).

While strivings for belongingness, meaning, and effectiveness may take different forms for each member, the conditions for membership are similar for each group. They require the member to:

1. contribute to the shaping and coherence of the group;
2. invest in it emotionally;
3. help move it toward a goal;
4. help establish its norms, and/or obey them;
5. take on some specific role or function;
6. help establish viable communication;
7. help establish a desired level of intimacy;
8. make contributions relevant to others;
9. make a place for each person;
10. acknowledge the group's significance.

Interaction between participants and the group conditions for membership

The form and the substance of an individual's interaction with his group are highly personal. The individual is expected to make a growing emotional commitment to the group while moving through the sequence of meetings. The reward for this growing commitment is increased security in membership and increased responsiveness from fellow members.

Depending on such factors as the type of group one is in, its composition, a person's motivations, and the leader's skills, the effects of his participation could be limited to feeling included, accepted, and transiently valued by others. They could, on the other hand, extend to understanding more clearly how others see one, and they could also include consideration of how one might replace unrewarding ways of interacting with more effective ones.

To be cognizant of the various factors operating on one in the experiential group requires considerable reflection along with emotional involvement. Without intellectual comprehension, the process is solely a matter of emotional pressures. With only intellectual comprehension, the process is sterile. It is thus desirable for participants to experience both emotionally and cognitively; to feel, but also to understand. The achievement of this balance is a difficult but necessary accomplishment if lasting significant benefit is to be realized.

The reader may wish to look ahead to Table 1, which schematizes the ways in which group effects interact with individual needs. The way in which these effects are experienced in a specific experiential group is due partly to the mix of personalities in the group, but also to the set of ideas or the ideology which guides the group as an experience (partly due to the influence of its leader). Let us consider in greater detail some group effects and the kinds of personal behavior they influence.

A. Achieving and maintaining cohesiveness

Group cohesiveness is the collective correlate of personal belongingness and leads to greater tolerance, deeper association, and concern for the other members; specifically (a) it binds members emotionally to a task and to one another; (b) it assures greater stability of the group despite frustrating circumstances; (c) it develops a shared frame of reference that allows for the diverse aims of group members. A negative view of one's belongingness reduces one's participation in the group, but valued membership leads to a greater investment in the values anchored in the group and to greater personal and collective productivity.

B. Conforming to group norms

Experiential helping groups promote expressiveness, warmth, frankness, and the like. These attributes become standards for member behavior. Norms in daily group life are usually taken from the broader society, but in many helping groups the convention is that they evolve more organically, can be revised or re-evaluated, and serve the group's own purposes. They operate as pressures on the member's actions. Presumably, the individual participant, having shared in their formation, or at least nominally accepted them, is committed to those norms. Norms endorsed if not developed by participants signify greater 'ownership' of the group experience and signify the group's 'otherness' from ordinary experiences and its specialness as a therapeutic one.

C. Reliance on consensual validation of personal perceptions

Another group effect is the press toward agreement. People often depend on others around them for their definitions of social reality (Sherif, 1963; Asch, 1951; Festinger, 1954). This is no different in the experiential helping group.

Indeed, especially in an emotionally charged group, each individual gauges the definition of the situation that other participants establish for themselves and compares it with his or her own to establish a personal framework of meaning. These groups typically attach more than usual importance to the assessments of individual participants toward each other and to the consensus process that integrates them. 'Feedback' itself is construed as a type of consensual reaction summary. One must also keep in mind the possibility that a group consensus could be determined on the basis of inadequate data or under the influence of a minority of extreme reactions. How the consensus is achieved and with what consequences for each participant is in itself significant. Ideally, all participants should be able to see themselves in the consensus and evaluate the part they played in arriving at it. This provides a counter to consensus becoming merely a mechanism for forcing increased conformity.

D. The expression of affective immediacy

An experiential group appears to facilitate emotional expressiveness in participants. Whatever else one hears about such groups, their emotionality is the one thing that nearly everyone is impressed by. Indeed, the position of many pioneers of psychotherapy was that the emotionalism of groups was primitive and uncontrollable. Freud and Jung, among others, held that groups were inherently unstable, suggestible, and vulnerable to charismatic leadership.

It is true that in most experiential helping groups hostile or affectionate feelings are evoked relatively easily and are expressed with fewer inhibitions than in other interpersonal situations. Although a freer expression of feeling seems to be thus fostered, other factors in the group militate against emotional 'binges.' For one thing, the unceasing concern for one's standing with others influences the participants to modulate personal outpourings. For another, reactions to their expressions should actually stimulate renewed self-inquiry rather than simple catharsis. Thus, they may ask themselves: 'How shall I deal with my feelings?' 'Can I really say what I feel?' 'Do I really feel this . . .?' or even, 'Would it be better to keep my feelings to myself?' An advantage of group sponsored affect is that 'contagion,' or the rapid spread of emotionality among members, may 'free up' participants who feel constrained about expressing their feelings. There is a disadvantage, however, in that it is also possible that individuals can be made to feel inadequate unless they express group approved emotions. Most people would probably agree that while unblocking the expression of feelings is a desirable development, emotionality 'upon demand' could lead to distortion of one's own real feelings.

E. Group perception of problem relationships

In what sense is it appropriate to talk about an experiential helping group as a problem-solving experience? These groups characteristically deal with problems of human relationships and the perceptions which determine them. To the problem 'How am I perceived?' the individual may be informed 'You come on too strong,' or might be told 'Your pompousness turns us off.' Through discussion of problem behaviors and their effects on an individual's relationship within the group, he or she might be encouraged to try modes of relating that are more adaptive. The assumption is that the problems of interactional behavior must be examined from the fresh vantage point of others' reactions. The experience of feedback provides alternative perspectives, and the differences in outlook may be used to consider alternative behavioral strategies. Although such feedback could lead merely to a change of tactics, it could also eventuate in useful re-examination of basic needs and interpersonal goals and the way one's interpersonal strategies help or hinder in achieving them.

F. Dominance alignments

Hierarchical relationships in real power terms are probably becoming somewhat less clear-cut, and are often sources of interpersonal stress in our society. In the group, members attempt to initiate, to mobilize, and to influence others. Performance of any of these reflects the individual's 'style' and characteristic problems in working with others. The flexibility of the group insures that leadership and influence positions rarely remain static. In fact, they facilitate shifts in who exercises power so that any member can try doing so. Such shifts are, in fact, most often achieved only with the help of leader intervention, since participants typically assume and try to keep positions of power that they are used to. With leader help, however, some flexibility in power ownership can be realized. This is important because often persons complain that they are victimized by institutions, by circumstances, or by people whom they cannot control. For such individuals, the chance to experience themselves as decision makers or power brokers contrasts with their accustomed self-perception as power victims.

It is possible to establish in experiential groups that no person is quite as important as is feared. On the other hand, power seekers must garner support from others, and their influence attempts—involving the giving and bartering of support and sanctions—are open to a group surveillance. In this way, the group demonstrates as well as enacts power and influence transactions of everyday experience.

G. Role differentiation

In a task-oriented group each member performs needed roles according to skills and abilities and in accordance with the mission of the group. In most helping groups the starting point for role differentiation is in personal behavior style. Thus, the roles of initiator, clarifier, harmonizer, and would-be leader immediately become salient in the experiential group. (There are, of course, others depending on the personalities that make up the group.) But the availability of roles does not mean that role interchange among members is easily achieved. This is because participants seek roles they are accustomed to, and because groups as collectives tend to fix individuals in consensually agreed-upon roles, heedless of personal needs or inclinations. Simply put, to characterize a member as 'our blocker,' 'this group's clown,' 'our expert,' or even 'our troublemaker' is to designate a 'constant' in the life of the group and thus to provide some element of predictability about it. It is therapeutically useful for individuals to try out different roles and for the group to permit them to do this without penalty. In most helping groups the distinction of 'task' and 'socio-emotional' roles established by Bales and Slater (1955) is of limited use, because the 'task' itself relates to social and emotional goals. One result is that the participant who gives full attention to feelings and attitudes is in the mainstream, whereas a 'get-the-job-done' task-oriented leader will be frustrated by an absence of conventionally concrete achievements. Consequently, the task-centered individuals feel at least temporarily disadvantaged. Their reorientation toward the unaccustomed realm of feelings is not a simple one, because they miss the role and function to which they have been accustomed in other groups.

H. Movement toward intimate disclosure

Objective 'change' indices following training show increases in levels of emotionality for most participants (Oshry and Harrison, 1966; Lakin et al., 1971). Whether this signifies a fundamental behavior change, temporary accommodation to a situational norm, or simple catharsis is not always clear. Most participants do attempt to be more 'open' with one another. Do these efforts to be open have long-term results? The members of therapeutic and expressiveness experiential groups appear to believe they do, and they push toward intimacy, directness, and expressiveness, each participant being enjoined to intensify this push. However, risk attends attempts to alter disliked behavior patterns. Probably no group succeeds fully in suspending critical judgment or in dispensing with interest in motives. The task in helping groups is not to achieve some absolute standards of revealing but rather greater comfort with greater openness with self and with others.

Table 1 summarizes effects that appear in experiential helping groups and pictures their relationships to personal response alternatives. The intention is to indicate that each group effect relates to personal response tendencies as a pressure, as an influence, and as an opportunity. The individual response alternatives (signifying an implicit range from 'positive' to 'negative') are shown on a line with the related group process. The interaction between process and response, is, of course, singular for each individual and an interaction may have objectively as well as subjectively rewarding or punishing consequences, depending upon the person's group and the interpretation of the person's group experience.

Table 1 Interactions between group effects and individual response alternatives in an experiential group

Group effects		Individual response alternatives	
A.	Achieving and maintaining cohesiveness	A1.	Feeling a part of group, experiencing belonging
		A2.	Losing oneself in group, giving up autonomy in order to belong
B.	Behaving in conformity with group norms	B1.	Awareness of participating in creating group norms
		B2.	Being pressured to abide by group norms
C.	Reliance on consensual validation of personal perceptions	C1.	Reality testing or correcting distortions
		C2.	Sharing illusions of group
D.	Expression of affective immediacy	D1.	Free expression of feelings
		D2.	Feeling inadequate unless expressing group approved emotions
E.	Group perception of problems	E1.	Unblocked thinking
		E2.	Forced to share problems with group
F.	Dominance alignments	F1.	Chance to feel influential
		F2.	Feeling manipulated
G.	Role differentiation	G1.	Achieving role flexibility
		G2.	Type-cast in a role
H.	Movement toward intimate disclosure	H.	Insight into personal blind spots
		H2.	Becoming shaken in belief in self

Following line A, we see that a person may experience the cohesiveness of the group (process A) with a positive response of confident belongingness or a negative feeling of being submerged or overwhelmed. With respect to B, conformity, participants could respond by becoming aware of their part in standard setting and, as a consequence, consciously determine their responsibility to the group; or they could bring their behavior into line with everyone else's by uncritical acceptance of group norms. Similarly, with respect to C, we see that although the achievement of consensus is unquestionably satisfying, there is the accompanying risk that reality could be distorted in order to achieve it.

Consider the range of possible responses to process D, expressing affective immediacy. One might feel liberated; but one could also be caught up in the prevalent emotional atmosphere of the group. Considering E, the group perception of problems, sharing interactional problems could provide perspectives hitherto unconsidered or, if excessively pressured, could heighten defensiveness or produce superficial 'insights.'

F, dominance alignments, could be, as we have seen, among the most dynamic relationships in the helping group. If one considers the range of potential benefits, the most significant one is that no one would remain permanently in a role that is at either extreme, that is, feeling constantly manipulated on the one hand, or able to dominate the group at will, on the other. It could happen, as implied by Table 1 that a negative result occurs, i.e. that one could become blocked. The cause might be the individual's own passivity, the particular composition of the group, faulty leadership, or all three factors.

Group process G, role differentiation, shows the way in which the group promotes greater flexibility in a given role or function, encouraging individuals to try themselves out in hitherto unaccustomed ways. As I have indicated, for its own reasons of security the group may stereotype the individuals and 'role lock' them into a pattern of behavior. This occurs because 'pigeonholing' members simplifies the cognitive problems in defining the group situation.

In regard to process H, movement toward intimate disclosure, one desirable result might be a greater intimacy and a consequent illumination of previously unappreciated aspects of one's effects on others. Such results are, of course, ultimately dependent on whether the group provides meaningful feedback. As we noted earlier, achieving greater intimacy and its consequent disclosures is not without the accompanying risk that the group shakes one's confidence in one's self-perception by virtue of the nature of the feedback that is given in response.

The interweaving of emotional and cognitive elements has advantages from the point of view of the participants. First of all, they find themselves intimately involved, no matter what the group. Secondly, since self-disclosure evokes not only deeper layers of feeling, but also evokes some deeper awareness of interpersonal problems, one is likely to learn new and possibly important things about oneself. The emotional and the cognitive processes are mutually reinforcing. Of course, persons who explicitly seek emotional release are frustrated by an emphasis on learning processes, while those who become involved in learning and thinking about their own interpersonal styles frequently are 'put off' by intense emotionalism. Because it is quite difficult to achieve a productive balance between these processes in the group, it is precisely here that the leader function is perhaps most significant.

The functions of the group leader

All experiential helping group leaders must cope with problems arising from the group context, i.e. accommodate the shifting tensions involving individuals and coalitions within the group. Some of these shifts are extremely rapid and may be confusing to the participant. Each leader has to help participants cope with their responses to him or her as an authority or dependency object. While leaders may 'facilitate' some interactions, they are likely to initiate some as well. The ratio of these two functions, facilitation and initiation, is an indication of how much the nature of the influence exerted is a function of both participant and leader initiatives. In broad ideological terms, many group leaders would agree that leader functions should be counterbalanced by member initiatives so that members can assume increasing responsibility for their own behaviors. Other than those groups that are conducted in an authoritarian way, most leaders encourage members to take on leadership functions or share with them the decisions to direct attention to specific persons, subgroups, or topics. The degree to which this idea is actually realized is dependent, too, upon group composition.

Satisfactions for the leader derive from facilitating growth and understanding in group members, but there are also stresses in this role. At the simplest level, there is strain in keeping track of the flow of interactional data. There is also frustration in maintaining the 'half in, half out' emotional balance, as well as the perspectives and the objectivity required of a leader. (The leader's prototypical position 'on the edge of the group's inner circle' is never tensionless.)

Let us explore leader aims in detail, since they influence how leaders behave. Some leaders favor emotional expressiveness whereas others strive for a balance between emotional and cognitive purposes. These positions are held with varying degrees of conviction about their validity. Some of the differences among group leaders appear to be so ideologically fixed that they are probably resistant to information that might invalidate them. What we can do here is to understand the rationales given for such ideological positions and their significance for what goes on in the group. The kinds of issues raised in a group depend only in part on the group composition and the expectations, wishes, or purposes of participants. They also depend on the leaders' interpretations of their groups' purposes. Thus, it is very important that some leaders stimulate more intense emotionalism than others and that some leaders appear to raise anxiety deliberately among their participants, but that others do their best to alleviate whatever anxiety arises. It seems very likely that such value differences also lead to differences in post-group effects on members.

We can imagine leaders who finish their orienting comments, and then invite the members to try to develop ways of interacting with each other. Their relative passivity generally produces two effects: (1) it becomes clear that non-conventional solutions are demanded for the dilemma of having to create agendas and relationships without guidance or rules; and (2) participants attempt in characteristic ways to ameliorate the structurelessness of the void. For instance, one person suggests introductions, but another may ask each member his motives for coming. A third proposes some presumably shared concern—the mutual strangeness—'to get us rolling' whereas a fourth wants to divide up the time so that each one can talk about his or her 'problem(s).' Meanwhile, a more hostile individual can begin by probing for prospective targets. Rarely is any suggestion unanimously adopted as a procedure. Any of the aforelisted suggestions could be at least partially successful in opening up interactional possibilities. Fundamental and coordinate processes are thus initiated: getting more deeply acquainted and building a common frame of reference, 'our group.' These will combine to serve as context for each person's behavior as a member. (It should be understood that many leader-directed groups and most self-help groups do not follow this model—they may follow prescribed formulae of interaction or ritual. It applies to various forms of helping groups that allow free interaction among members with emphasis upon self and interpersonal awareness and mutual feedback.)

How may we characterize the leaders' facilitative efforts beyond their initial orienting and encouraging attitude? The leader's probe, 'What do you think is going on here?' keeps the group alerted to interactional processes. Sometimes the probe concerns emotional aspects of the experience: 'What are we feeling now?' 'What is the atmosphere in here right at this moment?' 'How do we feel toward each other at this point?' Sometimes an immediate goal is questioned: 'What were you trying to accomplish in that last interaction?' 'I see that some of you shifted around the room—how come?' Sometimes the participants' attention is drawn to a particular condition in the group: 'Can we get clearer on why a person is seen as "in" or "out"?' 'How come everything anybody says in here gets dropped.' Subsequent interventions may be centered on individuals. 'How do we feel about the fact that Irving didn't want to come today?' Emphasis in the early phases is on the group experience; not that personal improvement is ignored, but the primarily collective experience establishes the frame of reference for individual ways of behaving. This common reference is the point of departure for subsequent feedback to the individual.

Feelings of cohesiveness fluctuate with other mood shifts. After a number of sessions participants know enough about each other to have some sense of the role each plays in the group's activities, and members' actions are therefore generally more predictable. With greater intimacy, there is also more self-disclosure. With these developments the leader becomes somewhat more active, sometimes helping individuals face the problems in their communications pattern, sometimes helping clarify issues in a relationship, but always calling for more resourcefulness from the group. Interventions are now as often directed to specific individuals as to the group as a whole. Role problems tend to emerge. Here the leader may attempt to delineate those that are self-induced and those that are imposed by the group. The leader's interventions might be phrased as follows: 'I see that we keep relating to Al as though he were the group's psychiatrist, even though he has pretty clearly said he doesn't want to be. How come?' 'Mary has been telling us that she doesn't feel the same as she did at the beginning of the group, but no one seems to want to hear her. Why is that?' He might try to elucidate intermember problems: 'Don, you and Ted are hinting that there is some sort of trouble between you. Want to let us in on it?' 'Sheila, you said you have "lousy" feelings toward Lucy. Then you suddenly switched away from that. Why?' Investigating the group response to individuals is exemplified in the following intervention: 'We have ignored Bobbie this session. Is that because he said we didn't mean all that much to him last session?'

As a group 'matures' there should be evidence of increasing understanding of underlying attitudes and feelings. For helping groups, a successful experience will be evidenced by progressively less defensiveness and the tolerance of relatively greater honesty. This honesty should be reflected in the personal feedback during this phase. However, the interactions of the group are never solely concerned with feedback, even though feedback undeniably leaves the deepest impression on individual participants.

If the group functions well, the leader's interventions mainly monitor, clarify, or supplement feedback when necessary. If the members have identified with the leader's concerns about constructive feedback, the leader can simply allow the process to flow. Of course, leaders still need to make sure that individuals are not pushed into unwanted feedback and that attention is allocated fairly. In general, the more the members can assume responsibility for these aspects of the experience, the less the leader should find it necessary to intervene. As a rule of thumb, the less active the leader during the feedback phase, the more the participants learn from their own experience. Always, the leader needs to restrain grossly inappropriate or potentially harmful interactions; but mainly helps with bogged-down affective exchanges or elucidates foggy ones.

The leader's activity continues to be concerned with maintaining intermember transactions as the context for the group's development at later stages. To this end the leader encourages ever wider participation and, typically, will have to remind members periodically of distinctions between content and process. In this fashion, skills in understanding the connections between manifest activity and topic and underlying dynamics and feeling are cultivated.

In such ways the members' attention is directed toward how things are being done in the group and the way emotional reactions influence what is being done. It is necessary to highlight these 'process' aspects because of our habitual concentration on 'content.' Once we are aware of these connections and mindful of such distinctions, it is easier for us to grasp how relationships between individual members interact with the group's total development. The context of group membership and the roles of each of the members then form the basis for meaningful interpersonal feedback.

During the later phases of a group experience, the content of discussion almost always becomes increasingly personal, reflecting deepening emotional ties between members. The mode of relating is now primarily, although not exclusively, through feedback. During these final phases of the experience, especially if participants are really managing their own interactions, leaders are faced with even more subtle choices for their own actions. They can fade into the background, or they can become more saliently active in interpreting feedback or elaborating on it. The notion that a group leader simply metamorphoses into being simply another group member (an idea that is sometimes advanced as an ideal outcome in experiential helping groups) is not really an option in professionally conducted groups.

Knowing differences in leader objectives means knowing in a general way what kind of interventions are likely to be made. For instance, a leader who thinks that emotional expressiveness is most important intervenes differently than does one who regards behavior strategies or group roles as more important. At an extreme, each emphasizes behaviors that are likely to be ignored by the other. Participants learn partly from what leaders do and how they act. In this sense, the emotionality a leader expresses (acceptingness, warmth, confrontingness, etc.) will be noted as a meaningful guideline for members. No leader can remain indifferent to this fact of his influence on members' behaviors. Leaders indicate interactions that should be noted and attended to. Further, they influence how these should be considered. When the leader suggests, 'Let's look at what's happening between A and B,' he or she is signaling the group that there is something useful in attending to a particular interaction and, further, that there may be some particularly useful way of viewing the interaction.

Participants see their leader as a symbolic authority figure, and this image almost always activates latent 'transference' fantasies. In practical terms this means that counterdependent persons will resist and resent what a leader says, no matter what, because they typically have problems with anyone in positions of leadership or authority. Others, just as reactively, will regard leaders as having infallible wisdom. Leaders may counter such irrational attitudes by sharing their guidance function with the participants, particularly, as the participants develop progressively greater skills in interacting in the group. It is useful to imagine the leader as observing and acting from a position just outside the circle of interactions, better able to see them clearly by virtue of slight detachment and professional experience, but very much attuned to the actions and feelings within the circle. The leader may take what is going on inside and reflect it in words and with descriptions of feelings the members can recognize. The 'good' intervention reflects an accepting understanding of the main threads of the feelings and actions of the people in the group and this understanding, in turn, encourages further efforts at deeper relating and greater understanding.

The leader and the feedback process

Feedback, the reflection of impressions to the participants by peers, is, as we have noted the most impactful aspect of experiential helping groups. It should take place in a manner that does not provoke excessive defensiveness and in terms that are as clear as possible. The way the leader handles feedback influences the way participants deal with their own reactions to each other. If the participants are able to voice their reactions to the leader and understand the relation between the leader's behavior and their reactions, they move toward being able to do the same with one another.

'Letting it happen' or 'making it happen'

The question of who determines the activity in the group could be put in this way: is the activity predominantly leader or member generated? This is the meaning of the ratio of initiations referred to earlier. Although the answer is rarely an 'either-or' issue, the ratio of leader and member initiatives is a revealing index. Does a leader rely on the group's natural dynamic processes? 'Letting it happen' means the leader acts as though the natural ingredients for corrective experiencing are implicit in the group's situation and that people will naturally express characteristic styles and be able to respond to each other in mutually helpful ways—with a minimum of direction. (Of course, leaders' functions are not completely passive. At the very least, they intervene when there is danger that a member might be hurt; they clarify obscure communications; and they rescue bogged-down or tangled interactions.) Perhaps we can understand this point better by contrasting 'letting it happen' with its contrast, 'making it happen.' In the latter case, the leader not only supplies a model of how the participants should behave but actually directs them in reacting or in experiencing emotion ('Wrestle Harvey,' 'Yell at Juan,' 'Hug Sarah.') Psychodramatically, such direction is successful, because markedly changed behaviors are almost immediately demonstrated. The fact is, however, that behaviors evoked in this way are often 'leader bound,' in the sense that they are perceived to occur by virtue of the leader's unique powers. (Again, highly structured programs, such as some self-help groups, must also be considered as exemplifying a 'Make-it-happen approach —although spontaneous supportive expressions must play some role in them too.)

Were the group a theatrical company, leader 'takeovers' would be unexceptional, for the goal is good performances. To what extent do all helping groups create an essentially theatrical representation of life's problems? The main roles taken by the group's members and the major themes, those of conflict and affiliation, are the classic themes of human interaction. The general trend of its 'plots' may thus be broadly predictable, but different people, different personalities, enact them differently. However, it is just these 'dramatic' variations on universal themes that endlessly fascinate us as human beings. We cannot help but wonder, 'Is A expressing what she *really* feels?' 'Does B *really* feel as he claims?' The boundary between authentic behavior and manipulation for 'effect' is a fuzzy one. For this reason, we are understandably wary about emotional behavior that seems contrived or artificial, even though we might participate in it ourselves. The leader's 'making it happen' must be considered in this light.

Genuineness is especially important to establish and to maintain. If the participants inwardly conclude, 'It's not really me making it happen but the leader, or the "set-up",' the authenticity of their experience may be undermined.

'Directive' and 'facilitative' leaders are rarely found as 'pure types,' but differences in tendencies along these lines develop on the basis of how leaders feel about autonomy–dependency conflicts in themselves and on the basis of competing gratifications from charismatic ('making it happen') and facilitative ('letting it happen') leadership styles. Some conflict is inescapable, because every leader manipulates at times as well as facilitates. Therefore it is essential that what the leader does should be clearly perceived as open to review by the group. Since the patterning of interactional elements is difficult to track, the leader must protect participants against his or her own manipulative tendencies by establishing early that the leader's own behaviors should be as closely queried as any participant's. (Programs of helping groups that rely upon high structure and little spontaneous interaction do not encourage questioning leadership.)

We have alluded to leader preferences. The inner satisfactions and frustrations of the leadership role depend to some extent on the ways in which a person prefers to relate to others. Some, for example, prefer an enduring, intimate relationship with people; they have a special affinity for listening to personal problems, for being on the receiving end of intense feelings, or perhaps for sharing strong feelings with others. Others like the challenge of facilitating interactions between others. They may especially enjoy getting participants to work together or bringing them together in a common bond of feeling. A person who cannot enjoy any of these types of activities will probably not like helping group leadership. In few other professional roles does one have the opportunity (and the demand) to become involved as a helper with such a range and variety of people so quickly. Not surprisingly, a major source of stress for group leaders is the difficulty of attending to and making sense of communications from many people at the same time. Glances, body shifting, and other nonverbal cues demand constant attention, as do the verbal communications to which we are so much more accustomed. Another kind of stress stems from the resentment of members at the leader's probes, for the leader seeks to bring to light concerns that participants are at least ambivalent about disclosing. Impatience resulting from incomprehension will also be channeled into resentment against the leader when participants have difficulty in integrating emotional and intellectual elements in helping groups.

Finally, the leader's protective behavior toward individuals who are emotionally vulnerable or less psychologically aware than other members is yet another source of irritation. Providing protection to a member in a group is a subtle operation at best. Sometimes the protection may be unwarranted; for instance, it can make a participant feel incompetent. A related problem is that attractions or antipathies between leader and individual members often assume exaggerated importance in the eyes of other members. Since symbolically the leader may represent 'father or mother figure,' 'boss,' 'elder brother or sister,' etc., there is always a potential reserve of emotional reactivity in the relationship between leader and participant. To keep this tendency in awareness and to facilitate subsequent understanding of it by the participants is another reason for remaining psychologically at the boundary of the group.

Ethical considerations in experiential helping groups

Ethical concerns have been aroused by instances of haphazard selection, recruitment by misleading advertising and exaggerated claims, and poor leader practices, which may have resulted in psychological casualties among participants. Some of these poor practices have proved to be eliminable simply through greater wariness on the parts of intending participants and sponsoring agencies. Others, however, are not easily resolved. For example, helping relationships with organizations or systems are ethically equivocal where the leader conducts the group experiences and also does evaluations with the same people. A person should do one or the other.

Another egregious problem is that of confidentiality. What about confidentiality? Complete confidentiality cannot be guaranteed in a helping group; the promise that it can comes to constitute a kind of pressure on individuals to behave in terms of a norm of disclosure for the abuse of which there may be no realistic safeguard. Participants are made uneasy by the group aspiration to a norm of complete honesty (complete candor leaves one vulnerable in almost any group). Some must conclude that they have failed in a test of disclosure, or to some extent feel driven to 'fake it' as a consequence. Leaders who insist on a norm of complete candor strain the credibility of experiential helping processes. No such norm is supported by the intuitions of human experience. The more productive issue is really the challenge of how much one can or wishes to trust others, i.e. 'How far do I dare trust these people with meaningful disclosures about myself and my feelings?' The risk and the potential for gain or benefit are then real enough and flow authentically from the interaction of group influences and personal responses.

Risk in experiential helping groups

What are the risks in experiential helping groups? The danger that has been most publicized is that of emotional breakdown. Reports of damaging incidents associated with group experiences include occurrences of incapacitating anxiety, depression, suicide, or institutionalization. One hears different 'casualty' figures, varying with the favorable or unfavorable predisposition of the evaluator toward experiential groups. In only a few cases are the means of evaluation reported. One reported range of 'casualties' extends all the way from .05% to 38% of participants—great variability indeed! (For other comment on possible risks involved in experiential groups, the reader is referred to the special supplement of the *American Journal of Psychiatry*, 1969, **126** (6), 91–107, as well as to Lieberman *et al.*, 1973).

Data collected by Lubin and Zuckerman (1969) suggest that the most stressful level in NTL (National Training Laboratory) training groups, with more or less balanced emotional and cognitive elements, is roughly comparable to anxiety experienced during a college course examination. In general, the number of instances where participants became disturbed was small in relation to the number of participants who actually found the anxiety positively stimulating.

Data collected by Lieberman (1970) and his colleagues (Lieberman *et al.*, 1973) revealed a casualty rate of only .08%, based on over 200 West Coast participants in various types of experiental groups (learning groups, encounter groups, and even leaderless, tape-guided groups), Some negative effects persisted beyond the duration of the experience itself. As it happens the highest casualty rate (14%) occurred in groups led by the most charismatic leaders. They were reportedly very active, highly intrusive, and personally disclosive. It seems that charismatic leadership, while perhaps group satisfying and self satisfying, can also be dangerous to at least some participants' welfare. There is another danger, less dramatic perhaps, but serious enough: it is the trivialization of participants' feelings through coerced production of emotional responsiveness.

Experiential helping groups for whom?

Attributes of persons who profit most from such group experiences have been described before, and present knowledge gives no reason to alter these criteria. They are: (a) a reasonably adequate sense of self and of reality; (b) defenses that are sufficiently permeable and relaxed to allow individuals to perceive accurately what others communicate to them; (c) the ability to convey thoughts and feelings with minimal distortion. In other words, those most likely to profit from such a group are persons capable of learning from experience. Accordingly, groups should reflect real-life complexities and should be based on the premise that the attitudes displayed could not realistically be other than a mix of favorable and unfavorable reactions and feelings. Simple catharsis or unconditional support, by themselves, do not represent the reality in which people live.

One view of experiential helping groups, in the light of ever increasing mobility and attenuating family ties is that they may be useful in preparing people for inevitable temporariness in relationships (Bennis and Slater, 1968). I find such a view uncongenial because of the added instability and stresses it seems to me to bring to bear on already taxed capacities for relating. For one thing, easy access to and egress from relationships is already painfully evident in widespread loss of communual feeling. For another, it seems to me likely that premiums would be placed on dissembling in such 'revolving-door' relating, thus increasing the value of purely manipulative behaviors. If this is so, using the experiential group to develop such skills might produce the paradoxical result that the end product of authenticity-seeking group experiences would be a technology of emotionality—a grotesque irony in view of the centrality of authenticity in the purposes of the helping group movement.

Looking to the future of helping groups

The experiential helping group movement is coming of age. It has been widely praised as the greatest innovation since psychoanalysis and just as emphatically criticized as cultistic. A 'coming of age' should be a time for realistically toting up assets and shortcomings as well as estimating the promise for the future. The potential in the helping group lies in the possibility that human relationships can be improved by means of systematic induction of awareness of what goes on between people, reinforced by actually experiencing and then reflecting on the process. The immediate reward must be the discovery by participants that they gain important understandings of themselves and others from the ways in which their group develops and from learning how to cope with problems within the developing group. The central concern of the helping group movement remains the sharpening of methods of understanding interactional processes. These positive possibilities can, of course, be diluted, even destroyed, by overclaim, poor leadership, or indefensible leader practices. There are encouraging signs that many people want a better understanding of the purposes to which experiential helping groups are applied and the processes by which they achieve their results. Although group interventions are virtually commonplace they are not well understood. A present plateau of conceptualization stands in marked contrast to the constantly increasing uses of groups for psychological helping. This paper is intended as a step toward an eventual integrated conception of experiential helping group processes and their effects.

References

Asch, S. E. (1951). 'Effects of group pressure upon the modification and distortion of judgments,' in H. Guetzkow (ed.), *Groups Leadership and Men*, pp. 177–190, Carnegie Press, Pittsburgh, Pa.
Bales, R. F., and Slater, P. E. (1955). 'Role differentiation in small decision-making groups,' in T. Parsons, R. F. Bales, J. Olds, M. Zelditch, Jr, and P. E. Slater (eds.), *Family Socialization and Interaction Process*, pp. 259–306, Free Press, Glencoe, Ill.
Bennis, W. G., and Slater, Philip E. (1968). *The Temporary Society*, Harper and Row, New York.
Festinger, L. A. (1954). 'Theory of Social Comparison Processes,' *Human Relations*, 7, 117–140.
Lakin, M. (1972). *Interpersonal Encounter: Theory and Practice of Sensitivity Training*, McGraw Hill, New York.
Lakin, M., Lomranz, J., Schiffman, H., Thompson, L., and Thompson, V. D. (1971). *Personal Change and the Group Laboratory Culture*, Unpublished manuscript.
Lieberman, Morton A. (September 1970). *Human Relations Laboratory Training: A Critical Evaluation*, Symposium, American Psychiatric Association.

Lieberman, M. A., Yalom, I., and Miles, M. B., (1973). *Encounter Group: First Facts*, Basic Books, New York.
Lubin, B., and Zuckerman, M. (1969). 'Level of emotional arousal in laboratory training,' *Journal of Applied Behavioral Science*, 5, 483–490.
Oshry, B. I., and Harrison, R. (1966). 'Transfer from here-and-now to the there-and-then: Changes in organizational problems diagnosis stemming from T-group training,' *Journal of Applied Behavioral Science*, 2, 185–198.
Sherif, M. (1963). *The Psychology of Social Norms*, Harper, New York.

Small Groups and Social Interaction, Volume 2
Edited by H. H. Blumberg, A. P. Hare, V. Kent and M. Davies
Published by John Wiley & Sons Ltd 1983

4.2   Self-Help Groups: Types and Psychological Processes*

Leon H. Levy   *University of Maryland—Baltimore County*

Although the evidence for their effectiveness rests largely upon testimonials, it seems clear that self-help groups have become a salient feature of the contemporary human services scene. . .

The difficulties entailed in the evaluation of the effectiveness of self-help groups are serious, if not insuperable. Few, if any, groups make any kind of systematic attempt to assess their effectiveness or keep records. . . . These problems become further compounded when dealing with other groups because of their frequently ephemeral existence and the variability in how different chapters of the same organization function. Moreover, most active members of self-help groups seem to find questions about their group's effectiveness difficult to comprehend—they *know* their group works—so it is difficult to enlist their cooperation in the kind of systematic effort that would be necessary to satisfy scientific standards.

Even though we may be unable to assess satisfactorily their effectiveness, however, the fact that self-help groups exist and continue to flourish suggests that they must either be meeting, or be seen as meeting, the needs of their members. Thus, for this reason alone they would seem to merit serious study. But additionally, because self-help groups tend to be pragmatically oriented and relatively free of the theoretical dogma to which most professionals are bound, it seems reasonable to assume that the techniques and approaches found to be used

* The research upon which this paper is based was supported by National Institute of Mental Health Research Grant MH24961. I wish to thank Ronald Curry, Robert Durham, Andrea Klein, Robert Knight, Valerie Potts, and Richard Wollert who served as research assistants and contributed materially to all aspects of the research. I would also like to express my gratitude to Dr Sandra Levy for her encouragement and helpful insights.
Reproduced by special permission from *The Journal of Applied Behavioral Science*, 'Self-Help Groups: Types and Psychological Processes,' by Leon H. Levy, Volume 12, Number 3, pp. 310–322, copyright 1976, NTL Institute. (Abridged by agreement with the author.)

by them are likely to be those which have proven their effectiveness in the hands of laymen, or, at the very least, are acceptable to them as ways of dealing with their problems. And to the extent that this is true, the study of the activities of these groups holds the promise of leading to improvements in professional practice as well as enhancing the natural support systems that exist in everyday life.

The study

This paper presents a preliminary report of our speculations on the psychological processes involved in the activities of self-help groups. These speculations are based upon observations made while attending meetings of various kinds of self-help groups, a scanning of the literature which these groups either publish or draw upon in their activities, and a review of the growing body of research and theoretical literature on such groups.

The study was limited to groups that dealt with problems which had a significant psychological component, either in explanations of the nature of the problem, such as alcoholism and child abuse, or in the possible concomitants or consequences of the problem, such as being a single parent or being terminally ill. Admittedly, the boundaries established by these criteria become faint and questionable in many instances. . .

Definition of a self-help group

Our working definition of a self-help group was one that satisfied the following five conditions:

1. *Purpose.* . . . to provide help and support for its members in dealing with their problems and in improving their psychological functioning and effectiveness.
2. *Origin and sanction.* . . . rest with the members of the group themselves, rather than with some external agency or authority.
3. *Source of help.* . . . relies upon its own members' efforts, skills, knowledge, and concern as its primary source of help, with the structure of the relationship between members being one of peers, so far as help-giving and support are concerned . . . professionals, [if any,] . . . are . . . in an ancillary role.
4. *Composition.* . . . members who share a common core of life experience and problems.
5. *Control.* . . . structure and mode of operation are under the control of members. . .

Method and sample

Our procedure in working with a group begins with an initial contact in which the purposes of our study are described and their cooperation is solicited. Complete confidentiality is assured the group. Where possible, two observers attend meetings of the group as nonparticipants. No notes or recordings are made at meetings since we learned early in our study that many groups felt that these activities would make their members feel uneasy. Immediately following each meeting, the observers prepare a report which consists of two parts: a narrative description of the meeting and a speculative analysis of the dynamics and processes operative during the meeting. After having attended anywhere from two to eight meetings, ... the observers then solicit either interviews with group members or distribute detailed questionnaires which group members are requested to complete anonymously and return in a self-addressed, stamped envelope. (The interview and questionnaire data will not be reported on in this paper.) The interviews and questionnaires cover the same topics and are concerned with group *members' attitudes toward the group, descriptions of how the group operates, the extent to which certain methods are used by the group, and what the respondents believed was most and least helpful in the group meetings.* ...

Variations in this procedure were necessary in several instances. ...

This report is based upon our observations of the following groups. ..

Type I (objective is conduct reorganization or behavior control): Two chapters each of Alcoholics Anonymous (AA), Take Off Pounds Sensibly (TOPS), and Parents Anonymous (PA), and one chapter of Overeaters Anonymous (OA).

Type II (members share a common status or predicament entailing some stress): Al-Anon, Emotions Anonymous (EA), Make Today Count (MTC), Parents Without Partners (PWP), and Recovery, Inc.

Type III (survival oriented—people whom society has either labeled deviant or discriminated against): A women's consciousness-raising group sponsored by the National Organization of Women (NOW).

Type IV (personal growth, self-actualization, and enhanced effectiveness): Two unaffiliated women's support groups, one chapter of La Leche League.

This listing by type is tentative and is not necessarily mutually exclusive. ..

Results

General observations

The most striking fact about the groups we observed was their variability and diversity of approach. For example, we found that among nationally organized self-help groups, the meetings of two different chapters were conducted similarly in some cases and very differently in others. ... While most groups' meetings were marked by a high degree of freedom of expression among their participants, those conducted by Recovery, Inc. were very formalized and controlled. Some groups had their own jargon and some did not. The meetings of most groups were led by their members; but those of a few, such as Parents Anonymous and Make Today Count, involved some form of shared leadership between their members and professionals. Different members appeared to perform clearly defined roles in some groups, while role differentiation was impossible to discern in others. The meetings of some groups appeared to be well organized and marked by a high decree of member involvement, while those of others could be best described as desultory. Thus, we are convinced that it would be extremely hazardous to make any unqualified generalizations about self-help groups, either with respect to their mode of functioning or their effectiveness.

Two other observations are worthy of note. The first is that the membership of most groups cuts across the various demographic dimensions along which social groups are usually divided. . . . The other observation of interest is that, with the exception of AA, the membership of all the other self-help groups was either exclusively or predominantly female. . . . Apparently, cultural factors have conspired to prevent men from affiliating with self-help groups. Since it seems unlikely that the problems with which these groups deal are any less prevalent among men than among women, either men are less able to publicly admit their need for help or they do not regard self-help groups as likely to be effective in meeting their needs.

Processes

In searching for formulations of genotypical processes which would account for the diversity of activities and methods we have observed in self-help groups, and which might also account for whatever effectiveness these groups might have, we attempted, insofar as possible, to avoid any theoretical preconceptions. Thus, we have been led to postulate the operation of 11 processes. Their functioning in any given group might take a variety of different forms, and we do not claim that they are all operative in all groups. Indeed, we would expect their presence to vary with the type of group, as will be apparent from their description below. Together, however, we believe that these processes may provide new insights into the helping process itself, which may transcend the differences between professional and nonprofessional, peer self-help approaches, as well as between individual and group approaches to intervention.

Processes with a behavioral focus. . .

1. *Both direct and vicarious social reinforcement for the development of ego-syntonic behaviors and the elimination of problematic behaviors.* The praise, applause, and sometimes tangible token rewards used by such groups as TOPS are the most obvious examples of the operation of this process. At the beginning of each TOPS meeting all members weigh in and their gains and losses in weight are announced to the whole group. . .

Viewed in its broadest sense, reinforcement is inherent in all social interactions. What makes it worthy of note in understanding self-help groups is that its use is focused and guided by the purposes of the group and its conceptualization of members' problems and the appropriate way of dealing with them. Moreover, its effects are likely to be more potent as membership itself in the group becomes rewarding, as it frequently does. . . .

2. *Training, indoctrination, and support in the use of various kinds of self-control behaviors.* This includes requiring members to monitor their own behavior and advice as to how and what they can do to control the problematic behavior or avoid situations likely to cue the behavior. . . . Research on cognitive dissonance suggests that this process may also be aided by the various kinds of public commitment rituals used by many groups regarding control over problematic behaviors and the initiation of desirable behaviors.

3. *Modeling of methods of coping with stresses and changing behavior* . . . this process may be found operating in the testimonial portions of meetings of many self-help groups . . . and in part it operates simply through the sharing of experiences. . . . A discussion at a PWP meeting in which several members told the group how they dealt with feelings of loneliness by writing letters to relatives or calling a friend whenever they felt 'down' illustrates modeling.

4. *Providing members with an agenda of (and rationale for) actions they can engage in to change their social environment.* Most typically found in Type III groups, such as Gay Liberation, this process was also found operative to some degree in some of the discussions of one of the PA groups studied by us and in one of the women's support groups. This process operates in two ways to aid individuals in distress: first, it externalizes the source of their distress, and second, it can result in an actual modification of their social environment so that it is more supporting and less stressful. . . . The relief a woman might gain, for example, from learning that her feelings of inadequacy are a consequence of the social and political arrangements of our male-dominated society rather than a reflection of some internal, psychological deficit of her own, cannot be underestimated—nor should the possible social and political changes that may occur as a result of this. At a less dramatic level, a mother in a PA group who follows the group's suggestion that she arrange for a baby-sitter to come in for 2 hours each day so that she can have some time for herself, away from her children, also illustrates the effects of this process.

Processes with a cognitive focus. . .

1. *Providing members with a rationale for their problems or distress, and for the group's way of dealing with it, thereby removing their mystification over their experiences and increasing their expectancy for change and help.* The truth value of this rationale is of less importance than is its acceptance by group members as a framework within which they can see order and change as possibilities where previously they were experiencing only chaos and a sense of fixity—a sense of

being trapped. Thus, for example, while the AA view of alcoholism and its treatment may be lacking in firm scientific support, and while professionals might find much of the Recovery, Inc. way of talking about emotional problems rather quaint, the important thing is that in both instances, for members who subscribe to them, they seem to provide an effective rationale for understanding their problems and for dealing with them. Groups vary . . . but we have found no group in which some kind of rationale could not be found, albeit at a very implicit level in some instances.

2. *Provision of normative and instrumental information and advice* . . . this, we believe, may be one of the most important functions served by group meetings . . . also one of the most prevalent.

3. *Expansion of the range of alternative perceptions of members' problems and circumstances and of actions which they might take to cope with their problems.* . . .

4. *Enhancement of members' discriminative abilities regarding the stimulus and event contingencies in their lives.* The report of a woman at a PA meeting in which she said that one thing that had helped her feel more secure was recognizing finally that her present husband was not like her previous one, who had been unreliable and brutal, is an example of the operation of this process. Another was a discussion in a women's support group about when it is appropriate to ask your husband for help. As group members attempt to understand and analyze one another's experiences—in a way frequently amounting to a functional analysis of the matrix of events in which their problems appear to be embedded—they begin to develop better analytic and discriminative abilities, thereby making it possible for them to gain better control over their behaviors and environment.

5. *Support for changes in attitudes toward one's self, one's own behavior, and society.* . . .

6. *Reduction or elimination of a sense of isolation or uniqueness regarding members' problems and experiences through the operation of social comparison and consensual validation.* . . . The sense of community that results from this process is not only intrinsically rewarding but it also serves to enhance the group's influence over its members, as studies in the relationship between group cohesiveness and influence have shown (Bednar and Lawlis, 1971; Lott and Lott, 1965). We believe that the emphasis on self-disclosure so central to many self-help groups operates in the service of this process, as does the very knowledge that the group itself is composed of others who share a common problem and a common purpose. The recitation of the Twelve Steps in AA meetings and in those of other groups patterned after AA may also be seen as a ritualized way of furthering this sense of community.

7. *The development of an alternative or substitute culture and social structure within which members can develop new definitions of their personal identities and new norms upon which they can base their self-esteem.* Although perhaps most obvious in self-help group communities such as Synanon, this process appears to

be operative to some degree in all groups, self-help and otherwise. Many of the members of self-help groups are suffering from what Goffman (1963) has called 'spoiled identities,' among other things. Whether branded as a mental patient, an alcoholic, or a child-abusing parent, the group provides members an opportunity to build a new identity, and hence, a new base from which they can face the world and their predicaments. This would seem to be particularly fostered through the operation of the 'helper principle' (Riessman, 1965), as a group member begins to find himself or herself in the role of helping a fellow member, as well as by the various milestones and offices which members achieve as they begin to cope successfully with their problems.

Although some of the changes that occur in members of self-help groups are clearly emotional, we have not found it necessary to postulate any processes which are specifically emotional in nature. . . .

Discussion: an integrative theory of intervention

There appears to be some degree of convergence between the processes we have described and those posited by other writers on self-help groups (Caplan, 1974; Hansell, 1975; Hurvitz, 1970, 1974; Katz, 1970; Trice and Roman, 1970). While such convergence is reassuring, the ultimate test of the utility of any theoretical formulation rests in the increased understanding it provides and in the empirical and practical implications that follow from this understanding.

Of the processes we have described, we may expect to find that some function most effectively within group settings, while others may function most effectively in the context of dyadic, professionally conducted psychotherapy. For example, it may be found that a professionally trained therapist in a dyadic exchange process may be more effective than any kind of group in helping individuals improve their discriminative abilities, while self-help groups are more effective than either individual therapy or professionally conducted psychotherapy groups in providing individuals with new bases upon which to rebuild their personal identities and improve their self-esteem. Thus, we believe that the evaluation of all the forms of psychological intervention in terms of the efficacy of the various processes found to be operative in them may provide the basis for an overarching integrative theory of intervention. Such a theory would allow for the selective and most effective use of all the modes of intervention available, and the most effective use of professional manpower possible.

As further research confirms and makes more precise our formulations of the processes operating in self-help groups, we see two other purposes to which they may be put. First, it seems conceivable that while it may never be possible to rigorously evaluate the effectiveness of intact self-help groups, some assessment of their effectiveness might be possible through the use of laboratory group analogues in which the effectiveness of each of the processes could be evaluated in terms of the functions they are presumed to serve. This would then make it possible to assess the effectiveness of any particular self-help group in terms of how effectively it implements those processes deemed necessary to achieve its purposes.

Secondly, it would seem possible that with further research, guidelines or manuals could be developed which would specify how groups should be structured and operated so as to facilitate the functioning of any particular set of processes. It may be, for example, that for certain types of groups (possibly Type I groups) the development of an explicit and detailed set of precepts to which members are asked to commit themselves in joining the group is very important, while for other types of groups (possibly Type IV groups) it is of less importance. Such guidelines could be used by laymen who wish to form a self-help group as well as by professionals who could serve as consultants to those who wish to establish or improve the effectiveness of their self-help groups.

We embarked on the study of self-help groups because we saw them as a potentially important mental health resource and we believed that they might help further our understanding of the fundamental nature of the helping process. While our observations have led us to believe that their effectiveness in helping their members is quite variable, it seems likely that this is not any more so than it is for other modes of intervention. Thus, while some of the hyperbole which has characterized many discussions of self-help groups may not be justified, our analysis of their functioning suggests that they may have a distinctive contribution to make to the mental health of our society. Therefore, efforts made to enhance their effectiveness and to determine how they might be integrated into a comprehensive mental health delivery system clearly seem justified.

Regarding the light that they might shed on the helping process, we would propose that the fact that the processes we have described as being operative in them are not unique to self-help groups gives them a certain degree of convergent validity. No doubt, additional processes will be necessary to comprehend all the activities engaged in by the entire gamut of modes of psychological intervention. But it would seem reasonable to assume that those processes which are found to be the most prevalent throughout all the modes of intervention are among the most fundamental. Thus we believe that with further refinement, the processes described in this paper may provide the foundation for a general theory of psychological intervention, with various modes differing in how these processes are implemented as well as in the operation of one or more processes unique to each mode.

References

Bednar, R. L. and Lawlis, G. F. (1971). 'Empirical research in group psychotherapy,' in A. E. Bergin and S. L. Garfield (eds.), *Handbook for Psychotherapy and Behavior Change*, pp. 812–838, Wiley, New York.
Caplan, G. (1974). *Support Systems and Community Mental Health*, Behavioral Publications, New York.

Goffman, E. (1963). *Stigma: Notes on the Management of Spoiled Identity*, Prentice-Hall, Englewood Cliffs, NJ.

Hansell, N. (1975). *The Person in Distress*, Behavioral Publications, New York.

Hurvitz, N. (1970). 'Peer self-help psychotherapy groups and their implications for psychotherapy,' *Psychotherapy: Theory, Research, and Practice*, 7, 41–49.

Hurvitz, N. (1974). 'Peer self-help psychotherapy groups: Psychotherapy without psychotherapists,' in Paul M. Roman and Harrison M. Trice (eds.), *The Sociology of Psychotherapy*, Jason Aronson, New York.

Katz, A. H. (1970). 'Self-help organizations and volunteer participation in social welfare,' *Social Work*, 15, 51–60.

Lott, A. J., and Lott, B. E. (1965). 'Group cohesiveness as interpersonal attraction: A review of relationships with antecedent and consequent variables,' *Psychological Bulletin*, 64, 259–309.

Riessman, F. (1965). 'The "helper" therapy principle,' *Social Work*, 10, 27–32.

Trice, H. M., and Roman, P. M. (1970). 'Delabeling, relabeling, and Alcoholics Anonymous,' *Social Problems*, 17, 538–546.

Small Groups and Social Interaction, Volume 2
Edited by H. H. Blumberg, A. P. Hare, V. Kent and M. Davies
Published by John Wiley & Sons Ltd 1983

4.3   Some Suggested Rules for Confrontation*

Gerard Egan   *Loyola University of Chicago*

In summary, the following rules may help to make confrontation in the group a constructive process:

1. Confront in order to manifest your concern for the other.
2. Make confrontation a way of becoming involved with the other.
3. Before confronting, become aware of your bias either for or against the confrontee. Don't refrain from confrontation because you are for him or use confrontation as a means of punishment, revenge, or domination because you are against him. Tell him [or her] of your bias from the outset.
4. Before confronting the other, try to understand the relationship that exists between you and him, and try to proportion your confrontation to what the relationship will bear.
5. Before confronting, try to take into consideration the possible punitive side effects of your confrontation.
6. Try to be sure that the strength or vehemence of your confrontation and the areas of sensitivity you deal with are proportioned to the needs, sensitivities, and capabilities of the confrontee.
7. Confront behavior primarily; be slow to confront motivation.
8. Confront clearly: indicate what is fact, what is feeling, and what is hypothesis. Don't state interpretations as facts. Don't engage in constant or long-winded interpretations of the behavior of others.
9. Remember that much of your behavior in the group, such as not talking to others, or expressing a particular emotion, can have confrontational effects.

10.   Be willing to confront yourself honestly in the group.

No set of rules will provide assurance that confrontation will always be a growth process in the sensitivity-training group. But groups can learn much from both the use and abuse of confrontation.

Small Groups and Social Interaction, Volume 2
Edited by H. H. Blumberg, A. P. Hare, V. Kent and M. Davies
© 1983 John Wiley & Sons Ltd

4.4 Comparative Analyses of Change Mechanisms in Groups*

Morton A. Lieberman   *University of Chicago*

Most accounts of how people find something of value to take away from group treatment are attributed to a limited set of discrete events and/or experiences. If we were to station ourselves outside the doorway of a psychotherapeutic group meeting, an encounter session, a women's conciousness raising group, or a group of widowers who belong to a mutual aid group, what would we hear as they left the session? A goodly proportion of those interviewed would tell us, in a variety of languages associated with a particular type of group, that something positive had occurred. If we inquired about the ways they had been helped, we would in all likelihood hear such words as 'I felt accepted for the first time in my life;' 'I was able to say things about myself that I had never told anyone else before; 'I finally understood what was bothering me and how it was I came to have such a difficulty;' 'I found people really understood my problem;' 'I reached out to others and they didn't move away from me;' 'I saw things in a new light;' 'I was able to get all of those angry feelings out.' Rarely would we hear a participant state that 'although I feel I am better, I am not sure what happened or how it is I came to feel better.'

Is this simple linkage by group participants between their felt change and their reports about the nature of the group learning context more than a common-sense labeling to reduce ambiguity? We rarely question the meaning of such linkages, taking them at face value as representing an important if not crucial perspective for understanding change procedures.

*Studies referred to in this paper were supported by: University of Chicago Cancer Control Center (PHS #3, R18-CA1640-0151); National Institute of Mental Health (Self-Help and Urban Problems: Alternative Help Systems, PHS #5, R01-MH30742); and a Research Scientist Award (Processes and Outcomes of People-Changing Groups, #1, K05-MH20342).

This paper critically reviews the findings from a series of 'change mechanisms' studies conducted by the author. Considered are methodological perspectives on data generation, as well as the effects of group contexts on client perceptions of beneficial mechanisms. In addition, I will examine change mechanism research from an epistemological perspective in order to test the limits of perceptually derived data for developing a change processes theory.

Interest in the characteristics of change mechanisms was apparent at the very beginning of systematic group treatment. During the 1950s Corsini and Rosenberg (1955) published the seminal paper on change mechanisms. Rather than our example of the researcher in the hallway, Corsini and Rosenberg raised the same question with professionals who conducted and theorized about group psychotherapy. Long lists of items were produced, from which a limited set of middle level abstractions were generated. The categories have remained remarkably stable—concepts such as altruism, universality, insight, catharsis, feedback are still the prime ideas that appear with an unending regularity in theoretical treatises, empirical studies, and everyday conversation of psychotherapists. The correspondence between theory, our experience as psychotherapists, and patients' reports reinforce the 'correctness' of such a view. We are at peace because our common-sense perceptions of the therapeutic world make theoretical sense and are echoed in the perception of those who are recipients of our treatment.

Problems of studying therapeutic mechanisms

The critical choice facing investigators is whether to use an external or internal frame of reference. They might choose to gather information relevant to change mechanisms by observing group participants, or they may choose to inquire directly about participants' personal experiences. Several considerations are worth noting. An external perspective provides a sensitive indicator of behaviorally imbedded transactions. For example, information exchanges leading to insight or perspective building can only reflect attempts by others in the group to provide such information. The observations cannot directly assess insight or the development of a participant's altered perspective. What observations can do best is to assay sensitively both the intensity and frequency of certain classes of interactive and self-behavior. If the investigator's hypotheses include notions that how often a thing happens is critical, then there is no question but that the observational mode is the method of choice.

Many of the events and experiences reflective of therapeutic mechanisms are not, however, behavioral. For example, universality expressed in terms of finding out that there are many others like oneself; learning that one's problems, feelings, and fears are not unique represents a state of mind and cannot be specifically linked to particular behaviors. Even for some behaviorally linked events, such as self-revelation, the indexing of this event may ultimately rest on the phenomenological set and not the observational one. Although often trivialized by experienced groupies who are past masters at revelations that have been practiced frequently, what is revealed is not specific information but rather the sense that the individual has said something or is able to say something that heretofore was hidden. Such consideration as well as the difficulty and cost involved in observations has led most investigators studying therapeutic mechanisms to a phenomenological approach.

Influences on change-mechanisms reports

Although phenomenological data can be developed quickly, are low cost compared to observations, and more adequately reflect the range of mechanisms that have been theoretically linked to change, they have their pitfalls. Lieberman has shown (Lieberman and Borman, 1979) that participants' reports of beneficial therapeutic mechanism were influenced by: the group therapist/leader; the group's ideology; specific properties general to all small face-to-face intensive groups; the complaint or affliction that brings the patient to a helping group; and finally, general societal values and beliefs about help. Information about change mechanisms was developed from comparisons among various group systems: group psychotherapy, encounter groups, conciousness-raising groups, and self-help groups.

The pronounced source of influence was that of professional leaders. Despite differences in ideology between formal group psychotherapy and encounter groups, these two settings shared remarkably similar respondent reports of helping experiences and events that sharply contrasted to those reported by participants in settings not containing professional leaders, such as conciousness-raising and self-help groups. Therapists of widely diverse theoretical persuasions appear to emphasize events and experiences that are under their control. We found that the provision of insight or other cognitive processes, feedback, the encouragement of the expression and experience of strong affect, self-disclosure and experimentation—are the common elements stressed by therapeutic and encounter group theory. Events and experiences reflecting these emphases appeared in the top reported items that patients reported were characteristic of their learning experience. They are subject to specific leader interventions, in contrast to, e.g. altruism which is not associated with a specific intervention. Evidence was found, although not with the same order of certainty, that ideological beliefs associated with particular self-help groups influenced the change events participants stress.

Beyond these influences, certain conditions characteristic of all intensive, change-oriented, small face-to-face groups have a profound influence on experiences reported as helpful. Individuals enter such settings in a high state of personal need and are required to share with others information and feelings that are ordinarily considered personal and private. Each participant is immediately faced with a number of strangers, frequently dissimilar to themselves except for one critical characteristic—the shared status of being a patient in a psychotherapy group, the shared societally devalued role or status in a conciousness-raising group, or the shared affliction in a self-help group. The basic group requirement is to share something personal, no matter how banal, about the real or perceived similarity of their suffering, whether it be behavior, roles, life crises, or the need for growth or change. The enactment of this requirement leads to high levels of cohesiveness, experienced instantaneous similarity, and the common perception that they are different from others outside of the refuge. These conditions—and the manner in which they are expressed in the uniquely created social microcosm of a group whose purposes are change and aid—lead directly to the normalizing and support experiences judged to be so highly useful by all participants no matter the kind of group. The requirement that some aspects of their painful affliction be shared in public leads not only to such normalizing and support experience but, in addition, provides a fertile context for making comparative judgments, a valued 'change mechanism.'

The particular dilemma or problem that brings a person to a group setting appears to influence the processes they perceive as helpful. To illustrate, Compassionate Friends is a setting where individuals who have lost offspring seek solace from this tragedy. Such a loss appears to confront individuals with fundamental questions about their existence and the need for a reappraisal of basic life values. Experiences and events associated with existential concerns occur in chapters of Compassionate Friends and are seen by the participants as a critical change mechanism. We have not observed similar reporting in a variety of other groups, even those professionally conducted by existential-oriented leaders.

These observations—about sources of influence on experiences participants report as being instrumental in helping them learn, grow, change, and obtain relief—call into question the nature and meaning of change mechanism data generated from self-reports. It is well nigh impossible to link phenomenological data with observed frequencies of such events. What then are we, as investigators, studying? Obviously, the reason we have been intrigued for over 30 years with an examination of events and experiences that are proximally linked to therapeutic change is the belief that such events are intrinsic to therapeutics and are not merely the product of particular conditions or influences. The goal has been to develop general theories of what it is about therapeutic settings that produce change in those who participate. This dilemma could be resolved if we were able to link patients' reports of events that were useful with objective measures of benefit. Such a finding combined with information that successful change mechanisms were those influenced by group leaders or group ideology would go a long way in diminishing our disquiet about the nature of the change mechanism data generated through self-reports.

Therapeutic mechanisms and outcome

This strategy was pursued in the Encounter Study (Lieberman *et al.*, 1973). Outcome classification into learners, unchanged, and negative reactions was based upon a wide variety of information: self-reports, third-party reports, therapists' reports, co-participants' reports, as well as a host of psychological tests representing changes (Time 1–Time 2) in attitudes, value orientation, coping styles, self-perception, self-esteem, conceptions of others, measures of inter-personal adequacy, and sociometric status in the group itself. The interested reader is referred to Ch. 3 of the aforementioned study for details. The Encounter Study provided an ideal setting for examining change mechanisms, since it was predicated on random assignment of participants to different types of learning environments created by different theoretical orientations. Included in our study were leaders who conducted Sensitivity Training, Gestalt, Psychodrama, Psycho-analytically oriented, Transactional analysis, Rogerian, Marathon, Synanon, personal growth, and leaderless groups that used a preselected tape program. This diversity was hypothesized to provide a range of therapeutic mechanisms.[1] Theoretical orientations, however, were neither predictive of leader behaviors nor participant experiences, but an empirically devised typology of group leaders did provide a model of leader style.

Our findings were: (1) wide variations in leader effectiveness; (2) some but small systematic differences in change mechanisms among participants under different leader types; and (3) considerable variation in change mechanisms among those who learned, those who remained unchanged, and those who experienced negative consequences. Most of the differences, however, in change mechanisms associated with outcomes are due to the negative change group. In other words, those who learned and those who were unchanged (but not negative) resemble one another on critical change mechanism. Furthermore, the Encounter Group data also reveal that the significant change mechanism differences among leader types are not the same ones that are critical to learning. Groups' differences in mechanisms explain 'failures in learning.'

Thus, our findings suggest from the macro-perspective provided by compara-tive analyses of various group change induction settings—self-help, encounter, psychotherapy, and conciousness-raising groups—that system properties do have a major influence on the type of events or experiences participants report as being useful. When we shift to examining one system, even when theoretical perspec-tives of the leaders differ widely, we are hard pressed to fine precise linkages among specific leader behavior, change mechanisms, and outcome. Leaders' influence on participants' reports of therapeutic experiences appear to reflect generalized expectations about therapy and professionals, rather than the product of particularistic therapist behavior. We were able to show some influence among the various leader types, but these were not the events that were critically related

SMALL GROUPS AND SOCIAL INTERACTION

to productive learning. In short, our findings from the Encounter Study suggest that we can be more articulate when leaders fail (their groups have a preponderance of negative outcomes). Most of the variance in our analyses presented in the encounter study comes from the failed leaders and the failed members.

How can we account for lack of substantive findings? Perhaps the global model of outcome used in the Encounter Study which rests upon the summation of a wide variety of specific change indices makes it difficult to connect mechanisms to outcome. Precision might be achieved if we were to specify particular outcome criteria, and determine whether there is a precise linkage between particular benefit and specific therapeutic mechanisms. This is a question raised in the next study presented.

Before proceeding, it should be noted that a limited set of mechanisms critical for learning could be isolated in the Encounter Study. They were cognitive experiences. Expression of anger, the experience of intense emotions, the receipt of feedback, and self-disclosure in and of themselves appeared not to differentiate markedly between those who learned and those who remained unchanged. Learners were people who could take the role of others, who could step into another person's shoes and feel with him or her, as well as get some useful analyses for their own cases. In short, learners appeared to be people who could maximize their time by rendering more from processes in which they are only indirectly, vicariously or empathically involved.

Testing the hypothesis of invariant relationship between change mechanisms and outcome

Our final study of change mechanisms examines the linkages between a specific type of benefit and change mechanisms. The data for this study were generated from a large-scale study on self-help groups involving several thousand individuals and eight self-help organizations. We chose three organizations for our test. All three organizations involved significant personal losses, widowhood for two of them (Theos and Naim), and child loss by parents (Compassionate Friends) for the third. Contained in a large-scale survey was a 31-item instrument indexing change mechanisms, administered subsequent to at least 1 year's participation. Members were asked how helpful, on a three-point scale, each of the 31 items had been in their learning. Categories representing change mechanisms used to generate the items were: Universality, Support, Self-Disclosure, Catharsis, Insight, Social Analysis, Advice–Information, Perspective, Feedback, Comparative–Vicarious Learning, Altruism, and Existential Experimentation (Lieberman and Borman, 1979).

A single change dimension that reflected a common central issue of participants in each of these three different self-help organizations was selected to assess outcome. After a year's participation in the group, participants were asked to indicate, on a series of scales, the ways they had changed. Separate factor analyses of the responses to this questionnaire for each of the self-help organizations (N's, Theos 491; Naim 187; Compassionate Friends 197) yielded a factor concerned with guilt and anger (low significance correlations, .20 range, were found between this factor and standard depression and self-esteem scales).

A general examination

Initially we examined the change mechanisms of these three rather distinct self-help organizations.[2] Table 1 shows the top ranked and bottom ranked mechanisms, i.e. those items that individuals indicated were very important or unimportant in being of help to them.

An examination of Table 1 indicates a rather remarkable correspondence among the three self-help organizations. The prototypical experience for almost all individuals in these three self-help groups is universality—the feeling that you are with others who have been through the same experience, that you are not unique. We have found this experience characteristic of all eight self-help organizations studied. This simple yet apparently powerful experience is the core to what it is members most value. At a theoretical level it bespeaks normalization, a process influencing perceptions that one's thoughts, feelings, and behaviors are not aberrant or unusual, but rather common to those who have experienced the affliction or the dilemma that brought them into the self-help group. Normalization is probably the prime and most immediate impact that self-help organizations have on their members. Three other mechanisms can be seen in the list of items characteristic of all the loss groups: support, comparative judgment, and altruism.

Equally instructive are those events or experiences that participants perceive as least helpful. Although the correspondence among the three systems is lower than for those items seen as helpful; the expression of strong negative emotions, the revelation of personal material, and the receipt of information or reactions from others (feedback) are not viewed by the majority of participants as helpful. The least helpful items are not a simple product of social desirability. Other types of groups such as encounter, sensitivity training, and to a certain extent, group psychotherapy, when studied in a similar fashion demonstrate that many of these unvalued items were perceived as among the most helpful (Lieberman et al., 1973).

These findings reflected in Table 1 suggest that there is a common prototypical experience in loss-oriented self-help groups. It does not of course tell us about the linkage between such events or experiences and the benefit individuals take away from such groups. To accomplish this we need to turn to our next analyses.

A comparison of high and low learners

Required was a division of our samples into those who showed high and low benefit attributable to the self-help group experience. We chose the aforementioned guilt dimension for this analysis since it represented a common and

Table 1 High and Low Change Mechanism

NAIM		Theos		Compassionate Friends	
Most helpful					
1. Being with other people who had been through the same thing (Un)	89%	1. Being with other people who had been through the same thing (Un)	79%	1. Finding out there are many others who have also lost a child (Un)	83%
2. Finding that I am pretty much like other people (Un)	79%	2. Learning that my problems, feelings, fears are not unique (Un)	77%	2. Being with other people who had been through the same thing (Un)	82%
3. Finding out there are many others who have also lost a spouse (Un)	76%	3. Finding out there are many others who have also lost a spouse (Un)	74%	3. Learning that my problems, feelings, fears are not unique (Un)	80%
4. When I hear others' pain I feel less sorry for myself (Comp)	68%	4. Getting a perspective on my problems (Cog)	69%	4. Sharing thoughts and feelings about my child's death (Un)	78%
5. Learning that my problems, feelings, fears are not unique (Un)	68%	5. Sharing thoughts and feelings about my spouse's death (Un)	67%	5. Getting a perspective on my problems (Cog)	72%
6. Feeling understood (Sup)	65%	6. Reaching out to others in need (Alt)	65%	6. Being able to say what bothered me instead of holding it in (Cath)	70%
7. When I listen to the experiences of others it helps put mine in perspective (Comp)	65%	7. When I hear other's pain I feel less sorry for myself (Comp)	65%	7. Reaching out to others in need (Alt)	67%
8. Reaching out to others in need (Alt)	64%	8. Feeling understood (Sup)	64%	8. Feeling understood (Sup)	64%
9. Helping others (Alt)	63%	9. Being supported and valued by the group (Sup)	64%	9. Knowing that I can call on another member when I am discouraged (Sup)	62%
10. Knowing that I can call on another member when I am discouraged (Sup)	61%	10. Knowing that I can call on another member when I am discouraged (Sup)	63%	10. Helping others (Alt)	62%
		11. Helping others (Alt)	61%	11. Seeing the ways that men and women grieve differently (Comp)	60%

Least helpful

#		%		%		%
1.	Venting my anger (Cath)	15%	Venting my anger (Cath)	20%	Venting my anger (Cath)	30%
2.	Understanding more about the causes of my problems (Cog)	24%	Feedback: others telling me what they think about the way I'm handling my loss (Cog)	32%	Feedback: others telling me what they think about the way I'm handling my loss (Cog)	34%
3.	Revaling things about myself (SD)	25%	Discussing how bereaved spouses are unjustly treated by society (Cog)	35%	Discussing how bereaved parents are unjustly treated by society (Cog)	38%
4.	Feedback: others telling me what they think about the way I'm handling my loss (Cog)	25%	Revealing things about myself (SD)	39%	Revealing things about myself (SD)	37%
5.	Discussing how bereaved spouses are unjustly treated by society (Cog)	28%	Understanding more about the causes of my problems (Cog)	41%	Others helped me face my situation (Sup)	43%

Notes: Un = Universality; Comp = Comparative Judgments; Sup = Support; Alt = Altruism; Cog = Cognitive; Cath = Catharsis; SD = Self-Disclosure important psychological dimension. Each individual in the three populations was given a score based on guilt dimension factor loadings. Those who decreased in guilt defined as that group of people who had scores one standard deviation below the group mean were defined as a high benefit group; those one standard deviation above the group mean, a slight increase in guilt, were defined as a low change group. For each of the three organizations, Naim, Theos, and Compassionate Friends, a separate linear discriminate analysis was computed. We chose this method since it maximizes differences, recognizing that such statistical procedures, without replication, are at best only suggestive. We asked the question: what events or experiences judged to be helpful would maximally distinguish the high and low learners. Table 2 shows the results of this analysis.

Contrasting Table 2 with Table 1 suggests that unlike Table 1 which showed similarity among the three groups, Table 2 shows that the particular sets of events distinguishing those who decreased in guilt and those who increased in guilt are unique for each system,[3] and it would be difficult to state that there is a common set of mechanisms related to guilt reduction.

What can we learn about change processes by examining the events and experiences cited by participants in each of the three systems that maximally discriminated between those who showed a reduction in guilt compared to those who showed a slight increase in guilt? To recast the question for analysis, we asked what unique experiences did those whose guilt was reduced have as participants? I will examine each of three groups in turn. For the widows in Naim (and occasional widower; sex differences were examined as a possible source of variation, none was found) the core experiences associated with guilt reduction were the sharing or revelation of troublesome feelings; normalization, not feeling out of place; and the redirection of anger by externalizing it, by seeing problems as being a product of an insensitive world as well as the more socially acceptable reaching out to others in need. Those change items seen as not characteristic for those who changed provide a clue to the underlying processes. The avoidance of hostile impulses by not venting anger as well as avoiding the aggressiveness implications of social comparison, was characteristic of those who showed no guilt reduction. The conversion of feelings outside of self as well as catharsis in a setting that signifies that their feelings and behaviors and thoughts are normal could certainly be seen as consonant with the general accepted theory of guilt and its reduction associated with spousal loss.

When we turn, however, to the other widowed organization, Theos, and examine Table 2 we find contrasting results. The normalization aspects are certainly there, but rather than the emphasis on expressivity, revelation, and externalization on to objects outside of self, we find an emphasis on cognitive mastery and the use of the group context for experimentation. Certainly it would be possible to see this set of experiences as consonant with some views of guilt, and many professionals in the area would not be uncomfortable with seeing such a set of therapeutic experiences as leading to guilt reduction. The dilemma, for

Table 2 Discriminant Analysis: High and Low Changers

NAIM		Theos		Compassionate Friends	
High changers					
1. Seeing that some things are caused by the insensitivity of others and are not my fault	.36	1. I don't feel like I'm a 'fifth wheel' when I'm at Theos	.47	1. Others helped me face my situation	.68
2. I don't feel like a 'fifth wheel' when I'm at NAIM	.52	2. Reaching out to others in need	.36	2. Others gave me hope	.49
3. Reaching out to others in need	.26	3. Seeing how others coped gave me ideas	.33	3. Revealing things about myself	.43
4. Being able to say what bothered me instead of holding it in	.33	4. Being able to try out new ways of solving my problems in a supportive setting	.31	4. Being supported and valued by group	.34
5. Sharing thoughts and feelings about my spouse's death	.30	5. Finding out there are many others who have also lost a spouse	.23		
		6. Understanding more about the causes of my problems	.23		
		7. Being supported and valued by group	.22		
Low changers					
1. Venting my anger	−.24	1. When I listen to the experiences of others it helps put mine in perspective	−.58	1. Venting my anger	−.42
2. When I hear others' pain I feel less sorry for myself	−.17	2. Getting a perspective on my problems	−.45	2. Expressing sorrow	−.38

researchers, for the development of general principles about change processes, was to find a reasonable explanation why the sets of unique experiences leading to guilt reduction in widowhood groups are so different. Frankly, no reasonable systematic explanation exists so far in our data. As we have described elsewhere (Lieberman and Borman, 1979) the ideology and characteristics of these two widowhood systems are distinct and there is no reason to assume that we should expect similarity in processes given the characteristics of the groups. However, the purpose of this present study was to test the idea that there exists some unique set of experiences that individuals have that can be linked to a specific outcome. The findings on the two widowhood groups would not support such a view, although *post hoc* explanations of the change mechanisms could fit into an understanding of guilt as a dynamic process and 'account' for how experiences could reduce guilt.

Among parents who have lost children, change mechanisms different from either of the two widowhood groups occur. Although normalization is common to all three, critical for guilt reduction in Compassionate Friends are existential considerations: the inculcation of hope and confrontation with the situation. Loss of a child (based on our observations and interviews) in which the losses were unexpected, accident and suicide, was uniformly accompanied by bitterness and fury at society, and the experience of isolation from everyone is a distinct psychological state different from what we have seen among our widows and widowers. Perhaps the dilemma facing those who have lost a child, and the consequent experience of acute guilt and responsibility can best be resolved through the confrontation with the ultimate meaning of their lives. Such a *post hoc* explanation could fit the particular circumstances of this group, but again we are faced with a set of observations suggesting that despite the appearance of such a fit, we are unable to provide reasonable generalizations regarding the linkage between change mechanisms and a specific type of change.

Although, as an examination of Table 2 reveals, the change mechanisms singled out by those who showed guilt reduction are not common across the three systems, at least one generalization can be made. An examination of the entire array of the items (not shown in Table 1 or 2) reveals that those who showed change were more likely to endorse, as being important, a larger number of change mechanisms than those who did not show such change. This finding is similar to the Encounter Study finding that high learners used a wider variety of change mechanisms than the unchanged. The method used in that study, critical incidents, provided after each group session was not open to the same type of bias possible in the self-help study change-mechanism data. In the latter study, the increased endorsement of a wide variety of change mechanisms may represent response bias, i.e. high endorsement of all scales. The Encounter Study data were not open to such potential artefact since only one critical incident was collected per group session.

Given the confluence of these two studies representing different populations and group conditions it seems reasonable to suggest that critical for learning in groups directed towards personal change and distress relief is an encounter with a diversity of change events. Therapeutic change does not appear to be maximized by the idiosynchratic match between an individual's specific group experience and particular events. Rather, it appears as if the sheer number of different kinds of experiences or events that a person will encounter in a change induction group will, on average, lead to the increased likelihood of change. The number of items endorsed as important by those who changed are more than twice the number endorsed by those who did not change.

Discussion

If such observation represents the current reality and our level of understanding of how individuals use a group context for change, learning, or growth, then it certainly could lead to alterations in how we conduct such groups. Therapists or leaders should under this view direct their attention toward maximizing a wide range of events or experiences thought to be therapeutic. In a sense this becomes a therapy of opportunity, attempting to take advantage of as many learning experiences of a different kind that he or she can for each particular member of a therapeutic group. Specificity, as it is usually understood with regard to kinds of experiences for particular types of people becomes less of an issue. Successful therapists from this point of view would be those who are able to create a wide range of learning experiences for patients.

What are the implications of our observations for the study of therapeutic mechanisms? Faced with such an array of findings, the easiest response is to raise the question of methods. The methods question can be raised in two distinct forms. As a question of technical issues: does the particular form of instrument used in these studies lead to artefacts—social desirability, lack of sensitivity of the instrument to the subtlety of change, and so on? The checklist method has been used in a variety of settings, and is open to stereotypical responses. The correspondence, however, with findings generated in the Encounter Study where much more sensitive, specific, and detailed measure was used suggests that technical considerations are not central.

The prime culprit lies in the specific type of data being collected: asking participants, whether it be in a standard checklist or in the more open-ended post-meeting form of questionnaire used in the Encounter Study, is open to powerful contextual influences. The influence of professional leaders or group ideology or the special demands of the affliction may override all other considerations. There may in fact be a unique set of events or experiences associated with change, but given the context of such studies, any approach that relies on the phenomenological data will be shaped more by the context than by the specificity of change. Perhaps participants are fundamentally incapable of reflecting sensitively upon particular experiences they have had in a change context. The subtleties of psychological experiences in a therapeutic setting may be 'pre-conceptual' and our demand as researchers for them to provide concepts flies in the face of their experiential reality. To state this another way, they can only provide us with what we have put in, and therefore what we end up studying are reflections of our own theories.

Notes

1. Two approaches, both relying on participants' perceptions, were used to assess the occurrence as well as the importance of various 'change mechanisms.' At the end of every meeting, each participant was asked to respond to a brief question—What was the most important event for you personally in the group today, and why was it important? The events were coded by raters into 22 different categories based upon the type of change mechanism, who was involved in the event, and what was the person's response to the event. The other major source of data was provided by a questionnaire administered at the termination of the entire series of meetings. This questionnaire assessed the relative importance of 14 different change mechanisms.

The mechanisms explored through the two methods included expressivity of both positive and negative feelings, self-disclosure, feedback, the experience of intense emotions both positive and negative, a variety of cognitive events or experiences—insight, information, and understanding—communion or similarity, altruism, spectatorism, involvement advice getting, modeling, experimentation with new forms of behavior, the inculcation of hope, and the re-experiencing of the group as a family.

2. These three self-help organizations and the chapters in them are distinct. We have elsewhere (Lieberman and Borman, 1979) described the ideology and structure of these three organizations. These three organizations differ in their stated goals as well as in their ideology. Differences were also noted in norms regulating them, the images the participants have of these three organizations, and to some extent the characteristics of the people who join them.

3. The 'predictive power' of the linear discriminate analysis is quite high, correctly identifying 76% of the participants in Naim, 77% in Theos, and 88% in Compassionate Friends, indicating that there are real differences at least in a statistical sense in their perception of important change mechanism between those who benefited, and those who did not. If such perceptions reflect actual experience, those who benefited had different experience in the self-help group than those who did not.

References

Corsini, B. and Rosenberg, B. (1955). 'Mechanisms of group psychotherapy: Processual dynamics,' *Journal of Abnormal Social Psychology*, 51, 406–411.
Lieberman, M. A., and Borman, L. D. (1979). *Self-Help Groups for Coping with Crisis* Jossey-Bass, San Francisco, pp. 194–233.
Lieberman, M., Yalom I., and Miles, M. (1973). *Encounter Groups: First Facts*, Basic Books, New York.

Small Groups and Social Interaction, Volume 2
Edited by H. H. Blumberg, A. P. Hare, V. Kent and M. Davies
© 1983 John Wiley & Sons Ltd

4.5 Person as Group

John Rowan   *Independent Consultant, London, UK*

One of the problems about studying groups is that most of the groups we study are temporary and have little purpose or identity. We get them together for our project, and then they disperse. It often seems to be true that the remarks of Sorokin (1956) still hold:

> The bulk of the groups studied represents incidental, semi-organized collections of students or soldiers, or workers, or dwellers in an establishment (room, apartment, several small houses, factory room, classroom, etc.), or of members of a street gang, and so on. Often the real purpose of researching is not disclosed to the members of these semi-nominal plurels. Instead, they are told some yarn as to why they are gathered together and have to answer the questions or participate in the discussion, and the investigators naively assume that their yarns fool the drafted or semi-drafted participants. Further, this incidental collection of individuals is often made up of complete strangers to one another, quickly corralled together in a pen of semi-organized discussion or interviewing.

This means, of course, that we do not know the people very well. Often we make a virtue out of this by observing only external behavior, but it now seems to me that this is a cop-out, and that we are never going to discover much about groups unless we know more about what is going on inside each of the group members.

As a result of these two problems—unreal groups and external views—many of our theories about groups are not actually very interesting. There is a boring accuracy about many of the recent studies, not to mention the long and uneventful history of Bales, and the whole tedious episode of the risky shift.

Of course one of the difficulties about doing anything different from this is that intact, well-functioning groups are usually too busy going about their own business to put up with researchers, their observations, their apparatus, and their interviewing. It is very time consuming to find such groups and gain access to them. It is even more difficult to get them to make any changes in what they do, for the benefit of the researcher.

It would be good if we could have access to a live group—a group of people with a common task which was real and important to them, who stayed together for a long period of time, with members joining and leaving, members changing under the impact of events, relationships developing and falling away—and the whole thing accessible at any time.

It would be good if this group were always available for experimental interventions to be made into it.

It would be even better if our study of this group turned out to be beneficial—that instead of just using the group, we were acting in a therapeutic way to it.

What I intend to argue here is that all of us have access to such a group. It is inside us, and it consists of our subpersonalities.

In saying this, I am not arguing that we are all abnormal dissociated personalities, as described so well by McKellar (1979); I am talking about people who are as normal as you and me.

It has long been pointed out that the personality can divide itself. Lewin (1936) had this to say:

> The degree of dynamical connectedness of the different parts of the person can be nearly equal within the whole region of the person, or certain regions can separate themselves to an especially high degree from the others and develop relatively independently. This can be observed in the normal person and it seems to be important for certain mental diseases.

Lewin was one of the first social scientists to talk in this way, though William James (1890) had put forward the idea in a rather general fashion. In terms of Lewin's theoretical model, it was quite possible to speak of separations between different subregions of the personality, and the distances between them. After the experiences of the 1960s, this concept of internal distances and the exploration of internal worlds has become a common experience. In the Gestalt therapy of Perls (1969) it is common for one part of the person to talk to another part, and for this dialogue to reveal conflicts and differences which are extremely important for the person.

There has been little research in this area, however. One of the few pieces of work which has been relevant is that by Gergen (1967) who shows very clearly that we modify our self-presentation, and also the way we actually see and experience ourselves, with different people in different situations. We are often quite unaware of what we are doing, and it feels to us as though we are being sincere and retaining our integrity all the way through. As he put it in another article (Gergen, 1972):

> The individual has many potential selves. He carries with him the capacity to define himself as warm or cold, dominant or submissive, sexy or plain. The social conditions around him help determine which of these options are evoked.

It is important to note that Gergen does not say *qualities*, he says *selves*. It is not just a question of different sides of a person, or different aspects of a person coming out, it is a fully fledged personality (what for clarity's sake I call a subpersonality) with a complete set of qualities and characteristics. This is because the attitude brought out by a particular situation or social frame (Goffman, 1974) is an habitual one, not just a one-off thing. It is many years now since Jung (1971) first pointed out that such an attitude could turn into an autonomous entity:

> When a man has an habitual attitude to certain situations, an habitual way of doing things, we say he is quite *another man* when doing this or that. This is a practical demonstration of the autonomy of the functional complex represented by the habitual attitude: it is as though another personality had taken possession of the individual, as though 'another spirit had got into him.'

What Jung meant by a complex was precisely a semi-autonomous system within the person, which could take over at times; the two commonest of these are the mother complex and the father complex. This idea has of course been taken over in another form by transactional analysis; but instead of *complexes* the term *ego states* is used. The most adequate theoretical statement of this idea (Berne, 1961) runs as follows:

> An ego state may be described phenomenologically as a coherent system of feelings related to a given subject, and operationally as a set of coherent behavior patterns; or pragmatically, as a system of feelings which motivates a related set of behavior patterns.... Repression of traumatic memories or conflicts is possible in many cases, according to Federn, only through repression of the whole pertinent ego state. Early ego states remain preserved in a latent state, waiting to be re-cathected.

This last sentence gives us the clue to the power of the subpersonality in suddenly taking over. Berne (1972) later likened it to the way in which a bull stops in mid-arena when the scientist who has implanted an electrode in his brain pulls a switch. He actually calls it 'the electrode' because it can be so dramatic and sudden:

> Many people know the instantaneous turn-off in the midst of sexual excitement, and have observed the smile which turns on and then instantaneously off as though someone in the smiler's head had pulled a switch. . . . The electrode got its name from a patient named Norvil who sat very still and very tense during his group sessions, unless he was spoken to. Then he answered instantly with a string of careful clichés . . . after which he crunched up again. It soon became clear that it was a strict Father Parent in his head who controlled him with the 'sit still' turn-off switch, and the 'talk' button that turned him on.

It is one thing to talk in metaphorical terms about a father in the head—we can all understand that—but another to talk in terms of getting to know this father better, becoming this father and speaking on his behalf, having dialogues with this internalized father. But it is this possibility which has been exploited by the psychotherapeutic school called psychosynthesis. Assagioli (1975) laid out the way in which this could be done, and developed specific techniques for working with these internal people, which he was the first to call *subpersonalities*:

> The organization of the sub-personalities is very revealing and sometimes surprising, baffling or even frightening. . . . Therefore, one should become clearly aware of these sub-personalities because this evokes a measure of understanding of the meaning of psychosynthesis, and how it is possible to synthesize these subpersonalities into a larger organic whole without repressing any of the useful traits.

Assagioli started his work in psychotherapy in 1910, but only became widely known during the 1960s. He started a worldwide organization, which is now strongest in the USA and in Holland and Britain. For a period it produced a journal called *Synthesis*, and in the first issue was published a complete Workbook on subpersonalities, written mainly by James Vargiu (1974). This contains a very good case history of a woman who discovered three subpersonalities, whom she named as the Hag, the Doubter, and the Idealist: in a therapy session which is fully described, she learned what each of these had to offer her, and how to integrate them, instead of having them interfere with each other's functioning.

In 1973 I discovered that I had such a group of subpersonalities inside me. There were six of them, and each had a name, and a separate identity, and his or her own way of looking at the world. After exploring this for some time on my own, I started to wonder if other people had anything like the same experience. (At this time I had read none of the literature mentioned above.) I got together 14 people who wanted to explore this thing with me, and we had a number of meetings.

One of the first things I was interested in was the number of subpersonalities within each person. Elliott (1976) suggests that each person has a dozen or so, and Vargiu says this:

> When people are first acquainted with the idea of working with subpersonalities, they often tend to do just that, becoming so fascinated with uncovering a teeming cast of thousands that the more fruitful work of understanding and integrating the central ones, is neglected.

It was interesting, therefore, to find after our first meeting that the mean number of subpersonalities was 6.5, with a range of from 0 to 10. After 7 years of further investigation, I am of the opinion that from 4–8 is the normal range, and that anything outside this bears traces of insufficient coverage or of duplication. Shapiro (1976) has done a great deal of work in this field since the early 1960s, and he comes to the conclusion that from 4–9 is the usual range—a strikingly similar result. This means that the group is usually of a suitable size for study—neither too small nor too big.

Another thing I was interested in was the question of the origin of the subpersonalities. Where do they come from? One obvious answer, of course, is that they come from the roles which we play. Berger (1966) has made a powerful case to the effect that the person is essentially a sociological phenomenon—he urges a dramaturgical perspective:

> This view tells us that man plays dramatic parts in the grand play of society, and that, speaking sociologically, he *is* the masks that he must wear to do so. ... The person's biography now appears to us as an uninterrupted sequence of stage performances, played to different audiences, sometimes involving drastic changes of costume, always demanding that the actor *be* what he is playing.

This view is now very common in sociology, and it has led to a great increase of interest in the small-scale interactions of social life. And it seems in Goffman's (1974) work that the emphasis is not so much on roles as on the social frames which evoke complete subpersonalities—bringing this approach much closer to those which I have mentioned already. He says:

> Although the pronoun 'I' certainly refers to the speaker, and although certainly the speaker is a specific biographical entity, that does not mean that the whole of this entity in all its facets is to be included on

each occasion of its being cited. For he who is a speaker might be considered a whole set of somewhat different things, bound together in part because of our cultural beliefs regarding identity.

There is clearly room here for a concept of subpersonalities. But it would seem quite wrong to reduce subpersonalities to roles—even habitual and ingrained roles. We have already seen how Jung (1968) has argued the case of the complex, something acquired in many cases in early childhood:

> It is just as if the complex were an autonomous being capable of interfering with the intentions of the ego. Complexes indeed behave like secondary or partial personalities in possession of a mental life of their own.

And more recently the object relations school (Klein, Winnicott, Fairbairn, Guntrip, etc.) have urged that internal objects are extremely important early formations:

> The figures with whom we have relationships in our phantasies are called appropriately, by Melanie Klein, 'internal objects' because we behave with respect to them, emotionally and impulsively, in the same ways as we do towards externally real people. (Guntrip 1961)

So there must be at least these two different sources of subpersonalities—regular roles and personal psychodynamics. But I believe that that there are more sources than this, and have now found at least these six:

*THE COLLECTIVE UNCONSCIOUS. If Jung (1971) is right, this is where the archetypes come from, and the Shadow often seems to emerge as one of the subpersonalities. Anima figures are also quite common. So it seems that we should allow this as one of the sources.

*THE CULTURAL UNCONSCIOUS. This is where the Patripsych comes from, as Southgate and Randall (1978) have described—the 'internal constellation of patriarchal patterns.' They go on to explain:

> By this we mean all the attitudes, ideas and feelings, usually compulsive and unconscious, that develop in relation to authority and control. . . . In general, men tend to internalise mastery and control. In general, women tend to internalise self-effacement and morbid dependency.

This is similar to what Steiner et al. (1975) have called the Pig Parent—an internalized form of cultural oppression.

*THE PERSONAL UNCONSCIOUS. The complexes described by Jung and the internal objects described by Guntrip and others come out as subpersonalities, as well as Berne's ego states and Perls's top dog and underdog. All these seem to derive from early experiences in the family, although as Grof (1980), Lake (1966), and Laing (1976) have pointed out, some of the traumas which can lead to the violent defense of splitting can happen at or before birth. Janov and Holden (1975) have tried to give a theoretical account of this linked to physiology.

*INTERNAL CONFLICTS. Two or more sides arguing within us (on the one hand I want to—but on the other hand—) may become repetitive enough and frequent enough and vivid enough to require an identity each before they can be worked out. Gestalt therapy (Fagan and Shepherd, 1972) and psychodrama (Greenberg, 1974) are full of this—Moreno apparently invented the technique of the 'multiple double' back in the 1920s. The Shapiro and the Vargiu work already mentioned certainly makes use of this category. Literary versions of this go back hundreds and thousands of years—a classic example in modern times is Hesse's *Steppenwolf*. Many examples are collected together in the excellent little book by O'Connor (1971), and McKellar (1979) has a good discussion of Jekyll and Hyde.

*ROLES. Different roles bring out different subpersonalities, as William James (1890) urged long ago. So do different social frames, as Goffman (1974) has outlined. This is probably the aspect which needs least arguing—it is quite obvious in the work of Lewin (1936) and Allport (1937) and many psychologists and sociologists before and since. Merton (1957) has written very well about the social deformation which roles impose on the person, and how 'trained incapacity' can be positively crippling.

*FANTASY IMAGES. We may identify with a hero or heroine, or with an admired group, and take on their characteristics. For example, in the 1970s I frequently came across hippie and revolutionary subpersonalities in the people I was working with. Klapp (1969) has an excellent discussion of how heroes and celebrities are used in a search for identity. These fantasy images may come from the past or future, as well as from the present. Watkins (1978) has shown how the psychotherapist can deliberately set up within himself or herself a fantasy image of the client, so as to be able to tune in to the client better; this is the deliberate setting up of a subpersonality for the purpose of developing resonance with the client. Most of the time, of course, it is not done in this deliberate way, but rather as an attempt to live up to some ideal, which in this case takes the form of an individual. Where a group is concerned, this may become very like the phenomenon of anticipatory socialization in relation to a reference group, as I have outlined elsewhere (Rowan, 1976).

Wherever the subpersonalities come from, however, they seem to interact, once established, as real people in some kind of interaction with the others—forming what the personal construct theorist Mair (1977) has called 'a community of self.' In other words, they form a group. Or as McDougall (1932) said 50 years ago:

I who consciously address you am only one among several selves or *egos* which my organism, my person, comprises. I am only the dominant member of a society, an association of similar members.

Recently Ogilvy (1977) has embroidered very fruitfully around this theme, relating it to broad social questions. It seems very much in the air (see Martindale, 1980).

But the question arises now—granted that the idea of an internal group makes sense, what can we do about it? I do not have any full or final answers to this question, but it seems a fair one, and we can at least make a start in answering it. From my own work in this area, a number of hypotheses have emerged, which seem to be checkable by going back and forth between this internal group and the external groups which are available. Let us just look at a few of them, to see whether this seems convincing.

1. Better decisions are made by bringing out the counterarguments and integrating them, than by allowing one side to dominate, or making some kind of mean compromise. This would fit with the work of Janis and Mann (1977) on decision making, and the more philosophical work of Follett (1941), and with the work on psychotherapy of Rogers (1961) and Perls (1969), as well as with the clinical work on subpersonalities already mentioned. The implications of this would be that one should deliberately look for countervailing viewpoints whenever one decision seems particularly attractive, or particularly unpleasant. This seems a very important hypothesis in the field of professional disillusionment, as Edelwich (1980) has suggested.

2. It is good to have a trained process observer at each meeting, to give feedback on *how* each person was acting and relating to others, as opposed to what they were saying. In this way dysfunctional relations and actions can be raised to awareness and thereby changed. This is fairly well established as a management technique, but as a form of self-awareness it has only been pushed by people like Gurdjieff (Ouspensky 1969) who are not in the orthodox stream at all. Assagioli (1975) and the other people who have worked with subpersonalities often mention the desirability of making deliberate use of a 'chairman' or an 'observer' figure to help with the work. It seems that each could gain from the other here.

3. Cohn (1971) suggested that 'disturbances take precedence' as a rule should be applied in good working groups; the same seems to apply to the internal group. We do better to pay attention to what is going wrong with us and do justice to it fully—feel it deeply—rather than trying to override it and carry on as if it did not matter to us. This idea can be checked out both in the group and in the individual context; or as we have now learned to put it, both in the external and in the internal group.

4. One of the things that seems to happen with great regularity in all sorts of psychotherapy is that people are released from the domination of their 'top dog' or 'superego' or 'critical parent' or 'bad breast,' etc. They do not need an internal autocrat any more. This seems to parallel some of the things which happen in groups, particularly in T-groups—for some very interesting thoughts in this area,

see Mann (1975). But what happens instead? What we need are some really good studies of how leadership changes within the internal group—I do not know of any at the moment. But my hypothesis would be that different leaders would be able to come forward at different times, in quite a healthy way—the person would be able to use the subpersonalities, rather than being used by them. Or it might be that the subpersonalities become much less separate and distinct, and the personality much more unified, along the lines of Jung's concept of individuation. I am slightly skeptical about the likelihood of the latter, because of the very strong social pressures within our very complex culture, which make it hard indeed to avoid some kind of role playing.

5. People in the group change and develop the more they are open to each other and trust each other, as Golembiewski and McConkie (1975) have described. But also in therapy this quality of mutual trust tends to grow between the subpersonalities—certainly this is the outcome of my own research into this area, and I think Vargiu, Shapiro and others would probably concur. Rogers (1961) has for long made the point that one of the major signs that therapy is working is that the person displays more self-trust. This seems to be a theme which could be very fruitfully explored using both the external and the internal group, and going back and forth between the two.

6. In the social world, it is very convenient to give one person one job; this is called the division of labor. But it has been pointed out often that this narrows people (Rowan 1976) and alienates them from their work, from other people, and from themselves. It is a distortion of the human being to make him or her merely a social functionary, and the process also makes it harder for the person to change and develop. A very striking instance of this, to which much attention has been drawn in recent years by the feminist movement, is the gender role. Jung (1959) has suggested that this is also true within the individual—the gender role has been so exaggerated in our culture that most individuals have within them an equally exaggerated representation, at the unconscious level, of the opposite sex; this is the notion of the anima or animus. One answer to this has been the concept of androgyny, as described by Bem (1977) and more recently, in a different way, by June Singer. But there are difficulties with this concept, as Miller (1976) rightly says:

> Likewise Jung's 'woman hidden inside the man' is not the same as its reverse. The idea remains a fanciful notion unless we ask seriously who really runs the world and who 'decides' the part of each sex that is suppressed. The notions of Jung and others deny the basic inequality and asymmetry that exists; they are also ahistorical.

There are at least three things involved in this area: sexual preferences; gender roles; and sexual identity as a man or woman. In order to tease out the very difficult distinctions which need to be made if we are to put right the injustices of the past without introducing cures which are worse than the disease, it seems the idea of going back and forth between the external group and the internal group could be of great value.

7. No one can represent or speak for a whole group. Even if information is gathered from all the members (which is often not done) the focal person still sees things from his or her own angle, and is *parti pris*. This is a hypothesis which originally came from group work, and which seems equally valid in the person-as-group situation. If I get into one of my subpersonalities, I invariably find it is richer and more complex than I would have expected, and has things to say which I could not have predicted. Similarly when I ask group members what they really think about some matter on which they have perhaps voted, I find that the vote often misrepresents their real position, which has many reservations and qualifications, perhaps to the extent that they do not really go along with the decision in any significant sense. This again seems to me something which could well be investigated in both contexts with advantage, results from the one reflecting back on the other.

8. The real structure of a group can be very different from its ostensible structure: in particular, it can be dominated by one strong character. However, if the external world changes, other characters may come to the fore—this is the understudy or standby or substitute phenomenon. It happens in genetics as well as in sociology and in psychology. It also happens in information theory, where what was background noise may become the message. This phenomenon can very readily be studied using the internal group, and the conclusions then tested with greater difficulty at the external group level. It is in this sort of investigation that the internal group is perhaps of greatest use.

These examples are of course just a few of the many which could be considered—other chapters in this book may suggest other topics which would benefit from this sort of approach, and the reader's own experience may bring others to mind.

What I have tried to do in this chapter is to suggest that in the internal group we have a resource which has hardly been tapped in the study of group processes. It is accessible without professional help, although a good therapist or group can help a good deal in helping one to become acquainted with one's subpersonalities. Certainly anyone who wants to work with them regularly would be well advised to have a support group of some kind, because some disturbing phenomena can emerge; dealing with the Shadow, for example, can be very unpleasant. But the experience is, taken all in all, an enriching one, and leads to much greater self-understanding, as well as to greater understanding of groups.

References

Allport, G. W. (1937). *Personality: A Psychological Interpretation*, Holt, New York.
Assagioli, R. (1975). *Psychosynthesis: A Manual of Principles and Techniques*, Turnstone Books, London.

Bem, S. L. (1977). 'Beyond androgyny: Some presumptuous prescriptions for a liberated sexual identity,' in C. G. Carney and S. L. McMahon (eds.), *Exploring Contemporary Male/Female Roles: A Facilitator's Guide*, University Associates, La Jolla, CA.

Berger, P. (1966). *Invitation to Sociology*, Penguin, Harmondsworth.

Berne, E. (1961). *Transactional Analysis in Psychotherapy*, Grove Press, New York.

Berne, E. (1972). *What Do You Say After You Say Hello?* Grove Press, New York.

Cohn, R. C. (1971). 'Living-learning encounters: The theme-centred interactional method,' in G. Blank *et al.* (eds.), *Confrontation: Encounters in self and Interpersonal Awareness*, Collier-Macmillan, London.

Edelwich, J. with Brodsky, A. (1980). *Burn-out: Stages of Disillusionment in the Helping Professions*, Human Sciences Press, New York.

Elliott, J. (1976). *The Theory and Practice of Encounter Group Leadership*, Explorations Institute, Berkeley.

Fagan, J., and Shepherd, I. L. (eds.) (1972). *Gestalt Theory Now*, Penguin, Harmondsworth.

Follett, M. P. (1941). *Dynamic Administration*, Pitman, London.

Gergen, K. J. (1967). 'To be or not to be a single self,' in S. M. Jourard (ed.), *To Be or Not To Be: Existential–Psychological Perspectives on the Self*, University of Florida Press, Gainesville.

Gergen, K. J. (May 1972). 'Multiple identity: The healthy, happy human being wears many masks,' *Psychology Today*, **5** (12), 31–35, 64–66.

Goffman, E. (1974). *Frame Analysis*, Harper & Row, New York. (See also Sub-Chapter 7.11.)

Golembiewski, R. T., and McConkie, M. (1975). 'The centrality of interpersonal trust in group processes,' in C. L. Cooper (ed.), *Theories of Group Processes*, John Wiley & Sons, London.

Greenberg, I. A. (ed.) (1974). *Psychodrama: Theory and Therapy*, Souvenir Press, London.

Grof, S. (1980). *LSD Psychotherapy*, Hunter House, Pomona.

Guntrip, H. (1961). *Personality Structure and Human Interaction*, Hogarth, London.

James, W. (1890). *The Principles of Psychology*, Henry Holt & Co., Dover, NY.

Janis, I. L., and Mann, L. (1977). *Decision Making: A Psychological Analysis of Conflict, Choice and Commitment*, The Free Press, New York.

Janov, A., and Holden, E. M. (1975). *Primal Man: The New Consciousness*, Abacus, London.

Jung, C. G. (1959). *Aion: Researches into the Phenomenology of the Self* (Collected works, Vol. 9 Part 2.) Routledge & Kegan Paul, London.

Jung, C. G. (1968). *Analytical Psychology: Its Theory and Practice*, Pantheon, New York.

Jung, C. G. (1971). (ed. Joseph Campbell) *The Portable Jung*, [chapter on Psychological Types], Viking (Penguin), New York.

Klapp, O. (1969). *Collective Search for Identity*, Holt, Rinehart & Winston, New York.

Lake, F. (1966). *Clinical Theology*, Darton, Longman & Todd, London.

Laing, R. D. (1976). *The Facts of Life*, Penguin, Harmondsworth.

Lewin, K. (1936). *Topological Psychology*, McGraw-Hill, New York.

McDougall, W. (1932). *Body and Mind*, Methuen [1911], London.

McKellar, P. (1979). *Mindsplit: The Psychology of Multiple Personality and the Dissociated Self*, J. M. Dent & Sons Ltd., London.

Mair, M. (1977). 'The community of self,' in D. Bannister (ed.), *New Perspectives in Personal Construct Theory*, Academic Press, London.

Mann, R. D. (1975). 'Winners, losers and the search for equality in groups,' in C. L. Cooper (ed.), *Theories of Group Processes*, John Wiley & Sons, London.

Martindale, C. (1980). 'Subselves: the internal representation of situational and personal dispositions,' in L. Wheeler (ed.), *Review of Personality and Social Psychology No. 1*, Sage, Beverly Hills and London.

Merton, R. K. (1957). *Social Theory and Social Structure*, Free Press, New York.

Miller, J. B. (1976). *Toward a New Psychology of Women*, Beacon Press, Boston (and 1978, Penguin, Harmondsworth).

O'Connor, E. (1971). *Our Many Selves: A Handbook for Self-Discovery*, Harper & Row, New York.

Ogilvy, J. (1977). *Many Dimensional Man*, Oxford University Press, New York.

Ouspensky, P. D. (1969). *In Search of the Miraculous*, Routledge, London (and 1949 and 1965, Harcourt Brace, New York).

Perls, F. S. (1969). *Gestalt Therapy Verbatim*, Real People Press, Moab, Utah.

Rogers, C. R. (1961). *On Becoming a Person*, Constable, London.

Rowan, J. (1976). *The Power of the Group*, Davis-Poynter, London.

Shapiro, S. B. (1976). *The Selves Inside You*, Explorations Institute, Berkeley. [*see also* 'A theory of ego pathology and ego therapy,' *Journal of Psychology*, **53**, 1962.]

Sorokin, P. A. (1956). *Fads and Foibles in Modern Sociology and Related Sciences*, Henry Regnery Company, Chicago.

Southgate, J., and Randall, R. (1978). *The Barefoot Psychoanalyst*, AKHPC, London.

Steiner, C., *et al.* (1975). *Readings in Radical Psychiatry*, Grove Press, New York.

Vargiu, J. G. (1974). Psychosynthesis workbook: Subpersonalities, *Synthesis 1*.

Watkins, J. (1978). *The Therapeutic Self*, Human Sciences Press, New York.

5 Living Together

Small Groups and Social Interaction, Volume 2
Edited by H. H. Blumberg, A. P. Hare, V. Kent and M. Davies
Published by John Wiley & Sons Ltd 1983.

5.1 Commitment and Community: Boundary Problems*

Rosabeth Moss Kanter *Goodmeasure, Inc., Cambridge, Massachusetts*

Boundaries define a group, set it off from its environment, and give it a sharp focus, which facilitates commitment. Strong communities tend to have strong boundaries—physical, social, and behavioral. What goes on within the community is sharply differentiated from what goes on outside. As with the secret societies described by Georg Simmel, events inside the community may even be kept hidden from outsiders and reserved for members alone to know, witness, and perform. One kind of boundary may help to define another. Physical boundaries, as of location and territory, might define those people with whom a person may legitimately engage in a relationship. Social boundaries may define behavioral ones, as in a monogamous marriage, where the two people who have defined themselves through the relationship behave toward each other in ways that they do not exhibit toward others.

With strong boundaries, it is clear who belongs to the group and who does not. The outside may treat members as a unit for many purposes. Passing in and out of the community, both for new recruits and for old members, may be relatively difficult. The definition of a communal group as an expressive unit concerned with interchanges between its members, as a group of people interested in mutual support and a shared way of life, indicates in part the importance of boundaries, because of their value in preserving the uniqueness of interaction between the specific set of people comprising the community.

Many of the commitment mechanisms that differentiated successful from unsuccessful nineteenth-century communes revolved around erecting and maintaining strong affirmative boundaries, which distinguished the group from its

*From Rosabeth Moss Kanter (1972). *Commitment and Community*, Harvard University Press, Cambridge, Massachusetts, pp. 169–175. Reproduced by permission of the author and publisher.

environment, so that members created for themselves psychic boundaries that encompassed the community—no more and no less—as the object of commitment and fulfillment. The commitment-generating problems of some unsuccessful groups can even be pinpointed as boundary issues, such as the fact that New Harmony let anyone in, exercising no selectivity and no socialization, or the fact that members of Brook Farm practically commuted to Boston. Many of the difficulties that successful groups later encountered stemmed in part from a weakening of the boundaries: hiring outside workers; educating children on the outside; increasing numbers of visitors; adopting the fruits of outside social change; and most important, engaging in expanded commerce and trade or decreased internal production and consumption, which destroyed the kind of self-sufficiency that itself constitutes a boundary.

Communes are conscious and purposeful in their attempt to separate from the larger society and create a special group. In the nineteenth century, conditions were such that distinct boundaries could be erected with relative ease. Physical isolation was possible, as well as a relatively self-sufficient farm and light industry economy. Technological needs were low, and contact with the outside minimized, so that a group could become institutionally complete, a comprehensive community comprised of all social institutions. Communication was slow, so that it was possible for a group to remain hidden, developing and maintaining a distinctive culture. Travel was generally confined to small geographic areas. There were fewer options for life in the society—from choice of career to choice of lifestyle—so that it was possible to find a homogeneous group of people who were willing to share beliefs, without the confusion and pressure of constant subjection to opposing views. Some commitment mechanisms even arose unintentionally: the distinctive language and dress style of such groups as Harmony and Amana were a function of the fact that they were immigrant groups with a transplanted culture, but could in the nineteenth century experience few pressures for assimilation.

Twentieth-century American society provides a very different kind of environment, one that is constantly intruding and penetrating the borders of groups, which contributes to the fact that the boundaries of most contemporary communes are weak and constantly shifting. Four characteristics of contemporary society are primarily responsible: urbanization, advanced technology, instant communication, and a white middle-class culture that is increasingly both national (fairly uniform across the country) and pluralistic and eclectic within the range of options provided nationally. More people live in cities and want to stay in cities, which has given rise to urban communes, a new phenomenon of this century, for evidence is lacking of any urban utopias in the last century. Advanced technology makes it less possible for any group to supply all or most of its needs by itself or for a small group easily to develop an economic base as a complete production unit. Thus, many communes today do not even attempt to constitute an economic unit, concentrating rather on being a family, which typifies the diminishment of scope characterizing a large proportion of the new communes. Institutional comprehensiveness is no longer as possible as it was in the nineteenth century. Instant communication means that new ideas and new stimuli can intrude constantly, increasing the difficulty of generating and maintaining a distinctive set of beliefs. Most communes today do not develop their own ideologies, and even when they do, they often borrow and incorporate bits and pieces from other people and other groups. The problems of ideological completeness, therefore—of any one group developing a unique, comprehensive ideology—are intensified.

These three factors—urbanization, technology, and mass communication—have supported the development of a national middle-class culture that is increasingly both uniform across regions and pluralistic in terms of styles available. People are more mobile—particularly the young, who are the ripest recruits for the new communes. As they move, they carry with them across the nation the counterculture of which communes are one part. In addition, people and places are increasingly interchangeable. If strong Utopian communities in fact resemble secret societies, then in the twentieth century most communes participate in a culture that has become too pervasive and widespread to develop such a secret, shared truth. Developing a distinctive culture, set off from that of the surrounding environment, is much more difficult today than in the nineteenth century; many contemporary communes choose not even to try, again retreating from their former scope. Rather than separating themselves from society, as did the communes of the last century, many become a link in a chain of the national counterculture, exchanging members with other communes. The fact that modern American culture is at the same time pluralistic and eclectic, surrounding the person with a much greater number of options than in the last century—with respect to careers, consumption, relationships—makes it harder for the individual both to make definitive choices (as of one group or one culture and lifestyle within that group) and to find one set of people with whom he can share every aspect of his life, since everyone else has the same large number of options from which to extract a lifestyle. The individual constructs his own social world out of the myriad choices confronting him, and the chance that many others will construct theirs in exactly the same way is much more limited than in the less diverse environment of the last century. Without a strong set of beliefs to indicate to the person why he should suspend his options, he generally continues to exercise them in the new communes. And most new communes, given the increased difficulty of placing limits on options, choose not to do so.

The boundary problems of today's communes are exacerbated by the fact that communes as a unique social arrangement lack definition and legitimacy in American society. For legal and official purposes, they must define themselves in terms of some other form such as a nonprofit corporation, a business, a church, an educational institution, or a family. Sunrise Hill set itself up as a trust fund; Synanon defined itself as a charitable foundation; the Fort Hill commune is organized into a holding corporation, 'United Illuminating.' Moreover, whereas the norms of the larger society indicate the ways in which legitimate social institutions are to be approached, there are not yet such established guidelines for communes. There are socially delimited ways of entering a family, for example—through marriage, birth, or legal adoption—but no similar guidelines for joining a commune. In America as a whole, strangers do not knock at the doors of residences asking for a place to sleep or inquiring whether they can become a member of that particular family, but they do approach communes with these requests. To some extent, communes are considered fair game for anyone, and their borders are easily penetrable.

Thus, it is more difficult today to develop strong boundaries than it was in the nineteenth century, and territorial or spatial limits no longer suffice to give a group coherence. Today's communes have had to develop other kinds of group-environment relations and other means of handling their boundary problems, for as Eric Berne pointed out, the existence of a group is in part dependent on being able to predict who will or will not be present and behaving in particular ways at specific events. That is, the very definition of a group is to some extent dependent on the existence of boundaries: 'constitutional, psychological or spatial distinctions between members and non-members.'

Boundaries transcend people, however; they also distinguish between events that occur within a group and those that do not. Boundary distinctions can be established on two principles, affirmative and negative. Affirmative principles define the group by what it accepts; negative, by what it rejects. Affirmative boundaries encompass only that which is accepted by the group; all events or people are excluded except those specifically included. A person is not 'in' unless the group defines him as 'in.' Norms are positive, specifically defining appropriate behavior and events. Negative boundaries, in contrast, encompass everything but what the group specifically rejects; all events or people are included except those explicitly excluded. A person is not 'out' unless the group defines him as 'out.' All behavior is permitted except that defined as inappropriate. Affirmative boundaries, then, are characteristic of secret societies in being exclusive and strict. Negative boundaries are characteristic of open societies in that they are inclusive and permissive. Affirmative boundaries are more conducive to building commitment than are negative boundaries.

Today's communes can be placed in two general categories, depending on the predominance of negative or affirmative boundaries. One set of communes, in line with today's diminishing scope and retreat themes, has primarily negative boundaries. I call these 'retreat' communes. They tend to be small, anarchistic, and easily dissolved, predominantly rural and youth-oriented. Some urban communes also fall into this category, since they choose to specialize in domestic life rather than to develop a complete set of social institutions. They limit their goals to relationships, and like the rural retreat groups, they tend to be permissive, inclusive, and temporary. But the rural communes tend to be more purposeful and organized than the urban ones, and also to have some minimal shared economy, which urban houses generally lack. Thus, urban communes must be considered a different phenomenon, representing alternative forms of the family rather than new communities.

The other set of communes has affirmative boundaries. Rather than shrinking into a small family or avoiding the issue of boundaries altogether, these communes choose interaction with the wider society through service. Their mission gives them the focus around which to erect affirmative boundaries. They are either urban or rural, tend to have a strong core group holding the community together, and incorporate in their structure ways of coping with the mobility and turnover characteristic of today. They may also be larger and more enduring than retreat communes. More traditional Utopias, such as the Bruderhof and Twin Oaks, and religious missionary communes are similar to the service communes in that they, too, have affirmative boundaries. In the twentieth century, however, affirmation alone may not be enough to give a group strength, and to the extent that a commune can define a special way in which it helps or transforms the larger social environment, it may gain added strength and ability to endure.

The distinction between retreat and service communes corresponds roughly to those made by other observers of the contemporary commune movement. Retreat groups tend to be what Bennett Berger called 'noncreedal,' in that they generally lack a shared ideology or creed; service communes more often are 'creedal.' Retreat communes tend to be solidarity-based and unintentional; service communes are generally ideology-based and intentional. Service communes are more similar to the Utopias of the past, and many of the lessons of the past apply to them. Retreat communes, in contrast, are part of the new contemporary movement to regain Eden.

Small Groups and Social Interaction, Volume 2
Edited by H. H. Blumberg, A. P. Hare, V. Kent and M. Davies
Published by John Wiley & Sons Ltd 1983

5.2 People Together: The Idea*

Clem Gorman

Communality is the key element is a communal situation, and it is best grasped intuitively and inductively. Although it can be described as an intention in the mind of someone who is a member of a group to behave in a cooperative, sharing, and perhaps loving way towards the other members of that group, there is no one clear and standard definition of communality. There are an infinite number of degrees of communality, springing from the individual and the group's level of commitment, emotional and environmental circumstances, personalities, means, etc. There is no archetypal, authentic commune in Britain because all are different and most are valid. . . .

Communality manifests itself differently in different types of communal projects . . .

In pragmatic communal projects the manifestation of communality has, perhaps, more subtle sources. The living of a communal life, or the solving of a common problem by communal means, is the basis for such projects, and very often communality manifests itself in such situations not as a by-product or expression of a belief but as an end in itself, the central and only activity for which the group came together. . . .

In all sorts of communal groups communality manifests itself as a product of the small scale, in contrast to the large scale which we might call the organisational or institutional scale. . . .

An image of a communal project could be a dozen or so people gathered together informally for a chat about how things are to be run for the next few days, or how a certain arrangement is to be made. . . .

These extracts are from Clem Gorman (1975). *People Together*, Paladin, Frogmore, St Albans, Hertfordshire, pp. 23–41. Reprinted by permission of the publisher, Granada Publishing Ltd.

... it could be said that the communal family tends to produce children who are less competitive, and less achievement-oriented than the nuclear family. Such a statement would need some pretty severe reservations. Many nuclear parents are aware of the dangers of offering the child an impossible model (e.g. rich, famous or very successful parents) and will seek to minimise the feeling on the child's part that he or she needs to fulfil himself and prove his or her worth as a person by achieving something similar to dad or mum. Again, many parents who have moved into a communal lifestyle of some sort will seek to maintain the nuclear family structure within that lifestyle; which will bring them into conflict with the communal project as a whole. ... in a communal situation sex loses its special importance, and ... jealousy and possessiveness are no longer needed. ...

Tribes and clans are of course communities, and in the sense that all members are taught and expected to manifest communal or tribal intention, they are communal groups. Nevertheless they could not be described as communal in the sense in which we use that term in the West today, the sense in which it is used throughout this book. Tribes are not chosen, they are born into. ...

Yet there is a tribal, or village form of communalism which, while normally based upon at least some degree of blood relationship, and while carrying into the future at least some of the taboos and religious beliefs of the past, has as its basis the free choice of members and an attitude of mind that is essentially socialist and communal rather than tribal and blood-based. This is Ujaama, the village socialism of Tanzania, and I quote here from an article on this movement which suggests the similarities between its philosophical premise and the philosophy of our communalism. The speaker is Julius Nyerere.

> We shall achieve the goals we in this country have set ourselves if the basis of Tanzanian life consists of rural economic and social communities where people live together and work together for the good of all, and which are interlocked so that all of the different communities also work together in co-operation for the common good of the nation as a whole ... The basis of rural life in Tanzania must be the practice of co-operation in its widest sense—in living, in working, and in distributing, and all with an acceptance of the absolute equality of all men and women.

Village socialism thus is seen as a form of economic organisation where each village aims at self-sufficiency, on the Chinese model, and where the guiding economic principle is cooperation. But it is much more than that; it is an attitude of mind, one which we can see is very close to the communal intention mentioned before. No matter what kind of economic unit is chosen as the basis of village socialism, Nyerere is aware that only if the members of the village, and the nation as a whole, maintain an attitude of cooperative intention towards each other, can the system survive. It is mental attitudes which make a system of social life, not economic or political systems; and nothing could be more true of communality.

Obviously such an attitude, in Tanzania with its special problems or in a British communal project with its special problems, precludes sexism of any kind. It is perhaps in this area that a number of communal projects in this country, hesitating to accept fully the theory of communalism, have got stuck in the mire of broken down internal relationships by clinging to some, but not all, of the sexist attitudes and habits they brought with them from their conditioning in the outside world. An attempt to compromise with the philosophy of communal life/work is fatal. Either by stages, or all at once, a communal group should be aiming to establish a fully communal intention among all members; attempting to maintain some sexist attitudes in an otherwise communal situation, has been shown by the bitter experience of many British projects to be disastrous for communal spirit. This is the subject of the relationships chapter. One point may be added here: in the early stages a communal project may still be a battleground of cultures, and in this situation it may sometimes be true (and has often proved true in practice) that women have to struggle to assert their position as fully equal members of the group. This may not always prove easy in a situation where nuclear couples continue in the commune.

Some communal practices, which are similar to practices in some tribal communities—such as the Polynesian—may be necessary to a full, non-sexist, non-nuclear communal life, not as things in themselves, or structures within which to herd the members of a group, and from which to exclude 'non-conformists' or scapegoats, but as manifestations of the communal intention in the mind of every member. There are collective childrearing and its corollary collective attribution of parenthood, collective marriage, collective use and attribution of space, and collective property holding. None of these can be truly said to have been fully implemented in any British projects over the past ten years, but this is not to say that they are theoretically wrong or even unattainable but that they must be long-term goals rather than overnight developments.

In theory it can be clearly seen how the adoption of these practices would necessitate putting an end to sexism, possessiveness, jealousy, and sexual repression. Where members are making love freely with whomever they choose there is no way, should it be wished, to keep a check on which male is the parent of which child. This effectively liberates women from allegiance to one man, in return for which they all have the allegiance of all the men in the communal group.

In the light of all this the theoretical enemies of communality can be easily identified. They are selfishness, jealousy, possessiveness, egotism, selfish individualism, and so on. But more, of course, than these manifestations, they are the absence of communal intention. . . .

What about the little things of daily life? If a member has made a commitment to communal intention does this mean that immediately, in all ways, he or she must think more of the group than of themselves? This would hardly seem reasonable. Even dirty dishes or socks in the bathroom could be tolerated by a group which believed that, deep down, the member cared about others but tended to forget in little ways. The principle of communality does not have to be formally applied in order to remain valid. It is more communal, often, in the ways and to the extent that it is not enforced.

Somehow a communal project must seek to enable its members to enjoy the freedom they want while maintaining the web of unity that the community itself needs. The slogan adopted by the Commune Movement—Do what you want that does not prevent someone else from doing what he or she wants—seems to cover the situation as well as any brief slogan can. . . .

In general it is true that communality allows a very flexible and varied range of options for individual members. Outside friends, personal idiosyncrasies, privacy, personal fulfilment—none of these are incompatible with communal living, and still less with non-residential communal projects. Communality is merely a different way of looking at relationships, leading to a different sort of commitment, a different sort of intention, and different sorts of relationships. It may in theory often be associated with an egoless consciousness, but it need not in practice. A communal situation can be as tight or as loose as the members want, and it is usually small enough for the members to be able to retain control of the group identity at all times. In fact, unlike a larger, institutional scale grouping, a commune can hardly be said to have an identity outside its members, not even a collective identity, still less an 'image.'

There is a well-known theory of human motivation which assumes that needs are arranged in a hierarchy of priority or potency. Needs lower in the hierarchy must be satisfied adequately before needs higher up may be satisfied. In particular, needs for belonging and security require satisfaction as a precondition of the satisfaction and fulfilment of needs for self-realisation. On this view, the realisation of one's potentials rests on a fulfilled sense of affiliation with others. From this perspective communality can be said to be a system of multiple aspiration with mutual security and individual self-fulfilment.

At either end of the spectrum whose extremes are conformity and anarchy, lie enemies to the communal aspiration. Any group which seeks to impose strict conformity to any one idea or interpretation must be storing up trouble for itself. So must any group which ignores collectivity for total individual selfishness. Paranoia, the genesis of conformist and anarchist pressures alike, is to be guarded against. If communality works it does so by creating a microcosm of society so open that the very thought of secrets, mistrust, fear, suspicion is impossible. If it even only half works, at least these feelings can be brought into the open as they occur.

Before finishing with theory of communality one idea, so often associated in people's minds with communality, should be considered; the idea that communal living in particular, and collective life and work in general, is an escape from the realities of life; i.e. struggle, work, sacrifice, and stability.

It is hard to disagree. It is also hard to see why anyone who wishes to escape those things should not do so. Certainly the Commune Movement itself is escapist; the very term 'alternative society' suggests escape. But there is a difference between escape from and escape to. Many young people who start out by escaping from—escaping from the drug scene, or suburbia, or careers—may find in communal living an escape *to*—escape to a healthier, more together, more hopeful life than they might otherwise have known.

It will always be true, and never more so than in these times, that many young people will want time to travel, to reflect, to meet others and seek adventure, outside the normal framework of society, before they decide what they want to do with their lives. It happened in Hermann Hesse's *Siddharta*, and it is unlikely ever to stop happening. One finds people in this situation in any commune at any given time. Communality satisfies something in the seeker, the wanderer, the restless searcher; communal houses in turn can protect such people from sleeping rough and wandering lonely, much as monasteries once did. These young people could be called escapists, as could the many single mums and people coming out of bad emotional or chemical trips, who turn up on doorsteps of communes. But for all of us at some time escape is a necessity if we are to survive. Escape can be a positive action sometimes. Anybody who tries to use a commune as a place in which to escape personal inner conflicts may soon find that a communal situation is as good a place as any to face up to them.

No chapter on the theory of communality is complete without a warning against over-reliance on theory and a mention of some of the pragmatic necessities that make life possible and easy. Grand theory is all very well, but we don't search for friends and lovers with this in mind. Humour, laughter, fun, sex, games, ceremonies, jokes, madness, and sheer silliness are essential ingredients in the communal pudding, and 'grand theory' must come to some arrangement with instincts and emotions. Try to get a group of people together without these saving graces, however much theory you may have worked out, however long you may have planned, and you will be bound to fail. Try a little madness and fun and although you may have no guaranteee that your communal project will work out all right, you will at least be sure that it has been worth trying. And at the bottom of it all, when all theories have been tried, there must be love.

Small Groups and Social Interaction, Volume 2
Edited by H. H. Blumberg, A. P. Hare, V. Kent and M. Davies
Published by John Wiley & Sons Ltd 1983

5.3 Kibbutz and Parental Investment

Joseph Shepher   *University of Haifa*

and

Lionel Tiger   *Harry F. Guggenheim Foundation, New York*

[The present selection begins with a brief description taken from the book *Women in the Kibbutz* (Tiger and Shepher, 1965) followed by the paper 'Kibbutz and parental investment,' which the authors wished to include in lieu of revising or reprinting a longer extract from their book.]

The way of life in the kibbutz*

Kibbutzim are collective rural communities in Israel. Infield ... calls them 'comprehensive' collectives, meaning that collectivism embraces every sphere of social life. Today [more than] 100,000 people live in some [250] kibbutzim. These communities differ in size, economic structure, geographic locality, political ideology and affiliation, religiosity, members' cultural backgrounds, and members' seniority in the kibbutz and in the nation. However, they are all more or less alike in a number of important ways:

1. There is far-reaching collectivization of production. Most members work together in collective work branches, with less than 10 per cent of the working population employed outside the collective framework. In one of the three kibbutz federations, the Ichud, only 4.5 per cent of all workdays was expended outside the kibbutz; these accounted for 5.6 per cent of gross income and for 1 per cent of the costs, which include all expenses of the outside workers such as food, transportation, lodging. ... Even those who work outside are registered in the general work-assignment list, and like all other members, work in the dining hall, kitchen, and on the night watch, according to a *corvée* system.

---

* Reprinted with permission, from Lionel Tiger and Joseph Shepher, *Women in the Kibbutz*, Harcourt Brace Jovanovich, New York, 1975, and Penguin, Harmondsworth, 1977, pp. 34–37 (part of Ch. 3, 'The way of life in the kibbutz'). For additional information and documentation, including footnotes which originally applied to this extract, readers are referred to the original book.

2. There is far-reaching collectivization of consumption. All members receive goods and services from the kibbutz, usually through collective institutions such as a communal dining hall serving three meals a day, a communal laundry, a communal clothing store that mends, irons, purchases, and—for part of the population (mainly women and children)—produces new clothing. There are communal cultural institutions, such as clubhouses and cultural centers and theaters, and communal health-care and educational services. House maintenance, landscaping, personal transport, and annual vacations are also organized collectively.

3. The socioeconomic role and level of performance of the individual kibbutz member bear no relationship to the goods and services he receives. The secretary and general manager, the highest administrative officers of the kibbutz, receive no more than anyone else, nor does a worker whose output is higher than his co-member's. Most economic rewards are provided in kind, such as food, shelter, and most clothing; only about 4 per cent of the money value of all goods and services is given in cash. And only episodic conditions such as illness and pregnancy are held to justify any deviations from this system.

4. Education is collective in the sense that the kibbutz, not individual parents, is responsible for it. Both the aims and the means of education are established by the kibbutz, and all children receive twelve years of education. Each child's talents (musical, artistic, etc.) are identified and cultivated in accordance with the decisions of the educational authorities and economic resources of the kibbutz.

5. Membership is individual and voluntary, and it usually follows a one year candidacy. It is granted by a two-thirds majority of the General Assembly. If the candidate is not granted membership, he is usually advised to leave, which most rejected candidates do; however, on rare occasions a new candidacy is allowed. Membership can be ended by the member or by a two-thirds majority of the General Assembly, but this is rare. Those who decide to leave the kibbutz receive a cash allowance fixed by the statutes of the kibbutz and its federation; this allowance grows with the number of years of membership and is usually enough for the person to start a new career.

6. The political system is direct democracy. A General Assembly consisting of all members (and in some kibbutzim candidates as well) is the highest political instrument. Every member has the same active and passive political rights, and one vote in the General Assembly, which must approve the annual plans of economic production and consumption. The Assembly also elects all important officials and committees and admits people to candidacy and membership. There is no party system. The criteria for election to office are fitness, talent, and experience of the individual. Every member may submit proposals for election either to the nominating committee or to the General Assembly itself. The right to make motions to the agenda and to question principal officeholders ensure each member direct access to the highest political institution. There are no judicial institutions; the kibbutz enjoys considerable autonomy in judging its members, and does so through the General Assembly and certain committees. Behavior

considered deviant by the kibbutz is dealt with internally; only the rare incidents of such major misconduct as fraud, larceny, and murder are handed over to the state police. Only one murder is known to have been committed within a kibbutz (by a candidate who had spent three months in the community), and only one act of embezzlement.

7. Each kibbutz and its members are incorporated in concentric institutions—the kibbutz federation, the General Organization of Labor (Histadrut), the Zionist movement, and the state of Israel. These affiliations reflect the basic value of service to the society as a whole. So do the few requirements for membership: the candidate must belong to the Histadrut, accept Zionism, and be an Israeli citizen. Each kibbutz is affiliated with one of the kibbutz federations, and federation offices are staffed by kibbutz members. Some decisions of the democratically elected bodies of the federation (congress, councils, and central committees) are binding on all kibbutzim, while others are considered merely advisory. Each kibbutz is part of the Workers' Economy (Chevrat Ovdim) of the Histadrut and collectively affiliated with it and with the World Zionist Organization through the Colonization Department of the Jewish Agency. Each kibbutz is incorporated in the state as an independent municipal unit.

Kibbutz and parental investment

On the 15 of September 1975, two books waited for the Israeli author in his mailbox at the University of Haifa: the first copy of *Women in the Kibbutz*, just arrived from New York and the heavy volume of E. O. Wilson's *Sociobiology: A New Synthesis* (1975). Shepher browsed with satisfaction through the pages of his recently published book with Lionel Tiger, but did not read it: he knew it almost by heart from the repeated proof readings. Instead, he started to study Wilson's book. When after several days, he finished Chs. 15 and 16 on parental investment, he was as though struck by lightning: the lightning of the feeling of overwhelming evidence. But it was too late. The Tiger–Shepher book was out and had run its course. Its three editions provoked some 40-odd reviews and created a scientific debate. Most of the reviewers praised the well organized data and the sophistication of their analysis but disagreed with the authors' interpretation. Especially the feminists—Bernard (1976), Shapiro (1976), Somerville (1979), and Syrkin 1976)—accused the authors with selectiveness of analysis of different data, of internal contradictions, and of biological determinism. Others, like Cohen (1976), Peres and Russkin (1977), Rosner and Palgi (1976) were more balanced in their criticism. Interestingly, none of the critics claimed that Tiger and Shepher were wrong in their *biological* argument, that their use of the vague concept of 'biogrammar' is theoretically vulnerable and guilty of group selectionist aberrations. Most sociobiologists praised the book and quoted it repeatedly: Wilson 1978) and van den Berghe (1979).

It is only fair that after 5 years, the authors themselves, should reconsider their own arguments and put them in the right theoretical dimensions. In fact, we, the authors, can hardly excuse our ignoring parental investment theory as the right theoretical framework for our argumentation by the synchrony of the publication of our book with that of Wilson's. All his enormous contribution to the formulation of sociobiological theory notwithstanding, E. O. Wilson was, to a certain extent, codifying earlier pieces of the theoretical framework: especially Hamilton (1964) and Trivers (1972). Whereas Hamilton's papers were published in a highly professional biological journal, Trivers's 1972 article was published in a volume much more accessible to social scientists—Campbell's (1972) *Sexual Selection and the Evolution of man (1871–1971)*. In fact, both authors read this volume during the hectic days of the writing of their own book, but seemingly did not realize the relevance of Trivers's paper (that was based mainly on ornithological evidence) to their own human case. Moreover, as are most social scientists, the authors were too slow in adjusting themselves to the new forms of evolutionary thinking and in keeping up with the burgeoning literature of the early 1970s. Be that as it may, it is never too late to admit one's shortcomings and to try to set them right.

Trivers's 1972 theory of parental investment is as simple as it is powerful. It is, in fact, a specific case of Hamilton's (1964) inclusive fitness theory. Hamilton, in his effort to answer the question, whether altruism is an evolutionary plausible strategy, convincingly proves that an animal can increase its fitness (the relative number of its surviving offspring) not only by breeding itself but by helping its close relatives to breed instead. This help—consentaneously called altruism—is proportional to the degree of relatedness of the benefactor to the beneficiary. The question whether an animal should breed itself or should act altruistically to its relatives is a question of individual strategy highly dependent on environmental factors.

Another problem of strategy arises between males and females in sexually reproducing species. In order to have offspring, a sexually reproducing creature has to combine its genes with those of the opposite sex. In some species, the offspring is created by the very fact of fertilization and no additional care is needed to bring the offsping to maturation. In others, different energetic efforts are needed to achieve the same purpose, such as gestation, feeding, protecting, teaching, etc. All these efforts may collectively be called parental investment, although in many species it is not the biological parents who perform them (the best examples are the Hymenoptera).

In most birds and mammals, parental investment is highly asymmetric. The greatest part of parental investment is done by the female and in some avian and mammal species, the male only contributes his sex cells. The disproportionate parental investment is the basis of different sexual strategies of males and females. Since the female usually is the high investor, she becomes a limiting resource for the low investor males. Males usually fight for females and the latter are cautious and selective. Males usually tend to mate polygynously, being able to benefit genetically from mating with every female, mainly because they count on the high investment of the female which would prevent her from deserting the offspring. On the other hand, females are not usually prone to being polyandrous because they cannot, thereby, increase their fitness. Consequently, it is hardly surprising that in the whole mammalian class, polygyny is usual; polyandry is highly exceptional. So it is with humans. More than 70 per cent of human societies are polygynous, whereas only 1 per cent are polyandrous.

Parental investment and inclusive fitness explain, not only male–female strategies, but also parent–child conflict and sibling conflict (Trivers, 1974) and several problems of courtship, kinship, and marriage (Chagnon and Irons, 1979; Symons, 1979).

Let us now review our findings in the light of the *pi* (parental investment) theory. We summarized them on pp. 262–263 of our book:

1. Early in kibbutz history, more than half the women worked for a considerable time in production. Then came a long, gradual process of sexual polarization of work. Today the sexual division of labor has reached about 80 per cent of maximum.

2. Sexual division of labor is more polarized in the second and kibbutz-bred generations than it is in the first generation, and more polarized in younger kibbutzim than in older ones.

3. Despite complete formal equality in political rights, women are less active in the General Assembly than men are, as measured both by their presence in the Assembly and by the incidence of their participation. Women are somewhat overrepresented in committees dealing with social, educational, and cultural problems; they are seriously underrepresented in committees dealing with economy, work, general policy-making, and security.

4. The higher the authority of an office or committee, the lower the percentage of women in it. At the highest level of the kibbutz, women make up only 14 per cent of the personnel.

5. Women seem to have special problems sustaining all-female work groups; they usually prefer mixed-sex groups or male leadership.

6. Men and women receive nearly the same number of years of education; in fact, women have a slight edge. Advanced schooling, however, differs in kind for each sex. Women are overrepresented in higher nonacademic education leading to such jobs as elementary-school teaching, kindergarten teaching, and medical nursing. Men are overrepresented in higher academic education leading to such jobs as agriculture, engineering, economics, and management.

7. From the ninth grade on, women consistently fall below men in scholarly achievement. This discrepency between sexes seems to be wider here than in comparable modern societies.

8. Although women, like men, are drafted into the army, the over-whelming majority of kibbutz women (like other Israeli women) do secretarial and service jobs there; few do characteristically male work or occupy command positions. The conception of the women's army as essentially a substitute unit, also providing back-up aid and encouragement for the fighting men, is completely accepted by the kibbutz women. There has, however, been a steady expansion of the range of noncombatant tasks for women.

9. Even the long, demanding Yom Kippur War did not sub-stantially change the division of labor in the kibbutzim even though almost half the men were called up by the army for a long period.

10. The family has risen from its initial shadowy existence to become the basic unit of kibbutz social structure. It now fulfills important functions in consumption and education, and there are demands for further expanding its function. Increased familization is indicated by high and growing rates of birth and marriage, and by a decreasing divorce rate. The status of singles, especially of women, is becoming more and more problematic, to the extent that the family, the kibbutz, and even the federations now try to help them marry.

11. The main instigators of familization are women, whose attitude toward familism is more positive than men's.

12. Attitudes toward equality have always been more egalitarian than actual behavior has. The discrepancy causes recurrent soul-searching within the kibbutzim and federations.

How is sexual division of labor connected with parental investment theory? Obviously, the higher pi of the female is energetically extremely demanding. The very asymmetry of parental investment between male and female is the foundation of sexual division of labor. Assuming that every individual has the ability to expend a limited and equal amount of energy to all the possible endeavors and purposes, the female, by investing generously in the offspring, has to forego investments in alternative tasks. Assuming that amount of energy expended is not limited but flexible because of possible time differences in energy investment, the female has to work more hours than the male if she wants to perform the same tasks in addition to those of her high parental investment. Thus, if we take the first assumption that is $\Sigma e_m = \Sigma e_f$ (total available energy is equal in both sexes) and we know that $pi_f > pi_m$ than the free energy fe of the male must be greater than that of the female. Thus

$$fe_m = \Sigma e - pi_m$$

and

$$fe_f = \Sigma e - pi_f$$

and since

$$pi_f > pi_m$$

therefore, obviously

$$fe_m > fe_f$$

In the case of second assumption, the total available energy will be a linear function of time:

$$\Sigma e_m = t_m e$$

where e is the unit of energy expended in t time:

$$\Sigma e_f = t_f e$$

and therefore, free energy:

$$fe_m = t_m e - pi_m$$
$$fe_f = t_f e - pi_f$$

therefore $fe_m = fe_f$ is possible only if $t_f > t_m$. Assuming that fe_m should be equal to fe_f, we have:

$$t_m e - pi_m = t_f e - pi_f$$
$$pi_f - pi_m = t_f e - t_m e$$

or:

$$\Delta pi = \Delta te$$

that is, the higher the difference in parental investment between the female and the male the higher will be the difference between the time she and the male have to work in order to have the same 'free energy.'

All this concerns the quantitative aspects of division of labor between the sexes. The size of pi depends on the number of children, their ages, and spacing of births: Δpi is uninfluenced by pi_m until after delivery, except the male's contribution to the female's feeding and, thereby, to the nutrition of the offspring. After delivery, Δpi is highly dependent on the propensity of the male to invest in the offspring directly or indirectly, although the flexibility of Δpi is much lower in preindustrial cultures where lactation is simply part of the natural order of things.

Sexual division of labor is not less dependent on asymmetry of parental investment from the qualitative point of view. Not only is the female able to expend less 'free energy' than the male, but the free energy she does expend, must be devoted to tasks, that in order to be fulfilled, have to be in close propinquity to the tasks of parental investment. Hence, the 'domestic' character of 'female' tasks. Guarding the fire, home making, cooking, washing, or alternatively any work that can be carried out without unduly moving, transferring or otherwise disturbing the baby.

Now all this assumes that only the two parents can share the parental investment. But parents can and do delegate their parental investment activities, first of all to relatives, such as siblings, grandparents, uncles, aunts, who themselves are interested in the well-being of the offspring according to Hamilton's inclusive fitness principle. Since in most cases, maternal investment is thereby alleviated, we usually speak of 'allomothering.' Allomothering can be part of inclusive fitness altruism, but it can be undertaken by an unrelated individual if she can profit thereby, by training herself in mothering for her future tasks.

In the case of the kibbutz, we witness *an institutionalized allomothering*. In the 'classical' collective system of housing (see pp. 56 and 162–165 of Tiger and Shepher, 1975) the parents spend from $1\frac{1}{2}$ to 3–4 hours per day with their child, according to the child's age: the older the child, the longer the time spent with him. The 'real' parental investment: feeding (after weaning), washing, dressing, toilet training, playing, teaching, walking was carried out mainly by a nurse or nurses, absolutely unrelated to the child (normatively, the policy was to prevent sisters, grandmothers, or aunts from working with the children in order to maintain the universalistic standards between the nurses and the children). During the night, the children sleeping in the children's houses, usually situated in the ecological heart of the kibbutz, were watched by a female night watch.

Such a far reaching delegation of parental investment to nonrelatives, especially in early childhood, is extremely rare in human societies. Under what conditions would one expect such a strategy? If the parental investment theory makes good sense, one has to hypothesize that such a strategy would be chosen only in extreme situations, in which all the energy is needed in order to provide the basic needs of life such as food, shelter, and security. Such situations arise for instance, in war, extreme difficulties in production, and scarcity of manpower. In the early kibbutz, all these elements were present, with two additional factors: this was a self-selected group of unrelated youngsters, and they believed that they could substitute friendship relations for family relations (see pp. 37–38, 59, and 206–210). Therefore, no relatives for allomothering were available. Even if there were, the ideology stemming largely but not exclusively, from the extreme situations and their having nicely adjusted to them, prevented 'nepotistic' allomothering. Not that the whole process of the collectivization was very smooth (see p. 161) and, at least partially, the origin of the Moshav Movement can be traced back to the disputes on parental investment in the first kibbutz (Bein, 1945; pp. 166–168, 230–232). Moreover, the general attitude was not to hasten with marriage and when married, to postpone having children (see pp. 206–210). Thus the group had decided to change the composition of total free energy available to all tasks except parental investment to:

$$\Sigma fe_1 = fe_m + fe_f = (\Sigma e - pi_m) + (\Sigma e - pi_f).$$

By having only a few children (let us assume 25 per cent of the women) we shall have:

$$\Sigma fe_2 = (\Sigma e - pi_m) + 0.75(\Sigma e - pi_m) + 0.25(\Sigma e - pi_f)$$
$$\Sigma fe_2 = 1.75(\Sigma e - pi_m) + 0.25(\Sigma e - pi_f)$$

whence it is obvious that: $\Sigma fe_2 > \Sigma fe_1$ where Σfe_1 represents a situation in which all adult females have children.

Moreover, instead of letting all the mothers freely invest in their offspring, the kibbutz instituted groups of five children nursed by a single nurse, thereby cutting total parental investment by 80 per cent and increasing the free available energy considerably. That was not easy either, but it was rendered possible because of the dire environmental conditions, the powerful ideology and the tight solidarity of the group.

From the point of view of the individual, this strategy was acceptable as long as he or she considered his or her attachment to the group as mentally, emotionally, and economically better for parent and offspring than in another social form. There were anticipated differences between males and females. The latter had more difficulties in accepting the strategy than the former obviously because of their higher initial parental investment. The long and obstinate fight to return to personal and not delegated parental investment is largely the fight of women.

Of course, not all members of the kibbutz were prepared to delegate parental investment to others. Many left the kibbutz and are still leaving because of the collectivistic parental investment strategy. Presently, the Kibbutz Artzi federation stood up in its convention against the pressure of legitimately introducing the familistic housing system of the children. One of the results: couples leave the kibbutzim of the Artzi federation and join kibbutzim of the ichud federation, where the housing system is familistic.

In view of the system of delegated parental investment, one can easily understand the quasi-underground existence of the family in the early kibbutz as well as the impressive process of gradual familization.

The nuclear monogamous family, as was known in the cultures where most kibbutz founders were socialized, is a result of high paternal investment in the offspring. The economic existence of the female and her children was dependent on the male's work. Bulwarked by religious sanctions, this created either a very strong social control negatively sanctioning males who neglected their paternal duties, and/or the romantic love complex largely the outcome of atomization of the productive system, the dependence of sexual outlet on marriage and the competition among males for the most desirable females. The traditional sexual division of labor between the providing male and the home-making, socializing female broke down in the early kibbutz. Everyone had to provide. There were few children and few home services. Hence, the nuclear family was also unimportant. Couples were slowly formed, there was a high rate of divorce and a lot of talk of

Table 1   Percentage of Single People Having Children

	Males		Females	
	%	N	%	N
Kibbutz Artzi	1.73	(17)	3.22	(17)
Ichud	3.69	(61)	3.73	(27)
TOTAL		78		44

free love. Marriages were informally contracted and even the privacy of the couple was intruded upon by the 'primus' custom (see pp. 207–210). Since the investment of the male was not needed or at least not individually, it was not necessary for the nuclear family to be an important and stable unit. This explains the comparatively large percentage of singles (not divorced or widowed!) both males and females who have children in the kibbutz (see Table 1).

Also a very large percentage of divorced and widowed persons have children (Table 2).

Obviously, if the parental investment is delegated to the collective, the marital status of the parents does not have a decisive impact on the socialization of the children.

But when the economic and security situation improved, and starting from the late 1930s, more and more children appeared (Shepher 1977, pp. 38–41), even the delegated system of parental investment created a sexual division of labor. Since an increasing number of women were extracted from the labor pool of production in order to handle the growing number of young children (nobody suggested that men should do this), and since the growing population needed more services, more women who wanted to be close to their children first reluctantly, and later willingly, agreed to supply the services of cooking, washing, ironing, mending, and health care.

But it was a change of degree; not of kind. It was not until the mid-1950s, after the War of Liberation was over, security was much better and the economic situation had greatly improved, that the twin process of polarization of sexual division

Table 2   Percentage of Divorced and Widowed Persons Having Children

	Males		Females	
	%	N	%	N
Kibbutz Artzi	91.04	(216)	95.84	(578)
Ichud	83.63	(181)	93.68	(595)
TOTAL		397		1173

(Computed from Tables 2, 50a, 51a.)

of labor and 'familization' gathered momentum. With the amazing force of an irresistible social movement, the women of the Ichud federation won their case: the familistic system of housing was legitimized in 1967 and today there are almost no kibbutzim left in the Ichud federation with the collectivistic system. The Kibbutz Meuchad federation followed and with the impending fusion between the two federations, the last obstacles were to be removed before the full introduction of the familistic system. The Kibbutz Artzi federation, in which such an 'iconoclastic' proposal could not even be mentioned earlier, was compelled to deal in its national convention recently, with the formal request of one of its kibbutzim to introduce the familistic system of housing. In spite of a very effective informal pressure of the young women in many kibbutzim, the convention rejected the request, trying to block the way of the growing Social Movement within its cohorts exactly as the Ichud federation did in 1950 and 1964 and probably with no greater chance of success.

The defenders of the ideology, mainly males, found consolation in the illusion that the change in the housing system is not more than a technical matter. But what happened was nothing but the *reindividuation of the parental investment*. Instead of 1–3 hours, mothers now spent 15 hours per day with their children. They bathed them, put them to bed, woke them up in the morning, bathed them again, dressed them, brought them back to the children's house, and visited them there once or twice during the day-care hours between 7.00 a.m. and 4.00 p.m. The nursing mother kept her baby at home 24 hours a day for the first 3 to 6 months and, only thereafter, brought it to the babies' house for the day. In acknowledgements of the fact that females take the greatest part of this new individual parental investment, the working hours of the mothers were formally cut by between 12.5 and 37.5 per cent, no matter where those mothers worked. Since most of them, however, worked in the children's houses, the cut is an obvious change in the direction of the individuation of parental investment. The corollaries of this sweeping change strengthened the nuclear family tremendously. The familistic system of housing necessitated a large apartment. Instead of the one to one and a half-room apartment allotted to a couple whose children spent the night in the children's houses, the new system provided the family with two to three bedrooms, a large living room complete with a kitchenette and an open or closed patio. The big apartment needed a lot of housework and the kitchenette was an attracting factor for the family to have its evening meals there instead of in the communal dining hall.

Having more housework, the woman needs more help from her mate. More paternal investment strengthens the nuclear family. All the indicators of its growing importance appear: the romantic love complex; early dating and early sex life of the young females; early marriage; great formal ceremonialism of the wedding; stability of the marriage; descending divorce rates; ascending remarriage rates; almost unbearable social status of singles, especially of females in the age of fertility; institutionalized and informal matching for singles; and rising fertility rates reaching a new modal average of four children per couple.

The males, indeed, invest much more than earlier, in their children and in the family home. Seeing his mate almost collapsing under her self-imposed heavy burden of 5 to 7 hours of work, housework, preparation of meals, nursing and nurturing the children, the male takes upon himself the heavy work of gardening, removing the garbage, bringing and taking the laundry and occasionally substituting for the tired wife by bringing food and washing the children, etc.

The strong nuclear family constantly attracts new functions to itself: it is a central unit of consumption, it has an important say in matters of education, it becomes a focus of *rites de passage* of all its members. Bowing to this general tendency, the kibbutz transfers functions, that were once characteristically collective, to the family: care for the children during Sabbath, care for the sick, and care for the aged. Especially in cases of manpower shortage, the kibbutz readily finds solutions in the general atmosphere of inclusive fitness and parental investment. This development pushes the kibbutz to the extreme limit of its uniqueness: it becomes more and more like the moshav shitufi, a kolchoz-like form of cooperation, where production is collective but consumption is individual.

In what sense is the present explanation superior to what we used in our book (see pp. 269–281)? First we used a very inarticulate and, even at the time of its English publication (1973), completely outdated biological paradigm, that of Count (1973). Count's essays on the biogram were first published in German and English (Count, 1958a,b). In his elaboration of the vague concept of biogram, Count (1973, p. 25) devotes two pages to the concept of 'parentalism' and actually speaks of parental investment but amazingly, he does not reach the conclusion that there might generally be some differences between the sexes in parental investment. Even in dealing with the mammalian biogram, he has only this to say:

> The peculiar mammalian physiological pattern of coitus–uterine gestation–lactation has its psychological corollary: The female always possesses a double reproductive orientation: an erotic orientation toward a male partner and a broody orientation toward her offspring; while the male possesses but one: an erotic toward a female partner. Hence the monopoly of familialism by the female sex.

Count completely misses the point: the problem is not single and double orientation, but basically higher female parental investment and high variability of male parental investment. The question is—generally and especially in the human case—under what conditions will a strategy of higher parental investment 'pay' for a male. Shepher (1978) tried to explain how the human male became a reluctant monogamist, deviating thereby from the usual mammalian pattern.

Tiger and Fox (1971, p. 6) criticized the concept of biogram: 'the total repertoire of possible behaviors of any species.' They argued that such a repertoire would be a static list, and in order to understand how the elements in the list are related, one had to know the rules that governed the relationships between the different items of the repertoire. These rules, being similar to those of the grammar of a language, can therefore be called 'biogrammar.' Thus the human biogrammar would be then the set of ground rules according to which the repertoire of universally human behavioral traits are organized.

Let us now return to *Women in the Kibbutz*. We presented our main argument on p. 272:

> We have already cited evidence that sex differences in political and economic activity are universal, that the care of young children is virtually everywhere a female monopoly, and that some widely argued explanations for this universality are weak, improbable, or partial. Our data show that although some 10 to 15 per cent of the women in the kibbutz express dissatisfaction with their sociosexual roles, the overwhelming majority not only accept their situations but have sought them. They have acted against the principles of their socialization and ideology, against the wishes of the men of their communities, against the economic interest of the kibbutzim, in order to be able to devote more time and energy to private maternal activities rather than to economic and political public ones. Obviously these women have minds of their own; despite obstacles, they are trying to accomplish what women elsewhere have been periodically urged to reject by critics of traditional female roles. Our biogrammatical assertion is that the behavior of these mothers is ethologically probable: they are seeking an association with their own offspring, which reflects a species-wide attraction between mothers and their young. Usually women have no choice but to have close contact with their children; in the kibbutz, the opposite is true. So, what kibbutz women choose to do may be significantly related to what other women elsewhere routinely do under similar circumstances, if also apparently more constraining ones. A single case cannot define a species, but given the experimental style of kibbutz society, the result is certainly revealing.

All this is true but the argument that kibbutz women act in an 'ethologically probable' way is a theoretically free-swaying assertion. Kibbutz women act as they do because they are mammals and, therefore, are predisposed to a high and direct parental investment. They, being cultural animals, are able to subdue this predisposition as long as the environmental situation makes such a postponement and suppression the only viable alternative. No sooner is the pressure removed, the behavior predictable through parental investment theory inexorably returns.

Then, too, in our handling the double phenomenon of polarization of sexual division of labor and familization, we argued that the two processes were parallel, but we did not show why. Parental investment theory explains both, and in fact, argues that the two phenomena are the different facets of the same process: the reindividuation of parental investment.

In summary, we rather agree with our own critics. We accept the data, but we criticize the interpretation, only for different reasons.

References

Bein, A. (1945). *The History of Zionist Settlement*, Masada, Tel Aviv (Hebrew).

Bernard, J. (1976). 'Maternal deprivation: a new twist,' *Contemporary Psychology*, **21**, 172–174.

Chagnon, N. A., and Irons, G. I. (1979). *Evolutionary Biology and Human Social Behavior*, Duxberry Press, North Scituate, Mass.

Cohen, Eric. (1976). Review in *American Journal of Sociology*, 708–709.

Count, Earl, W. (1958a). 'The Biological Basis of Human Sociality,' *American Anthropologist*, **60**, 1049–1085.

Count, Earl W. (1958b). 'Eine Biologische Entwicklungsgeschichte der Menschlichen Socialitat,' *Homo*, **9**, 129–146.

Count, Earl W. (1973). *Being and Becoming Human: Essays on the Biogram*, Van Nostrand Reinhold, New York.

Hamilton, W. D. (1964). 'The Genetical Evolution of Social Behavior,' *Journal of Theoretical Biology*, **7**, 1–52.

Peres, Y., and Russkin, L. (1977). Review in *Journal of Marriage and Family*, **39**, 627–628.

Rosner, M., and Palgi, M. (1976). 'Sexual equality in the kibbutz: a retreat or a change of significance?' in *Kibbutz*, 3–4, 149–185 (Hebrew).

Shapiro, J. R. (1976). 'Determinants of role differentiation: The Kibbutz case,' *Reviews in Anthropology*, 682–692.

Shepher, Joseph, (1977). *Introduction to the Sociology of the Kibbutz*, Ruppin Institute (Hebrew).

Shepher, Joseph. (1978). 'Reflections of the origin of the human pair bond,' *Journal of Social and Biological Structures*, **1**, 3.

Somerville, R. M. (1979). Review in *Contemporary Sociology*, **8**, 229–303.

Symons, Donald. (1979). *The Evolutionary Theory of Human Sexuality*, Oxford University Press, New York and Oxford.

Syrkin, Marie. (1976). Review in *The New Republic*. Nov, 25–27.

Tiger, L., and Fox, R. (1971). *The Imperial Animal*, Holt, Rinehart and Winston, New York.

Tiger, L., and Shepher, J. (1975). *Women in the Kibbutz*, Harcourt, Brace Jovanovich, New York.

Trivers, R. L. (1972). 'Parental Investment and Sexual Selection,' in B. Campbell (ed.), *Sexual Selection and the Descent of Man 1871–1971*, Aldine-Atherton, Chicago.

Trivers, R. L. (1974). 'Parent–Offspring Conflict,' *American Zoologist*, **14**, 249–264.

van den Berghe, Pierre. (1979). *Human Family Systems*, Elsevier, New York.

Wilson, E. O. (1975). *Sociobiology: a New Synthesis*, Harvard-Belknap, Cambridge, Mass.

Wilson, E. O. (1978). *On Human Nature*, Harvard University Press, Cambridge, Mass.

Small Groups and Social Interaction, Volume 2
Edited by H. H. Blumberg, A. P. Hare, V. Kent and M. Davies
Published by John Wiley & Sons Ltd 1983

5.4 New Wave Co-ops[1] (Ideas about cooperatives, and unusual ideas for possible consumer and producer co-ops in Britain)

Compiled by Nicholas Albery

(The following represent a selection from the 160 ideas included in the original work—see pp. 297–8 at the end of this sub-chapter.)

1. In some ways, of course, the whole concept of 'consumers' cooperatives' is up the creek. 'Consumer' is such an ugly word, 'one who wastes, destroys, uses up.' A bulk-buying co-op can just mean that the 7 lb jar of honey goes as fast as the 1 lb jar used to, because it's always there, encouraging greed. What are also needed are 'unconsuming co-ops,' 'living-better-on-less co-ops,' with people learning together to live frugally and to send 5% of their income to third world co-ops, etc., perhaps along the lines of the Lifestyle groups organized by the Dean of Bristol (see Organizations section, at the end of this report).

'Cooperatives' too is a dubious concept in some ways, often bringing out the worst committee-mindedness and bickering put-down mentality in people—if it is not established as a first principle that people within a co-op are free and encouraged to use their initiative, with minimum restraints, so that the co-op is experienced as enhancing the creativity of individuals, rather than as a bureaucracy holding people back.

2. In a neighbourhood it is essential before cooperatives are formed to discover the lie of the land and what's in people's heads already. One way we've found to do this is a cooperative newsletter coming out once a month or fortnight, produced by a different house each time—initially with no editorial content at all. This is important, as it allows the neighbourhood to feel less imposed on. A different couple of residents go round house to house each time, and collect a message from each person, if possible, however trivial the message, by encouraging the person to think of something—such as 'sewing machine wanted' or 'bike for sale,' or 'come to a party at my house on Sunday,' or a food co-op can give its news, and so on. The paper should be restricted in circulation to the immediate neighbourhood of about 60 households for intimacy's sake. Typed on stencils and duplicated, each issue then costs only a few pence.

3. Another way to discover what co-ops might be needed in an area would be to follow BIT's example[2] of setting up a 24 hour service advertising information and help on any subject—with a board outside saying 'We are prepared to tackle anything.' Then over a period of years self-help groups emerged as a natural process in the areas where BIT's activities had shown there to be a need.

4. The churches and the BMA (British Medical Association) should send circulars to priests and doctors respectively advising them how to assist in the launching of co-ops in their villages. Several successful co-ops, particularly in isolated rural areas, have been started up thanks to the efforts of the local doctor or priest. It would be good to spread news of their achievements among their fellows, in order to encourage more to do the same.

5. In any neighbourhood, the evolution of a cooperative feel can be accelerated if the residents can agree to pledge a regular commitment of, say, 20 minutes a week when they all work together on pressing community needs such as cleaning or gardening or redecoration work. The best time to schedule this work is before the general meeting, as it then becomes a traditional foreplay to the meeting, and creates a better atmosphere for the meeting, and tends to give status to those in the co-op who combine talk with action.

7. In Boston, the Cambridge Food Co-op is the size of a supermarket, with prices 15% lower, because members spend $2\frac{1}{2}$ hours a month helping to run it . . .

9. Nick Falk: 'Working class areas are full of warring communities, contrary to myth, so if setting up a cooperative, . . . the first thing done there will stamp it with an image—e.g. if it's language classes for people from Bangladesh . . . Perhaps the most successful way to use community space would be simply to lease it out to local groups . . .'

13. Big meetings are almost always a disaster, and need splitting down into smaller groups coming together again at the end . . .

14. Cooperatives which meet regularly for discussions of business, should also take the trouble to have sessions together to sort out their tensions and relationship problems. Not doing so has been the downfall of many groups . . .

22. . . . a bulk-buy club . . . can rapidly grow new dimensions. One instance is a bulk-buy food co-op . . . which led to a playgroup, women's march, self-help therapy, jumble sales and kids' club; and their hopes for the next stage included women going out together on social outings, babysitting schemes, a women's centre with self-health groups, legal aid, films, etc. . . .

26. Some people say there's a need for a wholefood co-op shop selling only local produce, or for barter. ('Who are being ripped off so that we can eat nuts, raisins and lentils? The third world undoubtedly.')

29. 'Co-op and mutual aid groups for old people. Besides cooperative food-raising and bulk-buying, the running of local employment bureaux, contacts for holiday exchanges, mutual instruction in skills and interests, swaps, a small monthly mag. "Over-60" centres at present tend to confine their work largely to entertainment and social activities.'

32. Just as tubes have alternate smoker and non-smoker carriages, one could have social or silent carriages on tubes or other public transport; and if one went in the social carriage one would know that it was OK to talk to one's neighbours. Likewise there could be discotheque compartments on the tubes, or drinking bars on the buses. ["Tubes" are urban underground railways.]

47. 'An idea for just a free space in the centre of the capital, a place with no rules, restrictions, forms to fill, money involved, where anyone can go at any time day or night with no need to ask or apologize, to rest, to be quiet or to seek company. It would need several dormitories and quiet rooms, as well as a central communal hall. One room devoted to silence. One can't say if it would tend towards a doss-house or a temple. Maybe a few residents, and an all night cafe. Perhaps libraries, theatres, clubs would evolve. It would need a nucleus of volunteers to keep it going.'

Christiania, the squatted 80 acre ex-army camp in Copenhagen is an example of such a free space and, despite being open to all comers, it seems to have attracted a bearable mix of junkies and disruptives on the one hand (who might otherwise be in institutions) and creative activists on the other. About 700 people have been living there for half a dozen years, and a series of workshops have taken root. Social pressure against undesirable behavior seems to be enough to stop the place falling apart. The constant threat of closure by the government has also been a great help in creating a sense of unity.

54. Witkar, the electric car co-op in Amsterdam . . . Witkar hope to build up to 15 termini and 100 cars by 1982 . . . This scheme grew out of the Amsterdam white bicycle idea, and will in future incorporate it, since the co-op member's car key will also work the bike padlocks at the terminus should the member prefer to go by bike. This will improve on the original white bike scheme, giving wide but not totally unrestricted access to the bikes. The present witkars have a range of only 4 to 10 kilometres, so a car with greater capacity would need to be produced for use in London.

Obviously, there would also be scope for a producer co-op to be the manufacturer of the vehicles over here . . .

59. 'A community-owned pub, re-funding hundreds of pounds a week of cheap beer profits back into the community. Plus home-brew available. Lead up to this with a monthly community dance with disco and local artists. "Change stems from very low-key activities based on community cooperation. The only potential revolutionary force is the working-class community where planners have not destroyed their culture. If a community meet regularly, hundreds of benefits come from increased solidarity." '

60. The following idea I successfully tested for one day in Notting Hill: a community pub, where every time you have a drink, you mark which of the community projects listed on the wall should receive the profit from the sale of your drink. Helps to make you believe that you are advancing the revolution by drinking. A busy pub could raise several hundred pounds a week in this way.

68. In Northern Denmark they have held 3-month-long tented alternative festivals which developed into mini-cities, and were an inspiration in cooperation and self-reliance to many people, and out of which groups forming permanent communities could grow.

71. The San Paolo University could be copied elsewhere: all it consists of is a prospectus listing all courses on offer and where they meet and how much they cost. It has no premises for students. Anyone can write in offering a course for inclusion in the regular prospectus, on any subject.

73. 'This is a mad beautiful idea for bringing people together. You know what yellow pages in the telephone book are but do you know what the pink pages are? Everyone in the city would be allowed so much space in the pink pages to say whatever they might wish to say, advertise, proclaim, etc., and these would be put in alphabetical order according to subject. Anybody could call up anyone—and both parties could decide where or if or when or why, etc., they go from there.'

75. . . . Creating an open communal garden out of wasteland in the inner city . . .

83. Suggestion for an alternative houseowners' association, geared to obtaining 100% loans for those with adequate income but little or no capital, who would undertake to:

(a) Buy a house of the recommended size and facilities.
(b) Use only a minimum amount of accommodation for themselves.
(c) Reserve one large room for communal use.
(d) Rent the remainder at cost, giving preference to those who would otherwise experience extreme difficulty in finding somewhere to live.
(e) Grow a certain amount of produce in the garden.

Such a scheme would cut through the whole assumptions of ownership and vacant possession; and it might shame middle-class owners of houses which are for the exclusive use of themselves and their kids, into freeing some of that space.

89. Just as the New Zealand government has provided marginal land for young people to set up 'Ohu' work cooperatives, so this government should give the opportunity to self-selected groups of people to set up as 'social experiments', new villages on fringe land such as ex-military establishments; on the agreement that the social history of the new villages be recorded in detail.

97. Local councils could be cooperatively run—just as you are summoned for jury service, so you could be summoned to become a councillor, maybe for a fixed term or for a fixed project, say a building project. Could the council be 50% regular councillors and 50% summoned citizens, with expert advisers?

108. 'Craft retail collectives importing direct from craft-producing co-operatives in the third world, and helping to initiate more self-help craft-aid projects from surpluses generated; thus cutting out exploitative middlemen.'

122. 'A good way to create a greater feeling of cooperation and self-reliance within a neighbourhood, and a spectacularly good way of fighting any attempt by central government to interfere adversely with one's neighbourhood, is to declare independence, and to become a nation in one's own right. . . .

The recommended method of declaring independence is as follows: hold a referendum of all inhabitants, and then, depending on the result, apply to the United Nations and possibly the EEC for membership. Call on the United Nations for a peace-keeping force in case of trouble with imperialistic Britain. Inform the media worldwide. Create a heraldic device and motto for the nation. Issue stamps (20p [40¢] a sheet is the cost price by colour Xerox). Make a rubber stamp for visitors' passports (the rubber stamp costs about £6 [$12].) Create as many institutions as possible, or as necessary for the good life, such as a national theatre and film institute.

The ideal size for a nation is about 100 to 200 citizens—any bigger and one's not likely to know all the ministers or to have easy access to them. . . .

New nations should of course strive for a cooperative constitution—in Frestonia, there are no subjects, everyone is a minister of state, no one is prime minister, and ministerial roles rotate every three months to give maximum experience of government to all concerned.

It is recommended that all new nations make contact with the Micropatrological Society ... They are in contact with 150 microstates throughout the world.

The advantages of announcing one's neighbourhood as a nation are manifold: people can take it on whatever level they like, as a joke, or deadly serious, as a symbol, as a publicity gesture, as a legal quirk, as a foretaste of the future, as a step in the right decentralist direction, etc. (As a safety measure, citizens who so wish can retain dual nationality).

In Frestonia, three near-derelict streets became world-famous overnight, TV companies from half a dozen nations swooped on the new republic, tourists began to arrive by the coachload. Tourism and the media made quite large sums available to the exchequer. But mainly, cooperation within the area was enhanced, and it is now more realistic to look towards the day when Frestonia will become a craft settlement, instead of the threatened industrial estate.'

126. 'Sociological holiday exchanges between, say, American sociologists and people from a housing estate in the East End, could prove very popular—so could squatting holidays.'

Further information

Nicholas Albery, 48 Abingdon Villas, London W8, can supply further information about many of the above ideas, if required. Further information is also available in the following:

Publications

Co-op Year 2000 (Ideas for encouraging innovation within Co-op Retail Societies.), £2 from M.A.C., 18 Victoria Park Square, London E2.

In the Making, a directory of cooperative projects, from 44 Albion Rd., Sutton, Surrey, UK. Also produce regular supplements. £1.40.

Turning Point, newsletter and meetings, £2 subscriptions, from Spring Cottage, 9 New Road, Ironbridge, Shropshire TF8 7AV, UK. New Age news.

Organizations

Communes Network, Redfield Community, Winslow, Bucks., UK; Newsletter, £4 subscriptions.

Lifestyle Groups, c/o Revd Horace Dammers, Dean of Bristol, The Cathedral, Bristol.

Urban and Economic Development Group (URBED), 359 Strand, London WC2. Have helped set up cooperative workshops in London.

Notes

1. Some of the ideas in this report are mine, but many are gathered from a variety of sources. I am particularly grateful to the seven people who attended my think tank of 14 November 1978.
This report was prepared for submission to the *Mutual Aid Centre*, 18 Victoria Park Square, London E2, which was set up by Michael Young to encourage the development of mutual self-help. The centre is involved in activities such as do-it-yourself centres for the repair and servicing of domestic appliances, a motorists' cooperative garage in Milton Keynes, and parents acting together to preserve small schools faced with closure. The centre also organized 'brain trains,' that is, 'study clubs' of commuters on morning trains into London. A full copy of the report is available from the author (address as above, under 'Further information') for £3.50.
2. [BIT was an information service in London.]

Small Groups and Social Interaction, Volume 2
Edited by H. H. Blumberg, A. P. Hare, V. Kent and M. Davies
Published by John Wiley & Sons Ltd 1983

5.5   Marx and Brown Rice*

Uhuru Collective   *Cowley Road, Oxford, England*

If any of us who have been running Uhuru these last two and a half years were involved in setting up a similar project elsewhere, we would think seriously about several issues that barely crossed our minds before we came here. So we might as well write them down for others to think about, since they may face similar issues.

There is a book that has been quite popular recently called *Zen and the Art of Motorcycle Maintenance*. The author, Robert M. Pirsig, argues that there is a major divide in Western society between people who are into Zen—and philosophy, and aesthetics, hallo birds hallo trees hallo sky, and perhaps relationships, but who are technologically incapable—and those who are into motorcycle maintenance, who understand the technology that maintains Western society. The book bore out some of our experiences at Uhuru.

There have been many painful tensions, as well as much laughter and a little peace, at Uhuru. Many of these strains were, admittedly, due to our personalities and to our not caring enough for each other, and so are of limited interest to others. But a fair number of the tensions which we thought of in personal terms were in fact due to the different aims or ideals that we held, or to the ways we had been differently brought up to behave. If we had realised this, we are now discovering, it would have been easier to discuss and resolve these tensions. In so far as conflicts did arise out of different ideas and upbringings they can be of interest—warnings—to others.

Apart from the Zen/technology split, there were the alternative lifestyle/mainstream politics dilemma, the male/female upbringing difference, the efficient executive/unselfconfident person clash or worse still failure to clash, the

---

* Reprinted from Uhuru Collective (1976). *A Working Alternative*, Uhuru, Oxford, pp. 16–25. Reproduced by permission of Uhuru.

home/open house incompatibility and more. If any of us were Robert M. Pirsig, we would write about these fascinatingly. As it is, here are some observations anyway. The first one, by the way, is that it is all more complex than these simplistic contrasts like Zen/technology make it appear: apart from the fact that all of us were male or female, none of us completely represented any of these rather extreme points of view or traits of character. It was rather that they were present to different degrees in all of us; and the tensions were often between different attitudes held by the same person rather than a clear person against person clash.

Home or open house

To start with something fairly straightforward: the use of living accommodation above a shop or cafe like Uhuru. We have had to decide whether to use it as

- a 'crash pad' for homeless or mentally messed up people
- a head-quarters for fund-raising campaigns
- a quite place to talk with claimants
- a common room where anyone helping in Uhuru can come to drink coffee and listen to records
- a home for the five or six people actually living there

(it has been all these things) and the use of upstairs is under constant discussion. The people who live there may need peace, solitude and space to create a 'family' atmosphere among themselves, particularly when they are tired out by working downstairs, and even more particularly when they are ill. If they do want this, the other uses of the place must be severely curtailed, and everyone must help with housework to make the place 'homely'; or else those who need such a home must for their own and everyone's benefit live out.

One sure recipe for getting to a place where you all resent each other, and thereby both alienate others who could help the project and diminish your own creativity in it, is to fail to recognise these different and incompatible ideals for the use of living accommodation and so, instead of working out an agreed policy in discussion, veer between extremes, muttering curses under your breath about your impossible friends. We did this for a time and it was awful. The tensions wore out some of us who were living there. We were inconsistent to our friends: some of us would invite people up, others would ask them to leave. As a result several people who wanted to be part of the project felt rebuffed and left. This was not only a case of a young lifestyle putting off older people, though that happened too; it was a case of a 'home' ideal, putting off those whom people upstairs did not want to be part of the 'family.' So, please, decide on a consistent policy *before* you collect six people with different views of the home all living in it!

And whoever you have living there, no matter how compatible they seem, there is no substitute for all getting together and talking frankly—particularly before it has got too bad. Otherwise the best of friends can get alienated from each other, as we have seen. It is often a succession of trivial irritations which build up bad feeling. No one can bring themselves to sound a harsh note by complaining about a trivial item—it sounds too niggly. But it's essential to find a way of doing it: things have gone much better when we have done so. . . .

Marx and brown rice

If the intellectual/practical split goes right through the left, so does the alternative lifestyle/mainstream politics dilemma. Too often the latter two seem to be in conflict when they could be complementary.

We waltzed cheerfully into setting up Uhuru without thinking too much about the degree of conflict between various ideologies on the left. But the group who ran Uhuru in its first year came from fairly different ideological backgrounds, and this led to initial difficulties. Dave, Tess, John C. and Graham for instance had got to know each other through the 'third world group' in the university. Connected with Third World First and the World Development Movement, this group had run lunchtime discussions, some street campaigns using theatre and leaflets to get over points to shoppers (for instance about the EEC's sugar importing policy), and fund-raising campaigns in fairly close connection with Oxfam. Dave, Tess and John had lived together in the summer of '73, and worked on decorating the shop together. Their lifestyle then was frugal but conventional—lunches of Wonderloaf and meat paste, as well as cheese and raw cabbage. Their understanding of the struggle against the policies which the Western system adopts both to the 'third world' and to the poor and powerless in Britain, was fairly conventional—supporting socialist[1] political campaigns. John was a research chemist, Tess had gone to university to study chemistry and had changed to politics and economics, Dave was researching a religious movement from a social scientific viewpoint—their mentality was rather biased towards science, rationalism, and efficiency. Personal actions, such as not eating South African oranges, they saw as relevant only if they were part of a political campaign, not for the sake alone of having a good conscience about what they consumed—since practically everything is tainted in the world trading system, and 'purity' would therefore require a hermit-like existence.

The others in that first year had been, or very soon became, much more involved in issues of personal liberation and an alternative lifestyle. Paul and Sue had been living in a commune situation in Manchester, working on the *Catonsville Roadrunner*. This paper had been working out connections between the spiritual life, non-violent political struggle, a libertarian or anarchist outlook and changes of lifestyle. Paul, Sue and Ana felt strongly the need for a style of everyday life more basically moral than the materialist life of conventional Western people. A wholefoods diet, a less bureaucratic style of organisation, and a caring communal life were important elements of this. For Bob and John S., in particular, supporting themselves by craftwork was also important. Bob began to teach Ana silver craft. In this outlook a number of spiritual and traditional beliefs and practices derided by rationalist Westerners were at least to be considered seriously, at best found to contain much wisdom—Christian faith, the I Ching and astrology, herbal remedies and acupuncture, and Eastern religions for example. All this was not seen as just a personal matter. Behind it lay a vision of long term social change: that the replacing of materialist values by a growing movement of people would challenge Western capitalism more effectively than any amount of conventional politics would. Paul particularly perhaps at that time, as most of us have since, combined an appreciation of these approaches to lifestyle with concern for political campaigning.

In the first months is was John S., Sue, Ana and Bob who worked most in the shop, and therefore their approach rightly suffused it. Upstairs since issues of diet, for instance, were of greater importance to those who were keen on an alternative lifestyle than to the others, it was the wholefoods diet which was followed by all. Further arguments for it was that it was cheap and interesting.

Looking back on it Dave, Tess, John and Graham to some extent suffered from culture shock in that first year. They learnt a new language (all the hip terms like 'suss', 'freak out', 'rip off'), a new diet (Dave for instance had cooked for himself cheaply the previous year without seeing a lentil, dried bean, or wholegrain, and had never heard of tahini, miso, or tamari), a new attitude to organisation and to people living in a house together. And the shop was all very different from what they had imagined it was going to be. For them there was the temptation to think, when coping with these things became difficult, 'We were the first in this project; if only we had not chosen the others it would be so much easier and less confusing.'

There were sore points at which these various ideological approaches seemed to clash: often small issues which aroused resentment out of all proportion because they arose from wider differences of outlook. They included debates on the sort of food we should sell in the shop; and whether some strongly held opinion about food or whatever was scientifically based or not, and whether it mattered. Then there was the point that people attending political meetings in the evenings needed punctual meals if they were not to go to the meeting hungry. Students who could only spare an hour or two from the library to work in the shop needed a rota system if they were to use their time effectively: otherwise they might turn up and find that they weren't needed, or else find that when they had to go there was no one to relieve them. More important issues included the fear that Uhuru's attempt to relate well to the local working class community, to ordinary shoppers and pensioners, which was essential to political and community work, was being thwarted by Uhuru's image as a 'freak' shop. A massive police drugs raid incidentally showed us how straight society viewed us (there wasn't anything for them to find—apart from Graham's sample of Percy Thrower compost and some vitamin C powder which they took for analysis thinking it might be cocaine—as they would have known if their prior investigation had been better, since we had a clear policy against drugs on the premises). Another problem area was that those who were more immersed in campaigns outside Uhuru sometimes took over the upstairs as a sort of campaign centre, which made life fairly impossible up there for the others. Those investing more of themselves in the place itself needed it to be more bearable, whereas those who could escape to flats, colleges, libraries could affort to let it become a mess.

But this should not discourage others! In the end we have all learnt a great deal and Uhuru has been a more interesting and valuable place as a result of the confusion as well as in spite of it. People starting new projects who are clear what they want had best decide to make that very obvious from the start and only take on those who agree with them. But if those who started Uhuru had done that they would have missed one of the most valuable lessons to have come out of the place for all of us. Namely that with a bit of give and take there need be no conflict between lifestyle politics and conventional politics, if both are followed in a way that avoids the pompousness that both sides are prone to—the feeling amounting almost to contempt of those who do not follow their path. Combined, lifestyle politics and campaigning to affect the power structures directly, can have a greater effect in challenging materialist values, culture and social organisation than either can alone. Having survived the turmoil we found the meshing of ideologies in a confined space had been wonderfully creative.

It is noticeable that those most into straight politics have often been shot to pieces in their personal lives—viz. Labour politicians with several houses and children at public[2] school, or New Left male leaders dominating 'their' women. People who concentrate on the purity of their personal lives and relationships, though, have often been too serene or too superior to muck into political organising. The women's movement has probably done more than anything to break this down—to relate political oppression and struggle to personal experiences and to the need for waging the battle in your own life as well as in the public arena. We would like to be able to practise this sort of synthesis ourselves, and the experience at Uhuru has helped all of us towards this. Most of us now are fairly different from what we were in that first year, having converged a lot in our ideas and become friends again.

Uhuru's political line?

In the end Uhuru has emerged as mainly vegetarian, no longer selling local crafts, but selling more whole foods than anything else, participating in left wing political campaigns and in community work. Where does this put us in the political spectrum?

None of the most committed Uhuru workers have yet belonged to the 'hard left' parties—the I.S., I.M.G., W.R.P., etc.—and only one has campaigned for the Labour Party while at Uhuru, though volunteers working in Uhuru have belonged to both poles. Our aims for society and our views on the means to reach them are more libertarian socialist than Trotskyist, it would probably be fair to say. At least we tend to react strongly against the authoritarianism of the self-styled 'vanguard' parties which insist on a joint line for their members. They often seem to hold a simplistic view of the efficacy of violent revolution. Indeed they tend to have so structuralist a view of society that they think that if only social structures are overturned people will inevitably be liberated. As a result the content of their personal relationships even within the party does not seem to be attended to enough. In addition they often seem to hold people who disagree with them (meaning the majority of the population including the working class) in contempt, being so sure they know exactly what is good for everybody else, and that they alone can fulfil it. Put together, these characteristics seem to us to hold a grave danger of authoritarian types and relationships flourishing in these political movements, leading to a trend to Stalinism after the revolution if such groups hold power—and how will that liberate people?

On the other hand most people at Uhuru have as little sympathy with those groups that emphasise love, religion, and individual morality to the neglect of political struggle. Such groups do not appreciate the realities of power, and the way in which materialist values are embodied in the social structure of our society. We are aware that people on the 'hard' left could and do make similar criticisms of us—that we are too charitable, too reformist, too alternativist, out of touch with the real needs for instance of the developing countries, whose problems cannot be touched by the growth of a few cooperatives, or of the British working class, for whom brown rice and shops run on voluntary and 'scab' labour are irrelevant.

Our dilemma is that of being uncertain about a real alternative road to political power to that of the tightly organised 'vanguard' party which waits and prepares for economic crisis. We want to see everyone grow in confidence and political understanding to the extent that if a crisis situation ever arises, when social structures are amenable to being overturned and rebuilt, then the people will be able to force the 'vanguard' to obey them; and if crisis does not arise, that people will nonetheless be able to make progress in democratising their industries, institutions and families. To that end we back the establishment of workers' cooperatives (in the 'third world' or in the Cowley Road, or anywhere else), mothers and toddlers groups, adventure playgrounds, claimants' unions, tenants' campaigns, trade union rejection of the Social Contract—indeed the whole range of community- and industry-based struggle, organisation and self-help, in so far as it does increase both awareness of the power that can be taken and commitment to the values of equality, cooperation, love, and the solidarity of the alienated and oppressed. Whether such activities do have such effects is often open to doubt. Our efforts are riddled with uncertainty about their value—it would probably be easier to be in an out-and-out vanguard party or alternative commune, where certainties give a sense of security.

And Uhuru's role in this libertarian struggle for people's power? We can be useful as a meeting place, a centre for information and discussion for all the left groups (including of course the Trotskyists—we are nearer to them than the criticisms above might suggest). We tend through our open image to involve people who would not go near a political party, but who gradually become politicised through Uhuru and move on to more overtly political action. We do have 5–6 people with half their week free for community/political activity, and when we organise ourselves well this can be very useful. In the long term there is much to be said for spreading the practice of a diet that does not waste the earth's resources, and it is worth some people running cafes and shops now to help that along, if that's the way they want to earn their living. Such a diet should be encouraged by any future socialist society, as should energy conservation, etc. It is not however our main aim to change people's diets or to conserve energy. We aim to be an unconventional form of politicisation, and are learning through experience.

Experts and others

(This section was written about Nov '74)
It's very easy to talk glibly about the evils of 'exploitation', hierarchical structures, and job specialisation. It is much more difficult to build a project that actually incorporates alternative approaches to work.

Uhuru definitely does see itself as a collective—using a weekly workers' meeting and occasional 'open meetings' as platforms for discussing all important topics and decisions. On the whole it works well, but it's important to highlight some of the problems:

(a) In order to be efficient, people persist in taking on jobs they're good at and find easy to do. It means they get into a routine, get less satisfaction from repeatedly doing the same job, don't learn how to do other things, and prevent other people from learning the job. It places people in a position of power if they have accumulated a specialist knowledge in one field, and fails to give them an understanding of what it is like to do other things and gain a wider sympathy for other people's point of view.

(b) In contrast to that it's annoying being unable to get really involved with a project because you have to constantly break off and take up other jobs.

(c) It's easy for a hierarchical situation to develop when volunteers take on the more mundane (but essential) jobs like washing-up, serving in the cafe, etc., while full-time people take the more interesting project work. There is a real danger that volunteers never get on the escalating ladder to more interesting involvement and see their commitment to Uhuru as a routine obligation to wash-up and clear the tables.

(d) If full-time workers don't share their accumulated knowledge and information they develop a position of strength which must help to alienate them from other people.

(e) It's easy to label people with particular areas of work. The person then feels that it *is* his/her responsibility and fails to get enough support when something goes wrong or he/she can't handle a particular problem.

(f) There's a problem that the people who initially set up the project hold expectations of the team enough flexibility or a sense of 'open progress'. Also those who financially set up the project must be careful not to use that 'economic strength' to any advantage.

(g) It takes just one member of the team to repress an emotional upset by throwing himself/herself into excessive amounts of work to pressurise everyone into feeling they're not working hard enough. The result: resentments and grudges build up, everyone is uneasy about relaxing, everyone does more work, and yet nothing more is achieved. Everyone has a different view on how much work is necessary, according to their other commitments. One has to explain these views to others and then stand by them and use leisure time in a constructive way. Projects are often made or broken according to the way people relax and share their spare time with each other.

We know we're on the right tracks when one worker gets up, does a little cooking in the morning, serves in the shop, helps wash the dishes, goes to give a talk at a school, handles some accounts before supper, and then sets the cafe up for a meeting in the evening. . . .

Notes

1. [In England, 'Socialist' often simply refers to the Labour Party.]
2. [That is, 'prep'.]

Small Groups and Social Interaction, Volume 2
Edited by H. H. Blumberg, A. P. Hare, V. Kent and M. Davies
Published by John Wiley & Sons Ltd 1983

5.6   Living the Revolution*

Susanne Gowan, George Lakey, William Moyer, and Richard Taylor

Movement for a New Society, Philadelphia

We have written a great deal in this book [Gowan *et al.*, 1976] about the vision of a better society and the need to generate a powerful movement in the direction of that vision. There is a danger, however, of becoming too fascinated with the goal, the vision, the ends of our action. We cannot be sure that our ends will be attained, whereas we can be sure that the revolutionary means we use are in keeping with the world which we envision for ourselves and our children.

If the great virtues and teachings of the martyrs, resisters and saints are relegated to a utopian or future-oriented condition, then indeed, they have little value for us at all. But the great heritage that this 'community of liberation' has left us is not some unreal, impossible dream. It is this: Love can, and must be lived today, despite the pain and difficulty of such life. Tomorrow will carry the tenderness and peace which we live now. Do not compromise today. It is all, dear brothers and sisters, that we have. [Guinan, 1973]

We are convinced that the American political economy must be radically transformed. We want to build a new society whose institutions will carry out the necessary work and will encourage the development of full, loving persons. But we are clear that such a new society will not evolve unless the agents of social change are doing all they can to become full, loving persons themselves. That kind of new society will not be sustained unless it is thoroughly infiltrated by loving and

* Reprinted from Susanne Gowan, George Lakey, William Moyer, and Richard Taylor (1976). *Moving Toward a New Society*, New Society Press, Philadelphia, pp. 282–296. Reproduced by permission of New Society Press.

joyous people whose commitment is to such values as justice, community, cooperation, simplicity, world equality, shared power, mutual well-being, and harmony with nature.

Economic and political structures can do much to enhance human dignity or to crush it, to enable love to find expression or to subvert it, but no system can automatically assure that humans will behave toward one another in a spirit of caring and justice. Ultimately, such behavior depends upon choices made deep within each person, and such choices are crucial if a real revolution for life is to come about. Inward and outward revolution, therefore, must go together. The revolution must be lived in personal and interpersonal relations, as well as struggled for in social, economic and political structures.

This is why we choose to live in the kind of community that we do. Realizing inherent dangers of a lifestyle that would 'retreat to the woods' or deal only with personal growth, the Philadelphia Life Center of the Movement for a New Society puts a great deal of effort into combining simple living, personal growth, and responsible relationships, with political and economic activism. That is, we see ourselves living in an evolving model for what we hope the new society might be.

It is our hope that in reading about the model, the readers of this book will think about ways that this and other communities may improve and flourish, new support systems might form and we might find new and better ways of living the revolution.

We do not offer the Life Center as *the* model of how to live the revolution, but one model which we hope people will seriously consider, evaluate, modify, and improve upon. We focus on the Life Center because it represents our most immediate experience.

We realize that what we write is limited by our own experience and background. At this writing, the Life Center is only four years old and we are mostly middle class, white, college-educated people with experiences in the peace and civil rights movements. Because of these limitations, we have found it necessary and valuable to be in dialogue with persons who are starting from other places and who experience limitations of their own. It is out of this experience and dialogue that we share our insights in the belief that anyone seriously committed to changing our sick society must consider changes in personal lifestyle and interpersonal relations so that they can 'live the revolution' in the present society.

The Philadelphia Life Center of the Movement for a New Society

The Philadelphia Life Center is a multi-generational support community for persons involved in fundamental social change training and activity. Beginning in 1971 as a group of about 35 persons, the Life Center has grown to about 125 persons living in seventeen houses located in West Philadelphia and all within easy walking distance of each other. We tie in with a network of other communities, work collectives, and training centers across the United States and in other parts of the world. The US part of the network is called *Movement for a New Society*.

Our community is enriched by the participation of activists from other countries, Japan, New Zealand, England, West Germany, Australia, India, Norway, France, have been some of the places from which Life Center participants have come. Usually the activists return to their own countries and provide living links to international movements. The travel is facilitated by the MNS Exchange Committee and contacts are maintained by the Committee of Correspondence, both located at the Life Center.

Some aspects of the Philadelphia Life Center/MNS

Households. The living arrangements are by households, autonomous units of 6–10 people with diverse interests and collective commitments. Houses are responsible for their own management and policies and are tied together only by an informal information network and support system.

Alternative Institutions. We have limited experience in alternative institutions here at the LC/MNS. However, one institution which we use a great deal (and have put a lot of thought into its operation) is the Community Associates, the print shop which printed this book. A five person collective, CA does commercial printing as well as the publishing of social change manuals, brochures, and books.

A food co-op has been in existence for about $3\frac{1}{2}$ years. LC members as well as people in the neighborhood can order produce and dry goods at more reasonable rates than is possible in stores.

Collectives. The Collectives are the working groups of the MNS. In Philadelphia we have 13 collectives working on a variety of concerns. Each collective, while in constant communication with other work groups in the network, is responsible for its own life and concerns. A collective will usually meet at least once a week to make decisions, develop strategy, discuss work to be done, and do personal sharing of what is happening with each of the members of the group.

The collectives in the Philadelphia area meet together regularly in a Regional MNS meeting where ideas and projects are discussed. It is here that support as well as questioning can take place. Philadelphia MNS collectives are: [Outreach Collective, Feminist Collective, Training/Action Affinity Group, Churchmouse Collective (focus on simple living and on issues of global justice that pose a challenge to the church), Orientation Week-end coordinating committee, an alternative food service, Philadelphia Namibia Action Group, a Macro-Analysis collective (research), a co-ordinating group for the training of organizers, B-1 Bomber Peace Conversion Collective, Committee of Correspondence, and Training Organizing Collective]. . .

Other groups and individuals in the MNS network develop their own styles and tasks, yet are committed as we are to nonviolent revolution. In Seattle, people are struggling against the institutions of sexism. . . . At the Eugene, Oregon, Life Center, emphasis is on tax resistance and opposition to nuclear power. . . . A San Francisco Life Center is under way, evolving a new model. . . .

A group exploring social change in the rural Southwest is the San Juan Collective. . . . In DeKalb, a group encourages the growth of macro-analysis seminars. . . .

In several parts of the country there are regional associations of MNS groups which get together for celebration and growth. To find out what the various MNS groups are doing, people subscribe to the MNS newsletter *Dandelion*, which appears about four times a year.

To get the *Dandelion* or find the nearest MNS group in your area, write to the Outreach Collective, 4722 Baltimore Ave., Philadelphia, PA 19143.

Training. By training, we mean preparing people for long-term social change, organizing and struggle. We have found it is important for social change people to have skills ranging from group dynamics to planning for and doing direct action.

There is a two-year program for social change organizers which is located in Philadelphia. Evolving out of a need to understand how we can systematically approach the developing of organizers and provide the support and challenging needed, the Philadelphia Training Program began in 1973 and is now working with its third group.

Another mode of training is the Medium Term Training Program, coordinated by the Medium Term Training Collective. This program is set up for persons living outside the Philadelphia area who come for a three day, one week, or two week training session. General skills shared are group dynamics, strategy skills, street speaking, direct action and campaign planning, conflict resolution, and others that the group defines.

Orientation week-ends provide an opportunity for people to visit the Life Center and have a somewhat abbreviated look at how training takes place. Included are short information sessions on the Life Center/MNS, a Macro-Analysis seminar, a nonviolence training session which provides an opportunity for the group to examine how we can learn to deal with personal as well as societal violence.

Other training takes place as collectives and individuals feel a need to get or share skills or insights. Much training also takes place in an informal manner as we develop new ways of interrelating and working.

Action. An important part of training/organizing is nonviolent direct action. From the beginning of PLC/MNS we have been training people for action. United Farmworkers demonstrations, Assembly to Save the Peace Agreement, and B-1

Bomber rallies are just some examples of actions that have been participated in or organized out of the community. Increasingly, Life Center folks have been working in our neighborhood and finding the need for local action such as a candlelight walk by neighbors through the surrounding area to show community solidarity and fight fear after a brutal crime in the neighborhood.

Connections to other groups. Many LC/MNS folks either work with other social change groups or have strong connections with them. We feel it is important to not only be in communication with but in an active process of learning from other people. Groups such as Wages for Housework (602 S. 48th St., Philadelphia, PA 19143) whose focus is the raising of consciousness about the exploitation of women's labor, provide constant input into our thinking about the effect of sex roles on our society. Other important relationships for our developing strategy are Children and Nonviolence (of the Friends Peace Committee), National Coalition for Social Change, American Friends Service Committee, War Tax Resistance, Friends Peace Committee, War Resister's League, and others.

Manuals. The last way that we will mention in which we hope to share our model is the growing body of writing available. Articles, pamphlets, and manuals are playing an important role in helping others to think about possible alternatives for themselves.

Most of the manuals, kind of 'do-it-yourself' pieces, are available from the Outreach Collective of the MNS.

Macro-Analysis Manual—a complete listing of readings and description of
   processes and exercises for the 22 week group self-education course. Macro is
   designed to help pull together the many aspects of social concern, economics,
   military, environmental concerns, third world relationships, into one 'big
   picture.' ($1.00 plus 18¢ postage)
A Manual for a Living Revolution or the 'Monster Manual'—A manual for
   organizers which includes tools of analysis, vision, strategy. There is also much
   about the role of trainer and many helpful suggestions about how to develop
   workshops suited to the needs of groups.
How to Work Collectively Manual—A manual describing the workings of one
   collective and processes that they developed in order to function more
   effectively and humanly. (Pamela Haines, 254 S. Farragut, Philadelphia, PA
   19143)

In process is a Direct Action Manual which will spell out step-by-step the components of a direct action campaign. Covers strategy design, dealing with press, police, and how to develop a collective working spirit that will sustain the campaign.

Some common assumptions

Within the Life Center/MNS there is a great diversity of interests, styles, and foci. Because the houses and work collectives all are autonomous there is an exciting and sometimes confusing variety of approaches to dealing with the problems and joys of everyday life. But we all share common assumptions and beliefs which allow and enhance the freedoms which exist and serve as guidelines for our growth.

Simplicity. Members of the PLC for the most part work only part time at income-producing employment, so as to leave larger blocks of time for social change work. Freed from the 9 to 5 treadmill and from the trap of 'working your way up the ladder' in jobs, community members can then consider their social change work their primary focus.

Simplification is aided by buying inexpensive clothing, getting food through our own co-op and garden, more efficient use of bicycles and public transportation whenever possible for travel, repairing our own homes, and sharing of household furniture and appliances.

Involved in the simplification of life style is a healthy respect for the needs of the individuals. Most community members have a room of their own and people learn that privacy is something that is easily attained in a sensitive household.

Skill sharing. Since it is our vision that in the new society we will have much less of the compartmentalizing of knowledge and skills that is so pervasive now, we act out our vision by skill sharing as much as possible. Everyone learns to plan and prepare meals, and in most houses to bake bread. Men learn the skills of household cleaning as well as women. Women of the community more and more are learning home repair.

The skills of working with groups, of public speaking, of folk dancing, of community organizing are shared also. No more, an elitist society of super-charged specialists who lay claim to a body of knowledge that is unavailable to many capable other people!

Anti-sexism. It is imperative in a society that is built upon the power and economically motivated tracking into sex roles that we must break this pattern in our daily lives. Women are strong, competent, and intelligent human beings. Men are gentle, feeling, affectionate, and playful. We all have all of those traits usually only attributed to the other sex. By giving each other emotional support as well as challenging sexist behavior we can grow to be more full human beings.

Elimination of sexist language is one small step in consciousness raising. Awareness of use of power in relationships is a critical step in the advancement toward a non-sexist society.

Children raised in the environment of a community in which men and women share equal work and responsibility and who are sensitive to needed changes in ways men and women perceive themselves, are growing up with a broader, freer vision of what it is to be a man or a woman.

Sexism is by no means eliminated in our community. Years of societal training have ingrained many destructive subtleties in all of us, but we are seeing the results of confrontation and challenging as well as loving support.

Egalitarianism. In the Life Center, we see that all community members share equally in responsibility for the life of the community. No one is the 'head of the group.' No one decides for all.

This does not, however, mean that no one ever takes specific responsibility for anything. Quite the contrary. This was one of the hard lessons of the Life Center. Just saying 'everyone is in charge' in reality often means 'no one is in charge,' and little gets accomplished. What needs to happen for an efficient egalitarian process to function is honest assessment of skills, talents, interests, then specific decisions, agreed upon by all concerned, about which persons will for a given *period of time* be responsible for a specific activity. This must be evaluated and carefully examined at intervals to see what adjustments or changes need to be made.

Cooperation and non-competition. In a community working at egalitarian processes, one of the most important elements is that of cooperation. Our society teaches us to compete, to be best, to win out over someone else. It is our hope at the Life Center that eventually this will disappear in our culture and we will see only cooperation and encouragement and we build that hope into our style of living.

'What can we do to help?' is a common question. Often the help is in the form of encouragement, specific affirmation that acknowledges appreciation of a person or of their ideas. Sometimes it is the loan of a typewriter from one collective to another. A group of folks will just show up to help a household which is moving or doing repairs. Sometimes the help is in the form of feedback.

A common form of assistance is the use of 'outside facilitators' for groups. A person who is not a member of the house (or collective) will come into a group for one or several sessions to facilitate discussions on difficult matters or to help with conflict resolution.

Affirmation. Support best comes about through recognizing all of those good things about people that exist in abundance. There is no such thing as too much affirmation. All of us need and thrive on real appreciation of ourselves.

We have learned that specific affirmative feedback is a powerful social change catalyst. Weekly house meetings incorporate time for hearing good things that are happening and most groups provide time for each individual to hear those things about her/himself that others really appreciate.

In an atmosphere of trusting affirmation, people then feel good enough about themselves, their work, and the people around them that they can hear feedback on needed changes as well as to surface problems they are having so that work might begin on those problems.

Feelings.   Feelings are important and it is our experience that any social change community dealing with the complexity of issues such as social justice, communal living, and responsible relationships must devise ways of helping folks to express their feelings in healthy ways. One method used in the LC/MNS is Re-evaluation Counseling, a form of peer counseling which helps people sort out old hurts from current realities. By identifying those old experiences that have angered, frightened, or hurt us and working on them in a counseling context, we are more able to see each situation in a new fresh light.

Certainly not all of the members of LC/MNS are in co-counseling, but insights and practices of 'RC' have permeated the thinking and processes of our groups. We have learned that it is important to affirm people's feelings, and to find appropriate outlets for negative feelings.

Querying.   Groups and individuals seeking to make decisions, evaluating directions, or struggling with problems might ask for help in the form of clearness or querying. Other people can come together with them and raise questions that would open up new ways of thinking.

It is assumed also, that as loving individuals, we have the responsibility to raise questions at any time with members of the community.

Study.   For the person truly interested in fundamental change, there is no substitute for careful thought and study. All of us must become involved in the most searching kind of study until we can begin to answer the basic questions of social change: 'How do you analyze what's wrong with the present society? What's your vision of a better society? What is your strategy for moving toward that better society? What should we be doing right now?'

We have already mentioned the national movement of study/action groups called 'Macro-Analysis Seminars.' The seminars are designed to help people develop social change actions out of a deep understanding of how the US political economy works and how it needs to be transformed. One of our first such seminars led directly into a nonviolent action campaign directed against US military and economic support of the Pakistani dictatorship of Yahya Kahn. Using a 'nonviolent fleet' of canoes and kayaks, we blockaded the ports of Boston, New York City, Philadelphia, and Baltimore against Pakistani ships, gaining the support of longshoremen who refused to load such ships. Because of the dramatic nature of these actions there was world-wide mass media coverage, giving us an opportunity to educate about an economic system which finds it necessary to give support to brutal dictatorships around the world.

Group dynamics. We have been working for the last four years to develop processes for groups which allow for healthy discussion without exclusion, and maximize the creative energy of any collection of people. We use consensus for making decisions, believing that in order for people to put whole-hearted effort into anything over a long period of time, they must feel themselves to be in a decision-making process where they are not going to be losers. Consensus is an exciting, egalitarian method of working toward a commonly accepted decision that can be acted on by all, not just a majority.

Other processes, carefully examine how women and men participate in groups, how we deal with feelings, and how goals and visions can be agreed upon.

Celebration. Celebration for us means many things. It means the basic attitude and appreciation for life which we hope would move all of us to meet the challenges of every new day. It means the festival atmosphere that surrounds holidays and calls us together as family. Christmas finds thirty or so people in a neighborhood park singing and dancing while decorating a 'people's' tree with homemade ornaments. Celebration can mean one house having a New Year's party for the children and adults on their block. It means the frequent 'get-togethers' for making music, playing soccer in the park, or for making applesauce. There are people for whom celebration means worship and the honoring of religious holidays.

Celebration has meant the calling together of the whole community when in deep sorrow over the loss of two beautiful and vibrant members, and rejoicing that we had known them.

It takes many forms, but basically it is affirming that life brings joy and hope. It is saying 'yes' to today so that we can move to tomorrow with the assurance that it deserves.

These are some of the elements that have been important here in the political community that we call our home. We are in a growing, changing, process. Much needs to be improved. We look forward to the time when our in-community communication is more efficient. We are moving now to be more in touch with other social change groups and their struggles. We are hoping to feel more rooted in and responsible for the geographic area in which we live. Our mistakes are part of our learning process and careful evaluation of what we have done well, not done well, or not done at all will yield more exciting change.

The common assumptions and the basic elements are only part of the story, however. The real sustaining force of revolutionary change is the spirit and vitality of those people involved in that change. Personal commitment, courage, love, discipline will be the backbone of the reshaping of our society.

More and more in social change organizations and networks throughout the United States and other countries, people are blossoming with new energy and hope. People are coming alive with the realization that by engaging in thoughtful, courageous, and ongoing struggle, we *are* the revolution!

References

Gowan, S., Lakey, G., Moyer, W., and Taylor, R. (1976). *Moving Toward a New Society*, New Society Press, Philadelphia.

Guinan, E. (ed.) (1973). *Peace and Nonviolence*, Paulist Press, New York.

6. Social Action and Social Change

Small Groups and Social Interaction, Volume 2
Edited by H. H. Blumberg, A. P. Hare, V. Kent and M. Davies
© 1983 John Wiley & Sons Ltd

6.1 A Social Technology–Economics Integration for Conflict Resolution*

Jacobo A. Varela

The work reported in this paper is concerned chiefly with applications. The writer, as an engineer turned social scientist, reached to social science in an endeavor to seek in the findings derived from pure research, material that would enable him and others to solve the many problems that occur when human beings interact in the course of daily life in their work and other situations. Although research is important, there is an urgent need for finding new ways with which to solve the many social problems that humanity faces.

The solutions proposed here therefore do not involve research. They constitute systems in which findings often from widely divergent areas are combined to create solutions to specific problems. As in engineering, medicine, and many other disciplines, although general solutions are available for certain types of problems (appendectomies for appendicitis), each individual case requires a unique solution adapted to that particular individual. Standardized solutions therefore applied across-the-board to all supposedly similar cases are not acceptable. This is typical of technology as contrasted to research. Technological problem solving and the scientific method as applied to research are two entirely different types of activity and should not be confused. The conditions required for a satisfactory technology of the social sciences have been spelled out in some detail elsewhere (Reyes and Varela, 1980). Very briefly, it can be stated that social technology creates systems' solutions and are based on idealizations of reality. Although often not of the rigor to satisfy fastidious researchers, they are nevertheless of practical value for solving problems. The nature of the solutions is determined by the nature of the problem rather than the particular theory preferred by the problem solver.

* A more extended version of this paper was presented in June 1981 at the XVIII Congress of the Interamerican Psychological Association, where the author was recipient of the Association's Interamerican Prize.

The approach of social technology is quite different from that of research or of theoretical untried formulations when dealing with conflict resolution. It is eminently practical. There has perhaps been too much stress on research in the social sciences with very little accompanying interest in actual application. Although initially research in the social area was started ostensibly to aid in problem solving it rapidly followed the course of pure research in which applications were felt to be demeaning.

This state of affairs, however, is not confined to social science. The emphasis on research to the detriment of applications has affected many other areas. It is even permeating such ostensibly practical fields as management and marketing. Klein (1980), on deploring a similar state of affairs in mathematics in which the field is rapidly receding from reality, states:

> Another inducement to take up problems of pure mathematics is the pressure on mathematicians from institutions such as universities to publish research. Since applied problems require vast knowledge in science as well as in mathematics, and since the open ones are more difficult, it is far easier to invent one's own problems and solve what one can. Not only do professors select problems of pure mathematics that are readily solved, but they assign such problems to their doctoral students so that they can produce theses quickly. . . Specialization has become so widespread and the problems so narrow that what was once incorrectly said of the theory of relativity, namely that only a dozen men in the world understood it, does apply to most specialties. . . The price of specialization is sterility.

The above, with little alteration could be said about the status of social science today. Although there is a huge depository of knowledge available, very little of this is being used to solve major or minor social problems. Most of what is being done in any area is totally disconnected from other areas. Reyes and Varela (1980) state: 'Problem solving requires that there be available a scientifically based technology. Technology without a good scientific foundation is ineffective. Science without a technology is useless.' This statement was echoed by Dr Jonas Salk in a recent TV interview: 'The next great breakthrough will come when we use the information we already have.'

A paradox

With respect to social problems, we are living a major paradox. The essence of this paradox is that while we have gained great insights into how social processes function, yet, when faced with concrete problems posed by specific situations, we tend to use the same old primitive procedures, disregarding the advances that are so easily accessible. It is as if Edison, after having invented electric illumination had continued his later research by candlelight. Economists in particular propose and implement on national scales action based on certain economic 'laws.' Such 'laws' have been formulated and are being sustained oblivious of the findings of social science. Many of these laws are therefore seriously flawed since they tend to be based on psychologically incorrect assumptions. Among these can be cited the 'law of diminishing marginal utility,' the 'law of supply,' the 'law of demand,' 'utility,' the assumption of transitivity of preferences, etc. It is not surprising to see therefore that the predictions of economists are most often unfulfilled and that their action seldom produces the predicted outcomes.

This is not to say that there is not some truth to the laws of economics. It is merely a comment to the effect that economic laws that disregard knowledge about human behavior are bound to be flawed.

The need to create solutions to problems is urgent. Time cannot be wasted in 'taking sides,' with economics or psychology. Both disciplines can contribute. Neither can alone be completely successful. There must be integration. The integration, as in any other discipline, can be achieved through tangible problem solving. Since our work along those lines has produced such integrative solutions, it seems fit to present at least one simple case of such problem resolution. It will show that there is a way to escape our social paradox.

Present approach to labor–management bargaining

As now generally practiced, management–labor relations, in particular as related to contract negotiation have been institutionalized into a petrified ritual anchored around such key terms as, 'preparation for negotiation,' 'the bargaining table,' 'confrontation,' 'trading points,' 'mediators,' 'ulcers,' etc. (The same holds for attempts at solving international conflict.) These and other aspects reflect a tacit acceptance of the inevitability of win–lose conflict (Sherif, 1962; Blake and Mouton, 1962). This fatalistic attitude is similar to that adopted by medicine with respect to pneumonia and other illness prior to the discovery of antibiotics. Before doctors merely waited for the 'crisis' to pass. Now they administer penicillin.

In the social and economic areas, we now possess much knowledge that properly integrated into meaningful solutions can be applied to the solution of conflict. However, before presenting an actual solution to a conflict based on these principles, some of these have to be spelled out and clarified.

The laws of supply and of demand

Basic to economics are the law of supply and the law of demand. The first states that the lower the price of a product or service, the greater will be the demand for that product (demand curve). Economics is a bit vague on this topic since demand is defined as desire for the product and immediatelly equated with amount of the product actually sold. The relationship is represented graphically as a linear function. The law of supply states that the lower the price, the less of that product will be made available (supply curve). These two laws are represented graphically as in Figure 1. The point at which the two curves cross determines the price and quantity of units actually traded. This is called the equilibrium point.

There is an insidious and incorrect assumption in both of these laws and their combined use. They both assume that since a change in price will tend to create a change in market conditions, such a change will actually occur. As the price decreases, the product will become more attractive and therefore more of it will be sold.

However, two steps are involved. The change in price may very well bring about a change in attitude, but this need not lead inevitably to buying behavior. Festinger (1964) stated 'it seems clear that we cannot glibly assume a relationship between attitude change and behavior.' Linn (1965) found that 'individuals with either positive or negative attitudes did not necessarily act in accord with these attitudes.' Therefore two steps are required. The first is to obtain a change in attitude. The second is to obtain a change in overt behavior.

If we therefore accept the laws of supply and of demand as possible indicators of attitude instead of actual behavior, we can, using other principles from social sciences, design a solution to a conflict in which the topic of wages is the only issue. In more complex cases in which other issues are involved but which can be judged even approximately on rating scales, more complex problem solution can be attempted. The discipline that achieves this is Social Technology. Examples of different types of solutions can be found in Varela (1971, 1974, 1976, 1977, 1978a, 1978b, 1981), and Reyes and Varela (1979 and 1980).

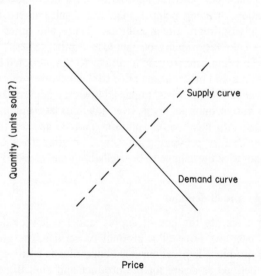

Figure 1   The economic laws of supply and demand

A case of conflict resolution (planning)

The union representatives of the eight plants of XYZ Co. met with the management team of negotiators to settle their differences over the basic hourly wage. The company paid $3.85. The union demanded $4.50. Matters had reached a crisis stage since the wage issue had been repeatedly relegated, both sides being unwilling to move from their final positions. The company stated that competition and economic considerations made any wage increase impossible. The union was adamant in requiring a 15% raise. One of the union representatives was enrolled in a Social Technology course and proposed to solve the problem using such a technology. The goal was to satisfy both parties while avoiding an impending strike.

It was decided to use the economic principles of supply and demand. However, they were used in the sense of attitudes as described above in order to see if an equilibrium point could be reached. The union representative, therefore, working with this author, and with her knowledge of the parties involved, expressed her opinion as to how the two parties stood with respect to the issue of wages. This was done by giving Likert-like scores to the different possible wages as perceived by the union and as perceived by management. These of course were the union representative's perceptions. The opinions as estimated by the representative are given in Table 1.

While it was felt that this preliminary estimate was probably close to the true feelings of the two contending parties, with an equilibrium point around $4.05, it was nevertheless felt that it would be necessary to obtain commitment from each of the parties on these estimates. Confronting the parties with these data at the bargaining table would probably provoke reactance (Brehm, 1966) which would lead to a desire on the part of both sides to restore freedom to think as they wished by denying the validity of these judgments. It was therefore felt that it was essential to obtain judgments from the parties separately. This would result in real commitment (Kiesler, 1971). Any later deviation from such commitment would lead

Table 1   Probable positions of the parties with respect to different wage proposals as expressed in Likert-type ratings

Hourly wage	Probable company reaction	Probable union reaction	Hourly wage	Probable company reaction	Probable union reaction
3.85	+1	−5	4.20	−7	+3
3.90	−1	−4	4.25	−8	+4
3.95	−2	−3	4.30	−9	+5
4.00	−3	−2	4.35	−10	+6
4.05	−4	−1	4.40	−11	+7
4.10	−5	+1	4.45	−12	+8
4.15	−6	+2	4.50	−13	+9

to cognitive dissonance. This would tend to restore the opinions freely given. It was also felt that each party was perceiving the other as being much more extreme and firm in its position than it really was (Stagner, 1956). It was also supposed that if the parties were to always sit at opposite sides of the table, the location would tend to emphasize the roles of 'us' v. 'them,' not conducive to problem solving. The meeting should at one moment be converted into a problem-solving rather than a conflict situation.

It was felt that the breakup of the 'us' v. 'them' mentality could be obtained by using material from research on proxemics, since on being asked to move from one locality to another, participants would tend to place some distance between themselves.

A case of conflict resolution (the implementation)

As soon as the meeting started, Mrs Smith, the union representative asked if she could meet alone with her group at that table since she needed to use a blackboard that had been placed at the head of the table for this and other reasons. Management immediately agreed and withdrew. Mrs Smith then asked the members to please now sit on *both* sides of the table so all could see the blackboard. As predicted, four of the union members rose and sat on the other side, but not contiguously, leaving also alternate vacant spots on their initial side. This left spaces vacant on both sides. It would allow management members to intermingle with the union representatives on their return.

Mrs Smith conducted the meeting in accordance with the procedure for group problem solving described in Varela (1971), obtaining definitions from the group as to how they felt that management and they would rate the different possible wage proposals. She obtained their estimates on the management position first and then proceeded to ask for their opinion as to how the union members would react. The results are shown graphically on Figure 2. They are shown in solid lines.

It is seen that the two lines cross at a wage of about $3.95. This is more promising than even Mrs Smith had hoped for. She then left the room stating that she would like to sound out management.

After dealing with other matters with the management team, she asked them to rate how they felt the union would feel with respect to the different wages and their willingness to strike if satisfaction was not obtained. There is no room here to describe how she led the conversation to the point where such a question could be asked. Having obtained this, she then asked management to rate how *they* felt towards the different wages and the possibility of having a strike. They did so. The results are shown in Figure 2 in dotted lines. From the graph, it can be seen that for management, the two lines cross at about $4.05. This is even more promising than Mrs Smith had supposed, based on her own perceptions of the attitudes as seen on Table 1. The two parties are seen as not being too far apart. It seems that

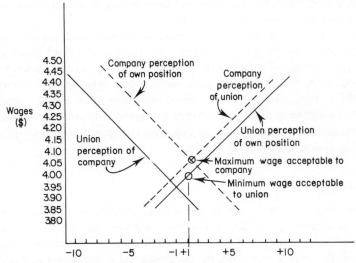

Figure 2 Perceptions of attitudes of self and other party towards possible wages

a settlement is possible between $3.95 and $4.05. It is even more interesting to note that the equilibrium point is higher for management than it is for the union. In other words, management seems to feel that there is a possibility for a settlement at a wage that is higher than the one the union is willing to accept.

With this knowledge in hand, Mrs Smith felt that she could bring the two teams back together, but not to discuss these curves. She had already planned that they would return to solve another though related problem. In that problem, there would be no two sides as defined by the win–lose situation. She could therefore ask the management team to sit anywhere they liked. They did so and sat in between the union representatives. This was the first step in breaking up the 'us' v. 'them' mentality.

The second step was to turn the meeting into a problem-solving discussion as described in Varela (1971) and to do this over a problem that was therefore not related to salaries. She therefore asked all of the members to join in deciding about what criteria should be used in order to select an industry for comparative purposes. It is to be noted that she did not ask what *industries* should be selected for this purpose. This might revert to a win–lose situation. On the other hand, by asking for criteria, in which no immediate connection with anyone else could be seen, she was turning the meeting into a real problem-solving situation. The group then mentioned several criteria such as type of product manufactured, location, size of the organization, etc. Mrs Smith then mentioned several industries that met the criteria and whose base salaries were within $4.05 and $4.10. At that point, the top management negotiator stated that $4.10 would be acceptable. Since this was higher than the least the union had been willing to accept, the entire committee immediately approved.

An agreement was drawn up and signed right there by both parties. They were both extremely satisfied with the results. The whole process had lasted less than 75 minutes. Months of acrimonious bargaining, perhaps even a strike, had been eliminated. Management reduced its dissonance provoked by offering more than the 'nothing' they had previously stated was their rock bottom position by persuading themselves that the $4.10 they had voluntarily offered was acceptable. They brought their private belief in line with the spoken statement (Festinger, 1957). The Union was of course delighted.

Conclusion

A combination of data from economics and psychology was very effective in solving an impending conflict. The supply and demand curves obtained from economics and interpreted as measures of attitudes, combined with findings on proxemics, dissonance reduction, the psychology of commitment and other findings, has produced a quick, mutually satisfactory, and viable solution.

This is just one of many cases, and a very simple one at that, in which social technology, to which principles of economics have been added, effectively solved a social problem that was considered to be rather intractable by all the parties involved.

Lack of space precludes presenting other very interesting aspects of the above solution as well as those used in solving much more complex problems. However, such concrete effective social action shows promise for possible further work in this and other areas.

References

Blake, R. R. and Mouton, J. S. (1962). 'The intergroup dynamics of win–lose conflict and problem solving collaboration in union management relations.' in M. Sherif (ed.), *Intergroup Relations and Leadership*, Wiley, NY.

Brehm, J. W. (1966). *A Theory of Psychological Reactance*, Academic Press, New York.

Festinger, L. (1957). *A Theory of Cognitive Dissonance*, Stanford University Press, Stanford.

Festinger, L. (1964). 'Behavioral support for opinion change,' *Public Opinion Quarterly*, **28**, 404–417.

Kiesler, C. A. (1971). *The Psychology of Commitment*, Academic Press, NY.

Klein, M. (1980). *Mathematics: The Loss of Certainty*, Oxford University Press, NY.

Linn, L. S. (1965). 'Verbal attitudes and overt behavior: a study in racial discrimination,' *Social Forces*, **43**, 353–364.

Reyes, H. and Varela, J. A. (1979). 'The Fundamentals of Social Technology,' Paper presented at the 40th Annual Meeting, Canadian Psychological Association, 14–16 June, Quebec, Canada.

Reyes, H. and Varela, J. A. (1980). 'Conditions required for a technology of the social sciences,' in R. Kidd and M. Saks (eds.), *Advances in Applied Social Psychology*, Lawrence Erlbaum Associates, Hillsdale, NJ.

Sherif, M. (1962). [See Blake and Mouton, 1962.]

Stagner, R. (1956). *Psychology of Industrial Conflict*, Wiley, New York.

Varela, J. A. (1971). *Psychological Solutions to Social Problems and Introduction to Social Technology*, Academic Press, New York.

Varela, J. A. (1974). 'Can social psychology be applied?' in M. Deutsch and H. Hornstein (eds.), *Applying Social Psychology*, Lawrence Erlbaum Ass., Hillsdale, NJ.

Varela, J. A. (1976). 'Social Logic,' Invited Address to XIV Interamerican Congress of Psychology, Miami Beach, Fla, Dec. (Published in Spanish in *Advances en Psicología Contemporánea* (eds., G. E. Finley and G. Marín), Trillas, Mexico.)

Varela, J. A. (1977). 'Social technology,' *American Psychologist*, **32**, 914–923.

Varela, J. A. (1978a). 'Attitude Change,' in H. Pick, H. W. Leibowitz, J. E. Singer, A. Steinshneider, and H. W. Stevenson (eds.), *Psychology: From Research to Practice*, Plenum Press, New York.

Varela, J. A. (1978b). 'Solving human problems with human science,' *Human Nature*, **1**, (10), 84–90, October.

Varela, J. A. (1981). 'The place of the /P–B/ matrix in marketing management,' in *Buyer Seller Interaction*, American Marketing Association, Chicago.

Small Groups and Social Interaction, Volume 2
Edited by H. H. Blumberg, A. P. Hare, V. Kent and M. Davies
© 1983 John Wiley & Sons Ltd

6.2 Group Processes in Successful Community Groups

Frederick D. Miller   *New York University*

Most traditional studies of voluntary groups have concentrated on describing members' characteristics (Turner and Killian, 1972). More recently, studies of social movement organizations have begun to concentrate on group organization and functioning (Gamson, 1975; Tilly, 1978). This paper presents a model of the organization of neighborhood block associations, particularly the factors that enable groups to maintain themselves and positively influence their neighborhoods.

In New York City, the basic unit of community organizing is the block association, a voluntary organization of the residents of a single block or group of contiguous blocks. Since 1968, more than 12,000 block associations have been formed in New York. The more than 2,000 currently active organizations address a wide variety of neighborhood problems. The present model is based on studies of more than 60 organized blocks, both interviews with leaders and observations of meetings and group activities (Miller *et al.*, 1980).

We wish to understand two aspects of organization success. One is the ability of an association to *maintain* itself—to mobilize resources and people, and to be able to raise and pursue issues. The second is the association's *effectiveness*—its ability to win demands, run successful programs, and positively influence local residents. Maintenance and effectiveness do not always coincide. An effective organization must maintain itself, but maintenance does not guarantee effectiveness. Some groups maintain themselves but have little positive influence.

Our research has identified three general variables that influence maintenance and effectiveness. These are: (1) tactical history—the types of issues the group addresses, the methods it uses, and the responses it receives; (2) resources available in the neighborhood—both the skills and resources of residents and the problems the neighborhood presents; and (3) organization structure—how the group makes decisions, recruits leaders and members, and mobilizes resources such as money and publicity. An outline of a model of the effects of tactics, resources, and structure on block association maintenance and effectiveness is presented below.

Tactical history

Block associations are usually started in response to a dramatic local problem. This can be a violent crime or a change in government services, such as the city cutting the number of garbage pickups or announcing plans to open a halfway house for juvenile offenders. A person or existing small group will call a meeting and start the organization.

In responding to such problems, block associations assume a role in 'neighborhood foreign relations' (Suttles, 1972), protecting the neighborhood and negotiating for goods and services with other neighborhoods and government agencies. Block associations have assumed a role left vacant by the decline of neighborhood-oriented political machines. The city government is often responsive to community groups in this role. The city seldom accedes to all demands, but is usually willing to talk, accept information, and compromise. Many groups then demobilize, having met the challenge to the neighborhood. Other groups maintain themselves, following through initial demands or broadening their activities to include other neighborhood matters.

Block associations usually first organize around 'reactive demands' (Tilly, *et al.*, 1975) by which people protest infringements of their traditional rights or goods. Reactive demands often arise in periods of social change. Reactive demands differ from 'proactive demands' that call for the recognition of new interests and rights.

Groups that do not demobilize must choose between concentrating on reactive demands to protect the neighborhood or broadening their agenda to include proactive demands for community development. This is a crucial transition. Groups that only raise reactive demands are at a tactical disadvantage. Because they are reacting, they have little control over what issues they fight or the time at which they fight them. These issues—crime, cutbacks—seldom allow final victories. Instead, the reactive group has to remobilize repeatedly around the same problems. Such remobilization appears to become increasingly difficult and encourages residents to consider individual withdrawal as an alternative to collective action (Orbell and Uno, 1972).

The proactive group can work in a much wider arena. Block associations provide free medical services, give scholarships, buy supplies for schools and parks, organize programs for the elderly, and run sports teams, among many activities. Such programs involve many residents in the association, thus increasing the likelihood of group maintenance. By picking accessible short-range goals, the group can demonstrably increase its effectiveness. Thus a proactive stance has tactical advantages. Yet many groups never adopt one.

Two explanations can be offered for why only some groups adopt a proactive stance. First, it is easier to get consensus about reactive issues than proactive ones. Few residents disagree about the desirability of stopping crime, but the difficulty in getting agreement about community improvements, particularly in racially or economically heterogeneous areas, can be substantial. Such disagreements can block the development of a proactive focus. Secondly, groups that have a difficult time pressing reactive demands may find it difficult to broaden to a proactive stance. If reactive battles have drained resources, there may be little left with which to pursue proactive issues. Additionally, an intense defensive struggle may dampen residents' ardor for community building.

Another tactical issue is the militance with which groups pursue demands. Block associations typify pluralist politics. They enable people to organize to get goods from the political system. As such, block associations integrate people into the political system. Militant tactics, such as demonstrations or even violence, often express a group's lack of integration. Such tactics may be effective for new or unrecognized organizations (Gamson, 1975). Established groups tend to rely on more moderate tactics: phone calls to friendly officials; lobbying; statements at public hearings; letters; and petitions. In general, more successful groups become more moderate in tone.

Neighborhood and resources

Tactical choices are influenced by the resources available to block associations in their neighborhoods. One important aspect of the neighborhood is its degree of ethnic and economic heterogeneity. Heterogeneity makes it more difficult to achieve consensus about goals and strategies. It is easier to maintain a group in a homogeneous neighborhood, where fewer issues encourage factional splits. When a group in a heterogeneous neighborhood manages to avoid factionalism, the diverse skills of its members may facilitate activities that affect more people. If a factional split occurs, the organization may dissolve or it may be maintained by one faction in opposition to other groups in the neighborhood. Such an outcome will greatly curtail the beneficial effects of the organization. Such cleavages are most likely to occur along socioeconomic status lines. These lines are confounded with race because race and income are correlated, but cleavages most clearly split middle class and poor or fully employed from underemployed.

A second important aspect of a neighborhood's resources is its residents' income and skills. One sign of a healthy block association is that many residents are involved. Wealth has a complicated effect on this. Money facilitates programs that involve purchasing things such as safety devices and trees, but money and the professional skills of well-off members can discourage mass involvement in the association. A wealthy block can purchase services instead of providing them through volunteer efforts. A skilled member, such as a lawyer, can often accomplish things, by working alone in the group's name, that another organization might approach by putting a petition together. Both tactics may be effective—for example, in forcing landlords to correct housing violations—but only the latter method involves many people. Organizations in wealthy areas are likely to depend on the efforts of a few experts rather than on mass participation. This lack of participation can interfere with group maintenance. When one or two of these active people leave the organization it often ceases to function.

Association structure

The ability of one or two people to run an organization raises the final issue, that of block association structure. Organizations differ in the extent to which they operate democratically. A democratic structure encourages the involvement of many residents and increases the likelihood of diverse points of view being represented. This may improve effectiveness, if the organization can represent all views. In practice, however, few organizations follow democratic procedures. Most block associations are enlightened autocracies whose leaders make decisions that are generally supported. These leaders usually are elected, but since elections seldom are contested, the leaders effectively are volunteers.

Three reasons can be offered for the absence of democracy. One is that members lack interest in day-to-day decision making. The second is that organizations require some centralization of power to maintain order in the absence of formal rules. A third reason, apparent in heterogeneous neighborhoods, is that an open airing of the cleavages within the organization could be divisive. This last reason poses a curious problem. Democracy functions most easily in homogeneous neighborhoods with few cleavages. This is where it is needed least. In areas where divisive issues arise, the threat that democracy will not work serves to limit democratic functioning. This in turn discourages people from regarding the block association as a means of achieving their ends.

Most block associations elect their leaders, but usually without opposition. Contested elections in block associations often signify divisive factionalism rather than healthy democracy. Leaders are an essential resource for groups. Regardless of their total membership, most block associations depend on the efforts of a few people. Such people are seldom willing to spend more than a few years devoting their spare time and energy to a community group. Leader turnover is a crucial problem for group maintenance. Most groups do not provide adequately for recruiting and training new leaders. A common reason for group decline is the inability to replace key leaders.

Prospect

This has been a very brief sketch of the roles of tactics, resources, and structure in influencing community group maintenance and effectiveness. It does throw some points for group research into relief.

1. Group dynamics—how groups operate—should be studied in field research.

Findings from laboratory groups—for example, on the effect of democracy—must be reconsidered in the light of findings from groups in the natural environment. Such factors as members' social class or their awareness of having an actual task to accomplish tend to be lost in laboratory studies.

2. In the absence of experimental studies that show causal relations, descriptive field studies that reveal regularities in group structure and action can be used to generate causal hypotheses. It would be particularly instructive to study how different groups handle the same problems under different circumstances.

3. The Lewinian tradition in social psychology would be well served by field studies that identify the problems faced by various groups and the costs and benefits associated with various solutions. Such findings would unite social psychological research with a potential application.

References

Gamson, W. A. (1975). *The Strategy of Social Protest*, Dorsey Press, Homewood, Ill.

Miller, F. D., Grega, D., Malia, G. P., and Tsemberis, S. (1980). 'Neighborhood satisfaction among urban dwellers,' *Journal of Social Issues*, **36**, (3), 101–117.

Orbell, J., and Uno, T. (1972). 'A theory of neighborhood problem solving,' *American Political Science Review*, **66**, 471–489.

Suttles, G. B. (1972) *The Social Construction of Communities*, University of Chicago, Chicago.

Tilly, C. (1978). *From Mobilization to Revolution*, Addison-Wesley, Reading, Mass.

Tilly, C., Tilly, L., and Tilly, R. (1975). *The Rebellious Century 1830–1930*, Harvard, Cambridge.

Turner, R. H., and Killian, L. M. (eds.) (1972). *Collective Behavior*, 2nd edn, Prentice-Hall, Englewood Cliffs.

Small Groups and Social Interaction, Volume 2
Edited by H. H. Blumberg, A. P. Hare, V. Kent and M. Davies
Published by John Wiley & Sons Ltd 1983

6.3   Resource Exchange Networks*

Seymour B. Sarason and Elizabeth Lorentz

Yale University

Students and resource exchange

There is no logical relationship between the principle of resource exchange and the formation of a network. Indeed, it appears that the most frequent manifestation of the principle takes place between two people with little or no consequences for the networks of either. When the principle is combined with network formation, it is usually because people have made a commitment to the value of the combination and wish to get others to see it in their self-interest. We know little about how frequently or under what conditions an exchange between two people gets articulated in a way so as to cause one or both of them to apply it elsewhere with other people. That articulation, we suggest, is crucial if the benefits of resource exchange are to be realized, because the nature of the articulation reveals the degree of clarity attained in regard to three factors: the values that should power the exchange, what it means for an individual's diverse potentialities, and the general significances of this type of exchange for dealing with social problems. To the extent that its articulation does not address these factors the maximum benefits to be derived from resource exchange will be limited, which is not to say there will be no benefits.

These introductory comments are stimulated by numerous examples of middle and high school programs that offer students the opportunity to be of some service to individuals and agencies in their community. We refer only to examples that have the following features: they are based on the belief that students are resources and that students can render a service; the students are not put in

*Reprinted from Seymour B. Sarason and Elizabeth Lorentz (1979). *The Challenge of the Resource Exchange Network*, Jossey-Bass, San Francisco, pp. 77–78, 160, 164–174. Reproduced by permission of Jossey-Bass Publishers.

'busywork' jobs but in those where they can acquire knowledge and skills; the settings in which the students are placed recognize the service students can perform and are prepared to give the students time and instruction; someone in the school oversees the program and has an active relationship with the students and the settings. The following is from a description of a program in the Shoreham-Wading River Central School District in Shoreham, New York (1977, pp. 1–6):

> A school serves a community by educating its children. If, in addition, by serving the community in other ways it can educate its children better, then the community is doubly blessed. Shoreham-Wading River Middle School, a public [State] school in suburban Long Island, teaches its eleven- to thirteen-year-old students by supplementing classroom instruction with responsibilities outside the school, usually for one hour each week. And, because they know their community service activities matter to everyone involved, the children live up to adult challenges of the Community Service Program.
>
> 'It makes me feel older than I really am to take over responsibilities I never had before. This is the very first time I have been able to prove what I can do,' reports a child whose school experience included work at a local nursing home. Many in this same project felt repulsion or fear when they began associating with old people. Unaccustomed to wheelchairs and the smell of disinfectant, they also had to face the hostility of an elderly patient who loudly claimed, 'Children don't belong in a place like this.'
>
> But kids and adults were transformed by their experience with the project; soon both old people and Middle Schoolers became comfortable with one another, developing mutual respect and even love. . . .

What is a resource exchange network?

We strongly believe that it is not until we have more and better descriptions of network formation, activities, and vicissitudes that we will better understand their actual and potential roles in society. We are not opposed to definitions and typologies, but we are aware that more often than not, and especially in regard to new research areas, definitions and typologies obscure more than they illuminate. Let us illustrate what we mean by discussing a provisional definition of the Essex Network:

> The Essex Network is an instance of a loose, informal, voluntary association of individuals whose interrelationships (their frequency and substance) depend on a few self-selected individuals seeking to make resource exchange a basis for existing and new interrelationships

so that membership expands, interrelationships are reshuffled, new clusters are formed around new self-selected individuals who will serve a role similar to that of those who brought them into the association. There are no geographical, substantive, educational, or status criteria for membership; no formal rules; and no time- or calendar-determined tasks. Members may or may not know each other, although each knows self-selected individuals and some members. They have access to each other; the most frequent way this access initially takes place is through the self-selected individuals; over time, access takes place more directly.

To determine whether something is an instance of a class of things requires that we look at as many instances as possible, permitting us to factor out features that are common, accidental, or unique. This, unfortunately, we cannot do, because descriptions of what might be appropriate instances do not exist. How would one decide what would be an appropriate instance? Take, for example, the two descriptions from *Uplift* [see Sarason and Lorentz, 1979, Ch. 3] ... From the very brief descriptions of the early phase of these projects, one might intuit (one does not really know) similarities to the Essex Network: self-selected leaders, informality, voluntary, resource exchange. However, in contrast to the Essex Network, there was from the very beginning a single, time-influenced task or focus that would require formal structure and roles and would, therefore, change the basis for interrelationships. There would be rules and obligations, if only because survival and success depended on earning more money than was spent. . . .

We do not have a ritualistic abhorrence of funding, but we have seen too many instances where seeking and obtaining public funds—a process in which one is aware (or is made aware) that one is competing for funds and that one must conform (or appear to conform!) to externally determined guidelines and criteria—have had disastrous consequences, especially for those groups committed to some kind of resource exchange rationale. This does not mean that these groups disappear. Many of them survive, in an organizational sense, but there is an obvious discrepancy between what they wanted to do and what they are in fact doing. Given the rationale of the resource exchange network, it should be apparent that the sources of and conditions for funding have to be given the most searching examination. In regard to the *Uplift* examples, our comments reflect a fear derived from the experience of countless people: You can win the battle of funding and yet lose the war of purpose and goals.

Let us take another example described in Chapter Three [of Sarason and Lorentz, 1979]: The Shoreham-Wading River report about how pupils in a middle school spend time each week in a community setting, not doing busy work but performing human service functions that are both necessary and educationally meaningful. There are again several points of similarity to the Essex-type network, the most obvious one being the theme of resource redefinition and exchange:

these young students can be helpful to less fortunate people, and the students need these experiences for their educational and personal development. What is also involved is a change in a school's perception of a variety of other community agencies and, in turn, a change in the latter's perception of the former. Another point of similarity is the voluntary basis of participation by students and agencies. A third point of similarity is the wide range of possibilities by which exchanges can occur.

Beyond these points, the similarities cease. Granted that resource exchange is a major goal, we are not dealing with an Essex-type network. To be sure, a network was formed, but its characteristics are not those of the Essex one. For example, one can say that the network is composed of students, some school personnel, directors of community agencies, and people with varying handicaps. The relationships between students and handicapped people are determined by school and agency personnel. It is not a goal of this network to facilitate resource exchange relationships among agencies, among handicapped people, or among students. Furthermore, if a major purpose is educational in the broadest sense (that is, to expand the student's understanding of self in relation to environment), one can ask, 'What is the student learning about the principle of resource exchange in society?' From the descriptions of the program, it appears that its success as an educational venture is judged by what students learn about themselves and others in the helping process—not, in addition, by what they have learned about their community. We can assume that school personnel and agency heads have grasped the idea of resource exchange but not its general potential or implications.

Here, again, we are not being critical. If more schools and community agencies engaged in such efforts, our educational system would be discernibly better than it is. Our comments are intended to underline two points: First, *resource exchange can be embedded in different types of networks* and, second, *for a network to exploit the potentials of resource exchange, resource exchange must be equal with any other purpose, and, therefore, must make it possible that interrelationships can be formed between any two people in the network.*

It could be argued that we are too quickly passing over the fact that a school's major responsibility is to students, and, although it can and should be part of a community network, there are limits of time, personnel, and responsibility to what a school can do. Put in another way, by virtue of being a formal organization with a legally based mandate, one should not judge a school by the degree to which it exploits a principle, such as resource exchange, that certainly is not clear in its mandate. This argument suggests that a formal and traditional organization such as a school is not conducive to the development of an Essex-type network. [Suffice it to say here, when we say 'Essex-type network' we are not asserting that the Essex Network is all it should or could be, but we are suggesting that the potentials in its rationale are of great practical significance. If formal organizations turn out not to be hospitable to the rationale, the question is why this is so and to what extent the rationale is absorbable.] . . . But this is precisely the kind of argument that for so long was a massive obstacle to redefining what a school is or could be and, therefore, ill prepared the school for dealing with the impact of social change on it. The Shoreham-Wading River School, others like it, and the efforts of the National Commission for Resources on Youth (see Chapter Two [of Sarason and Lorentz, 1979]) are all instances of resource redefinition and exchange in response to changes in society. They are also instances of redefinition of school-community relationships. So, when we suggest that schools may be able to become part of a community network in which resource exchange is a dominant feature (far more than it is now), it is not for the purpose of transforming them into Essex-type networks but to suggest that if they examined more closely the possible relationships between the resource exchange rationale and network development they would gain more for themselves and give more to others. What is instructive about the Essex Network is that its form is not related by chance to its function. It should be obvious by now that a resource exchange rationale can be expressed in different types of networks, but that does not mean that in any one instance the form of the network does justice to the rationale . . .

How does a resource exchange network come to be?

In addressing the question 'What is a resource exchange network?' and in trying to see similarities and differences among instances of them, we were comparing them from a cross-sectional, not a longitudinal, perspective. Each of them was at a different point in time in its history. Consequently, we cannot say that their current forms and functioning have characterized them in the past and will characterize them in the future. So, when we talk about different types of resource exchange networks, we cannot assume that their differences were somehow inherent in their beginnings. For example, most of what we know about organizations (their structure, administrative style, internal dynamics, and interorganizational relationships) comes from studies done long after these organizations were formed. As has been discussed in detail elsewhere (Sarason, 1972), we know very little about the context out of which organizations emerge and develop. Why do some organizations never grow up; that is, why do they go bankrupt? Why do so many organizations seem to be functioning inconsistently with their stated purposes? Why does it seem that 'organizational craziness' has become the norm?

In suggesting that these questions should be described and analyzed from a developmental perspective, with special emphasis on the prehistory and earliest phases of a setting, Sarason was not suggesting that the chronologically mature organization could be explained by knowledge of its gestation, birth, and infancy—just as some used to argue that adult personality was largely if not wholly explainable by early child–parent relationships. Sarason's argument had several parts. First, living as we are in an era in which the rate of creation of new settings is the highest in human history, we needed to focus on their earliest phases of settings in the hope of learning how they can develop to be more consistent with their stated purposes. Second, the new setting (like the new human organism) experiences a rate of change and transformation that will be greater than at any time in its future. Third, creating a new setting is an inordinately complex process, because it involves commitment, forging new relationships, garnering resources appropriate in quantity and quality, and dealing with interorganizational connections. Fourth, it is a process that generates changes in the leader that make it increasingly difficult for him or her to steer a course between the Scylla of indulging his or her personal needs and the Charybdis of conformity to externally generated pressures. Fifth, the tendency is both subtle and strong to protect the new setting by sharpening boundaries with other settings as well as among individuals and groups within the new setting. These are the major features of a new setting, Sarason maintains, to which one must look if one is to understand why new settings abort and disappear, or become so transformed that their initial rationale is hardly apparent, or change but consistently with their rationale. Explicit in his argument is the thesis that the differences one finds among chronologically mature settings obscures the recognition of the possibility that in the process of their creation they had many features in common and that the developmental transformations that occurred reflect an interaction between the demands of the process of creating a setting and characteristics of the larger society.

Sarason's conceptualization and description of the creation of settings are applicable to how resource exchange networks come to be. In fact, in his emphasis on the context out of which new settings emerge (the 'prehistory' and the 'before the beginning' stages), the new setting is seen as the resultant of the interaction among many types of networks, and by its very emergence it alters these interactions and initiates new ones. He emphasizes that the too frequent failure of those in the new settings to understand and deal with these network interactions, past and present, always has adverse effects. And in the emphasis on the significance of the leader, especially in regard to sensitivity to the universe of action alternatives appropriate to the setting's rationale, we see another key aspect for understanding how resource exchange networks come to be. It is not our purpose here to demonstrate, as we could, that how resource exchange networks come to be can be put in terms of the creation of settings . . . Our purpose has been to emphasize first, that, just as the frequency of setting creation requires that we understand the process better, so should the increasing popularity of the network stimulate efforts to describe and understand how networks come to be. Second, just as in the creation of settings the fact of limited resources is so poorly predicted and confronted, it is likely that one of the factors limiting the scope of resource exchange networks is in the looseness of the conceptual tie between their rationale and the fact of limited resources. Third, by focusing on how resource networks came to be we would, as in the case of the creation of settings, see more clearly how our individual ways of thinking, acting, and goal setting reflect our culture at the same time that that same culture is the major source of obstacles. And, fourth, by adopting a longitudinal approach to resource exchange networks we are less likely to be satisfied with static typologies and definitions, which, whatever their value, are poor guides for action.

In short, how resource exchange networks come to be will in our opinion turn out to be a more productive question than what a resource exchange network is. The second question is, of course, subsumed in the first, but the advantage of the first question is that it focuses attention on the connections between theory and practice: the natural history of, and the vicissitudes that occur in, the relationship between a resource exchange rationale and network formation and how this illuminates the fact that there are different types of resource exchange networks and, no less important, that many of these networks never develop because they die an early death. Any theory of resource exchange networks has to explain why some networks live and others die. The question 'What is a resource exchange network?' is not likely to come up with an explanation.

It is noteworthy that in the twentieth century the people who have contributed most to our understanding of individual behavior had a developmental approach. Freud, Gesell, Piaget, and Erickson are examples that come to mind. Binet should also be on the list, because he was quintessentially the clinical developmentalist, less enamored with typologies than with how individual differences come about (Sarason, 1976; Wolf, 1973). When people, especially in the United States, used his scales and developed typologies (*idiot*, *imbecile*, *moron*, and so forth), they were doing violence to Binet's developmental way of thinking and researching. The developmental approach to networks in general and resource exchange networks in particular hold the most promise for our understanding of ourselves and our society.

References

Sarason, S. B. (1972). *The Creation of Settings and the Future Societies*, Jossey-Bass, San Francisco.

Sarason, S. B. (1976). 'The unfortunate fate of Alfred Binet and school psychology,' *Teachers College Record* (Columbia University), **77** (4), 579–92.

Sarason, S. B., and Lorentz, E. (1979). *The challenge of the Resource Exchange Network*, Jossey-Bass, San Francisco.

Shoreham-Wading River Central School District (1977). 'Children and their community,' Middle School Friday Memo, No. 4–77, Randall Rd., Shoreham, NY 11786.

Wolf, T. H. (1973). *Alfred Binet*, University of Chicago Press, Chicago.

Small Groups and Social Interaction, Volume 2
Edited by H. H. Blumberg, A. P. Hare, V. Kent and M. Davies
Published by John Wiley & Sons Ltd 1983

6.4   From *Beyond the Fragments**

Sheila Rowbotham

[Participatory democracy]

Basically the women's movement accepts a form of 'participatory democracy' which has a long tradition from democratic religious groups to the American New Left of the late sixties and the anti-authoritarian currents in the student movement. The problems about participatory democracy are evident. If you are not able to be present you can't participate. Whoever turns up next time can reverse the previous decision. If very few people turn up they are lumbered with the responsibility. It is a very open situation and anyone with a gift for either emotional blackmail or a conviction of the need to intervene can do so without being checked by any accepted procedure. Participatory democracy only works if everyone accepts a certain give and take, a respect for one another's experience, a desire and need to remain connected. If these are present it can work very well. If they are not it can be a traumatic process. We have lived these difficulties in the history of women's movement conferences and the arguments about the Workshop Centre and Women's Day March. Despite obvious inadequacies though, 'participatory democracy' does assert the idea that everyone is responsible equally and that everyone should participate. It concedes no legitimating respect for permanent leaders or spokespeople.

It has been modified in the practice of the women's movement by women bringing in other concepts of how to organize from tenants' groups, trades' councils, trade unions or from the Labour Party, the CP and from Trotskyist and Maoist groups. Sometimes these have been met with a defensive suspicion and dismissed

* Reprinted from pp. 76–78, 132, and 134 of Sheila Rowbotham (1979). 'The Women's Movement and Organising for Socialism,' in S. Rowbotham, L. Segal, and H. Wainwright (eds.), *Beyond the Fragments: Feminism and the Making of Socialism*, Merlin Press, London. Reproduced by permission of the authors and publisher. Interested readers are encouraged to consult the original book.

simply as male dominated. But in cases when the women's movement has been stronger and more confident we have been able to meet these ideas and recognize the validity of some of their criticisms. The resilience of the women's movement has been partly because of this openness. In practice what we have been doing is adapting several forms of organizing to fit the particular circumstances we are engaged in. This does not remove the dangers of 'substitutionism,' or centres losing contact with local groups, or small groups of people doing all the work, or people not knowing what other people are doing. All the problems of democracy do not magically disappear. But it does make for an approach to organization which is prepared to test forms and discard or select according to the situation rather than asserting a universally correct mode. It also means that the 'movement' is perpetually outwards. As women encounter feminism they can make their own kinds of organizing depending on their needs. It is this flexibility which it is extremely important to maintain. It means that, for example, groups of women artists or groups of women setting up a creche or on the subcommitee of a trades council can decide for themselves what structure is most useful.

The women's movement shares with the 'anti-authoritarian' movements of the late sixties a commitment to a notion of democracy which does not simply recognize certain formal requirements of procedure. Obviously the danger of this is to reject completely any understanding of how these formal procedures have historically come to be used. When the dust of the first rush of enthusiasm settles it is often handy to have them. But if we simply respond to this by dismissing 'anti-authoritarian' movements as naive and just ignorant of the 'correct' political procedure, we miss an insistence which carries a deeper meaning of democracy. . .

[Consciousness-raising]

The consciousness-raising group assumes that our consciousness is changed in the realization that we share a common predicament. . . But the other aspect of consciousness-raising is that we experience a different kind of relationship with other women than we knew before. The ideal is an openness and trust, a recognition of other women's experience as well as our own. In practice we know consciousness-raising groups can become frustrating, as for example it is difficult sometimes to make general connections from personal experience. People feel other women know more than them, and are holding back. Mysterious silences appear in the meeting. It is sometimes hard to assert individual personal experience against a collective consensus which may appear because of hidden power structures. There are unstated ideological assumptions or an emotionally terrorizing morality. So consciousness-raising groups, like other political forms, are not magic. But they are still part of a crucial process of learning and feeling towards alternative relationships from those which predominate in capitalism. . .

Small Groups and Social Interactions, Volume 2
Edited by H. H. Blumberg, A. P. Hare, V. Kent and M. Davies
Published by John Wiley & Sons Ltd 1983

6.5 Leadership, Meeting Facilitation, and Conflict Resolution*

Lynne Shivers   *Movement for a New Society*

Leadership

Questions of leadership have presented endless problems to people seeking social change. Leadership has become confused with authoritarianism and the wielding of undemocratic economic and political power in our society. As a result, people often refuse to take on leadership responsibilities or imitate the styles of leadership around them. Neither results in viable political and social alternatives for our society.

Our experience has taught us that *leadership can best be understood as a set of functions* rather than as a personal trait. Dominating leadership is fulfillment by one person of many group functions and roles of leadership at the expense of, and with the cooperation of, other members. In group-centered leadership, all members take on responsibilities that often would fall to one person. The result is less centralized leadership, not vulnerable to the loss of a few members. When all group members share leadership responsibility, the group's cohesion and durability tend to increase.

Leadership is a composite of learnable skills through which the efforts of individuals are coordinated to accomplish group goals. These skills are used as appropriate in a given situation.

To exercise group leadership means:

○ to accept and clarify feelings of another without threat;
○ to aid the group's insight into its feelings and attitudes;
○ to relate emotions/feelings to the demands of the present situation;

---

* Based on sections from Resource Manual for a Living Revolution by Coover, Deacon, Esser, and Moore. See the notes at the end of this paper. Reproduced by permission of Ellen Deacon on behalf of the co-authors of the *Resource Manual for a Living Revolution*.

○ to state all sides of a controversy fairly and objectively;
○ to bring a group to a point for decision making without threat;
○ to recognize and interpret forces operating in a group;
○ to recognize and articulate themes noticed in discussion;
○ to sense the development of tension;
○ to coordinate the questions and steps a group needs to consider to reach a decision;
○ to collect thinking and restate it for group acceptance and action;
○ to encourage others to gain experience in and learn leadership skills.

To the degree to which participants recognize and learn these skills, they are in a position to decide to what extent they want to formalize leadership roles, to share and rotate them among the members, or to experiment with a variety of structures.

Decision making

When faced with the difficult decisions of building a new society, a group needs to take advantage of the resources of all its members. As we take control over our decision-making processes, we are learning several things:

1. *We need to understand the decision making process to have control over it.* There are a number of ways to acquire a better understanding.

(a) Take a few minutes to evaluate the decision making process of any group session. Some questions to raise to make the process visible are: How was the leader selected? What did the group want to accomplish? Does everyone in the group agree? What steps or structures were used to make decisions? How did they work? Have individuals clarified their own roles, so that group goals can be clarified?

(b) Recognize when the process breaks down and review task and maintenance functions to see which ones are not being performed.

2. *It is helpful to explore different theoretical processes of decision making,* e.g. totalitarian, voting, consensus, and to understand the advantages and disadvantages of each.

Experiment with different decision-making processes: consensus, majority vote, central director, hierarchy. We recommend either a general discussion or Fishbowl format. Evaluate the advantages and disadvantages of each structure, taking into account your own feelings and the morale of the group.

Typical communication patterns for the different decision-making processes can be illustrated as shown in Figure 1.

3. *It is important to demystify the abilities of some people to facilitate decision making.* Following each meeting, evaluate contributions of the facilitator in moving the group toward decisions and in dealing with the agenda. Also note

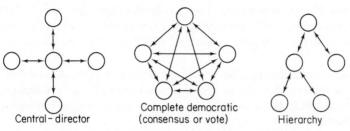

Central - director   Complete democratic
(consensus or vote)   Hierarchy

Figure 1   Patterns for decision-making processes

areas where improvement is needed. By articulating the functions that need to be filled, such as summarizing, coordinating, etc., more people can learn about these functions and specific ways of carrying them out. In addition, both experienced and inexperienced facilitators take turns facilitating in most of our regular meetings, so that the skills are learned and practiced by all. (Large or difficult meetings, of course, require experienced facilitators.)

Consensus decision making and why we prefer it

Consensus is a process for making group decisions without voting. Agreement is reached through a process of gathering information and views, discussion, persuasion, a combination of synthesis of proposals and/or the development of totally new ones. The goal of the consensus process is to reach a decision with which everyone can agree. Consensus at its best relies upon persuasion rather than pressure for reaching group unity.

Consensus does not necessarily mean unanimity. A group can proceed with an action without having total agreement. In the event that an individual or small group cannot agree with a given proposal and is blocking consensus, the facilitator may ask if the individual(s) are willing to 'step aside' and allow the group to act, or if they feel so strongly about the issue that they are unwilling for the group to act. If the individual(s) agree to step aside, their disagreements can be noted in the minute of the meeting, and the group is free to act on the decision. If the individual(s) are not willing to step aside, action is blocked unless a compromise or substitute agreement can be found. The group may agree to postpone the decision until a later time so that more information can be gathered, tempers can cool, participants have a chance to reflect on the options or discuss the issues in more detail, or a compromise can be worked out by the major disagreeing factions. Some large groups (with several hundred attending) use a modified consensus technique in which two or three persons are not enough to block consensus unless they object strongly.

The consensus method is an effort to achieve a balance between task and maintenance needs in the decision-making process, and is most suitable for groups whose members value their association highly. Many small groups actually use a kind of consensus process even if officially they take votes. In order to preserve the group unity and spirit, they take votes only when they feel sure that the group is nearly in complete agreement, and they take time to reconsider close votes.

Consensus decision making sometimes requires a great deal of patience. It is necessary to listen carefully to opposing views to reach the best decision. In spite of this drawback, the consensus method has the following advantages over a voting method:

O It produces more intelligent decisions, by incorporating the best thinking of everyone.
O It keeps people from getting into adversary attitudes where individual egos are tied to a proposal that will win or lose.
O It increases the likelihood of new and better ideas being thought up.
O Everyone has a stake in implementing a decision, because all have participated in its formation. Participants have more energy for working on projects with which they are fully in agreement.
O It lessens significantly the possibility that a minority will feel that an unacceptable decision has been imposed on them.

Facilitation of meetings

A good meeting will exhibit some of the following qualities, all of which can be encouraged by good facilitation: commonly understood goals; a sense of involvement and empowerment (the participants feel that the decisions are their decisions; that they are able to do what needs doing); a high level of energy and enthusiasm; a sense that it is a meeting of real people, not just of roles or recorded messages.

What is a facilitator?

A facilitator fills a role similar to that of a 'chairperson,' but never directs the group without its consent. He or she helps the members of the group decide what they want to accomplish in a meeting and helps them carry it out. He or she takes responsibility for reminding the group of its task, tests for consensus, and in general makes sure that the task and maintenance roles are being filled. The facilitator initiates process suggestions which the group may accept or reject, but at no time does he or she make decisions for the group or take on functions which are the responsibility of the group as a whole. A good facilitator helps participants be aware that *they* are in charge, that it is *their* business that is being conducted, and that each person has contributions to make to the group. It is to emphasize the mutual responsibility of the group and the democratic nature of the process that we use the word 'facilitator' rather than 'chairperson,' 'secretary,' or 'president.'

Selecting a facilitator

In a large meeting or when a meeting is expected to be difficult, a clearly desig-nated facilitator or co-facilitators is (are) needed. Co-facilitators take turns facilitating and support each other. When choosing a facilitator or co-facilitators, strive for a balance of the following:

O little (or less) emotional investment in the meeting;
O ability to encourage others to participate;
O a general overview of the task or goal;
O energy and attention for the job and courage to push the meeting along to meet time limits.

Preparation for meetings

1. Be aware of the physical arrangements—e.g. temperature, arrangement and comfort of chairs, ability to hear.
2. Think about how late-comers can be up-dated so meeting can continue uninterrupted.
3. Make sure that everyone is informed about the meeting time and place and has pre-meeting materials if necessary.
4. Arrange in advance for someone to present each agenda item, preferably the person who submitted the item.
5. If an item is expected to be complicated or produce tension, consider ahead of time helpful processes for discussions, such as breaking the item down and discussing component parts one by one.
6. Gather necessary materials such as written presentations, paper, pencils, marking pens, blackboard, chalk, and chairs.
7. Have an 'alternate' ready to facilitate in case of an emergency, or if the facilitator tires or needs to participate actively in the discussion.
8. For most meetings, it will be necessary to collect agenda items and plan a tentative agenda beforehand. Write a proposed agenda on a large wall chart or blackboard visible to everyone, or distribute copies to participants. This is helpful during the meeting and helps to democratize the process of agenda formation.

Tips on agenda formation

1. Select a process to gather the group, whatever is acceptable: introductions, excitement sharing, singing, brief game.
2. Make tentative judgments about priorities for the agenda. When should difficult items be discussed? If possible, create a balance of long and short items. Deal with difficult items after the group is warmed up but before it is tired.

3. Estimate the time needed for each item and put it on the agenda chart. Allotting time helps participants tailor their participation to the time available and gives a sense of progress to the meeting.
4. If the whole group needs to form the agenda, criteria should be determined ahead of time about how items will be included.
5. Think about what sort(s) of break the group might need.
6. Plan an evaluation of the meeting near the end.

Facilitating the meeting—beginning to end

1. Excitement sharing or other form of introductions.
2. Get agreement on who facilitates and for how long.
3. Agenda review and approval: (a) review the agenda, what will be covered and how; (b) ask for approval, corrections, additions; (c) determine the ending time.
4. Make sure someone is taking notes, if appropriate, and select a time-keeper, also if appropriate.
5. Use short agenda items, fun items, and announcements to break up the more taxing items.
6. Go through the agenda item by item. Applause, a few deep breaths, mutual congratulations, crossing off items are tension relievers.
7. Select a facilitator, date, time, and place of the next meeting.
8. Evaluate the meeting. Start with positive aspects, then aspects that need improvement. Don't get caught up in further discussion.
9. Try to end on a positive note or a feeling of cohesion—a song, silence, standing in a circle—anything that affirms the group and gives a sense of closure.
10. End the meeting on time. If the agenda takes longer than anticipated, renegotiate the time.

Facilitating group maintenance

Stay aware of group maintenance functions and remember to use affirmation and appreciations. Comment on special contributions of members. Try to maintain a relaxed but purposeful atmosphere. Suggest an unscheduled break if people are fidgeting, sleepy, or too depressed to function. In tense or trying situations, try humor, silence, some activity to refocus attention. Some groups might rebel at the suggestion of 'wasting time' on a game, but welcome a stretch break or informal hilarity.

General suggestions for facilitation

1. Bring out opinions: encourage the expression of various views; call attention to strong disagreements; ask people to speak for themselves and to be specific.

2. Help everyone to participate; don't let a few people monopolize; some people need help to be asked to speak more briefly or less frequently; small groups might be useful if much discussion is needed.
3. Keep the facilitator role neutral: step aside as a facilitator if you want to add personal opinions or take a stand on issues.
4. Keep discussion relevant: point out to the group when the discussion wanders off the topic; cut off discussion when repetition occurs.
5. Keep track of time; remind the group when time is up; be sure the timekeeper is alert.
6. Encourage individuals to pursue their own projects or ideas when the group is not interested in them.

Facilitation when consensus is sought

1. Encourage presentation of viewpoints, especially when they conflict. A real consensus develops only when differences are openly faced.
2. Listen carefully for agreements and hesitations: stating these points will help group morale and may lead to agreement of larger issues.
3. Test for agreement: state tentative consensus in question form, and be specific. Insist on a response from the group. If you doubt the consensus, ask members if they agree. Be suspicious of agreements reached too easily.
4. When there is no agreement: ask those disagreeing to offer alternative proposals. Or propose a break, allowing time for thinking. Or decide on a process to reach an alternative proposal, such as a working party. Or, you might ask the one or two people blocking consensus to step aside.

Problems that commonly arise in groups

Groups occasionally experience members who are filling their own needs but are unaware of how they affect the group. Some of these 'Individual Roles' are Blocker, Dominator, Cynic, Special-interest pleader, Recognition-seeker, Aggressor, Help-seeker. Group members will need to take the initiative to deal with these problems.

Certain common events often occur—which may be seen as problems—such as people coming in late, someone is dominating the meeting, some members are not participating at all, etc. A thorough knowledge of group dynamics, a capacity to respond openly, firmly, and gently to conflicts, and a willingness to take the initiative are all needed to respond to these problems.

Conflict resolution

Inevitably in group work, conflicts will arise for which there seems to be no quick and easy solution. The conflict may be between two participants or many people. By using various processes, we are discovering that conflicts can be clarified and resolved so that group members can continue to work together creatively and cooperatively.

The use of these conflict resolution techniques assumes the desire of both parties to resolve the conflict in a mutually acceptable way, and therefore must be distinguished from conflict with the government or an employer, or any conflicts where one party may choose to exercise legal authority and/or force to have its way rather than negotiate a solution satisfactory to both.

While we have used these techniques most often in ongoing groups, the principles and many of the techniques are applicable outside of meetings, in neighborhoods and in work places.

For successful conflict resolution, the following elements seem to be necessary:

O to allow enough time to deal with the conflict;
O to define the problem in terms that are clear and acceptable to all parties in the conflict;
O to deal with negative feelings in positive ways;
O to help people identify in concrete terms what makes them unhappy with the situation; distinguishing between feelings and reality;
O for each member of the conflict to identify his/her real needs;
O to allow an opportunity for individuals to unload feelings of hurt, fear, etc., in the presence of accepting people;
O to have at least one person give special attention to the process, someone uninvolved, if possible.

Some assumptions about conflict

Our thinking about conflict is based on the following assumptions:

1. Conflict is a natural occurrence.
2. Conflict is one way that individuals and communities grow.
3. Conflicts arise because people believe that they have incompatible goals.
4. Social structures frequently cause conflicts.
5. Conflicts should not be allowed to build up or be glossed over.
6. Conflicts have predictable dynamics and cycles.
7. Feelings are an integral component of conflicts.

Five important aspects of conciliation

There are no guarantees to handling conflicts, but we do recognize guidelines which have been useful:

1. Making contact between people who are in conflict.

2. Handling the feelings of the conflicting people.
3. Building trust—dissolving stereotypes, affirming the good aspects of people in the conflict, etc.
4. Getting the conflicting parties to agree to talk about the feelings and the issues.
5. Setting up guidelines for the discussion/negotiation.

Processes and techniques for conflict resolution

There are seven processes that we have found especially helpful in resolving conflicts. Numbers 3, 4, and 5 come out of the Parent Effectiveness Training field; numbers 6 and 7 come from the negotiation/mediation tradition.

1. *Clarifying of conflicts preventing consensus.* When one person shows consistent strong disagreement to a growing consensus, he or she takes time to write down his/her thoughts and feelings preventing agreement, as well as a proposal for solving the problem.

2. *Decision-making method based on Re-evaluation Counseling.* This method employs the process of emotional discharge (unloading hurts and other feelings by crying, laughing, raging, etc.) to deal with feelings that may be blocking clear thinking about the decision. People need to be committed to the process, which might take a fair amount of time to be completed or be effective. For further information about Re-evaluation Counseling, write to the Re-evaluation Communities, 719 Second Avenue North, Seattle, WA 98109, USA.

3. *'No-lose' Problem-Solving Process.* Based on Parent Effectiveness Training (see bibliography). This process is applicable for *any* two individuals, regardless of their ages. The process in intended to resolve conflicts in which real needs are being frustrated; it is not recommended as a method to resolve conflicts based on philosophical or value differences. Brief description of the process: (a) define the problem in terms of both people's needs; (b) restate the problem; (c) brainstorm alternative solutions; (d) evaluate alternative solutions; (e) decide on the best solution, acceptable to everyone; (f) implement the solution; (g) evaluate how it is working.

4. *Active Listening.* Active Listening is a process of rephrasing what a person says; the effect is to help the person move from frustration and anger to generating his or her own ideas about what steps should be taken.

5. *'I-Messages'.* This is a process of replacing negative and blaming statements that too often increase the conflict between people. The model basically goes: 'When (unacceptable behavior) I (speaker's feelings), because (consequences of the behavior to the speaker).' Essentially, the speaker is stating his/her feelings in a declarative way rather than transmitting them in a value-laden way.

6. *Support Person Role during Negotiations.* A person can play a valuable role as a support person to a party of a conflict. The support person helps by giving

emotional support to one party and asks clarifying questions before negotiations begin. The support person does not join the negotiating team and does not speak during the negotiating process, except during a break.

7. *Mediator/Facilitator for a Negotiation Process.* The person who guides the negotiating process; thinks about the process for resolving the conflict; identifies points of agreement, etc. This role involves a high level of skills, but it can be learned.

References and notes

This contribution is borrowed almost entirely from the *Resource Manual for A Living Revolution*, by Virginia Coover, Ellen Deacon, Charles Esser, and Christopher Moore, Published by the New Society Press in Philadelphia in 1977. The *Resource Manual* represents a good deal of thinking of members of the Life Center community in west Philadelphia as well as other 'Movement for A New Society' members across the US. Movement for A New Society and the Life Center began in 1971 as a decentralized network of collectives and communities committed to radical nonviolent social change. This is the 'we' which is occasionally used in the text.

The section in the contribution dealing with the facilitation of meetings is drawn substantially from Berit Lakey's pamphlet, *Meeting Facilitation, the No Magic Method.* Two small sections in the section on conflict resolution are from the booklet, *Building Social Change Communities* by the Training Action Affinity Group. Both sources are listed in the bibliography.

The author wishes to note that this contribution is a summary, basically, from the *Resource Manual*, with updating in the conflict resolution section. The pages of the *Resource Manual* summarized here are pp. 48–53, 61–72, and 88–98.

Bibliography

Working in groups

Center for the Study of Conflict Resolution. (1977). *A Manual for Group Facilitators*, CCR, 731 State St, Madison, WI 53706.
Chase, Stuart. (1951). *Roads to Agreement*, Harper Brothers, New York.
Hall, Edward. (1959). *The Silent Language*. Fawcett Premier, Greenwich, Conn.
Lakey, Berit. (1975). *Meeting Facilitation: The No Magic Method*, Movement for A New Society, 4722 Baltimore Ave., Philadelphia, PA 19143, USA.
Lippitt, R., Watson, J., and Westley, B. (1958). *Dynamics of Planned Change*, Harcourt, Brace and World, New York.
Luft, Joseph. (1970). *Group Processes, An Introduction to Group Dynamics*, National Press Books, 850 Hanson Way, Palo Alto, CA 94304.
Pfeiffer, William, and Jones, John. (1969–73). *A Handbook of Structured Experiences for Human Relations Training*, 4 volumes, University Associates Press, PO Box 615, Iowa City, IA 52240.
Thelen, J. P. (1954). *Dynamics of Groups at Work*, Univ. of Chicago Press, Chicago.
Vocations for Social Change. (No date). *No Bosses Here: A Manual on Working Collectively*, VSC, 353 Broadway, Cambridge, MA, 02139.
Woodrow, Peter. (1975). *Clearness Manual*, Movement for A New Society, Philadelphia.

Conflict resolution and crisis intervention

Coser, Lewis. (1956). *The Functions of Social Conflict*, The Free Press, Glencoe, Ill.

Curle, Adam. (1971). *Making Peace*, Tavistock, London.

Fisher, Roger. (1969 [1970]). *International Conflicts for Beginners*, Harper & Row, New York.

Gordon, Thomas. (1970). *Parent Effectiveness Training*, Wyden Press [McKay, New York].

Nierenberg, Gerald. (1975). *The Art of Negotiating*, [Dutton, New York, 1968; Cornerstone Library, New York, 1971].

Training/Action Affinity Group. (1979). *Building Social Change Communities*, Movement for A New Society, Philadelphia.

Wehr, Paul. (1979). *Conflict Regulation*, Westview, Boulder, CO.

Small Groups and Social Interaction, Volume 2
Edited by H. H. Blumberg, A. P. Hare, V. Kent and M. Davies
© 1983 John Wiley & Sons Ltd

6.6 HELP SCORES: A Guide to Promoting Change in Groups and Organizations

R. G. Havelock   *American University*

and

Marshall Sashkin   *University of Maryland*

The literature and research on the diffusion and acceptance of innovations has been very useful in providing general strategies for change (Havelock, 1969; Rogers and Shoemaker, 1971; Sashkin *et al.*, 1973). This same body of work, however, has not been used to the extent possible to provide more 'microscopic' guidance to the change agent faced with a specific client group. Some of the available literature describes characteristics that, while specific, are not alterable by any of the parties. Much of it, however, can be used by a change agent and client to optimize their approach to any specific change effort.

There are many change models available in the literature which can form the basis of successful strategies for change. For example, the social interaction model shown in Figure 1 (see Menzel and Katz, 1955–1956; Katz, 1957) and the research and development model (see Sashkin *et al.*, 1973, for a definition) center on the diffusion and acceptance of change or innovation in large social groups or collectives that are low on formal structure. Another set of models, typified by Lippitt *et al.*'s (1958) planned change model, shown in Figure 2, and Argyris's (1970) intervention theory model, focus almost entirely on the internal dynamics of the group or system undergoing change. This provides a useful group dynamics focus, but it ignores the larger scale societal diffusion of innovation process. Havelock's linkage model is based on the notion of a dialogue process which occurs between the 'user' or 'client' system and various types of 'resource' systems. The change agent acts as a linker to help the user–client, individual, group, organization, or society obtain and use the resources needed to satisfy internal needs. This process is shown in simplified outline in Figure 3.

In the linkage model the internal problem-solving process of the user is seen as the essential starting point, but the process of searching for and retrieving new

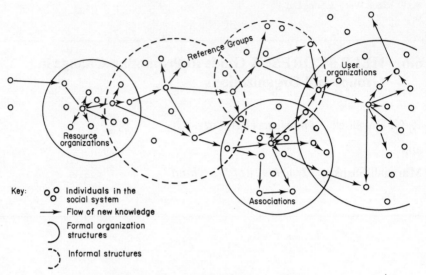

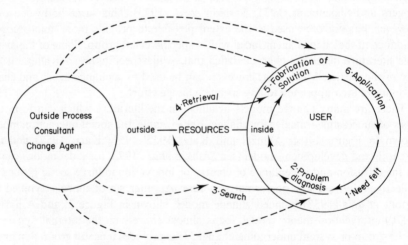

Key: ○○ Individuals in the
       ○ social system
      ⟶ Flow of new knowledge
      ⟩ Formal organization
          structures
      ⟩ Informal structures

Figure 1   The social interaction perspective

Figure 2   The problem solver strategic orientation

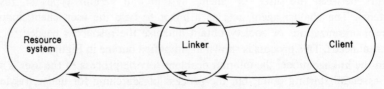

Figure 3   Linkage model

outside knowledge relevant to the problem-solving cycle is also spelled out in considerable detail. To coordinate helping activities with internal user problem-solving activities, the outside resource person (or system) must be able to recapitulate or simulate that internal process. Technically speaking, the resource person needs to develop a good 'model' of the user system in order to 'link' to it effectively. Clinically speaking, we could say that the change agent needs to have empathy or understanding; one must be able to put oneself into the shoes of the client.

At the same time, the user system must develop an adequate appreciation of how the *resource system* operates. In other words, users must understand and partially simulate such resource system activities as research, development, and evaluation.

In order to build accurate models of each other, resource and user systems must provide reciprocal feedback and must provide signals to each other which are mutually reinforcing. This type of collaboration will not only make particular solutions more relevant and more effective but will also serve to build a lasting relationship of mutual trust, and a perception by the users that the resource system is a truly concerned and competent helper. In the long run, then, initial collaborative relations build effective channels through which innovations can pass efficiently and effectively.

The linkage model incorporates aspects of the various models mentioned above, as well as of other models, but goes significantly beyond any of them. It is, in part, an individually-targeted approach to change in which key characteristics of individuals, both change agents and persons in the client systems are seen as critical. Yet it is additionally a group-centered approach in which the client is seen as an interconnected complex of individuals having certain important commonalities which earn them the collective description of 'system.' Let us look first at these two important elements of the linkage model, the focus on group commonalities and key characteristics or roles.

One overrriding characteristic of groups could be called 'commonality.' A group can be defined as a number of people who have something in common. Typically they have common backgrounds, common interests, common circumstances, common values, common problems, and, most of all, common needs. A social system is a group of people who have pooled their resources to satisfy needs they have in common. These common things bind them together psychologically so that 'mine' becomes 'ours' and 'self-interest' becomes 'our common interest.' This arrangement is usually very beneficial for all concerned, but sometimes it gets in the way when new ideas and new ways of doing things are introduced from outside. When this happens, the members of the group have to decide individually or collectively whether or not the new thing threatens the common good. At this point, all these common values, beliefs, interests, and backgrounds become potential *barriers*.

Social organization, by its very nature, is conservative and protective; it is supposed to keep some potential 'innovations' out, for the preservation of the common good, and when it lets them come in they are supposed to be 'acceptable,' which usually means 'what we are accustomed to.' Therefore, the structure of the group is a kind of filtering mechanism. Various members are needed to 'sniff out' new ideas, to expel dangerous ones, or to make the final decisions about 'acceptability' for the group as a whole. Sometimes different people are appointed or self-appointed to fill each of these filtering functions.

The first step for the change agent who wants to gain the acceptance of the group is to find out what kinds of barriers are most important and what kinds of filters are used to maintain the *status quo*. We cannot generalize too much beyond this, for all groups, because some are very open to new ideas while others will admit almost nothing new.

Diffusion of an innovation begins with the acceptance of the idea by a few key members of a community. From there on, it begins to spread more rapidly, usually through word-of-mouth contacts between friends, neighbors, and relatives. This person-to-person process is very effective; once it has started and there are clusters of people who accept the idea and are 'talking it up,' it gathers momentum. A chain reaction seems to be generated once this 'critical mass' of key individuals has formed, and there is a rapid upswing in the rate of acceptance until a large majority has been won over. Such a social diffusion process has been rather thoroughly documented in the empirical research literature of the diffusion of innovations (e.g. Rogers and Shoemaker, 1971). The pattern repeats itself with reasonable regularity across innovation types, settings, and adopting units. Three types of people play a significant part in generating group acceptance. These are the 'innovators,' the 'resisters,' and the 'leaders.' Because the characteristics of these three types of people have been studied extensively by social scientists, we are in a position to understand who they are and how they work regardless of the particular innovation with which we are concerned.

The innovators

The innovators tend to be intelligent and risk taking; they travel a lot, they read a lot, they depend on outside sources of information, and they are usually very receptive to influence by outside change agents. They also tend to be marginal to their home communities. They may be viewed as 'odd balls' or mavericks, and they do not usually have a great deal of direct power or influence. Hence, they can be both an asset and a liability to the change agent. These people will have commitment to a new idea and are willing to stand up and be counted even though they may be risking the scorn and ridicule of others, but if they have stood up too often for lost causes they may not be effective allies to any would-be change agent. Usually, inside members of inside–outside change agent teams can be recruited from this group, but their typically marginal status often makes them problematic as spokespersons or models for fellow system members.

The resisters

Many organizations also contain some members who assume the active role of resisters or critics of innovation. They are the defenders of the system the way it is, the self-appointed guardians of moral, ethical, and legal standards. Although these people are 'conservative' in a strictly logical sense, they may wear all kinds of labels from 'radical' and 'liberal' to 'reactionary.'

The leaders

Many studies of how groups accept innovations have singled out one very important social role which they have identified as the 'opinion leader.' Opinion leaders are found in any group or organization and they are a key to the acceptance of any innovation. Study after study has shown that there are certain influential people who are held in high esteem by the great majority of other group members. They are usually not the first people to try out new ideas, because they need to maintain their standing with their followers. The opinion leaders listen to both the innovators and the resisters so that they can better size up a developing situation. They watch the innovator to see how the idea works, and they watch the resister to test the social risks of adopting the idea. Indeed, in many cases they are eager to observe these changes because their continuance in power rests upon their ability to judge innovations. They want to be the champions of the *innovation whose time has come*. In other words, they must be able to adopt new ideas at the point at which those new ideas are ready to become popularly feasible.

Leadership of any kind has critical strategic importance in a change program whether that leadership be formal, informal, administrative, or elective. For example, the school superintendent, the principal, or the esteemed senior teacher will all have a great deal of 'opinion leadership' on a wide range of innovations. Some leaders act as *legitimators*, making the majority feel that it is all right to try something out without 'having the axe fall.' Others serve as *facilitators*, approving and rewarding the innovators and encouraging others to follow their example, getting clearance, providing funds and time, and generally making it easier to be an innovator. Still others serve as *gatekeepers*, opening up (or closing off) access to needed resources, funds, outside consultants, training courses, etc. The gatekeeper is often not the top person in an organization and a gatekeeping role may be function-specific, e.g. the business manager, the training director, etc.

It should, then, be clear that the key 'leader' role is really a set of roles that overlap in the sense that the people in such roles can all provide support for innovation, but that differ in the exact kind of support that can be given.

The linkage model synthesizes the knowledge base that has been developed concerning the process of innovation, through a focus on the group or social system, and the role and characteristics of the linker or change agent. The detail of such an integration can obviously not be presented in a brief paper, and the interested reader is referred to the following texts: *Planning for Innovation* (Havelock, *et al.*, 1969); *The Change Agent's Guide to Innovation in Education* (Havelock, 1973); and *Solving Educational Problems* (Havelock and Huberman, 1977).

Characteristics of change agents and clients

In this article we present a pragmatically focused distillation of research-based knowledge on the diffusion of innovation and change in groups and social systems. This is offered as a summary guide for change agents who would use the linkage model in planning for innovation. Our set of guidelines is summed up by the mnemonic, HELP SCORES, and is shown in Table 1. (As an initial step in diagnosing change readiness, change agents and client system members can rate their current conditions—using a seven-point scale for each of the defined variables. The authors have been developing this procedure, so far for training and consulting purposes.)

Homophily

One of the most basic characteristics that affects the success of a change effort is the degree to which the change agent is similar to the client in a variety of ways (age, culture, status, background, etc.). The technical term for this overall degree of similarity or alikeness is 'homophily.' The more homophilous the change agent and client, the easier it will be for the change agent to succeed, all other things being equal. While many change-agent characteristics such as age or sex cannot be changed simply to increase homophily, other characteristics are more easily altered, such as style of dress, speech patterns, or use of the client's cultural customs by the change agent. Analysis of weakness on the homophily dimension may also suggest to the change agent the need for teaming up with other agents, inside or outside the system, who possess the missing attributes.

Empathy

If one cannot always be similar to a client, the change agent *can* always attempt to *understand* the client. This is the quality of 'empathy.' Empathy is often confused with sympathy, the quality or attitude of compassion or charity for another. Actually, empathy refers to the skill of understanding what someone else is saying and feeling, regardless of one's own feelings. One does not have to agree with another person or feel the same as another in order to understand what the other is saying and feeling. Empathy is a learned skill and is one of the skills basic to effective change agentry. There are a number of empathy training programs and exercises now readily available (e.g. Milnes and Bertcher, 1980; Kinlaw, 1981).

Linkage

At the most rudimentary level linkage signifies the amount of contact or connection between the change agent and the client. The more contacts on every level the more likely a given change effort will succeed. Traditional approaches to change emphasized the neat packaging of a message to potential adopters, a sort of 'marketing' strategy which allows rapid connecting to a mass audience. Research, however, tells us that the more two-way interaction exists between change agent and client the more likely the change effort is to be effective. This kind of two-way exchange represents an ongoing linkage process between change agent and client. One important part of the linkage process is its collaborative nature. When change agent and client relate to the change process as one of shared and mutual efforts, change is more likely to be effective.

Linkage sounds simple, but is really a basic strategy concern that permeates everything the change agent does.

Proximity

Innovation and change are more likely when the 'target' or client and the change agent are close, physically and psychologically. Proximity implies ready access by one party to the other. Thus, *de facto* proximity can be achieved by a variety of technological devices—telephone, computer conferencing, two-way radio, etc.—*if* there does exist a basic psychological closeness. When such psychological proximity is lacking, physical proximity may be useful in developing it, but when both are absent it will be very difficult for the change agent to develop an effective change relationship. As a general rule, the more the change agent can do to be highly accessible to the client, the greater the likelihood of success.

Structuring

This factor refers to the quality of planning and organization that the change agent and client engage in, for the purpose of initiating and supporting change. Just as a formal organization requires structure, a 'temporary system' such as a planned change effort requires some degree of systematic planning, including a clear division of labor, an integrated or coordinated plan of action, and a timetable for action.

Successful change or adoption of innovation requires that the change agent be well organized, but structuring is more than just planning and organizing on the part of the change agent. Structuring involves the change agent in analyzing the client system in terms of how problems are approached, understood, and resolved, what the nature of the client's problem-solving process or cycle of activities is, and, especially, how the client is organized to receive and use new information. Structuring thus involves the change agent in working with the client collaboratively, using the client's approach to problems of change but trying at the same time to restructure this approach so that it becomes more effective and more likely to help facilitate the acceptance and continuance of the specific change or innovation that the change agent is concerned with.

While structuring is a relatively simple skill for the change agent to develop with reference to his or her own activities, the collaborative application of structuring to the client–change agent 'system' is more complex and difficult to learn. Change agents should also be cautioned against *over*-structuring a change effort, particularly if such structuring binds them into a single plan of behavior which cannot be altered as conditions change or as the client's concerns suggest adaptations.

Capacity

The more resources the change agent and client are able to put together and apply to the change process, the more likely it is that changes will be accepted and effectively implemented. Some clients—and some change agents—are either resource poor or are unwilling to invest resources (such as time, capital, and the application of skilled personnel).

The change agent can try to develop his or her social resources—expertise, referent power, experience, etc.—if 'concrete' resources are lacking. When the client is unable to contribute substantial resources to the change effort, this fact becomes part of the change problem. The least that a client can be asked to give, in terms of resources, is time, energy, and psychological involvement. When these are not present, the client is likely to be withholding by choice rather than need, and a 'red flag' should go up in the mind of the consultant.

Innovations or changes that are backed by heavy investment and extensive development are, in general, more likely to gain acceptance and succeed. Determining capacity requires a judgment by the change agent as to the degree to which resources exist and are being used to achieve change goals on the change agent's own part as well as on the part of the client. Low capacity is associated with failure of change efforts and the rejection of innovations by clients. When the change agent is limiting his or her contributions of resources, the question arises of whether the change agent really wants to be, or should be, involved in this particular project. When the client is limiting (rather than limited in) capacity, one of the change agent's first tasks is to determine why and whether this situation can be 'turned around' to the degree necessary for success of the change effort.

It is also important for the change agent to think about capacity in a rather complex multidimensional way. Capacity refers to the relative abundance of various resources in the change agent, in the client, and even inherent in the innovation itself. It includes financial capacity, human resource capacity, ideational or inventive capacity, and capacity in terms of intelligence, experience, or expertise of one kind or another. To some extent capacities are interchangeable such that low finances can be substituted with large amounts of human labor, etc. Unfortunately, there is a tendency for capacities of different types to mass together and to attract one another such that 'the rich get richer' and 'to those who hath, it shall be given.' Nevertheless, change agents should inventory both their own and their client's capacities, looking for strengths on which to build and weaknesses which need attending to.

Openness

This is simply the willingness to be influenced—to be helped or to change—by the client, but it also refers to the more subtle factor of the extent to which the change agent is willing to be influenced by the client. Openness, then, is not merely an important client attribute, it is also a critical change-agent characteristic. When a change agent is closed—cannot be influenced by feedback from the client—for whatever reason (e.g. conviction that one knows 'the' right way; obtuseness or insensitivity; etc.) then the client models this behavior and becomes less open to change—less influenceable. Openness is in one sense also a measure of *flexibility* on the part of both client and change agent.

The change agent should find it easier to deal with lack of his or her own openness than with the problem of lack of client openness. The latter issue is quite difficult to deal with. One way is for the change or innovation to be highly 'open' in the sense of being visible, desirable, demonstrable, testable, and having no hidden aspects. The greater the degree of client–change agent homophily, empathy, linkage, and proximity the more likely the client is to be open to change and to the change agent.

'Openness' can be seen partly as the inverse of 'structuring.' Too much or too little of either can be dangerous. Whereas a project should always remain flexible, it should not change direction with every slight stimulus from either the client or the environment. The challenge for the change agent is to develop open, flexible structures that allow deviation but can stay on course regarding the general objectives of the change effort.

Reward

The greater the likelihood of reward for success to the change agent and the more rewarding the change is shown to be for the client, the more likely that change will occur, and be successful. Change agents can enjoy a variety of rewards, including the obvious financial benefit of success but also extending to peer recognition, ego satisfaction, the satisfaction of a job well done, and the satisfaction which comes from helping others (altruism). For the client, rewards are more obviously tied to the benefits which derive from the specific change or innovation. However, extrinsic and secondary rewards are also important for clients. They, too, have peers and may, for example, be interested in projecting an image of 'progressiveness' or 'innovativeness.' Moreover, a client may find interaction with the change agent rewarding, as the change agent and client collaborate on the change effort. The process of communication itself can be rewarding as, for example, when one discovers interest and understanding expressed by another person in one's own self, opinions, problems, goals, etc.

Past experience as well as expected benefits will also condition the client group's acceptance of change. Clients who have had positive experiences with past changes or innovations are, reasonably enough, more likely to accept and effectively implement new changes and innovations. However, when the perception persists that long-run chances for benefits are low, the client will hardly develop much enthusiasm for the change.

One of the things a change agent should ask regularly is whether the rewards of being a change agent are still meaningful and adequate. It is quite possible for change agents to experience 'burn-out'—a loss of meaning and joy in what they are doing; nevertheless many continue because of obvious extrinsic rewards (status, money, etc.) or because they feel trapped by personal and professional obligations. When this occurs, one's effectiveness is liable to be seriously diminished. The change agent may, for example, unwittingly slip into a punishing rather than a rewarding style of relating to the client.

An inherently rewarding style of interaction between change agent and client, coupled with clear, immediate, and obvious client benefits (communicated or demonstrated by the change agent) maximizes the reward potential of change and thus increases the chances of success.

Energy

Earlier we referred to capacity in terms of available and used resources of the client and change agent. Energy is one such resource but is so important as to be worth separate consideration. By energy, we mean the willingness to expend one's own efforts, 'sweat and blood' so to speak, to create effective change. This means investing time, persisting in the face of problems, even when the work is long and laborious. Energy also refers to enthusiasm, overt commitment, dedication, and to energizing others, as well: inspiring and sustaining expectations of success in others.

Another form of this quality as it applies to change agents is 'charisma.' There is such a quality, above and beyond the normal expression and direction of energy, that can help even the most unlikely change or innovation succeed. It is not reasonable to expect a change agent to have or develop charisma; in fact, charisma can be dangerous when it leads clients toward inappropriately high expectations. However, the change agent can attempt to recruit charismatic members of the client system, who can then give 'testimonials' and generate support for change.

The innovation itself may possess energy, too—it may be inspiring, forceful, or point out obvious problems that could be resolved if changes were implemented.

Clearly some changes, such as a proposal for a new school or an entirely new product line, are more inherently energizing than others, such as a plan for a new edition of a textbook, the revision of a legal code or the adoption of some new computer software. The effective change agent invests and mobilizes energy wherever it is to be found.

Synergy

As often as it is said, it remains true that a 'whole' is often greater than the sum of its parts. This is the simplest statement of synergy, a condition that occurs when various elements of and participants in the change process act positively to reinforce one another to the extent that a new and substantially stronger foundation of support develops. Synergy is facilitated when the greatest number and diversity of change agents or change resources, and clients (or client system members) are involved in the change or innovation process. It also contributes to synergy when the innovation generates useful spinoffs, side-benefits, and variations, or simply when it is repeated in various ways. Further, the more of the preceding nine factors that are strongly positive and change supportive, the greater the synergy.

Synergy incorporates the critical notion of *timing* in the change process. If a planned intervention coincides with some natural event which heightens client awareness of the need, the likelihood of change is greatly enhanced. Thus 'crises' of various kinds, disturbances of the social or material environment which threaten the social equilibrium make 'cracks' in the system into which timely innovations can flow. Such cracks may also occur in the natural life cycle rhythm of people and organizations much as the annual salary review or the preparation of next year's budget at the beginning of a new fiscal year. Effective change agents learn to spot these teachable moments, coordinating their interventions to coincide with them.

With synergy we finally come to the notion that planned change is an orchestrated process. Influences come from the written word, from discussion, from concerns which are heightened, from persuasion from colleagues, from tough appraisal of the research evidence, from the experience of trial efforts, from the encouragement and persistence of the change agent, and from the charisma of leaders and informal leaders of opinion. If HELP SCORES is a way of packaging change factors for the change agent, synergy is the ribbon on the package, tying things together but also reminding us that a well orchestrated change effort is a lovely gift to the change agent and to the client alike.

Summary

Table 1 provides a summary recapitulation of the preceding discussion. Certainly there are additional change-agent and client characteristics and attributes that can facilitate the change process, for example, the credibility of the

Table 1   HELP SCORES—Definitions

H:	Homophily, the degree of similarity between change agent and client.
E:	Empathy, the level of understanding the change agent and client have of one another.
L:	Linkage, the extent to which the client and change agent are tied together in collaborative activities.
P:	Proximity, the physical and psychological closeness of the change agent and client.
S:	Structure, the extent to which clear plans have been made by the change agent and client so that a well-defined structure for the change effort exists.
C:	Capacity, the nature, variety, and amount of resources available to the client and change agent to use in furthering the change effort.
O:	Openness, the degree to which the change agent and client are willing to hear, respond to, and be influenced by one another.
R:	Reward, the nature and variety of potential positive outcomes of the change effort that might accrue to the change agent and client system.
E:	Energy, the amount of physical and psychological effort the change agent and the client are able and willing to expend on the change effort.
S:	Synergy, the variety of people, resources, energies, and activities involved and interacting in the change effort that mutually support success.

change agent as an expert, the status of the client, and the way change agent and client may relate in terms of complex social networks of interaction. Some of these factors are implicitly or explicitly included in the 10 we have reviewed, but the field of planned change is by no means well mapped, nor are change agents scientists acting within a precise cause-and-effect model. The characteristics we have chosen to review and emphasize in the mnemonic 'HELP SCORES' are those which current research tells us are the most—but not the only (nor always the most)—important ones.

References

Argyris, C. (1970). *Intervention Theory and Method*, Addison-Wesley, Reading, Mass.
Havelock, R. G. (in collaboration with A. Guskin, M. Frohman, M. Havelock, M. Hill, and J. Huber) (1969). *Planning for Innovation*, Institute for Social Research, the University of Michigan, Ann Arbor, Mich.
Havelock, R. G. (1973). *The Change Agent's Guide to Innovation in Education*, Educational Technology Publishers, Englewood Cliffs, NJ.
Havelock, R. G., and Huberman, A. M. (1977). *Solving Educational Problems*, UNESCO, Paris.
Katz, E. (1957). 'The two-step flow of communication: An up-to-date report on an hypothesis,' *Public Opinion Quarterly*, **21**, 61–78.
Kinlaw, D. (1981). *Helping Skills for Human Resource Development*, University Associates, San Diego.
Lippitt, R. O., Watson, J., and Westley, B. (1958). *The Dynamics of Planned Change*, Harcourt, Brace, New York.
Menzel, H., and Katz, E. (1955–56). 'Social relations and innovations in the medical profession; The epidemiology of a new drug,' *Public Opinion Quarterly*, **19**, 337–352.

Milnes, J., and Bertcher, M. (1980). *Communicating Empathy*, University Associates, San Diego.

Rogers, E. M., with Shoemaker, F. F. (1971). *Communication of Innovations: A Cross-Cultural Approach*, Free Press, New York.

Sashkin, M., Morris, W. C., and Horst, L. (1973). 'A comparison of social and organizational change models: Information flow and data use processes,' *Psychological Review*, **80**, 510–526.

Small Groups and Social Interaction, Volume 2
Edited by H. H. Blumberg, A. P. Hare, V. Kent and M. Davies
Published by John Wiley & Sons Ltd 1983

6.7 One Year of Prison Reform*

Tom Murton

On January 29, 1968, Claude Overton, manager of the Cummins Prison Farm, an installation of the Arkansas State Penitentiary, informed chief security officer Harold A. Porter that, because rain was expected in the afternoon, he would not be working the longline (inmate work force) after lunch. Porter therefore stopped by the infirmary about 1.15 p.m. to pick up Reuben Johnson, who had related a bizarre tale of inmates having been murdered and buried in the mule pasture known as Bodiesburg. A squad of Negro inmates marched through the pasture to a point selected by Johnson and proceeded to dig in three adjacent sites.

Livestock manager Frank Crawford and I were in the general area at the time when an inmate came up to us and matter of factly stated: 'Mr Murton, we've struck a coffin.' I moved to the site and supervised the excavation of three graves which yielded three mutilated bodies placed in the exact location and in the same condition as Reuben Johnson had indicated. Two were decapitated and the skull of the third had been crushed to the size of a grapefruit.

Within the hour, the remains of the three inmates had been dug up, preserved as evidence, the official agencies had been notified and the squad of inmates had moved triumphantly back to the barracks to relate events to the jubilant prison population. They left behind three gaping scars in the mule pasture—mute testimony to the degradation imposed upon the penal slaves of Arkansas.

The state's prison system had been operated on fear for a century, and most of the traditional methods had been used to instill it: beatings, needles under the fingernails, stompings, the 'hide' (a leather strap 5 inches wide and 5 feet long), starvation and an electric device whose terminals were attached to the genitals of the inmate while a trusty or 'warden' gleefully turned the crank. True, the prison

---

*Abridged from Tom Murton, 'One year of prison reform,' *The Nation*, 12 January 1970, pp. 12–15. Reprinted by permission.

had made a profit during the previous fifty years. The champions of the Arkansas prison system proudly boasted—and still do—that no appropriated funds were required to support the 'convicts.' But exploitation of inmates was effective only under the spur of threats, and the ultimate threat was murder. There is ample evidence that the illegal executions uncovered that January day were not isolated events.

The prison has survived the cycle of scandal and reform every twenty or thirty years and has resisted with equal success the occasional token objections from those who became 'concerned' about the treatment of prisoners. But that was before Winthrop Rockefeller became the first Republican governor of the state since Reconstruction. Rockefeller expressed understandable indignation over a state police report, prepared in August of 1966, which catalogued the cruelty practiced in the Arkansas prison system. As a candidate, he pledged elimination of corruption in state government, efficiency and 'to hire a professional penologist to run the state prison system.' [See 'Arkansas Prison Farm' by Robert Pearman, *The Nation*, December 26, 1966.] Rockefeller won the election with a mandate from the electorate to end the century of decadence in Arkansas.

A routine police investigation at another unit of the penitentiary system, Tucker Prison Farm, in January of 1967 had disclosed Superintendent Pink Booher sitting at his desk behind a Thompson sub-machine gun, ready to repel any attack from the inmates who had threatened to shoot him if he attempted to enter the prison proper. This was no idle threat because, in the Arkansas tradition, the total guard force consisted of inmates who were issued guns and instructed to watch over the other prisoners. At that time, only six hired staff and some forty-eight inmate guards were authorized at Tucker. That was one way to save money for the state.

Governor Rockefeller promptly dismissed the superintendent and three other staff members. And for the third time in less than a year, the Arkansas State Police was placed in command of some 300 inmates on the 4,500-acre prison farm.

As one of several consultants to the new state administration, I was called to Tucker to evaluate the situation. In the latter part of February 1967 I was hired as superintendent. The first thing that struck me was the atmosphere of total despair. The inmates did not smile, laugh or talk. Their eyes, their expressions and their demeanor were a vivid portrayal of hopelessness. We found that control of inmates, work assignments, promotion, food rations, bed assignments, visiting privileges, commissary privileges, furloughs, laundry and clothing procedures, parole eligibility, inmate funds, and the very survival of the inmate had always been delegated to a select few powerful inmates who operated the prison. The system had become ingrained because of lack of outside staff, an apathetic civilian population, indifference on the part of the Governor and the greed of both inmate trusties and various citizens who had a vested interest in the prison and its profits.

To make the system operable, the trusties had been granted certain privileges, including graft obtained from all inmate goods and services, freedom to sell liquor and narcotics, to gamble and lend money, to live in 'squatter shacks' outside the main prison, to spend the night with a female companion and to profit from the illegal traffic in prison produce.

Of the two staff members remaining at the time of my appointment, one resigned and the other was fired. That left me in command of a fifteen-man police detachment quartered at the prison, with no civilian staff and an 'uptight' inmate population. The first order of business was to arm the state troopers, who had been prohibited by the inmate guards from carrying arms. The power of the inmate guard force was so absolute that when Governor Rockefeller first visited the prison he was not allowed in until his bodyguard had surrendered his gun to an inmate at the front gate.

That spring, the legislature increased the authorized staff at Tucker from six to thirty-eight officers, and I immediately imported a cadre of officers with whom I had worked before. Our basic strategy was to treat the inmate with dignity—a concept heretofore unheard of in Arkansas. Trust was built up in the prison population by daily decisions which cumulatively demonstrated that the prison administration was actually committed to inmate welfare.

However, the real danger was in the inmate power structure, and an attempt to eliminate every aspect of that power would have been foolhardy because, in varying degrees, inmates determine the operation of *all* such institutions. We decided to accept the existence of inmate power, but to substitute, if we could, a legitimate form of self-government for the traditionally exploitive one.

The prison reforms received no assistance from the official agencies of criminal justice, the legislature, the prison board, the prison study commission, other state agencies or the public. As a result, the staff and inmates were drawn together in efforts to reform the prison while providing mutual defense against collective opposition from outside.

My sole authority was that granted by the Governor. Nevertheless, we were able in a few months to feed and clothe the inmates, hire competent staff, upgrade the agricultural programs, establish educational and vocational training programs, provide a rational religious counseling service (to replace forced church attendance under the gun), eliminate corruption, move the trusties into the barracks, and practically eliminate the rapes and other homosexual assaults.

Inmates were no longer required to act as servants for the staff: they no longer worked outside, tilling the soil for private citizens. Prison-grown food no longer went 'out the gate' into private hands; livestock management was upgraded by acquisition of new breeding stock and the institution of sound animal husbandry practices. And a host of minimal creature comforts were provided. We ultimately broke the convict power structure by eliminating the monetary exchange that had maintained the inmate economy, with the attendant gambling loan rackets and assaults.

I acknowledged that the inmates had information, not available to the professional staff, that could be effective in reforming the prison. One-half of the newly elected inmate council constituted the classification committee which determined work assignments, promotion and the ever critical decisions as to which inmates would be issued guns. It should be noted that no inmate whom the committee classified as minimum custody ever escaped during our administration.

The other half of the inmate council became the disciplinary committee. It proved much more effective than the administration in assigning punishments (I had abolished all corporal punishment). I sat with both committees and reserved the right of veto, but never had to exercise it. A form of responsible self-government was emerging.

Breaking the power structure produced great anxiety among the trusties and culminated in a rash of escapes. (Arkansas is one of the few states where the prison administration must be concerned with the escape of *guards*.) During the first half of my tenure at Tucker, we lost thirty-eight inmates; in the last half, only one inmate escaped. As the tensions eased, we were able to open up death row, where the ten condemned men—one white and nine black—had been confined to their cells under rigid security. Eventually, they were playing in ball games, performing work assignments with the white inmates, attending school, church and vocational classes, playing in the prison band and finally were eating in the dining hall.

One of the last innovations at Tucker, toward the end of 1967, was the inauguration of prison dances, to which inmates were allowed to invite their girl friends or wives (either, but not both). There were no incidents at these parties, no hurled insults, no drinking and no rape. One unplanned result of the relaxed atmosphere was the intermingling of staff and inmates as dancing partners and the unpardonable sin (in Arkansas) of interracial dancing.

By Christmas of 1967, a woman supervisor was able to work at the prison laundry, female employees ate in the prison dining hall, female teachers conducted classes inside the institution with no guard present and the staff and their families attended programs, sitting with the general inmate population. The most significant change was in the attitude of the inmates. Fear had disappeared, a new community had been created and despair had been replaced by hope. Our energies were no longer directed toward overcoming the inmate population, but toward coping with the state bureaucracy and dealing with our changing relationship with the Governor's office.

That was the situation at Tucker as my staff and I prepared to assault Cummins. The word is used advisedly because it became evident that it might be necessary to shoot our way into the prison to install me as superintendent of the entire prison system. The opposition from both inmates and officials at Cummins was so concerted that death threats had been made against both me and Harold Porter, who earlier had transferred to Cummins. The official police assessment of the situation was that I could not take over the superintendency without an armed force of about 1,000 men. Such a force, composed of state troopers, National Guardsmen and airborne troops, was made available.

I declined the help, preferring to choose for myself the back-up force with whom I would entrust my life. Consequently, I initially took over the institution—peacefully—with the help of a single man, inmate Sheriff 'Chainsaw' Jack Bell, who was serving a life sentence for killing a man by sawing off his head.

In a few weeks we managed to gain a semblance of control of the institution, dismissed the more hostile and brutal employees, changed key inmate guards, improved living conditions for both inmates and livestock, eliminated inmate services to the staff, stopped corruption in the medical services and modified procedures at the Women's Reformatory located at Cummins.

That institution of about forty women had constituted the 'lost souls' of the Arkansas prison system. They customarily were transported in the same transfer vans with the men and were routinely raped en route to the prison or to and from the state hospital. Many female inmates refused medical attention for fear of being raped on the way to surgery.

Negro inmates among the women had been forced to clip grass with their fingernails as 'therapy;' they received only scraps of food left on the table after the white inmates had finished eating. The sewing endeavors in the reformatory were primarily for the benefit of the matrons and their families. Exercise, dancing, talking during the evening, smoking, sitting on the bed, looking at a man (or worse yet, talking to a man) were all punished as serious offenses. The usual sentence was solitary confinement in a concrete cell, which had no plumbing, water or heat. If a prisoner rebelled, the head matron would call her husband, who would 'lay on the hide' as the inmate was held to the floor by trusties. One former superintendent had had a buzzer installed next to his bed. With it, he could summon his favorite girl friend from the nearby reformatory.

Mrs Frank Crawford, whom I placed in charge, promptly corrected the more obvious faults, as we had done at the other institution. We later took a bus load of female inmates to Tucker to participate in the dances. An inmate who had been taken to the State Hospital for childbirth, was allowed to bring her baby back to the prison and to keep him in the main dormitory in an area screened off as a 'nursery'.

A wedding was planned to legalize a common-law relationship between a pregnant inmate and her man. Mrs Crawford was to be the matron of honor; her husband Frank was to be best man; my visiting sister, Paula, was to play the organ; Jon Kimbrell, the Tucker chaplain, was to officiate; and I was asked by the prospective bride to give her away. The ceremony was to take place in the main prison auditorium on March 11, 1968. But events which took place four days before that date forced cancellation of the plans.

In thirteen months, we had revolutionized Tucker and were well on the way to doing the same at Cummins. We achieved what we did in spite of the hostile prison board (which hoped for my failure), the system of criminal justice (which blocked my efforts to prosecute those who stole from the prison), the legislature (which tried to censure me), the citizens of the area (who could no longer steal from the prison), the grand jury (which threatened to indict me for 'grave-robbing') and the trusties and staff (some of whom in both groups threatened to kill me).

We also had to withstand the sabotage of equipment sent to Cummins for 'repair,' the shooting of our livestock at night, the deliberate burning of our slaughterhouse, the refusal of Cummins officials to can our produce and the interference by state purchasing officials, consultants, the Governor's aides and other state officials. *All* reform achievements were accomplished under these adverse conditions.

The year 1968 promised to be different. We had gained the impetus of reform by the Tucker experience, and solving the Cummins problems was essentially a matter of time and strategy. Four of the five members of the old prison board resigned rather than confirm my appointment as permanent superintendent of the prison system. This action cleared the way for Governor Rockefeller to gain control of a state department for the first time since his election.

John Haley, his first appointee to the board a year previously, was elevated to chairman and four other men of seemingly progressive views were appointed in mid-January . . .

We waited in anticipation for Governor Rockefeller, through the board, to effect some of the changes beyond the power of the superintendent. Now the audit of prior prison management could be commenced; gains we had made at Tucker could be consolidated under the supervision of Robert Van Winkle; progressive bills could be prepared for the legislature; a contract could be signed with Tennessee correctional authorities for housing and care of female prisoners; federal funds could be obtained pursuant to grant requests then pending; livestock management could be brought into the 20th century; the inmates could be properly clothed and fed; the Cummins power structure could be broken; and a thorough investigation of the bodies in the mule pasture could be completed.

These were all within our grasp, but the board members, sensing no real support from the Governor, did not reach out to seize true prison reform. Instead, they chose to undermine every aspect of our work. Governor Rockefeller became frightened on the very threshold of success, and deferred to opponents who desired the prison system to remain as it had been. They, and his own advisers, convinced him that I was damaging the image of Arkansas and that his continued stay in office depended on my immediate removal.

The new prison board officially met with me for the first time on March 2, 1968 and informed me that I probably would not be appointed as commissioner to guide the new Department of Correction. Five days later, when the board again met with me, I was summarily fired and placed under house arrest. Although no reasons were given at the time, Governor Rockefeller and John Haley at a press conference the following day accused me, in part, of being a 'poor prison administrator' (although Haley had stated I demonstrated 'near genius' in revolutionizing Tucker); of knowing nothing about agriculture (ignoring my degree in agriculture, that I had farmed and also taught the subject); and of having ordered asparagus tips for the inmates (a grave accusation contrary to the facts).

[In the original article, details are given of various reforms being reversed, and of negative consequences.] ...

It was my stated conviction after leaving Arkansas that the prison had reverted to its evil ways. To refute the allegations, the commissioner granted me permission to make a personal inspection of all prison facilities in October 1969. Although I had been kept adequately informed of the decline of the prison, I was not prepared for what I found: both inmates and staff reported to me that conditions have returned almost to the level prior to our intervention. They speak of assaults, beatings by staff and inmates, extortion, liquor rackets, lack of clothing (some fifteen inmates were then working in the fields without shoes), threats on the lives of inmates, pistol whippings and shooting at inmates to speed up field work. The inmates uniformly report the food to be atrocious.

What discouraged me most was the evidence that the flickering light of hope we had ignited had been extinguished. The inmates look at the staff with distrust, suspicion and fear. Once more they shuffle silently to and from work, trapped in the futile, endless cycle of imprisonment, pondering the hopelessness of their plight and the mystery of how they were cheated of the promised emancipation from penal slavery ...

There is little doubt in my mind that Governor Rockefeller was committed to prison reform during his campaign of 1966 and even after his inauguration in 1967. But power structures can tolerate only a limited amount of integrity. There comes a time when the new administration discovers that its other objectives are threatened by the reforms that have been instituted to correct the deficiencies of the former system. Previous Arkansas administrations stand condemned of knowing about prison conditions but not caring. The Rockefeller administration is guilty of knowing, pledging true reform—and recanting for the sake of political expediency. It must share the greater burden of responsibility for what ultimately happens to the prisoners of Arkansas.

Small Groups and Social Interaction, Volume 2
Edited by H. H. Blumberg, A. P. Hare, V. Kent and M. Davies
Published by John Wiley & Sons Ltd 1983

6.8   From *The Miracle of Being Awake**

Thich Nhat Hanh

[Below are some extracts from a work which implies how group and other activities may be enriched by individual ways of being. Interested readers are encouraged to consult the original work. This view complements (a) material by other authors (e.g. see Chapter 4, above) who suggest how one's personal life can be enriched by group experience and (b) the work of many groups devoted to peace and freedom—see, e.g. The *World Peace Diary* (revised annually by Housmans, 5 Caledonian Road, London N1, U.K.).]

Washing the dishes to wash the dishes

... While washing the dishes one should only be washing the dishes, which means that while washing the dishes one should be completely aware of the fact that one is washing the dishes. At first glance, that might seem a little silly: why put so much stress on a simple thing? But that's precisely the point. The fact that I am standing there and washing these bowls is a wondrous reality. I'm being completely myself, following my breath, conscious of my presence and conscious of my thoughts and actions. There's no way I can be tossed around mindlessly like a bottle slapped here and there on the waves ...

If while washing dishes, we think only of the cup of tea that awaits us, thus hurrying to get the dishes out of the way as if they were a nuisance then we are not 'washing the dishes to wash the dishes.' What's more, we are not alive during

---

*From *The Miracle of Mindfulness! A Manual on Meditation* by Thich Nhat Hanh (1976). Beacon Press, Boston. Translated by Mobi Warren. Drawings © 1976 by Vo-Dinh. Copyright © 1975/6 by Thich Nhat Hanh. Reprinted by permission of Beacon Press and the author. (Abridged from pp. 3–12, 27–31, 39, 75–76.) Also published as *The Miracle of Being Awake*, Nyack, NY: Fellowship Books, 1975.

the time we are washing the dishes. In fact we are completely incapable of realizing the miracle of life while standing at the sink. If we can't wash the dishes, the chances are we won't be able to drink our tea either. While drinking the cup of tea, we will only be thinking of other things, barely aware of the cup in our hands. Thus we are sucked away into the future—and we are incapable of actually living one minute of life.

Eating a tangerine

... A tangerine has sections. If you can eat just one section, you can probably eat the entire tangerine. But if you can't eat a single section, you cannot eat the tangerine. Jim understood. He slowly put his hand down and focused on the presence of the slice already in his mouth ...

The essential discipline

More than 30 years ago, when I first entered the monastery, the monks gave me a small book called *The Essential Discipline for Daily Use*, written by the Buddhist monk Doc The from Bao Son pagoda and they told me to memorize it. It was a thin book. It couldn't have been more than 40 pages, but it contained all the thoughts Doc The used to awaken his mind while doing any task. When he woke up in the morning, his first thought was, 'Just awakened, I hope that every person will attain great awareness and see in complete clarity.' ... The book is comprised entirely of such sentences. Their goal was to help the beginning practitioner take hold of ... consciousness. The Zen Master Doc The helped all of us young novices to practice, in a relatively easy way, those things which are taught in the Sutra of Mindfulness. Each time you put on your robe, washed the dishes, went to the bathroom, folded your mat, carried buckets of water, or brushed your teeth, you could use one of the thoughts from the book in order to take hold of your own consciousness.

The Sutra of Mindfulness ... says, 'When walking, the practitioner must be conscious that he is walking. When sitting, the practitioner must be conscious that he is sitting ...' The mindfulness of the positions of one's body is not enough, however. We must be conscious of each breath, each movement, every thought and feeling, everything which has any relation to ourselves.

But what is the purpose of the Sutra's instruction? Where are we to find the time to practice such mindfulness? If you spend all day practicing mindfulness, how will there ever be enough time to do all the work that needs to be done to change and to build an alternative society? How does Allen manage to work, study Joey's lesson, take Ana's diapers to the laundromat, and practice mindfulness at the same time?

The miracle is to walk on earth

Allen said that since he's begun to consider Joey and Sue's time as his own, he has 'unlimited time.' But perhaps he has it only in principle . . . [If] he really wants 'unlimited time,' he will have to keep alive the realization that 'this is my time' throughout the time he's studying with Joey . . . [If] one really wants to keep one's consciousness alive (from now on I'll use the term 'mindfulness' to refer to keeping one's consciousness alive to the present reality), then one must practice right now in one's daily life, not only during meditation sessions.

When you are walking along a path leading into a village, you can practice mindfulness. Walking along a dirt path, surrounded by patches of green grass, if you practice mindfulness you will experience that path, the path leading into the village. You practice by keeping this one thought alive: 'I'm walking along the path leading into the village.' Whether it's sunny or rainy, whether the path is dry or wet, you keep that one thought, but not just repeating it like a machine, over and over again . . .

I like to walk alone on country paths, rice plants and wild grasses on both sides, putting each foot down on the earth in mindfulness, knowing that I walk on the wondrous earth. In such moments, existence is a miraculous and mysterious reality. People usually consider walking on water or in thin air a miracle. But I think the real miracle is not to walk either on water or in thin air, but to walk on earth. Everyday we are engaged in a miracle which we don't even recognize: a blue sky, white clouds, green leaves, the black, curious eyes of a child—our own two eyes. All is a miracle . . .

A day of mindfulness

Every day and every hour, one should practice mindfulness. That's easy to say, but to carry it out in practice is not. That's why I suggest to those who come to the meditation sessions that each person should try hard to reserve one day out of the week to devote entirely to [his or her] practice of mindfulness. In principle, of course, every day should be your day, and every hour your hour. But the fact is that very few of us have reached such a point. We have the impression that our family, place of work and society rob us of all our time. So I urge that everyone set aside one day each week. Saturday, perhaps.

If it is Saturday, then Saturday must be entirely your day, a day during which you are completely the master. Then Saturday will be the lever that will lift you to the habit of practicing mindfulness. Every worker in a peace or service community, no matter how urgent its work, has the right to such a day, for without it we will lose ourselves quickly in a life full of worry and action and our responses will become increasingly useless. Whatever the day chosen, it can be considered as the day of mindfulness.

To set up a day of mindfulness, figure out a way to remind yourself at the moment of waking that this day is your day of mindfulness. You might hang something on the ceiling or on the wall, a paper with the word 'mindfulness' or a pinebranch—anything that will suggest to you as you open your eyes and see it that today is your day of mindfulness. Today is your day. Remembering that, perhaps you can feel a smile which affirms that you are in complete mindfulness, a smile that nourishes that perfect mindfulness.

While still lying in bed, begin slowly to follow your breath—slow, long and conscious breaths. Then slowly rise from bed (instead of turning out all at once as usual), and nourishing mindfulness by every motion. Once up, brush your teeth, wash your face, and do all your morning activities in a calm and relaxing way, each movement done in mindfulness. Follow your breath, take hold of it, and don't let your thoughts scatter. Each movement should be done calmly. Measure your steps with quiet, long breaths. Maintain a half-smile.

Spend at least a half hour taking a bath. Bathe slowly and mindfully so that by the time you have finished, you feel light and refreshed. Afterwards, you might do household work such as washing dishes, dusting and wiping off the tables, scrubbing the kitchen floor, arranging books on their shelves. Whatever the tasks, do them slowly and with ease, in mindfulness. Don't do any task in order to get it over with . . .

For those who are just beginning to practice, it is best to maintain a spirit of silence throughout the day. That doesn't mean that on the day of mindfulness, you shouldn't speak at all. You can talk, you can even go ahead and sing, but if you talk or sing, do it in complete mindfulness of what you are saying or singing, and keep talking and singing to a minimum . . .

At lunchtime, prepare a meal for yourself. Cook the meal and wash the dishes in mindfulness. In the morning, after you have cleaned and straightened up your house, and in the afternoon, after you have worked in the garden or watched clouds or gathered flowers, prepare a pot of tea to sit and drink in mindfulness. Allow yourself a good length of time to do this. Don't drink your tea like someone who gulps down a cup of coffee during a workbreak. Drink your tea slowly and reverently . . .

> *Be a bud sitting quietly in the hedge*
> *Be a smile, one part of wondrous existence*
> *Stand here. There is no need to depart.*
> *This homeland is as beautiful as the homeland of our childhood*
> *Do not harm it, please, and continue to sing . . .*
>
> ('*Butterfly Over the Field of Golden Mustard Flowers*')

In the evening, you might read scripture and copy passages, write letters to friends, or do anything else you enjoy outside of your normal duties during the week. But whatever you do, do it in mindfulness. Eat only a little for the evening meal. Later, around 10 or 11 o'clock, as you sit in meditation, you will be able to sit more easily on an empty stomach. Afterwards you might take a slow walk in the fresh night air, following your breath in mindfulness and measuring the length of your breaths by your steps. Finally, return to your room and sleep in mindfulness.

Somehow we must find a way to allow each peace worker a day of mindfulness. Such a day is crucial. Its effect on the other days of the week is immeasurable. Ten years ago, thanks to such a day of mindfulness, Chu Van and our other sisters and brothers in the Tiep Hien Order were able to guide themselves through many difficult times. After only three months of observing such a day of mindfulness once a week, I know that you will see a significant change in your life . . .

The guard—or the monkey's shadow?

While practicing mindfulness, don't be dominated by the distinction between good and evil, thus creating a battle within oneself.

Whenever a wholesome thought arises, acknowledge it: 'A wholesome thought has just arisen.' And if an unwholesome thought arises, acknowledge it as well: 'An unwholesome thought has just arisen.' Don't dwell on it or try to get rid of it, however much you don't like it. To acknowledge it is enough. If you have departed, then you must know that you have departed, and if you are still there, know that you are still there. Once you have reached such an awareness, there will be nothing you need fear anymore . . .

Service

The service of peace. The service of any person in need. The word service is so immense. Let's return first to a more modest scale: our families, our classmates, our friends, our own community. We must live for them—for if we cannot live for them who else do we think we are living for?

. . . How can we live in the present moment, live right now with the people around us, helping to lessen their suffering and making their lives happier? How? The answer is this: We must practice mindfulness. . . .

I've written these pages for our friends to use. There are many people who have written about these things without having lived them, but I've only written down those things which I have lived and experienced myself. I hope you and our friends will find these things at least a little helpful along the path of our seeking: the path of our return.

Part III
Theoretical Perspectives

Introduction

When so much theory has been presented in earlier sections, it may seem invidious to choose a few papers to form a special section with a portentous title. However, there are many different general approaches to the study of small groups, and it is helpful to look at these outside the confines of specific issues like attraction or leadership or conflict.

We have tried to be reasonably eclectic, and because of this the papers are presented as one large chapter, for they could have formed various groupings according to different criteria. We have not been able to include as much as we would have liked: sociological social psychology is rather under-represented, there is no paper on the divisions of social psychology into 'psychological' and 'sociological,' and there is no discussion of cross-cultural issues in the study of small groups. Some suggested reading for these topics is to be found at the end of this introduction.

The first contribution, by Kent (sub-Chapter 7.1), is a brief synopsis of some important general theories in social psychology, most of which have been cited in earlier papers. It is designed for easy reference for the reader who may be unfamiliar with some of the assumptions, applications, and limitations of these theories. In the main, the theories are about individual rather than group processes, although they are relevant to what individuals do in groups.

Both the following papers are concerned with the patterning of outcomes of people in interaction, and both can be said to have their origins in the idea of social exchange (Thibaut and Kelley, 1959; Homans, 1961; Blau, 1964), although each represents a different, highly sophisticated, development from it. Hatfield's paper (sub-Chapter 7.2) is a very clear and concise overview of equity theory and research. At present, it can be argued that the emphasis in equity research is on the individual's restoration of equity rather than on the group processes by which systems of equity are evolved and sustained; because of this, some of the research has more in common with, for example, cognitive dissonance theory, than with many of the other papers in this section. However, there is no reason why more research effort should not be directed toward the group process aspects of the theory (see Homans, 1976).

For further reading on social exchange, see Gergen *et al.* (1980); for equity theory, see Berkowitz and Walster (1976).

Harrison and McCallum (sub-Chapter 7.3) have tackled, very successfully, the difficult task of expressing Kelley and Thibaut's Interdependence Theory in such limited space. It is a general theory for the analysis of social interaction, in which an 'interdependence matrix' is taken to represent the patterns of influence in a relationship. The 'effective' matrix, which is the immediate determinant of behavior, is a transformation of the 'given' matrix, and is partly a consequence of the attribution and self-presentation processes of the actors.

Had we not decided to include Hinde in the chapter on Roles and Relationships, that paper would have been found here. Readers interested in the taxonomy of interpersonal relationships should consult it (Volume 1, sub-Chapter

9.1), and Hinde (1979), in which both exchange and interdependence approaches are seen as only one type of principle for understanding the dynamics of relationships.

Hare's paper (sub-Chapter 7.4), which discusses a functional interpretation of interaction, provides a link between sub-Chapter 7.3, which concludes by stressing the importance of a functional analysis of social motivation, and the succeeding papers, which focus on what might be called group products, and the problems of group survival.

The paper by Hoffman and Stein (sub-Chapter 7.5) focuses on the dynamics of the problem-solving group and, like sub-Chapters 7.4 to 7.8, is concerned with the group process rather than the individual's social behavior. In this paper, the Hierarchical Model is described, and related to the process of leadership emergence.

In Zander's paper (sub-Chapter 7.6), he presents his work on the development of desire for the group's success, in terms analogous to the individual's desire for success, or achievement motivation. Desire for the group's success is enhanced in cohesive groups (see Shaw, Volume 1, sub-Chapter 2.4), and may even overcome the individual's fear of failure.

Whether or not the members of a group work together for group success is also the theme of Randall and Southgate's paper (sub-Chapter 7.7). Their analysis of creativity in self-managed groups is firmly psychoanalytical, although it combines two different lines of psychoanalytic thought to describe the 'creative energy cycle' of the self-managed group. They go on to discuss the issues which affect group creativity.

Schutz (sub-Chapter 7.8) in his paper, describes his theory of small groups and also outlines the experiences which led him to develop it from his earlier FIRO theory.

Holmes (sub-Chapter 7.9) applies a unique combination of Freudian and Piagetian approaches to the analysis of the functioning of both small groups and larger societies. In the present paper he takes the Freudian myth of the Primal Horde as the starting point for his closely argued analysis of leadership, authority, and ritual. The myth he regards as having no necessary historical validity, but as having interesting explanatory use. Although the myth itself is inherently sexist—inevitably so—it seems possible to regard Holmes's case as extending to a sexually neutral analysis of power.

The next two papers present different ways of describing interaction, both at the level of the group and of the participants. Bales (sub-Chapter 7.10) describes the theoretical background of his 'system for the multiple level observation of groups,' or SYMLOG, and how to use it. He sees the system as providing a means by which one can look both at the level of group process and at the level of the individual, at both levels permitting the statistical analysis of naturalistic data.

If Bales provides a way of describing 'reality,' as perceived by observers, and a means of comparing these observations, Goffman, in the penultimate paper (sub-

Chapter 7.11), discusses the problems of the nature of reality. According to his dramaturgical perspective, the participants in any activity perceive the activity as consisting of differently 'framed' episodes—'frame' used as in the sense of a film strip. When an actor takes on a role, something of the self is also 'given off;' Goffman sees the relation between person and role with respect to the framing of events.

Finally (sub-Chapter 7.12), we asked Steiner to comment on the outcome of his prediction that there would be a revival in the study of groups by the end of the 1970s (Steiner, 1974). As we found in our research for this book, there is plenty going on, although taken in relation to other aspects of social psychology, one could hardly say that the subject had become 'groupy.' However, although Tajfel's (1972) strictures that reductionism is prevalent in social psychology are still to the point—that is, attempts are made to explain human social behavior in terms of 'general laws of individual motivation'—it is also true to say that there is now a growing interest in explanation at the level of social process, which can be expected to stimulate research in the next decade. For a further discussion of current social psychology, see Pepitone (1981).

Further reading

For good coverage of sociological perspectives on social psychology, see Rosenberg and Turner (1981). For a symbolic interaction approach, Cicourel (Volume 1, sub-Chapter 9.2) and Denzin (1979). For discussion of the 'division' of social psychology, see House (1977) and Liska (1977). For cross-cultural research on small groups see Mann (1979) and Shuter (1977).

References

Berkowitz, L. and Walster, E. (eds.) (1976). *Equity Theory: Toward a General Theory of Social Interaction*, Academic Press, New York.

Blau, P. M. (1964). *Exchange and Power in Social Life*, Wiley and Sons, New York.

Denzin, N. K. (ed.) (1979). *Studies in Symbolic Interaction*, Vol. 3, Jai Press, Greenwich, Conn.

Gergen, K J., Greenberg, M. S., and Willis, R. H. (eds.) (1980). *Social Exchange: Advances in Theory and Research*, Plenum Press, New York and London.

Hinde, R. A. (1979). *Towards Understanding Relationships*, Academic Press, London.

Homans, G. C. (1961). *Social Behavior: Its Elementary Forms*, Harcourt, Brace, Jovanovitch, New York.

Homans, G. C. (1976). 'Commentary,' in L. Berkowitz and E. Walster (eds.), *Equity Theory: Toward a General Theory of Social Interaction*, Academic Press, New York.

House, J. S. (1977). 'The three faces of social psychology,' *Sociometry*, **40** (2), 161–177.

Liska, A. E. (1977). 'The dissipation of sociological social psychology,' *American Sociologist*, **12** (1), 2–8.

Mann, L. (1979). 'Cross-cultural studies of small groups,' in H. C. Triandis and R. W. Brislin (eds.), *Handbook of Cross-cultural Psychology*, Vol. 5, Allyn and Bacon, Boston, Mass.

Pepitone, A. (1981). 'Lessons from the history of social psychology,' *American Psychologist*, 36, 972–985.

Rosenberg, M., and Turner, R. H. (eds.) (1981). *Social Psychology: Sociological Perspectives*, Basic Books, New York.

Shuter, R. (1977). 'Cross-cultural small group research: A review, an analysis, a theory,' *International Journal of Intercultural Relations*, 1 (1), 90–104.

Steiner, I. D. (1974). 'Whatever happened to the group in social psychology?' *Journal of Experimental Social Psychology*, 10, 94–108.

Tajfel, H. (1972). 'Experiments in a vacuum,' in J. Israel and H. Tajfel (eds.), *The Context of Social Psychology*, Academic Press, New York and London.

Thibaut, J. W., and Kelley, H. H. (1959). *The Social Psychology of Groups*, Wiley and Sons, New York.

7 Approaches to the Study of Small Groups

Small Groups and Social Interaction, Volume 2
Edited by H. H. Blumberg, A. P. Hare, V. Kent and M. Davies
© 1983 John Wiley & Sons Ltd

7.1   An Outline of Some Theories

Valerie Kent   *University of London Goldsmiths' College*

Introduction to the theories table

Table 1 outlines some of the social psychological theories which are particularly relevant to other papers in this volume. While the comments are necessarily brief, they are intended to help the reader grasp some of the fundamental points of the theories. The table includes only theories from 'psychological' social psychology, and may therefore be particularly useful to readers with a sociological background and to psychology undergraduates.

The first column presents a rather cursory synopsis of the theory. The column headed 'References' gives a short selection of further readings; an early publication date indicates, generally, a seminal work, while the more recent references cover theoretical and empirical developments.

In the 'Assumptions' column, an attempt is made to relate the theories to some of the underlying issues in psychology, for example, innate versus acquired characteristics, the role of contemporary rather than historical factors in shaping behaviour, human nature as good or evil, free will versus determinism, the legitimacy of inferring unobservable mediating processes. Any one theory may address itself explicitly to perhaps only one of these issues. While only these points are listed, the reader might like to try to work out how a particular theory might stand in relation to the other issues above.

Some social psychological theories are advanced in order to explain social influence, while for others social influence processes are inherent because of the accounts they give of the acquisition, maintenance or change of behaviour. In the column headed 'Social influence,' the social influence processes implicit or explicit in the theories are given, using the distinctions made by Kelman (1961) between 'compliance,' 'identification,' and 'internalization.'

Table 1. Theories in social psychology

Theory	Statement	References	Assumptions	Social influence	Range
Learning Theory	Various uses and developments of learning theory from general psychology. Behavior derived from satisfaction of drives—innate or acquired. Responses shaped by reinforcement (often related to process of identification in social learning theories).	Bandura (1977)	Some drives innate, some acquired, but social behavior *not* innate—derived from drive reduction	Compliance, identification. Need external reinforcer prior to internalization (if this ever happens)	Attitudes, socialization, interaction, liking
Exchange Theory	Assumes people in interaction seek to maximize own outcomes (rewards minus costs), seen against a comparison level (CL) and CL of Alternatives. (Anything can be reward or cost, as perceived by individual: theory is therefore ultimately unfalsifiable.) Behavior shaped by anticipation of outcomes. Norms serve to regulate exchange, thus avoiding excessive use of personal power, disruptive to a relationship.	Homans (1961) Thibaut and Kelley (1959) Gergen *et al.* (1980) See also: Interdependence Theory (sub-chapter 7.3 below)	Behavior shaped by anticipation of outcomes; seek own maximum outcome. Relative power, status important	Compliance, identification—tends to imply a superficial level, though elastic enough to extend to internalized values. This last is rarely done.	All forms of social interaction. Aims to be general theory
Equity Theory	Developed from the above but stressing importance of perceived *justice* of outcomes. 4 propositions: (I) Individuals try to maximize outcomes. (IIA) Members will evolve systems of equitable apportionment of outcomes, thus maximizing collective reward. (IIB) Groups will generally reward members who treat others equitably and punish those who do not. (III) Individuals finding themselves in inequitable relationships become distressed—greater inequity leads to greater distress. (IV) Such distressed individuals try to restore equity—the more distress, the harder they try.	Berkowitz and Walster (1976) Hatfield (sub-Chapter 7.2 below)	People are innately selfish. Behavior shaped by maximization of outcomes, within the limits of perceived equity.	Compliance, perhaps identification—but processes and mechanisms do not really have a clear place in this analysis, although it is a 'cognitive' theory and includes internalization.	General, but business, exploiting, helping and intimate relations, in terms of main research areas so far.

| Self-perception | Bem, describing himself as a radical behaviourist, states that 'To the extent that internal stimuli are not controlling, an individual's attitude statements may be viewed as inferences from observations of his own overt behavior and its accompanying stimulus variables.' Theory developed to provide alternative explanation of dissonance phenomena (qv). Does not, in principle, *dispute* the phenomena, but says both 'self' and 'other' are making 'partial inferences from the same evidence.' Uses Skinner's idea of *tacts* and *mands*. | Bem (1972) Much work by attribution theorists is also relevant (see below) | That the concept of 'enduring attitude' is not valid or useful. Defines attitudes as self-descriptive statements, derived from social learning processes. Can be seen as intrapersonal and in a sense, cognitive, given emphasis on *inferring*. | Internalization. Learning of labels from 'verbal community.' | Forced compliance. Perception of own motivation and emotion. |
| Social Comparison | Two types of reality, physical and social—the latter more variable, and depends largely on perceived group consensus. 'Where the dependence on physical reality is low the dependence on social reality is correspondingly high. An opinion, a belief an attitude is "correct," "valid," and "proper" to the extent that it is anchored in a group of people with similar beliefs, attitudes and "opinions"' Festinger (1950). The group of people may only be *believed* to think thus—the reference groups may be stereotypes, and the person may have no real knowledge of them. | Festinger (1954) Schachter (1959) Suls and Miller (1977) | People seek to evaluate themselves against others. Behavior may change over time, and with place or role also, depending on reference group. | Identification. Contemporary social influence, interindividual. Reference person or group may be unaware that they serve this function. | Influence, communication, affiliation, interpersonal attraction. |

Table 1 *continued*

Theory	Statement	References	Assumptions	Social influence	Range
Cognitive consistency	Several developments of Heider's (1946) argument that people like to have internally consistent (to them) attitudes, beliefs, perceptions, etc. This theory of Cognitive Balance was extended to an inter-individual theory by Newcomb. In Osgood and Tannenbaum's Congruity Model, different evaluations of a message and its source were studied. Most research stimulated by Festinger's work (see below).	Heider (1946) Abelson *et al.* (1968)	People seek psychological consistency, to be able to cope with environment. Inconsistency must be noticed, and does not depend on logic, but 'psycho-logic'.	Identification may here lead to change in belief or behavior. Compliance may lead to internalization.	Attitude change, persuasion, interpersonal attraction.
Cognitive Dissonance	If, when considering two cognitive elements alone, the obverse of one implies the other, dissonance will occur. This is an aversive drive state and the individual will engage in efforts to reduce it. These efforts may, but not necessarily, lead to attitude change. Again, a theory of *psychological* consistency, not rationality. Forced compliance predictions have been modified by addition of variables specifying when dissonance will occur. These include: self-concept, commitment, size of consequences, and freedom of choice. Opposes learning theory in that it predicts that attitude change will be an *inverse* function of reward.	Festinger (1957) Aronson (1968) Zimbardo (1969) Collins and Hoyt (1972) and see Moentmann (1979) for a bibliography of dissonance research	Mixture of innate drive reduction theory and cognitive theory. Much depends on unspecified experience which gives rise to the individual's perception of what is consistent.	Argues that compliance may *lead* to internalization if minimum force is used, mediated by dissonance which arises because of inconsistency between beliefs and behavior. Attitude change is not the only means of dissonance reduction.	Forced compliance studies of attitude change, decision making, selective exposure to information, cognitive aspects of motivation.

Reactance	Another theory of social motivation with a drive reduction basis. Brehm argues that if a person perceives that his or her freedom of action is reduced or threatened, this gives rise to an aversive drive state, which he calls *reactance*. The person is thus motivated to reduce reactance; different routes may be taken to restore 'perceived freedom.' Steiner distinguishes between decision freedom (choosing what you want) and outcome freedom (getting what you've chosen)	Brehm (1966) Steiner (1970)	Drive reduction assumptions, mixed with cognitive orientation. Brehm suggests that the ability to achieve and maintain freedom of action served an evolutionary function.	Negative, in that perceived freedom may be *threatened* by attempts to influence. Justification of threat may serve to reduce reactance, and may be socially based.	Aggression, interpersonal attraction, group behavior, social influence and resistance to it. Frustration, power, socialization.
Attribution Theory	Also derived from Heider (1958). The person strives to cope with, to predict the environment. There are three criteria for external validity when the person attributes causes to entities: distinctiveness; consistency and consensus. The idea of attribution of *cause* is fundamental to the theory. Attributions need not be *correct* in terms of external yardstick, and erroneous or differential attributions are themselves subjects of research	Heider (1958) Harvey and Smith (1977) Harvey, Ickes and Kidd (1976, 1978) Gorlitz (1980)	Need to be able to predict environment, to find causes. Person's history may affect both the tendency to make, and type of, attributions.	Internalization, do things because seen as valid, correct, based on attribution of causes, from best info. available. *Note*: Influence may be *sought* if need to make better attributions is felt.	Informational influence. Person- and self-perception, attitude change, cognitive aspects of emotion and motivation, affiliation, achievement, reinforcement schedules, psychotherapy language.

Table 1 *continued*

Theory	References	Statement	Assumptions	Social influence	Range
Evaluative Response Contagion	Nuttin (1975)	Argues with both findings *and* theory on forced compliance, whether learning, dissonance or self-perception theory. After a systematic series of 13 experiments varying levels of financial rewards, giving non-monetary rewards (which might be relevant or not to the task) and also giving aversive consequences for a 'highly important' counter-attitudinal statement, he developed a new theory. Nuttin concluded that where an individual is 'perturbed' (e.g. by too high *or* too low a level of reward, or embarrassed, surprised, etc.), this leads to a 'contagion' of the induced evaluative response to the subsequent attitude measure and hence of attitude *response*. He, like Bem, is unhappy with traditional conceptions of attitude. He used non-lab. as well as laboratory procedures and follow-ups in the field to test his hypotheses.	Virtually a conditioning model. Here a response emitted when aroused, is highly likely to recur, whether source of arousal or 'perturbation' is produced by pleasant (+) or unpleasant (−) circumstances.	Internalization of behaviour when aroused (but it is response rather than attitude which is internalized). Nuttin would say it is a *specific* response only. More labile or susceptible to influence than concept of attitude.	Forced compliance. Nuttin argues that this is a special case of persuasion, namely self-persuasion and that the theory can apply to much wider aspects of persuasion.

In compliance, observable behaviour is changed because the agent of change can reward or punish the actor. Identification depends on the actor's perception that the source of influence is attractive and provides the opportunity for a satisfying self-defining relationship. With internalization, values, attitudes, beliefs are changed when a source is perceived to be credible, that is, both expert and trustworthy. These three processes of influence, as Kelman says, may not be distinguishable in practice, and may in any case, occur together.

The last column, 'Range,' simply lists some of the topics to which the theory has most notably been applied.

References

Abelson, R. P., Aronson, E., McGuire, W. J., Newcomb, T. M., Rosenberg, M. J., and Tannenbaum, P. H. (1968). *Theories of Cognitive Consistency: A Sourcebook*, Rand McNally, Chicago.

Aronson, E. (1968). 'The theory of cognitive dissonance: A current perspective,' in L. Berkowitz (ed.), *Advances in Experimental Social Psychology*, Vol. 4, Academic Press, New York.

Bandura, A. (1977). *Social Learning Theory*, Prentice-Hall, Englewood Cliffs, NJ.

Bem, D. J. (1972). 'Self-perception theory,' in L. Berkowitz (ed.), *Advances in Experimental Social Psychology*, Vol. 6, Academic Press, New York.

Berkowitz, L., and Walster, E. (eds.) (1976). *Equity Theory: Toward a General Theory of Social Interaction*, [Vol. 9 of *Advances in Experimental Social Psychology*], Academic Press, New York.

Brehm, J. W. (1966). *A Theory of Psychological Reactance*, Academic Press, New York.

Collins, B. E., and Hoyt, M. F. (1972). 'Personal responsibility for consequences: an integration and extension of the "forced compliance" literature,' *Journal of Experimental Psychology*, **8**, 558–593.

Festinger, L. (1950). 'Informal social communication,' *Psychological Review*, **57**, 271–282.

Festinger, L. (1954). 'A theory of social comparison processes,' *Human Relations*, **7**, 117–140.

Festinger, L. (1957). *A Theory of Cognitive Dissonance*, Row, Peterson, Evanston, Illinois.

Gergen, K. J., Greenberg, M. S., and Willis, R. H. (1980). *Social Exchange: Advances in Theory and Research*, Plenum Press, New York.

Gorlitz, D. (ed.) (1980). *Perspectives on Attribution Research and Theory*, Ballinger Publishing Company, Cambridge, Mass.

Harvey, J. H., Ickes, W. J., and Kidd, R. F. (eds.) (1976, 1978). *New Directions in Attribution Research*, Vol. 1, Vol. 2, Erlbaum, Hillsdale, NJ.

Harvey, J. H., and Smith, W. P. (1977). *Social Psychology: An Attributional Approach*, C. V. Mosby Company, Saint Louis.

Heider, F. (1946). 'Attitudes and cognitive organization,' *Journal of Psychology*, **21**, 107–112.

Heider, F. (1958). *The Psychology of Interpersonal Relations*, Wiley, New York.

Homans, G. C. (1961). *Social Behavior: Its Elementary Forms*, Harcourt Brace, NY.

Kelman, H. C. (1961). 'Processes of opinion change,' *Public Opinion Quarterly*, **25**, 57–78.

Moentmann, V. (1979). *Dissonance Theory: A Bibliography 1957–1978*. Publication of the Sonderforschungsbereich 24 Sozialwissenschaftliche Entscheidungsforschung, University of Mannheim, West Germany, Mannheim.

Nuttin, J. M. (1975). *The Illusion of Attitude Change: Toward a Response Contagion Theory of Persuasion*, Academic Press, New York.

Schachter, S. (1959). *The Psychology of Affiliation*, Stanford University Press, Palo Alto.

Steiner, I. D. (1970). 'Perceived freedom,' in L. Berkowitz (ed.), *Advances in Experimental Social Psychology*, Vol. 5, Academic Press, New York.

Suls, J., and Miller, R. L. (eds.) (1977). *Social Comparison Processes*, Hemisphere/ Halsted, Washington DC.

Thibaut, J. W., and Kelley, H. H. (1959). *The Social Psychology of Groups*, Wiley & Sons, New York.

Zimbardo, P. G. (ed.) (1969). *The Cognitive Control of Motivation*, Scott, Foresman and Co., Glenview, Ill.

Small Groups and Social Interaction, Volume 2
Edited by H. H. Blumberg, A. P. Hare, V. Kent and M. Davies
© 1983 John Wiley & Sons Ltd

7.2 Equity Theory and Research: An Overview[1]

Elaine Hatfield   *University of Hawaii at Manoa*

Equity: the theory

Propositions I–IV

Equity theory is a strikingly simple theory. It is composed of four interlocking propositions:

> PROPOSITION I: Individuals will try to maximize their outcomes (where outcomes equal rewards minus punishments).
>
> PROPOSITION IIA: Groups (or rather the individuals comprising these groups) can maximize collective reward by evolving accepted systems for equitably apportioning resources among members. Thus, groups will evolve such systems of equity, and will attempt to induce members to accept and adhere to these systems.
>
> PROPOSITION IIB: Groups will generally reward members who treat others equitably and generally punish members who treat each other inequitably.
>
> PROPOSITION III: When individuals find themselves participating in inequitable relationships, they will become distressed. The more inequitable the relationship, the more distress they will feel.
>
> PROPOSITION IV: Individuals who discover they are in inequitable relationships will attempt to eliminate their distress by restoring equity. The greater the inequity that exists, the more distress they will feel, and the harder they will try to restore equity.

Definitional formula[2]

Equity theorists (see Walster, 1975) define an equitable relationship to exist when the person scrutinizing the relationship—who could be Participant A,

Participant B, or an outside observer—concludes that all participants are receiving equal relative gains from the relationship; that is, when

$$\frac{(O_A - I_A)}{(|I_A|)^{kA}} = \frac{(O_B - I_B)}{(|I_B|)^{kB}}$$

where I_A and I_B designate a scrutineer's perception of Person A's and Person B's inputs, O_A and O_B designate his or her perception of Person A's and Person B's outcomes, and $|I_A|$ and $|I_B|$ designate the absolute value of their inputs (i.e. disregarding sign).[3,4]

Definition of terms

Inputs (I_A or I_B) are defined as 'The scrutineer's perception of the participants' contributions to the exchange, which are seen as entitling them to reward or punishment.' The inputs that participants contribute to a relationship can be either assets (entitling them to rewards) or liabilities (entitling them to punishment).

In different settings, people consider different inputs to be relevant. For example, in industrial settings, businessmen assume that such hard assets as capital or manual labor entitle one to reward; such liabilities as incompetence or disloyalty entitle one to punishment. In social settings, friends assume that such social assets as wit or kindness entitle one to reward, whereas such social liabilities as drunkenness or cruelty entitle one to punishment.

In addition to assessing what participants have put into their relationship, the scrutineer must also assess whether or not participants are getting the outcomes they deserve from the relationship. Outcomes (O_A or O_B) are defined as 'the scrutineer's perception of the rewards and punishments participants have received in the course of their relationship with one another.' The participants' total outcomes, then, are equal to the rewards they obtain from the relationship minus the punishments that they incur.

The exponents k_A and k_B take on the value of $+1$ or -1 depending on the sign of A and B's inputs and the sign of their gains (outcomes − inputs): k_A or k_B are $+1$ if I and (O − I) are both positive (or both negative); otherwise k_A and k_B are -1.[5]

Who decides whether a relationship is equitable?

According to the theory, equity is in the eye of the beholder. Observers' perceptions of how equitable a relationship is will depend on their assessment of the value and relevance of the participants' inputs and outcomes. If different observers assess participants' inputs and outcomes differently, and it is likely that they will, it is inevitable that they will disagree about whether or not a given relationship is equitable. For example, a wife—focusing on the fact that she works long hours, is trapped with no one to talk to all day, and is constantly engulfed by noise, mess, and confusion—may feel that her relative gains are extremely low. Her husband—focusing on the fact that she gets up in the morning whenever she pleases, and can see whom she wants, when she wants—may disagree; he thinks she 'has it made.' Moreover, an 'objective' observer may calculate the couple's relative gains still differently.

The psychological consequences of inequity

According to Proposition III, when individuals find themselves participating in inequitable relationships, they feel distress—regardless of whether they are the beneficiaries or the victims of inequity. The overbenefited may label their distress as guilt, dissonance, empathy, fear of retaliation, or conditioned anxiety. The underbenefited may label their distress as anger or resentment. Essentially, however, both the overbenefited and the underbenefited share certain feelings—they feel 'distress' accompanied by physiological arousal (see Austin and Walster, 1974a, b).

Techniques by which individuals reduce their distress

Proposition IV states that individuals who are distressed by their inequitable relations will try to eliminate such distress by restoring equity to their relationship. There are only two ways by which participants can restore *actual equity*—by altering their own or their partners' relative gains. For example, imagine that an unskilled laborer discovers that a contractor has been paying him less than the minimum wage. He can re-establish actual equity in four different ways: he can neglect his work (thus lowering his inputs); he can start to steal equipment from the company (thus raising his own outcomes); he can make mistakes so that the contractor will have to work far into the night undoing what he has done (thus raising the employer's inputs); or he can damage company equipment (thus lowering the contractor's outcomes). (The ingenious ways people contrive to bring equity to inequitable relationships are documented by Adams, 1965.)

Participants can restore *psychological equity* to their relationship by changing their perceptions of the situation. They can try to convince themselves and others that the inequitable relationship is, in fact, perfectly fair. For example, suppose that the exploitative contractor starts to feel guilty about underpaying his unskilled laborers. He can try to convince himself that his relationship is equitable in four ways: he can restore psychological equity by minimizing his workers' inputs ('You wouldn't believe how useless they are'); by exaggerating his own inputs ('Without my creative genius the company would fall apart'); by exaggerating his workers' outcomes ('They really work for the variety the job provides'); or by minimizing his own outcomes ('The tension on this job is giving me an ulcer').

Actual versus psychological equity restoration

At this point, equity theorists confront a crucial question: Can one specify when people will try to restore actual equity to their relationships, *versus* when they will settle for restoring psychological equity? From Equity theory's Propositions I and IV, one can make a straightforward derivation: people may be expected to follow a cost–benefit strategy in deciding how they will respond to perceived inequity. Whether individuals respond to injustice by attempting to restore actual equity, by distorting reality, or by doing a little of both has been found to depend on costs and benefits participants think they will derive from each strategy (see Berscheid and Walster, 1967; Berscheid *et al.*, 1969; or Weick and Nesset, 1968).

Equity: the research

Researchers have applied the Equity framework to four major areas of human interaction—exploiter/victim relationships, philanthropist/recipient relationships, business relationships, and intimate relationships. (See Walster *et al.*, 1978; Hatfield and Traupmann, 1980; or Hatfield *et al.*, in preparation, for review of this voluminous research.)

Let us consider a sampling of the kind of research that Equity theorists have conducted in the first of these areas—exploiter/victim relationships.

Exploiter/victim relationships

People have always been concerned with promoting social justice. It is not surprising, then, that early Equity theorists, who could have begun by investigating any of the four Equity propositions, in fact, focused on a single question: 'How do exploiters and their victims respond to injustice?'

Definition of terms. Researchers began by defining terms. They defined *exploiters* (or *harm-doers*) as 'People who commit acts that cause their relative-gains to exceed their partners'.' The *exploited* (or *victims*) are 'People whose relative-gains fall short of their partners'.'

Reactions of exploiters and their victims to inequity. (a) *Distress*: According to Equity theory (see Hatfield *et al.*, 1979):

> Proposition III: When individuals find themselves participating in inequitable relationships, they will become distressed. The more inequitable the relationship, the more distress they will feel (p. 101)

According to the theory, then, any time people take more than they deserve . . . or accept less, they should feel distress. On first glance one might think that people who receive far more than they deserve should be delighted, not distressed. The theory, however, predicts that they will feel both delight at receiving such a large reward ... mixed with the distress they feel at finding themselves caught up in an inequitable relationship. If inequitable relationships are distressing to exploiters, they should be doubly distressing to their victims. Equity theorists, then, predict that Equity will be related to contentment/distress as indicated in Figure 1.

Compelling evidence exists to support the contention that both exploiters and their victims *do* feel intense distress after an inequitable exchange. (See Austin and Walster, 1974a, b; Walster *et al.*, 1978; Hatfield, *et al.*, in preparation, and Utne *et al.*, in press, for a review of this research.) In one study, for example, Austin and Walster (1974b) investigated workers' cognitive, affective, and physiological reactions to equity and inequity. They tested the dual predictions that (1) workers will be more content (and less distressed) when they are fairly rewarded than when they are either over-rewarded or under-rewarded. Further (2) participants will be less distressed when they are over-rewarded than when they are under-rewarded.

Austin invited college students to participate in a psychological study of decision making. Each student was assigned to work on a task with a partner (actually an experimental accomplice). A third student (also an experimental accomplice)

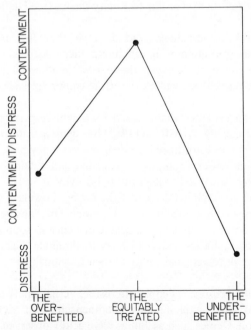

Figure 1 The predicted relationship between equity and contentment/distress

was designated 'decision maker' and told to pay the two students on the basis of their task performance. Since both students performed equally well, the 'decision' should have been a simple one—each student should have received $2.00. Sometimes, the decision maker did pay the student an equitable $2.00. Sometimes, however, by prearrangement, he did the unexpected: sometimes he overpaid her (i.e. gave her $3.00; $1.00 more than she deserved); other times he underpaid her (i.e. gave her $1.00; $1.00 less than she deserved). The student was then quizzed about how she felt about the way she had been treated. As predicted, equitably paid students were more cognitively and emotionally content than either overpaid or underpaid individuals. Also as predicted, overbenefited students were more content than underbenefited ones. The women who received $1.00 more than they deserved were slightly upset, those who received $1.00 less than they deserved were extremely upset.

Physiological data tended to substantiate the women's reports of how they felt about the decision. *Galvanic Skin Response* measures revealed that equitably treated workers were the most tranquil. Overbenefited women were slightly aroused; deprived women were even more aroused. (Additional evidence in support of this contention comes from Austin and Walster, 1974a, b; Walster *et al.*, 1978; Hatfield and Traupmann, 1980; Hatfield *et al.*, in preparation, and Utne *et al.*, in press.)

(b) *Restoration of Equity*: According to Equity theory (see Hatfield *et al.*, 1979):

> Proposition IV: Individuals who discover they are in inequitable relationships will attempt to eliminate their distress by restoring equity. The greater the inequity that exists, the more distress they will feel, and the harder they will try to restore equity. (p. 101).

Theoretically, an exploiter/victim could be taught to perform *any* action that reduces his or her anxiety. Aronfreed (1961) has demonstrated the wide variety of ways transgressors can learn to reduce their anxiety: they may find relief by confessing their sins, in self-criticism, by apologizing and making reparation to their victim, or in promising to modify their future behavior.

When we look at exploiters'/victims' behavior, however, we find that two classes of responses seem to occur most commonly (perhaps because they reduce anxiety most effectively). There is compelling evidence to support the Proposition IV contention that exploiters and victims try to eliminate their distress by restoring either actual or psychological equity to their relationships.

Restoration of actual equity.   People can restore actual equity to a relationship in a straightforward way—exploiters can compensate their victims; victims can insist on restitution. Cynics such as Junius have acidly observed that even 'a death bed repentance seldom reaches to restitution.' Such pessimism is not always warranted. Recent studies verify the fact that *harm-doers often do voluntarily compensate their victims* (see, for example, Berscheid and Walster, 1967; Berscheid *et al.*, 1969; Brock and Becker, 1966; Carlsmith and Gross, 1969; Freedman *et al.*, 1967; Walster and Prestholdt, 1966; Walster *et al.*, 1970).

Demands for compensation. Undoubtedly the victim's first response to exploitation is to seek restitution (see Leventhal and Bergman, 1969, and Marwell *et al.*, 1970). If victims secure compensation, they have 'set things right' and benefited materially. It is easy to see why this is a popular response.

Restoration of psychological equity. As we noted earlier, people can restore equity in a second way—they can distort reality and convince themselves that their unjust relationship is, in fact, perfectly fair. If exploiters and victims can minimize the exploiter's relative gains, or can aggrandize the victim's gains, they can convince themselves and perhaps others that their relationship is, in fact, equitable. Some distortions that harm-doers and victims use include: blaming the victim, minimization of the victim's suffering, or denial of responsibility for the victim's suffering.

Let us focus first on the exploiter's responses:

Blaming the victim. It is not unfair to exploit others if they deserve to be exploited. Thus, an obvious way by which exploiters can persuade themselves that their acts were equitable is by devaluing their victim's inputs. That harm-doers will often derogate their victims has been demonstrated by a number of researchers (see Berkowitz, 1962; Davidson, 1964; Davis and Jones, 1960; Glass, 1964; Katz *et al.*, 1973, Sykes and Matza, 1957; and Walster and Prestholdt, 1966). In a typical experiment, Davis and Jones (1960) found that students who were recruited to insult other students, as part of a research project, generally ended up convincing themselves that the students deserved to be ridiculed. Sykes and Matza (1957) found that juvenile delinquents often defended their victimization of others by arguing that their victims are really homosexuals, bums, or possess other traits that make them deserving of punishment. In tormenting others, then, the delinquents can claim to be the restorers of justice rather than harm-doers.

Minimization of the victim's suffering. If exploiters can deny that their victims were harmed, they can convince themselves that their relationship with the victim is an equitable one. Sykes and Matza (1957) and Brock and Buss (1962) demonstrate that harm-doers will consistently underestimate how much harm they have done to another. Brock and Buss, for example, found that college students who administer electric shock to other students soon come to underestimate markedly the painfulness of the shock.

Denial of responsibility for the act. If exploiters can convince themselves that it was not their own behavior, but rather the action of someone else (e.g. the experimenter or fate) that caused the victim's suffering, then their relationship with the victim becomes an equitable one. (The person who is unjustly assigned responsibility for reducing the victim's outcomes will now be perceived as the harm-doer, and it will be this third party's relationship with the victim, not the original harm-doer's relationship, that is perceived as inequitable.)

That harm-doers will often deny their responsibility for harm-doing has been documented by Sykes and Matza (1975) and by Brock and Buss (1962, 1964). In daily life, the denial of responsibility seems to be a favorite strategy of those who are made to feel guilty about exploiting others. War criminals protest vehemently that they were 'only following orders.'

* * *

But, it is not just exploiters who justify their unjust acts. Victims, too, have been found to justify their own exploitation. Sometimes, victims find that it is impossible to elicit restitution. Under such circumstances, the impotent victims are then left with only two options—they can acknowledge the exploitations and their inability to do anything about it, or they can justify their own exploitation. Often, victimized individuals find it less upsetting to distort reality and justify their victimization than to acknowledge that the world is unjust and that they are too impotent to elicit fair treatment [see Lerner and Matthews, 1967].

Victimized individuals have been found to restore psychological equity to the exploiter/victim relationship in several ways:

Concluding it was all for the best.   Sometimes victims console themselves by imagining that they were not really exploited, or by insisting that exploitation has brought compensating benefits. For example, there is evidence that when things are arranged so that people cannot win, they often convince themselves that they do not want to win. For example, Solomon (1957) set up an experimental game. A powerful player treated some players benevolently (benefiting them whenever he could) and others malevolently (depriving them whenever he could). As we would expect, the benefited players were more content than the frustrated ones. More interestingly, the players who were treated benevolently attached far more importance to doing well in the game than did the malevolently treated ones.

It will all come out in the wash.   Sometimes victims console themselves by concluding that in the long run the exploiter will be punished as he deserves ('The mill of the Lord grinds slowly, but it grinds exceedingly fine').

He who has deserves to get.   Or, victims may convince themselves that their exploiters actually deserved the enormous benefits they received. Recent data demonstrate that the exploited are inclined to justify their exploiter's excessive benefits. Jecker and Landy (1969), Walster and Prestholdt (1966), and Hastorf and Regan (personal communication, 1962) pressured individuals into performing a difficult favor for an unworthy recipient. They found that the abashed favor-doers tried to justify the inequity by convincing themselves that the recipient was especially needy or worthy.

Reformers who work to alleviate social injustice are often enraged to discover that the exploited themselves are sometimes vehement defenders of the *status quo*. Black militants encounter 'Uncle Toms' who defend white supremacy. Women's liberation groups lobbying for the Equal Rights Amendment must face angry housewives who threaten to defend to death the inferior status of women. Reformers might have more sympathy for such 'Uncle Toms' if they understood the psychological underpinnings of such reactions. When one is treated inequitably, but has no hope of altering the situation, denying reality is often less degrading than facing up to one's humiliating position.

Summary

The theory

Equity theorists agree that people try to maximize their outcomes (Proposition I). A group of individuals can maximize its collective outcomes by devising an equitable system for sharing resources. Thus, groups try to induce members to behave equitably: that is, they try to ensure that all participants receive equal relative outcomes:

$$\frac{(O_A - I_A)}{(|I_A|)^{k_A}} = \frac{(O_B - I_B)}{(|I_B|)^{k_B}}$$

They can do this in only one way: by making it more profitable to be good than to be greedy. They can reward members who behave equitably and punish members who behave inequitably (Proposition II). When socialized persons find themselves enmeshed in inequitable relationships, they experience distress (Proposition III) and are motivated to reduce such distress either by restoring actual equity or by restoring psychological equity to their relationships (Proposition IV).

The data

Equity theorists have collected evidence in support of Proposition III, namely, they have shown that:

1. Men and women feel most content when they are engaged in equitable relationships. Both the overbenefited and the underbenefited feel ill at ease. The more inequitable the relationship, the more uncomfortable participants feel. Participants are less distressed by inequity when they gain from it than when they lose from it.
2. People who discover they are in an inequitable relationship (and become

distressed) try to reduce their distress by restoring either actual equity or psychological equity to their relationships.

Cynics have expressed skepticism that exploiters will voluntarily compensate their victims to restore equity ... but the data suggest that they often do. It probably comes as no surprise that victims are generally eager to be compensated.

If compensation does not occur, both exploiter and victim have been found to restore psychological equity by aggrandizing the exploiter, minimizing the victim's suffering, or assuming that some outside power will intervene and set things right.

Notes

1. The research reported in this article was supported, in part, by a grant from the University of Wisconsin graduate school.
2. For a detailed explanation of the logic underlying this definition of Equity, see Walster (1975).
3. There is one restriction on inputs: The smallest absolute input must be $\geqslant 1$, that is, $|I_A|$ and $|I_B|$ must both be $\geqslant 1$.
4. Of course, other theorists have proposed other, related definitions of equity. See, for example, Alessio (1980), Harris (1976), Moschetti (1979), or Zuckerman (1975).
5. The exponent's effect is simply to change the way relative outcomes are computed: If $k = +1$, then we have $O - I/|I|$, but if $k = -1$, then we have $(|I|) \cdot (O - I)$. Without the exponent k, the formula would yield meaningless results when $I < O$ and $(O - I) > 0$, or $I > O$ and $(O - I) < 0$.

References

Adams, J. S. (1965). 'Inequity in social exchange,' in L. Berkowitz (ed.), *Advances in Experimental Social Psychology*, Vol. II, pp. 267–299, Academic Press, New York.

Alessio, J. C. (1980). 'Another folly for equity theory,' *Social Psychology Quarterly*, **3**, 336–340.

Alessio, J. C. (Unpublished manuscript). 'A method of measurement and analysis for equity research,' Paper presented at the Midwest Sociological Society Meetings.

Aronfreed, J. (1961). 'The nature, variety and social patterning of moral responses to transgression,' *Journal of Abnormal and Social Psychology*, **63**, 223–240.

Austin, W., and Walster, E. (1974a). 'Participants' reactions to "Equity with the World",' *Journal of Experimental Social Psychology*, **10**, 528–548.

Austin, W., and Walster, E. (1974b). 'Reactions to confirmations and disconfirmations of expectancies of equity and inequity,' *Journal of Personality and Social Psychology*, **30**, 208–216.

Berkowitz, L. (1962). *Aggression: A Social Psychological Analysis*, McGraw-Hill, New York.

Berscheid, E., and Walster, E. (1967). 'When does a harm-doer compensate a victim?' *Journal of Personality and Social Psychology*, **6**, 435–441.

Berscheid, E., Walster, E., and Barclay, A. (1969). 'Effect of time on tendency to compensate a victim,' *Psychological Reports*, **25**, 431–436.

Brock, T. C., and Becker, L. (1966). 'Debriefing and susceptibility to subsequent experimental manipulations,' *Journal of Experimental Social Psychology*, **2**, 314–323.
Brock, T. C. and Buss, A. H. (1962). 'Dissonance, aggression and evaluation of pain,' *Journal of Abnormal and Social Psychology*, **65**, 197–202.
Brock, T. C., and Buss, A. H. (1964). 'Effects of justification for aggression in communication with the victim on post-aggression dissonance,' *Journal of Abnormal and Social Psychology*, **68**, 403–412.
Carlsmith, J. M., and Gross, A. E. (1969). 'Some effects of guilt on compliance,' *Journal of Personality and Social Psychology*, **11**, 232–239.
Davidson, J. (1964). 'Cognitive familiarity and dissonance reduction', in L. Festinger (ed.), *Conflict, Decision, and Dissonance*, pp. 45–60, Stanford University Press, Stanford, Calif.
Davis, K. E., and Jones, E. E. (1960). 'Changes in interpersonal perception as a means of reducing cognitive dissonance,' *Journal of Abnormal and Social Psychology*, **61**, 402–410.
Freedman, J. L., Wallington, S. A., and Bless, E. (1967). 'Compliance without pressure: The effect of guilt,' *Journal of Personality and Social Psychology*, **7**, 117–124.
Glass, D. C. (1964). 'Changes in liking as a means of reducing cognitive discrepancies between self-esteem and aggression,' *Journal of Personality*, **32**, 520–549.
Hastorf and Regan. (1962). (Personal communication).
Harris, R. J. (1976). 'Handling negative inputs: On the plausible equity formulae,' *Journal of Experimental and Social Psychology*, **12**, 194–209.
Hatfield, E., and Traupmann, J. (1980). 'Intimate relationships: A perspective from Equity theory,' in Steve Duck and Robin Gilmour (eds.), *Personal Relationships I: Studying Personal Relationships*, pp. 165–178, Academic Press, London.
Hatfield, E., Traupmann, J., Sprecher, S., Utne, M., and Hay, J. (In preparation). 'Equity and intimate relations: Recent research.'
Hatfield, E., Utne, M. K., and Traupmann, J. (1979). 'Equity theory and intimate relationships,' in Robert L. Burgess and Ted L. Huston (eds.), *Social Exchange in Developing Relationships*, pp. 99–133, Academic Press, New York.
Jecker, J. and Landy, D. (1969). 'Liking a person as a function of doing him a favor,' *Human Relations*, **22**, 371–378.
Katz, I., Glass, D. D., and Cohen, S. (1973). 'Ambivalence, guilt, and the scapegoating of minority group victims,' *Journal of Experimental Social Psychology*, **9**, 432–436.
Lerner, M. J. and Matthews, Gale. (1967). 'Reactions to the suffering of others under conditions of indirect responsibility,' *Journal of Personality and Social Psychology*, **5**, 319–325.
Leventhal, G. S., and Bergman, J. T. (1969). 'Self-depriving behavior as a response to unprofitable inequity,' *Journal of Experimental Social Psychology*, **5**, 153–171.
Marwell, G., Schmitt, D. R. and Shotola, R. (1970). 'Sex differences in a cooperative task,' *Behavioral Science*, **15**, 184–186.
Moschetti, G. J. (1979). 'Calculating equity: Ordinal and ratio criteria,' *Social Psychology Quarterly*, **42**, 172–176.
Solomon, L. (1957). 'The influence of some types of power relationships and motivational treatments upon the development of interpersonal trust,' Research Center for Human Relations, New York University, New York.
Sykes, G. M., and Matza, D. (1957). 'Techniques of neutralization: A theory of delinquency,' *American Sociological Review*, **22**, 664–670.
Utne, M. K., Hatfield, E., Traupmann, J., and Greenberger, D. (Submitted for publication). Equity, marital satisfaction and stability.

Walster, E., Berscheid, E., and Walster, G. W. (1970). 'The exploited: Justice or justification?' in J. Macaulay and L. Berkowitz (eds.), *Altruism and Helping Behavior*, pp. 179–204, Academic Press, New York.

Walster, E., and Prestholdt, P. (1966). 'The effect of misjudging another: Overcompensation or dissonance reduction?' *Journal of Experimental Social Psychology*, 2, 85–97.

Walster, E., Walster, G. W., and Berscheid, E. (1978). *Equity: Theory and Research*, Allyn and Bacon, Boston.

Walster, G. W. (1975). 'The Walster *et al.* (1973). Equity Formula: A Correction,' *Representative Research in Social Psychology*, 6, 65–67.

Weick, K. E., and Nesset, B. (1968). 'Preferences among forms of equity,' *Organizational Behavior and Human Performance*, 3, 400–416.

Zuckerman, M. (1975). 'A comment on the equity formula by Walster, Berscheid and Walster (1973),' *Representative Research in Social Psychology*, 6, 63–64.

Small Groups and Social Interaction, Volume 2
Edited by H. H. Blumberg, A. P. Hare, V. Kent and M. Davies
© 1983 John Wiley & Sons Ltd

7.3 Interdependence Theory*

Wayne Harrison   *University of Nebraska at Omaha*
and

J. Richard McCallum   *Catawba College*

Imagine, for a moment, yourself as a child involved in a game. Your classroom teacher has taken several of your new classmates and you aside and seated you in a circle. He has delighted the group with the information that in the game extra minutes of recess may be won. He has told you little else other than that on each play of the game you are to choose a color, red or blue, and that your choice will in some way affect the number of minutes of recess you win. It is up to you otherwise to learn the rules of this strange game.

On the first play of the game you hold up your blue card—blue is your favorite color. Of your four classmates, two also choose blue. Ann and Tommy both choose red. Your teacher looks around the circle and says, 'Ann and Tommy each get four extra minutes of recess; the rest of you each get seven minutes.' Everyone claps their hands with pleasure, though a small frown briefly crosses Ann's features. On the second play of the game you and everyone but Tommy choose blue. Your teacher tells you that each of you except Tommy wins five minutes of recess; Tommy gets two extra minutes. Tommy sighs at this pronouncement. On the third play of the game all of you choose blue and are rewarded with three extra minutes of recess. You think to yourself, 'This isn't going in the right direction!' On the next several plays you experiment and discover that whenever you choose blue you receive more points than anyone choosing red. Tommy seems to have learned the same thing and has settled on blue

* The authors are among many who are grateful to John Thibaut and Harold Kelley for their contributions to the theory of social behavior. We are also greatly appreciative of John Thibaut's comments on this chapter.

as his choice. Following the tenth trial you and Ann exchange glances as you each choose red; you have both discovered a second rule to this game: the more blue choices by the group, the fewer minutes of recess for everyone. Another player, Sally, who you are certain is also aware of this, persists nonetheless in choosing blue. The game ends shortly; you are pleased with your 'winnings' but somewhat unhappy with everyone else in the group except Ann, who seems like someone you'd like. Tommy, however, isn't real sharp, and Sally—why Sally is downright mean.

The preceding social interaction may serve to illustrate the analytic concepts of interdependence theory. Many readers will be familiar with Thibaut and Kelley's *The Social Psychology of Groups* (1959), in which some of these concepts were introduced. Subsequent collaboration has resulted in *Interpersonal Relations: A Theory of Interdependence* (Kelley and Thibaut, 1978), in which a systematic theoretical framework is proposed. Kelley has further extended and refined some of these notions in his 1979 volume, *Personal Relationships: Their Structures and Processes*.

The scope of Thibaut and Kelley's theorizing is nothing less than the analysis of social interaction. Forms of interdependence (patterns of mutual influence) are analyzed by means of several structural indices. A taxonomy of forms of interdependence results, and some behavioral implications of the variety of patterns of interdependence are drawn. Individual differences in response to the problems posed by certain forms of interdependence are recognized in a discussion of the *transformation* of interdependence patterns by application of the relationship members' attitudes and values. This conceptualization leads neatly into consideration of processes of attribution and self-presentation and of negotiation and coalition formation.

Our aim in the present chapter is to introduce the reader to the analytic power of interdependence theory. Of necessity we shall be less technical and specific than is wholly desirable. Interdependence theory's virtues of systematism and scope make it also rather demanding. Darwyn Linder has marvelously expressed this in his review of the 1978 text, 'Reading this book is a little like drinking unblended, pot-still scotch whiskey: One must pay close attention and expend no little effort, but the rewards are more than adequate compensation' (1979, p. 564).

The story opening this chapter exemplifies several features of social interaction which Thibaut and Kelley suggest must be encompassed by any theory of social behavior. We shall discuss in turn their approach to each of the following characteristics of social behavior: (1) interdependence of outcomes; (2) responsiveness to others' outcomes; and (3) processes of attribution and self-presentation. Following this discussion, we shall focus more specifically on the application of the theory to the analysis of small groups.

Interdependence of outcomes

⟨Thibaut and Kelley conceptualize interdependence as the effects interacting persons have on each other. Effects or outcomes can be stated in terms of rewards received and costs incurred by the parties to a relationship, but for most purposes can simply be combined into a single scale of 'goodness' of outcome. The 'goodness' of an outcome is gauged by comparison with personal standards. Two such standards are proposed: the *comparison level* reflects the quality of outcomes that a participant expects or believes that he or she deserves; the *comparison level for alternatives* reflects the lowest level of outcomes the participant will accept given available opportunities in other relationships.⌋

The outcomes for the children participating in the described game are clear: extended recess time. This extra recess presumably constitutes an outcome above each child's comparison level (comparison level is largely a function of recently experienced outcomes), and is rewarding. There are no direct costs in this interaction, simply the potential for increased rewards. Of course the value attached to these rewards will surely differ by individual, and would be reflected in the scaled outcome values. For example, Tommy may love playing baseball during recess and find 15 extra minutes very rewarding; Ann's evaluation of 15 extra minutes of exercise may be less positive.

A conceptual tool which has proven useful for the analysis of interdependence is the outcome matrix. The simplest case of two interdependent persons, each with a pair of behavioral alternatives, can be represented in a 2 × 2 matrix. The four cells of such a matrix represent the four possible combinations of actions the interdependent persons could perform. The resultant outcomes for each person can be usefully displayed in the appropriate cells of the outcome matrix.

To begin our analysis of the children's interdependence we start with consideration of just two members of the group. Suppose that Ann and Tommy are the sole participants in the game. Their behavioral alternatives on each play are choosing either red or blue. Figure 1 contains the matrix representation of this two-person situation. For simplicity, we equate outcomes with minutes of recess in this example.

The numbers entered in the outcome matrix are typically scaled from a zero point equal to the comparison level for alternatives. The entries therefore indicate the degree to which each person is dependent upon the relationship. In Figure 1, positive values represent extra minutes of recess, scaled against the alternative of zero extra time available outside of the game. A major basis of the utility of this representation is that the *pattern* of entries in the outcome matrix represents the nature of the members' interdependence. Even the minimal matrix, the 2 × 2, permits the description of a diverse array of interpersonal situations, and is richly suggestive of the processes associated with them.

The nature of interdependence is such that each relationship member's dependence constitutes the basis for the other member's power, defining power as

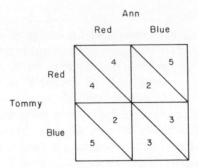

Figure 1   An outcome matrix

the range of outcomes through which one member can move the other. It is possible to characterize uniquely outcome matrices (i.e. relationships) in terms of the general level of outcomes available to the members, the individual preferences for behaviors, and two types of interdependent power. One form of power has been termed *fate control*, and represents the extent to which one person can, by varying his or her own behavior, affect the other member's outcomes regardless of what that member does. The second type of power is *behavior control*. To the extent that one member can, by varying his or her own behavior, make it desirable for the other member to vary his or her behavior, the former has behavior control over the latter.

The analysis of variance model provides an exact analog for these distinctions. A member's average possible outcome in a relationship is comparable to a grand mean. If the member's behavioral alternatives are represented as the rows of the outcome matrix, the member's *reflexive control* or personal preference among the possible actions is analogous to a row main effect. The interdependent partner's fate control over the member corresponds to the column main effect on the member's outcomes. Finally, behavior control is analogous to the analysis of variance interaction term.

The set of four matrices comprising the top half of Figure 2 illustrates the component analysis of Tommy's outcomes in the game relationship with Ann. Averaging Tommy's four possible outcomes yields a grand mean component of 3.5—the relationship is attractive (rewarding). Tommy's direct preference between the two game choices is his reflexive control (the row main effect component of his outcomes), in this case a small incentive in favor of blue. Ann's fate control over Tommy's outcomes (the column main effect component) is such that when she chooses red, he is benefited. Ann's fate control over Tommy's outcomes is twice the magnitude of his reflexive control over his own outcomes. There is no behavior control (incentive for acting in concert with or in opposition to Ann) in this example—no interaction term is necessary to represent Tommy's outcomes.

A dyadic relationship can be characterized by the pattern of outcomes, as represented by *bilateral reflexive control, mutual fate control*, and *mutual*

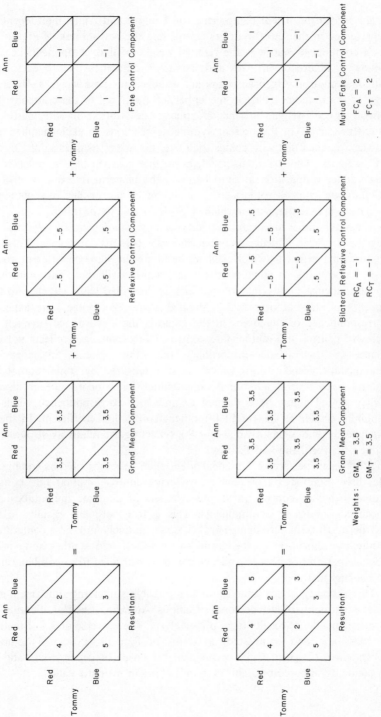

Figure 2 Component analysis of an outcome matrix

behavior control. These components of Tommy and Ann's interdependence are represented in the set of matrices comprising the bottom half of Figure 2. Below each component matrix is the relative weight of that component, i.e. the magnitude of difference in Ann and Tommy's outcomes due to each source of outcome control. Algebraic signs are attached to these weights—reflecting the sign of the outcome value in the upper left-hand cell of the component matrix. These signed weights permit a concise description of the nature of the interdependence. In the present symmetric relationship each member has more power over the other's outcomes than over his or her own (ratio of FC weight to RC weight). The essential problem in this relationship is reflected by the discordance (opposition in sign) between the bilateral reflexive control and the mutual fate control components. In acting in his or her own interests each member will take that action which is less favorable to the other.

The single most important property of any interdependent relationship is the degree of correspondence between the two persons' outcomes. This property captures the extent to which their interests are the same or different and implies how smooth or conflictual their interaction will be. The nature of the correspondence in any relationship can be described with reference to the components of the outcome matrix defined above. As noted, one aspect of the correspondence of outcomes in the game is the discordance between bilateral reflexive control and mutual fate control. Correspondence reflects not only this source of concordance–discordance but other sources in more complex relationships. Relationships which are characterized by some mutual behavior control have several additional potentialities for concordance or discordance. Kelley and Thibaut have defined an index of correspondence which is conceptually similar to the product–moment correlation coefficient. In the present example this index has a value of $-.80$, reflecting the relatively strong conflict of interest between Ann and Tommy.

All possible patterns of interdependence can be represented as combinations of the three components of bilateral reflexive control, mutual fate control, and mutual behavior control, in all possible sets of outcome magnitudes and concordances among the components. This is true both analytically, in that any interdependence pattern can be broken down uniquely into these components (this requires specification of the grand mean term), and synthetically, in that all possible patterns of interdependence can be constructed from combinations of the component matrices.

This property of the analysis makes possible something fundamentally desirable: a taxonomy of interpersonal situations. An exhaustive classification of forms of interdependence results from this analysis. The universe of 2×2 matrices can be classified (and contrasted) in terms of four properties: (1) mutuality of dependence; (2) degree of dependence; (3) bases of dependence; and (4) correspondence of outcomes. This system is of major heuristic value.

Responsiveness to others' outcomes

⌈The working assumption of interdependence theory is that behavior is not predictable from the structural properties of the relationship alone, but is predictable from these properties and the perceptions of the members of the relationship. The theory distinguishes the antecedents of the outcome matrix that is *effective* at the time the behavior occurs. This matrix, the *effective* matrix, is the immediate determinant of interdependent behavior and is itself predictable from facts about the participants and their situation.⌋

A critical conceptual development of the theory concerns the two sets of factors or processes that result in the *effective* matrix. As Kelley and Thibaut (1978) have conceived them:

> These [processes] operate successively in time, the second set acting on the products of the first. The distinction is facilitated by representing the first products in a *given* matrix. Thus we distinguish (a) a set of causal factors that generates a *given* matrix from (b) a set of processes *elicited* by the pattern of that matrix and acting to redefine it. The result of this redefinition is the *effective* matrix. (p. 16)

A *given* matrix, then, is a representation of the contingent outcomes determined by environmental factors in combination with such personal factors as needs and skills. The matrix is 'given' in the sense that the behavioral alternatives and their outcomes are strongly under the control of factors external to the interdependence relationship itself. There is no determinative relationship between the *given* matrix and the behavior it elicits. Outcomes defined locally (cell by cell), as in the *given* matrix, do not account for behavior in interdependent relationships. This is represented schematically in Figure 3.

The children's behaviors are in part, then, due to the contingent reward structure of the game in which they find themselves. The interdependent determination of minutes of recess won (environmental antecedent), together with each child's evaluation of those outcomes (personal antecedents), are summarized in the *given* matrix. Individuals respond to the *given* matrix (reward contingencies) that they perceive. This perception is not necessarily accurate. In our example, while Ann learnt both outcome contingencies, Tommy learnt only that blue always received more than did red.

The *given* matrix *per se* is only part of the influence on the actors' behavior. They react to the *pattern* of outcomes in this matrix. An actor might respond to the disparity between own and other's outcomes or to the possibility of alternating between differentially preferred cells. It is at this juncture that the *person* appears as a causal agent, responding to aspects of pattern to transform the *given* matrix into a new one, the *effective* matrix, which *is* closely linked to behavior.

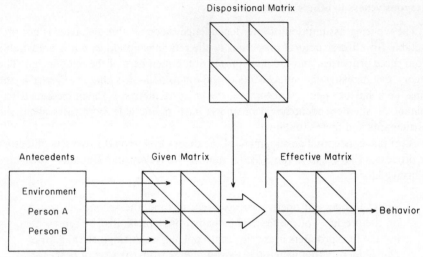

Figure 3   Antecedents of the *effective* matrix

The general theoretical perspective taken is one of problem solving. *Given* matrices are viewed as problems to be solved rather than as direct causes of behavior. Reactions to a particular *given* matrix will be diverse, themselves characterized by pattern and structure, and even involving redefinitions of the problem. Solutions to the problems of interdependence often require that behavior be freed from control by the immediate situation. This realization is embodied in the theory as a shift from a *given* matrix to an *effective* matrix—a *transformation* of the *given* matrix into one which may be said to control behavior.

The possible interdependence patterns can be thought of as problems. Thus, the taxonomy of relationships is a taxonomy of problems. Each type of pattern has its unique problematic aspects and implies the necessary elements of its solution. In truly interdependent situations both actors are faced with problems. For example, an interdependent relationship characterized primarily by mutual fate control poses a problem of *exchange*. Patterns characterized primarily by mutual behavior control pose problems of *coordination*.

The taxonomy of problems provides a basis for a functional analysis. In their experience with various interdependence problems and from the necessity of coping with them, people develop solutions to them. Social norms and individual rules are 'solutions' or adaptations to situations of social interdependence which are common or recurrent. These solutions to problems of interdependence are forms of *transformations*. Psychologically, transformations are ways in which a person reconceptualizes the *given* matrix. In so doing, an interdependent actor responds not to his or her own outcomes in each cell but to these outcomes viewed within the context provided by the partner's outcomes and by past and future interactions within the relationship.

Logically, transformations are the result of applying various mathematical operations and sequential rules to *given* patterns. Three general types can be distinguished. As delineated by Kelley and Thibaut (1978) these are:

> cases in which the person (a) gives some direct weight to his partner's outcomes in his decision-making criteria (outcome transformations); (b) attempts to be the first or second to act on a given occasion out of regard for the second actor (transpositional transformations); and (c) adopts a policy governing his successive choices over a series of interactions in the given matrix (sequential transformations). (p. 139)

A number of investigators (e.g. McClintock, 1972; Kagan, 1977; Wyer, 1969) have conceptualized social motives as, in effect, outcome transformations. Commonly identified motives include jointly maximizing one's own and one's partner's outcomes, maximizing the difference between one's own outcomes and one's partner's, and minimizing this difference. Adoption of one of these criteria is acting as if the *given* matrix were different, i.e. transformed.

An outcome transformation may be readily illustrated by considering Ann's reaction to the game. She has apparently recognized the critical features of the interdependence (strong discordant fate control), and responds to this by adopting a course of action which is counter to her immediate *given* interests. By making red choices she may hope to influence the others to act similarly so that all might receive consistently high outcomes. We may describe her *transformation* of the situation mathematically in terms of her own and the others' outcomes. For simplicity, let us consider just Ann and Tommy as in the Figure 1 matrix. Ann's transformation may be expressed, assuming equal weight to her own and Tommy's outcomes, as a *max joint* or simple sum operation on the outcomes. This transformation is illustrated in Figure 4. In this reconceptualization Ann finds mutual red choices most rewarding, and her behavioral choices are then made in the context of her redefinition of the relationship. Her actual outcomes are of course determined by the contingencies described in the *given* matrix, but

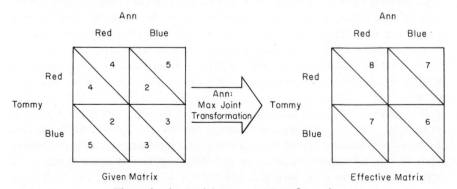

Figure 4   A *max joint* outcome transformation

she makes her choices *as if* the relationship were described by the right-hand matrix in Figure 4.

The two other types of transformations identified by Kelley and Thibaut are transpositional and sequential transformations. These capture certain temporal aspects of interactions. The former is illustrated by an actor recognizing the value of 'going first' and thereby preempting his or her partner's choice. This modification and those classified as sequential transformations are, like outcome transformations, responses to a *given* matrix which is thereby converted into the *effective* matrix.

While these logical and mathematical possibilities may be intriguing, an obvious question is why an interdependent person would act according to some transformed matrix rather than the *given* matrix. The answer is that transformations are *functional*. Two major functions can be distinguished. Acting in accord with a transformed perception of the interdependence relationship may permit the individual to achieve better outcomes in the *given* matrix than he or she would otherwise attain. Secondly, a transformed matrix may provide a basis for action where none exists in the *given* matrix; for example, application of a sequential (turn-taking) transformation to a matrix characterized by noncorrespondent outcomes. Individually-held interpersonal values and more widely-held social norms result from such experiences. Thibaut and Faucheux (1965), for example, have experimentally demonstrated the functional grounding of social norms in the requirements of interdependence. Such shared rules may then broadly guide subsequent transformations.

Transformations may be considered to be either prosocial or egoistic in nature. Certain conditions of interdependence may be posited to result in prosocial transformations. In accord with a functional analysis these are conditions in which it is mutually desirable to take some positive account of the partner's outcomes. Prosocial transformations provide a mutually satisfactory solution to problems posed by relationships characterized by intermediate levels of correspondence, i.e. when individual interests neither fully coincide nor are in complete conflict. Prosocial transformations provide no benefits to the participants in cases of high conflict of interest and cases of unilateral dependence.

Certain conditions elicit egoistic transformations; for example, adoption of a competitive orientation will result in superior *given* outcomes in those cases in which an actor's partner has made a stable prosocial transformation. This is to suggest that life's dilemmas and conflicts provide experiences for the learning and practice of distrust, competitiveness, and exploitation, as well as the prosocial motives.

This analysis indicates that interdependent relationships provide settings in which both prosocial and egoistic transformations are learned. Such learning involves discriminating among types of *given* interdependence patterns and among types of transformations currently or potentially applied by one's partner. The latter discrimination is of particular importance. Losses may result from being more prosocial than one's interdependent partner (being taken advantage of) or from failing to recognize a partner's willingness to make a mutually beneficial prosocial transformation (getting caught up in a competitive cycle). These opposing considerations create a constant tension between prosocial and egoistic transformations in certain relationships.

The preceding argument has been cogently summarized by Kelley and Thibaut (1978):

> Patterns of interdependence make possible and, indeed, even require the learning of value transformations. Because of their good consequences for him, in terms of his basic *given* outcomes, the individual learns to deal with the *given* pattern of interdependence as if it were a different pattern. This learning is reflected in his tendencies to apply action criteria that take account of the partner's outcomes and to follow certain rules of timing and sequencing in interaction. (p. 179)

Attribution and self-presentation

Interdependent persons have a strong interest in predicting one another's behavior. Such assessments are important in determining whether a relationship is likely to be worthwhile and, if so, for realizing the full potential of the relationship. Actors have an interest in accurately perceiving the other's *given* outcomes and in deducing the likely transformations of their partner. Similarly, the individual has an interest in conveying information about his or her outcomes in the *given* matrix to the partner, and in presenting some (not necessarily veridical, e.g. ingratiation) transformation tendencies.

These problems can perhaps be solved by frank and open discussion, but this is likely to occur only in highly correspondent relationships. Instead, the basic language for communicating these desires and tendencies is behavior within the relationship itself. The actions taken, and not taken, by the actor, and the consequences of these behaviors, provide the evidence of rewards and costs and of transformations. Thus, interdependence provides both the reason for communicating person attributes and the means of such communication.

Kelley (1979) has distinguished *interpersonal* dispositions. The grist for inferring or displaying dispositions of this type differs from the basis for other attributions and self-presentations. Interpersonal dispositions are those traits of an actor which govern transformations, e.g. being considerate or being aggressive, and are inferred from ways in which the actor's behavior departs from his or her direct outcomes. That is, the perceived transformation of the *given* matrix is the basis for the attribution of interpersonal dispositions. We submit, in elaborating slightly on Kelley's thinking, that a departure from the *given* matrix is not the direct basis of these attributions. Interpersonal dispositions are often inferred from the perceived unwillingness of an interdependent partner to make a (e.g. prosocial) transformation. An actor's failure to depart from his or her own direct outcomes is itself informative. The basis for interpersonal attributions is in the difference between the *effective* matrix and a matrix representing the expected transformation by a generalized other of the *given* values. To the extent that these two matrices differ are interpersonal dispositions attributed.

Kelley and Thibaut note that interdependence exists at the dispositional level as well. The display of certain traits may be itself rewarding, for example, being thought of as a cooperative person. For such a person interdependence with a competitive person may prove frustrating at the dispositional level. As revealed in Kelley and Stahelski's well-known work (1970a,b), cooperators paired with competitors in restrictive interdependencies must act 'competitively' in order to avoid being thoroughly exploited in *given* outcomes. There is noncorrespondence at the dispositional level in this relationship—the cooperator cannot satisfy this dispositional motive (without suffering consequences in the *given* matrix) at the same time that the competitive partner satisfies his or her dispositional motive. Figure 3 contains a dispositional matrix linked to the transformation process. This reflects the impact of interpersonal dispositions on the *given* interdependence problem, and the interdependence which itself exists at this level of analysis. It is at this point in the causal sequence leading up to social behavior that the person appears as a causal agent. The person who modifies the *given* incentive conditions through a sharp transformation appears, both to him- or herself and to others, as an active agent who is partially responsible for his or her own behavior.

The children's experience in playing the game is fertile ground for dispositional attributions. Your perception that Tommy did not fully realize the contingencies of the game led you to question his intelligence. Communication, both nonverbal and through choices made in the game, led to an appreciation of Ann's cooperativeness. She, like you, was willing to make a short-term personal sacrifice in the long-term interests of all. Finally, your perception that Sally was making a competitive transformation (or at least refusing to prosocially transform the situation) also occasioned certain attributions about her character.

The major tenets of interdependence theory are exemplified in the preceding discussion of interdependence of outcomes, responsiveness to other's outcomes, and attribution and self-presentation processes. We have often employed the dyad in illustration as our purpose has been clarity and simplicity of presentation. The theory itself is applicable to any interdependence, and we turn now to a brief consideration of its extension to the analysis of triads. From this discussion implications for the analysis of larger groups will be apparent.

Interdependence in triads

The extension of interdependence theory beyond dyadic relationships is informative for two reasons. First, the addition of a third person to the analysis tests the generality of the theoretical concepts in multiperson groups. A second and equally important consideration is that, even if the focus should remain on the dyad, its inclusion in a triad serves to represent the influences of the general social context within which dyadic relations exist.⟩

Analysis of triadic interdependence naturally proceeds with added complexity, but factorial experimental design remains a helpful analog. The behavior of the third person may be conceptualized as the addition of a third independent variable. Triadic interdependence corresponds to an analysis of variance with three independent variables (the behavioral choices of each individual) and three dependent variables (the outcomes experienced by each individual). The sources of outcome control may be represented by the seven sources of variance in such a design: three main effects, three two-way interactions, and one three-way interaction. The main effects represent the unilateral control exercised by each of the three individuals over their own and their two partners' outcomes. For example, considering the triad of Tommy, Ann, and Sally, Tommy's unilateral behavior potentially exercises reflexive control over his own outcomes and fate control over the outcomes of each of the two girls. The two-way interaction terms represent the sources of variance resulting from the various combinations of behaviors of each of the three dyads which comprise the triad. For example, the TA interaction term would express the effects of combinations of Tommy and Ann's behavior on the outcomes of all three members of the triad. Finally, the three-way interaction term expresses the effects of various combinations of all three children's behavioral choices upon the outcomes of each. This effect is the behavior control exercised over each person by the joint behavior of the other two.

This analysis is simplified when the triad is composed of *compounded* dyadic relations, as is the case in our example. The nature of each child's interdependence with each other child is the same. The multiperson interdependence is really just a compounding of these identical dyadic relationships. The simplification results from the fact that an actor's behavioral choice is the same in each dyad.

The analysis of triadic interdependence has many specific implications for understanding interdependence in multiperson groups; we shall make only a few general comments here. First, the components of interdependence retain their meaningfulness when extended to the triad and, by implication, beyond. Perhaps more importantly, the analysis points up the impact upon particular interdependent relationships of the social environment in which they are embedded. Observe the effect upon the dyad of its inclusion in a triadic relationship. On the one hand, the third person may act on the process by which the dyad copes with its pre-existing pattern of interdependence by pointing out coordination strategies or encouraging the adoption of particular transformations. On the other hand, the third party may, by his or her behavioral choices and the outcome control exercised, directly affect the actual pattern of interdependence in the dyad. Consequently, the effect of the third party's behavior may be either to facilitate or to interfere with the dyadic relationship by altering the degree of outcome correspondence or the viability of various transformations. The types of outcome control exerted by the third party illustrate the mechanisms by which the general social environment affects problems encountered in relationships and the processes available to deal with them.

An issue approached only impressionistically so far is the *dynamic* of social interaction: How do interdependent persons achieve stable solutions to the problems posed by the nature of their relationship? This is the issue of negotiation and, in small groups, coalition formation.

Negotiation and coalition formation

Mixed-motive patterns of interdependence present opportunities for negotiation and coalition formation with the end of improving the ultimate outcomes of the participants. Kelley and Thibaut propose a model of behavior in the dyad which posits three types of action in pursuit of higher outcomes. These are: (1) *independent action*, in which each person acts on his own without agreement with the partner; (2) *cooperative joint action*, in which the two persons act in an agreed-upon manner with the aim of providing both with better outcomes; and (3) *imposed joint action*, in which agreement is reached in the interest of preventing one of the partners from taking disruptive action in the relationship.

Which of these three types of action will be taken is determined primarily by the bargaining position defined by two pairs of outcomes in the particular pattern of interdependence. These bargaining positions are the independent action (IA) pair, which is the pair of outcomes each will receive through their most advantageous independent actions, and the threat (Th) pair, which results from each individual's efforts to establish a threat position from which to make demands upon the other. The remaining outcome pairs in the relationship are then classified relative to the IA and Th pairs, producing four categories of outcome pairs. These are *reward pairs* in which both persons have higher outcomes than in the IA pair, *A-complies* pairs in which Person A receives outcomes below that in the IA pair but above the outcomes in the Th pair, *B-complies* pairs in which this is true for Person B's outcomes, and the remaining nonviable pairs in which both receive outcomes below those available in the Th pair. The reward and compliance pairs may be ordered in terms of each person's preferences. Negoation then becomes a process of moving down these preference orderings until both persons arrive at the same outcome pair, which serves as the basis for agreement.

The negotiation model may be extended to the triad with the addition of a new type of action, *coalition action*. By forming a coalition a pair of individuals may establish new bargaining positions analogous to the IA and Th pairs but dependent upon coordinated action. In general, coalition formation in the triad follows the format of negotiation in the dyad with each individual moving down his or her preference ordering of triplets (rather than pairs). Each person's preference ordering of possible coalition positions takes into consideration both the coalition's power relative to the third party and the individual's power relative to the coalition partner. Individuals are hypothesized to seek coalitions which maximize on both criteria.

Conclusions

If the reader has followed us to this point we feel assured that he or she will recognize the systematicness of interdependence theory. It is a tightly woven fabric; appreciation of its warp and woof requires starting at the beginning and unraveling it slowly. We concur with Linder (1979) in advising that the compensations justify the effort.

We consider the fundamental contributions of interdependence theory to be two. One is the development of a taxonomy of interpersonal relationships. Kurt Lewin (1935) early recognized the unmet need for such a system. The outcome matrix has certain limitations as a conceptual device, but its power is unmatched to our knowledge in permitting the derivation of a systematic and exhaustive description of types of situations and the forces at work within them. A theoretical basis for comparison of vastly different social circumstances becomes possible through this analysis. The comparability is not restricted to the situation, but includes the personal and norm-based dispositions of the actors as well. Both environmental and person variables are expressible in this language.

A second fundamental contribution is the firm grounding of social motivation in a *functional* analysis. The crucible that is human socialization is encountering the variety of possible interdependence dilemmas, struggling with them, and learning adaptive strategies. Social norms and individual dispositions and values emerge from these trials. We learn that it is adaptive to be responsive to more than the immediate, situationally-determined outcomes. The potential for bringing order to the plethora of motives postulated by social psychologists, through identifying their developmental communalities in the requirements of social interdependence, is tremendously exciting. The path to such an achievement seems certain to us to pass through many of the concepts of interdependence theory.

References

Kagan, S. (1977). 'Social motives and behaviors of Mexican-American and Anglo-American children,' in J. Martinez (ed.), *Chicano Psychology*, pp. 45–86, Academic Press, New York.

Kelley, H. (1979). *Personal Relationships: Their Structures and Processes*, Lawrence Erlbaum Associates, Hillsdale, NJ.

Kelley, H., and Stahelski, A. (1970a). 'The inference of intentions from moves in the Prisoner's Dilemma game,' *Journal of Experimental Social Psychology*, **6**, 401–419.

Kelley, H., and Stahelski, A. (1970b). 'The social interaction basis of cooperators' and competitors' beliefs about others,' *Journal of Personality and Social Psychology*, **16**, 66–91.

Kelley, H., and Thibaut, J. (1978). *Interpersonal Relations: A Theory of Interdependence*, Wiley, New York.

Lewin, K. (1935). *A Dynamic Theory of Personality*, McGraw-Hill, New York.

Linder, D. (1979). 'An algebra of social interaction matrices,' *Contemporary Psychology*, **24**, 563–565.

McClintock, C. (1972). 'Social motivation—a set of propositions,' *Behavioral Science*, **17**, 438–454.

Thibaut, J., and Faucheux, C. (1965). 'The development of contractual norms in a bargaining situation under two types of stress,' *Journal of Experimental Social Psychology*, **1**, 89–102.

Thibaut, J., and Kelley, H. (1959). *The Social Psychology of Groups*, Wiley, New York.

Wyer, R. (1969). 'Prediction of behavior in two-person games,' *Journal of Personality and Social Psychology*, **13**, 222–238.

Small Groups and Social Interaction, Volume 2
Edited by H. H. Blumberg, A. P. Hare, V. Kent and M. Davies
Published by John Wiley & Sons Ltd 1983

Bd^{u}

7.4   A Functional Interpretation of Interaction*

A. Paul Hare   *Ben-Gurion University of the Negev, Israel*

Social interaction in small groups can be viewed from a number of different perspectives. The perspective with the longest tradition in small group research involves the use of category systems or ratings on behavioral dimensions to record the *process* or *form* of the interaction as it unfolds in a group. The best developed systems of this type are represented by the work of Bales and his colleagues who first used 12 interaction process categories to describe variation in task and social–emotional behavior in problem-solving groups (Bales, 1950). More recently they have shifted to the use of three dimensions (upward–downward, positive–negative, and forward–backward) for the analysis of movement in a three-dimensional social space (Bales, 1970; Bales *et al.*, 1979).

Another perspective has as its focus the analysis of the *content* of social interaction. The four basic categories of content are represented by the four functional problems of groups (values, norms, leadership, and resources). In the paragraphs that follow, reproduced with minor changes from two books (Hare, 1976, 1982), the definitions of the four functional categories are given together with some hypotheses concerning group development, conforming behavior, and group problem solving. Further applications of the functional perspective for the analysis of interpersonal choice, roles, and creativity, as well as comparisons with

*Portions of this paper are based on A. Paul Hare (1973). 'Group decision by consensus: reaching unity in the Society of Friends,' *Sociological Inquiry*, **43**, 77–80 (also in Hare, 1976, pp. 12–16) and on A. Paul Hare (1976). *Handbook of Small Group Research*, 2nd edn, pp. 54–57. (Copyright © 1976 by the Free Press, a Division of Macmillan Publishing Co., Inc.). Essentially, the present version of this paper has also been adapted from A. Paul Hare (1982). *Creativity in Small Groups*, Sage, Beverly Hills, CA. Adapted and reprinted by permission of all of the aforementioned publishers.

three- and four-dimensional theories of group process, exchange theory, and dramaturgical theory are also presented in the volume on *Creativity in Small Groups* (Hare, 1982).

Four functional categories

The present set of categories was proposed by Effrat especially for analysis of small groups. This is only one application of a comprehensive theory developed by Parsons and his colleagues for the analysis of social systems (Parsons, 1961; Effrat, 1968; Loubser *et al.*, 1976). A reader already familiar with functional theory from other sources should note that the definitions of the *adaptive* (A) and *goal-attainment* (G) sectors as they are used here differ in certain respects from Parsons's formulations.

The fundamental idea in functional theory is that all groups, whether small discussion groups or whole societies, if they are to survive, must meet four basic needs: (L) the member must share some common identity and have some commitment to the values of the group; (A) they must have or be able to generate the skills and resources necessary to reach the group goal; (I) they must have rules that allow them to coordinate their activity and enough feeling of solidarity to stay together to complete the task; and finally (G) they must be able to exercise enough control over their membership to be effective in reaching their common goal.

The formal names of the AGIL categories are: Adaptation, Goal-attainment, Integration, and Latent pattern maintenance and tension management (or simply pattern maintenance). These same terms, or more frequently their first letters, A, G, I, and L, will be used throughout the text. The term 'adaptation' does not precisely fit the present definition of this category. In Parsons's description of a social system the 'adaptive' area was the area in which the system related or 'adapted' to the outside environment or to other systems. In the present definition the emphasis is on the production of resources for internal use.

The relatively long title of the 'L' sector of 'Latent pattern maintenance and tension management' has several ideas packed into it. The central idea is that every group needs a set of values and that a pattern of activity must be maintained in line with these values if the group is to have integrity. The term 'latent' appears because members of most groups only have face-to-face meetings on occasion. During this period the group is 'manifest.' However, during the periods between meetings the group is 'latent.' Thus the process of pattern maintenance must be strong enough not only to set general guidelines for the group while the members are present but also to provide enough commitment so that the members will return for the next meeting. The idea of 'tension management' is included in the title because too much tension, especially that associated with the success or failure of work in the 'G' area can dissolve the group if the tension is not managed. In general, any activity that has to do with the initial selection of members for the

Table 1 Substructures, Generalized Media of Exchange, Value Principles, and Standards of Coordination for Four Functional Problems

A   G

(1) Adaptation (2) Economic (3) Money (4) Utility (5) Solvency	(1) Goal attainment (2) Political (3) Power (4) Effectiveness (5) Success
(1) Pattern maintenance (2) Familial and Religious (3) Commitments (4) Integrity (5) Pattern consistency	(1) Integration (2) Legal (3) Influence (4) Solidarity (5) Consensus

L   I

Key: (1) the functional problem
   (2) the substructure at the social system level
   (3) the generalized medium of exchange
   (4) the value principle
   (5) the coordinative standard

group, their initiation into the rights and duties of membership, and their commitment to the group activity falls in the 'L' area.

In a large social system, such as a nation, the four categories (AGIL) are represented by the economic, political, legal, and familial and religious substructures. For each of these substructures there is a generalized medium of exchange (money, power, influence, and commitments), a value principle that guides the action in this area (utility, effectiveness, solidarity, and integrity), and a standard of coordination for activity (solvency, success, consensus, and pattern consistency). A summary of these concepts is given in Table 1.

Thus an activity that seems to be primarily *economic*, such as raising money to be used for the general purposes of the group, where the focus is on utility with a concern for solvency, would be classified in the A or *Adaptive* sector. In contrast, an activity that seemed religious or familial, that had to do with forming basic commitments to the group, was concerned with its integrity, and was related to the consistency of its pattern of activity over time would be classified in the L or *Pattern maintenance* sector. In a similar way the other activities of a group would be classified as related to the other two functions, *Integration* or *Goal-attainment*. The content of each sector as it would appear in a small group is given in Table 2 in the set of functional categories for small group analysis.

Table 2   Functional Categories for Small Group Analysis

L PHASE	+	Seeks or provides basic categories or ultimate values Asks for or seeks to define: basic purpose or identity of group fundamental meaning of 'all this' general orientation basic obligations
	–	Seeks to deny, take away, or inhibit the development and recognition of values.
I PHASE	+	Seeks or provides solidarity or norms (as primary mechanisms of conflict management) Asks for or seeks to define: how the group can get along better, promote harmony, or decrease conflict what the specific norms governing relations should be
	–	Seeks to deny, inhibit, or prevent the formation of norms and movement toward group solidarity
G PHASE	+	Seeks or provides relatively specific direction, goal-definition, or problem solutions relevant to the group's goals. Asks for or seeks to define: relatively specific group goals (be careful to distinguish from values and norms) decisions which in effect are attainment of group goals
	–	Seeks to prevent or inhibit movement toward the group's goals
A PHASE	+	Seeks or provides facilities for goal attainment Asks for or seeks to define: how to get or increase (especially to generalize) resources, relevant information, or facts
	–	Seeks to deny, inhibit, or prevent the provision of facilities and relevant information

The cybernetic hierarchy of control

The 'cybernetic hierarchy of control' is a concept that was first used in the analysis of physical systems but it can also be applied to social systems. The basic idea is that a part of a system containing *information* will be able to control a part of a system containing *energy*. The classic everyday example is that of the rider with ideas about where to go (information) being able to control the direction of the horse (energy). In physical systems the thermostat that processes information about temperature is able to control the furnace that produces the heat or a computer is able to control the activity on an industrial production line (Effrat, 1976, pp. 666–669).

In the case of groups the highly generalized normative elements of the system guide and control the more specific elements of action. Thus within the total action system, the four system levels (cultural, social, personality, and biological, which correspond to the same fourfold paradigm—L, I, G, and A, respectively) are related to each other in a cybernetic hierarchy of control. The values represented by the culture are more controlling than the norms of the social system. The norms of the social system are in turn more controlling than the personality of the individual. Finally the personality characteristics play a more controlling part in social interaction than the biological traits and processes of the physical organism.

Within the social system (or any of the other system levels) the four functional areas, as indicated in Table 1, are controlling in the same order. The area of pattern maintenance (L) controls the integrative area (I), that in turn provides more control than the goal-attainment area (G). The adaptive area (A) ranks lowest in its influence on other parts of the system. One example of the application of the concept of the cybernetic hierarchy in the analysis of small groups is given near the end of this chapter where the various pressures toward conformity can be seen to be operating in this way.

Group development

The basic outline of the theory of group development presented here was suggested by Effrat and tested in the field in an analysis of a small regional development planning board in the Philippines (Hare, 1968), then by comparing it with other theories (Hare, 1973), and further elaborated with field experience in Curacao, Netherlands Antilles (Hare and Blumberg, 1977, pp. 281–282). In terms of the AGIL categories the typical sequence of development in small groups seems to be L–A–I–G with a terminal stage of L.

When the AGIL categories are applied to the description of a learning group, such as a classroom group, the forces at work seem to be as follows: the work of the group requires that the purpose of the group be defined (L); that new skills be acquired (A); that the group be reorganized so that the members can try out new skills without being too dependent on the leader (I); and that the group members work at the task (G). Finally, there is a terminal phase when the group is disbanded. The group returns to L to redefine the relationships between the members and the group, to distribute the remaining resources, and to consider the meaning of the group experience for the individual member.

The amount of time the group spends in each phase is determined by the activity of the leader (his or her direction or nondirection) and by the skills and emotional strengths of the members. Presumably the leader is ready for each stage at the outset, having been through the stages before. However, members come to the group with different degrees of problem-solving skills or preferences for different emotional modalities. Subgroups tend to form on the basis of skills and emotional modalities. If the subgroup with the appropriate skills and emotional state is large enough or strong enough, it can carry the whole group through that phase. If not enough members of the group are ready for a particular stage, more intervention by the leader may be necessary. Some groups never progress beyond the early stages and some recycle through the same stage several times before gaining enough closure on that stage to move on to the next.

The assumption that the group moves from phase to phase when a subgroup or leader is able to carry the movement needs further documentation in research since many of those who propose theories of group development do not discuss the *process* of development in any detail; rather they simply *observe* that one phase follows another. A typical comment is that of Schutz (1958, p. 171) concerning the affection phase: 'Finally, following a satisfactory resolution of these problems of control, problems of affection become focal.' Schutz does not tell us how the problems of control become resolved or by what process the group moves on to the next phase. However, it may not require much justification to assert that a group will face special problems at the beginning and at the end of its life. For example, at the beginning of a training group, when the leader fails to be assertive, Bennis and Shepard (1956, p. 420) observe: 'The ambiguity of the situation at this stage quickly becomes intolerable for some.' Or Mills (1964, p. 78), describing the termination of a group, says: 'The fact of separation forces a complex set of demands and issues.'

Phases within phases

Although the basic outline of four phases (LAIG) with a terminal stage of L may be enough for many purposes, it is also possible to identify the same sequence of phases (i.e. L–A–I–G) within each of the major phases and thus provide a better understanding of how groups move from one phase to the next as well as providing a way to integrate the observations of Shambaugh (1978) on emotionality and task activity.

The phases within the phases are most easily seen when the group requires some special equipment for its task and when the nature of the work requires clear role differentiation. Without going into all the details of the adventure, incidents from the voyage of the raft *Acali* from the coast of Africa to the coast of Mexico in 1972 (Genovés, 1979) can be used to illustrate each of these subphases. Although I did not sail with the raft, I was on hand as a participant observer during the preparations for sailing in Madrid and Las Palmas and during the debriefing at Cozumel on the coast of Mexico and the welcome in Mexico City at the end of the voyage (Hare, 1974).

In this case, as in many, the idea of the exercise began with one person. The development of the idea by one individual, or by a small set of persons who may become a subgroup of the 'founders' in the eventual small group (or large group for that matter) can be thought of as either a 'pre' stage of L or as a third level of analysis within the L stage (i.e. the stages within the L_1 stage). Santiago Genovés, the originator of this particular expedition had already served as a crew member on two previous voyages of rafts over the same route, RA I and RA II led by

Thor Heyerdahl (1972) and already had the basic information for the idea. Since the fact that one could drift on a raft from Africa to Mexico had already been established, Genovés had to give a new meaning to the voyage. As the idea occurred to him while the Vietnam war was in progress, he decided that he would bring together on the raft representatives of groups that might otherwise be in conflict as a demonstration of the possibilities for peaceful coexistence of Black and White, Muslim, Christian, and Jew, and Old and New World. Unfortunately by the time the expedition was ready to begin the Vietnam war no longer occupied the public mind. So the voyage was now labeled a scientific expedition to study sexual behavior, et cetera, et cetera. In the news conferences at the beginning of the voyage it was never too clear what the 'et cetera' stood for, although it presumably included taking samples of pollution in the sea. However, the press seems to have got the message since as the raft sailed from La Palmas one British newspaper carried the headline: 'Sex Raft Sails.'

One visible part of the L stage involved the final selection of the crew of 11 for the voyage. This took place at a convent in Madrid. It required several types of supplies and equipment (defined broadly): the convent and psychological tests, for example. The provision of these would be classified as L_a (or a subphase of A within the L phase). Also special roles were needed for the selection process: doctors, psychologists, graphologists, etc. These would be classified as L_i (or part of the subphase of I within the L phase). Thus the idea of selection of the crew (an L_l activity) required the provision of special equipment (L_a) and the formulation of special role relationships (L_i) to carry out the actual selection (L_g).

Once the crew had been selected they needed a raft that was fully equipped. Part of this A activity had been completed in England where the raft had been designed and built before being shipped to Las Palmas, however a distinct A phase was required to complete the work and prepare the raft for the sea voyage. This involved a whole set of ideas for construction and provisions (A_l), special tools (A_a), ship's carpenters and other specialized roles (A_i), and of course the work of fitting it all together (A_g).

While the A activity was in progress the I activity was underway as various crew members were given an orientation for their roles on board the raft (I phase). The final G phase was the actual voyage with the terminal L phase taking place at Cozumel where the group was debriefed by psychiatrists and matters of physical and mental well-being attended to before the group traveled to Mexico City to meet the press and to speculate about the meaning of the experience for their future lives.

If I were presenting this as an actual case, rather than an illustration, details of the subphases within the I and G phases could be added. As it happened the major role conflict within the group occurred just at the end of the I phase, where it seems most likely that the 'revolution within the revolution' will occur, as will be noted in the discussion that follows.

The general schema showing the progress through the phases within phases is

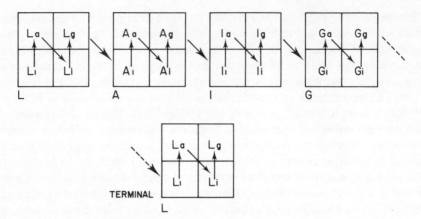

Figure 1   Subphases of group development

set out in Figure 1. The movement to any major phase is from the subphase 'g' in the prior phase. Thus once a group has completed its definition of its overall purpose and secured the commitment of members to the group (L_g) it is ready to proceed with the definition of the resources and skills that are required for the work (A_l). So the group moves from one major phase to the next. Once the G phase has been reached there could be several instances of different tasks (i.e. G_1, G_2, G_3, etc.) without any basic reorganization in the group. In the case of the raft *Acali* the first G was to cross the Atlantic Ocean and reach Barbados. There the raft was refurbished and a decision made to continue through the Caribbean Ocean to Cozumel. The crew was now experienced, but the advent of the hurricane season created additional problems. The second part of the trip was seen by crew members as a distinct task, or a second G.

Whether the task is to conduct an ocean expedition, to take part in a university course, or to join any new group, some people drop out at different stages and some try to reorganize the group. The dropouts are most likely to occur as the group moves from the subphases of 'i' to 'g' during the first two phases of L and A. In the first phase there are some persons who are attracted by the overall idea of the group but find that as the definition of the task is worked out in more detail, the group is not what they had in mind. Having developed relatively little commitment to the group at this stage, they drop out. Or, as in the case of the selection of crew members for the *Acali*, it is decided that they really do not fit in and are encouraged to leave.

Some persons may be satisfied with the purpose of the group but find that they are not satisfied when it is clear what the resources will be at the end of the A phase. They decide that there is not enough money to carry out the task as it was originally envisaged, or that the skill level in the group is not high enough, or that in some other way the group lacks resources. Although these persons have more invested in the group by this time, they may decide to drop out. If the members are satisfied with the level of resources they may stay on board until it becomes clear what the role distribution will be. Then they may discover that their own projected role is not satisfactory or that someone else seems to be taking over too much of the leadership function. At this point the dissatisfied members are more likely to decide to try to change the role relationships than they are to drop out. If they fail to make a move now there is nothing left but to carry out the task with the resources available and the roles as they have been designated. Since there must have been a majority of members or a minority of powerful members who have approved of the role definitions as they were developed, the work of reorganizing the group will be met with resistance. Hence the major conflict, or what in another context has been termed 'the revolution within the revolution,' is most likely to occur at this point in the group's development. For the *Acali* this conflict came to a head as the raft was being towed out to sea to begin the expedition. However the 'mutiny' was contained and the raft commenced its voyage, but not without further problems of role definition.

The terminal stage for some groups may not be clear-cut, groups may not die dramatically, but only fade away. However, in the case of the *Acali* the events were dramatic up to the very end. Bypassing all the histrionics that took place at Cozumel and Mexico City, a simplified version of the terminal stage for the *Acali* crew would center on the idea that they were no longer the *Acali* 'family' but would return to their statuses as separate individuals in different parts of the world (L_l). For the purpose of the 'debriefing' the group was isolated in a set of tourist lodges that had been rented for the occasion on Cozumel, complete with police guards to make sure that no unauthorized persons went in or out during the first week (L_a) and a professional staff of psychiatrists to conduct group and individual sessions with the crew members (L_i). The actual work of the terminal stage (L_g) included a series of confrontations between various subgroups of the crew and between some crew members and Genovés. Even 'mother nature' seemed to be joining in the upheaval since we experienced an earthquake during the second phase of the terminal stage that was held in Mexico City. However, eventually the crew members did board their planes and return to their everyday lives.

A further elaboration of the phases

Thus far the analysis of group development focuses primarily on the task side of the group through the *content* categories of AGIL. Since one of the 'tasks' of a group is to develop an appropriate structure for each phase of its activity, this method of analysis combines some of the behaviors that others, Tuckman (1965) for example, divide into 'group structure' and 'task activity.' With regard to two types of *process* categories, we would expect that the categories for 'task behavior' (observe, hypothesize, propose action) would appear at approximately the same rate throughout the life of the group as each functional problem is taken up in turn. With regard to the 'social–emotional' process categories (dominant–submissive, positive–negative, etc.) the relationship with the LAIG phases would be as follows: during the L phase the conforming–nonconforming dimension would be most salient, during the A phase, serious–expressive, during the I phase, positive–negative, and during the G phase, dominant–submissive.

It is now possible to combine the hypotheses concerning phases within phases with Shambaugh's (1978) generalizations concerning the accumulation of group culture and the oscillation between positive and negative feelings in the emotional area, as in Figure 2.

Moving from the top to the bottom of Figure 2, the first row of letters gives the indications of the limits of the major phases in the order L–A–I–G. For any actual group the phases will probably not be of the same length, and as indicated earlier, a group may recycle through a phase or not proceed beyond a given phase, however only the simplest model is given here. The second row of letters indicates the subphases.

Next is a line showing the 'zero' level of emotionality. When the graph is above the line the emotions are positive, when it is below the line the emotions are negative. Given the previous analysis of group development, positive feelings should reach a peak during each 'i' subphase. Then positive feelings would fall off during the 'g' subphase as the application of dominance (leadership) in the interest of the task either generates hard feelings or alternatively turns the group from a concern about interpersonal relationships. The low point of positive feeling might be expected to continue into the next subphase of 'l' (in the next major phase) but for different reasons. As the group members begin the task of defining 'the meaning of all this' for the particular subphase they will probably discover that subgroups within the group have different ideas, and until the unity in the group has been restored, negative feelings will be evident as subgroups defend their different

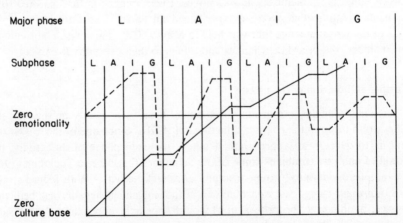

Figure 2   Relationship between phases and subphases of LAIG, accumulation
of group culture, and emotionality

points of view. This is probably where Bales *et al.* (1979) have observed the greatest degree of 'polarization' in their 'self-analytic' groups, with the greatest degree of 'unification' occurring during the 'i' subphase. Thus if one disregards the task content and focuses with Shambaugh on positive and negative feelings or with Bales on changes in group structure, one will observe a continual oscillation.

The bottom line in Figure 2 gives the 'zero' level of culture for the group. As in Shambaugh's analysis, culture 'builds' during the positive emotional periods and shows no growth during the negative periods. But now the categories for content (AGIL) give an additional insight into the process since it is primarily during the l, a, and i subphases that new points of view, understandings, practices, and norms are developed. During the g subphase the various resources (a) and norms (i) are used to carry out the task in line with the values agreed on at the beginning of the phase (l). We would not, therefore, expect much of an increment to the culture during the g subphase nor during the first part of the following l subphase while group members are still in disagreement over the overall guidelines for the next phase.

Pressures to conform

In the mid-1950s both Jahoda (1956) and Kelman (1958) outlined theories of conformity which illustrate an application of the cybernetic hierarchy of control in functional theory, although neither seemed to be aware of the similarity at the time. Jahoda's paper provides an example of four types of conformity which turn out to match A, G, I, and L.

At the time of Jahoda's research, civil liberties, especially centering on the loyalty oath, were a dominant issue in universities in the United States. Although Jahoda had conducted several surveys about this issue, she does not cite her own research evidence, but rather makes up an incident which she feels illustrates all the processes of conformity which are involved. She notes that any similarity with actual events is purely coincidental.

> A college president together with a faculty committee of four persons considers applicants for a new appointment. The best qualified man is one who is known to be a socialist. Each of the four faculty members initially favors his appointment. The president recommends rejection because of the candidate's unsuitable political views. He adds that such an appointment would furthermore seriously offend a benefactor of the college who is about to make a substantial gift to it. As it happens, in this fictitious example, all four members of the faculty go along with the president's recommendation and reject the candidate. (Jahoda, 1956, p. 236)

Since each of the faculty members went along with the president's recommendation, we might suppose that they were all equally conforming. However,

Jahoda suggests that we use our imagination to hold confidential conversations with each of them after the event. They turn out to have four different stories:

Faculty member A says: 'I feel awful. I still believe that we should not have considered the candidate's political views. But I couldn't stand up to the President. I admit I acted out of fear. The question of my promotion will come up next week.'

Faculty member B says: 'We had an interesting meeting. Originally I was quite opposed to the notion of considering a candidate's political views. But I changed my mind. The President made a very good argument against the inappropriateness of socialism for our country. He really convinced me of the mistake of deliberately exposing our students to an unrealistic idealist.'

Faculty member C says: 'I go to these meetings solely because I have been appointed to the committee. I really am not very much interested in these matters. But it is nice to sit together with the President and my colleagues. It makes me feel good to have close friendly contact with them. And if a group of nice people agree, I am the last to make difficulties. I think we did the right thing today.'

Faculty member D says: 'This was a really difficult decision for me. I still believe in academic freedom. But the argument that convinced me was that I know the college depends on getting the gift. After all you can fight for academic freedom only if you have a college that can pay its expenses. I decided to reject the candidate because the President was right when he said we would never get that gift otherwise' (Jahoda, 1956, pp. 233–237).

Jahoda then suggests that these four types can be explained by two underlying dimensions: first, whether the subject was moved by the argument or by pressure, and second, whether his belief was changed or unchanged as a result. This cross-classification is presented in Table 3.

The four types fit the AGIL scheme directly as we rotate Table 3

Table 3   Four Processes of Conformism

	Belief changed	Belief unchanged
Argument	L Consentience (Faculty member B)	A Convergence (Faculty member D)
Pressure (unrelated to issue)	I Conformance (Faculty member C)	G Compliance (Faculty member A)

Source: Marie Jahoda (1956). Adapted from 'Psychological issues in civil liberties,' *American Psychologist*, **11**, 236. Copyright 1956 by the American Psychological Association. Reprinted by permission of the author and the publisher.

counterclockwise one position: the process of convergence is related to adaptation (A) since it is based on facts, compliance to goal attainment (G) since it is based on the power of an authority, conformance to integration (I) since it is based on friendship ties, and consentience to pattern maintenance (L) since it is based on adherence to basic values. Following the cybernetic hierarchy of control we would expect conformity pressures of type L to be the most powerful, then I, then G, and last of all A.

Although Jahoda does not discuss these types in connection with the cybernetic hierarchy of control, her further examples and illustrations suggest reasons why the hierarchy of control might function as it does. Let us consider what it would take to change the minds of the four faculty members after their meeting with the president. The person who was convinced by the facts (A) should be the easiest to influence. Give him a new set of facts and he should reach a different decision. Next would come the person who complied through threat of loss of promotion (G). If he was actually promoted, or if in some other way the threat could be removed, he should be free to change. More difficult to change would be the person who enjoyed being with a friendly group (I). Even in another situation, this group might remain as a positive reference group and provide an anchorage for his opinions. If he were placed in a new group, the new group would have to appear more salient to him if he were to change. Finally the most difficult to change would be the person who has actually taken over the beliefs of the president (L). Since he now considers the beliefs his, it becomes a matter of his own integrity to maintain them.

Kelman (1958) identified only three processes, which he called compliance (G), identification (I), and internalization (L). A separate 'A' process was not described. He defines his processes in terms similar to Jahoda's. He then continues by offering some hypotheses concerning the conditions under which each type of behavior is performed. The hypotheses are as follows:

1. When an individual adopts an induced response through compliance, he tends to perform it only under conditions of surveillance by the influencing agent.
2. When an individual adopts an induced response through identification, he tends to perform it only under conditions of salience of his relationship to the agent.
3. When an individual adopts an induced response through internalization, he tends to perform it under conditions of relevance of the issue, regardless of surveillance or salience.

The propositions of Kelman's add something to our understanding of how the cybernetic hierarchy of control actually works. It is not that information is more controlling than energy in some abstract way, but that the information, in the form of values, is carried within the individual while the factors which depend on energy are external. Beginning at the top, the values (L) are the most powerful, since once they are internalized, the individual carries them with him. Next come the norms representing reciprocal role relationships (I). Once adopted through identification, they can be called up whenever the other person is present or whenever the relationship is 'salient' for some other reason. Next in order comes the response to the power of a task supervisor (G), since it will only be effective while the supervisor is present. Last would be the power of money or another energy source as a means of influence in the adaptive area. Although Kelman does not include this type of influence in his experiment, it should have the least power because money only insures a response at the moment it is exchanged. Once the deal is closed, the vote is purchased, or whatever form of influence was sought is obtained, the money has no continuing influence. For the next round, more money must be produced if the influence is to be maintained. In a similar way, other sources of high energy tend to be consumed in use.

Unfortunately few experiments consider more than one variable at a time, so that it is difficult to find evidence to support the hypothesis that four types of influence on conformity are ordered according to the L, I, G, A hierarchy. Kelman's (1958) experiment demonstrates that variables of the L, I, and G types have an influence on attitude change (see also Leet-Pellegrini and Rubin, 1974), and experiments by Kiesler and colleagues give evidence that commitment to continue in a group (L) is a more powerful influence on conformity than attraction to the group (I) (Kiesler and Corbin, 1965; Kiesler *et al.*, 1966; Kiesler, 1969, 1971).

Asch's experiments (1955) on judging lengths of lines provide the best illustration of the cybernetic hierarchy. He showed that individuals could be influenced by a coached majority giving incorrect answers, but that this effect would be countered by having at least one person agree with the subject. Further, the majority would have some influence no matter how extreme its opinion appeared to be. However, over 60% of the subjects held out against the majority. Many of these subjects said that they typically held out for their own opinions or that they considered the judgments an individual task. These results illustrate the hypothesis that a variable related to pattern maintenance (defining the task as one of individual judgment) was more powerful than an integrative variable (having a partner). The integrative variable was in turn more powerful than a goal-attainment variable (majority pressure). Finally, the adaptive variable (modifying the length of the line) was the least powerful.

The results of the Milgram (1963) experiments were similar. Although the effect of the shocks was unambiguous (A), the authority of the experimenter was much more powerful as an influence (G). This power could in turn be modified if one other subject appeared to defy the experimenter (I). Finally, the value the subject placed on not harming another human was the most effective deterrent (L).

Group size in relation to the functional problems

One way to look at the effects of increasing or decreasing group size is to consider the effects in relation to the four major functional problems of groups:

pattern maintenance, adaptation, integration, and goal attainment. The effects of changes in group size are, in turn, similar to the effects of certain changes in leadership style, communication network, or mode of reaching individual and group goals. Each of these aspects of a group is often considered to be an 'independent' variable in reviews of the research literature on group dynamics. Yet in relation to their effects on a group's ability to meet its functional needs, the variables can be seen to be interrelated. If one compares the following:

Large groups v. small groups
Authoritarian leadership v. democratic leadership
Centralized (wheel) communication networks v. decentralized (circle) communication networks
Groups where members are in competition v. those where members cooperate

the major results are always the same. For large groups, authoritarian leadership, centralized communication networks, and groups in which members are in competition, one finds an increase in productivity coupled with low satisfaction for the average member. (The central person is usually quite satisfied.)

Stogdill (1974, p. 413) in his *Handbook of Leadership* provides two clues to understanding the relationship between these 'variables' in his summary of theory and research on leadership. In relation to group size he finds two major generalizations concerning leadership, one that 'large groups make greater demands on the leader' and the other that in a large group it is 'more difficult for a randomly selected member to acquire leadership.' Thus the greater demands on the leader in the large group tend to make the person more authoritarian and use a more centralized communication network. The members in turn are in competition for the scarce resources of the group including the attention of the leader and the rewards that come from sharing the leadership position. Although one can vary leadership style, communication network, and mode of reaching individual and group goals without changing the actual size of the group (although the number and nature of the subgroups may vary), one cannot vary group size without having an effect on the other three 'variables.'

In terms of the four functional problems an increase in group size (or a comparable change in leadership style, communication network, or mode of interaction) tends to (1) reduce members' feelings of *identity* with the group and commitment to its values, (2) provide a greater pool of *skills* and *resources* so that the probability of finding an elegant solution to the problem may be greater although the average member contribution may be less, (3) require a clearer definition of the *norms* and a greater degree of *role differentiation* if the group is to make the best use of its resources, while group *solidarity* is more difficult to maintain, and (4) require more *control* on the part of the leadership to coordinate the role activity of the members as they use the resources to reach the goals that are consistent with the values of the group.

Creating small group processes in large groups

Given the ways in which large groups differ from small groups in their handling of the four functional problems, is there any way that large groups can maintain their advantage in productivity without the loss of commitment and satisfaction on the part of the average member? Usually in a small group, of five members for example, there is enough time to explore in some depth the opinions and feelings of each member of the group and to take them into consideration when reaching a group decision. But with a group several times as large, say 20 or 30 members, there is a tendency to consider the opinions of only the most vocal and high status members and to use some form of majority decision, sometimes leaving a dissatisfied minority that is nevertheless supposed to remain committed to the group goal.

One decision method that tends to preserve the small group process even in groups of considerable size is that of *consensus*. In contrast to majority vote, a group using consensus attempts to combine the best insights of all members to find a solution that incorporates all points of view. A set of guidelines for using consensus is given below (Hare, 1980 pp. 141–142). The guidelines are presented as positive and negative aspects of the sequence of phases in group development expressed in terms of functional theory (i.e. L–A–I–G . . . L).

Although the guidelines can be used by groups in which the leadership functions are shared by all group members, it is helpful to designate two specialized roles. One is a *coordinator* whose main task is to help the group formulate a consensus for each decision. The other is a *recorder* who records the consensus on each decision as it is reached and reads it out to the group for their approval or correction. By being clear about the wording of each decision as the group moves along, some misunderstandings are removed that occur with the more usual method of taking minutes of a meeting to be approved at the next meeting of the group. If the usual practice is followed some group members may have already been acting upon different interpretations of the group decision in the interval between the first meeting and the one at which the minutes of the meeting are approved.

Guidelines for decisions by consensus

(L) *Do:* Secure agreement to follow the rules for consensus, i.e. look for a solution that incorporates all points of view or is best for the group at this time.

Avoid: A zero-sum solution or using majority vote, averaging, or trading as conflict reduction devices.

(A) *Do:* Give your own opinions on the issue. Approach the task on the basis of logic. Seek out differences of opinion to obtain more facts, especially from low status members.

Avoid: Arguing for your own opinions.

(I) *Do:* Address remarks to the group as a whole. Show concern for each individual opinion.

Avoid: Confrontation and criticism.

(G) *Do:* Although the main function of the group *coordinator* is to help the group formulate a consensus and the main function of the group *recorder* is to record each decision as it is reached, all members should help formulate statements about solutions to which all can agree. Even if there appears to be initial agreement, explore the basis of agreement to make sure there is agreement at a fundamental level.

Avoid: Changing your mind *only* to reach agreement.

(L) *Do:* If consensus is reached, make it clear that each group member is responsible to apply the principle in new situations.

Avoid: Pressing for a solution because the time for the meeting is over. If consensus is not reached, postpone the decision until another meeting and do more homework on the problem.

Summary

A basic assumption of the functional perspective is that every social system or group has four problems to solve if it is to survive. In the small group the solutions to these problems are represented by the values (L) that give meaning to its activity, the norms (I) that specify the role relationships between members, the leadership (G) that provides the control of the work of the group, and the resources (A) that are necessary to do the work. A second assumption is that the four functional areas are related to each other in a 'cybernetic hierarchy' in the order L, I, G, and A, with L being the most controlling and A the least.

In terms of the four functional categories groups appear to develop in a four phase sequence of L–A–I–G with a terminal phase of L. First the purpose of the group must be defined and the commitment of members secured (L), then resources and skills must be provided or acquired (A), next roles must be developed and a sufficiently high level of morale achieved (I), and then the group is ready to work on the task with the coordination of leadership (G). At the end of the group's life there is a terminal phase in which the group returns to L to redefine the relationships between members as the group is disbanded.

In a more elaborate version of the L–A–I–G sequence one can observe the same sequence of phases within each of the major phases. Some persons may drop out of a group as it nears the completion of the first two phases of L and A. However, the 'revolution within the revolution' is most likely to occur near the end of the I phase if some members are dissatisfied with the leadership or the role distribution, since by this time they have become committed to the idea of the group and the resources are adequate. If change does not occur at this point there is nothing left to do but to carry on the work.

For the analysis of the pressures on individuals to conform in groups the theories of Jahoda and Kelman suggest reasons why different types of variables might have different effects. Their work can in turn be understood in terms of the four functional categories (AGIL) and the cybernetic hierarchy. For example, one can urge conformity on the basis of common values (L), for the sake of friendship (I), because a majority or someone in authority dominates the scene (G), or because of the facts of the case (A). From the cybernetic hierarchy one would expect L variables to be most persuasive and A variables to be least persuasive. Values (L) once internalized will be the hardest to change, next are norms (I) represented by reciprocal role relationships that are effective as long as they are salient, next comes the power of the majority or an authority (G) that is effective only under the conditions of surveillance, and last comes the influence of facts or money (A) that is only effective at the time of the exchange.

In comparisons of the productivity of large groups with small groups; authoritarian leadership with democratic; centralized communication networks with decentralized, and competition with cooperation, the results are similar. For large groups, authoritarian leadership, centralized communication networks, or groups in which members are in competition, one finds an increase in productivity coupled with low satisfaction for the average member. An increase in group size, for example, reduces commitment (L), provides more skills and resources (A), requires more role differentiation while solidarity is harder to maintain (I), and requires more control on the part of the leadership (G).

One way to preserve the commitment and solidarity of the small group in a large group that has more resources, without using a form of centralized controlling leadership, is to use the method of consensus for decision making rather than majority vote or some form of averaging individual opinions. Guidelines for the use of consensus are presented that have the effect of combining the best insights from all group members in a solution that incorporates all points of view or is accepted by the members as the best solution for the group at that time.

References

Asch, Solomon E. (1955). 'Opinions and social pressure,' *Scientific American*, **193** (5), 31–35.
Bales, Robert F. (1950). *Interaction Process Analysis: A Method for the Study of Small Groups*, Addison-Wesley, Cambridge, Mass.
Bales, Robert F. (1970). *Personality and Interpersonal Behavior*, Holt Rinehart & Winston, New York.
Bales, Robert F., Cohen, Stephen P., and Williamson, Stephen A. (1979). *SYMLOG: A System for the Multiple Level Observation of Groups*, Free Press, New York.
Bennis, Warren G., and Shepard, Herbert A. (1956). 'A theory of group development,' *Human Relations*, **9**, 415–437.
Effrat, Andrew (1968). 'Editor's introduction,' [Applications of Parsonian theory], *Sociological Inquiry*, **38** (Spring), 97–103.
Effrat, Andrew (1976). 'Introduction,' [Social change and development] in J. J. Loubser, R. C. Baum, A. Effrat, and V. M. Lidz (eds.), *Explorations in General Theory in Social Science*, pp. 662–680, Free Press, New York.

Genovés, Santiago (1979). *The Acali Experiment: Six Women and Five Men on a Raft Across the Atlantic*, Times Books, New York.

Hare, A. P. (1968). 'Phases in the development of the Bicol Development Planning Board,' in S. Wells and A. P. Hare (eds.), *Studies in Regional Development*, pp. 29–64, Bicol Development Planning Board (Philippines).

Hare, A. P. (1973). 'Theories of group development and categories for interaction analysis,' *Small Group Behavior*, **4** (3, August), 259–304.

Hare, A. P. (1974). 'Rafting across the Atlantic: Social science adrift,' Paper presented at meetings of Association for Sociology in Southern Africa, Durban, July.

Hare, A. P. (1976). *Handbook of Small Group Research*, 2nd edn, Free Press, New York.

Hare, A. P. (1980). 'Consensus versus majority vote: A laboratory experiment,' *Small Group Behavior*, **11**, (2, May), 131–143.

Hare, A. P. (1982). *Creativity in Small Groups*, Sage, Beverly Hills, Calif.

Hare, A. Paul, and Blumberg, Herbert H. (eds.) (1977). *Liberation Without Violence: A Third Party Approach*, Rex Collings, London.

Heyerdahl, Thor (1972). *The RA Expeditions*, New American Library, New York.

Jahoda, Marie (1956). 'Psychological issues in civil liberties,' *American Psychologist*, **11**, 234–240.

Kelman, Herbert C. (1958). 'Compliance, identification, and internalization: Three processes of attitude change,' *Journal of Conflict Resolution*, **2**, 51–60.

Kiesler, Charles A. (1969). 'Group pressure and conformity,' in J. Mills (ed.), *Experimental Social Psychology*, pp. 233–306, Macmillan, New York.

Kiesler, Charles A. (1971). *The Psychology of Commitment: Experiments Linking Behavior to Belief*, Academic Press, New York.

Kiesler, Charles A., and Corbin, Lee H. (1965). 'Commitment, attraction, and conformity,' *Journal of Personality and Social Psychology*, **2**, 890–895.

Kiesler, Charles A., Zanna, Mark, and de Salvo, James (1966). 'Deviation and conformity: Opinion change as a function of commitment, attraction, and presence of a deviate,' *Journal of Personality and Social Psychology*, **3**, 458–467.

Leet-Pellegrini, Helena, and Rubin, Jeffrey Z. (1974). 'The effects of six bases of power upon compliance, identification, and internalization,' *Bulletin of the Psychonomic Society*, **3** (1B, January), 68–70.

Loubser, Jan J., Baum, Rainer C., Effrat, Andrew, and Lidz, Victor M. (eds.) (1976). *Explorations in General Theory in Social Science: Essays in Honor of Talcott Parsons*, Vols. I and II, Free Press, New York.

Milgram, Stanley (1963). 'Behavioral study of obedience,' *Journal of Abnormal and Social Psychology*, **67** (4), 371–378.

Mills, Theodore M. (1964). *Group Transformation*, Prentice-Hall, Englewood Cliffs, NJ.

Parsons, Talcott (1961). 'An outline of the social system,' In T. Parsons *et al.* (eds.), *Theories of Society*, pp. 30–79, Free Press, New York.

Schutz, William C. (1958). *FIRO: A Three-Dimensional Theory of Interpersonal Behavior*, Holt, Rinehart, New York.

Shambaugh, Philip W. (1978). 'The development of the small group,' *Human Relations*, **31** (3), 283–295.

Stogdill, Ralph M. (1974). *Handbook of Leadership: A Survey of Theory and Research*, Free Press, New York.

Tuckman, Bruce W. (1965). 'Developmental sequence in small groups,' *Psychological Bulletin*, **63** (6), 384–399.

Small Groups and Social Interaction, Volume 2
Edited by H. H. Blumberg, A. P. Hare, V. Kent and M. Davies
© 1983 John Wiley & Sons Ltd

7.5 The Hierarchical Model of Problem-Solving Groups

L. Richard Hoffman

Graduate School of Management, Rutgers University

and

R. Timothy Stein   *A. T. Kearney, Inc.*

The Hierarchical Model (Hoffman, 1979, Ch. 13) describes the dynamics of problem-solving groups within a structural framework. Although the model encompasses many aspects of group functioning, the present chapter will introduce only its basic assumptions and dimensions. The model's utility for understanding the dynamics of group functioning will be illustrated by two types of studies: (1) the process by which problem-solving groups adopt solutions to task problems; (2) and the process by which leaders emerge in newly formed groups.

Basic to the model is the conception of a group as a loosely linked system of people that functions along several dimensions simultaneously. The group's structure is defined by a boundary and three intersecting dimensions, as shown by the cube in Figure 1. The boundary, represented by the faces of the cube, is drawn with dashed and solid lines to symbolize, respectively, its permeability to some aspects of the environment and its impermeability to others (Hemphill and Westie, 1950). Certain information, tasks, and values are acceptable to the group from the outside while others may be resisted or denied. Some members may be actively involved in the group's activities, while others may belong only nominally. The 'size' of the group is determined by the amount of resources and energy it can mobilize through its members to accomplish its goals. In any group the members are only partially included (Katz and Kahn, 1978), in that their membership in other groups, their own self-interest, and their sense of privacy may conflict with their total commitment to the group.

The Hierarchical Model posits three interacting dimensions of group activity that function simultaneously to maintain the boundary and to conduct transactions across it. The Task–Maintenance distinction is the traditional one between

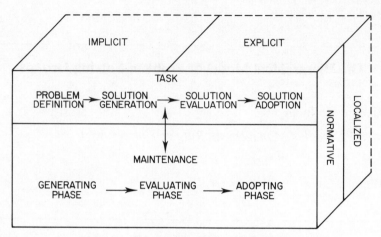

Figure 1   Sketch of the Hierarchical Model

the group's interaction with the environment and its internal membership requirements. The arrows shown on the cube between the two levels of this dimension
represent the interaction between the two levels. For example, a group can use the
status of its members as the basis for deciding on solutions to task problems
(Torrance, 1955). Activity at the task level can also have an impact on group
maintenance. Task success can increase cohesiveness (Zander, 1977), while
unresolved disagreements about the task can lead to dislike and distrust (Maier
and Hoffman, 1965).

The Normative–Localized dimension reflects the extent to which activities are
under normative control or are extremely individual. At the normative extreme
activities conform to the rules which govern all members of the group. Members'
behaviors that are highly idiosyncratic and not a product of the group as a social
system are at the localized extreme. Behaviors which meet the expectations of a
clique or a coalition fall in between.

The intersection of the Task–Maintenance and the Normative–Localized
dimensions indicates that groups have norms for both task and maintenance
activities. The presence of norms to govern the maintenance functions is so well
documented as to require little more than mention (e.g. Blau, 1964). The
Hierarchical Model provides a way of identifying more precisely the effects of
particular maintenance norms on the group's task activities (Hoffman, 1979, Chs.
12 and 13).

Less well recognized are the norms that regulate task activities. The rules of
formal problem-solving techniques, like brainstorming (Osborn, 1957), are considered to be group norms. Members may conform to or deviate from the rules
with varying degrees of approval or disapproval by the other members.

By the Explicit–Implicit dimension the model indicates that a group's activity may be explicitly acknowledged by the members or occur without public recognition. For example, the members can decide that the group needs a leader, discuss that need, and vote one member into office. Or a leader may emerge implicitly as the group complies with the suggestions of one member and permits him/her to direct the group's activities.

The Explicit–Implicit dimension interacts with both of the other dimensions. While a task or a maintenance activity is the explicit focus of the group at a particular time, other functions occur implicitly at the same time. For example, while a group is evaluating possible solutions to a task problem, the members are evaluating each other's abilities, developing feelings of like or dislike for each other, increasing or decreasing the leader's power, etc. (Hoffman, 1979, Chs. 11 and 12).

The intersection of all three dimensions of the model can be illustrated by examples from a few of the cells defined by the cubic representation in Figure 1. For a group to decide to use the brainstorming procedure to solve a problem would be an explicit task norm. If members refrain from mentioning in the leader's presence, errors made by others, they may be operating on an implicit maintenance norm to protect each other from the leader's wrath.

The dynamics of the Hierarchical Model are expressed through the concept of valence (Lewin, 1935). Valence is a force to adopt or reject a particular cognition (Hoffman, 1979, Chs. 1 and 2). Each norm or value, each belief about how the group should function, and each potential activity of the group has valence for each member individually and for the group as a whole. Valence values may be either positive or negative and will vary in magnitude. Both sign and magnitude can change through experience, becoming more positive with confirming or rewarding experiences and more negative with disconfirming or punishing experiences. In newly forming groups, valences for certain norms and beliefs may be close to zero. For example, the valence for solutions to a previously unknown problem in a typical experimental group may be assumed to be zero. However, even in such groups certain norms and beliefs which reflect the organization or society in which the group and its members are embedded will have high valence values initially. For example, the presence of a woman in an otherwise white-male group may activate high-valent beliefs about her lower status in the group (Berger et al., 1972). If she subsequently behaves deferentially to the other members, their valence for her lower status will increase. Conversely, if she makes valuable contributions to the group, the others' valence for her lower status may decrease and might even result in her attaining valence as a group leader.

In ongoing groups the valences for certain norms and beliefs are likely to have high values (either positive or negative) as a result of the groups' previous interactions. For example, a group may have high valence for a norm that no problem is worth discussing unless the leader is there to certify the decision. The members, therefore, fail to work on a problem important to the group.

The process of accumulating valence for a belief is an implicit one, but the group acts as if it is responding to the underlying valence process. For example a group does not usually discuss changes in the valence status of alternative solutions to a problem. But the solutions it adopts and rejects explicitly usually reflect the valences of the alternatives being considered.

To understand the problem-solving process, we must first extend our description of the group's boundary. The boundary is maintained in quasi-stationary equilibrium by habitual, repeated interactions with the environment. The group has a 'problem' when its equilibrium is substantially disturbed; i.e. when its habitual methods are inadequate to restore the equilibrium. Disturbances may arise from the task environment, as when an engineering group at General Motors receives new governmental regulations to reduce permissible pollution from cars. Or the disturbance may be internal, as when a group member is dissatisfied with the group's unwillingness to listen to his/her suggestion. The group then becomes motivated to restore the equilibrium by solving the problem.

Solving the task problem

The solution-adoption process

The Hierarchical Model assumes that a group passes through phases in the problem-solving process either explicitly or implicitly. For purposes of discussion the phases may be described as:

1. *Defining* the problem or setting goals
2. *Specifying* the barriers to be overcome
3. *Generating* alternative solutions
4. *Evaluating* the solutions
5. *Adopting* a solution

The number of phases will vary from group to group and from problem to problem, depending on the complexity of the problem definition. The valence for restoring the boundary provides a general force on the group toward adopting a solution.

Although these phases have been recognized by others (e.g. Bales and Strodtbeck, 1951), the Hierarchical Model makes two important departures from tradition. The first is that groups do not necessarily start at the *Defining* phase and move sequentially through to the *Adopting* phase. A group may begin its deliberations by evaluating a single solution—'Shall we hold a Christmas party?'—and adopting it without ever considering alternatives. The group may build valence implicitly for a particular definition of the problem as it justifies this solution, but only to the extent necessary for its adoption. The problem may never be defined explicitly so that alternative solutions to it might be generated and evaluated. A call for more discussion to define the problem might create antagonisms in the group, since it works against the general force to restore the group boundary.

Nevertheless, there are times when the group may 'move backward' in the sequence to set new objectives or to define the problem more adequately. A member might recognize that only a limited number of alternatives had been considered and suggest that the group ought to reconsider the problem definition. Or an impasse might be reached in a conflict between two high-valence alternatives, which would lead to an examination of the assumptions underlying each of them and an improved definition of the problem (Hoffman, 1979, Ch. 1).

These two methods for causing the group to 'move backwards' in the problem-solving sequence illustrate another important distinction made by the Hierarchical Model, based on the Explicit–Implicit dimension. Groups typically move from the generating phase toward adopting a solution by accumulating valence implicitly for particular solutions. As the solutions are being evaluated, one or more passes the minimum amount necessary for adoption, the adoption threshold. If only one solution's valence surpasses the adoption threshold, it will continue to accumulate valence and be adopted. If more than one solution's valence exceeds the adoption threshold, the one with the highest valence accumulation will be adopted.

However, when two or more solutions have approximately equal supra-threshold valence, conflict occurs. The conflict may be resolved in one of several ways. More favorable arguments are made for one solution, thus adding positive valence to it. Negative aspects of the other solution are brought out, thus decreasing the group's valence for that solution. The merits of a third solution may be brought out, causing its valence to surpass the adoption threshold. Such an alternative may have been offered at an earlier time and be re-evaluated as a 'compromise' solution. Or the new solution could be the product of the group's implicit or explicit return from the evaluating phase to the generating phase. One of the marks of a truly mature group is its ability to recognize such conflicts as necessitating a return to a prior phase *and* a willingness to do so. Conflict-generated solutions are frequently creative solutions to the problem, incorporating the advantages of each of the alternatives, but reducing their disadvantages (Hoffman, 1979, Chs. 1 and 12).

Conflict between alternative solutions may also be resolved by explicit or implicit processes usually associated only with the maintenance level. For example, a formal leader may generate valence implicitly for a preferred solution because he/she rightfully holds the floor longer than the other members. The members, too, may add valence to the leader's solution to curry favor with the leader (Hoffman, 1979, Chs. 11 and 12). A very powerful leader may quite explicitly end the evaluating phase by declaring that the obvious superiority of one of the two solutions makes further discussion unnecessary. Such a resolution of conflict is almost unheard of in laboratory groups, since the power of even experimenter-appointed group leaders is limited.

Our description of the solution-adoption process is not intended to imply a unanimous movement of the members to restore the group's boundary. The Hierarchical Model does not postulate identical valences for solutions at the group and individual levels. Rather, the model proposes that the members' individual valences for the various solutions determine their commitment to them. For example, a group may generate sufficient valence to adopt a solution while one or more members individually may have low or negative valence for it. Consequently, the intense motivation to implement the decision felt by the members who caused the solution to be adopted is not matched by those who hold low valence for that solution. The latter members subsequently may even sabotage the decision.

Empirical evidence

The Hierarchical Model's propositions concerning the solution–adoption process have been subject to empirical test with a variety of laboratory groups. While these studies are reported in detail in *The Group Problem-Solving Process* (Hoffman, 1979) some typical results are shown in Table 1 and Figures 2(a) and 2(b). Table 1 shows the relationship between the valence index for solutions discussed by a group and their status (adopted/not adopted) at the end of the session. The data are from two studies in which drastically different problems were assigned to the groups (see Hoffman, 1979, Chs. 2 and 4). The valence index in each case is the algebraic sum of the number of positive minus the number of negative comments made about a solution during the problem-solving discussion (Hoffman, 1979, Appendix B).

Several points are to be noted in the data presented in Table 1. First, the cumulative valence of every solution adopted by groups to both problems exceeded 15. For a group to adopt a solution to a problem previously unknown to it, the number of favorable comments made about the solution must exceed the number of unfavorable ones by at least 15, a value which we call the adoption threshold. When members have worked on a problem before the meeting, a positive pre-discussion valence thus generated would lower the observed value for the adoption threshold (Hoffman, 1979, Ch. 5).

Although passing the adoption threshold is a necessary condition for adoption, it is not sufficient. Most adopted solutions accumulate much more valence by the end of the discussion. In fact, the strong relationship between the magnitude of the valence index and the proportions of solutions adopted indicates that the more valence a solution gains, the greater is its likelihood of being adopted. The mean valence value for adopted solutions to the two problems in Table 1 was approximately 45.

Plotted in Figure 2 are the solution valences accumulated by five solutions during the problem-solving discussions of two groups represented in Table 1. Although these groups have worked on radically different problems, the plots are similar and typical in two respects. The solution with the highest valence was

Table 1 Valence Index and Adoption of Solutions

Valence index	STUDY I (N = 44 groups) Percent of Solutions				STUDY II (N = 43 groups) Percent of Solutions		
	Principal*	Adopted Subordinate	Not adopted	Number of solutions	Adopted	Not adopted	Number of solutions
≥40	81.8	6.1	12.1	33	80.0	20.0	35
30 to 39	50.0	16.7	33.3	12	58.3	41.7	12
15 to 29	26.2	35.7	38.1	42	36.4	63.6	22
1 to 14	0.0	2.6	97.4	302	0.0	100.0	28
−9 to 0	0.0	0.0	100.0	134	0.0	100.0	52
−10 to −19	0.0	0.0	100.0	1	0.0	100.0	51
≤−20	0.0	0.0	100.0	0	0.0	100.0	15
				524			215

* Many groups, although asked to produce a single solution, solved the problem by combining two of our separately coded solutions as a single one. In all but one instance, one of the two solutions was described in great detail, while the other was added on, usually to satisfy a dissenting member. The detailed solution was labeled the principal adopted solution and the other, the subordinate.

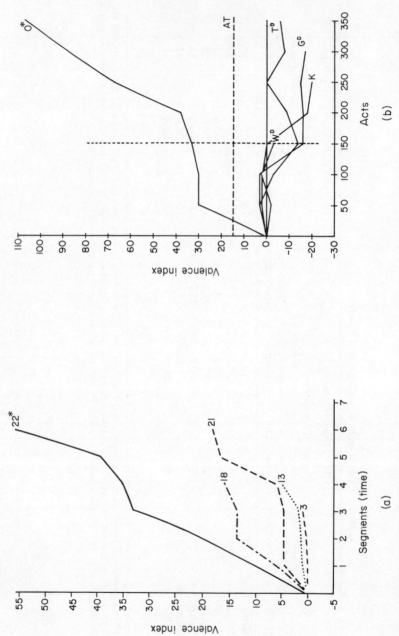

Figure 2 Accumulation of valence for solutions in two groups. Numbers in Figure 2(a) and letters in 2(b) identify the solutions discussed. Asterisks indicate the principal adopted solution. In Figure 2(b) the superscript D marks the verbally discarded solutions; the vertical line marks the announced end of the rejection phase; AT: adoption threshold

adopted in both groups, as it was in over 80% of the groups in both studies. Also, the solution finally adopted was the first to surpass the adoption threshold (15), which was also true of about two-thirds of the groups on both problems. Once a solution has passed the adoption threshold, it is difficult to unseat. However, the time at which the to-be-adopted solution will pass the adoption threshold is unpredictable. In some groups the adopted solution passed threshold in the first quarter of the discussion period, while others waited until the last quarter. The remaining groups were evenly distributed between those two points. Neither the amount of discussion generally nor the amount of discussion about a particular solution is correlated with its valence accumulation (Hoffman, 1979, Ch. 6).

Figure 2(b) illustrates the distinction between implicit and explicit phenomena. The vertical line shows the point at which the group announced that it has finished the rejection phase, during which the members decided to discard certain solution possibilities—those marked by a superscript D in the figure. Unlabeled solutions were retained for further consideration. It is clear from Figure 2b that Solution O has already been chosen implicitly by the group. Its valence of 32 exceeds the adoption threshold (15), whereas Solution K's valence is zero. The statement ending the rejection phase did not acknowledge this group's preference for Solution O over Solution K. However, as seen by the rapid valence accumulation for Solution O following the announcement, the preference already existed, although it took 200 more acts before the solution was finally adopted.

To summarize the solution–adoption process: as the group suggests, evaluates, and gains support for different solutions it builds valence for them. After the valence index for one solution passes the adoption threshold, it becomes a strong candidate for adoption. If further discussion of that solution is more favorable than unfavorable, it continues to gain valence until its valence is substantially greater than the valence of any other solution. It is then adopted by the group. Adoption may occur with or without members' acceptance. Acceptance is dependent primarily on each member's valence for the adopted solution. When adoption has occurred, the group has restored its task-level boundary with the experimenter by producing a solution. However, to the extent that some members are dissatisfied with the decision, it may have residual maintenance problems.

Emergent leadership as a maintenance problem

The emergence process

Although laboratory groups exist for only a short period, they must develop an interpersonal structure suitable to performing the group task. According to the Hierarchical Model the group has a maintenance problem in addition to its manifest task problem. Many groups solve the maintenance problem implicitly through the emergence of one member as leader; others fail to resolve it completely, but nevertheless manage to produce a solution to the task acceptable to the experimenter. Since the maintenance problem is an implicit one, the leadership valence model (Stein *et al.*, 1979), has been developed to describe the emergent leadership process in a manner analogous to the solution valence model just discussed.

The group's problem in selecting a leader is twofold: (a) 'What functions have to be performed by the group to accomplish the task?' and (b) 'What member is best able or most desirous of performing those functions and of guiding and encouraging others to perform them?' The leadership valence model posits that the group will generate valence for a particular definition of the leadership role and for the concept of a particular member as the leader during its problem-solving discussion.

The model assumes that the problem-solving phases described earlier also occur implicitly when the group solves its leadership problem. Since the members themselves form the complete set of possible 'solutions,' the group begins its interactions in the generating phase. In the beginning of a leaderless group of strangers, whose members are homogeneous with respect to status-related characteristics, all members have zero valence as leaders. When differences in status characteristics are present, they provide a basis for an initial attribution of leadership potential and pre-meeting leadership valence (Berger *et al.*, 1972).

During the generating phase[1] the members perform a variety of behaviors that indicate their willingness and ability to help solve the problem and to control the group. These behaviors also begin to define the leadership role, because the group receives the implicit message that the function performed is necessary, in the speaker's view, to accomplish the task. The members' positive responses to these attempts to influence them contribute additional positive valence to both the definition of the leadership role and to the person as leader. Disagreements with a member's suggestions and failure to follow them, generate negative valence toward both that member as leader and that type of behavior as part of the group's leadership norm. More complicated responses might add positive valence to the function but negative valence to the person as leader, or vice versa.

Built into the model and the methodology developed for scoring leadership valence (Pearse *et al.*, 1980) is the assumption that a reciprocal dominance–submission relationship is established between leaders and members. On the dominance side, positive leadership valence points are assigned for (a) helping to identify and solve task problems, (b) directing and controlling group procedures and structures, and (c) acts of dominance over others (e.g. interrupting). Behaviors which divert the group from task accomplishment or promote interpersonal conflict are scored with negative points. Acts of support and assistance of others (socio-emotional leadership) have been found to be independent of task leadership in laboratory groups and are not included in the valence count (Stein and Heller, 1979). A member also receives positive valence when another member conforms to or shows agreement with his/her influence attempt. In a similar manner, a member scores negative valence points when others disagree or fail to comply with his/her suggestion. Submitting to others (e.g. yielding to interruptions) is scored as negative valence. Finally, statements of self-enhancement and self-devaluation are scored with positive and negative points respectively.

The quality of some members' influence attempts and interpersonal relations may meet with consistent disagreement from the other members. The negative valence accumulated from antagonists may drop the poor performers' total valence below the rejection threshold, reflecting the low probability that these members will be adopted as leaders.

If a member is successful in influencing others, that member will accumulate enough valence to pass the candidacy threshold and the evaluating phase begins. Analogous to the adoption threshold found for solution valence, the candidacy threshold is the amount of leadership valence necessary for a member to be considered seriously for adoption as the group's leader. If only one member's valence passes the candidacy threshold, that member will become the leader. When more than one member gains sufficient valence to pass the candidacy threshold at about the same time, a leadership conflict is generated. Methods for resolving this conflict include the increased dominance of one candidate, withdrawal of the other, a coalition between the two candidates, or the emergence of a third candidate. The conflict is often not resolved in laboratory groups, since they are able to terminate their discussion (and the group) by solving the task problem. When the leadership conflict is associated with a dispute over two solutions, the dispute about the solutions is resolved by taking a vote on the solution to be adopted, capitalizing on the high valence for majority rule that exists in our society.

An emergence threshold is defined as the amount of valence necessary to adopt a person as the implicit leader. If no one surpasses the emergence threshold, the group remains locked in a leadership conflict and functions without an adopted leader. The adoption phase begins after one member's leadership valence has passed the emergence threshold. At that point the group has implicitly adopted a leader who usually continues to earn valence points and to consolidate his/her position. His/her repertoire of behaviors enlarges as he/she now has the power to play out the role he/she feels is appropriate for a leader (Hollander, 1978).

While we have labeled the behaviors which contribute to leadership valence as task-facilitating and controlling, the emergent leader does not necessarily promote group performance. Just as groups often produce an incorrect solution to a problem through the solution valence-adoption process, the members may also adopt a leader who is ineffective in facilitating the group's performance. They may misidentify the task requirements, misevaluate the leader's ability, or lack the ability or motivation themselves to resist the leader's attempts to control them. In the absence of external feedback concerning the leader's true task-facilitating abilities, the group must rely on its own internal criteria and direct experience with the leader.

Although a leader of a group may emerge, the members' acceptance of such a leader may vary considerably from person to person. We expect the acceptance to be a function of the member's contribution to the leader's total valence through that member's submission to or rejection of the leader's initiations.

Empirical evidence

Data have been collected from laboratory, problem-solving groups to test the leadership valence model. Coding has been completed for some of these groups and preliminary results are useful for illustrative purposes. Figures 3(a) and 3(b) show the leadership valence accumulations for the members in each of two groups and their associated post-meeting leadership ratings. These groups were selected because they had members whose ratings distinguished them from the rest of the group. It is clear that in both groups the rank orders of the cumulative leadership valence scores and the mean leadership ratings are identical. However, the differences among valence scores are not directly proportional to the differences in the ratings.

Nevertheless, the pattern of leadership emergence appears early in both groups. In Group 9, Member 1, who was perceived as the clear leader by the members, was differentiated early by the valence measure, showed a sharp rise between segments 6 and 9, and continued his dominance until the end. The other members also became more differentiated as the discussion proceeded, with Member 4 asserting greater leadership toward the end, although still subordinate to Member 1.

Group 16 took more time to sort out its leadership structure, despite its shorter overall discussion. However, by segment 6, Member 4 had differentiated himself from Member 2 and continued his greater valence accumulation to the end. Member 2's later ascendance would appear to be in support of Member 4 in domination over Members 1 and 3.

Although the statistical analysis is not complete, an upward shift in the slope of the emerging leader's valence curve suggests a possible candidacy threshold. The existence of an emergence threshold is not obvious in these graphs. However, the failures of Members 1 and 3 in Group 16 to continue to acquire leadership valence during the latter part of their meeting is matched by their low leadership ratings. Nobody's leadership valence dropped below zero, which would indicate true rejection of the member as leader. Very negative reactions to a member would not be expected in a newly formed, temporary group, since any mildly negative feelings could be contained for the 40 or 50 minutes of the experiment. By ignoring the initiations of certain members, the group can signal effectively its unwillingness to have them as leaders without risking their withdrawal from the group.

These separate analyses of valences in the solution-adoption and leadership emergence processes show promising support for the Hierarchical Model. They also lend themselves to an obvious examination of the interaction between these two processes, which is also planned. However, the principal promise of the

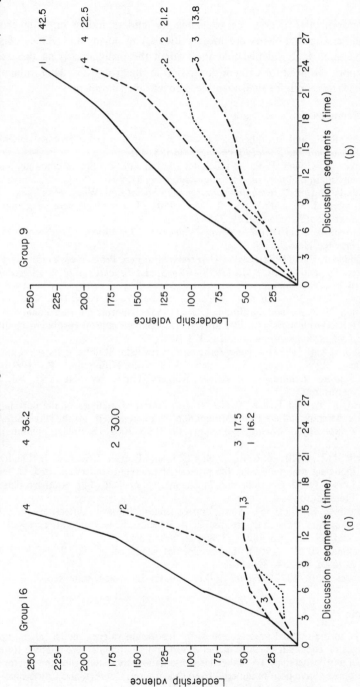

Figure 3   Accumulation of leadership valence by the members of two groups

Hierarchical Model is its relevance for understanding ongoing groups, whose maintenance problems are more critical. The norms and values of such groups have such high valence that they affect the problem-solving process implicitly, without the need for explicit discussion in the group. The Hierarchical Model can guide the search for their identification and measurements.

References

Bales, R. F., and Strodtbeck, F. L. (1951). 'Phases in group problem-solving,' *Journal of Abnormal and Social Psychology*, **46**, 485–495.

Berger, J., Cohen, B. P., and Zelditch, M., Jr (1972). 'Status characteristics and social interaction,' *American Sociological Review*, **37**, 241–255.

Blau, P. M. (1964). *Exchange and Power in Social Life*, Wiley, New York.

Hemphill, J. K., and Westie, C. M. (1950). 'The measurement of group dimensions,' *Journal of Psychology*, **29**, 325–342.

Hoffman, L. R. (1979). *The Group Problem-Solving Process: Studies of a Valence Model*, Praeger, New York.

Hollander, E. P. (1978). *Leadership Dynamics*, Free Press, New York.

Katz, D., and Kahn, R. L. (1978). *The Social Psychology of Organizations*, 2nd edn, Wiley, New York.

Lewin, K. (1935). *A Dynamic Theory of Personality*. McGraw-Hill, New York.

Maier, N. R. F., and Hoffman, L. R. (1965). 'Acceptance and quality of solutions as related to leaders' attitudes toward disagreement in group problem-solving,' *Journal of Applied Behavioral Science*, **1**, 373–385.

Osborn, A. F. (1957). *Applied Imagination*, rev. edn, Scribner's, New York.

Pearse, R. W., Cooley, S. H., Stein, R. T., and Hoffman, L. R. (1980). *Manual for Scoring Leadership Valence*, Rutgers University, Newark, NJ. Unpublished manuscript.

Stein, R. T., and Heller, T. (1979). 'An empirical analysis of the correlations between leadership status and participation rates reported in the literature,' *Journal of Personality & Social Psychology*, **37**, 1993–2002. (See also, Volume 1, sub-chapter 10.1).

Stein, R. T., Hoffman, L. R., Cooley, S. J., and Pearse, R. W. (1979). 'Leadership valence: modeling and measuring the process of emergent leadership,' in J. G. Hunt and L. L. Larson (eds.), *Crosscurrents in Leadership*, pp. 126–147, Southern Illinois University Press, Carbondale, Illinois.

Torrance, E. P. (1955). 'Some consequences of power differences in permanent and temporary three-man groups,' in A. P. Hare, E. F. Borgatta, and R. F. Bales (eds.), *Small Groups*, pp. 482–492, Knopf, New York.

Tuckman, B. W. (1965). 'Developmental sequence in "small groups",' *Psychological Bulletin*, **63**, 384–399.

Zander, A. F. (1977). *Groups at Work*. Jossey-Bass, San Francisco.

Note

1. In the original presentation of the leadership valence model (Stein *et al.*, 1979), the stages of Tuckman's (1965) model of group development were adapted to the problem of emerging leadership. To make this presentation consistent with the Hierarchical Model, the phases have been renamed—from Orientation, Conflict, and Emergence—to Generating, Evaluating, and Adopting respectively.

Small Groups and Social Interaction, Volume 2
Edited by H. H. Blumberg, A. P. Hare, V. Kent and M. Davies
Published by John Wiley & Sons Ltd 1983

7.6 Team Spirit vs. The Individual Achiever*

Alvin F. Zander   *University of Michigan*

A manager who over-rewards individual effort can spoil it all. A worker may strive harder for the success of his group than for himself. A unified group that can set its own goals develops its own aspirations and will rise to meet them.

Most people would agree these days that organizations run on individual achievement. With few exceptions, it seems, we consider teamwork and pride in one's group to be either old-fashioned notions or sources of restraint on individual effort. Even in athletics, the traditional bastion of esprit de corps, individual aspiration appears to be gaining the upper hand as superstars leave their championship teams for monetarily greener pastures. Selfless commitment to a group goal, we assume, is an outmoded value, obsolete in business firms where the only thing members have in common is their employer.

Most psychological research reflects this emphasis on the individual. 'Need for Achievement' (often called N-Ach, or Ms for *motive for success*) has been one of the most studied variables in our field. David McClelland, a pioneer in this area, has even attempted to show that the rise of great civilizations depended on the citizens having high aspirations for individual achievement. Psychologists have seen no need for comparable research on a 'need for group achievement.' But a great deal of recent research, both in large organizations and in group dynamics laboratories, shows that teamwork and team spirit never die, and are often more important than individual achievement.

In many organizations, I have seen people work harder for small work teams than for themselves. The success of these organizations, moreover, whether they

---

*Reprinted from *Psychology Today Magazine*, November, 1974, **8** (6), pp. 64–68. Copyright © 1974 Ziff-Davis Publishing Company.

be businesses, Government agencies or factories, often depends upon this teamwork.

A couple of years ago, for example, I had the opportunity to study assembly-line groups in a slipper factory. Each line was composed of six to eight women who sat behind each other and sewed different parts to slippers moving by on a belt. At the end of the line the completed products fell into a box and were counted on a meter. The management set each group's daily production goal and told them how they did, but did not base their salary on how many they completed or whether they met the goal. Yet when I asked them a series of questions to determine whether they placed more importance on their own or their group's success, they overwhelmingly felt the group to be more important.

Teamwork in breweries and business

I found a similar situation in a Swedish brewery, where I asked the members of work groups the same kinds of questions. These men worked in groups of six to 10 on a wide variety of tasks that ranged from driving trucks to research and plant management. Most rated their concern for their group's achievement as high as for their own, while expressing much less concern for the success of the company as a whole. I also found that in United Fund organizations, the executive board members felt more pride in their local organization's success than in their personal efforts. And in spite of the individual athletes who make headlines when they strike off for themselves, team spirit is the rule rather than the exception in sports. In fact, both amateurs and professionals generally feel that a team can't become a winner without it.

Self-centered striver

Because most leaders and administrators ignore or underestimate the importance of teamwork and group spirit, there has been little research on work groups. While desire for group success appears to be a promising source of energy for a social group, we know surprisingly little about what makes its members want to succeed or what creates a sense of group pride. Most textbooks on management and administration assume that the organization man is a self-centered striver. Even when such a person works hard for the company, many managers and psychologists presume his interest lies primarily in taking care of himself. Rarely has anyone seriously considered that members value group success so strongly that this desire increases their effort.

The first laboratory experiments my students and I conducted on this problem established clearly that groups with stronger team spirit perform better than those with less. As we progressed, we began to see similarities in the ways our groups performed and the ways that the Achievement Motivation theory of John W. Atkinson and N. T. Feather predicted individuals would perform. So we developed a model to explain team spirit, patterned after Atkinson and Feather's model to explain individual striving. Our group model then guided our subsequent research strategy.

Atkinson and Feather propose that when a person has an opportunity to choose a goal and to decide how hard he will work for it, the final decision depends on two conflicting tendencies: his need for achievement and his fear of failure. They believe these tendencies form enduring dispositions, which can be measured by analyzing the stories their subjects make up about a set of pictures from the Thematic Apperception Test. Basically, the two opposing tendencies work like this: People with strong motives for success (high Ms) tend to choose goals that are challenging—neither so easy as to make success certain, since then it wouldn't be much of an achievement, nor so difficult as to make failure certain. People with strong motives to avoid failure (high Maf), on the other hand, tend to choose goals at the extremes of difficulty—either too easy, so they will be assured of success, or too difficult, so they can say, in effect, 'I made a noble effort, but I never really had a chance anyway.' All decisions about goals, then, represent a compromise between the individual's two motives and his evaluation of how rewarding it would be to succeed.

Groups, we suggest, operate in a similar manner. When members have a strong desire for their group to succeed (high Dgs) they tend to choose 'realistic' goals and work hard for them. When they have a strong desire to avoid failure (high Dgaf) they tend to choose either very easy or very hard goals, and may not work as much. Like their individual counterparts, groups with low Dgs tend not to perform as well as groups with high Dgs. Similarly, groups with strong desire to avoid failure perform more poorly than groups with low Dgaf. To say that a *person* has a strong desire for group success simply means that he will feel satisfied if his group accomplished its goal; likewise, a strong fear of failure means that he will feel embarrassed if his group does not succeed.

The main difference between group achievement motivation and individual achievement motivation lies in our assumption that the desire for group success is not a permanent trait of individuals, but rather a motive that develops in particular situations. Since group achievement motivation has strong effects that are separate from the effects of individual achievement motivation, many of our laboratory experiments have aimed at discovering what particular circumstances nourish its development.

In one experiment, we attempted to induce a strong sense of unity in some of our subject groups (high-school boys) by telling them that their abilities and temperaments were well matched, that they were a team, and by asking them to choose a group name. In other groups we tried to develop a weaker sense of unity by addressing them as individuals, and telling them they did not match up well. When we asked the boys to set performance goals for themselves on a 'Communications Coding Test,' members of the strong group consistently set more realistic and challenging intermediate goals than members of weak groups, who tended to choose very easy or very difficult goals. Thus a sense of unity is one factor that prompts a group's wish for success and improves its actual performance.

Leaders, goals, and dominos

In another experiment we asked groups of boys to make certain patterns with dominos as quickly as they could. In each group we designated one boy as a leader who had to put his piece in the proper place before the other members could add theirs. When we asked them to specify goals, we found that the boys with more important, central positions chose realistic goals more regularly than those in less important, peripheral positions.

We found a similar situation in local United Fund organizations. Board members who held central positions in their groups expressed more concern for the success of their agency than did members in more peripheral positions. A second important factor that increases team spirit and desire for success, then, is having increased responsibility for one's group's outcome.

In order to test the effects of the desire to avoid failure, we designed a somewhat different experiment. We tried to arouse Dgs in some groups by giving them poker chips when they met their goals and Dgaf in other groups by taking chips away from an initial pile of 30 when they failed. We explained that we would count their total chips at the end of the test as the group score. The Dgs groups generally chose more reasonable goals than the Dgaf groups. Working conditions that emphasize the negative consequences of failure, we may infer, actually reduce performance.

One of the surest ways a group can develop a strong fear of failure is for it to have failed often in the past. Some of our earliest experiments showed that repeated failure leads group members to see themselves and others as less helpful, to feel less responsible for their group's outcome, and to say that it was less important for them to belong to the group. All of these effects tend to decrease Dgs and maintain a vicious cycle of failure. Groups that set their own goals can sometimes climb out of this cycle by reducing their goal to a level they can reach, although they often resist such an admission of defeat. But groups that do not exercise effective control over their own goals do not even have this way out.

Which Funds worked, and why

We recently examined in detail a real-life example of repeated failures among United Fund organizations. Half of the 46 groups we studied had failed to reach their fund-raising goals for the past four years in a row. The others had been successful in all of the previous four years. Officers in the failing Funds did not lower their goals, presumably because of community pressure to aim at meeting their needs fully. We discovered that the board members of these Funds felt differently about their organizations than members of successful Funds.

Members of the failing groups worked longer hours, enjoyed their work less, had less pride in their organization and in their personal efforts, blamed volunteers to a greater degree, and thought success was less important. In setting goals, they preferred to beat their previous year's performance rather than to meet their set goal, and would have chosen to eliminate goal-setting altogether, if possible. Failure clearly laid the groundwork for future failure: so long as they could not meet their quota, motivation dropped and efficiency decreased, contributing to another poor performance, another cycle of failure, and more difficult goals. Successful Funds, on the other hand, set challenging goals, harder than any they had yet attained, but not impossible. Success bred stronger motivation and increased efficiency, which in turn led to further success and an upward spiral of performance.

Forcing group failures

Research on other organizations often shows that managers tend to set unrealistically high goals for their workers. If the same process we've found in our laboratory and the United Fund operates in corporations and public agencies, these managers may be forcing their workers into failure. Regardless of the goal a manager sets, a group will develop aspirations of its own. By setting the official goal too high, an ambitious manager may actually induce the groups he or she supervises to set their own aspirations below the level they are capable of attaining.

The simplest and perhaps most effective road out of this bind is to include workers in the goal-setting process, which will moderate management's hopes. It is then very important to combat, as much as possible, the negative consequences that usually follow from revising goals downward to reachable levels.

Management must also provide accurate and continual feedback to groups about their performance. We have found that without feedback, many groups naturally overestimate their output and consequently set goals much higher than they can reach. This tendency alone can sometimes initiate a cycle of failure.

As we concluded our series of experiments on the conditions that facilitate Dgs or Dgaf, we still faced one major question: How could we be sure these group-oriented motives act independently of motives for individual achievement and fear of failure? Some of our colleagues had already suggested that we may have simply created conditions that tapped individual motives and thereby raised or lowered performance. To settle this issue, we designed a couple of fairly complex experiments.

In the first, we formed 16 groups of high-school boys, each with one high on motive to succeed, one high on motive to avoid failure, and one who scored intermediate on both measures. As in an earlier experiment, we asked them to arrange dominos in various specific patterns, with one central person always placing his domino before the other two could place theirs. Half of the time the high-Ms person occupied the central position, while the high-Maf person took it the other half. We reasoned that if the two behaved differently in the peripheral position, but similarly in the central position, then the group situation must be responsible for inducing the high-Maf person to act like a high-Ms person when he occupied the central role. This was precisely what happened.

The high achievers acted as expected in both positions; they chose realistic but challenging goals. The high fear of failure boys acted as expected when they occupied peripheral roles, choosing goals either too high or too low. But they acted like high achievers when they moved into central positions. This shows clearly that in appropriate circumstances, group responsibility and spirit can overcome the effects of personal motives.

Poker chips and group success

In the second experiment, John Forward tried to create conditions that would bring individual and group motives into conflict. We reasoned here that if group motives have independent effects, our subjects would feel tension when the two motives conflicted. We repeated an earlier experiment in which we set up a reward condition (we gave poker chips for success) and a cost condition (we took chips away for failures), with subjects we had selected for either high Ms or high Maf. As we expected, the high Ms subjects reported more tension in the cost condition, where achieving personal success and avoiding group failure would call for different goals; while the high-Maf subjects reported more tension in the reward condition, where avoiding personal failure conflicted with achieving group success.

These experiments show that when a person works in a group, his behavior and attitudes result from two different sets of motives: those that form part of his enduring personality, and those that arise in a particular circumstance. These motives may match and amplify each other, or they may come into conflict. But our evidence suggests that when they do collide, a strong sense of group involvement can overcome personal fear of failure or lack of achievement motivation.

Since group motives develop in some circumstances and not in others, people in positions to influence the structure of organizations can do much to nourish them. The most important step would be to shift control downward wherever possible, giving those who do the work more real say about how much they do and how they do it. This in effect places each member in a more central position, transferring more responsibility for the group's success or failure on his shoulders.

Each group should be able to evaluate its own performance, and on the basis of its past efforts and the organization's present needs, have a strong voice in setting current goals. Then members will react to the results of the group's work not as another piece of interesting information, but as a source of satisfaction or dissatisfaction, which cannot help but influence their future performance. Satisfaction feeds the desire for more, and the successful group usually chooses to raise its goals progressively upward.

Open channels, close rapport

It is also essential to keep channels of communicatic
members, perhaps with regular meetings or discussions. G(
only aids evaluation and goal-setting, but helps the membe
as a group and see that others have strong commitments t

I once studied a mirror factory in which the workers, who were su ᵕ.ᵍ .
motivated, were quite satisfied nevertheless with their production goals being set
by the number of orders the company received. The sense of teamwork I observed
seemed to be promoted mainly by the workers' involvement in other group and
company decisions. In particular, groups held regular meetings to discuss ways of
cutting costs and improving production.

Unlike assembly lines or annual fund-raising organizations, many groups have
no set of tasks to repeat, and many do not produce a single product the group as a
whole has responsibility for. It is more difficult to develop group pride in such
conditions; good communication among members and frequent, reliable feedback
become essential.

While we did not test the hypothesis directly in our experiments, we came to
suspect that the presence of other strong motives may weaken Dgs.
Organizational structures that emphasize and reward individual achievement tend
to splinter rather than unify groups. Similarly, when a group exists mainly to
determine how many dollars each member will take home in his pay envelope, as
in group incentive plans, group pride may not develop at all.

Man doesn't live by N-Ach alone

In spite of the theories of psychologists, administrators and educators, our
society does not run on individual achievement motivation alone. I fear that our
beliefs that it does have led us to assume that people who can't cut the mustard on
their own initiative can't cut it at all. We have designed our schools, businesses,
and public agencies primarily for individual achievers, and lost the valuable contributions others could make in different circumstances. And by operating our elementary schools on the 'succeed on your own or not at all' motto, we may be
depriving many of our children of the success experiences they need to develop
individual initiative and to overcome fear of failure. By creating conditions that
nourish group desire for success and then by rewarding group accomplishments, I
believe many of our institutions could become more flexible and more involving
for a larger part of our population.

For more information ...

Forward, John and Zander, Alvin F. (1971). 'Choice of Unattainable Group Goals and
    Effects on Performance,' *Organizational Behavior and Human Performance*, **6** (2),
    184–199.

der, Alvin F. (1971). *Motives and Goals in Groups*, Academic Press, New York.

ander, Alvin F. and Forward, John (1968). 'Position in group, achievement motivation and group aspirations', *Journal for Personality and Social Psychology*. **8**, 282–288.

Zander, Alvin F., Forward, John, and Albert Rosita (1969). 'Adaptation of board members to repeated failure or success by their organizations', *Organizational Behavior and Human Performance*, **4**, 56–76.

Zander, Alvin F, and Medow, Herman (1963). 'Individual and group levels of aspiration', *Human Relations*, **16**, 89–105.

Zander, Alvin F., and Ulberg, Cyrus (1971). 'The group level of aspiration and external social pressures', *Organizational Behavior and Human Performance*, **6**, 362–378.

Small Groups and Social Interaction, Volume 2
Edited by H. H. Blumberg, A. P. Hare, V. Kent and M. Davies
Published by John Wiley & Sons Ltd 1983

7.7 Creativity in Self-Managed Groups*

Rosemary Randall   *Milton Keynes, Buckinghamshire*
and
John Southgate   *Polytechnic of North London*

The question of creativity and destructiveness in groups can be a critical one for collective, cooperative, or self-managed organizations. The experimental organization structures adopted, the voluntary membership, the political and personal importance of the work all seem to lead both to possibilities of greater creativity than more traditional organizations allow, but also to destructiveness that can be hard for the group to contain and survive.

In 1977 we undertook some research at Loughborough University looking at these problems and in this paper we summarize some of the theoretical conclusions we arrived at. (A fuller version can be found in Southgate and Randall, 1980, and in the cartoon manual, *Co-operative and Community Group Dynamics*, Randall *et al.*, 1980.) It is our view that creativity in a group has a particular dynamic that is rooted in the sexual drive. Furthermore we argue that group creativity is much more likely to take place in a self-managed group because members are able to have greater control over the satisfaction of their desires. The contradiction for self-managed groups, however, is that operating as they do without some of the repressive constraints of conventional organizations and in an environment that is frequently hostile, the possibilities of destructiveness are also increased.

At the risk of oversimplifying one can divide group theorists into two major and opposing camps. There are the optimists and the pessimists. Group theorists from the human relations school emphasize group rationality and creativity (see for example Bennis *et al.*, 1970, or Bradford *et al.*, 1964) while those from the psychoanalytic tradition concentrate more on the group's potential for regressive,

---

* With permission of the authors and publishers we are reprinting—as Figure 1—pp. 6 and 7 of Randall, Southgate, and Tomlinson (1980). (The illustration is by Frances Tomlinson.)

irrational behaviour, emphasizing the necessity of leadership that can harness and direct the otherwise explosive and destructive forces (see for example Rice, 1965). Neither view takes much account of class or the politics of group organization. And although one view emphasizes the creative aspects of group life and the other the destructive aspects there is no possibility of a direct connection between them since they start from such different assumptions.

The theory we propose, developed on the basis of fieldwork observation, is an analysis of group creativity that connects the psychoanalytic work of Bion (1968) on groups with Reich's (1940) orgasm theory. Bion's views of creativity are those of traditional psychoanalysis. What he calls the 'basic assumption' group—the expression of infantile anxieties and part-object relations—is inevitable and omnipresent. It has to be controlled by the emergence of the sophisticated or 'w' group which for Bion is a rational and ego-related phenomenon. ('w' stands for work.) The creative 'w' group is not an alternative to the basic assumption group but a means of controlling it. However, other than to remark that it operates on the basis of cooperation rather than valency he gives little indication as to its dynamics.

It seems to us there is more to creativity in groups than Bion allows and that it does have discernible dynamics. Fundamentally these show the creative expression of the basic libidinal drive, the same drive which in distorted, repressed, and destructive form finds expression in the basic assumption group. We describe this creativity as follows.

A group that is working creatively goes through an observable cycle of activity. It begins with a *nurturing* phase. Here group members work to make themselves feel comfortable with each other and familiar with the task. It is a phase of preparation. Only when all members feel included, when plans have been made and the necessary resources gathered can this phase be satisfactorily moved out of. The nurturing phase gives way to an *energizing* phase which builds up slowly as the group engages on the task in hand. The early part of an energizing phase is usually characterized by fairly detailed work. This is gradually surpassed as the energy in the group rises and activity intensifies. The energizing phase culminates in a *peak*. This is usually an experience of terrific energy and pleasure for the group. Individual identity tends to be submerged in the experience of the group as a whole. Typically the peak brings with it the emergence of something new. In a practical manual task this would be the completion of whatever was being constructed. In a meeting it would be the point at which a satisfactory decision was reached. In an intellectual discussion it would be the point at which a new idea clarifies. The peak is followed by a slow *relaxing* phase. People admire the new creation, congratulate themselves and each other, celebrate, wind down, clear up. The energy of a group that is working creatively can be pictured graphically in the way shown in Figure 1. We called this energy cycle the creative orgasmic cycle because in our view it is typical of the flow of libidinal energy in any creative activity—individual or group.

Reich (1940) describes the normal flow of sexual energy as a four-beat process of mechanical tension—electrical charge—electrical discharge—mechanical relaxation which he called the orgasm formula. In our view all creative energy follows this same sexual flow and can be observed in any kind of pleasurable activity from the most mundane and simple to the most complex and extraordinary.

Sexual energy is of course subject to frustration and repression and this is as true of the group as of the individual. It can be as hard to achieve a satisfying and pleasurable creative cycle in a group as in two-person sexual relating. Present-day frustrations as well as effects of previous repression will have their effects. Although there are similarities, however, the two situations are not the same. In sexual relations one is generally dealing with the interaction between two individuals, with two-person compatibilities and incompatibilities, two-person disturbances. Those individuals' particular histories and characters will be of particular importance. In group activity we confront not merely the complications of a multi-faceted interaction where individuals bring into play their particular anxieties and creative abilities but factors that are specific to the group itself. Present-day, environmental factors have far greater importance in determining whether or not a creative cycle will take place. Actual frustration of desire rather than the historical frustration which has given rise to particular behaviour patterns has far more importance. Individual control is less. Curiously the possibilities of both creativity and pathology are greater. Individuals who in their personal sexual relationships are severely inhibited can sometimes participate more easily in creative group activity where they have less responsibility for the total outcome. Individuals who are in general more liberated sexually can in a group find themselves pulled into regressive behaviour they would not experience in other circumstances. The determining factors are usually those affecting the group as a whole rather than those affecting specific individuals. When the desires of the group as a whole are frustrated pathological behaviour is possible whether or not it is present in the character and history of individuals.

It follows from this that we see the basic assumption processes, that Bion describes, as primarily pathological. The three modes that he identified were the dependent, the fight–flight, and the pairing group and they bear an interesting relationship to the creative-orgasmic cycle. They can be seen as the dark shadows of creative processes, sharing some of the same roots, acting as solutions to some of the same desires but resulting in a very different experience and outcome for group members. The dependent group is the dark shadow of the nurturing phase. Here, instead of offering one another sustenance and engaging on preparation for the task, members cling passive, complaining, and dependent to a leadership that is conceived of as possessing magical abilities to satisfy all needs, instantly and without effort. The fight–flight group is the shadow of the energizing phase. Here leadership is typically with the most paranoid member or members. Energy is violent and destructive. The group turns in frustration on itself, persecuting

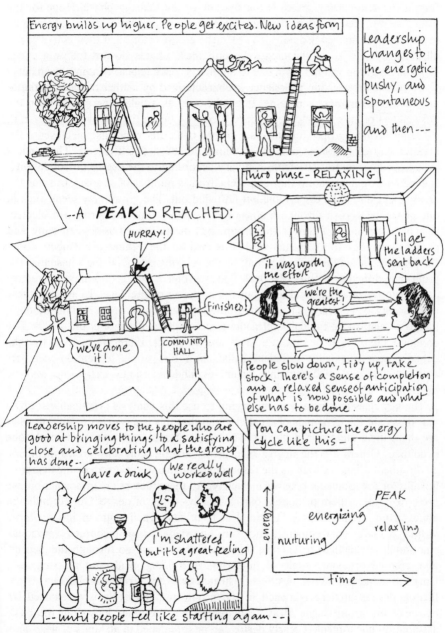

Figure 1

members randomly. The peak is replaced by splits and expulsions as the group fragments. The pairing group is the shadow of the relaxing phase. Hope for the future is embodied in the leadership pair. Success is promised, often in Messianic terms, at some unspecified date. The pair, the group's aims, and their activities are all idealized. Unlike in the creative group these phases do not follow a cycle. Typically a group will flip from one to another as each fails to contain the anxiety.

Of course most group experience is characterized by neither of these extremes and is altogether more mundane. It can be seen as a balancing act between the possibilities of creative and destructive process—hence the title we have given it, the 'intermediate' group. Intermediate groups can differ widely, some closer to the creative end of the spectrum, others closer to the destructive end. The point a group occupies on this spectrum will vary according to the degree of frustration it is experiencing, frustration that can come from a number of sources. In some the creative cycle may be discernible but flattened out. The group may seem stuck in one phase, or to rush through a phase too fast. Sometimes nurturing is neglected. A typical example of this is the group that meets for a business meeting and plunges straight into its agenda with no regard for the feelings of members about the process. In another group it may be the relaxing or energizing phase that the group has difficulty with or the peak that is avoided. One group may be creative at a cognitive or a practical level but not at the emotional level. In another these factors may be reversed. The permutations and variations seem infinite although there do seem to be typical intermediate groups. (See Randall *et al.*, 1980). The common factor is that although there are no peaks, there are no real troughs either. There is usually sufficient satisfaction for people to remain members although the level of complaints, grumbles, and occasional explosions may be high.

The key question for any group trying to use this analysis practically is, given that these are the dynamics of creativity and that this is a process to aim at, what are the critical factors in achieving it? Organizational structure is obviously one candidate. Others are the degree of neurosis among individual group members, environmental factors such as the resources available to the group or the degree of hostility or acceptance it receives in society. All these factors are important but we prefer to look at them through a particular lens—that of desire. Our formulation about group creativity is in its simplest form that when a group has a *shared desire*, a safe environment, and the knowledge and resources (practical, emotional, intellectual) to achieve the desire, then it will go through the pleasurable creative-orgasmic cycle of nurturing, energizing, peak and relaxing as it works to achieve it. When desire is frustrated or where group members have conflicting desires anxiety is raised in the group and the cycle is threatened. *In extremis* the group turns away from reality and becomes locked in the basic assumption phenomenon. Clearly desire can be threatened in all kinds of ways and, as we point out elsewhere (Southgate and Randall, 1980), is anyway not an unambiguous term. In practice, however, there are four questions we would ask about any group:

1. Is its organization structure such that desire can be satisfied?
2. Are its environment and resources conducive to desire being satisfied?
3. Is labour organized in such a way that desires can be satisfied?
4. What is the effect of the group's emotional–symbolic life on desire?

The traditional, highly structured and bureaucratic organizations that most people work in are not established to satisfy the desires of most of those who work in them. Workers are there to fulfill functions of the organization, not satisfy their own desires. The frustration and destructiveness this might be expected to engender is controlled through a mixture of economic sanctions and both overt and covert repression. The answers to our four questions are likely to be negative. Self-managed groups on the other hand are usually established to satisfy the desires of their members and, subject to external constraints, to establish appropriate organization structures and organize their own labour. Frustrations to their creativity will come firstly from the environment and from lack of resources. Just as significant, however, are the effects of lifting repression and raising the expectation that desire can be satisfied. The potential of this for engendering destructive processes should not be underestimated as members are likely to express and seek gratification for all kinds of conflicting desires beyond those the group can realistically satisfy. It is likely too that people will unconsciously seek gratification for desires that relate more to their own internal conflicts and repression. In a more traditional organization these are less likely to find direct expression or to affect the work of the organization because of the built-in repressive constraints.

The problems then for self-managed groups, whether they are formally constituted cooperatives or less formal collectives of people working together, is to find ways of exploiting this greater potential for creativity while protecting themselves against the possibilities of destructive processes.

References

Bennis, W. G., Benne, K. D., and Chin. R. (eds.) (1970). *The Planning of Change*, Holt, Rinehart & Winston, New York.
Bion, W. R. (1968). *Experiences in Groups*, Tavistock Publications, London.
Bradford, L. P., Gibb, J. R., and Benne, K. D. (eds.) (1964). *T-Group Theory and Laboratory Method*, John Wiley and Sons Inc., New York.
Randall, R., Southgate, J., and Tomlinson, F. (1980). *Cooperative and Community Group Dynamics . . . or your meetings needn't be so appalling*, Barefoot Books, London.
Reich, W. (1940). *Function of the Orgasm*, Farrar, Straus and Giroux Inc, New York.
Rice, A. K. (1965). *Learning for Leadership*, Tavistock Publications, London.
Southgate, J., and Randall, R. (1980). *The Psychodynamics of Self-managed Groups*, Loughborough University Management Department Working Paper No. 51.

Small Groups and Social Interaction, Volume 2
Edited by H. H. Blumberg, A. P. Hare, V. Kent and M. Davies
© 1983 John Wiley & Sons Ltd

7.8   A Theory of Small Groups

Will Schutz

History

In 1958 the FIRO theory of interpersonal behavior was published (Schutz, 1958). The theory was presented in a quasi-scientific form, using axioms, undefined terms, and postulates. The theory asserted that there were three basic interpersonal needs: Inclusion, Control, and Affection, and that these needs were necessary and sufficient to understand all of interpersonal behavior.

Inclusion, the IN–OUT dimension, was defined as the area of human contact. Human preferences for inclusion varied from oversocial—a condition where a person feels anxious when alone—to undersocial, where a person feels anxious in the presence of other people. Control, the TOP–BOTTOM dimension, was defined as the area of power, control, and influence. People's preferences varied from autocratic—a condition where a person feels anxious when not in control—to abdicratic, where a person feels anxious when in control. Affection, the NEAR–FAR dimension, was defined as the area of intimacy with one other person. People's preferences varied from overpersonal—a condition where a person feels anxious when not dealing intimately—to underpersonal, where a person feels anxious when getting close to someone.

The theory presented several postulates:

1. *Group Development* asserted that all groups of whatever size develop by dealing, in this order, with Inclusion then Control then Affection. Group members separate from each other by going through these phases in the opposite order.

2. *Group Compatibility* presented several ways of computing the degree of ability of people to work together by considering their reciprocal role preference—a high controller, for example, is compatible with someone who

wants to be controlled—and their atmosphere preferences—people who like an atmosphere of high affection, for instance, get along well.

3. *Relational Continuity* specified that adult patterns were direct reflections of childhood relations and these relations were directly predictable using measures of Inclusion, Control, and Affection.

To measure these notions and accumulate data relevant to them, a series of FIRO scales was devised (Schutz, 1966). FIRO-B a measure of behavior, has since become a widely used instrument. The other scales are the FIRO-F (feelings), FIRO-BC (behavior for children), COPE (defense mechanisms), LIPHE (relations with parents), MATE (relations between two people), and VAL-ED (educational values).

Since 1958 many changes have occurred in the theory. The most illuminating way to describe the changes and to present the present form of the theory is to describe the author's evolution during these two decades. This will make clear the basis of the present form of the theory.

Author's evolution

If the reader will pardon the departure from academic protocol, I find it easier to write this section in the first person.

FIRO was published just as I was at the height of my academic period. I was just completing teaching and research at Harvard and moving to a similar position at the University of California at Berkeley.

Through these academic years I never felt fully comfortable. I felt phony. In my classes I assigned the second best book in the field, while I read ahead in the best book and lectured from it. I never felt that I knew anything until I became involved in groups, encounter groups. After that I did not feel phony because I was teaching what I personally had experienced. I was no longer repeating a textbook. I could now say something that I knew in a more complete, holistic, way rather than just having read about it. I became fascinated with groups, and for the next 25 years I have been leading groups in one way or another all around the world.

In 1967 I went to the Esalen Institute in Big Sur, California. Esalen was devoted to developing the Human Potential Movement. The Esalen Institute was co-founded by Michael Murphy after he went to India and spent 18 months at the Ashram of Sri Aurobindo. Michael came back very excited and wanted to create a Western Yoga, to combine the best of the East and the West.

Partly as a reaction to the overemphasis on the intellectual in education that was characteristic of the West and partly as an attempt to combine the wisdom of the East with the scientific virtues of the West, the Esalen Institute arose. Attracted by this concept and by the many interesting men who were participating: for example, Alan Watts, Aldous Huxley, Arnold Toynbee, and Bishop Pike, many people appeared at Esalen and a movement began, the Human Potential Movement as it was later to be called.

My journey crossed Esalen's journey at an early point in their growth and, through that crossing, the academic background from which I came became greatly expanded. The first contributor to this expansion was psychedelic drugs. At that time, I tried LSD and most of the known psychedelics, because that was what people were doing in those days. Psychedelics helped me to shake loose from the rigidity of my academic training.

I had studied philosophy by that time and was influenced heavily by Hans Reichenbach, who was my teacher at the university. I had associated myself strongly with his scientific wing of philosophy, logical empiricism. At the other end of the corridor in the philosophy building were those 'softheaded' people, the mystical and spiritual philosophers. We scientific philosophers 'knew' they did not know anything. They talked about people being in tune with the universe and crazy things like that.

But then I took psychedelics. All of a sudden I found *myself* vibrating with the universe and crazy things like that. I began to realize that maybe those softheads knew something, that maybe there were other ways of finding truth. The 'trips' opened me to the other ways in which people could be investigated, and motivated me to study a number of other fields. The body, for example, became very important, and so did the spiritual quest, and so did esoteric activities like reading the Tarot, throwing the I Ching, and astrology. Many things that I had eschewed as a scientist, 'knowing' that they were not worth while, all of a sudden became worthy of consideration.

I experienced many fascinating approaches to understanding human beings, both individually and in groups. Most of these approaches were totally unknown to me. They were never mentioned in all of my doctoral training, nor did I discover them in 15 subsequent years of teaching. Each of these techniques seemed to have so much to offer that I felt embarrassed that the path to knowledge that I had steadfastly and rather successfully followed was so thin and resourceless relative to what I was being exposed to.

Aside from the encounter and other interpersonal approaches the methods to which I was exposed may be classified as follows:

Body methods

Except for enjoying sports, I had rarely given any thought to the body especially as an integral part of the whole person. Nor did I understand what 'bodymind' (Schutz, 1971) referred to. Rolfing (Rolf, 1977) was my first introduction to understanding how feelings are locked in the body, how muscle tensions surround incomplete experiences, how body structure reveals personal history. The work of Wilhelm Reich (Reich, 1949; Lowen, 1976) had developed into bioenergetics, a fascinating integration of body and mind into psychotherapy.

Then other techniques such as Alexander (Barlow, 1973), Trager, and especially Feldenkrais (1973) continued to expand my conception of the human organism. Feldenkrais pointed out that we know our bodies so poorly that we only use a tiny fraction of their capacity. He then invented exercises to increase, almost magically, our capacities.

Energy methods

From the Far East came acupuncture (Veith, 1966) and approaches derived from it, which presented the conception of looking at people as distributions of energy. Human beings are seen as energy fields and may be cured by working with their energy. Interaction between people could be regarded as the overlap of energy fields. Yoga and some of the martial arts, aikido (Yamada, 1974), T'ai Chi (Huang, 1977) present methods for using the energy model with strikingly effective results.

Spiritual approaches

To my amazement, I, a scientist, found myself taking seriously many spiritual and mystical approaches to understanding human behavior. These approaches took the form of techniques such as meditation, chanting, astral projection, psychic reading, and channeling spirits. Psychosynthesis, a neglected approach devised by an Italian contemporary of Freud, Roberto Assagioli (1975), presented a theory that attempted to integrate the spiritual with the psychological. I even found myself going to India to see Bhagwan Shree Rajneesh (1976) to experience this force personally.

As I progressed through my Alice-like journey my scientific side reasserted itself. The approaches were dizzying. There must be some unifying thread that integrates them all. To my amazement and delight, as I explored what I had experienced I discovered that there was a unity. No matter where I began the exploration, through encounter groups, the body, energy, or spiritual disciplines, if I allowed myself to become deeply immersed in the journey, I always seemed to come out at about the same place. There did seem to be a set of principles toward which all approaches, more or less, converged.

These principles (presented below) provide the basis for revising and expanding the FIRO theory and for giving the theory its present form (Schutz, 1980). (New measures (Schutz, 1983b) have been devised to reflect the theoretical changes.)

The nature of individuals

Limitlessness

People are limitless. The only limitations we have are the limits of belief. It has been and is constantly being demonstrated that what we hold to be limits, simply are not. Before Roger Bannister, we believed that a man could not run a mile in less than 4 minutes. Psychics violated physical laws by bending spoons and by moving objects with their minds. Biofeedback helps people to control their 'involuntary' nervous sytem. What we take to be the laws of nature are being violated constantly. In fact, we are capable of anything.

Holism

We are whole persons. Holism means that we function as a unitary organism. Our intellectual, emotional, physical, spiritual, social, and aesthetic sides are part of a whole. Holistic Health (New Dimensions Foundation, 1980) is demonstrating how the mind causes and can alleviate disease. How we play a sport is a direct manifestation or our emotional and intellectual selves (Gallwey, 1976).

Choice

We all choose our own lives and always have. We choose our behavior, our feelings, our health, our responses, everything. We act as if we are the victims of outside sources. Then we can blame. This concept of choice totally recasts many of the common beliefs of group behavior. Group pressure, for example, does not exist unless someone chooses to feel pressure. Likewise no one can manipulate a person unless that person allows the manipulation. Many of our sacred group terms become obsolete, terms such as 'group pressure,' 'manipulation,' 'using,' 'hurting people's feelings,' and 'brainwashing.' These are all terms we use to blame others for a self-created experience.

The aim of individuals

It follows from the choice principles that each individual may choose any aim he or she wishes. We choose, here, that an individual's aim is joy (Schutz, 1967) defined as the feeling that comes from unfoldment, the realization of all that individual is capable of. Feelings of pleasure and joy arise from developing and using the capacities inherent in the human organism. Displeasure arises when these potentials are blocked and irritability or boredom accompanies the lack of use of these capacities.

The evolution of individuals

A framework for understanding how individuals evolve requires a *mechanism* through which this evolution occurs, and *content* areas dealt with in the course of evolution.

Completion

Evolution may be looked upon as a series of energy cycles. Completion of these cycles is called growth or learning or maturation. When the cycles are blocked or not completed, individuals develop illness or emotional problems or body tensions. Developing fully requires experiencing the complete energy cycle. An energy cycle begins with some type of imbalance—discomfort, anxiety, desire, wonder— something that serves to *motivate* a person to change his or her state so as to satisfy the imbalance either by reducing the discomfort or anxiety or by satisfying the desire or wonder. People then mobilize their resources to reduce the imbalance. They *prepare* themselves to do something by thinking, planning, and preparing their body for some kind of movement. Discharge comes next, expressing in *action* the behavior for which they have prepared. Action leads to a rebalance, or *feeling*, determined by how close the action came to satisfying the motivating imbalance.

Difficulties arise when the energy cycles are not completed. Blockages, that is, denial or distortion, occur at each point in the cycle and affect all levels of being: interpersonal, intrapsychic, physical.

Dimensions

There are three basic areas of human endeavor that account for more, if not all, of the behavior in which we are interested. These are the dimensions of the FIRO theory except that there have been some changes over the past few years.

The dimensions of Inclusion and Control remain as they were described above. The dimension of Affection, however, has been replaced by Openness (Schutz, 1983a). The concept of Affection contained a strong element of feeling and these three dimensions were to describe the behavior level.

Openness, the OPEN–CLOSED dimension, is defined as the area relating to self-disclosure or the willingness to reveal thoughts, feelings, and experiences to other people and to the self. People vary in their preferences from over-openness: anxiety over not revealing everything to everyone, to under-openness: anxiety about revealing anything personal to anyone, the feeling of vulnerability.

Using this framework, human evolution looks like this:

Self-inclusion. Mobilizing all parts of a person so as to function in an integrated fashion is the first stage in human functioning. This ability to perform as a whole person is called *presence.*
Self-control. Once mobilized, the individual then learns to express himself or herself *spontaneously*, that is, freely without going to excess. Having an accessible repertoire of behaviors and feelings without inappropriate restrictions is the ideal.
Self-openness. The final stage is to be open to and *aware* of oneself. This entails being willing to know all about one's being. This stage leads to the mechanism which underlies the whole evolutionary quest, truth.

Truth

The truth does, in fact, make you free. In order to function optimally, on the levels of body, self, couple, group, organization, nation—it is essential to tell the truth. Untruthfulness leads to physical ailments, loss of energy, boring or destructive relationships, stressful organizations, and international tensions. Truth is the grand simplifier. Recent experience supports the view that the untruthful life is severely limited. If one is to reach full realization, truth is essential.

Truth means whatever is. My truth means whatever is happening in my experience, including my thoughts, feelings, memories, sensation, movements. Whatever parts of my truth I choose to let myself know is my *awareness*. For social or religious or other reasons, I usually do not let myself know all of my truth. The part that is blocked is called my *unconscious*. I, therefore, create my own unconscious. It is simply all of the things that I choose not to be aware of.

I choose to tell you a certain amount of what I am aware of. To that degree, I am *honest*. Honesty is the degree to which I tell you of that which I am aware. To be truthful, I must be both aware and honest.

Summary of theoretical perspective

1. Most interpersonal issues in groups stem from not telling the truth. Truth telling reduces issues to logical puzzles which are usually much simpler issues to solve than issues imbedded with unresolved interpersonal and personal conflicts.

2. Assuming that everyone is choosing everything they are doing reverses our view of many group phenomena. If someone is being scapegoated or is generally not happy in a group situation we now seek to learn why the person is choosing to be in that situation and why the group is colluding to keep that person in the situation.

3. The unconscious is not looked upon as a mysterious or primordial entity. It is simply the parts of a person's experience that they have chosen not to know. It is therefore quite feasible to choose to know it if one chooses to.

4. The assumption that a group is limitless leads an investigator to go beyond what used to be felt as limitations. The belief that anything is possible, leads to more adventuresome experimentation.

5. The Holistic assumption leads to a stronger focus on the body as an integral part of group behavior. It leads to teaching group leaders body reading and a deeper understanding of interpreting the body, its tensions, illnesses and what they mean (Schutz, 1980). It also leads to alerting group members to these phenomena. One pertinent example is that truth is revealed through a lack of body tension while lies usually manifest through various unpleasant body feelings.

References

Assagioli, R. (1975). *Psychosynthesis*, Turnstone Books, London.
Barlow, W. (1973). *The Alexander Technique*, Gollancz, London.

Feldenkrais, M. (1973). *Awareness through Movement*, Harper, New York.

Gallwey, T. (1976). *The Inner Game of Tennis*, Random House, New York.

Huang, A. (1977). *Embrace Tiger, Return to Mountain*, Bantam, New York.

Lowen, A. (1976). *Bioenergetics*, Penguin, New York.

New Dimensions Foundation. (1980). *The New Healers: Healing the Whole Person*, and/or Press, Berkeley, CA.

Rajneesh, B. (1976). *Way of the White Cloud*, Rajneesh Foundation, Poona, India.

Reich, W. (1949). *Character Analysis*, Orgone Press, New York.

Rolf, I. (1977). *Rolfing: The Integration of Human Structures*, Rolf Institute, Boulder, Colo.

Schutz, W. (1958). *FIRO: A Three-Dimensional Theory of Interpersonal Behavior*, Holt Rinehart, New York. Reprinted as *The Interpersonal Underworld*, Science and Behavior Books, Palo Alto, Calif.

Schutz, W. (1966). *The FIRO Awareness Scale*, Consulting Psychologists Press, Palo Alto, Calif.

Schutz, W. (1967). *Joy*, Grove, New York.

Schutz (1971). *Here Comes Everybody: Bodymind and Encounter Culture*, Harper and Row, New York; now published by Irvington, New York, 1983.

Schutz, W. (1980). *Profound Simplicity*, Bantam, New York; also Turnstone Books, London.

Schutz, W. (1983a). *The Human Element*, Tenspeed Press, Berkeley, Calif.

Schutz, W. (1983b). *The Schutz Measures: An Integrated System for Assessing Elements of Awareness*, Consulting Psychologists Press, Palo Alto, Calif.

Veith, I. (trans.) (1966). *The Yellow Emperor's Classic of Internal Medicine*, University of California Press, Berkeley, Calif.

Yamada, Y. (1974). *Aikido*, Wehman, Cedar Knolls, New Jersey.

Small Groups and Social Interaction, Volume 2
Edited by H. H. Blumberg, A. P. Hare, V. Kent and M. Davies
Published by John Wiley & Sons Ltd 1983

7.9 Freud, Piaget, and Democratic Leadership*

Roger Holmes   *London School of Economics and Political Science*

In an earlier paper (Holmes, 1976, Ch. 1) it was suggested that the ambivalence that Freud maintained was felt to all leaders, necessitated for its resolution the assumption of a 'third force' or 'Authority'—an Authority that endowed a leader with a right to his position. It was further argued that the requirements of an adequate Authority would make a class society based on birth, rather than a democratic society based on ability, ultimately more probable. These assumptions were not fully spelled out. It now remains to show in greater detail how an 'irrationally' based leadership can become secure from resentment. In doing so I shall invoke an idea—that of the attitude of the leader to his position—which has so far been almost wholly neglected in the literature.

'Attitude to the position' breaks down into two component attitudes—attitudes to the position itself and attitudes to one's right to occupy that position. The former is seen, for instance, when Elliott Jaques (1956) argues the need for joint consultation on the grounds that the managers felt that just 'as a manager' they did not have, in a democracy, the 'right' to implement a policy that had not been sanctioned by the work force at large. 'Being a manager' was not enough in itself, and it was on these grounds that he argued the necessity of joint consultation as a legitimizing agency.

The more impressive the position one occupies, the greater the enhancement. Elliott Jaques's managers did not think highly enough of 'being managers'. A king who genuinely believes in his divine right is in a totally different position psychologically from one who does not; here, as in loyalty to the institutions, or for that matter belief in one's God, the bigger the distance between the individual and the object of his reverence, the greater the benefit.

*Abridged from Holmes (1976, Ch. 2), by permission of the author and the publisher.

The second component of 'attitude to position' is that individual's feeling of 'right' to occupy that position. Such a 'right' is nearly always granted on the ground of fulfilling certain requirements—a mediaeval king on grounds of primogeniture, a priest on grounds of ordination, which, in turn is based on having met certain attitudinal and other demands. Those who feel they have the 'right' to their position have a clear start over those who feel they are trespassing. Indeed, for the latter an attitude of reverence for the position will detract from their effectiveness. The trouble with Macbeth, for instance, was that he thought too highly of kingship and his trespass was all the greater in consequence.

The leader in the most favourable position, then, is the one who both reveres his position and believes in this right to his incumbency—the Sergeant Major who believes in the 'dignity of his rank' and who feels that appointment through the 'due' processes is itself enough to bestow the right—for frequently 'right' devolves from some cherished source. The leader in the least favourable position is the man who reveres his rank but who feels he has not got the 'right' to occupy it. Somewhere in the middle must come those who have no strong feelings about the position they occupy.

Of course attitude to position is only one of three desiderata—the leader must also have the required ability and personality characteristics. If a mediaeval king such as Edward II was unable to keep order he was deposed even if his murder had to be camouflaged by a peculiarly atrocious crime. Indeed, it is possible that, as the demands on the leader become more arduous, so will the right 'abilities' and 'personality characteristics' become more important. In an emergency, birth is no substitute for ability; the army is more democratic in wartime and the warrior tribe will need a warrior at its head.

All this is straightforward—but what is the implication? If abilities become more important in a leader when abilities are needed, abilities will also become less important when abilities are not needed. The fewer the abilities needed the more must some belief in a more or less arbitrary 'right' supervene. This 'right' could be democratically or undemocratically based, but it is, of course, my contention that the latter is the more likely. Indeed, the whole thesis might be condensed into the assertion that the fewer the abilities needed to be a leader, the more exclusive a possession of a privileged class will it become. Where anyone could be a leader, leadership will be at its most irrational and most exclusive. This is, after all, no more than is summed up in this country by the position of the monarchy. For if we accept what, in the first paper, I called the 'building blocks of caste'—that we only expect our due, that behaviour and aspiration can be dependent variables, that our idea of due can itself be based on the social attributes of sex, age, birth, etc., then everything will depend on this last point, on whether the social attributes will indeed become the first basis of reward.

Once this is established, all will follow; once birth is seen as the criterion of worth, birth will perpetuate itself, since those who are controlled will identify with a force that allows them to keep their rivals (those 'as good as they are') under control.

It seems plausible to assume that such a class society would perpetuate itself, but why should it develop in the first place? Why should the social mobility of our own times congeal into the stagnancy of a system where merit is assessed on social attributes? In the first paper I assumed, of course, that change will cease to lead to yet further change. Given this flat assumption, I am left with the conclusion that less and less ability will be needed to act as a leader, and that more and more leader (and indeed follower) behaviour will become ritualized, stylized, 'good in itself'—a form of ceremony, the product, and the cause of continuity.

The more irrational and the more arbitrary, the more 'intrinsic', does the basis of leadership become (in that, for instance, it is based solely on birth) and the more irrational and the more arbitrary does the content of leadership become (in that it largely consists in the quasi-ceremonial implementation of preconceived actions), the more will leader effectiveness—and acceptability—become dependent on the past of the leader and follower alike—on earlier training and upbringing.

If the work of a leader in a static society becomes less and less exacting, by the same token it becomes more and more constricting. As ritual supervenes, as innumerable sequences of action become cut off from their extrinsic, instrumental purposes and enshrined in the tradition of the society, so will the leader find himself as much a slave to the values that are the source of his legitimacy as anyone else. In one sense, of course, the leader will have more 'power' than his subordinates but in another sense he will not. Has the actor who plays Hamlet more freedom than the actor who plays Fortinbras? Has the Sergeant Major more freedom—whether attitudinal or behavioural—than the recruit?

In my first paper the leader–follower relationship was schematically represented as shown in Figure 1.

The leader directs the follower and is in turn directed by the 'Authority', an 'Authority' that owes its legitimacy to the belief of both leader and follower. With the growth of ritual—or of any standardized behaviour—we arrive at something approaching Figure 2.

Here the 'Authority' directly affects the follower, as well as coming through the leader. The follower also knows what he is supposed to do, and the base of the triangle—the influence of the leader on the follower—becomes redundant.

And this, in Freudian terms, is as it should be—the 'Authority' must rule the ruler and the ruled. A leader can never be accepted who is not himself subordinate.

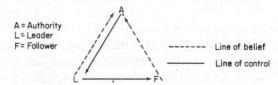

A = Authority
L = Leader
F = Follower

------- Line of belief
———— Line of control

Figure 1   The leader–follower relationship

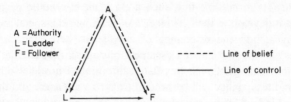

Figure 2   The leader–follower relationship: the development of ritual

This revenge of the subordinate is subtle and difficult to escape. It may be the leader, who often will feel the need to break free; he will be both more constricted and yet less in need of emotional support. He will have greater leisure and better opportunities for education and discussion. No wonder he will be the first to treat the values of his society with detachment and even cynicism. It would not be too surprising if he reacted against the call of omnipresent duty and used his more advantageous position in the network of responsibilities, to express his personal cupidity, his private resentments and aggressions, his unauthorized (we might say, id-iosyncratic) assertions and cruelties.

This behaviour on the part of the leader would give the ruled a legitimate complaint—a complaint that the traditional values were not heeded by their 'betters'. This kind of complaint can be peculiarly difficult to ignore and even more difficult to refute. The trouble with Luther, from the Pope's point of view, was that he took Christianity too seriously—and continued to do so despite secular blandishments. And was not Luther quite right? After all, the purpose of all moral behaviour is control—and being moral and conformist is something anyone can be.

All this makes good sense in Freudian terms. The dilemma of social living, as stated in my first paper, was the problem of how to succeed without allowing others to succeed as well in one's wake. The son tries to usurp the father's place without the retaliation of the father, or (and this is more to the point here) from the other sons. Equally, the son tries to possess the mother without incurring his father's wrath and his brothers' competition.

The solution to this dilemma lay in subordinating oneself to a code (or 'Authority') that was equally binding on the self and others. 'Since I cannot succeed myself, no one shall be allowed to succeed as well.' At one blow one has both expiated one's own guilt and gained control: for, having subordinated oneself to the current morality, one is then free to express one's aggression blamelessly, self-righteously—and anonymously. The 'law', 'God', 'public opinion', 'necessity'—or in whatever guise the 'Authority' may be found—can be evoked instead.

Whether or not the result will necessarily be a class society based on birth as argued here, is, of course, open to doubt. What is less in doubt, I think, is that, unless the process is arrested by (a) conflict or (b) the manifestly greater usefulness of one course of action over another (i.e. those factors that encourage means–end behaviour) more and more behaviour will become ritualized and 'morally encrusted' and 'leadership' will become absorbed into the system—a system that allows the complete control of everyone by all.

It will be a system in which the leadership will be used by the followers even more than the followers will be dominated by the leader. The leader will both provide that enhancement to the follower that only social distance can give and will act as a weighty weapon in the battle that really rages—the pre-occupation of each with the other's behaviour. Our leaders, like our gods, are created to enhance (the self) and to control (others).

Hence the enormous appeal of ritual to the subordinate. 'Ritual' is activity that is valued for its own sake—activity that is dominated by an 'Authority' and creates its own aura of veneration. We create an object of veneration that we may impress—and control. The leader becomes entrammelled in the very source of his legitimacy, he becomes emasculated by the basis of his stature. The creation of ritual, too, is a move in that warfare of power that must express itself 'legitimately'. To our democratic minds the existence of a parasitic elite that does nothing to 'deserve' its position is an anathema. Looked at from another point of view, they are the docile pawns of their followers' beliefs.

With my argument so clearly demonstrated, it seems sad to admit that it hardly ever applies; docile proletariats and ritualistic, or, for that matter, well-behaved leaders are not all that much in evidence. Why is this so? There are two reasons for this, of which only the second will be discussed.

The first reason is simply that the leadership may be strong enough to ignore the good will of those it controls. So far I have only been concerned with consent—the conditions under which a follower will accept his superiors as legitimate. If a leader is strong enough he can happily remain indifferent to such feelings, maintaining his position by a judicious use of force and patronage. This type of situation is perhaps not quite as important as might be expected, at least if the Freudian thesis is accepted, for if jealousy is the first social emotion, and the prime pre-occupation of one and all is that others 'as good as them' are equally treated, there will be a constant drift from rule by force to rule by consent. It might be called a 'drift to legitimacy'.

The second reason why my argument may be irrelevant is very different, and much more important. It is, of course, that the flat plateau of technical stagnation has not been (and will not be) reached and that the rule of the leader, far from being reduced to a recital of ceremonial legitimations, will involve exceptional abilities and exceptional personality characteristics. It is possible that new situations will continually have to be met; new decisions will have to be made without the crutch of precedent, but the resting instead on the intellectual and nervous resources of the individual.

It is with the problem of leadership under these conditions that this section will be largely concerned. How, when this task is at its most arduous, can a leader justify his position? For, by a cruel paradox, he cannot rely solely on the social attributes of what he is if the result of his actions leave clearly and grossly much to be admired. It is only those who have no demands made upon them who have no need to justify themselves.

We have come back to the problem of 'extrinsic' and 'intrinsic' grounds for holding beliefs which has been discussed. The leader who has to make decisions is measured by results, by his effectiveness in a situation. It is the entry of the situation as a third force that completely alters the relationship of the leader to his followers. For the situation challenges the leader; it allows him to be shown up to the follower. The 'situation' may well become so challenging that it imposes severe demands upon him. To the extent that the leader becomes exposed to the sanction of 'failure', so does his entire relationship to his follower undergo a change.

For, if a leader fails, he reveals his qualitative similarity to other lesser human beings. The whole force of the leader resides in that in some way he is seen as larger than life. This is why he is accorded 'veneration' and 'respect'. This is welcomed by the follower for neither enhancement nor control can come from those that are no better than we are. If he fail, even the most desirable of social attributes may not save him. Indeed, if he is a 'gentleman' this need not prevent his incurring the odium of failure—on the contrary, 'being a gentleman' itself may become suspect. The capital of social attribute, rather than helping him, may itself be threatened. But the situation may be worse than this. The leader may not be a gentleman. In taxing times more leaders are promoted on merit than in calmer times, leaders tend to be without the prop of desirable social attributes at the time they need them most. What then can this leader do? How can he justify his position to those who were erstwhile as 'good as him'? The position of this leader is peculiarly difficult; not only does he very frequently not have the customary social attributes, not only must he use his abilities, but also, he may very well call from his subordinates activities without justification or legitimation in precedent. This does not apply, or not nearly to the same extent, to other kinds of leaders. Thus, a traditional leader, who is not called upon to meet a new situation, may very well be acceptable to the followers in that all that is asked of them is that they engage in prelegitimated acts. This the followers will welcome because it allows them to control the leader. But this does not apply to the leader in times of change; he may not only lack the right social attributes, but he may be forced to demand of his men actions that have not previously been accepted as 'right'.

Since a leader in this position cannot invoke the 'Authority' of precedent, or ritual or of custom, he is driven to invoke a new 'Authority'—an 'Authority' that does not owe its persuasiveness to the legitimacy inherent in sheer repetition. And what can this 'Authority' be? The leader must confront the root cause of his difficulties and invoke these same difficulties as a new and radically different form of legitimation—the leader must invoke the situation itself. This, surely, is the psychological justification for what is known as democratic leadership. The leader must say, 'Look, it is not I that ask this of you, but the situation that demands it.' In a sense the leader must never ask for obedience to himself alone—even the 'traditional leader' as we have seen, is not free, and must say that the 'law' or that 'custom' demands it. This is true enough, but there is still a considerable difference between the position of the leader who is a 'traditional leader', and the 'leader in times of change'. At least the 'traditional leader' is able to fuse into the custom he embodies, he can allow the 'Authority' to 'emanate' from him, thus confounding his personal aura with the aura he 'serves'. But the 'Authority' of the 'leader in times of change' has a different effect. To the extent that the situation is a reality that demands attention, so is the leader not separate from his followers like the King at the ritual of the coronation is separated from his subjects; he is, on the contrary, placed on the same level.

The whole force of the 'objective situation' lies in that it unites the leader and his followers. He must show his qualitative similarity, in that he demonstrates that he too is subject to harsh empirical laws—laws that, unlike custom, will favour no man. 'We are in this together; I, too, must work and suffer'—the similarity of the leader to his followers, not his difference, is stressed.

Whence, then, the leader's 'qualitative difference'? This too, as I have argued throughout, is necessary. He must, alas, earn this status, through his competence and through the help he can give his subordinates. In that his subordinates may very well need help, they may be the more open to gratitude, but the leader must earn it none the less. In particular he must help his subordinate against the outside forces that hinder and challenges his 'group', even if those 'forces' be the leader's own superiors.

It is not surprising, then, that the leader who doubts the adequacy of his abilities will attempt a retreat into the inscrutable; for if no reasons are given, the rightness of his actions cannot be gainsaid. Another way of concealing incompetence is to attempt to concentrate decision making into his own hands, thus again breaking the 'contract' with his critical and reluctant subordinates. For, by a final twist of the knife, the 'democratic leader' is not only expected to give reasons and show his dependence on the situation, he is also expected to delegate. Where the 'situation' rules as the legitimizing agency, it legitimizes one and all: it is the man who knows who should be consulted, the man who has special skills who must be trusted.

All this can arguably be inferred from Freud's views on groups, but it is none the less gratifying to find a psychologist with a completely different orientation substantially agreeing with this distinction between 'Authority based on precedent' and 'Authority based on the situation'. The psychologist is Jean Piaget; in my opinion the only figure in psychology of comparable stature to Freud. Piaget is more concerned with the development of the abilities than with the emotions, but in one book, *The Moral Judgment of the Child* (Piaget, 1960), he deals with the emotional growth of young children. In this book he argues that the transfer from the acceptance of an 'Authority' based on tradition to the acceptance of an 'Authority' based on situational factors is not just something that happens on a social scale, it is also something that occurs in the life of every individual.

The child's earliest morality is the 'morality of constraint'. The child accepts his ideas of right and wrong from the parent—a parent who is seen as omniscient and above circumstance. The environment in which the parent operates being outside the child's comprehension, the child is free to see the parent as an unmoved mover. The parent is indeed seen in some way as dominating and controlling the entire world—and as a result a two-part rather than a three-part relationship supervenes: the child–parent, not the 'child–parent–environment'. Since there is no 'environment' to act as a yardstick, the parent's pronouncements—whether on matters of value or on matters of fact—are judged by their source rather than their content.

From about the age of five onwards, the child begins to interact—or 'co-operate'—with equals. Dealing with equals is different in two important ways from dealing with parents or superiors. In the first place, there is no barrier of social distance, and secondly, since they share the same environment, the source of others' opinions and beliefs is understood: the fellow child is seen as a dependent variable. The position of the other is understood, because the forces acting upon him are understood. This introduction of the environment as the third force quite changes the relationship: it allows the child to assess the content of his fellow's communications, and also to identify with him on the basis of a perceived common lot. This 'taking the role of the other' is not only necessary for the development of intelligence (in that intellectual operations are based on the ability to see the same data from more than one point of view), but also allows the emergence of a new morality—the morality of 'good' rather than the morality of 'duty'. The morality of 'good' is based on an awareness of the meaning of the situation to another, on an appreciation of both the person and his circumstances. The morality of 'duty' is based on the acceptance of an external fiat, as binding as it is inflexible and arbitrary.

The similarity with the two kinds of leadership discussed in this paper should be immediately apparent. What should be equally apparent is why so many leaders prefer to replace the parent than to replace the colleague. How nice to be believed and obeyed for what one is, and not to have to give reasons! (Even if one has to be totally imprisoned within one's own myth as a consequence.) What a comedown it is for a leader to shed his pretensions to ontological superiority and allow himself to be seen as a fellow human whose powers are not qualitatively different from others!

A 'mature' individual, then, prefers an egalitarian leader; it is the adult who is still fixated at an early stage of emotional development who prefers his oracle intact. But how 'mature' are we? Piaget contends that this development from 'constraint' to 'co-operation' will not take place when the child (a) is not exposed to contrary information and (b) remains in awe of the source of truth. 'Co-operation' will only grow where there is a clash of opinions; if we are insulated from contrary currents, it will not occur to us to change our views.

> There can be no doubt that this phenomenon is peculiar to our civilization . . . In our societies the child escapes from the family circle and comes in contact with an ever-increasing number of social circles which widen his mental outlook. Whereas in so-called primitive communities, adolescence is the age of initiation, therefore of the strongest moral constraint, and the individual, as he grows older, becomes more and more dependent. [Piaget, 1960, p. 99.]

Second, the child must escape the awesome source. Boys can discuss the rules of marbles 'intelligently' only when there are no older boys who play marbles. We will believe unless our gods withdraw.

> And if, at a given moment, co-operation takes the place of constraint, or autonomy that of conformity, it is because the child, as he grows older, becomes progressively free from adult supervision. This came out very clearly in the game of marbles. Children of 11 to 13 have no others above them in this game since it is one that is played only in the lower school. [Piaget, 1960, pp. 98–99.]

But will our gods withdraw? Piaget contrasts our western societies, with their complex cross-currents of emotional belief and factual orientations, with the simpler, homogeneous savage societies where all believe the same truths and subscribe to the same code. It is competition and the clash of interests that has characterized our own society and led to such decay of the 'morality of constraint' as there has been. But this development could equally well be reversed, if, for any reason, conflict or competition ceased to be a live force and wider areas of social life become entrammelled with precedent and agreement.

Thus with Piaget, directly, and with Freud, by inference, a society structured by social distance is seen as the 'natural society': the state to which society will return unless there are forces that constantly reassert equality and doubt. Whether or not the social distance be based on birth rather than merit, lot or conviction is, of course, another matter. In the 'first assumption' given here I have assumed that it will be. This is perhaps not so important. What may be more important for this argument is not the origin of any ruling caste there may be, but how secure and unchallenged it can manage to become and how 'socially distant' it remains. The importance of the leader remaining secure and retaining at least some 'social distance', even in the egalitarian society of today, will be the last point taken up and will, it is hoped, form a fitting coda.

Neither of the two descriptions of leadership given so far fits the actual kind of leader who appears to be appreciated in western industry today. What a worker wants from a 'good boss' has been summarized (see Viteles, 1954, Chs. 8 and 17, and see Kahn and Katz, 1960) and fits neither the picture of the remote socially distant parent nor that of the egalitarian colleague. The crude fact would seem to be that many subordinates, when it comes to their leaders, want to have their cake and eat it. They want someone who is secure enough and distant enough to act as a reasonable source of psychological support, to be strong enough so that he remains above the fray which he must adjudicate, and yet, at the same time, they want someone who is 'democratic', who consults and gives reasons.

But he need not always consult or delegate—only if the subject matter is new (as is evidence by the 'resistance to change' studies) (Viteles, 1954, Ch. 9) or is within the abilities of the subordinate. If the topic is too difficult for the subordinate, delegation is, not surprisingly, unwelcomed, and if the topic (or something like it) has been met before, the subordinate may very well be willing to grant his leader his trust. The leader may gain a 'zone of indifference' in Barnard's term (Barnard, 1938) and so will be free to take his onerous decisions in solitude. The subordinate, in other words, wants it both ways. He wants someone to take the difficult decisions and to leave him a voice in the easier ones; he wants someone who is strong enough to be an effective protector and judge while remaining approachable enough to understand his point of view. The leader must be both parent and servant.

Who is most likely to fill this exacting role? Who will be grand enough to enhance and control while yet remaining human enough to consult and to understand? Who will value his subordinates and yet not be dependent upon them? It is perhaps the last and cruellest paradox of the entire discussion that it is arguably the 'non-democratic' leader who is most likely to be 'democratic' in his behaviour. This is possible because the word 'democratic' has two meanings—meanings which seem directly antithetical to one another. On the one hand, a 'democratic' leader can be one who has been promoted on merit, and who does not owe his position to privilege; on the other, a 'democratic' leader can be an approachable leader, a leader who accepts the need for his instructions to be understood, a leader who asks for contributions and gives reasons for praise and blame. One leader is democratic by derivation, the other is democratic by behaviour. The assumption being made here is that, provided he is sufficiently competent, the leader who is undemocratic in the first sense will be the more democratic in the second sense—the man of privilege will be the man of the people.

'The man of privilege' may well be superior to the 'man of the people' on three counts. In the first place he will be in a better position to support his own subordinates, for the purely fortuitous reason that his own superiors will be more likely to take him seriously than they would someone who is not 'one of them' (Pelz, 1951, 1952). Second, he may be the more ready to delegate and consult. Since he cannot be dispossessed by his subordinates, he will have nothing to fear from them. Rather than worry unduly about being 'shown up' by their competence, he will welcome their contributions. He can afford to co-operate since there is no need to compete.

Finally and crucially, such a leader, particularly if his leadership has been foreseen and the right steps have been taken, may well accept his own right to lead. He is less likely to be trammelled by doubts over the legality of his position, and he will therefore attain that independence from his subordinates that all who occasionally have to take unpopular decisions must have. As a result he will be free to implement dispassionately what is after all the source of his subordinates' consent—the law, the 'Authority'.

And what is the lot of the 'democratically elected' leader, the leader who has no edge of intrinsic social superiority over his followers? Attempting to deal with subordinates who want both a protector and a servant, dominated by a 'situational authority' that may very well reveal the weaknesses of the only qualities on which he can base his claim to a higher status, the leader may well become little more than the hardest working and the most harassed member present. Some may attempt a retreat into dignity, leaving themselves open to the danger of the industrious subordinate who, like a latter-day mayor of the palace, may gain real power. Others may abandon the sacrifice necessary to gain the consent of their followers and attempt to manipulate them by an appeal to the wholly extrinsic incentives of money and fear.

And what is the result of this 'extrinsic manipulation'? If it fails, the followers will unite against their leaders, impose, by restricting output, their own local norms and evolve their own 'unofficial' leaders. In brief, they will attain their own 'Authority'. The 'official leadership' (namely management) will now be outside the moral orbit of the followers, their status will be that of an enemy in wartime—the enemy that it is meritorious to attack. The followers, with a scapegoat to hand on which to blame each other's shortcomings, may at last attain that harmony of group life and lack of social distance between leader and follower we are so often assured is the basis of mental health in industry. And if it succeed? Success is particularly likely where, by instilling strong competition, the followers are pitted one against the other. Where the rewards and penalties are high, each follower threatens the other, and the leader can withdraw, allowing his subordinates to pace one another.

It is not within the purview of this paper to discuss the advantages or disadvantages (from the leader's point of view) of encouraging such competition in subordinates, but, what can be said (and what forms an amusing conclusion to the whole discussion) is that rather than leading to democratic, egalitarian or 'spontaneous' behaviour, in some ways it resembles in its effects the very worst forms of an unduly rigid class structure.

For what happens? Wispé and Lloyd (1955) have described the effects of such competition in the relations between life insurance salesmen. Here all are 'equal' and yet all are a possible help or hindrance to the other. As a result, beneath the friendliness, a formality and a rigidity of behaviour is found that serves to keep the salesmen distant from one another rather more effectively than would be a barrier of rank. There was a desire for formalized structured relationships, for only then could they allay the 'permeating anxiety which results from the intense competition through which the agents must live and their inability to meet it efficaciously'. The authors continue, 'the desire for structured personal interaction is thus a defence mechanism which attempts to control the behaviour of these individuals in the system who have the authority to initiate negative sanctions'.

Put in another way, the salesmen do not form a 'group', they do not identify with one another because they cannot control one another. They cannot control one another because the 'natural' source of control, namely the leader, has abdicated his responsibilities. In playing off one against the other, the leader loses all claim to the loyalty of his followers, he becomes one more obstacle to be manipulated and deceived. Under reasonable conditions the followers will retaliate in kind, forming their own group and their own authority, but if their cupidity or their fear is played upon too insistently to make this possible, they may very well end up by hating one another with the peculiar hatred we have for competitors who remind us of our own weakness.

From now on, each forms his own society and each is forced to carry the burden of being his own leader. Each is his own tiny city state, at war with one and all. For where there are no superiors there are no equals. And that is no more than Freud said in the beginning.

References

Barnard, Chester I. (1938). *The Functions of the Executive*, Harvard University Press, Cambridge, Mass.

Holmes, R. (1976). *Legitimacy and the Politics of the Knowable*, Routledge & Kegan Paul, London.

Jaques, Elliott. (1956). *The Changing Culture of a Factory*, Tavistock, London.

Kahn, R. L., and Katz, D. (1960). 'Leadership practices in relation to productivity and morale,' in D. Cartwright and A. Zander (eds.), *Group Dynamics: Research and Theory*, pp. 554–570, Row, Peterson, Evanston, Ill.

Pelz, D. C. (1951). 'Leadership within a hierarchical organization,' *Journal of Social Issues*, **7** (3), 49–55.

Pelz, D. C. (1952). 'Influence: a key to effective leadership in the first-line supervisor,' *Personnel*, **51**, 57–60.

Piaget, J. (1960). *The Moral Judgment of the Child*, Routledge & Kegan Paul, London.

Viteles, Morris S. (1954). *Motivation and Morale*, Staples Press, London.

Wispé, L. G., and Lloyd, K. E. (1955). 'Some situational and psychological determinants of the desire for structured inter-personal relations,' *Journal of Abnormal and Social Psychology*, **51**, 57–60.

Small Groups and Social Interaction, Volume 2
Edited by H. H. Blumberg, A. P. Hare, V. Kent and M. Davies
Published by John Wiley & Sons Ltd 1983

7.10 SYMLOG: A Practical Approach to the Study of Groups*

Robert F. Bales *Harvard University*

The term SYMLOG ... is an acronym for something hard to describe: 'A *SY*stem for the *M*ultiple *L*evel *O*bservation of *G*roups.' It is not easy to describe SYMLOG simply, because it is in fact something new in the world. It is easier to describe what it is for. It is a set of methods for the study of groups—groups of many kinds, but basically small natural groups, such as families, teams, or classroom groups, where the personalities of the specific persons involved and their relationships with each other are the focus of interest.

SYMLOG is a 'system' for the study of groups in the sense that it consists of a number of different parts, integrated to serve the purpose of making a particular group easier to understand and work with. Although it is a large and complex system in its entirety, it has the great virtue of being very flexible in its application and can be made very simple. One may use only a small part of it for a given study and still have the advantages of being able to relate the findings to a working body of theory and methods that have been used in other similar studies.

The SYMLOG System is designed so that in its most compact reduction it can be applied by a single person in the study of a single group in any setting, without the use of any special apparatus. This may be done through the use of what is called the SYMLOG Adjective Rating Form (see Table 1), which may be used to help recall and describe, retrospectively, the characteristic behavior of any group of individuals one has seen in interaction with each other. The ratings may easily

---

* Reprinted with permission of Macmillan Publishing Co., Inc. from *SYMLOG: A System for the Multiple Level Observation of Groups* by Robert F. Bales, Stephen P. Cohen, and S. A. Williamson. Copyright © 1979 by The Free Press, a Division of Macmillan Publishing Co., Inc. Adapted from pp. 3, 11–17, 21–24, 54, 164–175.

Table 1　The SYMLOG Adjective Rating Form

Your Name _____　Group _____

Name of person described _____　Circle the best choice for each item:

		(0)	(1)	(2)	(3)	(4)
U	active, dominant, talks a lot	never	rarely	sometimes	often	always
UP	extroverted, outgoing, positive	never	rarely	sometimes	often	always
UPF	a purposeful democratic task leader	never	rarely	sometimes	often	always
UF	an assertive business-like manager	never	rarely	sometimes	often	always
UNF	authoritarian, controlling, disapproving	never	rarely	sometimes	often	always
UN	domineering, tough-minded, powerful	never	rarely	sometimes	often	always
UNB	provocative, egocentric, shows off	never	rarely	sometimes	often	always
UB	jokes around, expressive, dramatic	never	rarely	sometimes	often	always
UPB	entertaining, sociable, smiling, warm	never	rarely	sometimes	often	always
P	friendly, equalitarian	never	rarely	sometimes	often	always
PF	works cooperatively with others	never	rarely	sometimes	often	always
F	analytical, task-oriented, problem-solving	never	rarely	sometimes	often	always
NF	legalistic, has to be right	never	rarely	sometimes	often	always
N	unfriendly, negativistic	never	rarely	sometimes	often	always
NB	irritable, cynical, won't cooperate	never	rarely	sometimes	often	always
B	shows feelings and emotions	never	rarely	sometimes	often	always
PB	affectionate, likeable, fun to be with	never	rarely	sometimes	often	always
DP	looks up to others, appreciative, trustful	never	rarely	sometimes	often	always
DPF	gentle, willing to accept responsibility	never	rarely	sometimes	often	always
DF	obedient, works submissively	never	rarely	sometimes	often	always
DNF	self-punishing, works too hard	never	rarely	sometimes	often	always
DN	depressed, sad, resentful, rejecting	never	rarely	sometimes	often	always
DNB	alienated, quits, withdraws	never	rarely	sometimes	often	always
DB	afraid to try, doubts own ability	never	rarely	sometimes	often	always
DPB	quietly happy just to be with others	never	rarely	sometimes	often	always
D	passive, introverted, says little	never	rarely	sometimes	often	always

be tabulated and analyzed without the benefit of any complicated mathematics or statistics—and without any computer programs. This means that a practicing group therapist, a classroom teacher, an administrator, or in fact any interested group member, a parent or other member of a family for example, can use the basic methods and theory of the SYMLOG System.

Theoretical background

Although the connections cannot be analyzed in detail, some of the more closely related theories can at least be mentioned. The system is an immediate outgrowth of the senior author's earlier work. *Personality and Interpersonal Behavior* (Bales, 1970), which in turn is a continuation of the effort begun in the observation method titled *Interaction Process Analysis* (Bales, 1950). Those works and the present one contain elements from a considerable number of theories in psychology, sociology, and related fields.

The assumptions made in the present work about motivation, the general nature of personality, the powers of the ego, and the importance of the various mechanisms of ego defense, as well as many of the concepts of the nature of interpretation and its place in therapy come from psychoanalytic theory (S. Freud, 1900, 1933; A. Freud, 1936).

The concepts of the nature of the individual perceptual evaluative field have their source partly in gestalt psychology, as represented in both Lewinian field theory and the group dynamics school (Lewin, 1951; Cartwright and Zander, 1968). The theory of polarization and unification is closely related to various theories of social cognition: balance theory (Newcomb, 1953; Heider, 1958), congruity theory (Osgood and Tannenbaum, 1955), dissonance theory (Festinger, 1957), consistency theory (Abelson *et al.*, 1968), and attribution theory (Kelley, 1971), although the relationships to these various cognitively oriented theories are complex and far from adequately worked out.

On the more sociological side the present theory has much in common with symbolic interaction theory (Mead, 1934; Blumer, 1969; Goffman, 1959) in the emphasis given to the importance of the self-image and the individual definition of the situation, and in the stress on the communication of 'meaning' in the manner and content of social interaction, rather than on the physical substrate of behavior.

Small group interaction theory as it has grown out of the laboratory tradition has been important in providing many of the concepts of role differentiation, leadership, and small group structure in other respects, as well as groundwork in the actual observation and classification of social interaction (Hare, Borgatta, and Bales, 1965; Hare, 1976; Shaw, 1971).

Social exchange theory (Thibaut and Kelley, 1959; Homans, 1961; Blau, 1964, 1968) is represented at the small group level in the concepts that the behavior and content presented to each other by the participants in interaction constitute rewards and punishments or have both benefits and cost, which the participants over time attempt to adjust into a mutually rewarding exchange, though the theory does not assume that the efforts will reach a stable equilibrium or that a stable state, if found, will be one of unification rather than one of polarization or dissolution of the group. The *relativistic* nature of the costs and benefits individuals perceive by comparing their lot with that of others in the same social interaction field, is also assumed, as emphasized in reference group theory (Merton and Kitt, 1950) and in social evaluation theory (Pettigrew, 1967).

In general sociology there is a theoretical conflict as to how much emphasis should be given to the influence of common values and norms of participants in a social interaction field and how much to the conflicts of interest between the various participants and to differences in their relative power. This problem, often represented as a conflict between adherence to structural–functional theory (Parsons, 1951) and adherence to conflict theory (Dahrendorf, 1959), receives a kind of answer, perhaps, in the present approach, where both unification and polarization are recognized, but the relative preponderance of the two is determined empirically and may be different for each social interaction field.

The elements of the SYMLOG System, both in theory and methods, from the general fields of personality study, clinical psychology, and individual and group psychotherapy, as well as the fields of group training, organization development, social group work, and family therapy, are too numerous even for specific mention. Perhaps it will be useful to recognize, however, that one of these fields, the field of family therapy, is only beginning to make its impact felt on existing theory and methods in psychology and sociology. In the opinion of the present author, the work of family therapy is full of important potentials. The works of Bowen (1971) and Minuchin (1974) have been of particular interest to the present author, especially with regard to the concepts of 'triangles' of interpersonal relationships within families and how they may be dealt with, which are closely related to the concepts of polarization and unification in the present work, and the various ways in which polarizations may be neutralized.

Systematic multiple level field theory (the name offered for the basic theory of the SYMLOG System) is not an eclectic assembly of elements from these many sources, however, but a newly developed and integrated whole based on new methods of observation and expressed in a new language and set of concepts. It was not in fact developed by a careful fitting together of deductions from these various sources but grew inductively from a long continued effort to understand social interaction from observation, to construct measuring instruments for recording and analyzing the dynamics of small groups and for feedback of useful information to participants. It has been a 'grounded theory' (see Glaser and Strauss, 1967) from the first. The theory of the SYMLOG System can be understood and used appropriately without knowledge of its many connections with other theories. Potential users of the methods . . . need not be intimidated by the fact that they know little, perhaps, of the long list of theories and fields mentioned.

The theory of SYMLOG gives emphasis equally to the dynamics of groups and to the dynamics of individual personalities of group members. It gives an articulate way to get back and forth from a consideration of each individual personality to a consideration of the dynamic field properties of the total group-and-situation constellation.

Getting back and forth from a view of each individual separately to a view of the inclusive group constellation of individuals is made possible in the present theory by the fact that, according to the theory, the *same dimensional system* (see Figure 1) is appropriate for both levels. The theory provides the means for the observation and measurement, the conceptualization and representation, of *each individual perceptual field*, as well as the *inclusive social interaction field* (see Figure 2) constituted by the behavior and interaction of the individuals. The same kind of dimensional representation, a *Field Diagram*, is used for both types of fields. A 'social interaction field' includes all the individual perceptual fields that in various ways mirror it and help to make it up.

The orientation of multiple level field theory is psychoanalytic in many respects, but psychoanalytic theory does not provide the conceptual means for representing adequately the interpersonal and total inclusive group levels of social

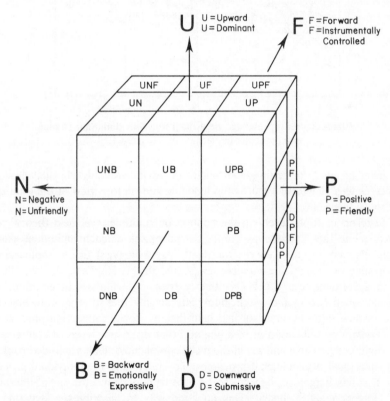

Figure 1 The SYMLOG three-dimensional space, showing classes of directions or locations, defined by logical combinations of the six named reference directions. (The cube is seen from an outside point. The directions are named from a reference point at the intersection of the three dimensions, looking forward.)

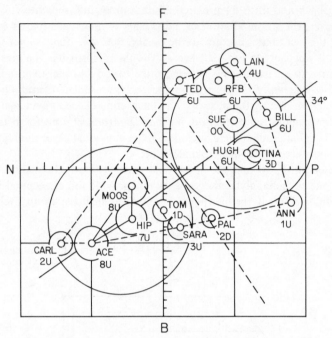

Figure 2   Group average field diagram, with dominant triangle
and perimeter (expansion multiplier = 1.843)

processes or a way of getting from a view of the individual level of psychological
processes to a view of the pairs of individuals and on to a view of the total inclusive social interaction field.

The term 'multiple levels' in the context of 'multiple level field theory' refers
partly to the fact that the psychological processes of each individual exist 'in
depth.' Psychoanalytic theory, as a 'depth' psychology, strongly emphasizes the
importance of recognizing multiple levels, and in this emphasis the two theories
are in agreement. But SYMLOG theory tries to formulate, in addition, what
happens when two or more individuals interact together in relation to objects of
common orientation ('images'). It is held that the social interaction process *adds*
new levels of complication of meaning and that these new levels of complication,
as individuals perceive and act in the more complicated field, are folded back into
their individual psychological processes. To understand the individual processes
once this has happened, one has to be able to understand the social interaction
field. Psychoanalytic theory gives no good way to describe the structure and
dynamics of the social interaction field. In SYMLOG theory there is a way.
Figure 2 is a Field Diagram based upon the average of all individual members'
subjective perceptions (and evaluations) of the field. It contains a set of
inscriptions (such as a tracing of the 'reference circle' and the 'opposite circle,' the

'line of balance,' and others) representing the SYMLOG theory of the structure and dynamics of that particular social interaction field, from which new inferences can be made, as we shall later see.

In the SYMLOG System, the measurements for the construction of both the individual perceptual fields and the inclusive social interaction field are based on the observation of individual acts of social interaction, whether the observations are made by members or nonmembers; whether the observations are made in a time-ordered series, act by act, as in SYMLOG Interaction Scoring, or by global retrospective recall, as in SYMLOG Ratings.

The social interaction field is an inclusive representation of the data of all individual fields. It is derived from a combination of all subjective views, including that of the researcher. When one wishes to look at the summary result of the ways in which the subjective views tend to converge, one may make a diagram of the *group average field*, as shown in Figure 2. One does not depend upon an average, however, since each individual field is unique and diverges from the others in important respects. In order to take this into account one looks at individual perceptual fields in *alternation*. In the 'alternation' mode of analysis, the subjective meaning of an act to the member who performs the act is translated by the researcher–theorist into the subjective meaning it probably has for each of the other participants taken separately. The meaning of their reactions, in turn, are translated back into the subjective view of the first. The members' ratings of each other give the means of making these translations.

Multiple level field theory, is closely related to gestalt field theory, realizing in many respects. I believe, the aspirations of Kurt Lewin and his school, but it differs from Lewin's field theory (see Lewin, 1939, 1947, 1951) in several important ways. Multiple level field theory is based on the observation of specific acts of social interaction as its primary grounding in empirical reality. Hence, the social interaction field is 'operationally defined' from the beginning, whereas the gestalt field theorists have tended to begin with an abstract concept of the individual psychological field or 'life space' apart from any means of measurement. For experiments, they have selected plausible operational definitions for the measurement of the variables they feel they need to represent for a particular experiment. They have not as a rule proceeded inductively to build general purpose measuring instruments based upon observation that can be applied in any situation of social interaction.

Because multiple level field theory is based on the observation of specific acts of social interaction, the measurement of its variables is anchored in time. In SYMLOG Interaction Scoring, every bit of evidence about the state of a variable or the structure of a dynamic field is obtained from some act of recording some piece of behavior that was observed to occur at some particular identifiable time. It is true that in retrospective Rating there is a collapsing of time, and one may lose track of just when some act observed occurred. But even so, the rating is based upon actual observation. It takes a lot of observation and a long time to get the amount of information necessary to construct the representation of a 'field,' either an individual perceptual field or an inclusive social interaction field. Lewin aspired to an a-historical theory dealing with the dynamics of the present field (for which physics was his model), and implicitly made the unfortunate assumption that one could obtain measurements of all the variables in the 'present' field without paying enough attention, perhaps, to the fact that measurement of many variables takes a long time and can be defined only by time-anchored or historical events. Lewin did not want to get bogged down in a historical definition of variables. And he wanted to escape the concrete 'phenotypical' conception of variables. Without formulation of the 'phenotypical' component, however, one cannot make empirical measurements.

SYMLOG field theory is also different from gestalt field theory in that it takes account of *multiple fields*. SYMLOG field theory keeps in perspective (1) *each individual perceptual field* at a given time, (2) the *multiple level behavior* of each separate individual at a given time, (3) the *process of interaction* between individuals *over time*, (4) the developing relationship of *each individual* to *each other individual* in the group, (5) the overall pattern of the inclusive group constellation or *social interaction field* during a given time period, and (6) the dynamic *changes over time of the social interaction field*. This can be done because of the explicit methods of measurement and representation.

Lewin's theory, like Freud's, was constructed from the perspective of the single individual. The concept for this perspective in Lewin's theory is the 'life space'; in Freud's theory it is the personality consisting of the interaction of its major parts, 'Ego, Super-Ego, and Id.' The extension of the individual perspective to *each of many individuals in social interaction with each other* was never accomplished, in either case.

Lewin's concept of the 'life space' was extended without any essential modification to serve as a kind of '*group* life space.' The group was treated as a *point* in the space, and the group was said to 'locomote' as a point through the space toward a single goal. The extension of the individual life space to the group was mostly metaphorical and introduced a host of logical and conceptual problems.

Freud's concept of 'Ego, Super-Ego, and Id' was also metaphorically extended (informally by others) to serve as a classification of the kinds of roles individuals play in a group. The results, while provocative and not entirely without value, remained unfortunately metaphorical and vague.

Neither Freud nor Lewin started from a concept of social interaction as a primary reality, and neither developed general methods of measuring it. As a result, in both cases the empirical grounding of the variables remained ambiguous, and the multiple-individual, multiple-level combination of perspectives was never clearly achieved. There were no suitable general measurements upon which the necessary concepts could be based.

Perhaps it needs to be said that, although SYMLOG field theory is based upon observations of 'behavior' in the broad sense (including the content of things said), it is not a variety of 'behavioristic' theory, if by 'behavioristic' one means a theory that rules out of consideration the subjective views of the persons interacting. On the contrary, social interaction field theory is strongly phenomenological in taking into account the subjective view of the actor (each of them), in paying attention to many subjective elements of behavior and regarding them as real determinants, in emphasizing the actor's unique 'definition of the situation,' and in emphasizing the prominent role of the levels of meaning and symbols. In these respects SYMLOG field theory is very similar to 'symbolic interactionism.' The present approach departs from the more extreme phenomenology of some symbolic interactionists, however, who tend to emphasize the subjectivity, uniqueness, and variability of meaning in the perception and behavior of each individual to such an extent that it seems hopeless to try to use any kind of systematic method, any standardized approach, or to look for any general tendencies.

SYMLOG field theory is case-oriented and naturalistic (in that sense, 'clinical') in spite of the considerable use of measurement, statistics, and geometry. The Field Diagrams look clean, cool, and precise, but they represent evanescent and uncertain subjective views of behavior and meaning, the real stuff with which one deals in working practically with people. The SYMLOG System provides extensive means for recognizing and conceptualizing individual differences between persons, general characteristics of the individual personality, and inconsistencies of direction of motivation, values, and behavior within the same personality, as well as consistencies. In using the system, one recognizes and characterizes unique properties of each group of individuals in interaction. In making SYMLOG interaction observations and in analyzing Field Diagrams, one pays attention to all the pair relationships in the group, as well as to the overall pattern characteristics of the group as a whole. In making observations at the image level and the value judgment level, and in making the Field Diagrams appropriate to these levels, one recognizes and portrays the relationships of persons to psychologically significant symbols and objects of common orientation. The SYMLOG System allows the tracing of changes through time of all the variables it measures.

Such a degree of inclusiveness is possible because of the complex of elements recognized in the original observation and description of the smallest unit observed in SYMLOG Interaction Scoring—the single act of the single individual. The observation of the single act of a single individual is the building block of all the more complex ways of analyzing patterns of behavior, whether patterns characterizing the individual personality or patterns characterizing the inclusive social interaction field. Acts are observed, recorded, sorted, counted, and aggregated in different ways to detect complicated patterns.

But the idea of an atomistic building block is only half of what is required. The other necessary conception is that the single act of the single individual is a complex, multiple-level entity in itself, compounded of many causal determinants, mirroring in microcosm the social interaction field in which it occurs. The description of the single act, using the SYMLOG Scoring format, calls for the description on different levels of a number of different characteristics of the same act. The levels include the 'behavioral' elements, the 'image content' presented in communication, and the evaluative attitude of the actor about the image, or the 'value judgment.'

For certain purposes, then, the researcher–theorist regards the single act as a unit—each counts as one unit. Single acts are added together with other single acts to get larger aggregates and to describe larger patterns. For other purposes, however, the researcher–theorist regards the single act itself as a multiple level pattern of subunits or characteristics, which can be examined one by one in fine detail.

The way in which *each act* may be observed and assessed in terms of the multiple levels of behavior it contains is described in the SYMLOG Interaction Scoring Manual. SYMLOG *Rating* may best be understood as a simplified global version of the operations performed in SYMLOG *Scoring*. The theoretical heart of SYMLOG is evident only in the Scoring method, not in the Rating.

The act of Rating (or Scoring) of the behavior of another person or of the self is best regarded as *still another level* of behavior of the rater. This seems especially clear when the information is to be returned to the group for their discussion. As a group member, one performs the Rating (or Scoring) in the expectation that each person rated will know how one describes him or her, and one expects that person will react in some way. This makes a difference in the way one rates or scores. The same pressures come to bear on Rating behavior as on other interactive behavior, only with some modifications in the strength of some of the pressures. The behavior of the person rated is measured by the behavior of the person rating. 'Measuring' is also behavior. Consequently, one does not expect anybody's ratings or scores to be independent of his or her personality or location in the social interaction field. The observer, whether Scoring or later Rating, is a part of the total field. A group member's ratings of the other members' behavior is a part of his or her own behavior, and the Ratings give information about the rater as well as about other members and about the social interaction field as a whole. The ratings of each person must be analyzed. Every person's ratings are 'subjective.'

There is no 'objective' view of the total field. One approaches what is ordinarily meant by 'objectivity' by putting together and averaging or in some other way combining the 'subjective' views of as many persons as one can.

A three-dimensional space

In order to understand the Field Diagram and the meaning of the location of the member 'images' plotted upon it as shown in Figure 2 it is necessary to take a short detour to grasp the meaning of the three dimensions of the SYMLOG theory and the way in which they may be used to constitute a three-dimensional 'space,' as shown in Figure 1. It is possible to describe the quality of behavior—more specifically, of any act of interpersonal behavior—by reference to three dimensions. The dimensions, described in adjectives that apply to behavior, are: (1) Dominant vs. Submissive, (2) Friendly vs. Unfriendly, and (3) Instrumentally Controlled vs. Emotionally Expressive. Each 'dimension' has two ends, qualitatively the opposite of each other. Each dimension may also be thought of as having a zero point in the center, at the origin of the two opposite directions.

For the sake of more easily grasping the logical relationships of the 'directions' we want to visualize, we may think of the three dimensions in relation to each other as if they were the dimensions of an actual physical space. Figure 3 is a perspective drawing of a three-dimensional cube, which may be thought of as enclosing the three-dimensional space we want to visualize. The labels on the directions indicate how the behavioral descriptive names are translated into names descriptive of directions in the physical space model, U, D, P, N, F, and B. The spatial names of the dimensions are U–D (for Upward–Downward), P–N (for Positive–Negative), and F–B (for Forward–Backward). The letters on the smaller cubes, made up of various combinations of the directional names, U, D, P, N, F, and B, give the names of directions in between the main ones. There are twenty-six directional names in all. These twenty-six directions are taken as the basis for the more fine-grained definitions of the variables of the SYMLOG system, as shown in [Table 1].

Each of the adjective rating items shown in Table 1 is labeled with a combination of letters, e.g. 'U,' 'UP,' 'UPF,' which indicates the direction in the three-dimensional space the items is designed to measure. A comparison of each adjective rating item with its corresponding direction (or vector) in the three-dimensional space as shown in Figure 1 will give a rapid intuitive understanding of the heart of the SYMLOG System.

Once the SYMLOG three-dimensional space is understood, the Field Diagram in Figure 2 is easily understood. The Field Diagram shows a *two*-dimensional plane as it would be seen if one were looking into the cube from the top. The Field Diagram is also calibrated with a numerical scale on each direction and is divided at the zero point—and again halfway out along each direction for more convenient measurement—but the *logic* of the space is given by the cube model of Figure 1.

The location of each individual in the two dimensions P–N and F–B is derived from the ratings and is shown as a point on the Field Diagram, as in Figure 2. The point proper is enclosed with a very small circle (called the core circle), to make it more easily visible. The summary ratings of the individual's behavior on the two dimensions P–N and F–B are thus shown by the location of the point in the plane of the diagram. The summary rating of the individual's behavior on the U–D dimension is shown by the relative size of the outer circle inscribed around the point. The larger the outside circle, the more dominant the behavior; the smaller the circle, the more submissive, as seen by the rater. The numerical location in the U–D dimension is written below the name of each member.

The format of the SYMLOG message (By Robert F. Bales and Stephen P. Cohen)

The observer, sitting and watching the group (optimally, but not necessarily, from an observation room), has a supply of observation sheets, as shown in Table 2. On the back of the first page the observer draws a large diagram of the table with members' names written in at the proper places. (If members' names are not yet known, they may be designated temporarily by number or by some other temporary sign.) Sometimes it is necessary to revise the space diagram, if people change their positions. In many meetings, however, a single diagram will do well enough for the whole meeting. The main purpose of the diagram is to fix the names of the group members in the mind of the observer, so that group members can be identified quickly.

The name of the observer is written at the top of each page. The designation of the group, the date, and the page number are also written at the top of each page.

The observer writes a series of 'messages' on the form. A single sheet has space for twenty messages. Since messages are usually written at a rate of about one per minute, and by good scorers considerably faster, four or five pages will usually be necessary for a single hour's meeting.

A 'message' is written as a communication between the observer and the group member designated in the message as the ACTOR. It is assumed that the message will later be read by the appropriate group member. It is assumed that other group members and observers will also read the message. Like a telegram, the message is short, but it must be understandable to the persons who will read it.

The SYMLOG message constitutes the formulation of the observer's judgment that an event significant to the group process has just taken place. The observer wishes to record this significant occurrence for the log of the group and for feed-back to the member of the group who initiated the interaction event. Each message may be said to have the unwritten preamble, 'The following significant event (or series of behaviors constituting a significant interaction event) has just taken place in the group.'

Suppose at the first meeting of the group, only a minute or two after the begin-ning of the meeting, one of the members of the group, TOM, makes a pleasant social remark to break the ice. The message written by an observer in the SYMLOG format might read something like this:

10 TOM GRP ACT UP a really friendly group PRO UP (in) GRP

Each part of the message is put in its appropriate column on the form. The first column is headed TIME. The '10' in our illustrative message is written in the TIME column and indicates that the act took place at ten minutes after the hour.

Table 2 The SYMLOG Interaction Scoring Form

Observer _____ Group _____ Date _____ Page_____

Draw a diagram of the physical location of group members on back of page 1

Time	Who Acts	Toward Whom	Act/ Non	Direc- tion	Ordinary Description of Behavior or Image	Pro/ Con	Direc- tion	Image Level

The word TOM is the abbreviation for the group member's name and it is written under the heading WHO ACTS. The word GRP is the abbreviation for the group as a whole as the addressee of the communication, and it is written under the heading TOWARD WHOM. The two columns are thought of as ground together, and specify the ACTOR and the RECEIVER of the ACT. The headings may be read together: WHO ACTS TOWARD WHOM.

The next element of the message is the technical word ACT written under the heading ACT or NON. It means in this instance just about what it seems to mean, namely that TOM acts or behaves overtly in a way apparently intended to communicate with others. The technical word NON stands for nonverbal behavior. If the behavior appears to the observer as not necessarily intended to communicate but nevertheless gives signs of the ACTOR's attitudes and feeling, then the behavior is classified as NON.

All communications are conveyed through behavior in the broad sense, and all behavior is classified as either ACT or NON. The term ACT refers to acts of intended communication. Behavior at the ACT level also has nonverbal components and accompaniments, which help the RECEIVER and the observer to understand the meaning of the communication. Unless the nonverbal components give a different (and perhaps unconscious or unintended meaning), the ACT classification is enough. So ACT means intended overt acts of communication toward the other, *including their nonverbal components*, so long as the nonverbal components do not give a different or contrary meaning.

The nonverbal behavior of the ACTOR at any time may be regarded as important and, if so, should be scored. When there are nonverbal signs that contradict the intended meaning of an ACT, then it is especially important to write an additional message that gives the NON meaning. If there is not sufficient time, it is more important to write the message giving the NON meaning than the ACT meaning. There are many instances when the ACTOR gives nonverbal signs without intending to communicate, and the observer should constantly remain alert to the nonverbal behavior, since it may be unobtrusive but nevertheless very important.

The next element of the message is written under the heading DIRECTION, which means the DIRECTION of ACT or NON, and in our illustrative message the code written there is 'UP.' This code term in this case actually consists of the two subelements, 'U' and 'P'. The first element, U, stands for the term 'Upward,' which means 'Ascendant or Dominant.' The second element of the code, P, stands for the term 'Positive,' which means 'Friendly.' The code term UP combines these two meanings and uses them as a qualitative description of the behavior. Thus the message says that TOM acted toward the group as a whole in a way the observer judged to be more or less ascendant or dominant, but at the same time friendly. . .

The final three elements of the message format are concerned with what kind of IMAGE is presented in the *content* of what the ACTOR says (as distinguished from the direction of his *behavior*, with which we have been dealing so far).

Suppose TOM had said, 'You know, this seems like a really friendly group.' In these words he presents an *image* of what 'the group' is, or might be. He almost makes a suggestion that if other people in the group agree with him, as he senses they will, then they might try to make it even more friendly. The words 'a really friendly group' carry some impression of genuine feeling and seem to coalesce into something we might call an 'image,' a kind of compact picture of an emotionally toned 'thing,' to which a name has been given, so that it can now be discussed and reacted to by all members. This is (approximately) what an IMAGE is.

An IMAGE is *a picture of an emotionally loaded focus of attention*. Sometimes attention may focus on a tangible physical object brought into the group, or some object in the immediate environment, but more often a set of words or a name of some kind is used as the means of focusing attention. More exactly speaking, an 'image' is something that exists in the mind of an individual. It is a 'picture' in the mind of the individual that comes from some 'perception' of some outside 'object' or from some set of memories and feelings that are aroused by a set of words. The observer cannot see the psychological entity inside the ACTOR, of course, but one can usually locate the set of words around which the attention seems to focus or the physical objects or events to which the ACTOR and the RECEIVERS are paying attention.

The description under the title ORDINARY DESCRIPTION OF BEHAVIOR OR IMAGE is a few words in uncoded language, preferably some of the words used by the ACTOR. The number of words used must be few, however, as in our example, 'a really friendly group,' since the remaining spaces of the message format are used to classify the IMAGE and the actor's attitude toward it. In rare cases the actor may act out the image in mimicry, without words. In this case, the observer describes the imitative behavior. Sometimes the observer records a nonverbal or other act with no IMAGE, for example, a sigh or a smile. In this case, the behavior is described under the heading ORDINARY DESCRIPTION OF BEHAVIOR OR IMAGE.

The column of the observation sheet immediately following the description of the BEHAVIOR OR IMAGE is headed PRO or CON. This is a judgment by the observer as to whether the IMAGE is something the ACTOR is *in favor* of (PRO), or *against* (CONTRA, or CON). In our example, the word 'really' preceding the word 'friendly' seems to imply a favorable feeling. The classification of the ACTOR's attitude toward the IMAGE is thus PRO. If the observer cannot make out what the attitude of the ACTOR is toward the Image, a question mark is put in the column. It is quite common for a person to act in a friendly way toward the other person to whom he is talking while both refer to an image of some third person or object about which they both feel negatively. The ACT or NON classification refers to the attitude of the ACTOR toward the *RECEIVER*, whereas the PRO or CON classification refers to the attitude of the ACTOR toward the *IMAGE* (or some element or aspect of the IMAGE).

The IMAGE in a given case may be an image of the self. When a person talks about SELF, for example, either PRO or CON attitudes may be expressed about those images. The term ACTOR does not mean the same thing as the term SELF. The term ACTOR refers to the person in the capacity of acting, behaving (including thinking and feeling), as seen from the perspective of the *observer*. The observer attributes the act to 'the ACTOR.' The ACTOR is the observer's name for the mental processes within the acting person's mind that are supposed to be psychologically *acting upon the images in that same person's mind.* On the other hand, the term SELF is the observer's name for the IMAGE the ACTOR may have of self. Thus, in SYMLOG language, it makes perfectly good sense to write that the ACTOR expresses a PRO or CON attitude about the SELF.

SYMLOG language implies that an Image or a field of images is only a *part* of the mental process of the person, and that there is another part that is *acting upon the IMAGES* in the person's mind. The name for that part is the ACTOR. The term ACTOR is a term for something we do not really understand. It is what is sometimes called a 'primitive,' or an 'undefined' term. Although we cannot define it except as a kind of unknown part of the mental process, there is no difficulty for the observer in writing down the *name* of the person WHO ACTS. All the observer supplies is the name of the person perceived as acting.

In our example, TOM's attitude toward the image is rendered: PRO UP (in) GRP. This means that he is in favor of some UP *element in* the group. When the message is written on the observation form, the word 'in' is omitted, as indicated by the parentheses, but it is understood to be there, and in reading the message it is included, since it is needed to complete the meaning. In this case, we translate TOM as saying that he is in favor of *ascendant friendly behavior* on the part of everybody in the group. He is not presumably in favor of *everything* that the GRP could be or could mean. For example, he is probably *not* in favor of the negative behavior that may also appear as an element of the group. He is, in effect, saying, 'I propose that we adopt a *norm* of friendly behavior in this group.' The particular *element in* the general image of the group that he is in favor of is just one of the many possible elements that could be a part of the general concept or image of 'the group.' Somebody else may be CON UN in GRP, that is, against dominant unfriendly behavior. Somebody else may recommend instead, PRO F in GRP—i.e., serious problem solving. TOM is in favor of (PRO) the *UP* element in the GRP.

The SYMLOG language, by use of the terms PRO and CON, permits the observer to record the kinds of *Value Judgments* individuals make and recommend to each other. Hence, the language gives the means of recording and describing the development of 'group norms,' since essentially what we mean by a 'group norm' is a PRO or CON value judgment about an element in some general image upon which members seem to agree.

At this point we may begin to see more clearly what is meant by the 'Multiple Level' observation of behavior. It means the observation and recording of both the simple and the more complex levels of behavior in the *same message* about the *same act or piece of behavior.* The method assumes behavior to be multiple leveled and provides a way to record each of several levels. What are these levels, so far?

The simplest two levels, ACT and NON, we have grouped together and called the *Behavioral Level*, or simply *Behavior.* Sometimes it is convenient to speak of interpersonal behavior on these two levels as 'interaction,' 'social interaction,' or 'the social interaction level.'

The next level recognized by the SYMLOG terminology is a global level of content presented in communcation called the *Image Presented.* As we shall see, there are several major classes of images, classified in a rough sort of way in terms of decreasing degrees of association with the self-image. These global types of IMAGES, which we also call 'levels' are: images of SELF, images of the OTHER, images of the GROUP, images of the SITUATION, images of SOCIETY, and images from FANTASY. Any image presented by the ACTOR is classified by the observer into one of these six global types, and this, of course, is the meaning of the final column on the observation form, headed IMAGE LEVEL. In our example, there is no difficulty in seeing that TOM's IMAGE of a 'really friendly group' is an image of the GROUP. The technical term GROUP means simply the present interacting group of persons, or sometimes more specifically the membership group, if some person present is regarded as not a member.

But a SYMLOG description of an *Image Presented* is never left as just a global classification of the IMAGE LEVEL, as SELF, OTHER, GRP, etc. The global Image is always supplied with a qualifying adjective, which points to the specific *element in* the global IMAGE on which the actor is focusing attention. Thus, it is the UP *element in* the group, and not simply 'the group' that TOM is recommending in his PRO statement. One of the major assumptions and simplifications of the SYMLOG language is that an important meaningful aspect of any IMAGE may be grasped and expressed by focusing attention on the way it 'acts,' as if it were a kind of behavior entity in its own right. Since in this metaphorical sense it 'acts,' the directional classification appropriate for the 'acts' of persons can be used to describe this action element. An IMAGE is thus a cognitive representation in the mind. An important emotional potential of it can be understood by determining for what kind of 'act' it stands. The way it 'acts' is the ELEMENT we choose for further specifying the IMAGE. The UP ELEMENT in GRP is the friendly ascendant behavior that is one of the ways in which the group (or its members) can act.

The DIRECTION of the ELEMENT is always combined with the classification of the global IMAGE in order to give the classification of the specific ELEMENT of the IMAGE. Thus, the ACTOR may refer to U in SEL (ascendance or dominance in the self) of UP in GRP (some element in the present group that acts in an ascendant or dominant and friendly way) and so on. The DIRECTION OF ELEMENT column on the message format is used for one of the twenty-six directional designations. The final column, headed IMAGE LEVEL, is used for the global image designation.

The class or level of IMAGE called OTHER, abbreviated OTH, is always converted into the name of the specific other meant. The image class OTHER refers *only to persons in the present participating group*, and these persons always have code names. In recording the message, the *code name of the particular person* is always supplied instead of the general term OTH. (This need not be done in the case of a reference to an image of the SELF, since the reader of the record knows that the name of the person referred to as SEL is always the same as the name of the person given as the ACTOR. But since there are often a number of OTHERs in the group, the name of a given OTHER must be specified to make it clear who is meant.) The combination of the specific *name* of the OTHER referred to with the *element* of that person's behavior given by the DIRECTIONAL qualifier thus gives the observer the power to be quite specific in reporting the attitudes and feelings that group members have about themselves and about each other. This is very relevant, of course, in a self-analytic group, where a great deal of the content is of just this kind.

The level of *Image Presented* is thus a very large set of possible sublevels and specific images. The presentation of an image by the ACTOR may be regarded as an aspect of behavior on a higher or more complex level than the 'behavioral' level, because it is a content reference that *stands for* other acts of behavior, both past and expected to come. We may say that the image communicates 'meaning' and 'feeling' from the ACTOR to the RECEIVER (and to the observer), about some entity that is not simply the ACT of the ACTOR. The ACT may be said to 'carry' the IMAGE, and the image 'carries' a meaning (the specific element of the image).

And now we may observe that a still higher level of behavior is assumed to exist in the distinction of PRO or CON. This level may be called the level of *Value Judgment*. It is not only the case that the ACTOR constitutes IMAGES and their ELEMENTS in his mind and communicates them to the RECEIVER. The ACTOR also makes value judgments about the ELEMENTS of the IMAGES and tries to change images so that they mean something different both for the ACTOR and for the RECEIVERS. The ACTOR may make a value judgment that puts a negative value on an IMAGE that a moment earlier was regarded as positive. The ACTOR may decide and say that the self as ACTOR does not like ascendant behavior in the SELF as a person (CON U in SEL). The ACTOR may decide and say that the self as ACTOR does not like friendly behavior in the OTHER (CON P in JOHN). This kind of value judgment may supersede the more spontaneous liking or disliking of the element of the image. The ability to make such value judgments is the level referred to in psychoanalytic theory of personality as the 'superego.' SYMLOG language permits the observer to record the highest-level value judgments that the ACTOR makes of the ELEMENTS in the IMAGE, as well as the lower-level semantic meaning (the DIRECTION) of the ELEMENT.

We may summarize by saying that SYMLOG recognizes three *major sets* of levels of behavior. These are (1) *The Behavioral Levels*; (2) *The Levels of Image Presented*; and (3) *The Levels of Value Judgment*.

The *Behavioral Levels* include two sublevels, ACT and NON. The *Levels of Image Presented* include six sublevels, SEL, OTH, GRP, SIT, SOC, and FAN, each of which is combined with a set of twenty-six directional specifiers, and two of which (SELF and OTHER) are subdivided into the names of each of the persons in the group. The *Levels of Value Judgment* are subdivided into PRO or CON (or '?') and the PRO or CON judgments are applied to each Element of an Image. In the SYMLOG message each piece of communication is described at all three major sets of levels if they appear. This is the meaning of the name, Systematic Multiple Level Observation of Groups. The person may ACT toward an OTHER without presenting an IMAGE. Or the person may ACT and present an IMAGE without communicating a value judgment PRO or CON. Or the person may ACT and communicate a value judgment, PRO or CON, about an ELEMENT in an IMAGE.

Summary

A concise summary of the elements of the message format and some scoring hints follow. Strictly speaking, each message is considered to include the name of the observer, the designation of the group, and the date in addition to the elements of the message we have just described. For convenience, this general heading is recorded only once, at the top of the first observation sheet. The elements of the message may be defined more exactly as follows:

> *Observer*: A short code, usually not over four letters representing the observer's name, e.g. John Doe may be represented as JD, or JOHN. Each observer indicates the abbreviation he or she wants to use, the instructor or investigator then compiles the list, checks to eliminate any duplications, and issues the standard list of abbreviations with names attached for use by observers and group members.

> *Group*: A short code to represent the group being observed. It might be Group A or B, Red or Blue—whatever the group is called.

> *Date*: The date on which the session observed is occurring, represented by numbers for the Month, Day, and Year in that order, e.g., 9/26/78. Slashes are used to separate the numbers.

The rest of the message, following the above three elements, may be called the 'body' of the message. The elements of the body of the message may be defined as follows:

> *Time*: A two-digit number representing the minute from the beginning of the hour period in which the session occurs. For example, if a session is scheduled at 9:00 a.m., the time 9:10 a.m. is designated by

the two-digit number, 10. If the scheduled time of the beginning of the meetings is 9:00 a.m., then the time 10:01 a.m. is designated by the number 61, and so on consecutively for succeeding minutes. A digital clock is necessary to obtain sufficient accuracy to coordinate the observations of more than one observer. (Without a digital clock observers tend to round to the nearest five-minute mark.) Accuracy by minute, and proper sequence within the minute, are important in comparing the observations of different observers, and for proper recall of actual events.

Who Acts (Actor): A short code name representing the name of the group member who is making the communication and whose behavior is being observed. The same names are used as the names for the persons as observers. (Each group member indicates the abbreviation he or she would like to use; the instructor checks for duplications and issues the list of standard abbreviations, with full names attached.) It is necessary to avoid use of the same code name for two different persons, of course.

Toward Whom (Receiver): The other person (or the group as a whole) to whom the actor is talking or toward whom the actor is acting. The group as a whole may be indicated as the Receiver with the use of the abbreviation GRP, if this seems most appropriate. The name of the specific person, as designated by the code name (see above) is ordinarily used. If the communication is addressed to some person outside the group (rare) the abbreviation OTH may be used.

ACT or NON: The classification of the communication at the Behavioral Level, either as ACT (an overt act toward the other intended to carry a communicated content) or as NON (an unintended nonverbal sign of emotion, feeling, or attitude, given off previous to or during the actor's overt intended communication, or instead of overt communication, as shown in facial expression, tone of voice, bodily movement, position, or posture). The same piece of behavior may be described by two messages, one at the ACT level and one at the NON level, if the directions are different. If the directions are the same, the message at the ACT level suffices.

Direction of Act or Non: The directional classification of either Act or Non (whichever has been specified) in terms of twenty-six directions (or twenty-seven if 'Ave' is counted). The direction describes the behavior qualitatively. . . The direction of the behavior at the ACT or NON level is *independent* of the direction of any element contained in an IMAGE. The direction of ACT or NON describes the ACTOR's attitude toward the RECEIVER (as seen by the Receiver). (The direction of an ELEMENT in an IMAGE describes the way the IMAGE is imagined to act toward the ACTOR.)

Ordinary Description of Behavior or Image: A few words in ordinary English, the actor's words if feasible or a paraphrase, to tell the reader the content the observer is selecting as an IMAGE. (The *global* classification of the image selected is given in the last column, and the direction of the specific element in the image is given in the next to last column.) If the behavior classified at the ACT or NON level carries no IMAGE beyond itself, the space headed ORDINARY DESCRIP- TION OF BEHAVIOR OR IMAGE is used to describe in ordinary language what the ACT or the Nonverbal Behavior sign was. The ordinary language description of the behavior or image is critically important in feedback, since members always want to be able to recognize what it was that the observer was scoring, and they cannot tell otherwise.

Pro or Con: One of these two codes, or a question mark, is written to indicate whether actor appears to be in favor of (PRO) or against (CON) the directional element of the IMAGE selected for attention. Value judgments PRO or CON are treated as independent of the direction of the element of the image. They are 'higher-order' positive or negative judgments of the directional elements. Thus, the actor may express a PRO value judgment about an element that may be ACT N or, vice versa, the actor may express a CON value judgment about an ACT P element. A PRO or CON statement is usually more or less equivalent to a proposal for a group norm—a suggestion as to what value judgments others should also make.

Direction of the Element of the Image: An element selected from a global image is described by the directional term that seems best to express the meaning it has for the actor. Sometimes this is apparent from context, tone of voice, etc., sometimes not. Often the meaning is similar for the actor and for the other group members. If one supposes the actor gives an image a particular meaning not the same as other group members give it, the meaning for the actor is the one chosen. The DIRECTION OF THE ELEMENT, in other words, is the direc- tion ACTOR seems to assign to the element.

Image Level: The observer may well have a list of the six levels as a reminder of the various classes of IMAGES: SEL, OTH, GRP, SIT, SOC, and FAN. Images are assumed to have different psychological qualities according to these general classes. Brief definitions are given below.

> *SEL*: Images of the SELF, that is, the self of the actor, as visualized by the actor. The term SEL is written in the message, and the reader determines who is meant by looking to see who is given as ACTOR. An image of the self is given by a remark that

indicates a characterization of the self or some element of it by references to own behavior, thoughts, feelings, or by the use of adjectives or trait names. When a situational, societal, or fantasy image is presented that the actor seems to accept, or claim, as a part of the self-image, the IMAGE is classed as SEL. Thus, 'I come from an upper-class family,' would probably be scored PRO U in SEL.

OTH: Images of particular members of the immediately interacting group, *other* than the actor. The term OTH is *not* written in the message. Rather, *the abbreviated name of the group member meant is given*. The OTH in question may be same as the RECEIVER of the ACT or it may not. An image of an OTHER is given by a remark that indicates a characterization of that other person, or some aspect or element of the person; by references to behavior, thoughts, or feelings of the other; or by the use of adjectives or trait names. Images of non-group members are classified as either in the SITUATION, in SOCIETY, or in FANTASY. However, when the actor uses images from the situation, society, or fantasy in order indirectly to characterize some person in the group, the IMAGE is classified as OTHER and the name of the person is given. Thus, 'John says he comes from an upper class family,' would probably be scored (PRO or CON) ? U in JOHN.

GRP: Images of the present interacting GROUP, considered as a collectivity, that is, as constituting a higher-order entity. The GROUP in this sense can be described in somewhat the same terms as a person, that is, by references to characteristic or normative behavior, thoughts, feelings, or by the use of adjectives or trait names describing some particular aspects of or element in the GROUP. Note that 'GROUP' is an IMAGE and that images exist in the minds of the individual actors. When the actor uses images from the situation, society, or fantasy in order indirectly to characterize the GROUP, the IMAGE is classified as GRP. Thus, 'We may as well give up. We don't have any power in this situation,' would probably be scored PRO D in GRP.

SIT: Images of objects or aspects of the SITUATION immediately external to the interacting membership group and constituting its immedaite environment. Includes the task or tasks, if any, but also all of the freedoms, possibilities, and psychologically significant features of the immediate environment for provoking or supporting any kind of behavior, thoughts, or feelings. The situation, the immediate environment, is described in terms of these meanings it has for the members—the images they construct of it, rather than in the observer's terms. References to persons outside the membership group, but who interact to some degree with it (for example the observers), may be classified as images of the SITUATION. For example, 'Those observers, sitting in judgment, make me nervous,' would probably be scored CON UNF in SIT.

SOC: Images of the SOCIETY within which the group and its immediate situation exist. Elements of the society in this global sense may be publicly known persons, groups, occupations, social classes, institutions, or any element of the society as defined and referred to by the actor. The directional description of an element is often that meaning which it has for the majority portion of society, but if the actor's definition of it seems to be different, the actor's meaning is taken. Images of elements in SOCIETY are often vague, abstract, stereotyped, ideological, and prejudicial, and the direction assigned depends upon the actor's attitude. Images of other societies and international relations are included in SOC. Thus, 'The international situation is a mess' might be scored CON UNB in SOC.

FAN: Images that seem to arise in the imaginal processes or the FANTASY of the actor, or seem to have a strong emotional meaning for the actor though based upon actual experience. Classification of an image as FAN does not imply it has no factual basis—it means that its present significance for the actor is given by its fantasy-arousing potential. The actor may not think of the image as one from fantasy; the actor may think of it as purely factual. In case of conflict as to whether to classify an IMAGE in FAN or in some other class, the FAN classification is preferred. The use of the term FANTASY in SYMLOG is much broader than in ordinary definition. Any report of doings of the ACTOR in contexts other than the group are scored as FAN, because they are assumed to function as arousers of fantasy in other group members, who have no direct access to the outside life of the ACTOR.

As a final comment on the set of components contained in the message format, we may note that all of them, with the exception of the natural language description of the BEHAVIOR or the IMAGE, are written in code words of three or four letters and in a standard order. This, of course, is needed for further operations of sorting, counting, and preparation of various statistics.

Although the message of the individual observer is made available to the individual group member, and as such may give an important insight, much of the power of the method depends upon the aggregation of the observations over time and over all members of the observation team. In this adding together, the peculiarities and biases of individual observers tend to cancel each other out, and their similarities and common perceptions tend to emerge. These common perceptions and interpretations are perhaps more convincing to the group members than single messages. This statistical approach provides an important element of 'objectivity' in a process that begins with individual 'subjective' judgments.

It is often true in psychology and sociology that in providing for a statistical approach one may lose the possibility of a 'naturalistic' approach—that is, the possibility of looking at the individual act in its full context and in relation to many levels of determinants. In SYMLOG, however, the naturalistic approach is preserved. One can recapture the memory of the individual act, locate it on the sound record, compare the observations of different observers, and examine it at its various levels of meaning. One can analyze it 'in depth' as usual in the 'clinical' approach. But, in addition, one may obtain statistical information about the frequency with which observers have picked up similar aspects of behavior. The present method thus integrates a 'statistical' with a 'naturalistic' approach, and its use may be turned in either direction, as needed.

References

Abelson, R. P., Aronson, E., McGuire, W. J. Newcomb, T. M., Rosenberg, M. J., and Tannenbaum, P. H. (eds.) (1968). *Theories of Cognitive Consistency: A Sourcebook*, Rand McNally, Chicago.

Bales, Robert F. (1950). *Interaction Process Analysis*, University of Chicago Press, Chicago.

Bales, Robert F. (1970). *Personality and Interpersonal Behavior*, Holt, Rinehart & Winston, New York.

Blau, Peter M. (1964). *Exchange and Power in Social Life*, Wiley, New York.

Blau, Peter M. (1968). 'Social exchange,' in D. L. Sills (ed.), *International Encyclopedia of the Social Sciences*, Vol. 7, pp. 452–458, Macmillan, Free Press, New York.

Blumer, Herbert (1969). *Symbolic Interactionism: Perspective and Method*, Prentice-Hall, Englewood Cliffs, NJ.

Bowen, Murray (1971). 'Family therapy and family group therapy,' in Harold Kaplan and Benjamin Sadock (eds.), *Comprehensive Group Psychiatry*, Williams & Wilkins, Baltimore.

Cartwright, Dorwin, and Zander, Alvin (1968). *Group Dynamics, Research and Theory*, 3rd edn, Harper & Row, New York.

Dahrendorf, Ralf (1959). *Class and Class Conflict in Industrial Society*, Stanford University Press, Stanford, Calif.

Festinger, Leon (1957). *A Theory of Cognitive Dissonance*, Row, Peterson, Evanston, Ill.

Freud, Anna (1963). *The Ego and the Mechanisms of Defense*, International Universities Press [1946], New York.

Freud, Sigmund (1900). *The Interpretation of Dreams*, in James Strachey (ed.), *The Standard Edition of the Complete Psychological Works of Sigmund Freud* (24 vols.), vols, 4, 5, Hogarth [1953], London.

Freud, Sigmund (1933). *New Introductory Lectures in Psychoanalysis*, in James Strachey (ed.), *The Standard Edition of the Complete Psychological Works of Sigmund Freud* (24 vols.), Hogarth Press [1953], London.

Glaser, Barney G., and Strauss, Anselm L. (1967). *The Discovery of Grounded Theory: Strategies for Qualitative Research*, Aldine, Chicago.

Goffman, Erving (1959). *The Presentation of Self in Everyday Life*, Doubleday Anchor Books, Garden City, NY.

Hare, A. Paul (1976). *Handbook of Small Group Research*, 2nd edn, Free Press, New York.

Hare, A. Paul, Borgatta, Edgar F., and Bales, Robert F. (eds.) (1965). *Small Groups, Studies in Social Interaction*, rev. edn, Knopf, New York.

Heider, Fritz (1958). *The Psychology of Interpersonal Relations*, Wiley, New York.

Homans, George C. (1961). *Social Behavior: Its Elementary Forms*, Harcourt, Brace & World, New York.

Kelley, Harold H. (1971). *Attribution in Social Interaction*, General Learning Press, Morristown, NJ.

Lewin, Kurt (1939). 'Field theory and experiment in social psychology,' *American Journal of Sociology*, **44**, 868–897.

Lewin, Kurt (1947). 'Frontiers in group dynamics,' *Human Relations*, **1**, 2–38, 143–153.

Lewin, Kurt (1951). *Field Theory in Social Science*, Harper & Brothers, New York.

Mead, George Herbert (1934). *Mind, Self, and Society*, University of Chicago Press, Chicago.

Merton, Robert K., and Kitt Alice S. (1950). 'Contributions to the theory of reference group behavior,' in Robert K. Merton and Paul F. Lazarsfeld (eds.), *Continuities in Social Research: Studies in the Scope and Method of 'The American Soldier,'* pp. 40–105, Free Press, New York.

Minuchin, Salvador (1974). *Families and Family Therapy*, Harvard University Press, Cambridge, Mass.

Newcomb, Theodore M. (1953). 'An approach to the study of communicative acts,' *Psychological Review*, **60**, 393–404.

Osgood, Charles E., and Tannenbaum Percy H. (1955). 'The principle of congruity in the prediction of attitude change,' *Psychological Review*, **62**, 42–55.

Parsons, Talcott (1951). *The Social System*, Free Press, New York.

Pettigrew, Thomas F. (1967). 'Social evaluation theory: Convergences and applications,' in *Nebraska Symposium on Motivation*, pp. 241–311, University of Nebraska Press, Lincoln.

Shaw, Marvin E. (1971). *Group Dynamics: The Psychology of Small Group Behavior*, McGraw-Hill, New York.

Thibaut, John W., and Kelley, Harold H. (1959). *The Social Psychology of Groups*, Wiley, New York.

Small Groups and Social Interaction, Volume 2
Edited by H. H. Blumberg, A. P. Hare, V. Kent and M. Davies
Published by John Wiley & Sons Ltd 1983

7.11   Conclusions from Frame Analysis*

Erving Goffman   *University of Pennsylvania*

I

1. This study began with the observation that we (and a considerable number of theys) have the capacity and inclination to use concrete, actual activity— —activity that is meaningful in its own right—as a model upon which to work transormations for fun, deception, experiment, rehearsal, dream, fantasy, ritual, demonstration, analysis, and charity. These lively shadows of events are geared into the ongoing world but not in quite the close way that is true of ordinary, literal activity.

Here, then, is a warrant for taking ordinary activity seriously, a portion of the paramount reality. For even as it is shown that we can become engrossed in fictive planes of being, giving to each in its turn the accent of reality, so it can be shown that the resulting experiences are derivative and insecure when placed up against the real thing. James and even Schutz can be read in this way. But if that is comfort, it comes too easy.

First, we often use 'real' simply as a contrast term. When we decide that something is unreal, the reality it isn't need not itself be very real, indeed, can just as well be a dramatization of events as the events themselves—or a rehearsal of the dramatization, or a painting of the rehearsal, or a reproduction of the painting. Any of these latter can serve as the original of which something is a mere mock-up, leading one to think that what is sovereign is relationship, not substance. (A valuable watercolor stored—for safekeeping—in a portfolio of reproduced masters is, in that context, a fake reproduction.)

---

*Erving Goffman (1974). *Frame Analysis: An Essay on the Organization of Experience*, Harper & Row, New York, and Penguin, London, pp. 560–576. Copyright © 1974 by Erving Goffman. Reprinted by permission of the publishers. Reprinted by permission of Penguin Books Ltd.

Second, any more or less protracted strip of everyday, literal activity seen as such by all its participants is likely to contain differently framed episodes, these having different realm statuses. A man finishes giving instructions to his postman, greets a passing couple, gets into his car, and drives off. Certainly this strip is the sort of thing that writers from James on have had in mind as everyday reality. But plainly, the traffic system is a relatively narrow role domain, impersonal yet closely geared into the ongoing world; greetings are part of the ritual order in which the individual can figure as a representative of himself, a realm of action that is geared into the world but in a special and restricted way. Instruction giving belongs to the realm of occupational roles, but it is unlikely that the exchange will have occurred without a bordering of small talk cast in still another domain. The physical competence exhibited in giving over and receiving a letter (or opening and closing a car door) pertains to still another order, the bodily management of physical objects close at hand. Moreover, once our man goes on his way, driving can become routine, and his mind is likely to leave the road and dart for moments into fantasy. Suddenly finding himself in a tight spot, he may simultaneously engage in physically adroit evasion *and* prayer, melting the 'rational' and the 'irrational' as smoothly as any primitive and as characteristically. (Note that all these differently framed activities could be subsumed under the term 'role'—for example, the role of suburbanite—but that would provide a hopelessly gross conceptualization for our purposes.)

Of course, this entire stratified strip of overlapped framings could certainly be transformed as a whole for presentation on the screen, and it would there be systematically different by one lamination, giving to the whole a different realm status from the original. But what the cinematic version would be a copy of, that is, an unreal instance of, would itself be something that was not homogeneous with respect to reality, itself something shot through with various framings and their various realms.

And by the same argument, a movie showing could itself be seen as part of the ordinary working world. It is easily possible to imagine the circumstances in which an individual attended the movies and became involved in its offering as one phase of an evening's outing—a round that might include eating, talking, and other actualities. Granting this, one can imagine the circumstances in which the moviegoer might compare the reality of the evening's round with watching a TV drama in which such an evening was depicted. Contariwise, in court, establishing an alibi, our individual could avow that he really had gone to the movies on a particular evening in question, and that doing so was for him an ordinary, uneventful, everyday thing to do, when, in fact, he had really been doing something else.

2. But there are deeper issues. In arguing that everyday activity provides an original against which copies of various kinds can be struck, the assumption was that the model was something that could be actual and, when it was, would be more closely enmeshed in the ongoing world than anything modeled after it.

However, in many cases, what the individual does in serious life, he does in relationship to cultural standards established for the doing and for the social role that is built up out of such doings. Some of these standards are addressed to the maximally approved, some to the maximally disapproved. The associated lore itself draws from the moral traditions of the community as found in folk tales, characters in novels, advertisements, myth, movie stars and their famous roles, the Bible, and other sources of exemplary representation. So everyday life, real enough in itself, often seems to be a laminated adumbration of a pattern or model that is itself a typification of quite uncertain realm status.[1] (A famous face who models a famous-name dress provides in her movements a keying, a mock-up, of an everyday person walking about in everyday dress, something, in short, modeled *after* actual wearings; but obviously she is also a model *for* everyday appearance-while-dressed, which appearance is, as it were, always a bridesmaid but never the bride.) Life may not be an imitation of art, but ordinary conduct, in a sense, is an imitation of the proprieties, a gesture at the exemplary forms, and the primal realization of these ideals belongs more to make-believe than to reality.

Moreover, what people understand to be the organization of their experience, they buttress, and perforce self-fulfillingly. They develop a corpus of cautionary tales, games, riddles, experiments, newsy stories, and other scenarios which elegantly confirm a frame-relevant view of the workings of the world. (The young especially are caused to dwell on these manufactured clarities, and it comes to pass that they will later have a natural way to figure the scenes around them.) And the human nature that fits with this view of viewing does so in part because its possessors have learned to comport themselves so as to render this analysis true of them. Indeed, in countless ways and ceaselessly, social life takes up and freezes into itself the understandings we have of it. (And since my analysis of frames admittedly merges with the one that subjects themselves employ, mine, in that degree, must function as another supportive fantasy.)

II

1. In looking at strips of everyday, actual doings involving flesh-and-blood individuals in face-to-face dealings with one another, it is tempting and easy to draw a clear contrast to copies presented in fictive realms of being. The copies can be seen as mere transformations of an original, and everything uncovered about the organization of fictive scenes can be seen to apply only to copies, not the actual world. Frame analysis would then become the study of everything but ordinary behavior.

However, although this approach might be the most congenial, it is not the most profitable. For actual activity is not merely to be contrasted with something obviously unreal, such as dreams, but also to sports, games, ritual, experimentation, practicing, and other arrangements, including deception, and these activities are not all that fanciful. Furthermore, each of these alternatives to the everyday is different from the others in a different way. Also, of course, everyday activity itself contains quickly changing frames, many of which generate events which depart considerably from anything that might be called literal. Finally, the variables and elements of organization found in nonliteral realms of being, albeit manifest and utilized in distinctive ways in each of these realms, are also found in the organization of actual experience, again in a version distinctive to it.

The argument, then, is that strips of activity, including the figures which people [see in] them, must be treated as a single problem for analysis. Realms of being are the proper objects here for study; and here, the everyday is not a special domain to be placed in contrast to the others, but merely another realm.

Realms and arrangements other than the ordinary can, of course, be a subject matter of interest in their own right. Here, however, another use is claimed for them. The first object of social analysis ought, I think, to be ordinary, actual behavior—its structure and its organization. However, the student, as well as his subjects, tends to take the framework of everyday life for granted; he remains unaware of what guides him and them. Comparative analysis of realms of being provides one way to disrupt this unselfconsciousness. Realms of being other than the ordinary provide natural experiments in which a property of ordinary activity is displayed or contrasted in a clarified and clarifying way. The design in accordance with which everyday experience is put together can be seen as a special variation on general themes, as ways of doing things that can be done in other ways. Seeing these differences (and similarities) means seeing. What is implicit and concealed can thus be unpacked, unraveled, revealed. For example, on the stage and on radio we have come to expect that a performer will externalize the inner state of the character he is projecting so that continuity of story line can be assured, so that, indeed, the audience will know at every moment what is going on. But precisely the same sort of intention choreography can be found in daily life, most evidently when an individual finds he must do something that might be misconstrued as blameworthy by strangers who are merely exercising their right to glance at him before glancing away.

2. As a paradigm case, take three or four flesh-and-blood individuals performing an actual task in one another's immediate presence—in short, an everyday strip of activity. What can frame analysis find to say about the scene and its participants?

First, the tracks or channels of activity. Assume that there is a main activity, a story line, and that an evidential boundary exists in regard to it. Assume at least four subordinate tracks, one sustaining disattended events, one directional, one overlaid communication, and one matters for concealment.

Second, the laminations. The strip under question presumably has none. Neither a keying is present nor a deception. Certainly such straightforwardness is possible. But one should see that it is not likely for a very long period of time. And often effort will have had to be exerted to ensure even this. The absence of laminations is to be seen, then, as something worth seeing.

Third, the question of participation status. A two-person chat sustained in a sequestered place implies, on first analysis, a full sharing of ratified participation status and, overlaid, an exchange of speaker and recipient roles.

But expand on these possibilities. Add a third participant, and allowance must be made for the speaker addressing the participants as a whole or singling out a particular other, in which latter case one is forced to distinguish between addressed and unaddressed recipients. (Then it can be seen that an unaddressed recipient, especially a chronic one, may stand back somewhat from ordinary participation and view the speaker and his addressee as a single whole, to be watched as might be a tennis match or a colloquy onstage.) With a third participant the possibility has also been created for a two-person collusive net and a distinction between colluders and excolluded. Add, instead, a third person who is a nonparticipating stranger and one has the bystander role whose performer is cut off from the others by civil inattention. Script the two-person arrangement or either of the three-person arrangements and perform it on a stage and one then has, in addition, the performer–audience roles.

Simple enough. But now see that these expanded possibilities can be drawn upon in order to quicken our sense of what can enfold within an actual, fully sequestered, two-person talk. As already considered at length, the possibility of collusive communication can occur in two-person talk, in the form of either self-collusion through which one participant performs gestural asides during the other's turn at talk, or (as it were) collusive communication, involving both participants playing both colluder and excolluded roles. Also one participant can style the externalization of his response so that the other is encouraged to perceive it but act as if he hasn't, thereby encouraging the latter to contribute two ways of functioning, not one, in effect expanding the two-person arrangement into something more complicated. And when a speaker replays a strip of experience for the delectation of his listener, the latter (and the speaker to a degree) may stand back and function not unlike an audience; the listener *and* the speaker can show appreciation for what the speaker presents before them.

In brief, arrangements which articulate multiperson interaction may be folded back into two-person talk, there to be given a structural role. And as spoken narrative forces simultaneously occurring events into a temporal sequence, and as cartoon strips force temporally sequenced events into a spatial sequence, so living interaction may itself be somewhat coerced by those sustaining it so that sequencing is more marked than it might otherwise be and timing of turns more nicely determined by a hidden effort to allow clear scorekeeping. It is thus that a child who falls and scrapes his knee may wait until he crosses the street to his parent before bursting into tears that are as hot and fresh as these things get. It is thus that an adult may puncture a conversation with a burst of laughter,[2] a spurt of anger, a sudden interruption, a downward look of chagrin and embarrassment—or any other genuine flooding out—and somehow manage in effect to time this rupture so that it neatly occurs at a juncture in the other's talk that would best allow an unseen audience an unimpaired view, a completed hearing, of what it is that called forth this response. And here instead of our following the usual practice of 'sequentializing' what is actually concurrent, we allow ourselves to see as overlapping what has actually been managed sequentially—thereby deeply enlisting framing practices in the general conspiracy to sustain beliefs about our human nature, in this case, that behind our civil niceties something undisciplined, something animallike, can there be found.

3. Given this perspective, one can turn to the central but very crude concept of participant (or player or individual), for again the comparative approach allows us to address assumptions about ordinary activity that would otherwise remain implicit. And one can begin to see, for example, that the body itself and how it functions in a frame is an issue that warrants systematic treatment.

Start with a board game such as chess. The dramatic focus is two opposing sets of figurines destined to move against each other in regulated ways. Behind this interaction of moves are two players, each of whom stands to gain or lose by the outcome, each of whom diagnoses what moves his side should make, and each of whom physically manipulates—animates—the pieces on his side.

It should be obvious how differently from this chess can be arranged and yet be, overall, the same game. The figures may be actual persons on a courtyard square. The diagnostic, cognitive function may be performed by a committee or a computer. The manipulation may be performed by third parties in response to voiced commands, or by an electrical arrangement, or by the figure itself in the case of courtyard matches. When the game is played only 'for fun,' then each of the two parties exercising the cognitive function presumably gains or loses whatever is going by way of psychic stakes. But if there is money at stake or national pride, or team score, then, of course, parties other than the two mentioned can directly participate as principals, that is, as backers, partners, and so forth. So, as already suggested, the following functions: figures, strategists, animators, principals.

Two points should be mentioned about chess. Although the several functions discussed can be performed by different entities, our very notion of player assumes that a full overlay will be present and that this needs no thinking about. Second, the role of the human body is here very limited. It is the pieces that cut the swath. Ordinarily a body is used only to maneuver the pieces, and this operation is ordinarily seen as unproblematic, routine, of no consequence. A polite request with instructions and one's own move can be physically made by the opponent. It is the cognitive function that is problematic.

Take now a brawling street fight between two men. Again it is possible to define each fighter in terms of multiple functions, for example, the principal or party with something at stake and the strategist who decides which moves to make. Easier than before, one can see that these functions could be segregated. (Professionalize the fight and a trainer-coach will share in the cognitive function, and backers, if not owners, will share in the gain or loss.) But in addition there is a rather obvious yet instructive contrast to chess. Instead of chess pieces as the figures, the human body serves that function. And whereas a chess piece draws its attributes, its powers, from the rules which tell us how it may move, and is in that sense unproblematic, a human (or animal) fighter draws its powers—strength, technique, exertion—from within, and it is these powers, perhaps even more than the cognitive ones, that are at issue.

When one turns to organized, equipment sports like tennis, fencing, or hockey, again one or more bodies per side figure as figures, except that here each body employs an extension thereof—a stick, club, bat, or whatever. These devices are used in an extremely efficient, instrumental way, which only very long practice can ensure, so that, incidentally, the plane within which the body operates becomes restricted in the matter of how exertion is channeled. Furthermore, the effort and skill involved make no sense unless one agrees on the special and peculiar goals of the game, the precisely defined measurements of the equipment (along with the obligation to restrict oneself to their use, and this within the rules), and mere markings as outer boundaries of the field of play. The actions induced in sports contests have thus an arbitrary, artificial character.

The dance might now be mentioned. Here the choreographer seems to claim much of the strategic function. Again, of course, the body figures largely, but this time in no way as a utilitarian task performance. The purpose is the depiction of some overall design, including bodily mimed feeling and bodily symbolized fate, and although muscle and bone and training and stamina are certainly required, and problematically so, all this is exerted for pictographic ends. Boxers, of course, can display grace and economy of movement, as can tennis players, but this must be a by-product, at most a marginal concern, the main one being physical, describable in terms of a state to be accomplished in whatever way seems most effective at the time—within the rules, that is.

When one turns to ceremony and ritual, another combination of elements is found. On the face of it, no decisionmaking function is operative, the whole having been scripted by tradition, lore, and protocol. Again the figures involved are bodies, but although some practice may be required in performance of the ritual, proper execution can easily become routine and unproblematic. And again, utilitarian procedures are not involved; the controlling, open intent is a kind of symbolization, a special kind of rounded, well-formulated representation.

Imagine now a high school debate. Two teams are involved, each with two or more players. What is put at play is verbally presented arguments, these judged on standards of content and delivery. The delivery itself is certainly a problematic and important feature, and certainly control of voice, monitoring of speech, and other physical acts are involved. But the body as a whole has dropped out. The individual is expected to debate on his feet, but if he needs a wheelchair he can still participate fully.

Now look at everyday activity, especially that involving face-to-face talk. It might be thought that as in a high school debate only arguments and competence to express matters verbally will be in play. But that is much too narrow a view. Verbal commitments are made which have real consequence in the future. Signaling is facilitated through which close collaboration in physical tasks becomes possible. Interpersonal rituals are performed.

And as a by-product of his doings, the doer provides gleanings of, for example, his personality, social status, health, intent, and alignment to others present. Therefore, in the case of most strips of ordinary, unstaged activity, it seems perfectly possible to show that although the bodily behavior of the actor is learned and conventional, that indeed a set piece is being run through, the action is nonetheless perceived as direct and untransformed. Ordinary body movements are seen not as a copy, as in the case of the faked emotional displays of con men, or as a symbolization, as in the openly enacted emotional displays of some native mourners, but, to repeat, as a direct symptom, expression, or instance of the doer's being—his intent, will, mood, situation, character. This 'directness' is a distinctive feature of the frame of everyday activity, and ultimately one must look to frames, not bodies, to obtain some understanding of it.

Ordinary behavior, then, is taken as a direct instance of, or a symptom of, underlying qualities and therefore has an expressive element, but symbolization—say, in Susanne Langer's sense of the term—is not taken to be centrally involved. Yet, of course, postures are struck and appearance is tailored, and this is a symbolizing action more akin to what is found in the dance than what is generated in other frames. And furthermore, behind expression and symbolization will often be found some threat, distant or close, of physical force, and some inclination, encouraged or not, to direct sexual contact, both of which imply still other roles for the body. Moreover, it is characteristic of everyday interaction that the immediate source of these emanations from the self will continuously shift: now the eyes, now the hand, now the voice, now the legs, now the upper trunk.

One can see, then, that in everyday interaction, the body figures in a limited but nonetheless very complicated way, and this one sees by checking back to the role it plays in other frames of activity.

4. Consider now the human nature said to ground the behavior of he who participates in ordinary doings. Again approach this comparatively, starting this time with the emotional self-response displayed by figures in various frames.

In stage and movie performances it is apparent that a well-trained and highly committed actor will be willing to take the part of an emotionally effusive character or an extremely self-contained one, depending only on what the script calls for. In the former case, he will be willing (in character) to break down under assorted pressures, flaunt his problems and feelings, beg for mercy, cry, groan, curse, and generally carry on in a manner he might well find quite unsuitable in real life—because of both the manners of his social group and his own particular version of them. Furthermore, on the stage he is willing to emote before a much larger number of people than would witness these outpourings in ordinary life were he there to indulge them; and moreover this larger group looks right at him instead of tactfully disattending.

In presented contests, again it is often the case that a more expansive display of emotion, especially chagrin, is allowed than in the sportsman's everyday life. (Indeed, each sport seems to provide a conventionalized use of its own equipment for this purpose, as when a baseball bat is thrown to the ground after a strikeout, or a tennis ball is hit into the backwire after a return has been muffed.) But these outbursts tend to be located just after the taking of a move, try, or turn, for at that moment the individual has ceased to be active in his player capacity, and what he does bears on that realm no more than does the applause or boos from the onlookers—which response he can elect to disattend. If a ballplayer throws down his bat during a pitch, he is a faulty player; if he throws it down after he has struck out, he is merely commenting on himself as a player during a moment of time-out in the play, a time when the players on the field are not in play either. So although the graphically displayed anguish of a golfer who misses an easy putt *looks* to be like the emotional volubility of a stage actor's performance of an excitable character, the difference is syntactical, bearing on the structure of experience.

A musician during a performance presents still another picture. He (like a conductor) is allowed to follow the physical act of performing with a parallel and supportive show of effortful disarray, for after all, he is modeling sounds, not comportment. But should he make a mistake, his preferred strategy is disattendance. If he is part of an ensemble, any stopping on his part to engage in chagrin, anger, embarrassment, and so forth would throw the whole into further disarray—even if he himself is temporarily not playing. If he is performing solo or with accompaniment he can make a point of stopping everything and beginning the troublesome passage again, but he can do this only once or twice a performance, and when he does he must be very sure to treat the whole contretemps as something manageable with distance and a twinkle so that it is not his full, literal self that has entered into the failure but only an expendable version of it. And what the twinkle says is that he knows the audience will be willing to collaborate in his momentary frame break, that they won't worry about his being really out of control or that he might think that they think that his little intransigence is disrespectful. Observe that what here calls for a virtuoso frame break, a performance that has to be exquisitely styled if it is to come off, is a commonplace achievement in everyday interaction. For there no audience is present with lofty expectations, and very often no one but the flubber himself is held up by his emotional self-response to the flubbing.

Now look again at the performance of popular songs. The story line typically involves some drama of the heart. As suggested, the story is typically told in first-person singular. As in stage productions, the animator and the figure are seen as technically different, but in the case of popular singing, some inner bond unites the two. In fact, the more the animator's life (as the audience knows it) qualifies for the plight that is being sung about the more 'effective' is the result. 'Sincerity' here means singing as though the lyrics were true of oneself. In any case, singers routinely trot out the most alarming emotional expression without the lengthy buildup that a stage play provides. Thirty seconds and there it is—instant affect. As a singer, an individual wears his heart in his throat; as an everyday interactant he is likely to less expose himself. As one can say that it is only *qua* singer that he emotes on call, so one can say that it is only *qua* conversationalist that he doesn't. Neither comment tells us about persons as such; both tell us about figures in frames.

The notion of emotional self-response is one part of 'emotional expression.' Another has to do with unintentional self-disclosure. The doctrine associated with the frame of everyday actual behavior is that the actor has incomplete control over his emotional expression. He may attempt to suppress this source of information about himself or falsify it, but in this (we presume) he can never be fully successful. Thus, he can willfully tell an outright, boldface lie, but can hardly fail to show some expression of guilt, hesitation, or qualification in his manner. It is felt that his nature itself ensures this. He who can be utterly false in his address to others can be thought to be 'psychopathic' or, God forgive us, 'sociopathic,' and in any case if we strap wires to him, the polygraph—our cosmological defense in depth—will show that he really doesn't contradict human nature.

In sum, as natural persons we are supposed to be epidermally bounded containers. Inside there are information and affect states. This content is directly indexed through open expression and the involuntary cues always consequent upon suppression. Yet when the individual engages in bluff games such as poker, one finds that he either blocks off almost all expression or attempts the most flagrant, expressively ramified deceptions—the kind which would give him a very bad reputation were he to attempt unsuccessfully such a display in his actual, literal activity.[3]

An answer is apparent. Incapacity to perfectly contrive expression is not an inheritance of our animal or divine nature but the obligatory limits definitionally associated with a particular frame—in this case, the frame of everyday behavior. When the frame is shifted, say, to bluff games, and this frame gives the player the assurance that his dissembling will be seen as 'not serious' and not improper, then magnificently convincing displays occur, designed to attest to holdings and intentions the claimant in fact does not possess. In brief, we all have the capacity to be utterly unblushing, provided only a frame can be arranged in which lying will be seen as part of a game and proper to it. And the same virtuosity can be elicited when the deceiver knows that what he is participating in is really an experiment, or in the best interests of an obviously misguided recipient, or as an illustration of how someone else carried on. It appears, then, that 'normal honesty' is a rule regarding the frame of ordinary literal interaction, which rule, in turn, is a particular phrasing of a more general structural theme, namely, that the party at play has something to conceal, has special capacity and incapacity for doing so, and labors under rulings regarding how he is to comport himself in this regard.

5. And at the heart of it? The individual comes to doings as someone of particular biographic identity even while he appears in the trappings of a particular social role. The manner in which the role is performed will allow for some 'expression' of personal identity, of matters that can be attributed to some-

thing that is more embracing and enduring than the current role performance and even the role itself, something, in short, that is characteristic not of the role but of the person—his personality, his perduring moral character, his animal nature, and so forth. However, this license of departure from prescribed role is itself something that varies quite remarkably, depending on the 'formality' of the occasion, the laminations that are being sustained, and the dissociation currently fashionable between the figure that is projected and the human engine which animates it. There is a relation between persons and role. But the relationship answers to the interactive system—to the frame—in which the role is performed and the self of the performer is glimpsed. Self, then, is not an entity half-concealed behind events, but a changeable formula for managing oneself during them. Just as the current situation prescribes the official guise behind which we will conceal ourselves, so it provides for where and how we will show through, the culture itself prescribing what sort of entity we must believe ourselves to be in order to have something to show through in this manner.

Take your auctioneer. He proves to be a 'character.' He is not in awe of what has been entrusted to him. He comments wryly on one or two of the articles he is obliged to knock down, showing he is slightly cynical about the sellers, the buyers, and what is being sold. He emcees, he editorializes, he wheedles and teases. He upbraids the assembly for bids not forthcoming. He declines to let well enough alone; he ever so slightly puts the whole enterprise on. (None of this, admittedly, prevents him from seriously touting the major items and may, in fact, provide a basis for his credibility here.) So this auctioneer seems a special fellow, except that in auctioneering a tradition, as well as the opportunity, exists for this sort of thing, and many of those who take on the role also take on the irreverent personal style encouraged in this particular business endeavor. So, too, your air stewardess. She can serve coffee with no more than a distracted half smile on making the offer and a facial flick when withdrawing the pot, wrapping the service in no more ritual than is available at every counter in America. But instead I have seen the following:

> Speaking lightheartedly as if announcing a novel possibility, and gesturing with the pot, the stewardess asks a middle-aged male in an aisle seat if he wants coffee. He nods yes. Apparently knowing she was nearing the end of a run, she sneaks a peek over the edge of the pot and gives a warning *moue*, reducing her age to the point at which it would be appropriate for the passengers in sight to take up her perspective on events in neglect of their own. She pours, finds the cup is just filled, shakes the pot with a mock serious effort to free the last drop, jokingly breaks frame with a conspiratorial adult laugh, thrusts the pot a shade in the direction of the female passenger who is next in line, withdraws it covetously while raising her face and tightening her mouth in mock hauteur, and says aloud, 'I gotta go back for more.'

The feeling the man might have had that, after all, he had come in for the dregs on his turn, and of his seatmate, that, after all, she had just missed an unpostponed turn, have been stirred, faced, and reframed as the required backdrop for what is to be taken in good humor, a girlish effort to push a slightly ludicrous adult role down a hill. A coalition against seriousness is induced so that remonstrances against the taste and temperature of the coffee can just as well be invoked by the server as by the served. Obviously she is a good kid, the sort who enjoys her work, is full of life, and loves people. She has a nice personality. Except she did not invent this way of no-contesting a transaction, nor, probably, could she ham it up in less favorable circumstances. Her age, sex, and appearance supply one part of the mix, her job the other. All the girls in her training class were encouraged to warm the world in the same way, and many succeed in flight in doing so. Thus, auctioneering and stewarding provide more than roles; they provide particular ways of not merely performing them, particular ways of keying literal events. In sum, whenever we are issued a uniform, we are likely to be issued a skin. It is in the nature of a frame that it establishes the line for its own reframing.

6. And 'oneself.' this palpable thing of flesh and bone? A set of functions characteristically superimposed in ordinary, literal doings but separated in all manner of ways in other realms of being. So, too, the persons we have dealings with. And if these functions—functions such as principal, strategist, animator, figure—are separated in extraordinary realms of being, why shouldn't analyses be able to separate them in ordinary reality? As Merleau-Ponty, for example, has tried:

> It is not sufficiently noted that the other is never present face to face. Even when, in the heat of discussion, I directly confront my adversary, it is not in that violent face with its grimace, or even in that voice traveling toward me, that the intention which reaches me is to be found. The adversary is never quite localized; his voice, his gesticulations, his twitches, are only effects, a sort of stage effect, a ceremony. Their producer is so well masked that I am quite surprised when my own responses carry over. This marvelous megaphone becomes embarrassed, gives a few sighs, a few tremors, some *signs of intelligence*. One must believe that there was someone over there. But where? Not in that overstrained voice, not in that face lined like any well-worn object. Certainly not *behind* that setup: I know quite well that back there there is only 'darkness crammed with organs.' The other's body is in front of me—but as far as it is concerned, it leads a singular existence, *between* I who think and that body, or rather near me, by my side. The other's body is a kind of replica of myself, a wandering double which haunts my surroundings more than it appears in them. The other's body is the unexpected response I get from elsewhere, as if by a miracle things began to tell my thoughts, or as

though they would be thinking and speaking always for me, since they are things and I am myself. The other, in my eyes, is thus always on the margin of what I see and hear, he is this side of me, he is beside or behind me, but he is not in that place which my look flattens and empties of any 'interior'. [Merleau-Ponty, 1973, pp. 133–134].

—only neglecting to apply to these references to self the analysis they allow him to apply to other.

References

Hausner, M., Nash, J. F., Shapley, L. S., and Shubik, M. (1964). 'So long sucker, a four-person game,' in M. Shubik (ed.), *Game Theory and Related Approaches to Social Behavior*, pp. 359–361, Wiley, New York.
Jefferson, G. (1974). 'Notes on the sequential organization of laughter,' unpublished paper.
Merleau-Ponty, M. (1973). *The Prose of the World* (ed. C. Lefort; trans. J. O'Neill), Northwestern University Press, Evanston, Ill.
Schutz, A. (1962). 'Symbol, reality and society,' in *Collected Papers*, Vol. 1, Martinus Nijhoff, The Hague.

Notes

1. See Schutz (1962, p. 328). Here again I am grateful to Richard Grathoff.
2. Here see Jefferson (1974).
3. A nice case is provided by the game 'So Long Sucker,' in which the rules and playing are organized so that subsets of players must form working coalitions, and each player, if he is to win, must betray his coalition and join another, which, too, he must betray, and so on. Apparently the game doesn't usually get finished because of the refusal of players to continue. Until the game blows up, however, one obtains a remarkable expressive show of assurances by each player that he will remain loyal to the coalition he is about to enter, when indeed all along he knows this will not be possible. See Hausner, *et al.* (1964, pp. 359–361).

Small Groups and Social Interaction, Volume 2
Edited by H. H. Blumberg, A. P. Hare, V. Kent and M. Davies
© 1983 John Wiley & Sons Ltd

7.12 Whatever Happened to the Touted Revival of the Group?

Ivan D. Steiner

University of Massachusetts—Amherst

For about a decade after the Second World War many social psychologists attempted to treat the individual as a participant in larger social systems. What a person did was presumed to reflect the state of the group within which he was operating, the behaviors of other participants, and the constraints that the system put upon the individual's actions. Consequently, the group was seen as an important subject for investigation; to ignore it was to overlook critical elements in the equation that determined human conduct. But by 1955 enthusiasm had waned, and social psychologists were increasingly inclined to find causes within the single organism. Dissonance, attitudes, and attribution became key concepts, and an intense examination of the individual's cognitive and affective processes was substituted for the study of individuals in groups. To be sure, research on groups did not totally cease, but it received little attention from social psychologists during the 1960s and early 1970s.

My Katz/Newcomb lecture of 1973 provided an opportunity to speculate about the fate that had befallen the group. Even during the golden years theory concerning the group had lagged behind empirical research; a propensity to see the group as an aspect of the individual's life space, instead of a unit with its own dynamics, had limited conceptual development and drawn attention away from the systematic qualities of the collectivity. Post-war research had concentrated on person-to-person processes and had often lost sight of the wholeness of the social unit within which interpersonal transactions occurred. Furthermore, the goal of investigative rigor had led experimenters to chop behavioral sequences into very small pieces, to examine behavior in highly contrived situations, or to rely heavily upon the use of experimental accomplices whose programmed behaviors dominated the course of events. The whole had been shattered into so many fragments that wholeness was difficult to detect, or *mutual* responsivity had been legislated out of existence. By 1955 group research and theory appear to have reached a plateau beyond which they did not progress. Much had been learned about portions of a total process, but no very satisfactory conceptualization of the group as a functioning unit had been created.

Several reasons for failure to rise above the plateau of the 1950s could be cited. Collaborative efforts by sociologically and psychologically trained social psychologists, which had occurred with promising frequency during the post-war years, were largely discontinued during the late 1950s as scholars of both persuasions retreated to their home bases. This development left both camps poorly prepared to take the next steps forward. Psychologically trained investigators were seldom entirely comfortable about moving away from the internal dynamics of the individual, and their sociological brethren, though free of such restraints, sometimes had limited experience in conducting programmatic experimental research.

Continued progress was also inhibited by pragmatic considerations. Research on the group was very difficult to perform. It usually required that several subjects be observed simultaneously, often necessitated the use of two or more experimenters, and seldom could be completed in a short period of time. There were easier ways to do a Ph.D. dissertation and to survive in the academic community after doing one.

But in 1973 none of these conditions seemed sufficient to explain the declining interest in the group. After all, most of them were no more prevalent in 1955 than they had been before the post-war surge in groupy research began. Perhaps a decade of work had yielded such meager results that scholars had despaired of success. But that seemed an unlikely explanation because social psychologists who had never aspired to chart the workings of groups also tended to become more individual-centered during the late 1950s. The study of attitudes and attributions was wedded even more closely than before to the cognitive and affective processes of the individual, and dissonance theory which emphasized *intrapersonal* harmony dominated the research of the 1960s. Such sweeping changes could hardly be blamed on frustrations experienced when attempting to treat the group as an object of study. Something else must have been happening to prompt so many theorists to regard the individual as a comparatively self-contained system.

My hypothesis concerning that 'something else' was based on the assumption that social scientists (or, at least, social psychologists) are responsive to the *Zeitgeist* of their time. When society is peaceful and serene the occasional deviants are highly conspicuous and thought to be in need of an internal overhaul. Their attitudes and attributions ought to be adjusted; their cognitive and emotional processes require fine-tuning. Thus when most people are behaving as they should, and society as a whole is functioning pretty well, social psychologists can be expected to concentrate their attention on the dynamics of single individuals. But when turmoil is endemic and clusters of people are moving in different and opposing directions, attention is drawn to groupy issues such as leadership, cooperation and competition, deindividuation, collective decision-making, social facilitation, task performance by groups, and mob behavior. In times of trouble social psychologists can be expected to put the individual back into the group, and perhaps even consider the group itself to be an important object of scientific study. But neither tranquility nor turmoil should have instantaneous effects. Social psychologists move slowly and one should anticipate it will take them 8 to 10 years to read the mood of the day, wind up their current projects, and become immersed in something new. They should become individual-centered about 10 years after the advent of tranquility, and groupy about a decade after turmoil sets in.

My hypothesis was consistent with recent American history. The Great Depression had certainly been a time of turmoil, and it was followed by the groupy social psychology of the 1940s. By contrast, the Eisenhower years were singularly serene, and a decade later the group had begun its current hibernation.

Of course, it is not very good science to test one's hypothesis against the events that have prompted its creation. And four data points do not constitute very strong proof of an enduring principle. But I was overwhelmed by the beauty of my discovery and proceeded to extrapolate my hypothesis into the future. The late 1960s had brought a bewildering array of conflicts to the surface. There were protests against the Vietnam War, draft-card burnings, assassinations, race riots, feminist revolts, student rebellions, and violence at the Chicago convention of the Democratic Party. The future seemed clear enough, so I boldly predicted that the group would rise again. By the late 1970s, I contended, social psychology would be groupy once more.

Oral predictions are usually safe enough; if they are not soon forgotten one can at least deny having made them. But I rashly published a written version of my talk (Steiner, 1974), and am now forced to acknowledge that my foresight was somewhat faulty. Although there has been a detectable resurgence of groupy research, the increase has been small by comparison with the upsurge of the late 1940s and early 1950s. For the most part social psychology has remained a discipline that examines the activities, cognitions, and feelings of single individuals. The dynamics of human behavior are still generally conceived to be lodged deep within the actor himself.

Before attempting to explain why my prediction was not very solidly confirmed, I would like to cite a little evidence suggesting that it was not totally wrong. Mostly wrong, perhaps, but not wrong beyond a reasonable doubt. We must, after all, be wary of making either type-one or type-two errors.

Evidence of modest revival during the late 1970s

One way of detecting change in an area of theory and research is to determine what participants themselves have said about it at various points in time. And a convenient way of locating such testimonials concerning group research is to consult the periodic evaluations that are published in the *Annual Review of Psychology*. In their 1967 review of group dynamics Gerard and Miller (1967) concluded that none of the new ideas of the previous 3 years had catalyzed or focused the activities of researchers as had the work of Sherif, Lewin, Asch, Heider, or Festinger during the period following the Second World War. Instead, the recent contributions had primarily been devoted to bolstering or refining old contentions. Six years later in an appraisal of developments since 1967 Helmreich *et al.* (1973) reported being impressed by the quantity of data but depressed by the general lack of excitement and new formulations concerning the group. The accomplishments of the period seemed to these authors to exemplify a psychological Gresham's Law in which bad research drives out good. Thus two successive reviews concluded that the group had fallen on bad times, was dormant, or worse. But the next entry in the series (Davis *et al.*, 1976) contended that interest in small group interaction was increasing, and attributed this change to a growing concern with the practical problems of their day. Their 503-item bibliography listed a great profusion of contributions during the period 1973–1975. Either the group was awakening from its hibernation or these critics had misjudged the work they reviewed.

Other evidence of revived interest in the group is probably more subjective than the appraisals of Davis *et al.*

In 1980 the *Journal of Personality and Social Psychology* was divided into three parts, and I became the editor of the section on Interpersonal Relations and Group Processes. While the incoming stream of manuscripts (about 20 per month during the first year) cannot be mistaken for the floodtide, there has been no reason to conclude that the group has become extinct. We cannot know how many people are *reading* the published papers, but we can be sure that quite a few aspiring authors are *writing* about groups and interpersonal processes. Even if the research reported in each submission entailed only 200 hours of work—probably a gross underestimate—each month's crop of manuscripts represents 500 days of toil. And this reckoning ignores the efforts of uncounted investigators whose findings failed to reach the .05 level, or who for whatever reason decided that their product was not publishable or should go to any of several other appropriate journals.

It is difficult to categorize the diverse manuscripts that are being submitted nowadays, but a few trends can be detected. Group influences on individuals' behaviors and judgments are being examined by research into deindividuation, diffusion of responsibility, the impact of audiences of varying sizes, and the role of spectators as determinants of self-monitoring. A surprising number of investigators are conducting longitudinal studies of the development of dyadic relationships, and others are endeavoring to chart the processes by which pairs of persons (usually spouses) resolve, or fail to resolve, conflicts. Direct observation of face-to-face interactions appears to be focused primarily on nonverbal or paralinguistic aspects of communication, but such research is both plentiful and precise now that sophisticated electronic gear has become more widely available. Group decision-making is being examined by studies of mock juries, and there have even been experimental investigations of the development of norms, power relationips, and reward systems across 'generations' of groups. Studies of negotiation processes are guided by models of ever-increasing complexity, and the conditions that favor equity over equality in the distribution of group payoffs continue to command attention.

Of course, not all of the manuscripts I see are very exciting, creative, or methodologically respectable. A few would probably have to be classed as mistakes. But an encouraging number are of a quality that would have alleviated the depression Helmreich *et al.* experienced when they reviewed publications appearing during the interval from 1967 to 1972.

Social psychology did become more groupy by the late 1970s, but the change was much less pronounced than I had anticipated. And because the 'base line' that prevailed when I formulated by prediction was very low, the change that followed does not provide very clear support for the rationale on which my forecast was based. If the temperature is 20 degrees below zero when a man asserts that he knows tomorrow will be warmer because his nose itches, he will probably be right. But we are unlikely to accept his itch as a theoretically significant predictor of meteorological events. My arguments concerning the *Zeitgeist* may only have been a fortuitous itch that happened to forecast (rather weakly) the future, without having any logical connection with it.

Why didn't social psychology embrace the group?

Hindsight is generally better than foresight, so perhaps I can explain why my prediction of 1973 was not very strongly supported. The excuses I can offer are still tied to the *Zeitgeist*, but they reflect an altered appraisal of conditions that have prevailed since the late 1960s. Unfortunately, this reassessment focuses almost totally on the American scene and on American social psychology. Because I feel incompetent to cope with the rest of the world, I must expose myself to the charge of American arrogance by assuming that what really mattered happened here. A more cosmopolitan approach would probably permit a better analysis.

It cannot be claimed that events of the late 1960s and early 1970s were not sufficiently tumultuous to produce a wholesale revival of the group. The Vietnam War, Watergate, and other occurrences combined to turn Americans against one another and against 'the system.' Clusters of people opposed one another, and disharmony was evident on all sides. Naturally-occurring events appear to have manipulated my independent variable as successfully during the late 1960s as they had during the Great Depression. But the dependent variable had not manifested much effect. Social turmoil had not proven to be a powerful predictor of groupy social psychology.

In cases such as this it is customary to look for other variables that may have mediated the impact of the independent variable. What conditions prevailed in the instance when strong effects were observed, but not when effects were minimal?

Although the turmoil created by the Great Depression was probably no less widespread than that of the late 1960s, it was certainly less dramatically publicized. In the pre-television era people were not so thoroughly exposed to the conflicts of the times. Evidence that society as a whole was divided was not so apparent, and people were not exposed to a daily procession of demonstrations, denunciations, and protests. To be sure, the breadlines pictured in daily newspapers were testimony to the scope and seriousness of unemployment, but the Great Depression was not ordinarily depicted as a matter of group against group. Families, communities, and organizations struggled to survive in the face of adversity, but the visible enemy was generally 'hard times' instead of other families, communities, and organizations. This interpretation was nurtured by President Roosevelt who assured us that the only thing we had to fear was fear itself, and whose administration launched numerous programs to alleviate financial difficulties. Although these actions were not universally approved, the government could hardly have been viewed as apathetic or unresponsive; on the contrary, it seemed to be the friend and guardian of Americans and their institutions. Furthermore, the Depression was followed by a war from which the country emerged victorious and strong. The post-war years were an era of optimism during which an emerging social psychology had reason to trust in the fundamental solidarity of society, and an incentive to examine the processes by which groups remain productive and cohesive in the face of adversity. Relationships inside the group seemed more critical than relationships among groups or in society as a whole.

By contrast, the turmoil of the late 1960s heightened conflict among groups, ideological camps, and sections of the population. ('Don't trust anyone over 30.') Moreover, the government often appeared to be one of the vying parties, and was frequently regarded as unsympathetic, inept, or corrupt. After two and a half decades of confidence and rising aspirations, the 1970s brought a new economic era, characterized by confusion, uncertainty, and volatility (Katona, 1980). The Vietnam War had produced the first major American military defeat, and it was followed by the Watergate affair. Doubts concerning the future of the society were prevalent in many quarters, and the 'me generation' of the 1970s emphasized independence and personal satisfaction over collective security and solidarity. Groups were indeed coming apart, but the problems of the day seemed unlikely to be solved by strengthening the family, building new community ties, assembling more effective work crews, or devising better ways of handling interpersonal conflicts.

The foregoing interpretation of cases in which turmoil *did* and *did not* lead to a highly groupy social psychology suggests a revision of the hypothesis I propounded in 1973. Turmoil leads social psychologists to focus on the group instead of the individual *provided the causes of the turmoil are not thought to reside in society as a whole and/or are not believed to be largely unalterable.* Perhaps this amounts to saying that social psychologists are inclined to study groups when the group rather than society seems to need attention. When both society and groups are functioning rather smoothly, there are always lots of individuals whose internal processes deserve to be examined.

Of course, the turmoil of the late 1960s and early 1970s was not ignored by social psychologists. For many, the problems of society were too urgent to be postponed while the business of the laboratory went on as usual. But many social psychologists questioned the relevance of their craft to the events of the real world. Years of research into the processes of individuals had produced few guiding principles that seemed useful when the goal was to understand, predict, and perhaps control a society in disarray. Crash programs of research to discover ways of dealing with mass movements, unresponsive governments, student rebellions, feminist revolutions, and racial uprisings were out of the question. Few social psychologists were prepared by training and experience to conduct such investigations, very substantial monetary support would have been necessary, extensive collaboration with other disciplines would have been required, and a sense of emergency made such efforts seem too little and too late.

A widely publicized crisis of confidence in social psychology began in the late 1960s; some observers would probably contend it still endures. A few scholars discontinued research in favor of outright activism; many continued their previous lines of work; most were at least stimulated to question the fruitfulness of recent lines of inquiry.

The plight of the discipline was explained in several ways. Its commitment to investigate practical problems (Lewin, 1946) had been neglected (Bickman, 1976; Helmreich, 1975, Ring, 1967; Weissberg, 1976), it had relied too exclusively on experimental-laboratory methods borrowed from the physical sciences (Buck-Morss, 1977; Proshansky, 1976; Smith, 1972), or it had failed to discover enduring laws of human behavior because the underlying principles do not, in fact, endure (Gergen, 1973).

Other diagnoses held that social psychology had floundered because it had attempted to treat the individual in isolation from the situation in which he operated (Altman, 1976; Pepitone, 1976; Proshansky, 1976; Sampson, 1977; Secord, 1976; Stokols, 1976). The arguments of these critics could be construed to favor a return to the group as the unit for study. But most of these observers were proposing something more ambitious than that: the unit of analysis should include the norms and institutional arrangements that are relevant to the ongoing behavior, the physical setting in which action occurs, and (in some cases) pertinent historical, economic or ideological circumstances within the larger society. Putting the individual back into the group was hardly enough; he or she should be located in a larger system of events provided by his or her social, temporal, intellectual, and physical context. It was a very big order that went well beyond anything I had anticipated in 1973, and it was probably responsible in part for recent interest in the creation of environmental and organizational psychology programs at American universities.

Social psychologists who might have been inclined to study groups were inhibited by certain other events of the 1970s. The period following the Second World War had been one of academic expansion as hordes of ex-GI's returned to the campuses. Professors who wished to wander from the beaten path could usually obtain funds for doing so, and they had little reason to believe that adventurous enterprises might endanger their job security. But the 1970s were very different. The population of students leveled off and then declined in response to demographic changes. The recession of 1974, skyrocketing energy costs, and rapid inflation eroded the budgets of funding agencies and universities alike. Retrenchment became the dominant theme of administrators, though it was more often preached than practiced. The old slogan, 'publish or perish,' acquired new credibility, especially for younger scholars, and even seasoned veterans sensed the importance of impressing their departmental personnel committee. It was not the time to plunge into new or uncertain lines of research, even if funds were available.

It is a plausible hypothesis that academicians tend to espouse the traditional concerns of their disciplines when jobs are scarce. House (1977) noted that the alliance of psychologists and sociologists that had promoted a groupy social psychology during the expansive post-war period had largely been dissolved by the late 1950s. Psychological social psychologists became more narrowly psychological, while colleagues from sociology departments struggled to establish their respectability within the parent discipline. Although it seems unlikely that academic hard times were primarily responsible for the initial decline of groupy social psychology, they undoubtedly made its revival more difficult. Nowadays both psychologists and sociologists seem more firmly anchored to their own departments.

The uncertain future

My limited success as a prognosticator has undermined the confidence I or anyone else can have in my ability to foresee the future. Experience has indicated that the broad societal forces that shape social psychology are more complex than I had believed in 1973. And the present state of the world provides only vague clues concerning how those forces will operate during the next decade or so. But I will nevertheless offer a few immodest predictions.

Current American enthusiasm for environmental and organizational psychology will level off as investigators discover that such massive units are even more difficult to research systematically than are groups, and as the paucity of integrative theory becomes increasingly apparent. Some of the present enthusiasm will probably be directed back to the group which, in the meantime, may be expected to maintain its recently renovated status as an object of study. However, departmental allegiances will dictate that much of the future research on group processes will occur outside of psychology and sociology departments. As has been true during the last few years, many contributions will be made by persons in schools of business or education, by researchers employed in industry, or by investigators in the field of family therapy. Perhaps military agencies will manifest renewed concern about group performance and morale. Although recent issues of the American Psychological Association's *Monitor* have advertised a surprising number of academic jobs for persons trained in group research, I cannot foresee a sizable or immediate increase of interest within the departments that fostered earlier work on the group.

Eventually the group will rise again, but eventually may be a long time. Soothsayers ought not to specify precise dates.

References

Altman, I. (1976). 'Environmental psychology and social psychology,' *Personality and Social Psychology Bulletin*, **2**, 96–113.

Bickman, L. (1976). 'Fulfilling the promise: A response to Helmreich,' *Personality and Social Psychology Bulletin*, **2**, 131–133.

Buck-Morss, S. (1977). 'The Adorno legacy,' *Personality and Social Psychology Bulletin*, **3**, 707–713.

Davis, J. H., Laughlin, P. R., and Komorita, S. S. (1976). 'The social psychology of small groups: Cooperative and mixed-motive interaction' in M. R. Rosenzweig and L. W. Proter (eds.), *Annual Review of Psychology*, pp. 501–541, Annual Reviews, Inc., Palo Alto, California.

Gerard, H. B., and Miller, N. (1967). 'Group dynamics,; in P. R. Farnsworth (ed.), *Annual Review of Psychology*, pp. 287–332, Annual Reviews, Inc., Palo Alto, California.

Gergen, K. J. (1973). 'Social psychology as history,' *Journal of Personality and Social Psychology*, **26**, 309–320.

Helmreich, R. (1975). 'Applied social psychology: The unfulfilled promise,' *Personality and Social Psychology Bulletin*, **4**, 548–560.

Helmreich, R., Bakeman, R., and Scherwitz, L. (1973). 'The study of small groups,' in P. H. Mussen and M. R. Rosenzweig (eds.), pp. 337–354, Annual Reviews, Inc., Palo Alto, California.

House, J. S. (1977). 'The three faces of social psychology,' *Sociometry*, **40**, 161–177.

Katona, G. (1980). *Essays on Behavioral Economics*, Institute for Social Research, University of Michigan, Ann Arbor.

Lewin, K. (1946). 'Action research and minority problems,' *Journal of Social Issues*, **2**, 34–46.

Pepitone, A. (1976). 'Toward a normative and comparative biocultural social psychology,' *Journal of Personality and Social Psychology*, **34**, 641–653.

Proshansky, H. M. (1976). 'Comments on environmental and social psychology,' *Personality and Social Psychology Bulletin*, **2**, 359–363.

Ring, K. (1967). 'Experimental social psychology: Some sober questions about frivolous values,' *Journal of Experimental Social Psychology*, **3**, 113–123.

Sampson, E. E. (1977). 'Psychology and the American ideal,' *Journal of Personality and Social Psychology*, **35**, 767–782.

Secord, P. F. (1976). 'Transhistorical and transcultural theory,' *Personality and Social Psychology Bulletin*, **2**, 418–420.

Smith, M. B. (1972). 'Is experimental social psychology advancing?' *Journal of Experimental Social Psychology*, **8**, 86–96.
Steiner, I. D. (1974). 'Whatever happened to the group in social psychology?' *Journal of Experimental Social Psychology*, **10**, 94–108.
Stokols, D. (1976). 'Social-unit analysis as a framework for research in environmental and social psychology,' *Personality and Social Psychology Bulletin*, **2**, 350–358.
Weissberg, N. C. (1976). 'Methodology or substance? A response to Helmreich,' *Personality and Social Psychology Bulletin*, **2**, 119–121.

Cumulative Name Index

Volume numbers (1 and 2) are followed by a colon plus page numbers. If a name is not on an indicated page, it could be part of an 'et al.' - check the references (on pages indicated) at the end of the sub-chapter.

Cumulative Subject Index

Volume numbers (1 and 2) are followd by a colon plus page numbers.
This index is based partly on author-specified terms; some entries
might not be exhaustive for the work as a whole.